PENGUIN BOOKS

LIFE AND DEATH IN SHANGHAI

Nien Cheng was born in Peking, her father a vice minister in the Navy. She met her husband, Kang-chi Cheng, in 1935 in England, where both were studying at the London School of Economics. After the Communists overthrew Chiang Kai-shek in 1949, the Chengs decided to remain in Shanghai, where Kang-chi Cheng served as general manager of Shell, the only multinational oil company to stay on after Mao Tse-tung's triumph.

When her husband died of cancer in 1957, Shell hired Nien Cheng as a special adviser; she worked for Shell until the company pulled out in 1966, the year Mao launched the Great Proletarian Cultural Revolution. In August 1966, Nien Cheng's house was ransacked by the Red Guards; a month later she was arrested and taken to No. 1 Detention House in Shanghai, where she would remain in solitary confinement for nearly seven years. In the more liberal era following Mao's death in 1976, Cheng was "rehabilitated" and declared a victim of wrongful arrest. She was allowed to leave China in 1980 and settled first in Ottawa, Canada, where she started writing *Life and Death in Shanghai*. Since 1983 she has lived in Washington, D.C., where she completed the book.

LIFE AND DEATH IN SHANGHAI

Nien Cheng

PENGUIN BOOKS

PENGUIN BOOKS
Published by the Penguin Group
Viking Penguin Inc., 40 West 23rd Street,
New York, New York 10010, U.S.A.
Penguin Books Ltd, 27 Wrights Lane, London W8 5TZ, England
Penguin Books Australia Ltd, Ringwood,
Victoria, Australia
Penguin Books Canada Limited, 2801 John Street,
Markham, Ontario, Canada L3R 1B4
Penguin Books (N.Z.) Ltd, 182–190 Wairau Road,
Auckland 10, New Zealand

Penguin Books Ltd, Registered Offices:
Harmondsworth, Middlesex, England

First published in Great Britain by Grafton Books 1986
First published in the United States of America by
Grove Press, Inc., 1986
Published in Penguin Books 1988

5 7 9 10 8 6

LIBRARY OF CONGRESS CATALOGING IN PUBLICATION DATA
Cheng, Nien, 1915– .
Life and death in Shanghai/Nien Cheng.
p.   cm.
Reprint.   Originally published: New York:
Grove Press, 1987, c1986.
ISBN 0 14 01.0870 X
1. Cheng, Nien, 1915– . 2. China—History—Cultural revolution,
1966–1969—Personal narratives.   I. Title.
[DS778.7.C445   1988]
951.05'6'0924—dc19
[B]   87-25643
CIP

Printed in the United States of America by
R. R. Donnelley & Sons Company, Harrisonburg, Virginia
Set in Baskerville

To Meiping

AUTHOR'S NOTE

THIS BOOK is a factual account of what happened to me during the Cultural Revolution. The events are recorded in chronological order, just as they occurred. Every word spoken at the time, the reader will soon understand, was vitally important. Indeed, my survival depended on what was said to and by me. I had ample time again and again to recall scenes and conversations in a continuing effort to assess their significance. As a consequence, they are indelibly etched on my memory, and my book, including the words quoted as direct discourse, is as nearly as possible a faithful account of my experiences.

With some reluctance, I use in this book the now standard pinyin system for the transliteration of most of the Chinese names. Among the few exceptions are such old, familiar forms as Hong Kong (pinyin: Xianggang) and Kuomintang (Guomindang), and my husband's, my daughter's, and my own name (Zheng), which I prefer to continue to spell in English as I have done for more than fifty years.

Contents

I
THE WIND OF REVOLUTION

1	Witch-hunt	3
2	Interval before the Storm	37
3	The Red Guards	69
4	House Arrest	96

II
THE DETENTION HOUSE

5	Solitary Confinement	125
6	Interrogation	145
7	The January Revolution and Military Control	170
8	Party Factions	202
9	Persecution Continued	243
10	My Brother's Confession	277
11	A Kind of Torture	301
12	Release	334

III
MY STRUGGLE FOR JUSTICE

13	Where Is Meiping?	357
14	The Search for the Truth	383
15	A Student Who Was Different	410
16	The Death of Mao	444
17	Rehabilitation	479
18	Farewell to Shanghai	504

Epilogue	537
Index	545

I

THE
WIND OF
REVOLUTION

Witch-hunt

THE PAST IS FOREVER with me and I remember it all. I now move back in time and space to a hot summer's night in July 1966, to the study of my old home in Shanghai. My daughter was asleep in her bedroom, the servants had gone to their quarters, and I was alone in my study. I hear again the slow whirling of the ceiling fan overhead; I see the white carnations drooping in the heat in the white Qianlong vase on my desk. Bookshelves line the walls in front of me, filled with English and Chinese titles. The shaded reading lamp leaves half the room in shadows, but the silk brocade of the red cushions on the white sofa gleams vividly.

An English friend, a frequent visitor to my home in Shanghai, once called it "an oasis of comfort and elegance in the midst of the city's drabness." Indeed, my house was not a mansion, and by Western standards, it was modest. But I had spent time and thought to make it a home and a haven for my daughter and myself so that we could continue to enjoy good taste while the rest of the city was being taken over by proletarian realism.

Not many private people in Shanghai lived as we did seventeen years after the Communist Party took over China. In this city of ten million, perhaps only a dozen or so families managed to preserve their old lifestyle, maintaining their original homes and employing a staff of servants. The Party did not decree how the people should live. In fact, in 1949, when the Communist army entered Shanghai, we were forbidden to discharge our domestic staff lest we aggravate the unemployment problem. But the political campaigns that periodically convulsed the country rendered many formerly wealthy people poor. When they became victims, they were forced to pay large fines or had their income drastically reduced. And many industrialists were relocated inland with their families when their factories were removed from Shanghai. I did not voluntarily change my way of life, not only because I had the means to maintain my standard of living, but also because the Shanghai municipal government treated me with courtesy and consideration through its United Front Organization. However, my daughter and I lived quietly, with circumspection. Believing the Communist Revolution a historical inevitability for China, we were prepared to go along with it.

The reason I am so often carried back to those few hours before midnight on July 3, 1966, is not only that I look back with nostalgia upon my old life with my daughter but mainly that they were the last few hours of normal life I was to enjoy for many years. The heat lay like a heavy weight on the city even at night. No breeze came through the open windows. My face and arms were damp with perspiration, and my blouse was clammy on my back as I bent over the newspapers spread on my desk reading the articles of vehement denunciation that always preceded action at the beginning of a political movement. The propaganda effort was supposed to create a suitable atmosphere of tension and mobilize the public. Often careful reading of those articles, written by activists selected by Party officials, yielded hints as to the purpose of the movement and its possible victims. Because I had never been involved in a political movement before, I had no premonition of impending personal disaster. But as was always the case, the violent language used in the propaganda articles made me uneasy.

My servant Lao-zhao had left a thermos of iced tea for me on a tray on the coffee table. As I drank the refreshing tea, my eyes strayed to a photograph of my late husband. Nearly nine years had passed since he died, but the void his death left in my heart remained. I always felt abandoned and alone whenever I was uneasy about the political situation, as I felt the need for his support.

I had met my husband when he was working for his Ph.D. degree in London in 1935. After we were married and returned to Chongqing, China's wartime capital, in 1939, he became a diplomatic officer of the Kuomintang government. In 1949, when the Communist army entered Shanghai, he was director of the Shanghai office of the Ministry of Foreign Affairs of the Kuomintang government. When the Communist representative, Zhang Hanfu, took over his office, Zhang invited him to remain with the new government during the transitional period as foreign affairs adviser to the newly appointed mayor of Shanghai, Marshal Chen Yi. In the following year, he was allowed to leave the People's Government and accept an offer from Shell International Petroleum Company to become the general manager of its Shanghai office. Shell was one of the few British firms of international standing—such as Imperial Chemical Industries, Hong Kong–Shanghai Banking Corporation, and Jardines—that tried to maintain an office in Shanghai. Because Shell was the only major oil company in the world wishing to remain in mainland China, the Party officials who favored trade with the West treated the company and ourselves with courtesy.

In 1957, my husband died of cancer. A British general manager was appointed to succeed him. I was asked by Shell to become his assistant with the title of adviser to management. I worked in that capacity until 1966.

Successive British general managers depended on me to steer the company clear of the many pitfalls that often surrounded a capitalist enterprise maintaining an office in Maoist China. It was up to me to find ways to resolve problems without either sacrificing the dignity of Shell or causing the Chinese officials to lose face. My job was to manage the staff and act as liaison between the general manager and the Shell Labor Union, analyzing the union demands and working out compromises. I drafted the company's more important correspondence with the Chinese government agencies, which had to be in the Chinese language. Whenever the general manager went on home leave or to Beijing for talks with Chinese government corporations, I acted as general manager. I thought myself fortunate to have a job I could do well and enjoyed the distinction of being the only woman in Shanghai occupying a senior position in a company of world renown.

In the spring of 1966, Shell closed its Shanghai office after negotiating an "Assets against Liability Agreement" with a Chinese government agency. We handed over our assets in China, and the Chinese government agency took over our staff with the commitment to give them employment and provide retirement pensions. As a member of management, I was not included in the agreement; its scope was limited to our staff who belonged to the Shell Labor Union, a branch of the Shanghai Labor Union, which is a government organization for the control of industrial and office workers.

When the agreement was signed, my daughter, a young actress of the Shanghai Film Studio, was performing with her unit in North China. I thought I would make a trip to Hong Kong when she came back. But while I was waiting for her return, the Cultural Revolution was launched. My daughter's group was hastily summoned back to Shanghai by the film studio to enable its members to take part in the Cultural Revolution. Since I knew that during a political movement government officials were reluctant to make decisions and that work in government departments generally slowed down, if not came to a complete standstill, I decided not to apply for a travel permit to Hong Kong and risk a refusal. A refusal would go into the personal dossier that the police kept on everyone. It might make future application difficult. So I remained in Shanghai, believing the Cultural Revolution would last no longer than a year, the usual length of time for a political campaign.

The tea cooled me somewhat. I got up to go into my bedroom next door, had a shower, and lay down on my bed. In spite of the heat, I dropped off to sleep. The next thing I knew, Chen-ma, my maid, was gently shaking me to wake me up.

I looked at the clock on my bedside table. It was only half past six, but sunlight was already on the awning outside the windows, and the temperature in the room was rising.

"Qi and another man from your old office have come to see you," Chen-ma said.

"What do they want?" I asked her drowsily.

"They didn't say. But they behaved in a very unusual manner.

They marched straight into the living room and sat down on the sofa instead of waiting in the hall as they used to do before the office closed."

"Who is the other man?" I asked as I headed for the bathroom. Qi, I knew, was the vice-chairman of our office branch of the Shanghai Labor Union. I had often conducted negotiations with him as part of my job. He had seemed a nice man: reasonable and conciliatory.

"I don't know his name. He hasn't been here before. I think he may be one of the guards," Chen-ma said. "He's tall and thin."

From Chen-ma's description, I thought the man was one of the activists of the Shell union. We had no Party members. From the way the few activists in our office behaved, I knew they were encouraged to act as watchdogs for the Shanghai Labor Union. Since I had no direct contact with the activists, who were mostly guards or cleaners, I learned of their activities mainly from the department heads.

There was a knock on the door. Lao-zhao, my manservant, handed Chen-ma a tray and said through the half-open door, "They say the mistress must hurry."

"All right, Lao-zhao," I said. "Tell them I'll be down presently. Give them a cold drink and some cigarettes."

I did not hurry. I wanted time to think and be ready to cope with whatever was coming. The visit of these two men at this early hour of the morning was unusual. However, in China, when one had to attend a meeting to hear a lecture or political indoctrination, one was seldom told in advance. The officials assumed that everybody should drop everything whenever called upon to do so. I wondered whether these two men had come to ask me to join one of their political indoctrination lectures. I knew the Shanghai Labor Union was organizing classes for the ex-staff of Shell so that they could be prepared for their assignment to work with lower pay in government organizations.

While I ate toast and drank my tea, I reviewed the events leading to the closure of the Shell office and reexamined my own behavior throughout the negotiations between the company and the Chinese government agency. Although I had accompanied the general manager to all the sessions, I had not taken part in any of the discussions. It was my job only to observe and advise the general manager afterwards, when we returned to our office. I decided that if I was asked questions concerning Shell I could always procrastinate by offering to write to London for information.

I put on a white cotton shirt, a pair of gray slacks, and black sandals, the clothes Chinese women wore in public places to avoid being conspicuous. As I went downstairs I reflected that those who sent the men to call on me so early in the morning probably hoped to disconcert me. I walked slowly, deliberately creating the impression of composure.

When I entered the living room, I saw that both men were sprawled on the sofa with a glass of orangeade untouched on the table in front of each of them. When he saw me, Qi stood up from force of habit, but when he saw that the activist remained seated, he went red in the face with embarrassment and hastily sat down again. It was a calculated gesture of discourtesy on the part of the other man to remain seated when I entered the room. In 1949, not long after the Communist army entered Shanghai, the new policeman in charge of the area in which I lived had made the first of his periodic unannounced visits to our house. He brushed past Lao-zhao at the front door, marched straight into the living room, where I was, and spat on the carpet. That was the first time I saw a declaration of power made in a gesture of rudeness. Since then, I had come to realize that the junior officers of the Party often used the exaggerated gesture of rudeness to cover up their feeling of inferiority.

I ignored Qi's confusion and the other man's rudeness, sat down on a straight-backed chair, and calmly asked them, "Why have you come to see me so early in the morning?"

"We have come to take you to a meeting," Qi said.

"You have been so slow that we will probably be late," the other man added and stood up.

"What's the meeting about?" I asked. "Who has organized it? Who has sent you to ask me to participate?"

"There's no need to ask so many questions. We would not be here if we did not have authority. All the former members of Shell have to attend this meeting. It's very important," the activist said. In a tone of exasperation, he added, "Don't you know the Great Proletarian Cultural Revolution has started?"

"What has a cultural revolution got to do with us? We worked for a commercial firm, not a cultural establishment," I said.

"Chairman Mao has said that everybody in China must take part in the Cultural Revolution," Qi said.

They both said rather impatiently, "We are late. We must leave at once."

Qi also stood up. I looked at the carriage clock on the mantelpiece; it was a quarter past eight.

Chen-ma was waiting in the hall with my handbag and a navy blue silk parasol. As I took them from her I smiled, but she did not smile back. She was staring at me anxiously, obviously worried.

"I'll be back for lunch," I tried to reassure her.

She merely nodded.

Lao-zhao was standing beside the open front gate. He also looked anxious but said nothing, simply closing the gate behind us.

The apprehension of my servants was completely understandable. We all knew that during the seventeen years of Mao Zedong's rule innumerable people had left their homes during political campaigns and had never come back.

There were few people in the streets, but the bus was crowded with solemn-looking passengers. It took a circuitous route, so that we did not get to our destination until after nine o'clock.

A number of young men and women were gathered in front of the technical school where the meeting was to be held. When they caught sight of us approaching from the bus stop, a few ran into the building shouting, "They have come! They have come!"

A man came out and said to my escorts irritably, "Why have you been so long? The meeting was called for eight o'clock."

The two men turned their heads in my direction and said, "Ask her!" before hurrying into the building.

This man now said to me, "Come this way." I followed him into the meeting room.

The large room was already packed with people. Among those seated on narrow wooden benches in front of the assembly, I saw Shell's physician and other senior members of the staff. The drivers, guards, elevator operators, cleaners, and clerks sat behind them among a large number of young people who were probably the students of the school. Quite a number stood in the aisles and in the space at the back of the hall. Hot sun streamed into the stifling room through bare windows, but very few people were using their fans. The atmosphere in the room was tense and expectant.

Although we had worked in the same office and seen one another daily for almost nine years, not one of the senior staff greeted me or showed any sign of recognition when I brushed past them to take up the seat allocated to me in the second row. Most of the men averted their eyes; the few whose gaze met mine looked deeply troubled.

I wondered what these men had been through in the months since Shell had closed its office. They were the real losers in the "Assets against Liability Agreement" reached between Shell and the People's Government agency authorized to take them over. Nearly all the men had been with Shell for a very long time, some since the 1920s. During the Japanese occupation of Shanghai, some of them made the long and arduous journey from Shanghai to the company's office in the wartime capital of Chongqing, abandoning home and family; others remained in the city and suffered great economic hardship rather than work for the Japanese oil company that had taken over Shell's premises. Most of the men were nearly sixty and approaching retirement. The agreement specified that they were all to be given jobs in Chinese organizations. What was not mentioned was that they would not be given jobs commensurate with their former positions in Shell but would be employed as clerks or translators at a low rate of pay with much-reduced retirement pensions. None of them had dared to oppose the terms of the agreement since it was what the government wanted them to accept. Both the last general manager and I tried to obtain assurances from the union chairman, but we were told that every member of our staff was pleased with the terms of the agreement.

At my last meeting with the Shell union chairman, he had said to me, "Everybody is extremely pleased at the prospect of being freed from the anomalous position of working for a foreign firm. They all look forward to making a contribution to socialism as workers of a government organization." That was the official line, in which even the union chairman himself could not possibly have believed. Senior members of the staff who came to my office during those last days would shake their heads and murmur sadly, *"Meiyou fazi!"*—a very common Chinese phrase meaning, "Nothing can be done," or "It's hopeless," or "No way out," or "There's no solution."

From nine o'clock to lunchtime, when the meeting might be adjourned, was more than three hours. The room was bound to get a great deal hotter as time went on. I knew I had to conserve energy while waiting for events to speak for themselves. The narrow wooden bench was just as uncomfortable as the one I had sat on during the war in a cave in Chongqing while Japanese planes rained incendiary bombs on the city. Perspiration was running down my face. I opened my bag to get a handkerchief. I saw that Chen-ma had put in it a small folding fan made of sandalwood with a painting of a peony on silk done by my painting teacher. I took it out and fanned myself to clear the air of the unpleasant odor of packed humanity.

Suddenly there was a commotion at the rear. Several men dressed in short-sleeved shirts and baggy cotton trousers came through the door at the back and mounted the low platform. One of them came forward to a small table covered with a white cloth while the others sat down in the row of chairs behind him. One could no longer assess a man's station in life by his clothes in China because everybody tried to dress like a proletarian, a word the Chinese translated as *wuchanzhe*, which meant "a man with no property." To look poor was both safe and fashionable for the Chinese people. So, while I could not tell the approximate rank or position of the man in charge of the meeting, I thought he must be an official of the Shanghai Labor Union.

"Comrades!" he said. "Our Great Leader Chairman Mao has initiated and is now personally directing the Great Proletarian Cultural Revolution. With our Great Helmsman to guide us, we shall proceed to victory without hindrance. The situation is excellent for us, the proletariat!

"The Great Proletarian Cultural Revolution is an opportunity for all of us to study the Thought of Mao Zedong more thoroughly and diligently than ever before so that our political awareness is sharpened. Only then can we truly differentiate between those who are in the ranks of the People and those who are on the side of the Enemy.

"The enemies of socialism are cunning. Some of them raise

the red flag to oppose the red flag, while others present us with smiling faces to cover up their dirty schemes. They cooperate with the imperialists abroad and the capitalist class within to try to sabotage socialism and lead the Chinese people backwards to the misery and suffering of the old days. Should we allow them to succeed? Of course not! No! A hundred times no!

"It's seventeen years since the people of Shanghai were liberated. Yet, until recently, foreign firms remained in our city. Their offices occupied prominent locations, and their cars sped through our streets. The foreigners and the few Chinese who forgot their national identity and worked with them swaggered around with insolence. We all know these firms were agents of the imperialists, who hoped to continue their exploitation of the Chinese people. We could not tolerate this state of affairs, so we have closed their doors and thrown out the foreigners. Most of the Chinese on their staffs have been contaminated, and their way of thinking is confused. But we must also recognize the fact that some of them are downright reactionaries. It's our job to implement our Great Leader Chairman Mao's policy of educating and reforming them. For several months we have conducted political indoctrination classes for them. But no one can be reformed if he himself does not come face to face with reality and recognize and admit the facts of his own mistakes. Self-criticism and confession are the first steps towards reform. In order to make a real effort at self-criticism, a man must be helped by the criticism of others. Today's meeting is called to criticize Tao Feng and to hear his self-criticism.

"You all know who Tao Feng is. For nearly thirty-five years he was a faithful running dog of Shell Petroleum Company, which is an international corporation of gigantic size with tendrils reaching into every corner of the world to suck up profit. This, according to Lenin, is the worst form of capitalist enterprise.

"Capitalism and socialism are like fire and water. They are diametrically opposed. Tao Feng could not have served the interests of the British firm and remained a good Chinese citizen under socialism. For a long time we have tried to help him see the light . . ."

I was surprised to learn that Tao Feng, the former chief accountant of our office, was the target of the meeting, because I had always thought the Party looked upon him with favor. His eldest son had been sent to both the Soviet Union and Czechoslovakia for advanced studies at the government's expense in the fifties, and the young man had later joined the Party. I knew that when a student was selected to go abroad, the Party always made a thorough investigation of his background, including his father's character, occupation, and political viewpoint. Tao Feng must have passed this test at the time his son was sent abroad. I could not understand why he had now been singled out for criticism.

Since the very beginning of the Communist regime, I had carefully studied books on Marxism and pronouncements by Chinese Communist Party leaders. It seemed to me that socialism in China was still very much an experiment and no fixed course of development for the country had yet been decided upon. This, I thought, was why the government's policy was always changing, like a pendulum swinging from left to right and back again. When things went to extremes and problems emerged, Beijing would take corrective measures. Then these very corrective measures went too far and had to be corrected. The real difficulty was, of course, that a state-controlled economy stifled productivity, and economic planning from Beijing ignored local conditions and killed incentive.

When a policy changed from above, the standard of values changed with it. What was right yesterday became wrong today, and vice versa. Thus the words and actions of a Communist Party official at the lower level were valid for a limited time only. So I decided the meeting I was attending was not very important and that the speaker was just a minor Party official assigned to conduct the Cultural Revolution for the former staff of Shell. The Cultural Revolution seemed to me to be a swing to the left. Sooner or later, when it had gone too far, corrective measures would be taken. The people would have a few months or a few years of respite until the next political campaign. Mao Zedong believed that political campaigns were the motivating force for progress. So I thought the Proletarian Cultural Revolution was just one of an endless series of upheavals the Chinese people must learn to put up with.

I looked around the room while listening with one ear to the speaker's tirade. It was then that I noticed the banner on the wall that said, "Down with the running dog of imperialism Tao Feng." The two characters of his name were crossed with red X's to indicate he was being denounced as an enemy. This banner had escaped my notice when I entered the room because there were so many banners with slogans of the Cultural Revolution covering the walls. Slogans were an integral part of life in China. They exalted Mao Zedong, the Party, socialism, and anything else the Party wanted the people to believe in; they exhorted the people to work hard, to study Mao Zedong Thought, and to obey the Party. When there was a political campaign, the slogans denounced the enemies. Since the beginning of the Cultural Revolution, the number of slogans everywhere had multiplied by the thousand. It was impossible to read all that one encountered. It was very easy to look at them without really seeing what was written.

The man was now talking about Tao's decadent way of life resulting from long association with capitalism. It seemed he was guilty of having extramarital relations, drinking wine and spirits to excess, and enjoying elaborate meals, all acts of self-indulgence frowned upon by the Party. These accusations did not surprise me, because I knew that when a man was denounced, he was depicted as totally bad and any errant behavior was attributed to the influence of capitalism.

When the man had thoroughly dissected Tao's private life and exposed the corrosive effect of capitalism on him, his tone and manner became more serious. He turned to the subject of imperialism and aggression against China by foreign powers. To him Tao's mistakes were made not because he was a greedy man with little self-control but because he had worked for a firm that belonged to a nation guilty of acts of aggression against the Chinese people more than a hundred years ago. He was talking about the Opium War of 1839–42 as if it had taken place only the year before.

Though he used the strong language of denunciation and often raised his voice to shout, he delivered his speech in a leisurely manner, pausing frequently either to drink water or to consult his notes. He knew he had a captive audience, since no one would dare to leave while the meeting was going on. A Party official, no matter how lowly his rank, was a representative of the Party. When he spoke, it was the Party speaking. It was unthinkable not to appear attentive. However, he had been speaking for a long time. The room had become unbearably hot, and the audience was getting restive. I looked at my watch and found it was nearly twelve o'clock. Perhaps the speaker was also tired and hungry, for he suddenly stopped and told us the meeting was adjourned until one-thirty. Everybody was up and heading for the exits even before he had quite finished speaking.

Outside, the midday sun beat relentlessly down on the hot pavement. In the distance, I saw a pedicab parked in the shade of a tree. I ran to it and gave the driver my address, promising him double fare to encourage him to move away quickly.

The man who had led me into the building in the morning dashed outside, shouting for me to stop. He wanted me to remain there and eat something from the school kitchen so that I would not be late again. So anxious was he to detain me that he grabbed the side of the pedicab. I had to promise him repeatedly that I would be back on time before he let go.

My little house, shaded with awnings on the windows and green bamboo screens on the verandah, was a haven after that hot, airless meeting hall. The back of my shirt was wet through, and I was parched. I had a quick shower, drank a glass of iced tea, and enjoyed the delicious meal my excellent cook had prepared for me. Then I lay down on my bed for half an hour's rest before setting out again in the pedicab, which I had asked to wait for me.

When I got to the meeting hall I was a little late, but by no means the last to arrive. I found a seat in the second row next to a pillar so that I could lean against it when I got too tired and needed support. I had brought along a shopping bag in which I had put a bottle of water and a glass, as well as two bars of chocolate. Secure in the knowledge that I had come well prepared, I settled down to wait, wondering what the speaker was leading up to.

The hall gradually filled. At two o'clock, the same number of men mounted the platform and took up their positions. The speaker beckoned to someone at the back. I was astonished to see Tao Feng being led into the room wearing a tall dunce cap made of white paper with "cow's demon and snake spirit" written on it. If it had not been for the extremely troubled expression on his face, he would have looked comical.

In Chinese mythology, "cow's demon and snake spirit" are evil spirits who can assume human forms to do mischief, but when recognized by real humans as devils they revert to their original shapes. Mao Zedong had first used this expression to describe the intellectuals during the Anti-Rightist Campaign of 1957. He had said that the intellectuals were like evil spirits in human form when they pretended to support the Communist Party. When they criticized the Party's policy, they reverted to their original shapes and were exposed as evil spirits. Since that time, quick to adopt the language of Mao, Party officials had used the phrase for anyone considered politically deceitful. During the Cultural Revolution it was applied to all the so-called nine categories of enemies: former landlords denounced in the Land Reform Movement of 1950–52; rich peasants denounced in the Formation of Rural Cooperatives Movement of 1955; counterrevolutionaries denounced in the Suppression of Counterrevolutionaries Campaign of 1950 and Elimination of Counterrevolutionaries Campaign of 1955; "bad elements" arrested from time to time since the Communist Party came to power; rightists denounced in the Anti-Rightist Campaign of 1957; traitors (Party officials suspected of having betrayed Party secrets during imprisonment by the Kuomintang); spies (men and women with foreign connections); "capitalist-roaders" (Party officials not following the strict leftist policy of Mao but taking the "capitalist road"); and intellectuals with bourgeois family origins.

Often the phrase was shortened to just "cows," and the places in which these political outcasts were confined during the Cultural Revolution were generally referred to as "cowsheds." As the scale of persecution expanded, every organization in China had rooms set aside as "cowsheds," and the Revolutionaries of each organization had full power to deal with the "cows" confined therein. Inhuman treatment and cruel methods were employed to force the "cows" to confess. In many instances, they fared worse than those incarcerated in regular prisons.

How changed Tao Feng looked! When we were working in the same office, he was always full of self-assurance. Now he looked nervous and thoroughly beaten. He had lost a great deal of weight and seemed years older than only a few months ago. The young people behind me snickered. When Tao was brought to the platform, the crowd at the back stood up to have a better view and knocked over some benches. So a man pushed a chair forward on the platform and told Tao Feng to stand on it. When Tao climbed onto the chair and stood there in a posture of subservience in his tall paper hat, the snickers became uncontrolled laughter.

Someone in a corner of the room, obviously planted there for the purpose, stood up. Holding the Little Red Book of Mao Zedong's quotations (so called because of its red plastic cover), which everybody had to have by his side, he raised it high in the air and led the assembly to shout slogans.

"Down with Tao Feng!"

"Down with the running dog of the imperialists, Tao Feng!"

"Down with the imperialists!"

"Down with the capitalist class!"

"Long live the Great Proletarian Cultural Revolution!"

"Long live our Great Leader Chairman Mao!"

The sound of laughter was now drowned in the thunder of voices. Everybody got to his feet shouting and waving the Little Red Book of Mao's quotations. I had not brought along my copy. Embarrassed by my oversight, I was slow to get to my feet. Besides, I was shocked and surprised to see Tao Feng raising his fist and shouting with gusto the same slogans, including those against himself. By the time I had collected my fan, my bag, my bottle of water, and the glass from my lap, placed them on the bench, and stood up, the others had already finished and had sat down. So I had to pick up my things again and resume my seat. The man sitting next to me was glaring at me with disapproval. He shifted sideways away from me as if he feared contamination by my bad behavior.

When the crowd had demonstrated its anger at and disapproval of the culprit, he was allowed to come down from the chair. As he bent his head to step down, the paper hat fell off. There was renewed laughter from the young students. Tao stared at the man in charge of the meeting with fear in his eyes, obviously afraid of being accused of deliberately dropping the hat. He heaved a sigh of relief when another man picked it up and placed it on the table.

The man in charge of the meeting called upon other members of the company's staff, including the two men who had come to my house in the morning and some junior clerks in Tao Feng's accounting department, to come forward to speak. One by one they marched to the platform and expressed anger and indignation, repeating the same accusations against Tao Feng made by the speaker during the morning session. The scope and degree of criticism was, I knew, always set by the Party official. It was just as ill advised to try to be original and say something different as not to criticize enough. The Chinese people had learned by experience that the Party trusted them more and liked them better if they didn't think for themselves but just repeated what the Party told them. The criticism of Tao Feng by other members of our former staff went on for a long time. All those who were allowed to speak were workers or junior clerks. None of the senior members of our former staff participated. They sat silently with heads bowed.

Finally the man in charge of the meeting took over again. He told the audience that after several weeks of reeducation and "help" by activists, Tao had finally recognized the fact that he was a victim of capitalism and imperialism. Turning to Tao, the man asked in a voice a stern schoolteacher might have used to address a pupil caught in an act of mischief, "Isn't it so? It was the high salary paid you by the foreign imperialists that turned you into their slave! You sold yourself to them and were ready to do any dirty work for them because of the high salary you received and the money they promised you. Isn't this the case?"

There was a hush in the room as everyone waited for Tao's reaction. But there was no dramatic, tearful declaration of repentance. He merely nodded his head, looking more dejected than ever.

I thought Tao Feng very stupid to agree that he had sold himself for money, because this admission could open the way to all sorts of more serious accusations from which he might find it difficult to disentangle himself. It seemed to me it would have been much better and certainly more truthful to explain that Shell paid its Shanghai staff the same salary after the Communist Party took over the city as it had done before. Since the government did not intervene, naturally the question of reducing the pay of the staff did not arise. What he could also have said tactfully was that working for a foreign firm did not carry with it the personal prestige enjoyed by government workers serving

the people—a point the Party officials would have found hard to
refute.

"Tao Feng will now make his self-criticism," the man announced.

Still in a posture of obsequiousness and without once lifting
his eyes to look at the audience, Tao took a few sheets of paper
from his pocket and started to read a prepared statement in a
low voice devoid of emotion. He admitted humbly all the
"crimes" listed by the speakers and accepted the verdict that his
downfall was due to the fact that he did not have sufficient
socialist awareness. He expressed regret for having worked for
a foreign firm for more than thirty-five years and said that he had
wasted his life. He declared that he was ashamed he had been
blinded by capitalist propaganda and enslaved by the good
treatment Shell had given him. He begged the proletariat to
forgive him and give him a chance to repent. He mentioned the
fact that his son was a Party member and had been educated
abroad at government expense. His own life of depravity, he
said, was an act of gross ingratitude to the People's Government. He assured the assembly that he now recognized the
dastardly schemes of the foreign capitalists and imperialists
against Communist China and would do his best to lay bare their
dirty game in order to show his true repentance. He said he was
in the process of writing a detailed confession of criminal deeds
he had committed for Shell, which he would present to the
officials "helping" him with his reeducation.

It was a long statement full of self-abuse and exaggeration. At
times his voice trembled, and sometimes he opened his mouth
but no words came. When he turned the pages, his hands shook.
I did not believe his nervousness was entirely due to fear, since
he must have known that he was not guilty of any real crime.
After all, Shell had remained in China because the People's
Government had allowed, even wanted, it to be there. And I
knew that the company had been scrupulously correct in observing Chinese government regulations. Tao must have known this
too. I thought his chief problem was mental and physical exhaustion. To bring him to his knees and to make sure that he
submitted readily, those who "helped" him must have spent
days, if not weeks, constantly questioning him, taking turns to
exert pressure on him without allowing him to sleep. It was

common knowledge that in these circumstances the victim broke down and submitted when he was on the verge of physical collapse and mental confusion. The Maoists named these inhuman tactics "exhaustive bombardment." Many people I knew, including my own brother, had experienced it during the Anti-Rightist Campaign of 1957. The Party officials remained in the background while the activists carried out their orders. When there was excessive cruelty that resulted in death, the officials would disclaim responsibility for an "accident" resulting from "mass enthusiasm."

When Tao had finished, the speaker told the audience that he would be watched to see if his words were spoken in true sincerity. He added that his was only the first meeting of its kind to be held. There were many others like Tao to be dealt with, and Tao himself might speak again. Here he paused momentarily and swept the audience with his eyes. Did I merely imagine that his gaze seemed to linger for a fraction of a moment in my direction? He concluded that it was the duty of the proletariat to cleanse socialist China of all residue of imperialist influence and punish the enemies of the people. Again I thought he turned his gaze in my direction.

I certainly did not think I was important enough for this whole show to have been put on solely for my benefit. But if it was, it failed to frighten me. The emotion my first experience of a "struggle meeting" generated in me was one of disgust and shame that such an act of barbarism against a fellow human being could have taken place in my beloved native land, with a history of five thousand years of civilization. As a Chinese, I felt degraded.

There was more shouting of slogans, but everybody was already on his feet moving towards the door.

The same man who tried to keep me from going home for lunch was waiting in the passage. He said to me, "Will you come this way for a moment? Some comrades would like to have a word with you."

I followed him to one of the classrooms, where the students' chairs and desks were piled up in one corner. The man in charge of the meeting and another one who had been on the platform were seated by the teacher's desk. There was a vacant chair. They motioned me to sit in it.

"Did you hear everything at the meeting?" the man in charge asked me.

I nodded.

"What did you think of the meeting? I believe this is the first time you have attended one of this kind."

Obviously I couldn't reveal what I really thought of the meeting, nor did I want to lie and flatter him. So I said, "May I ask you some questions that have been in my mind the whole day?"

He looked annoyed but said, "Go ahead."

"What organization do you represent? What authority do you have to call a meeting like this? Besides the ex-staff of Shell, who were the others present?"

Clearly he resented my questioning his authority. Making a visible effort to control himself, he said, "We represent the proletarian class. The meeting was authorized by the committee in charge of the conduct of the Proletarian Cultural Revolution in Shanghai."

I asked him to explain the purpose of the Proletarian Cultural Revolution. He said that it was a revolution to cleanse Chinese society of factors that hindered the growth of socialism. He repeated an often quoted saying of Mao Zedong: "If poisonous weeds are not removed, scented flowers cannot grow." He told me that everybody in China without exception had to take part in the Great Proletarian Cultural Revolution.

"You must assume a more sincere attitude and make a determined effort to emulate Tao Feng and do your best to reform," he said.

"I'm not aware of any wrongdoing on my part," I said, my voice registering surprise.

"Perhaps you'll change your attitude when you have had time to think things over," said the second man. "If you try to cover up for the imperialists, the consequences will be serious."

"What is there to cover up? Every act of the imperialists is clearly recorded in our history books," I answered.

The man raised his voice. "What are you talking about? We are not concerned with what happened in the past. We are talking about now, about the firm you worked for. Tao has already confessed everything. We know the Shell office in Shanghai 'hung up a sheep's head to sell dog's meat' [a Chinese expression meaning that the outward appearance of something is not the same as the reality]. We are also clear in our mind about the important role you played in their dirty game. You must not take us for fools."

"I'm completely at a loss as to what you're referring to," I said. "As far as I know, the company I worked for never did anything either illegal or immoral. The People's Government has an excellent police force. Surely if anything had been wrong it would have been discovered long ago."

Both men glared at me. Almost simultaneously they shouted, "You are trying to cover up for the imperialists!"

I said indignantly, "You misunderstand me. I'm merely stating the facts as I know them. Why should I cover up for anybody? Shell's Shanghai office is closed, and the British general manager has left. No one needs my protection."

"Yes, yes, the British general manager has gone, but you are still here. You know just as much as he did. Your husband held the post of general manager for many years. After he died you joined the firm. You certainly know everything about it."

"It's precisely because I know everything about the Shanghai office of Shell that I know it never did anything wrong," I said.

The other man intervened. "I suggest you go home now and think things over. We'll call you when we want to speak to you again. What's your telephone number?"

I gave them my number and left the room.

Outside, it was already dusk. There was a pleasant breeze. I decided to walk home on the tree-lined sidewalks by a round-about route to get some exercise and to think things over.

When I passed the No. 1 Medical College, I saw my friend Winnie emerging from the half-closed gate, followed by a number of her colleagues. We waved to each other, and she joined me to walk home, as she lived in the vicinity of my house.

"Why are you out walking at this time of the evening?" Winnie asked me.

"I've just attended a struggle meeting. I've been told to take part in the Proletarian Cultural Revolution."

"Is that because Shell has closed its Shanghai office? Tell me about it."

"I will. Can you join me for dinner?" I asked her. It would be good to hear what Winnie had to say about my experience. She had been through quite a number of political movements and was more experienced than I was in dealing with the situation, I thought.

"All right. I'll phone home from your house. Henry comes home very late these days. He has to pay a price for being a professor whenever there is a political campaign. Professors always seem to become the targets," Winnie said. Henry, her husband, taught architecture at Tongji University.

"Is Henry in trouble?" I inquired anxiously.

"No, not so far, thank God," Winnie replied, taking a comb out of her bag to smooth her hair. "Your servants will have a fit if they see me coming to dinner looking so disheveled."

Though she was over forty-five and had three sons, Winnie had kept her slim figure and managed to look attractive in the ill-fitting Mao jacket and baggy trousers she was obliged to wear as a teacher of English and Latin at the medical college. After getting a degree in English literature at a New England women's college, she and her husband, a graduate of Britain's Cambridge University, returned to China at the end of the Sino-Japanese War. Henry was appointed professor of architecture at Tongji University and soon became dean of the department. But in those days of galloping inflation, the salary of a professor could not keep pace with rising prices. To supplement the family income, Winnie gave Chinese lessons to Europeans living in Shanghai. Disillusioned by the inability of the Kuomintang government to cope with pressing postwar economic problems and institute reform, they welcomed the Communist takeover in 1949 as an opportunity for peace and stability.

In those days, because of the Kuomintang blackout of all news about the Communist area, very few Chinese living in Shanghai had any real understanding of Marxism, the Chinese Communist Party, or Mao Zedong. Almost no one knew about the persecution of intellectuals carried out in Yanan in 1942 or the periodic witch-hunts for "spies of the Kuomintang and the imperialists" in the Communist Party and army. The only source of information for Chinese intellectuals about the Chinese Communist Party before 1949 had been the glowing accounts written by some Western journalists and writers who made fleeting visits to the Communist-held area of China. Most of these men were liberal idealists. They were impressed by the austerity, discipline, and singleness of purpose of the Communist leaders, but they did not have a deep understanding of either the character of these men or the philosophy that motivated them. When the Communist Party intensified its propaganda effort through its underground in Kuomintang-governed cities prior to the final military push to take over the country, its promises of peaceful national reconstruction, of a united front including all sections of Chinese society, and of a democratic form of government sounded an attractive alternative to the corrupt and ineffectual rule of the Kuomintang. And the Chinese intellectuals accepted the propaganda effort as a sincere and honest declaration of policy by the Chinese Communist Party.

After the Communist army took over Shanghai, women were encouraged to take jobs. Winnie became a teacher at the medical college in 1950. In the following year, Mao Zedong, anxious to put all universities under Party control, initiated the Thought Reform Movement. Winnie and Henry had their first rude awakening. Although they both survived this campaign more or less unscathed, they suffered the humiliating experience of having to make self-criticism of their family background, their education abroad, and their outlook on life as reflected in Henry's architectural designs and in their teaching methods. Repeatedly they had to write their life histories critically; each time, the Party representative demanded a more self-searching effort. At the end of their grueling and degrading experience, Henry was judged unfit to continue as dean of the architectural department, which was now to use exclusively Soviet materials for teaching. Both Chinese traditional work and architectural designs from the West were scorned as feudalistic and decadent.

After the Thought Reform Movement was concluded in 1951, Party secretaries were appointed to every level of university administration. They controlled every aspect of the life and work of the teaching staff, even though the majority of them had little education and had never been teachers. Henry and Winnie lived in premises assigned to them, accepted the salary given to them, did their work in the way the Party secretaries wanted. These two well-educated, lively, and imaginative young people, full of goodwill towards the Communist regime, were reduced by Mao Zedong's suspicion and abuse of the intellectuals to teaching machines. But they were the fortunate ones. Many others from universities all over China did not fare as well. Some were sent to labor camps, while others were thrown out of the universities altogether.

When the Korean War ended, Mao Zedong's witch-hunt for dissidents temporarily relaxed. Prime Minister Zhou Enlai, aware of the plight of the Chinese intellectuals, tried then to improve their condition. As a result of a more lenient policy, Henry and Winnie were given a more spacious apartment near my home. There were also fewer constraints placed on their professional activities. Winnie often dropped in to read the books and magazines I was able to have sent from Hong Kong and England through the office or to listen to my stereo records.

In 1956 Mao Zedong launched the campaign "Let a Hundred Flowers Bloom and Let a Hundred Schools of Thought Contend." The Party secretaries in every organization, and even Mao himself, urged the people to offer frank and constructive criticism of the Communist Party. Believing the Party sincere in wishing to improve its work, tens of thousands of intellectuals and more than a million Chinese in every walk of life poured out their grievances and suggestions. But Winnie and Henry refrained from speaking out. They escaped persecution when Mao Zedong swung his policy around in 1957 and initiated the Anti-Rightist Campaign. He labeled all those who had offered criticism "Rightists." Many of them lost their jobs, became nonpersons, and were sent to labor camps; others had their pay reduced and were demoted in rank. The treachery of Mao Zedong in repeatedly inviting frank and constructive criticism and then harshly punishing those who gave it completely cowed the Chinese intellectuals, so that China's cultural life came to a virtual standstill.

When Winnie and I reached my house, the front gate swung open before I pressed the bell. Lao-zhao was standing there anxiously waiting for my return. He told me my daughter had telephoned to say that she was not coming home for dinner.

"Please tell Cook Mrs. Huang is staying for dinner," I said to Lao-zhao and took Winnie upstairs to my bathroom.

Lao-zhao laid the table for two with white embroidered linen table mats. A bowl of white carnations was in the center of the dining table.

"Cook said it's steamed mandarin fish with a green salad. Is it all right?" Lao-zhao asked me. I was usually served either

Chinese- or European-style cooking, depending on what my cook was able to obtain at the market.

I looked at Winnie inquiringly, and she said, "That's fine. I love mandarin fish."

After we had sat down, Winnie looked up at the large painting of a female figure in pale blue by the famous painter Lin Fengmian, who was once the head of the Hangzhou Academy of Art. This painting was the decorative centerpiece of my blue-and-white dining room. It went well in color and style with the blue-and-white Xuande plate and Kangxi vase displayed on the blackwood sideboard.

"Have you heard? Lin Fengmian is in serious trouble," Winnie told me.

I was surprised. I knew the painter was earning large sums of foreign exchange for the People's Government, which bought his paintings for a paltry sum but sold them in Hong Kong for twenty or thirty times the amount.

"He is accused of promoting the decadent art form of the West. But a more serious charge is that he has maintained contact with people outside China and has given information to captains of foreign ships calling at Shanghai. The foreigners were observed coming to his home by his neighborhood activists."

"Well, his wife and daughter are in Brazil. Actually I know for a fact that the ships' captains came to buy his pictures," I said.

"Many other painters are in trouble too. Your old teacher, Miss Pang, is also being criticized. It's said she once painted a branch of the *meihua* tree [a flowering tree that blooms in late winter or early spring] hanging down rather than upright to symbolize the downfall of the Communist Party."

I laid down my fork and said to Winnie, "They are mad. In the paintings by old masters the *meihua* tree is often depicted hanging over a cliff. It isn't anything she has invented."

"Well, you know how it is. The Party officials in her organization have probably never seen any paintings by the old masters. Party officials in charge of artists are not required to know the difference between watercolors and lithographs. And most of them don't know."

Our conversation was so disheartening that it depressed our

appetites. We couldn't do justice to the delicious meal my cook gave us.

When we were drinking tea in the drawing room, I told Winnie about the struggle meeting I had just attended. After thinking it over, she said, "It seems you are going to be treated just like us now that Shell has closed its Shanghai office. No one outside China will know what happens to you."

"What do you think is the purpose of their getting me to attend the meeting?" I asked her.

"To frighten you, of course."

"I'm not easily frightened."

"That, I think, they don't know. All they know is that you are a rich woman who has led an easy life and who has never been involved in any political campaign before. They probably think you are easily frightened. As a rule they underestimate our courage."

"Why do you think they want to frighten me? What for?"

"That's very hard to say at this juncture. Whatever it is, be prepared for unpleasantness. Be alert and keep your mouth shut. Don't say anything inadvertent, whatever the provocation."

"What about yourself? How are you getting on?" I asked her.

"I'm worn out. We spend all our time at meetings or writing Big Character Posters. Classes have been suspended. Several professors and medical experts have already been denounced. The situation seems even more serious than in 1957 at the beginning of the Anti-Rightist Campaign."

"Are you likely to become an object of criticism?"

"Of course one can't be sure. But I don't think I'm important enough. I've been a junior lecturer for sixteen years, without promotion or a raise. I always humbly ask my Party secretary for instructions and never indulge in the luxury of taking the initiative. I carry out his instructions even when I know he is wrong. At indoctrination meetings I never speak unless told to do so. Then I simply repeat whatever was said by our group leader or the Party secretary. I think my behavior can be considered impeccable. Anyway, in the last analysis, the more senior you are the more likely you are to get into trouble. 'A big tree catches the wind' is a true saying."

"What about Henry?"

"I'm worried about Henry. I think he will be denounced as a 'cow's demon and snake spirit' like all the other professors and will be struggled against," Winnie said helplessly. Then she closed her eyes and sighed.

"I thought he never did anything apart from teaching or spoke a word outside the classroom anymore," I said.

"It's true. He has learned a lesson from all his friends who were labeled Rightists. But he's a full professor, for one thing. Moreover, his family used to be very rich. And his sister is in Taiwan."

"But you have no contact with his sister. You don't write to her."

"That doesn't matter. She is there and she is Henry's sister. If the Party wants to make an issue of it, we can't stop them."

Lao-zhao came in to fill our teacups.

"Cook would like to have a word with you before he goes home," Lao-zhao said.

"All right. Ask him to come in," I told him.

Both Cook and Lao-zhao came in.

"The vice-chairman of the Shell Labor Union, Qi, came again tonight just before you returned. He asked us to give you a message," the cook said.

"What did he say?"

"He told us to tell you to be careful when you talk to the Party officials. He said that after you left the meeting, they complained that you were rude to them. Qi wants you to know that the Party officials were annoyed," the cook said.

"Qi is a good man," Lao-zhao chipped in.

"A good man? You should have seen him denouncing Tao Feng at the struggle meeting!" His ugly performance was still in my mind.

"He can't help it. He had to do what he was told. If he weren't a good man, he wouldn't have bothered to come to give you this warning," Lao-zhao countered, defending Qi.

"You are right, Lao-zhao. I'll remember to be careful. It's good of Qi to have bothered to come. Thank you both for telling me this," I said to Lao-zhao and the cook.

After the servants had withdrawn, Winnie said, "They are right. You must be careful. It doesn't pay to offend the men directly in charge of you during a political campaign. They have absolute power to decide your fate. If they send you to a labor camp, you will have to go."

"How can they send me to a labor camp? Winnie," I said, "I don't even work for the government. Besides, I haven't broken the law!"

"Don't be naive! They can if they want to. You live here. You can't get out of the country. The only good thing about not working for the government is that they can't cut your pay."

Winnie got up to leave. I accompanied her to the front gate.

"Why didn't you go to Hong Kong when Shell applied to close the office last year?" Winnie asked me.

"How could I request such a thing? The general manager needed me during the negotiations. He didn't know the language. The whole thing was conducted in Chinese. I couldn't leave him holding the fort alone. Shell has treated me well. I couldn't let them down when they needed me," I said.

"I hope they appreciate your sense of duty. They can't help you now. You should have gone."

"I hope you and Henry will both come through this as well as you did the Anti-Rightist Campaign."

"I sometimes feel a real premonition of disaster," Winnie said sadly. "Think of all the years we spent just trying to survive!"

We stood outside my front gate to bid each other goodbye. After taking a few steps, Winnie turned and said to me, "I may not be able to come again until things clarify. Phone me if you need me."

"I understand. Take care of yourself!" I said.

"You too!" she said and waved.

After closing the front gate, I walked towards the house under a cloudless sky. A thousand stars were sparkling in space. It was a beautiful summer night.

Feeling tired and depressed, I went to my room to get ready for bed. My daughter came home while I was lying on my bed unable to sleep, with scenes of the day's events passing in front of my eyes.

"Mommy, Mommy!" she called as she mounted the stairs two steps at a time, just as she had as a teenager. I called out to say that I was in my bedroom. Chen-ma followed her into my room with a glass of milk and a plate of sandwiches on a tray.

"Goodness! I'm famished! I've had nothing to eat since breakfast." She picked up the glass and drank the milk. I saw that her fingers were stained with ink.

"Look at those fingers! Are you going to eat your sandwiches with inky fingers? You are already a twenty-three-year-old young lady, but you behave like a ten-year-old. In the old days, girls of your age were married and had two or three children already," scolded Chen-ma. As Chen-ma had been with us since my daughter was a small girl, she could chide her as an old servant would.

"Well, this isn't the old days anymore, dear Chen-ma, old-fashioned lady!" Meiping protested and went into my bathroom to wash her hands.

Chen-ma placed the sandwiches on the table and turned to leave the room. She said to me, "You don't have to worry about Lao-zhao, Cook, and me. We'll always stand by you."

"Thank you, Chen-ma, for your concern for me. Please tell Lao-zhao and Cook not to worry," I answered, deeply touched by her remark.

"We worry about you because you are alone. I wish the master were still with us," she murmured and shut the door behind her.

Chen-ma really was old-fashioned. In time of crisis she believed firmly in the superior ability of the male sex. In fact, I had been thinking of my husband as I lay on my bed in the darkened room before my daughter came back. For the first time since he died, I did not regret his death. I was thankful that he was to be spared the insults and persecution that would surely be directed against him if he were still alive.

With the bathroom door closed and the water running, my daughter did not hear our conversation. She was apparently having a shower.

My daughter Meiping was an attractive and intelligent young woman. In the course of growing up in Communist China, she had seen the disappearance of a society in which children of the educated and affluent had enjoyed many advantages. In its place was formed not an egalitarian society in which everyone enjoyed equal opportunity and status but a new system of discrimination against children like herself and their families. In each stage of her young life, she had been handicapped by her family background. For instance, to be admitted into a good middle school, she had to pass the entrance examination with marks of 80

percent, while children of workers and peasants got in with a
pass mark of 60.

"This is unfair!" I had exclaimed at the time, indignant that
my child was being discriminated against. "What is the reason
for such an unfair regulation?"

"Don't worry, Mommy! I can do it! I can get eighty! It isn't
hard," piped the twelve-year-old.

"It isn't fair!" I was still fuming.

"But, Mommy, the teacher told us the children of workers and
peasants have to do housework or cook the evening meal after
school. And their parents can't help them with homework. The
treatment I get is fair if you consider all that." She had learned
to be philosophical at a young age.

This kind of discrimination followed her in everything she
tried to do. Whenever she encountered it, she was made to feel
guilty and ashamed of her family background. She, and other
children like her, just had to try harder than the children of
workers and peasants. They learned from an early age that the
"classless" society of Communism was more rigidly stratified
than the despised capitalist system, where a man could move
from the lower to the upper class by his own effort. Because my
daughter had to try harder, she did well. In the prestigious No.
2 Municipal Girls' Middle School, she was a student leader and
won honors and prizes. She seemed happily adjusted and had
many friends, among them several children from working-class
families. Although she was by nature loving and generous, I
thought it was mainly the feeling of guilt instilled in her by
Communist propaganda about the rich exploiting the poor that
created in her the desire to help these children. She would bring
them home to share her food, help them with their studies, and
even go to their homes sometimes to assist them with their
chores. While I thought her activities rather commendable,
Chen-ma disapproved heartily, especially when she loaned her
clothes to other girls and then brought home the dirty laundry
for Chen-ma to wash.

From early childhood, she had shown an interest in music. We
bought her a piano and arranged for her to have private lessons
after school. When she was ten years old she became a member
of the Children's Palace in Shanghai, a sort of club for specially
selected schoolchildren who earned good marks in studies and

behavior. There she acted in plays and took part in musical activities. Being bilingual, she became one of the young interpreters whenever the Children's Palace had English-speaking visitors from abroad. Having learned to swim as a toddler in Australia, she was the unofficial swimming instructor of her class. When she was fifteen and in middle school, she was selected by the Shanghai Athletics Association for training with the Shanghai Rowing Club during the holidays and became cox for the first women's rowing team of Shanghai.

Although we lived in the midst of periodic political turmoil and were saddened by the personal tragedies of some of our friends and neighbors, I never had to worry about my daughter. I took it for granted that she would go to one of the better universities, be given a fairly good job upon graduation because of her good marks, and marry a nice young man. Her pay at work would be insignificant, but I could supplement her income with an allowance, as many other parents were doing in China.

I had hoped that after graduation she would be assigned a job in Shanghai so that she could live at home. But I couldn't be sure of that. I knew that young people with family backgrounds like hers were often deliberately sent to distant regions of China where living conditions were backward and extremely poor. This had happened to some of my friends' children. As I watched my daughter grow from a lanky teenager into a beautiful young woman, I wondered what was in store for her. However, when I felt optimistic, I would dream of converting the third floor of the house into a self-contained apartment for her and her family. The prospect of nursing a grandchild was immensely comforting to me. I gazed happily into the rosy future of my dream and could almost feel the warmth of the little creature in my arms.

It had been somewhat of a surprise when my daughter told me that two well-known film actresses, concurrently teachers in the newly established Film School of Shanghai, had approached her to suggest that she try for the entrance examination as a specially selected "talent." I could see she was flattered that she had been chosen. But I had hoped for something different for her, some work in which her intellectual power rather than her physical attributes would be an asset.

"The film school is on Hongqiao Road near the old golf club.

I can come home easily for weekends. And the two teachers told me all graduates will be given jobs in the Shanghai Film Studio. Actually the school is a subsidiary of the film studio. It has sent talent scouts all over the country to select students for the entrance examination. There is bound to be a big response because everyone wants to live in Shanghai," Meiping said.

"But do you really want to be a film actress?" I asked her.

"I don't mind. I can do it. It isn't hard." This was her standard response to any problem.

"I'm sure you can do it. But do you want to?" I believed this to be an important point. To be happy one should do the job one wants to do.

"Well, I never think of what I really want to do. It's no use thinking that way when I know the government is going to assign me a job. Thinking about what I really want to do only leads to disappointment. None of my friends think that way either," she said. "I'll just enjoy doing whatever the government wants me to do. If I try hard enough to do a job well, I generally end up liking it."

I suppose my daughter's attitude was sound under the circumstances. But could a man assigned to carry night soil as his lifelong occupation make himself like the job by working hard at it?

"So you have decided to try for the entrance examination?" I asked her.

"Yes, if you agree. The teachers spoke to me officially. It would be hard to say no without appearing unappreciative. Besides, I like the idea of working in Shanghai. I'd hate leaving you alone here and coming home only once a year for a few days at Chinese New Year," my daughter said.

"Yes, yes, darling, that's certainly an important point to consider. I would hate you to go into the interior to work." I agreed with her wholeheartedly.

So she went to the film school. Three years later she graduated and was given a job with the Shanghai Film Studio, which was run by the Bureau of Films of the Ministry of Culture.

The acting profession was somewhat glamorous even in Communist China, but those who worked in it did not receive higher pay or enjoy better working conditions than factory workers or teachers of the same age group. The function of an actress was primarily to bring entertainment to the masses, so besides appearing in films, she often gave performances in factories, rural communes, coal mines, and oilfields, traveling far and wide with her unit all over China. It was an arduous life. But she thought her experience enriched her understanding and knowledge of her own country and its people, and believed she was rendering service to them by giving them entertainment. For her, that was a meaningful way of life.

As she munched her sandwiches, she told me about the day's events at her film studio.

"I spent the whole day writing Big Character Posters for the Great Proletarian Cultural Revolution. We were told that the more Big Character Posters one writes, the more revolutionary enthusiasm one demonstrates, so everybody wrote and wrote until the notice board and all the wall space in our section were completely covered."

"Was that why you didn't come home for dinner?"

"We gave up having lunch and dinner to show our revolutionary zeal. Actually everyone was hungry, but nobody wanted to be the first to leave."

"What did you write about?"

"Oh, slogans and denunciations against those who had been labeled 'cow's demon and snake spirit,' and all China's enemies such as Taiwan, Japan, Britain, the United States, and the Soviet Union."

"How do you know what to write? Do you make things up?"

"Some people do. But I think that's too dangerous. Most of us get materials from our section leader. I concentrate on enemy countries. The section leader allows me to because she thinks I know more about other countries since I was born abroad. I don't want to write about individuals. I don't know much about the life of any of the denounced people, and I don't want to lie and insinuate. The older actresses, actors, directors, and scriptwriters have to write their own self-criticism. A lot of them are being denounced. From time to time, they are led out by the activists to be struggled against at struggle meetings or just to stand or kneel in the sun with their heads bowed."

"How terrible!" I exclaimed.

"Yes, it's terrible. I'm sorry for them. I heard that most of them are Jiang Qing's enemies from the old days. I heard that

Chairman Mao has given his wife Jiang Qing full power to deal with everybody in the field of art," my daughter said.

"Hasn't she been putting on modern Beijing operas?"

"Yes, it seems she has been in disagreement with the leaders in the Cultural Department for some time. In any case, I heard that the actresses who got better parts than she did in the old days when she was an actress in Shanghai have all packed their bags in preparation for going to labor camps. It's said she is very cruel and jealous. But it's best not to talk about her at all."

"Surely that's farfetched. She is the number one lady of China now. Why should she care about a few old actresses?"

"Perhaps they know too much about her past life. They say that before she went to Yanan and married Chairman Mao, she had a lot of lovers and even several husbands."

"Chairman Mao had several wives too. Why shouldn't she have had several husbands? She sounds like a proper Hollywood film star," I laughed. "You have been brought up in China, so you have a puritanical outlook on such matters. Tell me, how about yourself? Are you likely to get criticized?"

"Mommy, don't be silly. I'm not important enough. I'm just one of the masses. Of course, my family background and my birth abroad might get criticized. Wasn't it lucky I was born in Australia rather than in the United States or Britain?"

"Certainly no one can say Australia is an imperialist country."

"No, most people at the film studio think it's still a British colony where the people are oppressed. They don't know the Australians are really British and only the kangaroos are the natives." My daughter laughed heartily.

She finished her sandwiches and got up to go to her own room. Casually she asked, "What did you do all day, Mommy?"

"I was called to attend a struggle meeting against the former chief accountant of our office. It seems I also must take part in the Cultural Revolution. I might even become a target of attack," I told her.

"Oh, my goodness! This is extremely serious. Why didn't you tell me before?" Meiping was shocked by my news. She sat down again and urged me to tell her everything. After I had described my experiences of the day, she became very worried. She asked, "Was your office all right? Has it ever done anything wrong?"

"No, of course not," I told her.

"Why did they single out the chief accountant? Perhaps he infringed the foreign exchange regulations on behalf of the firm? Or perhaps you didn't pay your taxes?"

"We paid our taxes, all right. Certainly we were most meticulous in observing the foreign exchange regulations."

We were both puzzled but agreed it was useless to speculate. I urged her to go to bed. After remaining silent for a while longer, she said good night and left the room. She seemed a changed girl, much older than when she came in.

I switched off the light but remained wide awake. I was thinking that the Proletarian Cultural Revolution was also my daughter's first experience of a political movement. I wondered how it was going to affect her future. After some time, my bedroom door was gently pushed open. I switched on the light.

"Mommy, I can't go to sleep. Do you mind if I go down and play the piano for a while?" Meiping asked, standing in her pajamas in the open doorway.

"I'll come with you," I said, getting out of bed and following her downstairs.

Fluffy, Meiping's large Persian cat, was on the terrace outside. When he saw us, he mewed to get in. I opened the screen door. Meiping stepped out and picked him up to carry him into her study. She put Fluffy down, opened the lid of the piano, and proceeded to strike a few chords. Turning to me, she asked, "What shall I play?"

"Anything at all, but not revolutionary songs."

She started to play one of Chopin's nocturnes and murmured to me, "All right?"

I made an affirmative sound. Fluffy was stretched out at Meiping's feet under the piano. It was a scene of domestic peace and tranquility but for an invisible threat hanging in the air.

2

Interval before the Storm

IN THE WEEKS FOLLOWING that first meeting, I was called by the same men for several interviews. Our conversations varied very little from the first occasion. Once they asked me to provide them with a list of all the Americans and Europeans I had known, together with their occupations and the place and circumstance in which I had met each one. Another time they asked me to write about the activities of our office. But when I handed them the pages I had written, they barely glanced at them. While exhorting me to denounce my former employer, they did not ask me any concrete questions about the company. They never went beyond insinuating that Shell had done something wrong and that I was a part of whatever the crime was.

Indeed, I had the impression that the men were marking time, waiting for instructions from above before going any further. Actually, unbeknownst to me and to the Chinese people, the delay in activating the movement was due to a fierce struggle among the leaders of the Chinese Communist Party. The point of contention was who should conduct the Cultural Revolution: the established Party apparatus or a special committee of Maoists appointed by Mao Zedong as chairman of the Central Committee.

It was later revealed that early in August, at a Central Committee meeting, Mao had written a Big Character Poster entitled "Fire Cannonballs at the Headquarters." In it he made the extraordinary accusation that the government administration (headed by Liu Shaoqi as chairman of the People's Republic) and the Party Secretariat (headed by Deng Xiaoping as chief party secretary) were the headquarters of China's capitalist class because, he said, their policies protected and served the interests of the capitalist class. This was a very serious and shocking charge against the entire Party apparatus and the administrative organization of Communist China. Mao was able to make the accusation against Liu and Deng because he controlled the armed forces through his protégé Lin Biao, who was the defense minister. Attempting to salvage his own position under the circumstances, Liu Shaoqi made a pro forma statement of self-criticism, saying that his economic policy of allowing private plots for the peasants and free markets to meet the needs of the people in the cities had encouraged the revival of capitalism in China and represented a retreat from the road of socialism. Perhaps Liu Shaoqi believed he could save Mao's face by such an admission. The fact remained that Liu Shaoqi's economic policy rescued China from economic collapse after the disastrous failure of Mao Zedong's Great Leap Forward Campaign in 1958–60. However, Liu's admission of guilt was to prove a tactical mistake. It placed him at a great disadvantage and opened the way for the Maoists to escalate their attack against him and his followers in the government.

Mao's victory at the Central Committee meeting led to the appointment of a special committee of left-wing Maoists to conduct the Cultural Revolution. As time went on and the Party and government apparatus became paralyzed under the attack of the Red Guards and the Revolutionaries, this committee became the highest organ of government. Its members, including Mao's wife Jiang Qing, enjoyed extraordinary power and were all elected to the Party Politburo. Throughout the years of the Cultural Revolution, Jiang Qing made use of her position as Mao's wife to become his spokeswoman and representative, supposedly transmitting Mao's orders and wishes but in fact interpreting them to suit herself. A ruthlessly ambitious woman who had been kept out of Chinese political life for decades, she would now tolerate no opposition, imaginary or otherwise. Tens of thousands of Party officials, artists, writers, scientists, and common people who fell under the shadow of her suspicion were cruelly persecuted. Scores of them died at the hands of her trusted "Revolutionaries."

At this August Central Committee meeting, Defense Minister Lin Biao emerged as Mao's most ardent supporter. His eulogy of Mao was contained in the meeting's final communiqué, published in the newspapers. Lin claimed that Mao was "the greatest living Marxist of our age," with one stroke placing Mao ahead of the Soviet leaders, including Stalin, as the true successor of Lenin. During the entire ten years of the Cultural Revolution, even after Lin Biao was disgraced, this claim was maintained by the Maoists.

One day, soon after the publication of the communiqué of the Central Committee meeting, Mr. Hu, a friend of my late husband's, called on me. Because in China male friendship usually excluded wives, after my husband's death his friends ceased coming to our house. Only Mr. Hu continued to appear on Chinese New Year's Day to pay me the traditional courtesy call. He generally stayed only a short time, inquiring after my daughter and me and wishing us good health and happiness in the new year. He always mentioned my husband and told me how much he had esteemed him as a man and how much he had valued his friendship. Then he would take his leave, placing on the table a red envelope containing a tip for my servants, an old custom observed by only a few conservative people in China after the Communist Party took over. I was amused by his visits and thought Mr. Hu rather quaint but charmingly sentimental.

When Lao-zhao announced him, I was surprised. But I told Lao-zhao to usher him to the drawing room and serve tea.

Mr. Hu had been the owner of a paint factory. His product was well known in China and was exported to Hong Kong and Southeast Asia. After the Communist army took over Shanghai, he continued to operate under the Communist government's supervision. In 1956, during the Socialization of Capitalist Enterprises Campaign, his factory was taken over by the government, which promised all the capitalists an annual interest of 7 percent of the assessed value of their enterprises for ten years. Though the assessed value of the enterprises was only a fraction of their true worth, the capitalists had no alternative but to accept. Because of his technical skill, the government invited Mr. Hu to remain with his factory as chief engineer and assistant manager when Party officials took over.

A well-educated Chinese, Mr. Hu was quite untouched by Western civilization. He wrote excellent calligraphy; his conversation was sprinkled with traditional literary allusions. He was not bothered by the antiforeign attitude of the Communist regime because his own knowledge and interest did not go beyond the borders of China. On the whole he fared better during political campaigns because Party officials were less suspicious of people like Mr. Hu who had no foreign contacts than they were of those who had been educated abroad. His philosophical attitude towards the loss of his own factory and his ready acceptance of a subordinate position never ceased to amaze me. My husband once told me that while most capitalists found the Party officials assigned to their factories extremely difficult to deal with, Mr. Hu managed to establish a friendly relationship with the Party secretary who had superseded him as head of his factory.

"I hear you are involved in this latest political movement, the Great Proletarian Cultural Revolution. I wonder how you are getting on," Mr. Hu said, explaining the reason for his visit.

"Not very well, I'm afraid. The Shanghai office of Shell is being investigated. I have been questioned, and I had to attend a struggle meeting against our former chief accountant. The men who talked to me seemed to imply there were some irregularities in the firm's activities. But they won't say what they mean. I'm really rather puzzled. I have never been involved in a political movement before."

Lao-zhao brought in the silver tea set, my best china, and a large plate of small iced cakes, as well as thinly cut sandwiches in the best British tradition, something I reserved for my British and Australian friends who understood the finer points of afternoon tea. This was Lao-zhao's idea of treating Mr. Hu as an honored guest. As he placed the tray on the coffee table in front of the sofa, the telephone in the hall rang and he went out to answer it. He came back almost immediately and said, "It's those people again. They want you to go over there right now for another interview."

"Tell them I'm busy. I will go tomorrow," I said.

Lao-zhao went out. I could hear him engaged in a heated argument on the telephone. Then he came back and said, "They insist you must go at once. They say it's very important."

"May I ask who is calling? If it is important, don't delay going because I'm here," Mr. Hu said to me.

"It's those officials who have been questioning me," I told him.

"Oh, you must go at once. How can you refuse to go when those people call you! Please make haste. I'll stay here and wait for you. I want to know more about your position. I owe it to your husband, my dear old friend, to give you some advice. It's my duty. You are inexperienced in dealing with those men. They are mean and spiteful. You must not offend them," Mr. Hu said. He appeared really worried.

I was glad that he was going to wait for me, because I very much wanted to hear what he had to say about the Cultural Revolution and the recent Central Committee meeting. I left the house just after four. When I returned at eight, Mr. Hu was still there. As I walked into the house, he came out of the drawing room to welcome me back and beamed with pleasure and relief.

"I'm sorry I have been so long."

"Do sit down and rest. Tell me, how did it go?"

Lao-zhao brought me a cup of hot tea. While sipping it, I described to Mr. Hu my interview with the Party officials.

In addition to the usual two men, there had been a third person present who might have been their superior. Perhaps to impress this new man, they were even more unpleasant than usual. When I entered the room, one of them said sternly, "Why didn't you want to come?"

"I was busy. You should have telephoned this morning."

In the past, one of them had always motioned me to sit down. But today they just let me stand.

"We are not conducting a dinner party. We are conducting an investigation. Whenever we need to talk to you, you just have to come immediately," he said with a sneer.

I decided to sit down anyway.

"Look at this long list of your foreign friends! How come you have so many foreign friends? You must like them and admire their culture." He looked at me accusingly. Then he went on,

"You said they were all friendly towards China and the Chinese people and that some of them were born here and spent their childhood years here. You claim some of them admire Chinese culture and speak our language. Yet included here are men whose ancestors made fortunes in the opium trade. They used to own factories, warehouses, ships, everything under the sun, in China. Now they have lost them all. So how could they have friendly feelings towards the People's Government? Yes, they might have liked China when the Kuomintang was here, when they exploited the Chinese people as much as they wanted and were able to amass huge fortunes. But they definitely cannot like China now. And you talked about the diplomats having friendly feelings for China. That's even more ridiculous! Diplomats are spies sent here by their governments to gather information to be used against us. How could they feel friendly towards us? It's no use your pasting gold on their faces to make them look like benevolent Buddhas. They are our enemies. But they are your friends. Now it is quite clear where you stand, isn't it?"

"I got to know these people not because I went out of my way to seek their acquaintance or friendship. Most of them I met when my late husband was a diplomat or when he was in charge of the Shanghai office of the Ministry of Foreign Affairs in the old days."

"The Shanghai office of the Ministry of Foreign Affairs of the reactionary Kuomintang government! Your husband was a senior official of the reactionary Kuomintang government, and later he became the general manager of a foreign capitalist firm," he said sarcastically. "Your husband's career was nothing to be proud of."

"He became the general manager of the Shanghai office of Shell with the approval of the Shanghai Industry and Commerce Department of the People's Government. The department had to accept his power of attorney for the appointment. As for being an official of the Kuomintang government, he stayed in Shanghai in 1949 instead of going with the Kuomintang government to Taiwan. Doesn't that show he supported the Communist Revolution and was ready to welcome the establishment of the People's Government?"

"There might have been other reasons why he stayed. We will deal with his case later. Now we want you to denounce British imperialism and confess everything you did for Shell as their faithful agent."

"Everything I did for Shell was in accordance with the laws and regulations of the People's Government," I declared emphatically.

The new man had not spoken but smoked incessantly, filling the room with the smell of bad tobacco. Now he tossed the butt of his cigarette on the floor and crushed it with his foot. He looked at me steadily for a few seconds to intimidate me before saying, "Have you lived a completely blameless life? All your life you have been associated with foreigners, especially the British. Do you mean to say that you have never done anything or said anything that was not altogether correct?"

"Whether I did or said anything incorrect or not, I know for a certainty that I never did anything against the People's Government," I said firmly.

"That's for us to judge. At least you now admit the possibility that you might have done or said something that was incorrect," he said with a smile.

"Nonsense! I admitted no such thing!" I said.

The new man seemed to me more subtle than the other two. Though he spoke in a quiet voice instead of shouting, I was sure he was looking for an opportunity to trick me. Now he changed the subject, saying, "Give a résumé of the activities of your office."

I gave a brief account of our work at the office. When I had finished speaking, the man said, "What you have just told us is almost exactly what you have already written. I believe you took the trouble to memorize what you had written. Why this precaution?"

"What I have told you and what I have written are just the same because facts are the same, no matter how many times you talk about them," I said. This interview seemed to have gone on a long time already. I thought of Mr. Hu waiting for me, so I looked at my watch.

"Are you in a hurry to be gone? Perhaps you find this conversation uncomfortable?" The man was enjoying himself, twisting words and situation to suit his purpose.

"I just think you are wasting your time," I said.

"We are not afraid to waste time. We're patient. It took us, the

Communist Party, twenty-two years to overthrow the Kuomintang government. But we succeeded in the end. When we set out
to achieve our goal, we pursue it to the end."

There was dead silence. We had reached an impasse. Suddenly the man who spoke at the struggle meeting reverted to his
former tactics. He shouted, "We won't let you get away with it!
You must provide us with a list of the things you did and said
that were wrong, in order to show your sincerity in changing
your standpoint. Otherwise, the consequences for you will be
serious. We know for a certainty you are a spy for the British!"

This was the first time any of them had actually used the word
"spy." Hitherto they had merely hinted at it. Perhaps in the heat
of the moment the man exceeded their instructions, for the
other two glanced at him in surprise.

I laughed at his outburst and said calmly, "You are quite
wrong. I am no more a spy for anybody than you are."

The new man said quickly, "Perhaps there are things you did
or said that you don't remember offhand. Why don't you go
home and think about it? Write down everything you did and
said, no matter how trivial or insignificant. We will give you
plenty of time. What about two weeks?"

"Two years will make no difference. I don't intend to make up
any story," I told them.

"Well, let's say two weeks. It's painful to admit mistakes. But
it has to be done. Our Great Leader compared confession to
having an operation. The operation is painful, but only after it
is done can one become a new man. You want to be a good
citizen of our socialist state, don't you? Then you mustn't lag
behind the others. We want you to confess, not because we don't
know the facts already, but because we wish to give you a chance
to show your sincerity."

I wanted to tell him that he was mad, but I bit my lip and
remained silent, hoping not to prolong the senseless dialogue.

He took my silence as a sign that I was ready to do what he
wanted, so he dismissed me by saying, "It's getting late. Go
home and think about what I have said. We will call you in two
weeks' time."

With anger and indignation boiling inside me, I walked out of
the building. There were no pedicabs. After waiting at the bus
stop for a long time, I had to walk home.

Mr. Hu listened to my story in silence. Lao-zhao came in to announce dinner. My cook had prepared an excellent meal of Chinese dishes because he knew Mr. Hu did not enjoy European cooking. During the meal we did not talk about the unpleasant subject of the Cultural Revolution but discussed my daughter's and his children's activities. We were both proud and pleased that our children seemed to have done well in socialist China in spite of the handicap of their family background.

When we were seated again in the drawing room, I asked Mr. Hu a question that had been in my mind all the time I was with my inquisitors.

"These men gave me the impression that they wanted a confession from me even if I made it up. Could that be the case?"

"Oh, yes, yes. They don't care whether it's true or not as long as they get a confession. That's what they are after."

"But what's the point? Won't they themselves get awfully confused if everyone gives a false confession?" I was genuinely puzzled.

"To get a confession is their job. If they fail, they may be accused of not supporting the movement. The result is that whenever a political movement takes place, many people are attacked and many confessions are made. Later, when the turmoil is over, the sorting out is done. Some of those wrongfully dealt with may be rehabilitated."

"How long do they have to wait for rehabilitation?" I asked.

"Maybe a couple of years. Maybe it never happens. In each organization three to five percent of the total must be declared the 'enemy' because that is the percentage mentioned by Chairman Mao in one of his speeches."

"How terrible!" I exclaimed.

"Yes, it's really bad. There isn't really such a high percentage of people who oppose the People's Government. To fill their quota, the Party officials often include people whom they dislike, such as those who are disgruntled and troublesome, in the list of enemies. But no individual should make a false confession, no matter how great the pressure is." Mr. Hu said this with great seriousness. He looked at me steadily, as if to make sure I got his message, and added, "That has always been my policy during each political movement."

I understood that this was the advice he had come to give me.

He did not say outright, "You mustn't give a false confession,
no matter how great the pressure," because in a Chinese household the well-trained servant always remained within earshot
ready to be of service, especially when there was a guest. Mr. Hu
did not want Lao-zhao to hear him telling me not to confess. He
was a cautious man, and he trusted no one.

"There always comes a time when a man almost reaches the
end of his endurance and is tempted to write down something,
however untrue, to satisfy his inquisitors and to free himself
from intolerable pressure. But one mustn't do it. Party officials
will never be satisfied with the confession. Once one starts confessing, they will demand more and more admissions of guilt,
however false, and exert increasing pressure to get what they
want. In the end, one will get into a tangle of untruths from
which one can no longer extract oneself. I have seen it happen
to several people." Mr. Hu was still speaking in the third person
and did not say, "You mustn't."

His advice was timely and valuable. I was grateful to him for
taking the trouble to come and moved by his friendship for my
late husband, which was his motive for stretching out a helping
hand to me. When he thought I understood what he had come
to say, he spoke of political movements in general terms. He told
me that he was a veteran of many such movements and had
learned by bitter experience how to deal with them.

"What do you think of the communiqué of the Central Committee meeting?" I asked him.

Mr. Hu shook his head and sighed. After a moment he said,
"Chairman Mao has won. It's not unexpected." Then he added,
"The beginning of a political movement is always the worst
period. The hurricane loses its momentum after a few months
and often fizzles out after about a year."

"A year! What a long time!" I said.

Mr. Hu smiled at my outburst and said, "What's a year to us
Chinese? It's but the blinking of an eye in our thousands of years
of history. Time does not mean the same thing to us as to the
Europeans, whom you, of course, know well."

"I'm accused of being a spy because they think I know the
British well."

"Their accusation is only an excuse with which to fool the
masses. Sooner or later they will hit at everyone they do not

trust, and they probably think now is a good time to deal with you."

Mr. Hu got up to leave, asking me to telephone him whenever I wanted to see him to talk things over. As a final piece of advice he said, "Nearly all lower-ranking Communist Party officials suffer from an inferiority complex. Although they have power over us, somehow they have a deep feeling of inferiority. This is unfortunate, because some of them feel they need to reassure themselves by using that power to make our life uncomfortable or to humiliate us. When you are being questioned, be firm but be polite also. Don't offend them. They can be mean and spiteful. They can also be very cruel."

"It's not in my nature to be obsequious. But thank you for the warning. I shall remember it," I said.

I was so wrapped up in my own problems that only then did I think of asking him about himself.

Mr. Hu said philosophically, with an air of resignation, "I have joined the ranks of the workers. Another person has been appointed to my old job. When I tendered my letter of resignation to the Party secretary, I told him that I felt my class status as a former capitalist rendered me unsuitable for a responsible executive position."

The thought that he was now working as an ordinary worker in his own factory appalled me. But he was without bitterness.

"It's not so bad," he said. "In the Soviet Union, when the Communist Party took over, I believe all the capitalists were shot. I'm still alive, and I'm able to look after all three generations of my family. I asked the Party secretary to assign me to the most unskilled menial job. So now I am just a coolie, pushing drums of raw materials or carting coal. No one can be envious or jealous of a man doing work like that. You know, when I asked him for such a job, the Party secretary seemed to be quite sorry for me. We used to get on well together."

I recalled that my husband had told me that the reason Mr. Hu and his Party secretary got on well together was that Mr. Hu did the work and the Party secretary got the credit. Their factory won the Red Flag for good management and high production figures year after year.

"Did you not do all the work for him?"

"Yes, yes, I suppose I did most of the work. But I had spent my whole life building up that factory. In 1930, when I started, I had only a few workers. In 1956, when I handed the factory over to the government, there were fifteen hundred of them. And we ran a laboratory as well as a training center for young technicians."

"Why do you want to be a coolie? Surely with your knowledge and experience you could do more useful work even if you must be a worker."

He made a negative gesture with his hand. "To be a coolie at times like this is not bad. We coolies work outside the plant and take our breaks in a shed. If anything should go wrong, no one can accuse me of sabotaging the machinery inside the plant. An ex-capitalist is always first on the list of suspects during a political campaign, when everyone is jittery."

With that sagacious remark he took his leave. When he shook hands with me, he said, "Keep fit and try to live long. If you live long enough, you might see a change in our country."

From my servants' attitude and the quality of the meal served to Mr. Hu, I knew that they welcomed his visit. When I went upstairs to my bedroom, Chen-ma was there laying out my dressing gown and slippers. She advised me to listen to any advice from Mr. Hu, who was, she declared, a good friend and a gentleman.

To talk to someone sympathetic had been comforting. I was now more than ever resolved not to write anything false to satisfy the demand of the Party officials.

A few days without hearing from my persecutors restored my good humor somewhat. My daughter's birthday was on August 18. I decided we should have a small dinner party to celebrate the event and to dispel some of the gloom that had descended on the household. I asked my daughter to invite a few of her friends, and I phoned my old friend Li Zhen and asked her to join us.

I first met Li Zhen in the autumn of 1935 when I arrived in London as a student. She had just graduated from the Royal College of Music. Shortly afterwards she married a Chinese government official and returned with him to China. She became a professor at her old school, the Shanghai Conservatory of Music, where she was the head of the piano department. Her husband, Su Lai, the son of a rich Chinese merchant in Hong

Kong, had received a liberal education in a British school and university. His hatred for the colonial atmosphere of Hong Kong in which he grew up and the glowing reports of a new Soviet society from the pens of prominent British writers and educators, which flooded British universities in the early thirties, combined to produce a profound effect on his character. He became a fiercely patriotic nationalist and at the same time a believer in Marxism.

When the Communist army marched towards Shanghai, Su Lai was jubilant, declaring that a new era of national resurgence and honest government was about to dawn in China. He refused to go to Taiwan with the Kuomintang government, tried to persuade his friends to do the same, and welcomed the Communist takeover with enthusiasm. In 1950, during the Thought Reform Movement in the universities, Li Zhen, his wife, lost her position as head of the piano department at the Conservatory of Music. Su Lai was surprised to find that the Party member appointed to take her place could not read music. A worse blow came in 1953 when Mao Zedong launched the Three and Five Antis Movement against corruption and bribery, aimed at the Shanghai industrialists and officials like Su Lai who had worked for economic agencies of the Kuomintang government. Although all the evidence pointed to his honesty, Su Lai became a target. He was confined to his office, where Party officials took turns questioning him. And struggle meetings were held against him.

A man like Su Lai was beyond the understanding of the average Chinese Communist, who believed the desire for revolutionary change to be the exclusive right of the poor and downtrodden. However, because of the Korean War and the boycott of China by the United States, the People's Government was anxious to develop trade with Hong Kong. Su Lai's wealthy relatives in the British colony used this opportunity to secure his release by negotiating directly with Beijing. The Shanghai authorities had no choice but to allow him to leave for Hong Kong with his two children when Beijing acceded to his family's request.

Frustrated in their attempt to punish severely the rich man's son who had dared to assume the proud mantle of Marxism, the local Communist officials in Shanghai refused to grant Li Zhen an exit permit, using the pretext that her work with the Conservatory of Music required her to remain in Shanghai. She never saw her husband alive again. However, when he died in Hong Kong in 1957, in the more liberal atmosphere generated in China by the Eighth Party Congress in 1956, Li Zhen was given permission to attend his funeral and to see her children. She remained in Hong Kong until 1960, when she was invited back to Shanghai by the Conservatory of Music, to which she had a lifelong attachment. In the meantime, her children had been taken to Australia by an uncle.

When Li Zhen returned to Shanghai, the city was suffering from a severe food shortage as a result of the catastrophic economic failure of the Great Leap Forward Campaign launched by Mao Zedong in 1958. Long lines of people were forming at dawn at Shanghai police stations, waiting to apply for exit permits to leave the country. This was such an embarrassment for the Shanghai authorities that they viewed Li Zhen's return from affluent Hong Kong to starving Shanghai as an opportunity for propaganda. I read of her return in the local newspaper, which normally reported only the visits of prominent Party officials or foreign dignitaries. The Shanghai government hailed her as a true patriot and appointed her a delegate to the Political Consultative Conference, an organization of government-selected artists, writers, religious leaders, prominent industrialists, and former Kuomintang officials whose function was to echo and to express support for the government policy of the moment, to set an example for others of similar background, and to help project an image of popular support for Communist Party policy by every section of the community. In return, the government granted members of this organization certain minor privileges, such as better housing and the use of a special restaurant where a supply of scarce food could be obtained without the surrender of ration coupons.

The Communist officials always rewarded a person for his usefulness to them, not for his virtue, though they talked a lot about his virtue. Li Zhen had become a member of the Political Consultative Conference six years earlier, when China was suffering severe economic difficulties and food shortages. Now that they were a thing of the past, Li Zhen's usefulness to the Communist authorities was over. Besides, the Party liked people to show gratitude with a display of servile obedience and verbal glorification of its policies. Li Zhen was quite incapable of either. In fact, she told me that she found attending meetings boring and maintained silence when she was expected to pay homage to Mao's policies on music and education. Her lack of enthusiasm for her role as a member of the Political Consultative Conference could not have failed to irritate the Party officials.

These thoughts were in my mind when I telephoned her. I was very pleased when she accepted my dinner invitation with alacrity.

When I got up in the early morning of August 18, my daughter's birthday, Chen-ma was not in the house. A devout Buddhist, she always went on this day to the temple at Jing An Si to say a special prayer for Meiping, of whom she was very fond. Thinking that I would disapprove of these temple visits because I am a Christian, she generally slipped out of the house early and returned quietly, hoping I would not notice her absence. I pretended to know nothing about it and never mentioned it to her.

While I was in the dining room doing the flowers, she returned. I heard her talking to the cook in the pantry in an unusually agitated voice. When she came into the hall, I saw that she was wiping her eyes with her handkerchief.

"What's happened, Chen-ma?" I called to her.

She was silent but came into the room. "What's happened at the temple?" I asked her.

She sat down on a dining chair and burst into tears. "They are dismantling the temple," she said between sobs.

"Who is dismantling the temple?" I asked her. "Not the government, surely!"

"Young people. Probably students. They said Chairman Mao told them to stop superstition. They also said the monks are counterrevolutionaries opposed to Chairman Mao."

"What did the monks do?"

"Nothing. The students rounded them up. Some were beaten. When I got there I saw them prostrate on the ground in the courtyard. There was a large crowd of onlookers. One of them told me that the students were going to dismantle the temple and burn the scriptures as they had done at other places. I actually saw some of the students climbing onto the roof and throwing down the tiles," Chen-ma said while wiping away her tears.

"Please, Chen-ma, you mustn't be too upset. You can worship

at home. The Christian churches have been closed for several years now. The Christians all worship at home. You can do the same, can't you? In any case, you mustn't cry on Meiping's birthday."

"Yes, yes, I mustn't cry on Meiping's birthday. But I was upset to see such wanton destruction." She tucked her handkerchief away and went out of the room.

Then the cook came in to complain that several items of food I had asked him to get for the party were unobtainable. He added that at the food market he and other cooks were jeered for working for wealthy families.

"I suppose they didn't like to see you buying more things than they could afford. Please don't let it bother you. As for the party, please just use whatever you were able to get at the market. I'm sure you will be able to put together a good meal for Meiping's birthday," I tried to reassure him.

While I could understand my cook's experience at the market as the result of class hatred generated by massive propaganda against the capitalist class, which to the general public was simply "the rich people," I was puzzled by what had happened at the temple, which was operated by the state. The monks there were in fact government employees. If the government had decided to change its policy, it could have closed the temple and transferred the monks to other forms of employment, as it had done earlier during the Great Leap Forward Campaign. Actually the temple at Jing An Si was a showplace for official visitors from Southeast Asia, to create the impression that China tolerated Buddhism. I remembered reading in the newspaper that the temple was reopened after the Great Leap Forward Campaign and the monks brought back again. I wondered why the students had been allowed to do what they were doing and whether the Shanghai municipal government was aware of what was going on at Jing An Si.

At six o'clock Li Zhen arrived. With her snow-white hair and calm smile, she always seemed the epitome of scholarly authority, tranquility, and distinction. Only her old friends like myself knew that behind her serene exterior was such great sensitivity that she could be depressed or elated by events that would have left an ordinary person relatively unmoved.

Li Zhen was a great artist and an able teacher. From time

immemorial, China's tradition of respect for teachers gave them a special place in society. A good teacher who had devoted his life to education was compared to a fruitful tree, a phrase certainly applicable to Li Zhen, whose many former students worked as concert pianists, accompanists, and teachers all over China. Several had won international piano contests and received recognition abroad. I was very fond of Li Zhen and greatly admired her total devotion to music and her students. Since her return from Hong Kong, we had seen a great deal of each other. She would often bring her music and spend an evening with me listening to my records. I knew she often felt lonely and missed her children. Fortunately, since Liu Shaoqi had become chairman of the People's Republic in 1960 and Mao Zedong had retired from active administrative work, China had had no large-scale political upheavals until now, so that Li Zhen had been able to keep in touch with her children in Australia by correspondence.

After Lao-zhao had served us iced tea, I asked Li Zhen, "How is everything with you at the conservatory?"

"I'm afraid it's not good," she said sadly. "All classes have stopped. We are supposed to devote our entire time to the Cultural Revolution. Everybody has to write Big Character Posters. Professors like myself also have to write self-criticisms and read other people's Big Character Posters against us."

"Are there many against you?" I asked her anxiously.

"More are written against professors than against others. I don't know whether I have more than other professors. I haven't counted them. But so far, no struggle meeting has been arranged against me. My personal history is comparatively simple. I have never done any other work than being a teacher at the conservatory."

"Have there been many struggle meetings against other professors at the conservatory?"

"Yes, there have been several. One was against a former member of the Kuomintang, and another was against a former Rightist. The others are from other departments, so I don't know their personal history. These two are people who had already been denounced in former political movements," Li Zhen explained. "I hate struggle meetings. Somehow, everybody behaves like savages."

"Do you think you will be safe?"

"I have never opposed the Communist Party. I am entirely nonpolitical. When I graduated from the conservatory, I went to England to study. When I came back, I returned to the conservatory to teach. There is nothing about me the Party doesn't know. I should be safe, shouldn't I? But I don't know what may happen. There is something about this political campaign that seems different from previous ones."

"What is different?" I asked her.

"It's the attitude of the Party officials. In former political campaigns they were cocksure. They went into it boldly, full of confidence. This time, they seem nervous, almost as if they don't really want to do anything. The fact that they have limited their attack to people who have been denounced already seems to indicate they don't want to expand its scope. Perhaps after the failure of Mao's Great Leap Forward Campaign the Party officials are no longer certain Mao is always right to rely on political campaigns for progress."

What Li Zhen told me was very interesting. At that juncture we did not know, of course, that the Proletarian Cultural Revolution was in fact a struggle for power between the Maoists and the more moderate faction headed by Liu Shaoqi and Deng Xiaoping. It later became known that the chief Party secretary at the conservatory belonged to Liu Shaoqi's faction. He was murdered by Jiang Qing's Revolutionaries when she decided to install one of her favorite young men as the conservatory's Party secretary.

"The writing of Big Character Posters advocated by Mao seems to me a great waste. At the conservatory, a great deal of paper and thousands of writing brushes and bottles of ink have already been used. Yet when we needed extra lights in the classroom or additional musical instruments, there was never any money for them," said Li Zhen.

"What do the Big Character Posters say against you?" I asked.

"The usual criticism about my education in England, my sending the children to Australia, and my teaching method. When we were friendly with the Soviet Union, we were urged to teach Western music and train students to take part in international competitions. After we broke with the Soviet Union, Chairman Mao started to criticize Western music. We had to use

Chinese compositions exclusively for teaching. But there are so few Chinese compositions. Half my time was spent looking for teaching materials. It's hard enough to carry on as a teacher already. Now my students are made to turn against me. Do you know, one of them told me quietly that they had to write posters against me to protect themselves?"

"Exactly. You mustn't mind it. Don't let it hurt you! The poor young people have to do it."

"I feel very sad. It is almost as if my whole life is wasted," Li Zhen sighed.

"Don't be depressed by it! During the Great Leap Forward Campaign of 1958, the students in Meiping's school from capitalist families all had to criticize their family background. I told her to go ahead and criticize me. She did. The teacher and her fellow students all applauded her. It's only a formality. It's just acting. Don't let it bother you."

"I'm afraid I can't laugh it off like you do," Li Zhen said. "It's so unfair!"

"Doesn't your position as a delegate to the Political Consultative Conference give you some protection?" I asked my friend.

"I hear the Maoists want to abolish that organization. They call it an organization of radishes, red on the outside but white inside. They claim that while all the delegates talk as if they support the Communist Party, in actual fact they oppose the Party."

"Is that true?"

"Who knows? When the penalty for speaking one's mind is so great, nobody knows what anybody else thinks," Li Zhen said. I had to agree with her. In fact, after living in Communist China for so many years, I realized that one of the advantages enjoyed by a democratic government that allows freedom of speech is that the government knows exactly who supports it and who is against it, while a totalitarian government knows nothing of what the people really think.

When I told her that I too was involved in the Cultural Revolution, her reaction was the same as Winnie's. She said, "Now that Shell has closed their Shanghai office, the Party officials probably feel that they should use the opportunity of this political campaign to frighten you so that they can control you more easily in future." But she did not think the persecution against me would be serious. "They can't save money by reducing your salary since you get no pay from the government. They can't fire you from your job since you don't work for them. I can't see that there is much they can do to you except to give you a fright."

"I hope you are right," I said.

"You know, I feel so discouraged that I sometimes think I can't go on," Li Zhen said.

"Why don't you ask to retire? Lots of people retire before they are sixty and take a cut in pension to avoid politics."

"I might just do that when the Cultural Revolution is over," Li Zhen said.

My daughter arrived with four of her young friends: Kong, a handsome male actor from her film studio whose father was a very famous film director of the thirties; a violinist with the municipal orchestra named Zhang; Sun Kai, a mathematics teacher at a technical college who was Meiping's special boyfriend; and my goddaughter Hean, who had been Meiping's childhood friend in Australia. They were all keenly interested in music and often gathered at our house to listen to our stereo records.

The young possess an infinite capacity to be cheerful. Although all of them came from the type of family likely to be adversely affected by the Cultural Revolution, no mention was made of it. They laughed and chatted about music and books throughout the meal. When Meiping took what remained of her large birthday cake into the kitchen to share with the servants, even Chen-ma recovered her usual good humor. I heard her scolding Meiping fondly for licking chocolate from her fingers. When the meal was over, the young people retired to Meiping's study to indulge in their favorite pastime of playing records on her record player.

Li Zhen and I went into the garden. Lao-zhao arranged two wicker chairs on the lawn, put cushions on them, lit a coil of mosquito incense, and placed it on a plate between the chairs. Then he brought us chrysanthemum tea in covered cups. Soothing music from a violin concerto came through the window. I settled deeper into the chair and gazed up at the starlit summer sky.

"You really have a comfortable life. You manage to enjoy the best of the Western as well as the Chinese world, don't you?"

Li Zhen said. "I wonder if that's what irritates the Party officials."

"Maybe. Those questioning me certainly seem to hate me. Do you think they really believe it is our fault that the workers and peasants in China are poor?"

"I think they are just envious. People can't all live in the same way. I have a big apartment. It's allocated to me by the conservatory. That shows they don't expect everyone to live in the same way," said Li Zhen. She seemed more relaxed now.

"Of course, you're different. You have done so much for the country. Hundreds of young people have passed through your hands. Each one of them carried with him something you taught him. Isn't that wonderful?" I truly admired my friend.

"I don't hear anyone in the conservatory say that about me. It's always how I taught decadent Western music to poison the minds of the young. They don't stop to think that I couldn't have done it if the government had forbidden it. All our teaching materials had to be passed by our Party secretary before we could use them for the students. And they seem to forget that they used to urge me to teach Western music in the early fifties when China was friendly with the Soviet Union." Li Zhen was indignant and distraught. I wished I hadn't mentioned her work again. To try to cheer her up, I asked about her children.

"They seem so remote, especially now that they're married," she said.

"Don't you long to see them?"

"Oh, I do! But what's the use thinking about it now? The government may never give me a passport to travel to Australia. The children certainly won't come here."

"Perhaps you shouldn't have come back from Hong Kong," I said.

"At the time it seemed the best thing to do. I am very attached to the conservatory, you know. I was trained there and I have worked there. It is really the most important thing in my life apart from the children. Many of my colleagues were fellow students when we studied there together. They all wrote to me. My students wrote to me. The Party secretary wrote to me. Everybody said I was needed at the conservatory, so I came back."

"What did Su Lai's family say about your decision?"

"After Su Lai died, they weren't very concerned about me. Most of them have now settled in Australia. They are a close-knit family. The uncles think of Su Lai's children as belonging to the family rather than to me. Of course, if I weren't able to make a living myself they would look after me. But I found the atmosphere a little stifling."

Li Zhen's last few words were drowned in a sudden burst of noise from drums and gongs in the street. Lao-zhao came into the garden and said, "There's a parade of students passing the house."

The young people also came outside. Standing on the terrace, Kong, the young actor, said, "It's probably the Red Guards. A few days ago, Jiang Qing received their representatives at the Great Hall of the People in Beijing. That means the Chairman approves of the Red Guard organization."

"Who organized them in the first place?" I asked him. "I have never heard of an organization called the Red Guard."

"It's something new for the Cultural Revolution, encouraged by Jiang Qing, I heard. Someone told me she actually quietly organized some students from Qinghua Middle School and then pretended it was the spontaneous idea of the students. Since she is the Chairman's wife, the idea caught on. Now, acting as the Chairman's representative, she has given the Red Guards official recognition." Kong laughed and added, "My father used to say she was a mediocre actress in the old days. She seems to have improved." (Subsequently, when Jiang Qing dealt with her "enemies" in the film world, Kong's father had a terrible time and barely survived the ordeal. Kong himself was not given a part in any film production for years because of his father.)

Next day, I read in the newspaper that on August 18 Mao Zedong had reviewed the first contingent of the Red Guards in Beijing. On the front page was a large photograph of Mao wearing the khaki uniform of a People's Liberation Army officer, with a red armband on which the three Chinese characters for "Red Guard"—*hong wei bing*—were written in his own handwriting. From the gallery of Tiananmen Square (the Gate of Heavenly Peace of the Forbidden City), he had smiled and waved as he received a thunderous ovation from the youngsters gathered below. His special message to the Red Guards was to carry the torch of the Cultural Revolution to the far corners of China and to pursue the purpose of the Revolution to the very end. Young people all over China received this message from the man they had been brought up to worship as a call to arms. At that early stage of the Cultural Revolution the declared target was still only the "capitalist class," and it was there that the Red Guards focused their attack.

Group after group of young students continued to pass our house that evening, beating drums and gongs and shouting slogans. Meiping and her friends went out to watch the parade; Li Zhen and I retired to my study. The noise from the street was so loud that we couldn't talk. While we listened, I seemed to hear "Protect Chairman Mao" among the slogans shouted by the Red Guards. When Meiping came back alone, she told us that the students were carrying Mao's portrait and shouting, "Protect Chairman Mao" or "We shall protect Chairman Mao with our lives."

"Who is supposed to be threatening him?" I asked. None of us could think of an answer. In his lofty position as a demigod, Mao seemed beyond human reach.

Just as I was thinking of Stalin in the last years of his life, when he suspected so many people of attempting to kill him, Li Zhen said, "One of the symptoms of senile dementia is suspicion, and the other is paranoia."

"Oh, God!" I murmured.

Li Zhen, my daughter Meiping, and I stood in my study staring at each other speechlessly. We were rather frightened because suddenly the awesome reality that everybody in China, including ourselves, was at the mercy of Mao's whims struck each of us forcibly.

After a while, Li Zhen said, "I must go. No doubt we will know about everything as time goes on."

"I'll see Auntie Li home," said Meiping. "I don't think there are any buses. The streets have been taken over by the paraders."

I went with them to the front gate. Teams of teenagers holding colored flags with slogans and carrying portraits of Mao were passing down the street in front of my house. They were preceded by others beating drums and gongs. Every few yards a leader read out slogans written on a piece of paper, echoed loudly by the others. All the young paraders wore armbands of red cotton on which was written "Red Guard" in imitation of Mao's style of handwriting. The parade looked to me well organized and carefully directed, not something the young people could have done on their own. There was the hand of authority behind it, I thought.

Li Zhen and I said goodbye to each other. She walked away with Meiping, who was pushing her bicycle beside her. I stood there watching them until the parading youngsters hid Li Zhen's snow-white hair from my view.

That was the last glimpse I ever had of my dear old friend. A month later, when I was under house arrest, she committed suicide after a particularly humiliating experience. The Red Guards placed a pole across the gate of the conservatory less than four feet from the ground and made Li Zhen crawl under it to demonstrate that she was "a running dog of the British imperialists" because of her education in England. They then held a struggle meeting to compel her to confess her "love for Western music." She was found dead the next day, seated by her piano, with the gas turned on. The note she left behind held one sentence: "I did my best for my students."

The servants had already retired, so I waited downstairs for my daughter to get back. When she returned, we mounted the stairs together in silence. On the landing, she put her arms around me to hug me good night. There was much I wanted to say to her, some words of love and reassurance, but I felt choked with a deep feeling of sadness and fear that I could not explain.

"Well, this certainly is the one birthday I won't forget," my daughter said good-humoredly.

After she had gone into her bedroom, I closed the windows to shut out the noise from the street. The sound was muted and seemed further away, but without the cool evening breeze the house was very hot. Parade after parade passed outside. The resolute footsteps and emotional shouting voices of young men and women fired with revolutionary fervor continued to penetrate the walls.

I went into my study, took a book from the shelf, and tried to read. But I was restless and could not concentrate. Wandering aimlessly from room to room, I rearranged the flowers, throwing away the dead ones and putting water into the vases. I straightened the paintings on the walls and picked up ivory figures to examine the delicate carvings. All the time the parades went on outside. Even when a parade did not pass down the street by my house, I could hear the sound of the drums and gongs. After wandering around the house, I went finally to Meiping's room to see how she was. There was no answer to my light tap on the door. I opened it gently and found my daughter already asleep. Her black hair was spread on the white pillow, and her sweet young face was peaceful in repose. The light from the gap in the door fell on a snapshot of my husband in a small silver frame on her bedside table. I closed the door softly.

These were the two people in the world closest to my heart. One had died. The other was alive, and her life was just unfolding.

"Take good care of yourself and look after Meiping. I am sad to have to leave you both so soon."

I could hear again the weakened voice of my husband speaking these words before he lapsed into a deep coma from which he never awakened. That was nearly nine years ago. He had charged me to look after our daughter. I had done just that and watched her grow with joy in my heart. She was intelligent, beautiful, and warmhearted. I never had to worry about her. But now, with the start of the Cultural Revolution, a dark cloud had come over our lives. As I tried to look into the future, a deep feeling of uncertainty overwhelmed me. For the first time, I felt unable to control the direction of my own life and guide my daughter. That frightened me.

To face problems and changes with determination and optimism was the way I had lived. When my husband died in 1957, I was shattered by my loss and, for a time, felt half-dead with grief myself. But I found that taking positive action to cope with problems one by one was therapeutic and good for the renewal of courage.

In old China, women who lost their husbands lost their own identity. They became virtually nonpersons, subjected to ridicule and gossip by the neighbors. Although the new marriage law passed by the People's Government in 1952 protected women in general and forbade discrimination, the old prejudice against widows and unmarried older women persisted. Chinese society seemed to be offended and embarrassed by the sight of a woman trying to stand on her own.

When I started working at the Shell office, members of the

senior Chinese staff were dismayed that a woman with no administrative experience was put in charge of them. I had to prove myself over and over again to earn their respect and confidence. There was nothing I enjoyed more than meeting challenges and overcoming difficulties. And I was pleased and proud that I was able to maintain our old lifestyle in spite of losing my husband. Never in my life had I found myself in a situation so puzzling as the Cultural Revolution. I knew for a fact that whenever a Chinese national was appointed to a senior position in a foreign firm, the Department of Industry and Commerce of the Shanghai municipal government must give permission. Since the police kept a dossier on everybody, the government should know everything about me. There seemed no valid reason for the sudden accusation against me. While Winnie, Li Zhen, and Mr. Hu all seemed to think my being the target of persecution not unexpected, I did not know how best to conduct myself in the days ahead except to resist firmly all efforts to make me write a false confession. That would inevitably bring me into confrontation with officials of the Party. What would be the outcome of such confrontation? How would it affect my daughter's life? Standing outside her bedroom, I was so deeply troubled and felt so helpless that I invoked the guidance of God in a special prayer.

In the days after Mao Zedong reviewed the first group of Red Guards in Beijing and gave them his blessing, the Red Guards in Shanghai took over the streets. The newspaper announced that the mission of the Red Guards was to rid the country of the "Four Olds": old culture, old customs, old habits, and old ways of thinking. There was no clear definition of "old"; it was left to the Red Guards to decide.

First of all, they changed street names. The main thoroughfare of Shanghai along the waterfront, the Bund, was renamed Revolutionary Boulevard. Another major street was renamed August the First to commemorate Army Day. The road on which the Soviet Union had its consulate was renamed Anti-Revisionist Street, while the road in front of the former British consulate was renamed Anti-Imperialist Street. I found my own home now stood on Ouyanghai Road, named to commemorate a soldier who had given his life trying to save a mule from an oncoming train. The Red Guards debated whether to reverse the system of traffic lights, as they thought red should mean "go" and not "stop." In the meantime, the traffic lights stopped operating.

They smashed flower and curio shops because they said only the rich had the money to spend on such frivolities. Other shops were examined, and goods they considered offensive or unsuitable for a socialist society they destroyed or confiscated. Their standard was very strict. Because they did not think socialist man should sit on a sofa, all sofas became taboo. Other things, such as innerspring mattresses, silk, velvet, cosmetics, and clothes that reflected fashion trends of the West, were all tossed onto the streets to be carted away or burnt. Traditionally, shops in China had borne names that were considered propitious, such as Rich and Beautiful for a fabric shop, Delicious Aroma for a restaurant, Good Fortune and Longevity for a shop that sold hats for older men, Comfort for a shoe shop, Happy Homes for a furniture shop, etc. When the government took over the shops in 1956, the names had not been changed. Now, condemned by the Red Guards, they had to be changed to something more revolutionary. Uncertain what alternative would be acceptable, managers of a large number of shops chose the name East Is Red, the title of a song eulogizing Mao Zedong, which during the Cultural Revolution took the place of the national anthem. The Red Guards had removed the goods displayed in the windows of the shops, and Mao's official portraits replaced them. A person walking down the streets in the shopping district would not only be confused by rows of shops bearing the same name but also have the uncanny feeling of being watched by a hundred faces of Mao.

Daily, my servants reported to me all these incredible actions of the Red Guards. I became so curious that I decided to venture out to see for myself.

I had in a bank in the shopping district two fixed deposits that had matured. I decided to cash one of them so that I would have some extra money in the house, since experience told me that shortages of food and everything else always followed political upheavals. To keep alive, one had to resort to the black market, where prices were astronomical. I remembered my cook paying 50 yuan for a piece of pork that was 2 or 3 yuan in normal times, after the failure of Mao's Great Leap Forward Campaign.

Both Lao-zhao and Chen-ma suggested that I should be suitably dressed for going out, as the lady next door had had an unpleasant encounter with the Red Guards, who had confiscated her shoes and cut open the legs of her slacks when she went out to visit a friend. So before setting out from the house to go to the bank, I put on an old shirt, a pair of loose-fitting trousers borrowed from Chen-ma, and my exercise shoes. As the August sun was strong, Chen-ma handed me the wide-brimmed straw hat my daughter had brought back from the country after working in a rural commune in a program for students to help the peasants.

The streets were in a ferment of activity. Red Guards were everywhere. There were also many idle spectators. At this stage of the Cultural Revolution, the "enemy" was the capitalist class, so the majority of the population felt quite safe. To them the activities of the Red Guards were spectacular and entertaining. Many of them were strolling through the streets to watch the fun.

Groups of Red Guards were explaining to clusters of onlookers the meaning and purpose of the Cultural Revolution. I listened to one group for a little while and was puzzled and surprised to hear the Red Guard speaker telling the people that they would be "liberated" by the Cultural Revolution. Hadn't the people been liberated already in 1949 when the Communist Party took over China? Was that liberation not good enough, so that the people had to be liberated again? It almost seemed to me that the Communist Party was engaging in self-criticism. But that was unthinkable. I dismissed what I had heard as unimportant, perhaps merely a slip of the tongue by the young speaker. In fact, to liberate the proletariat again became the theme of the Cultural Revolution. Mao was to claim that his opponents in the Party leadership, headed by Liu Shaoqi and Deng Xiaoping, had revived capitalism in China. However, this was not revealed until much later in the year.

Other Red Guards were stopping buses, distributing leaflets, lecturing the passengers, and punishing those whose clothes they disapproved of. Most bicycles had red cards bearing Mao's quotations on the handlebars; riders of the few without them were stopped and given warning. On the sidewalks, the Red Guards led the people to shout slogans. Each group of Red Guards was accompanied by drums and gongs and large reproductions of Mao's portrait mounted on stands. At many street corners, loudspeakers were blaring revolutionary songs at intervals. In my proletarian outfit of old shirt and wide trousers, I blended with the scene and attracted no special attention. I walked steadily in the direction of the bank.

Suddenly I was startled to see the group of Red Guards right in front of me seize a pretty young woman. While one Red Guard held her, another removed her shoes and a third one cut the legs of her slacks open. The Red Guards were shouting, "Why do you wear shoes with pointed toes? Why do you wear slacks with narrow legs?"

"I'm a worker! I'm not a member of the capitalist class! Let me go!" The girl was struggling and protesting.

In the struggle, the Red Guards removed her slacks altogether, much to the amusement of the crowd that had gathered to watch the scene. The onlookers were laughing and jeering. One of the Red Guards slapped the girl's face to stop her from struggling. She sat on the dusty ground and buried her face in her arms. Between sobs she murmured, "I'm not a member of the capitalist class!"

One of the Red Guards opened her bag and took out her work pass to examine it. Then he threw the pass and her trousers to her. Hastily she pulled on the trousers. She did not wait for them to give back her shoes but walked away quickly in her socks. Almost immediately the same Red Guard seized a young man and shouted, "Why do you have oiled hair?"

I did not wait to see the outcome of this encounter but went straight to the bank. In China, every bank was a branch of the People's Bank, which belonged to the state. There was no brass railing or small windows. The tellers sat behind a plain wooden counter to deal with the depositors. I approached one of the women and placed my withdrawal slip on the counter in front of her.

Before I left the house, I had considered how much cash I should withdraw. The two deposits past the maturity date were for 6,000 yuan (approximately $2,400) and 20,000 yuan (approximately $8,000). The cost of living in China was low, as were wages and salaries. In 1966, 6,000 yuan was a large sum of money; 20,000 yuan represented a small fortune. The bank was really a department of the government. Those who worked there were charged with the task of encouraging savings so that money could be channeled to the state. During political campaigns the tellers had the power to refuse payment of large sums of money to depositors even when the deposits had matured. Sometimes they would demand a letter of approval from the depositor's place of work to certify the reason for the withdrawal. To avoid a possible rejection of my request to withdraw my money, I decided to cash the lesser sum of 6,000 and to renew the 20,000 for another year. But I had no difficulty whatever. The teller handed me the cash without uttering a single word, and before I had finished counting the bank notes, she had already picked up her knitting again. Although the walls of the small bank were covered with Cultural Revolution slogans and a number of Big Character Posters, the atmosphere inside was a contrast to the tension generated by the Red Guards on the streets.

As I stepped once again onto the sun-baked sidewalk, I rather regretted that I had been too timid to try to cash the larger sum. At the same time I was glad I had encountered no difficulty. I headed for home, but when I turned the corner, I was almost knocked down by a group of excited Red Guards leading an old man on a length of rope. They were shouting and hitting the poor man with a stick. I quickly stepped back and stood against the wall to let them pass. Suddenly the old man collapsed on the ground as if too tired to go on. He was a pitiful sight with his shirt torn and a few strands of gray hair over his half-shut eyes. The Red Guards pulled the rope. When he still did not get up, they jumped on him. The old man shrieked in pain.

"Dirty capitalist! Exploiter of workers! You deserve to die!" shouted the Red Guards.

My heart was palpitating wildly. The sudden and unexpected encounter with the group of Red Guards and the proximity of the suffering old man combined to give me a fright and made me think of Mr. Hu. I wondered how he was faring. Nearly two weeks had passed since he visited me. I thought I really ought to telephone him to see if he was all right. I slipped away and hastened towards my house. The streets were now even more crowded than an hour before. The Red Guards were seizing people indiscriminately. There were loud screams of protest and tearful pleading from the victims. When I saw that they were seizing women with permanent waves and cutting their hair off,

I was really thankful that Chen-ma had given me the large straw hat to cover my curly hair. There were quite a number of policemen on the streets, but they were just watching.

It was a relief to leave the busy shopping area behind me. The residential streets were more peaceful. However, when I turned into my street, I saw a large crowd of people in front of my house. They were looking at a Big Character Poster pasted on the front gate of my neighbor's house across the road. He was the chief engineer of the Shanghai Aluminum Company, formerly a Swiss firm, taken over a few years earlier by the Chinese government. Workers of the plant had put up the poster denouncing him as a "running dog of Swiss imperialism." Beside the poster was a smaller one written in a childish script. It was signed by my neighbor's two small children, who had joined in the denunciation of their father and vowed to sever their relationship with him. This unusual poster from an eleven-year-old and a ten-year-old was the reason for the crowd.

When Lao-zhao opened the gate for me, I asked about the poster signed by the children. Lao-zhao told me that my neighbor's servant had told him that it was the father's idea, to save his children from persecution.

The Red Guards' activities intensified by the hour. The very next day they entered the house of my neighbor across the street. His wife refused to open the front gate and turned the garden hose on the Red Guards to prevent them from entering. They simply smashed the gate down, snatched the hose from her, and drenched her with water. Then they knocked her down and beat her for resisting their revolutionary action. Her children tried to defend their mother and got into a fight with the Red Guards. They were denounced as "puppies of the running dog of Swiss imperialism" and made to assist the Red Guards in burning their father's books.

Day and night the city resounded with the loud noise of drums and gongs. News of looting and the ransacking of private homes all over the city reached me from different sources. I tried to reach Mr. Hu by telephone without success. It was the same with my other friends. The violence of the Red Guards seemed to have escalated. I heard of victims being humiliated, terrorized, and often killed when they offered resistance. Articles in the newspapers and talks by leading Maoists encouraged the Red Guards and congratulated them on their vandalism. They were declared to be the true successors to the cause of the proletarian revolution and exhorted to be fearless in their work of toppling the old world and building a new one based on Mao's teachings.

I felt utterly helpless. There was nothing I could do to prevent the destruction of my home and the loss of all my possessions. My daughter became very worried. More than once, she talked about our not being able to live on her small salary. I decided the time had come to tell her about my bank accounts in Hong Kong and elsewhere, which would be more than sufficient to cover our living expenses. Actually I myself was more worried about her status after the Cultural Revolution. If there was to be a new society in which descendants of capitalist families were to become a permanently unprivileged class in China, like the untouchables in India, her life would be unthinkable. To me this was of more importance than the loss of our material possessions.

To take care of the servants, I decided to give them the 6,000 yuan I had obtained from the bank right away, before the Red Guards came to our house. At first they refused to accept the money, reiterating their wish to remain to look after Meiping and myself. They also offered to hide my jewelry and valuables in their homes. Not wishing to implicate them in my own difficulties, I refused. I called Chen-ma, Lao-zhao, and Cook to my study and discussed with them how best to divide the money among the three of them. Because the gardener was not a full-time employee and came only occasionally, I decided to give him only 400 yuan. Chen-ma offered to take less than the other two because, she said, "They have to take care of their wives." After I had divided the money, I placed the 400 yuan for the gardener in an envelope, intending to give it to him the next time he came to work.

I told my servants that if they were afraid, they could leave anytime. When the Cultural Revolution was over, if I was financially able, I would give them additional money, for they had all been with me for a very long time.

After that had been done, I waited for the Red Guards.

3

The Red Guards

As the tempo of the Proletarian Cultural Revolution gathered momentum, all-night sessions of political indoctrination were often held in different organizations. On the evening of August 30, when the Red Guards came to loot my house, my daughter was at her film studio attending one of these meetings. I was sitting alone in my study reading *The Rise and Fall of the Third Reich,* which had come in the last batch of books from a bookshop in London with which I had an account. Throughout the years I worked for Shell, I managed to receive books from this shop by having the parcels sent to the office. Since the Shanghai censors always passed unopened all parcels addressed to organizations, and since Shell received an enormous amount of scientific literature for distribution to Chinese research organizations, my small parcel attracted no undue attention.

The house was very quiet. I knew Lao-zhao was sitting in the pantry as he had done day after day. Chen-ma was in her room, probably lying in bed wide awake. There was not the slightest sound or movement anywhere, almost as if everything in the house were holding its breath waiting helplessly for its own destruction.

The windows of my study were open. The bittersweet perfume of the magnolia in the garden and the damp smell of the cool evening air with a hint of autumn pervaded the atmosphere. From the direction of the street, faint at first but growing louder, came the sound of a heavy motor vehicle slowly approaching. I listened and waited for it to speed up and pass the house. But it slowed down, and the motor was cut off. I knew my neighbor on the left was also expecting the Red Guards. Dropping the book on my lap and sitting up tensely, I listened, wondering which house was to be the target.

Suddenly the doorbell began to ring incessantly. At the same time, there was furious pounding of many fists on my front gate, accompanied by the confused sound of hysterical voices shouting slogans. The cacophony told me that the time of waiting was over and that I must face the threat of the Red Guards and the destruction of my home. Lao-zhao came up the stairs breathlessly. Although he had known the Red Guards were sure to come eventually and had been waiting night after night just as I had, his face was ashen.

"They have come!" His unsteady voice was a mixture of awe and fright.

"Please keep calm, Lao-zhao! Open the gate but don't say anything. Take Chen-ma with you to your room and stay there," I told him.

Lao-zhao's room was over the garage. I wanted both of them out of the way so that they would not say anything to offend the Red Guards out of a sense of loyalty to me.

Outside, the sound of voices became louder. "Open the gate! Open the gate! Are you all dead? Why don't you open the gate?" Someone was swearing and kicking the wooden gate. The horn of the truck was blasting too.

Lao-zhao ran downstairs. I stood up to put the book on the shelf. A copy of the Constitution of the People's Republic caught my eye. Taking it in my hand and picking up the bunch of keys I had ready on my desk, I went downstairs.

Although in my imagination I had already lived through this moment many times, my heart was pounding. However, lifelong discipline enabled me to maintain a calm appearance. By the time I had reached the bottom of the staircase, I was the epitome of Chinese fatalism.

At the same moment, the Red Guards pushed open the front

door and entered the house. There were thirty or forty senior high school students, aged between fifteen and twenty, led by two men and one woman much older. Although they all wore the armband of the Red Guard, I thought the three older people were the teachers who generally accompanied the Red Guards when they looted private homes. As they crowded into the hall, one of them knocked over a pot of jasmine on a *fencai* porcelain stool. The tiny white blooms scattered on the floor, trampled by their impatient feet.

The leading Red Guard, a gangling youth with angry eyes, stepped forward and said to me, "We are the Red Guards. We have come to take revolutionary action against you!"

Though I knew it was futile, I held up the copy of the Constitution and said calmly, "It's against the Constitution of the People's Republic of China to enter a private house without a search warrant."

The young man snatched the document out of my hand and threw it on the floor. With his eyes blazing, he said, "The Constitution is abolished. It was a document written by the Revisionists within the Communist Party. We recognize only the teachings of our Great Leader Chairman Mao."

"Only the People's Congress has the power to change the Constitution," I said.

"We have abolished it. What can you do about it?" he said aggressively while assuming a militant stance with feet apart and shoulders braced.

A girl came within a few inches of where I stood and said, "What trick are you trying to play? Your only way out is to bow your head in submission. Otherwise you will suffer." She shook her fist in front of my nose and spat on the floor.

Another young man used a stick to smash the mirror hanging over the blackwood chest facing the front door. A shower of glass fell on the blue-and-white Kangxi vase on the chest, but the carved frame of the mirror remained on the hook. He tore the frame off and hurled it against the banister. Then he took from another Red Guard a small blackboard, which he hung up on the hook. On it was written a quotation from Mao Zedong. It said, "When the enemies with guns are annihilated, the enemies without guns still remain. We must not belittle these enemies."

The Red Guards read the quotation aloud as if taking a solemn oath. Afterwards, they told me to read it. Then one of them shouted to me, "An enemy without gun! That's what you are. Hand over the keys!"

I placed my bunch of keys on the chest amidst the fragments of glass. One of them picked it up. All the Red Guards dispersed into various parts of the house. A girl pushed me into the dining room and locked the door.

I sat down by the dining table and looked around the room. It was strange to realize that after this night I would never see it again as it was. The room had never looked so beautiful as it did at that moment. The gleam of the polished blackwood table was richer than ever. The white lacquered screen with its inlaid ivory figures stood proudly in one corner, a symbol of fine craftsmanship. The antique porcelain plates and vases on their blackwood stands were placed at just the right angle to show off their beauty. Even the curtains hung completely evenly, not a fraction out of line. In the glass cabinet were white jade figures, a rose quartz incense burner, and ornaments of other semiprecious stones that I had lovingly collected over the years. They had been beautifully carved in intricate designs by the hands of skilled artists. Now my eyes caressed them to bid them farewell. Having heard from Winnie that the painter Lin Fengmian was in serious trouble, I knew that his painting of a lady in blue hanging over the sideboard would be ruthlessly destroyed. But what about the other ink-and-brush painting by Qi Baishi? He was a great artist of the traditional style. Because of his having been a carpenter in early life, he was honored by the Communist Party. Would the Red Guards know the facts of Qi Baishi's life and spare this painting? I looked at it carefully, my eyes lingering over each stroke of his masterful brush. It was a picture of the lotus, a favorite subject for Chinese artists because the lotus symbolized purity. The poet Tao Yuanming (A.D. 376–427) used the lotus to represent a man of honor in a famous poem, saying that the lotus rose out of mud but remained unstained.

I recited the poem to myself and wondered whether it was really possible for anyone to remain unstained by his environment. It was an idea contrary to Marxism, which held that the environment molded the man. Perhaps the poet was too idealistic, I thought as I listened to the laughter of the Red Guards overhead. They seemed to be blissfully happy in their work of destruction because they were sure they were doing something to satisfy their God, Mao Zedong. Their behavior was the result of their upbringing in Communist China. The propaganda they had absorbed precluded their having a free will of their own.

A heavy thud overhead stopped my speculations. I could hear the sound of many people walking up and down the stairs, glasses breaking, and heavy knocking on the wall. The noise intensified. It sounded almost as if the Red Guards were tearing the house down rather than merely looting its contents. I became alarmed and decided to try to secure my release by deception.

I knocked on the door. There was such a din in the house that no one heard me. I knocked harder and harder. When I heard a movement outside the door, I called out, "Open up!"

The handle was turned slowly, and the door opened a narrow gap. A girl Red Guard in pigtails asked what I wanted. I told her I had to go to the bathroom. She let me out after cautioning me not to interfere with their revolutionary activities.

The Red Guards had taken from the storeroom the crates containing my father's books and papers and were trying to open them with pliers. Through the open drawing room door, I saw a girl on a ladder removing the curtains. Two bridge tables were in the middle of the room. On them was a collection of cameras, watches, clocks, binoculars, and silverware that the Red Guards had gathered from all over the house. These were the "valuables" they intended to present to the state.

Mounting the stairs, I was astonished to see several Red Guards taking pieces of my porcelain collection out of their padded boxes. One young man had arranged a set of four Kangxi winecups in a row on the floor and was stepping on them. I was just in time to hear the crunch of delicate porcelain under the sole of his shoe. The sound pierced my heart. Impulsively I leapt forward and caught his leg just as he raised his foot to crush the next cup. He toppled. We fell in a heap together. My eyes searched for the other winecups to make sure we had not broken them in our fall, and, momentarily distracted, I was not able to move aside when the boy regained his feet and kicked me right in my chest. I cried out in pain. The other Red Guards dropped what they were doing and gathered around us, shouting at me angrily for interfering in their revolutionary activities.

One of the teachers pulled me up from the floor. His face flushed in anger, the young man waved his fist, threatening me with a severe beating. The teacher raised her voice to restore order. She said to me, "What do you think you are doing? Are you trying to protect your possessions?"

"No, no, you can do whatever you like with my things. But you mustn't break these porcelain treasures. They are old and valuable and cannot be replaced," I said rather breathlessly. My chest throbbed with pain.

"Shut up! Shut up!" A chorus of voices drowned my words.

"Our Great Leader said, 'Lay out the facts; state the reasons.'" I summoned all my strength and yelled at the top of my voice to be heard.

The teacher raised her hand to silence the Red Guards and said, "We will allow you to lay out the facts and state the reasons." The Red Guards glared at me.

I picked up one of the remaining winecups and cradled it in my palm. Holding my hand out, I said, "This winecup is nearly three hundred years old. You seem to value the cameras, watches, and binoculars, but better cameras, better watches, and more powerful binoculars are being made every year. No one in this world can make another winecup like this one again. This is a part of our cultural heritage. Every Chinese should be proud of it."

The young man whose revolutionary work of destruction I had interrupted said angrily, "You shut up! These things belong to the old culture. They are the useless toys of the feudal emperors and the modern capitalist class and have no significance to us, the proletarian class. They cannot be compared to cameras and binoculars, which are useful for our struggle in time of war. Our Great Leader Chairman Mao taught us, 'If we do not destroy, we cannot establish.' The old culture must be destroyed to make way for the new socialist culture."

Another Red Guard said, "The purpose of the Great Proletarian Cultural Revolution is to destroy the old culture. You cannot stop us!"

I was trembling with anxiety and frantically searching my mind for some convincing argument to stop this senseless destruction. But before I could utter another futile word, I saw another young man coming down the stairs from the third floor with my blanc de chine Goddess of Mercy, Guanyin, in his hand. I turned to him and asked uneasily, "What are you going to do with that figure?"

He swung the arm holding the Guanyin carelessly in the air and declared, "This is a figure of Buddhist superstition. I'm going to throw it in the trash."

The Guanyin was a perfect specimen and a genuine product of the Dehua kiln in Fujian province. It was the work of the famous seventeenth-century Ming sculptor Chen Wei and bore his seal on the back. The beauty of the creamy-white figure was beyond description. The serene expression of the face was so skillfully captured that it seemed to be alive. The folds of the robe flowed so naturally that one forgot it was carved out of hard biscuit. The glaze was so rich and creamy that the whole figure looked as if it were soft to the touch. This figure of Guanyin I always kept in its padded box, deeming it too valuable to be displayed. I took it out only when knowledgeable friends interested in porcelain asked to look at it.

"No, no, please! You mustn't do that! I beg you." I was so agitated that my voice was shrill. The Red Guard just fixed me with a stony stare and continued to swing his arm casually, holding the Guanyin now with only two fingers.

Pleading was not going to move the Red Guards. If I wanted to communicate, I must speak their language. The time had come to employ diplomacy, it seemed to me. If the Red Guards thought I opposed them, I would never succeed in saving the treasures. By this time, I no longer thought of them as my own possessions. I did not care to whom they belonged after tonight as long as they were saved from destruction.

"Please, Red Guards! Believe me, I'm not opposed to you. You have come here as representatives of our Great Leader. How could I oppose the representatives of Chairman Mao? I understand the purpose of the Cultural Revolution. Did I not surrender the keys willingly when you asked for them?" I said.

"Yes, you did," conceded the teacher with a nod. The Red Guards gathered around us seemed to relax a little.

Somewhat encouraged, I went on. "All these old things belong to the past era. The past is old. It must go to make way for the new culture of socialism. But they could be taken away without immediate destruction. Remember, they were not made by members of the capitalist class. They were made by the hands of the workers of a bygone age. Should you not respect the labor of those workers?"

A Red Guard at the back of the group shouted impatiently, "Don't listen to her flowery words. She is trying to confuse us. She is trying to protect her possessions."

I quickly turned to him and said, "No, no! Your being in my house has already improved my socialist awareness. It was wrong of me to have kept all these beautiful and valuable things to myself. They rightly belong to the people. I beg you to take them to the Shanghai Museum. You can consult their experts. If the experts advise you to destroy them, there will still be time to do so."

A girl said, "The Shanghai Museum is closed. The experts there are being investigated. Some of them are also class ene- mies. In any case, they are intellectuals. Our Great Leader has said, 'The capitalist class is the skin; the intellectuals are the hairs that grow on the skin. When the skin dies, there will be no hair.' The capitalist class nourishes the intellectuals, so they belong to the same side. Now we are going to destroy the capi- talist class. Naturally the intellectuals are to be destroyed too."

The quotation of Mao she mentioned was new to me, but this was no time to think of that. I pursued my purpose by saying, "In that case, consult someone you can trust, someone in a position of authority. Perhaps one of the vice-mayors of Shang- hai. Surely there are many private collections in the city. There must be some sort of policy for dealing with them."

"No, no! You are a stupid class enemy! You simply do not understand. You are arguing and advising us to consult either other class enemies or the revisionist officials of the govern- ment. You talk about official policy. The only valid official policy is in this book." The young man took his book of Mao's quota- tions from his pocket and held it up as he continued, "The teachings of our Great Leader Chairman Mao are the only valid official policy."

Changing the direction of my argument, I said, "I saw a plac- ard saying, 'Long Live World Revolution.' You are going to carry the red flag of our Great Leader Chairman Mao all over the world, aren't you?"

"Of course we are! What has that got to do with you? You are only a class enemy," a girl sneered. She turned to the others and warned, "She is a tricky woman. Don't listen to her nonsense!"

Getting really desperate, I said, "Don't you realize all these things are extremely valuable? They can be sold in Hong Kong for a large sum of money. You will be able to finance your world revolution with that money."

At last, what I said made an impression. The Red Guards were listening. The wonderful prospect of playing a heroic role on the broad world stage was flattering to their egos, especially now that they were getting intoxicated with a sense of power.

I seized the psychological moment and went on. "Please put all these porcelain pieces back in their boxes and take them to a safe place. You can sell them or give them to the museum, whatever you consider right, according to the teachings of our Great Leader."

Perhaps, being an older person, the teacher felt some sense of responsibility. She asked me, "Are you sure your collection is valuable? How much would you say it is worth?"

"You will find a notebook with the date of purchase and the sum of money I spent on each item. Their price increases every month, especially on the world market. As a rough estimate, I think they are worth at least a million yuan," I told her.

Although members of the proletarian class did not appreciate value, they understood price. The Red Guards were impressed by the figure "one million." The teacher was by now just as anxious as I was to save the treasures, but she was afraid to put herself in the wrong with the Red Guards. However, she found a way for the Red Guards to back down without loss of face.

"Little revolutionary generals! Let's have a meeting and talk over this matter." She was flattering the Red Guards by calling them "little revolutionary generals," a title coined by the Maoists to encourage the Red Guards to do their bidding. The Red Guards were obviously pleased and readily agreed to her suggestion. She led them down the stairs to the dining room.

I knelt down to pick up the remaining winecups and put them in the box. The Guanyin had been left on the table. I took it and went upstairs to the large cupboard on the landing of the third floor, where I normally kept my collection. I saw that all the boxes had been taken out. On the floor there were fragments of porcelain in colors of oxblood, imperial yellow, celadon green,

and blue-and-white. My heart sank at the realization that whatever my desperate effort might now achieve, it was already too
late. Many of the boxes were empty.

The third-floor rooms resembled a scene after an earthquake
except for the absence of corpses. But the red wine spilled out
of broken bottles on white sheets and blankets was the same
color as blood.

Because we lived in a permanent state of shortage, every
household with enough living space had a store cupboard in
which we hoarded reserves of such daily necessities as flour,
sugar, and canned meat. Each time I went to Hong Kong I also
brought back cases of food and soap to supplement our meager
ration, even though the import duty was astronomical. The Red
Guards had emptied my store cupboard. Flour, sugar, and food
from cans they had opened lay on top of heaps of clothing they
had taken out of cupboards, trunks, and drawers. Some suitcases
remained undisturbed, but I could see that they had already
dealt with my fur coats and evening dresses with a pair of scissors. The ceiling fan was whirling. Bits of fur, silk, and torn
sheets of tissue paper were flying around.

Every piece of furniture was pulled out of its place. Tables and
chairs were overturned, some placed on top of others to form
a ladder. As it was summer, my carpets had been cleaned, sprinkled with camphor powder, rolled up, and stored in an empty
bedroom on the third floor. Behind the largest roll of carpet, I
found a shopping bag stuffed with two of my cashmere cardigans
and several sets of new underwear. It seemed a thoughtful Red
Guard had quietly put them away for personal use.

In the largest guest room, where the Red Guards had carried
out most of their destructive labor of cutting and smashing, a
radio set was tuned to a local station broadcasting revolutionary
songs based on Mao's quotations. A female voice was singing,
"Marxism can be summed up in one sentence: revolution is
justifiable." There was a note of urgency in her voice that compelled the listener's attention. This song was to become the
clarion call not only for the Red Guards but also for the
Proletarian Revolutionaries when they were organized later on.
I thought of switching off the radio, but it was out of my reach
unless I climbed over the mountain of debris in the middle of
the room.

I looked at what had happened to my things hopelessly but indifferently. They belonged to a period of my life that had abruptly ended when the Red Guards entered my house. Though I could not see into the future, I refused to look back. I supposed the Red Guards had enjoyed themselves. Is it not true that we all possess some destructive tendencies in our nature? The veneer of civilization is very thin. Underneath lurks the animal in each of us. If I were young and had had a working-class background, if I had been brought up to worship Mao and taught to believe him infallible, would I not have behaved exactly as the Red Guards had done?

The struggle over the porcelain had exhausted me. My chest still throbbed with pain. I wondered whether a rib had been broken. Examining my chest in the bathroom mirror, I saw a large bruise on the right side. I went down to the second floor looking for somewhere to lie down and rest. I opened the door of my own bedroom. It was in the same state of disorder as the third floor. Through the open door of my study, I saw my jewelry laid out on the desk. Since the Red Guards were still in the dining room discussing what they were going to do with the porcelain, I quickly withdrew to avoid the suspicion that I was attempting to recover anything. I turned the handle of my daughter's bedroom door to find the room as yet undisturbed. The strong breeze from the open window was tossing the gauze curtain. Crossing the room to secure it to the loop, I chanced to look down and was attracted by the sight of bright, leaping flames in the garden. I saw that a bonfire had been lit in the middle of the lawn. The Red Guards were standing around the fire carelessly tossing my books onto the flames. My heart tightened with pain. I turned my back to the window and closed my eyes, leaning against the windowsill for support. Hoping to shut out what I had seen and heard during the last few hours, I tried to escape to my inner self for a moment of peace and prayer.

Suddenly, a girl Red Guard appeared in the doorway and switched on the light. "What are you doing here? Who told you to come here? Are you up to any tricks?" She bombarded me with questions but did not wait for me to answer before she said, "Come along! We need you."

I followed her to my study. Several Red Guards were gathered around my desk. Seated on the chair was a thin girl with bobbed hair in a faded blue cotton blouse that she had outgrown. In a society where food was at a premium, those who had to depend entirely on official rations, without recourse to perks or the black market, generally acquired a pinched look. She was just such a girl. I supposed she came from a working-class family living on a tight budget, without either of her parents being smart enough to become a Party member. She sat there tensely with head bowed, and I guessed that the others, who fell silent when I entered the room, had been questioning her. One of the male teachers was standing next to the girl. He said to me, "Pull up a chair and be seated."

Several Red Guards brought chairs from my bedroom next door, and both the teacher and I sat down. I was directly opposite the girl on the other side of my desk. As I took my seat, she looked up and hastily threw me a nervous glance that was half-frightened and half-appealing. On the desk in front of me was my jewelry case, and some of the jewelry was on the blotting pad.

"Is this all the jewelry you have? Look it over and tell us if everything is here," the teacher said.

Opening the case, I saw that several rings and bracelets and a diamond watch were missing. The teacher asked again, "Is it all here, your jewelry? Speak the truth. We are going to check with your servants too. Have you hidden some? Some of the capitalist families have tried to hide their jewelry among flowers in the garden."

It was a tense moment. The boys at the other end of the room removing records from the record cabinet stopped to wait for my answer too. I understood the situation fully. They all suspected the girl, who had probably been left alone for a short moment, of having secreted some pieces of jewelry. In fact, that was probably exactly what she had done. If I lied to protect the girl and if my servants, who knew what jewelry I had, did not, I would be laying myself open to charges that I had hidden my jewelry. There was no choice for me but to tell the truth. Yet the girl looked so pitiful that I hated having to incriminate her.

"The main pieces are here. The most valuable ones, such as this jade necklace and this diamond brooch, are here. A few pieces are missing, but they are not the most valuable." I tried to minimize the girl's predicament.

"What is missing?" the teacher asked impatiently.

"A watch, several rings and gold bracelets."

"What is the watch like? What make is it? Is it like this one?" The teacher stretched out his wrist, and I saw that he had on an imported Swiss watch, a status symbol in Communist China. He thought I had a man's watch like most other Chinese women, who tried to achieve equality by being the same as men. But I had never followed the new fashion.

"No, the missing watch is a small one with diamonds and a platinum strap. It's French. The name of the maker is Ebel."

"I hope you are not lying. How come you had such an unusual watch? Swiss watches are the best, aren't they?" While the teacher was speaking to me, he gestured to a Red Guard to go to the drawing room downstairs to see if such a watch was among the cameras and binoculars. The Red Guard soon came back and shook his head.

"The Ebel watch was bought in Hong Kong when my late husband and I were there in 1957. It was his last gift to me. Please ask Chen-ma. She knows all about it and is familiar with all my things, including my jewelry."

No one said anything more. The poor girl was almost in tears; her pale face looked so sad and frightened. The teacher asked me about the rings and bracelets. As I described them, an idea occurred to me. The floor of my study, especially around my desk, was knee-deep in paper-wrappings, tissue paper wrinkled into balls, old magazines torn to pieces, many old copies of the airmail edition of the London *Times* in shreds, exercise books, note pads, and unused stationery from my desk drawers. Mixed with all these were also stacks of books waiting to be carried to the garden fire. When I finished describing the missing jewelry, I said, looking at the girl in front of me, "All of you have made such a mess with all these papers and books on the floor. Perhaps the missing watch, rings, and bracelets have dropped among the debris."

The girl's pale face reddened. In an instant, she disappeared under the desk. The other Red Guards followed suit. The teacher remained in his seat, contemplating me with a puzzled frown. It seemed to me he saw through my game but did not understand my motive for covering up for the thief. Confucius said, "A compassionate heart is possessed by every human being." This was no longer true in China, where in a society pledged to materialism, men's behavior was increasingly motivated by self-interest. The teacher probably thought I hoped to gain favor from the Red Guards.

After searching among the papers, the Red Guards recovered the rings and bracelets. The girl was smiling. But there was no watch. Probably someone else had taken it.

In my bedroom next door, the Red Guards were hammering on the furniture. Right in front of me, they were breaking my records. I stood up and said to the teacher, "These records are classical music by the great masters of Europe in the eighteenth and nineteenth centuries. They are not the forbidden music of the dancehalls and nightclubs. Western music of this kind is taught in our music academies. Why not preserve the records and donate them to the Music Society?"

"You live in the past," he said. "Don't you know that our Great Leader has said that Western music of any kind is decadent? Only certain passages of certain compositions are all right, not the whole of any composition."

"Isn't every section of any composition an integral part of the whole?" I murmured.

"Shut up! In any case, do the peasants and workers want Chopin, Mozart, Beethoven, or Tchaikovsky? Of course not! We are going to compose our own proletarian music. As for the Music Society, it's disbanded."

The night seemed interminable. I was so tired that I could hardly stand. I asked the teacher for permission to rest for a while.

"You may go to your daughter's room. She is an independent film worker earning a salary of her own. Her room is not included in our revolutionary action."

I returned to my daughter's room and lay down on her bed. It was still dark, but through the window I could see the faint light of dawn on the eastern horizon. I closed my eyes and slowly drifted off to sleep.

When I woke, the sun was streaming into the room. The house was a great deal quieter. There was the sound of a news broadcast from a radio, but there was no longer the noise of furniture being dragged about overhead. I had a shower in my daughter's bathroom and dressed in her slacks and shirt. Outside the room, I found the Red Guards sitting on chairs and on the stairs eating hot buns sent to them from their school. There seemed fewer of them, and none of the teachers was in sight. I went down the stairs to the kitchen to look for breakfast.

The cook was there removing food from the refrigerator, which, he told me, the Red Guards wanted to take away. I asked him to make some coffee and toast.

I sat down by the kitchen table, and the cook placed the coffee percolator, toast, butter, and a jar of Cooper's marmalade in front of me.

A pretty girl with a lithe figure and two long plaits over her shoulders came into the kitchen and sat down on the other side of the table, watching me. After I had drunk the coffee and put the cup down, she picked it up. There was still some coffee in it. She put the cup to her nose and sniffed.

Making a face of distaste, she asked me, "What is this?"

"It's coffee," I said.

"What is coffee?"

I told her that coffee was a beverage rather like tea, only stronger.

"Is it foreign food?" She put the cup down with a clatter.

"I suppose you could call it foreign food." I picked up another slice of toast and started to butter it.

She looked at the butter and picked up the jar of marmalade with its label in English. Then she leaned forward in her seat and stared at me with her large black eyes blazing. "Why do you have to drink a foreign beverage? Why do you have to eat foreign food? Why do you have so many foreign books? Why are you so foreign altogether? In every room in this house there are imported things, but there is not a single portrait of our beloved Great Leader. We have been to many homes of the capitalist class. Your house is the worst of all, the most reactionary of all. Are you a Chinese, or are you a foreigner?"

I smiled at her outburst. My house must have seemed rather different from the others they had looted. At the beginning of the Cultural Revolution, Lao-zhao did suggest that I hang up a portrait of Mao Zedong. But so many people had the same idea that we couldn't find a single one in any shop and had to give up. However, I thought I might try to help this pretty girl see things in their proper perspective.

"Do you eat tomatoes?" I asked her.

"Of course I do!" she said. Tomatoes were common in Shanghai. When the harvest was in, the price dropped to a few cents a catty (a catty being a little over a pound in weight). Every adult and every child in Shanghai ate tomatoes either as fruit or vegetable.

"Well, the tomato is a foreign food. It was introduced into China by foreigners. So was the watermelon, brought from Persia over the silk route. As for foreign books, Karl Marx himself was a German. If people didn't read books by foreigners, there would not have been an international Communist movement. It has never been possible to keep things and ideas locked up within the national boundary of any one country, even in the old days when communication was difficult. Nowadays, it's even more impossible. I'm pretty sure that by now people all over the world have heard that Chinese high school students are organized as Red Guards."

"Really?" she said and became thoughtful. It was apparent that I had opened a new horizon for her. After a while, she said, "You are good at making things clear. Have you been to a university?"

I had a mouthful of toast, so I just nodded. She looked wistful. "I had hoped to go to a university when I finish high school. But now there won't be any university to go to. All of us young people will have to become soldiers."

"You are a girl. You won't have to be a soldier."

"It's much worse for girls!" She sounded depressed.

"In any case, there won't be a war, so you don't have to worry." I tried to console her.

She turned quickly to look at the door and shot a glance of apprehension at the cook, who was bending over the sink washing vegetables. Putting a hand on my arm, she warned in a whisper, "Don't say that! It's dangerous to say that! Our Great Leader has already told us to prepare for a People's War against the American imperialists, the Soviet revisionists, and the reactionary Kuomintang in Taiwan. You must not speak such peace propaganda and oppose what was said by our Great Leader!"

I smiled at her and nodded in agreement.

The kitchen door opened. A boy poked his head into the room to ask the cook whether the refrigerator was ready. The girl

quickly removed her hand from my arm and stood up. Although
the boy had already withdrawn, she said in a firm, loud voice,
"You are a class enemy. I'm not going to listen to your nonsense."

She turned to leave. But at the door she looked back and gave
me a sweet smile.

At the sink, the cook said, "Not all of them are young fools!"

Remembering that his youngest son was a high school student, I asked him whether the boy also belonged to the Red
Guard organization.

"Oh, yes! How could he not join? He would have been looked
upon as a renegade and punished. Besides, young people always
want to do exactly what other young people are doing. But when
he comes home my wife searches him to make sure he hasn't
taken anything that doesn't belong to him."

"Is there a lot of that kind of thing going on?"

"Yes. The temptation is there. Some parents even encourage
the youngsters to take things. But I'm not going to let my son
be turned into a habitual thief," the cook said.

"What about the children from capitalist families?"

"They are having a hard time. They are made to feel like
outcasts and required to draw a line between themselves and
their parents. Young people can be very cruel to each other, you
know. There has been an increasing number of suicides."

Outside the kitchen, I saw a man who had not been present
with the Red Guards the night before. I could tell by his air of
self-assurance that he was a Party official, perhaps a veteran of
the Civil War, as he was obviously over forty.

"I'm a liaison officer of the municipal government," he introduced himself to me. "It's my job to inspect the revolutionary
action of the Red Guards. Have you been beaten or ill treated?"

It was a pleasant surprise to learn that the Shanghai municipal
government was endeavoring to check the excessive behavior of
the Red Guards. This attempt at moderation was to be very
quickly curtailed by the Maoists in the Party leadership in Beijing. The work of the liaison officer was short-lived. But when
he spoke to me he was unaware of his own impending downfall,
and his manner was authoritative.

"No, not at all," I said to him. "These Red Guards carried out
their revolutionary action strictly according to the teachings of

our Great Leader Chairman Mao. I have been allowed to eat and sleep." The Red Guards standing around us beamed.

He declared, "That's good. It's not the purpose of the proletarian class to destroy your body. We want to save your soul by reforming your way of thinking." Although Mao Zedong and his followers were atheists, they were very fond of talking about the "soul." In his writing, Mao often referred to the saving of a man's soul. During the Cultural Revolution, "soul" was mentioned frequently. Several times, Defense Minister Lin Biao stood on the balcony of Tiananmen to speak on behalf of Mao Zedong to the Red Guards gathered below about allowing the revolutionary spirit to touch their "souls" in order to improve themselves. While no one could ask Mao Zedong or Lin Biao what exactly they meant when they talked about a man's "soul," it greatly taxed the ingenuity of the Marxist writers of newspaper articles who had to explain their leaders' words to the people.

Then the liaison officer raised his arm and swung it in a circle to embrace the whole house. "Is it right for you and your daughter to live in a house of nine rooms with four bathrooms when there is such a severe housing shortage in Shanghai? Is it right for you to use woolen carpets and have each room filled with rosewood and blackwood furniture when there is a shortage of wood and basic furniture for others? Is it right for you to wear silk and fur and sleep under quilts filled with down? Is it right for you to have three servants to wait on you?"

He looked at me for a moment. When he saw I was not going to argue with him, he went on. "As I said a moment ago, it is not our objective to destroy your body. You will be allowed enough clothing and basic furniture to carry on a normal life, but you won't be allowed to maintain a standard of living above that of the average worker."

He looked at me again for my reaction. Seeing none, he continued. "It's now quite warm, but winter will be here soon. The Red Guards will take you upstairs to pack a suitcase of clothing for yourself. Pick a warm padded jacket. You won't have central heating in this house again. Coal is needed for industry. It's not for the luxury of the capitalist class."

He went into the dining room and closed the door. I followed a Red Guard to the third floor to pick up warm clothes from the debris. A male Red Guard who had been there the night before but had gone away in the morning returned to the house. He came up the stairs two steps at a time and said to the girl helping me, "Incredible! It's incredible! You know what I found when I went home? They are looting my house! How can they do this? My father and grandfather are both workers."

Indeed, this was extraordinary. We stopped sorting the clothes and asked him to explain.

"It's my aunt. During the Japanese invasion, she lost everything when the Japanese soldiers burned her area of Nantao City. She borrowed money to open a fruit stall after the war. She did quite well and made a living for herself and her children, but she gave it up two years ago when she got too old to manage it. Now they say she is a capitalist because she had a private business of her own. Our home is being looted because she is now living with us since her children are not in Shanghai."

The young man was full of indignation and almost in tears. The incident was a terrible blow to a self-righteous and proud Red Guard who was the third generation of a working-class family. It was also an eye-opener for me. Apparently, I decided, there were capitalists and capitalists, and none were more equal than others. If owners of fruit stalls were included in the category, the Red Guards in Shanghai had a big job to do.

More Red Guards joined us to hear the young man's story. I noticed that a couple of them slipped away quietly afterwards, no doubt going home to investigate.

Thinking of my daughter, I asked the Red Guards for her winter clothes.

"She is not included in our revolutionary action. We did not go to her room," they replied.

"But her winter clothes are not in her room. They were put away for the summer up here," I told them.

Evidently mellowed by his own family's experience, the boy whose home was looted volunteered, "We must pack a couple of suitcases for her too."

My daughter and I were each allowed a suitcase of clothes and a canvas bag with bedding.

The work of destruction accomplished, the Red Guards were getting things ready for removal. By the afternoon, there were no more than a dozen of them left in the house. One of them called me to the dining room.

The liaison officer and two of the teachers were seated by the dining table, which was strewn with old letters my grandfather had written to my father when the latter was a student in a naval college in Japan, before the 1911 revolution that made China a republic. They were included among the family papers brought to my house after my widowed mother passed away in Nanjing in 1962. I had never opened the boxes because they were to be sent to my brother in Beijing. Being the eldest son, he was the rightful heir. I could see that the paper and the envelopes were yellow with age, but the brush-and-ink handwriting of my grandfather had not faded.

After motioning me to sit down in a vacant chair, the liaison officer pointed to the letters and asked me, "Have you read these letters from your grandfather to your father?"

"My father showed them to me when I was in my teens, a long time ago," I told him.

"Your grandfather was a patriot even though he was a big landlord. He sent your father, his eldest son, to Japan to learn to become a naval officer because China suffered defeat in the naval battle against Japan in 1895. He also took part in the abortive Constitutional Reform Movement. When that failed, he returned to his native province and devoted himself to academic work. Do you respect your grandfather?"

I thought the liaison officer very brave to say my grandfather was a patriot even though he was a big landlord, because all big landlords were declared enemies of the state and shot during the Land Reform Movement in 1950. No attempt was made to verify whether any of them was a patriot. I remembered my father saying at the time that it was fortunate my second uncle, who managed the family estate, had died some years before the Communist takeover, so that my grandfather in heaven was spared the indignity of having one of his sons executed.

All Chinese revered their ancestors. Although I had never seen my grandfather, I loved him. So I said to the liaison officer, "Of course I respect and love my grandfather."

"Then why did you choose to work for a foreign firm? Don't you know the foreigners have never had any good intentions towards us? They exploited the Chinese people for economic gain or tried to enslave us politically. Only the scum of China work for foreigners. You should know that. You were offered a job teaching English at the Institute of Foreign Languages. But you preferred to work for Shell. Why?"

I couldn't tell him that I had made the decision to work for Shell because I was afraid to get involved in the new political movement initiated by Mao Zedong. In 1957 when I was called upon to make the choice of either going to the Foreign Language Institute to teach or accepting the job with Shell, the Anti-Rightist Campaign was in full swing. It was a campaign primarily aimed at the intellectuals, especially those trained in foreign universities and suspected of harboring ideas hostile to Communism. Many of my friends and acquaintances had been denounced and persecuted. Some were sent to labor camps; a few went to prison. All the universities and research organizations, including the Foreign Language Institute, were in a state of turmoil. Under such circumstances, it would have been asking for trouble to join the teaching staff of the Foreign Language Institute. I did not regret accepting the job with Shell even though I was aware that working for a foreign firm carried with it neither honor nor position in Chinese society.

"You were probably attracted by the pay you got from the foreigners?" he asked. I realized at once that I was on dangerous ground. It was the common belief in China, the result of persistent propaganda, that members of the capitalist class would do anything for money, criminal or otherwise.

"No," I said. "I already had a great deal of money. It was mainly the working conditions at Shell, such as shorter hours, the use of a car, etc. I suppose I am lazy," I added, feeling a gesture of self-criticism was called for. Laziness was another characteristic attributed to the capitalist class.

He stood up and looked at his watch. "There are several more places I have to go," he said. "You had better think over the things you did for the foreigners and be ready to change your standpoint to that of the people. It's not our policy to destroy the physical person of the members of the capitalist class. We want you to reform. Don't you want to join the ranks of the glorious proletariat? You can do so only after being stripped of your surplus belongings and changing your way of life. It's the objective of the proletarian revolution to form a classless society in which each individual labors for the common good and enjoys the fruit of that labor, and where no one is above anyone else."

It was an attractive and idealistic picture. I used to believe in it too when I was a student. But after living in Communist China for the past seventeen years, I knew that such a society was only a dream because those who seized power would invariably become the new ruling class. They would have the power to control the people's lives and bend the people's will. Because they controlled the production and distribution of goods and services in the name of the state, they would also enjoy material luxuries beyond the reach of the common people. In Communist China, details of the private lives of the leaders were guarded as state secrets. But every Chinese knew that the Party leaders lived in spacious mansions with many servants, obtained their provisions from special shops where luxury goods were made available to their households at nominal prices, and sent their children in chauffeur-driven cars to exclusive schools to be taught by specially selected teachers. Even though every Chinese knew how the leaders lived, no one dared to talk about it. If we had to pass by a special shop for the military or high officials, we carefully looked the other way to avoid giving the impression we knew it was there.

It was common knowledge that Mao Zedong himself lived in the former winter palace of the Qing dynasty emperors and had an entourage of specially selected attractive young women as his personal attendants. He could order the Red Guards to tear up the Constitution, beat people up, and loot their homes, and no one, not even other Party leaders, dared to oppose him. Even this liaison officer, a very junior official in the Party hierarchy, could decide how many jackets I was to be allowed from my own stock of clothes and how I was to live in future. He could make all these arbitrary decisions about my life and lecture me or even accuse me of imaginary crimes simply because he was an official and I was just an ordinary citizen. He had power, but I had none. We were not equals by any stretch of the imagination.

After the liaison officer had left my house, the Red Guards learned that no trucks were available that day for them to take away the loot, so they put my jewelry and other valuables in Meiping's study and sealed the door. They also charged my servants to watch me so that I could not take back any of my things.

It was late afternoon when the last Red Guard passed through the front gate and banged it shut. Lao-zhao and the cook tried to clear the debris that covered the floor of every room—pieces of broken glass, china, picture frames, and a huge amount of torn paper. I told them not to remove or discard anything in case something the Red Guards wanted was lost and we were accused of deliberately taking it away. They just cleared a path in the middle of each room and swept the debris into the corners.

When I went up to my bedroom to inspect the damage, I found Chen-ma already there, sitting at my dressing table staring at the mess around her. I told her to help me pick up the torn clothes and put them in one corner so that we might have some space to move about in. My bedspread was soiled with the foot-prints of the Red Guards. When Chen-ma and I took it off, we saw that they had slashed the mattress. On the wall over my bed, where a painting of flowers had hung, someone had written in lipstick, "Down with the Running Dog of Imperialism!" The Red Guards had punched holes in the panels of the lacquered screen. Hanging on the frame of the screen were strips of colored paper with slogans such as "Long Live the Dictatorship of the Proletariat" and "Down with the Capitalist Class." I folded the broken screen and put it in the passage outside, slogans and all. Then I picked up the crushed white silk lampshades while Chen-ma swept up the broken pieces of the porcelain lamps.

In the bathroom, soiled towels lay in a heap. The bathtub was half full of colored water because the Red Guards had emptied all the medicines from the medicine cabinet into it. I reached in to pull the plug and let the water out.

Suddenly the front doorbell rang again. Lao-zhao rushed up the stairs shouting, "Another group of Red Guards has come!"

Hastily I wiped my stained hands on a towel and came out to the landing. I said to him, "Keep calm and open the gate."

"Cook is there," he said breathlessly.

I walked downstairs. Eight men dressed in the coarse blue of peasants or outdoor workers stood in the hall. Though they were middle-aged, they all wore the armband of the Red Guard. Their leader, a man with a leather whip in his hand, stood in front of me and said, "We are the Red Guards! We have come to take revolutionary action against you!"

The situation was so absurd that I couldn't help being amused. "Indeed, are you the Red Guards? You look to me more like their fathers," I said, standing on the last step of the staircase.

The leather whip struck me on my bare arm just above my elbow. The sharp pain made me bite my lip. The men seemed nervous; they kept looking over their shoulders at the front door.

"Hand over the keys! We haven't time to stand here and carry on a conversation with you," their leader shouted.

"The keys were taken by the Red Guards who came here last night."

"You are lying!" The man raised his whip as if to strike me again, but he only let the tip of the whip touch my shoulder.

Another man asked anxiously, "Have they taken everything?"

"No, not everything," I answered.

One of the men pushed me and my servants into the kitchen and locked us inside. He remained outside guarding the door while the others collected a few suitcases of things from the house. They departed so hurriedly that they forgot to let us out. The cook had to climb out of the kitchen window into the garden in order to get into the house to unlock the kitchen door.

Chen-ma went back to my bedroom to try to make me a bed for the night. I sat down by the kitchen table to drink a cup of tea the cook had made for me. He sat down on the other side of the table and started to shell peas.

"What's going to happen next?" he asked. "There is surely going to be lawlessness and disorder. Anybody wearing a red armband and calling himself a Red Guard can enter anybody's home and help himself."

"The Red Guards have put up a Big Character Poster on the front gate. Shall I go out and see what it says?" Lao-zhao asked me.

"Yes, please go and see."

Lao-zhao came back and told me that I was accused of "conspiring with foreign nations," which during the Cultural Revolution meant that I was a "foreign spy." Strictly translated, the four Chinese characters, *li tong wai guo,* meant "inside communicate foreign countries." It's probably considered normal and innocuous anywhere else. But in Maoist China communicating with foreign countries other than through official channels was a crime.

I was thinking how the Chinese language lent itself to euphe-mism when I heard my daughter opening and closing the front gate and pushing her bicycle into the garage.

"Mei-mei has come home! She will be upset!" both Lao-zhao and the cook exclaimed. (Old servants in Chinese households often gave pet names to the children. Mei-mei was what my servants had called my daughter since she was a little girl.)

I composed myself to appear nonchalant and got up to meet her.

She opened the front door and stood there, stunned by the sight of chaos. When she saw me, she rushed forward and threw her arms around my shoulders and murmured, "Mommy, oh, Mommy, are you all right?"

"Don't be upset," I said in as cheerful a voice as I could manage. "When the Cultural Revolution is over, we will make a new home. It will be just as beautiful, no, more beautiful than it was."

"No, Mommy, no one will be allowed to have a home like we had again," she said in a subdued voice.

We mounted the stairs in silence with our arms around each other's waist. I accompanied her to her bedroom. At least there everything was still just as it had been. I sat down in the armchair while she went into her bathroom. When we came out, Lao-zhao had already cleared a space in my study and laid out a folding bridge table in preparation for dinner. The cook had managed to produce a noodle dish with a delicious meat sauce served with green peas. I did not know how exhausted and hungry I was until I started to eat.

While we were eating, I told my daughter that the liaison officer had said that I would be left basic furniture and utensils necessary for a simple life, the same as that of an ordinary worker. I would ask for the second floor of the house and give the rest to the government for other families. We would have my bedroom and bathroom, Meiping's bedroom and bathroom, and the study. It would be enough for us. To be able to plan and look ahead was good. I was already resigned to a lower standard of living. It would be a novelty and probably quite pleasant not to have too many things to look after. The human spirit is resilient, and I was by nature optimistic.

I noticed that as I talked about my plan for the future, Meiping became visibly more relaxed. She told me that in addition to appointing liaison officers to supervise the Red Guards, the Shanghai Party Secretariat and the municipal government had passed a Ten-Point Resolution stressing the importance of protecting cultural relics and pointing out that it was against the Constitution to ransack private homes. Lao-zhao stopped what he was doing to listen, and Chen-ma came out of my bedroom and clapped. They were comforted by this piece of good news. But what I had seen of the behavior of the Red Guards and what they said about revisionist officials in the government made me skeptical of the extent to which the Ten-Point Resolution was enforceable.

I knew my daughter was worried about me, as she kept looking at me anxiously. To put her mind at ease, I told her how I had lost all my possessions in Chongqing during the Sino-Japanese War.

"It happened in Chongqing in the summer of 1941. Daddy and I were about to leave for Canberra with the first group of Chinese diplomats and their families to open the new Chinese legation there. Two days before we were scheduled to leave, we had a prolonged and severe air raid. A bomb landed on the tennis court right in front of our house. The blast tore off the roof, and part of the house collapsed," I said.

"Goodness! Where were you?" my daughter asked.

"I was in the shelter under the house. Daddy was in the shelter at his office. The shelters in Chongqing were deep caves dug into mountainsides, very deep and quite safe."

"Did you lose everything in the house?"

"Fortunately we had put the packed suitcases under the stairs when the alarm sounded. The stairs collapsed and buried the suitcases underneath. We managed to dig three of them out. Of course they were in a terrible state. When we got to Hong Kong we had to buy everything all over again. We didn't have time to get the furniture out of the rubble. To this day, I have no idea what happened to it," I told her. "So you see, we did in fact lose almost everything we had."

"You never told me any of this."

"It happened such a long time ago, before you were born, when I was not much older than you are now. I had actually forgotten all about it. It was the looting by the Red Guards that made me remember it again."

"Oh, Mommy, how could you have forgotten something terrible like that? You lost everything!"

"Yes, I did forget. But it was wartime. People were being bombed out all over the place. Bad experience is more bearable when you are not the only sufferer."

"I'll never forget how our house looks today, not in a million years," my daughter said.

"It's always best to look ahead and not backwards. Possessions are not important. Think of those beautiful porcelain pieces I had. Before they came to me, they had all passed through the hands of many people, surviving wars and natural disasters. I got them only because someone else lost them. While I had them, I enjoyed them; now some other people will enjoy them. Life itself is transitory. Possessions are not important."

"I'm glad you are so philosophical," she said, smiling for the first time since she had come home. "Of course, we must not let our happiness be dependent on possessions. We still have each other. We can be happy together even if we are poor."

"We won't be poor. I have already told you about the assets abroad. We will always be better off than most others in China. You are worn out. I can see dark shadows under your eyes. You had better try to get some rest."

Meiping sat on in silence for a while longer, lost in thought. When she stood up, she declared, "Mommy, we will weather the storm together. I still believe in the future of our country. Things will change. They can't always be unfair like this. There are good leaders in the Party, such as Premier Zhou and many others."

"Well, I wonder what they are doing now, allowing so many innocent people to suffer."

"Don't lose heart! Surely they will do something when the time comes. I love China! I love my country even though it is not always good or right," my daughter proclaimed in a firm voice.

Her words brought tears to my eyes. I also had a deep and abiding love for the land of my ancestors even though, because of my class status, I had become an outcast.

4

House Arrest

I WOKE TO THE SOUND of a heavy downpour. After a while the rain settled into a steady drizzle. The wet garden, littered with ashes and half-burned books, was a sorrowful sight. I stood on the terrace contemplating this depressing scene and wondering what to do.

The morning passed slowly. There was no sign of the Red Guards. I wandered around the house aimlessly. There was no book to read. On the bookshelves covering two walls of my study only the four slim volumes of *The Collected Works of Mao Zedong* and the small book of his quotations in the red plastic cover remained. I couldn't do any sewing or knitting; the Red Guards had so messed everything up that I did not know where my knitting wool or needles and thread were. I couldn't write a letter or draw a picture; all the paper and envelopes were torn, and I did not know where my pen was. I couldn't listen to the radio, as the radio sets in the house were locked up with the "valuables." I could only sit there staring at the huge pile of debris in each room that we didn't dare to remove.

In the afternoon the rain stopped and the sun came out. Several parades passed the house, but none of the Red Guards came back. Lao-zhao brought me the *Shanghai Liberation Daily*, which always came out in the afternoon though it was a morning paper. On its front page, in bold type, was reprinted a lead article from the *People's Daily* in Beijing, the official organ of the Central Committee of the Communist Party. Since all Chinese newspapers were government-owned and voiced government policy, especially the *People's Daily*, I recognized the importance of this article and read it carefully. Written in stirring revolutionary language, it seemed superficially to be aimed at stimulating hatred for the capitalist class and rallying the masses to join in the activities of the Cultural Revolution. But I noticed that the article also made the claim that officials of the Party and government administration in many parts of China had pursued a capitalist line of policy opposed to Mao Zedong's teachings. The writer called these unnamed officials "capitalist-roaders." The "revolutionary masses," the article said, must identify these enemies, because "our Great Leader Chairman Mao trusts the revolutionary masses and has said their eyes are bright and clear as snow."

The article warned the "revolutionary masses" that the capitalist class was cunning, and alleged that its members hoarded gold and secreted weapons in their homes so that when an attack against China came from abroad they could cooperate with the enemy to become a fifth column. It praised the revolutionary action of the Red Guards, calling them "little revolutionary generals." In conclusion, the article mentioned the existence of a "countercurrent" against the Cultural Revolution and the Red Guards. It warned everybody to beware of this countercurrent and to avoid being influenced by it. Those "capitalist-roaders" who had a consistent "revisionist" outlook and tried to "protect" the capitalist class would be dealt with by the "revolutionary masses" and be swept away onto the rubbish heap of history.

The article was frighteningly irresponsible because no clear definition was offered either of the "revolutionary masses" who were to identify the enemies and punish them or of the "capitalist-roaders" who were to be the victims. The article left me in no doubt that Mao Zedong and his specially selected committee to conduct the Cultural Revolution intended to expand the scope of their attack and increase the degree of violence against those they had listed as victims. The chilling tone of the article could not be ignored. Since a lead article in the *People's Daily* was to be obeyed immediately, the tempo of the Cultural Revolution in Shanghai was sure to accelerate. The Party Secretariat and the municipal government would be quite unable to implement the Ten-Point Resolution. I expected the Red Guards to come back soon, and I expected their attitude to become even more hostile and intransigent. I thought it was only fair to urge my servants to leave my house and go back to their own homes.

The cook said that since he did not live in, he could come and go freely until the Red Guards told him to stay away. Lao-zhao said, "I'm not afraid to remain. You need someone to go to the market to buy food. It's not safe for you to go out. I am from a poor peasant family. My son is in the army and is a Party member. We are the true proletariat. The Red Guards have already smashed and confiscated everything. What else can they do? If they tell me to leave, I must go. Otherwise, I will stay." Chen-ma wept and said she wanted to stay with my daughter.

At a time like this, the loyalty of my servants was something very noble. I was deeply moved. I did not insist on their leaving immediately, because having them in the house was better than waiting for the Red Guards alone. However, after the cook had bought me some paper from the market, I wrote to Chen-ma's daughter, who lived in another province. I told her to come and get her mother. I felt more responsible for Chen-ma than for the cook and Lao-zhao.

When my daughter came home with the news that the municipal government building was besieged by Red Guards demanding the immediate withdrawal of the Ten-Point Resolution, denounced as a document offering protection to the capitalist class, I was not surprised. She also told me that a longtime associate of Jiang Qing, Mao's wife, had been appointed to conduct the Cultural Revolution in Shanghai.

"His name is Zhang Chunqiao. Someone at our film studio said that he was a journalist in Shanghai in the thirties when Jiang Qing was an actress. Those in the studio who used to know them both are terrified. Some of them have packed their bags in preparation for going to jail. They seem to believe Zhang Chunqiao will put them under detention to prevent them from talking about him and Jiang Qing in the thirties. Mommy, do you think those innocent actresses and actors will really go to jail?" My daughter was both puzzled and shocked by what she had heard at her film studio. Not knowing anything about Shanghai in the thirties, I had no idea what Jiang Qing and Zhang Chunqiao were afraid of or what the actresses and actors at the film studio knew about them that was so dangerous.

"Can you stay at home tonight?" I asked, as I hoped to spend a quiet evening with her to talk over the situation.

"I'm afraid not, Mommy. I really dashed home just to see how you are and whether the Red Guards had come back. The others are all remaining at the studio. An urgent meeting has been called to discuss an important article in the *People's Daily*. I was told it was written by someone close to Chairman Mao, so it is very important and represents Chairman Mao's viewpoint," she said hurriedly and looked at her watch. "Goodness! I must run!"

Lao-zhao brought her a bowl of noodles and said, "Eat some of it. It has been cooled. You can't go without food."

My daughter took the chopsticks and put some noodles into her mouth, swallowed, and said to Lao-zhao, "Thanks a lot. I really must go."

She gave me a hug and dashed out of the house. I had much to say to her, but there was no time to say anything.

Lao-zhao brought me his transistor radio so that I could listen to the evening news. Every station I could get was broadcasting the lead article of the *People's Daily*. The announcer read it in the excited, high-pitched voice I would come to know well during the following years. I left the radio on in the hope of hearing some other item of news, but there was nothing else. By the time I fell into an uneasy sleep, I had listened to the article so many times that I almost knew it by heart.

The next morning, the cook brought the news that there was very little food at the market, as the peasants from the surrounding countryside, who used to bring in vegetables, fish, and shrimp had answered Chairman Mao's call and joined the ranks of the "revolutionary masses" to take part in the Cultural Revolution. They had come into the city in large numbers and occupied several hotels in the business section of Shanghai. Their leaders demanded, and got, from the frightened hotel managers free food and service. As news of the luxury of hot running water, innerspring mattresses, and carpeted floors filtered back to the communes, women and children accompanied the men to the city to seize the opportunity for a free holiday. In the meantime, Red Guards were arriving at the railway station from Beijing and other northern cities to "exchange revolutionary experiences" with the Shanghai Red Guards. At the same time, the Shanghai Red Guards were traveling to Beijing in the hope of being reviewed by Chairman Mao. The Red Guards commandeered trains and ships for their transport, leaving normal passengers and goods stranded at stations and wharves. Nobody dared to oppose the Red Guards. Since the mention of "capitalist-roaders" in the lead article of the *People's Daily,* the officials were paralyzed with fear.

The denunciation of its Ten-Point Resolution put the Shanghai municipal government on the defensive. To avoid giving any further cause for complaint, it provided free meals for the incoming and outgoing Red Guards. Food stalls were set up at the railway station and wharves. All the shops making steamed buns and the former White Russian bakeries, now state-owned, were mobilized to produce buns and bread for the Red Guards. Determined to find fault with the Shanghai officials, the Red Guards denounced the Western-style bread made by the bakeries as "foreign food" and refused to eat it. At the same time, factory workers decided to join the "revolutionary masses" by organizing their own Cultural Revolution groups. To embarrass the Shanghai officials, they made extravagant economic demands. To protect themselves and win support, the officials authorized payments of bonuses and benefits to the workers. After only a few days, the cash reserves of the local banks were exhausted. The workers whose demands were not met became so infuriated that they joined the Red Guards in attacking the municipal government and its leading officials. Behind all these activities of the Red Guards and the workers against the municipal government was the hand of Zhang Chunqiao, who directed their revolutionary activities from the comfort of a suite of rooms at the Peace Hotel, which became the temporary headquarters of the Maoist leaders when they came to Shanghai, until the Shanghai Party Secretariat and the municipal government were toppled by the Revolutionaries in January of the following year.

A few of my daughter's friends were high school teachers. Because they also wore the red armband, they could drop in to see us without attracting undue attention. Lao-zhao also took the opportunity of the lull in the Red Guards' activities against me to visit his friends and mingle with the crowds on the streets. The cook's son, a factory worker, paid his father a visit and told him the conditions at his place of work. The stories they related were so astonishing and the reluctance of the Shanghai Party and government officials to exercise their power was so unusual that I began to wonder whether there wasn't something more to the Cultural Revolution than its declared purpose of destroying the remnants of the capitalist class and purifying the ranks of officials and intellectuals.

One day Xiao Xu, a schoolteacher friend of Meiping's, came to our house to see her when she was away at the film studio. He told me that the Red Guards had dismantled the Catholic cathedral's twin spires, which were a landmark in Shanghai. During the night, he said, the Red Guards had broken into the Shanghai municipal library and destroyed a large number of valuable books. When they went to the historical museum, they failed to break down the strong iron gate. So they went to the home of its director and dragged the old man from his sickbed to a struggle meeting.

"The old man is now in the hospital. Some say he has died already. The Red Guards are getting quite wild. I think you should take Meiping and try to escape to Hong Kong," he said.

"Do you think Meiping would want to go?" I asked him this question because once when he was at our house, just before I was to make a trip to Hong Kong, both he and my daughter said they would never want to live as second-class citizens in colonial Hong Kong.

"The situation is different now. After the Cultural Revolution, young people from non-working-class family backgrounds will have no future in China at all. In the past, if we worked twice as hard as the young people of the working class and expected no advancement, we could have a reasonably happy private life. In the future, we will be like the untouchables in India, whose children and children's children suffer too. The only way out is to escape. You have many friends abroad. Why don't you take Meiping and go?" he urged me.

"I think it's too late to escape now. You know the penalty for attempting to escape to Hong Kong is very serious, something like ten or twenty years in prison," I said.

"It's not too late. I have made some investigations. The whole railway system is in a state of confusion. No one buys a ticket or has a travel permit anymore. Red Guards are going all over the country by just getting on a train. No one asks any questions. I have been to both the station and the wharf. There are no ticket collectors at either place. No one in authority at all."

"I think the moment I got on a train I would be recognized and dragged off or beaten."

"You can both be disguised as Red Guards. I will get you some red cloth for armbands, and I will write the three characters for 'Red Guard' for you. I have done quite a few of these for our students," he said.

"I think I'm too old to be taken for a Red Guard."

"All you have to do is to have your hair cut short, take the book of quotations by Chairman Mao in your hand, and pretend to be absorbed in it. You can even wear a cap to cover your hair. If anyone should question you, you can say you are a teacher. As for Meiping, she can easily pass for a Red Guard," he said impatiently.

When I shook my head again, he declared, "You are foolish not to try. In any case, talk it over with Meiping when she comes home."

(I saw Xiao Xu again in Hong Kong in 1980, when I came out of China. He told me that he was turned back at the border when he tried to reach Hong Kong by train. But later he swam to Macao, and after a few years he got to Hong Kong, where he worked hard and saved money. In 1980 he was the part-owner of a toy factory in Kowloon that exported toys to many parts of the world. Since conditions in China had changed for the better after Mao died, he was thinking of making a trip to Shanghai to visit his mother.)

I was in the bathroom when I heard the sound of furious hammering on the front gate again. Halfway down the stairs, I came face to face with a little girl about fifteen years of age. She was dressed in a khaki-colored uniform, with a cap sitting squarely on her head. The edge of the cap covered her eyebrows so that her eyes peered from underneath it. Her small waist was gathered in by a wide leather belt with a shiny buckle. In her hand she carried a leather whip.

"Are you the class enemy of this house? How well fed you look! Your cheeks are smooth and your eyes are bold. You have been fattened by the blood and toil of the peasants and workers. But now things are going to be different! You'll have to pay for your criminal deeds! Come with me!" From her accent I knew she was a Red Guard from Beijing.

I followed her downstairs. Several boys and girls in similar attire were in the hall by the door of the dining room. She went into the room, and I followed her.

"Kneel down!" one of the boys shouted. Simultaneously his stick landed on my back. Another boy hit the glass door of a cabinet. It broke. He swung the stick around and hit the back of my knee. The decision of whether or not to comply with the kneeling order was taken out of my hands. I collapsed on the floor.

"Where is the cash?" one of them asked.

"The Red Guards who were here before took it."

"Did they take all of it?"

"No, they left a few hundred yuan for me to live on."

"Where is it?"

"In a drawer in my desk."

The boy kicked my leg as he passed me and went upstairs with the others. The girl with the whip was left to watch me. She swung her whip back and forth in the air, missing my head by a fraction each time. The others came down again with the drawer and tipped the bank notes onto the dining table. They told me to turn around and face the wall. I could hear them counting the notes.

There was the sound of more people entering the house. I wondered if the front gate had been left open, but I heard a man's voice ordering Lao-zhao to call Chen-ma and the cook to the hall. Then he said to someone, "Take them upstairs and question them."

The Red Guards went into the hall, and then they all came into the dining room.

"Here she is," someone said.

"You may go now. We will deal with her ourselves," said the same person who had spoken before.

I heard the Red Guards leave the house, hitting the walls and the furniture with their sticks and whips as they went out. They banged the front door so hard that the house shook.

"Stand up! Come over here!" the man yelled.

I stood up and turned to face the new intruders. The man who spoke was of medium height, slightly built, wearing a pair of tinted spectacles. There were two other men and a woman in the room. Although they all wore the cotton trousers and ill-fitting shirts and jackets of the working class, they spoke like people of some education. On their armbands were the three Chinese characters for "Revolutionaries."

They all sat down in a half-moon facing where I stood. The man said to me, "You are the class enemy of this house. You are guilty of conspiring with foreign powers. It's written on the Big Character Poster on your front gate. Do you deny it?"

"Of course I deny it! Who are you anyway? What do you want?"

"We are the Proletarian Revolutionaries."

"Never heard of such a title," I said.

"You are going to hear a lot about us. We are the Revolutionaries who represent the working class, which is the ruling class in China," he said with a lift of his chin.

"Isn't the working class in China represented by the Chinese Communist Party?" I asked.

"Shut up! We don't have to justify ourselves to you. You are an arrogant class enemy! You have no right to discuss who represents the working class in China. We are responding to Chairman Mao's call to take part in the Great Proletarian Cultural Revolution. That's quite good enough," said the woman.

"You are a class enemy and a running dog of the Anglo-American imperialists. You went to an American-endowed university in Beijing and then to a British university in London, so you were trained from an early age to serve the imperialists," the man said.

I remained silent, as it seemed pointless to talk to them.

"Is it because you are ashamed that you do not speak?" the woman asked me.

"Why should I be ashamed? Many graduates of Yanjing University have become leaders of the Communist Party. To have been a student there doesn't mean I am a running dog of anybody. The London School of Economics was a left-wing college founded by the Fabian Socialists of Britain. In fact, it was there that I first read the *Communist Manifesto* by Marx and Engels," I told her.

"Ha, ha, ha! What a joke! A class enemy and a running dog of the imperialists has read the *Communist Manifesto*! The next thing you are going to say is that you want to join the Communist Party," the man with the tinted glasses said sarcastically.

The woman said, "Lenin denounced the Fabian Socialists as reformers. They were not true socialists because they did not advocate revolution by violence. Don't try to ingratiate yourself with us. Your only way out is to come clean."

"I'm a law-abiding citizen," I declared. "I worked for a foreign firm and had no access to government secrets. I do not know any foreign governments, and they do not know me."

Another man said, "You do know and are on friendly terms with a number of foreign government officials."

"You needn't get so excited. All the senior staff of foreign firms are spies. You are not the only one," interjected the third man.

"Why should foreign governments trust us?" I asked them. "What hold have they got over people like us who live in China?"

"Ah! Nearly all of you have money abroad. You don't deny you yourself have money abroad," the man said.

"That's a hold on you. They can confiscate your money," added the woman.

"You don't understand. Governments abroad cannot interfere with the banks. They cannot confiscate anybody's deposit," I told them.

"Why do you keep money abroad anyway? Why should an honest Chinese want to keep money abroad?"

"I make trips to Hong Kong and have to pay my food and hotel bills when I am there. I'm not allowed to take my Chinese money with me, as you know. There is foreign exchange control. Each time I go out of China, I am allowed only five U.S. dollars. Besides, I have to bring money into China to buy coal and other things from the Overseas Chinese Store," I explained. "I have some money abroad, but I have a lot more money in Shanghai. I have this house. I have my only child here. She is worth more than anything in the world to me. She is a member of the Communist Youth League. Why should I oppose the Communist Party and the People's Government?"

"You would oppose the Communist Party even if your daughter were a Party member. It's your class instinct," said the man with the tinted glasses, who seemed to be their leader.

Several other men and women came into the room, followed

by my servants. The man looked at them. The newcomers shook their heads. Evidently they had not got what they wanted from my servants.

The man with the tinted spectacles assumed a severe tone of voice and asked me, "Where have you hidden your gold and weapons?"

"What gold and weapons?" I was surprised by his question until I remembered the lead article of the *People's Daily*. It had accused members of the capitalist class of secreting gold and weapons in order to form a fifth column when foreign powers invaded China.

"You know what gold and weapons! You had better come clean."

"I have no gold or weapons. The Red Guards have been here. They went through the entire house. They did not find any gold or weapons."

"You are clever. You hid them. Our Great Leader told us that the class enemies are secreting gold and weapons. He can't be wrong."

"We are going to find the gold and weapons. If you don't come clean, then you will be severely punished," said their leader. "Come along! They must be somewhere in this house."

I wondered whether they really believed the lead article or whether they just had to appear to believe it. The fact was that soon after the Communist takeover in 1949, possession of fire-arms was declared illegal. Those who had them had to hand them over to the government and were subject to a house search by the police. Former Kuomintang military and police personnel were arrested and "reformed" in labor camps. Their families all had to move out of their homes. Therefore, it seemed utterly absurd to say some Chinese could still have weapons in their homes in 1966.

However, the Revolutionaries took my servants and me all over the house. They ripped open mattresses, cut the upholstery of the chairs and sofas, removed tiles from the walls of the bathrooms, climbed into the fireplace and poked into the chimney, lifted floorboards, got onto the roof, fished in the water tank under the ceiling, and crawled under the floor to examine the pipes. All the while, they watched the facial expressions of my servants and myself.

I had lost track of time, but darkness had long descended on the city when they decided to dig up the garden. The sky was overcast, and it was a dark night. They switched on the lights on the terrace and told Lao-zhao to bring his flashlight. When they came to the coal shed, my servants and I were told to move the coal to a corner of the garden they had already searched. The damp, ash-covered lawn had been trampled into a sea of mud; all the flower beds had been dug up, and spades were sunk into the earth around the shrubs. They even pulled plants out of their pots. But they found nothing, for nothing was there to be found. The Revolutionaries, my servants, and I were all covered with mud, ashes, and sweat.

In the end, physical exhaustion got the better of their revolutionary zeal. We were told to go back to the house. They were fuming with rage because they had lost face by not finding anything. I knew that unless I did something to save their face they were going to vent their anger on me. If only I could produce something in the way of gold, such as a ring or a bracelet. I remembered my jewelry sealed in Meiping's study.

"The Red Guards put my gold rings and bracelets in the sealed room. Perhaps you could open the room and take them and let the Red Guards know," I said to the woman.

"Don't pretend to be stupid. We are looking for gold bars," she said.

We were standing in the hall. The man with the tinted glasses had removed them to reveal bloodshot eyes. He glanced at my servants cowering by the kitchen door, and he looked at his fellow Revolutionaries around him. Then he glared at me. Suddenly he shouted, "Where have you hidden the gold and weapons?" and took a step towards me threateningly.

I was so weary that I could hardly stand. Making an effort, I said, "There simply aren't any. If there were, wouldn't you have found them already?"

The fact that he had been proven wrong was intolerable to him. Staring at me with pure hatred, he said, "Not necessarily. We did not break open the walls."

He stood very close to me. I could see every detail of his sneering face. Although I found him extremely repulsive and would have liked to step back a pace or two, I did not move, for I did not want him to think I was afraid of him. I simply said slowly, in a normal and friendly voice, "You must be reasonable. If I had hidden anything in the walls, I could not have done it alone. I would have needed a plasterer to put the walls back again. All workmen work for state-controlled businesses. They would have to report to their Party secretary the sort of work they did." I was so tired that it was a real effort to speak.

The man was beside himself with rage, for I had implied that he was unreasonable. His face turned white and his lips trembled. I could see the bloated veins in his temples. He raised his arm to strike me.

At that very moment, Meiping's cat, Fluffy, came through the kitchen door, jumped on the man's leg from behind, and sank his teeth into the flesh of the man's calf. Screaming with pain, the man hopped wildly on one leg, trying to shake the cat off. The others also tried to grab Fluffy, but the agile cat was already out of the house like a streak of lightning, through the French windows we had left open when we came in from the garden. We all rushed outside. Fluffy was sitting on his favorite branch of the magnolia tree, out of reach. From this safe perch, Fluffy looked at us and mewed. The wounded man was almost demented. With his trousers torn and blood streaming down the back of his leg, he dashed to the tree and tried to shake it. Fluffy hopped up to a higher branch, turned around to give us all a disdainful glance, ran onto the roof of my neighbor's house, and disappeared into the night.

We came in again. In the drawing room, the man sat down on the sofa the Red Guards had broken and he had slashed not long ago. When I asked Chen-ma for some Mercurochrome or iodine, she reminded me that the Red Guards had already poured everything away.

The Revolutionaries were greatly embarrassed by the rather unheroic appearance of their leader, who was now wiping his leg with a handkerchief, completely deflated. Tactfully my servants withdrew into the kitchen. I was left there to witness his discomfiture. One of the women pushed me out through the connecting door between the drawing room and the dining room, saying, "We don't need your help or sympathy. You keep a wild animal in the house to attack the Revolutionaries. You will be punished. As for the cat, we will have the neighborhood committee look for it and put it to death. You are very much mistaken if you think by making your cat bite us we will give up. We are going to look further for the gold and weapons." She turned the key in the lock and went around to the hall to lock the other door also. Again, I was incarcerated in the dining room.

Do they really believe I have gold and weapons? I wondered. Or do they merely have to carry out the order of Chairman Mao to search for them? Surely they had done enough, in the latter case.

I heard Lao-zhao calling me in a low whisper in the garden. I went to the window and saw him standing outside.

"The cook has gone to the film studio to tell Mei-mei not to come home tonight. Is it all right?"

"Thank you, Lao-zhao. It's very thoughtful of you. It's best she is not here."

Suddenly there was the sound of hammering on the front gate again. Lao-zhao hurried away to open it. He came back to tell me that the Red Guards who first looted my house had come back.

"Please go to your room and take Chen-ma with you," I told him, anticipating more trouble.

There was the sound of many people running up and down the stairs, and there was loud shouting. Angry arguments seemed to have broken out overhead, followed by fighting. There was nothing I could do. I resigned myself to the possibility of the total destruction of my home. Pulling three dining chairs together, I lay down on the cushions. I was so exhausted that I dozed despite the loud noise.

After daybreak, several Red Guards and Revolutionaries threw the door open. It seemed that their dispute, whatever it was, was resolved. A girl shouted, "Get up! Get up!"

A woman Revolutionary told me to get something to eat in the kitchen quickly and then "come upstairs to do some useful work." I went into the downstairs bathroom to wash my hands. Looking into the mirror over the basin, I was shocked to see my disheveled hair and puffy white face, with smudges of mud on my forehead and cheeks. Stepping back, I saw in the glass that my clothes were spattered with mud. In fact, I looked very much like a female corpse I had seen long ago being dug out of the debris on a Chongqing street after an air raid during the Sino-Japanese War. The sight of that dead woman had haunted me for days. She seemed so finished, unable to do anything or even to make the smallest gesture of protest against the unfairness of her own fate. The recollection of her dead body now made me resolve to keep alive. I thought the Cultural Revolution was going to be a fight for me to clear my name. I must not only keep alive, but I must be as strong as granite, so that no matter how much I was knocked about, I could remain unbroken. My face was puffy because I had not drunk any water for a long time and my one remaining kidney was not functioning properly. I had to remedy that immediately.

In the kitchen, I drank two glasses of water before eating the bowl of steaming rice and vegetables Lao-zhao provided me. It was amazing how quickly food turned into energy and how encouraging was a resolute attitude of mind. I felt a great deal better already.

A Red Guard opened the kitchen door and yelled, "Are you having a feast? What a long time you are taking! Hurry up, hurry up!"

Lao-zhao and I followed the Red Guard up the stairs. Chen-ma also joined us. We found that the Red Guards and the few remaining Revolutionaries required our help in packing up my belongings so that they could be taken away. Anxious for them to be out of the house, I helped readily. The presence of the Red Guards and the Revolutionaries was more intolerable to me than the loss of my possessions. They seemed to me alien creatures from another world with whom I had no common language.

In the eyes of the Red Guards and the Revolutionaries, Lao-zhao was not a class enemy, even though they probably thought him misguided and lacking in socialist awareness to work for me. They chatted with him freely; I could see Lao-zhao was doing his best to appear friendly too. While we were sitting on the floor packing up the things that had been scattered everywhere, I heard the Red Guards excitedly discussing their forthcoming journey to Beijing to be reviewed by Chairman Mao. The few who had taken part when Mao reviewed the Red Guards from the gallery of the Tiananmen Gate in Beijing on August 18 were describing their experience with pride. They spoke of the role of the army in organizing their reception in Beijing, in providing them with accommodations and khaki uniforms, and in drilling them for the review. It was the army officers who had selected the quotations and slogans the youngsters were to shout.

I was interested in what the Red Guards were saying. It seemed the army was working behind the scenes to support and direct the Red Guards' activities.

When everything was packed, the trucks came. But to my great disappointment the Red Guards did not leave the house when the trucks drove away.

A woman Revolutionary said to me, "You must remain in the house. You are not allowed to go out of the house. The Red Guards will take turns watching you."

I was astonished and angry. I asked her, "What authority have you to keep me confined to the house?" Disappointment so overwhelmed me that I was trembling.

"I have the authority of the Proletarian Revolutionaries."

"I want to see the order in writing," I said, trying to control my trembling voice.

"Why do you want to go out? Where do you want to go? A woman like you would be beaten to death outside. We are doing you a kindness in putting you under house arrest. Lao-zhao will be allowed to stay and do the marketing for you. Do you know what's going on outside? There is a full-scale revolution going on."

"I don't particularly want to go out. It's the principle of the matter."

"What principle? Since you don't want to go out, why argue with me? You stay here until we decide what to do with you. That's an order."

She swept out of the house. I was furious, but there was nothing whatever I could do.

I was given the box spring of my bed to sleep on. A change of clothes and a sweater hung in the empty closet. The suitcase containing my winter clothes and the green canvas bag with a quilt and blankets for the colder days were in a corner of the room. Besides the table and chairs in the kitchen, I was left with two chairs and a small coffee table. The Red Guards detailed to watch me sat on these two chairs outside my room, so that I had to sit on the box spring on the floor. Every now and then one of them would open my door to see what I was doing. The only place where I had some privacy was my bathroom.

My daughter was allowed to live in her own room, but I was not allowed to go in there or to speak to her when she came home, which was very seldom, as she had to spend more and more nights at the film studio taking part in the Cultural Revolution. In the evenings, I would gently push the door of my room open, hoping to catch a glimpse of her as she came up the stairs. When she did come home and we managed to look at each other, I felt comforted and reassured. Generally I would sleep peacefully that night.

Lao-zhao went to market to purchase food, but neither he nor my daughter was allowed to eat with me. The Red Guards had a rotation of duty hours so that they went home for their meals. At night, one or two of them slept on the floor outside my bedroom on a makeshift bed.

Two days after I was placed under house arrest, Chen-ma's daughter came to get her mother. We had a tearful farewell. Chen-ma wanted to leave me a cardigan she had knitted, but the Red Guards scolded her for lack of class consciousness and refused to let her hand it to me.

"She won't have enough clothes for the winter. She isn't very strong, you know," Chen-ma pleaded with the Red Guards.

"Don't you realize she is your class enemy? Why should you care whether she has enough clothes or not?" a Red Guard said.

Chen-ma's daughter seemed frightened of the Red Guards and urged Chen-ma to leave. But Chen-ma said, "I must say goodbye to Mei-mei!" Tears were streaming down her face.

One of the Red Guards became impatient. She faced Chen-ma militantly and said, "Haven't you stayed in this house long enough? She is the daughter of a class enemy. Why do you have to say goodbye to her?"

When I put my arms around Chen-ma's shoulders to hug her for the last time, she burst into loud crying. The Red Guards pulled my arms away and pushed Chen-ma and her daughter out the front door. Lao-zhao followed them out with Chen-ma's luggage, and I heard him getting a pedicab for them.

Longing to know what went on outside, I avidly read the newspaper that Lao-zhao left on the kitchen table each day. One evening when I went into the kitchen to have my dinner, I saw a sheet of crudely printed paper entitled *Red Guard News* on a kitchen chair. The headline said, "Hit back without mercy the counterattack of the class enemies," which intrigued me. I longed to know more. There was no one about, so I picked up the small sheet and secreted it in my pocket. Later, in the quiet of my bathroom, I read it. After that, I kept a lookout for any crumpled piece of paper left by the Red Guards. These handbills produced by the Red Guards were mostly full of their usual hyperbole about the capitalist class and the revisionists. However, in the course of denouncing these enemies they revealed facts about certain Party leaders that had hitherto been kept from the general public. I was particularly interested in reports that certain officials in the Shanghai municipal government and the Party Secretariat were attempting to "ignore" or "sabotage" Mao's orders. The extent of conflict caused by policy differences within the Party leadership seemed far greater than I had thought. Being uncensored, these Red Guard publications and handbills inadvertently exposed some of the facts of the power struggle in the Party leadership and contributed to the breakdown of the myth that the Party leaders were a group of dedicated men united for a common purpose.

After a week indoors, I asked the Red Guards how long I was supposed to go without outdoor exercise and requested that I be allowed to use the garden. After making a telephone call, they allowed me into the garden to walk around or to sit on the steps of the terrace with Fluffy on my lap. The "sin" of biting a Revolutionary leader did not seem to be regarded as important by the young Red Guards. They would often play with Fluffy too.

Soon Meiping realized that I was fairly often in the garden, especially in the early morning. Whenever she came home at night, she would throw notes there, rolled into a small ball for me to pick up when I went down for my daily exercise next morning. But when it rained during the night, as it often did in September, the paper got wet and disintegrated when I tried to unroll it. She could not say much on a tiny strip of paper, but her messages of "I love you, Mom," "Take care of yourself," "We will be brave and weather the storm together, dear Mommy," etc., gave me great comfort and tempered my feeling of isolation.

If Lao-zhao happened to be in the kitchen when I went for my meals, a Red Guard would follow me there to make sure we did not converse. But Lao-zhao and the Red Guard would chat with one another. After a while I found that much of what Lao-zhao said was information for my ears also. For instance, one day he said to a Red Guard, "Do you beat up your teachers often?"

I was astonished by Lao-zhao's question, because when the Red Guards came to loot my house on the night of August 30 they seemed quite friendly with their teachers. I waited breathlessly for the answer.

The Red Guard said casually, "We beat them up when they are found to have capitalist ideas or when they insist we study and not have so many revolutionary activities. Some of them do not seem to understand the importance of carrying on with the Cultural Revolution. They still believe in the importance of learning from books. But our Great Leader Chairman Mao told us, 'Learn to swim from swimming.' We should learn from taking part in revolutionary activities and from active labor. We don't need the old type of school anymore. Those teachers who still believe in books obviously oppose our Great Leader, so we must treat them as enemies."

Another time, Lao-zhao asked the Red Guard, "Did you go to surround the municipal government building?"

"Of course! And this wasn't the first time or the last time either. The entire Shanghai municipal government is rotten with revisionism."

It was from Lao-zhao's conversations with the Red Guards and from their handbills and publications that I gained the impression that daily thousands of new revolutionaries were flocking to join the Red Guards and workers' organizations that had sprung up "like bamboo shoots after the spring rain." Whether hoping for personal gain or merely fearful of being thought politically backward, people felt compelled to become a part of the Proletarian Cultural Revolution.

The ransacking of the homes of members of the capitalist class and the attack on the intellectuals inflated the egos of the Red Guards and the Revolutionaries and whetted their appetite for violence. They were impatient to go further. It seemed to me that the Maoist leaders used this psychological moment to direct their anger and channel their energy towards pressuring the Shanghai Party Secretariat and municipal government, both of which were accused of protecting the capitalist class and oppos-

ing Mao's policies. It was alleged that for years Mao's orders
were deliberately ignored. But officials of the Shanghai Party
Secretariat and the municipal government were not novices of
the political game. They were experienced Communists who
had survived many political storms and purges. And they were
not unfamiliar with Mao's tactics. Since Mao used the masses,
they decided to use the masses themselves. Speedily they organized their own Red Guards and Revolutionaries to take part in
the Cultural Revolution. They vied with the Maoist Red Guards
and Revolutionaries to gain control of the situation in Shanghai.
To succeed, each group had to be more red, more revolutionary, more cruel, and more left in their slogans and action. Thus,
not only was it at times extremely difficult to identify a particular
group until the bloody civil wars broke out, but also the so-
called capitalist class and the intellectuals were confronted by
two contesting groups that competed in dealing the heaviest
blow to demonstrate their authenticity.

As the violence escalated and the scope of the Cultural Revolution expanded to include an ever increasing number of class
enemies, a new slogan was coined to emphasize the undesirabil-
ity of children of capitalist families. It said, "A dragon is born
of a dragon, a phoenix is born of a phoenix, and a mouse is born
with the ability to make a hole in the wall." In short, since the
parents were class enemies, the children would naturally be class
enemies too. Though I thought it rather astonishing in a country
pledged to materialistic Marxism that a slogan should be based
entirely on the importance of genetics, I had no time or heart
to dwell on it. Soon after its publication, my daughter Meiping
was removed from the ranks of the "masses" and placed in the
"cowshed" with all those in the film studio denounced as class
enemies. The "cowshed" earned its name from the fact that Mao
Zedong had characterized all class enemies as "cow's demons
and snake spirits." In the "cowshed" the victims spent their time
writing confessions and self-criticisms over and over again in an
effort to purge themselves of heretical thinking contrary to Mao
Zedong Thought. I was informed of this situation through Lao-
zhao's conversation with one of the Red Guards. In a loud voice,
just outside my bedroom, he asked the Red Guard's permission
to take bedding and clothing to my daughter in the so-called
cowshed of the film studio because she could no longer come

home. Later, when I went into the kitchen for my evening meal, which I could not swallow but pretended to eat in order to find out about my daughter's condition, Lao-zhao did not disappoint me. As soon as I sat down, he talked about Meiping to the unsuspecting Red Guard.

"I saw her when I went to the film studio to give her the things. She looked quite well and seemed cheerful. She told me she was writing self-criticism about her background and class origin. She also said all those in the cowshed were very friendly. In fact, she seemed quite all right and is taking everything philosophically. But why should she have to write self-criticism? She is a member of the Communist Youth League, and everywhere she went she got citations of merit. She is sympathetic and friendly towards the proletariat. Once she even saved the life of a poor peasant woman by rowing her in a boat through the creeks to the county hospital when the woman was suddenly taken ill."

"She was born abroad into a family like this. Of course she has to write self-criticism," the Red Guard said to Lao-zhao. "She is probably a radish: red outside but white within. In any case, the Communist Youth League is disbanded. The general secretary of the Youth League, Hu Yaobang, is a revisionist."

Shortly afterwards, a group of Revolutionaries from the film studio came to ransack her room and took away what was left of her things. I was desperately unhappy with the new turn of events. I could keep my spirit buoyant when the attack was directed at me alone, but now that she had also become the object of persecution I suffered from deep depression.

In the late afternoon of September 27, I was taken by a Red Guard and a Revolutionary to the same school building I had gone to in July. A large gathering was already there waiting for us. This time I was the object of the struggle meeting, attended not only by the Red Guards and the Revolutionaries who had come to my house but also by the former staff of Shell and the men handling their indoctrination who had questioned me. The man with the tinted spectacles was in charge.

The room was arranged differently. Instead of rows of chairs facing the platform, the seats were in an irregular circle. I was told to stand in the middle, with a Red Guard on each side. The man with the tinted glasses was quite a fluent speaker. He, too, started with the Opium War, giving a vivid description of how the invading fleet of Britain bombarded the Chinese coast. His account, full of inaccuracies and aimed at creating hatred for me, made me personally guilty for Britain's action against China over a hundred years ago. He spoke as if it were I who had led the British fleet up the Pearl River. Then he declared that Shell was a multinational firm with branches in all parts of the world. He said that Lenin had stated that such companies were the worst enemies of socialism. He told the audience that from time immemorial, under the pretense of selling kerosene to the peasants, Shell had sent salesmen deep into the rural areas of China to gather information useful to the imperialists. He also gave figures to show the enormous profit the company had made with its China trade and called it the "commercial exploitation of the Chinese people." He told the audience that the British imperialists were more subtle than the Americans. The United States government openly opposed the People's Government of China and protected the Kuomintang in Taiwan; the British gave the People's Government diplomatic recognition while voting with the United States at the United Nations to prevent the People's Government from taking China's seat.

He turned to an account of my family background, telling the audience that I was the descendant of a big landlord family that owned 10,000 mou of fertile agricultural land (there are roughly 6 mou to an acre). Unlike the liaison officer of the municipal government who had said my grandfather was a patriot, he now told the audience that my grandfather was a dirty landlord and an advocate of feudalism because in the history books he wrote he praised several emperors. Furthermore, he said, evidence had been found among his papers that he was a founder and shareholder of the Hanyehping Steel Complex, which included the Anyuan coal mine, where the Great Leader Chairman Mao once personally organized the workers in their struggle against the capitalists. This accusation was supposed to give concrete proof that my grandfather and Chairman Mao were on opposing sides; in fact, the two men belonged to two different generations. He went on to say that my father was a senior official of the prewar Beijing government and spent many years in Japan in his youth. He reminded everyone that Japan had been guilty of aggression against China and in eight years of war and occupation had killed ten million innocent Chinese men, women, and children. Carefully he avoided mentioning that my father went to Japan in the early years of this century, long before the Japanese invasion of China in 1937; instead he tried to create the impression that my father went to Japan in spite of what Japan did to China. Pointing at me, he said that I went to England when I was twenty years old and was trained by the British to be "a faithful running dog" in one of their universities. My late husband was described as a "residue of the decadent Kuomintang regime" who was fortunate to have died and escaped judgment by the Revolutionaries.

Throughout his speech, the audience showed their support and agreement by shouting slogans. Added to the usual slogans of the Cultural Revolution were a number accusing me of being a "spy" who conspired with foreign powers against China, and others simply denouncing me as a "running dog" of the British.

When the man with the tinted spectacles had finished speaking, the Red Guard who had led the other Red Guards into my home shouted into the microphone a description of its "luxury." Another Red Guard told how I had tried to "undermine" their "revolutionary activities" by fighting with them to preserve "old culture." A Revolutionary spoke of my stubborn arrogance and accused me of deliberately keeping a "wild animal" in the house to attack the Revolutionaries.

Members of the ex-staff of Shell were then called upon to provide further evidence against me. I could easily see how frightened they all were, and I wondered what they must have gone through. The men who got up to speak were white, and their hands holding the prepared statements shook. None of them looked in my direction. There was very little substance in what they said, but every sentence they uttered contributed to the picture that I enjoyed a warm and friendly relationship with the British residents of Shanghai. A web of suspicion was carefully woven. One of the office elevator operators declared that the British manager always stepped aside to let me get into the elevator before him. A driver testified that whenever the manager and I shared a car, the manager always allowed me to get in first. This was supposed to demonstrate my value and importance to the "British imperialists," because in Communist China a senior man would not dream of letting his female assistant get into a car or an elevator before him.

Other members of the staff spoke of files kept in a room next to the manager's office, not accessible to anyone but the manager and myself. A senior member of the staff who had been with Shell for many years said that geological maps of areas of China with possible oil deposits were routinely kept at the office because they were of value to the imperialists. Another speaker read out excerpts allegedly taken from reports written by Shell branch managers in various parts of China during the civil war of 1946–49, when the armies of the Kuomintang and the Communists were locked in a bitter struggle. Troop deployments of both sides were mentioned in these reports. This was supposed to repudiate my claim that Shell was interested only in commerce.

My late husband came in for severe criticism too. It was alleged that whenever the interest of Shell clashed with the interest of the state, both my husband and I stood on the side of Shell. All the statements were a mixture of fact and fiction, misrepresentation and exaggeration, calculated to mislead the ignorant minds of the gullible and the uninformed.

The meeting dragged on. Night had long ago fallen. But the drama of my misfortune was so absorbing that none of the Red Guards or the Revolutionaries left the room. The majority of them, I thought, were stunned by what they believed to be the exposure of a real international spy. Others simply had to pretend to believe in the allegations. I could see that the men who were running the show were gloating with success.

Years later, I was to learn that the date of this struggle meeting had been postponed several times because the organizers had hoped to get my daughter to take part in my denunciation. Despite enormous pressure, she refused repeatedly. But National Day, October First, was approaching. The Maoist leaders ordered the Revolutionaries in Shanghai to produce concrete results to celebrate the day in a mood of victory. It was in response to this order that the men in charge of my case decided to hold the meeting without my daughter.

When the man with the tinted glasses judged that sufficient emotion had been generated among those present, he complimented the men and women who took part in my denunciation for their high level of socialist awareness. He also had a good word to say for our former staff members, declaring that most of them had emerged from their reeducation with clearer heads.

But he issued a warning to those whose heads were still foggy, calling upon them to redouble their efforts at self-criticism to shake off the shackles of capitalism.

Turning to me, he said, "You have listened to the mountain of evidence against you. Your crime against the Chinese people is extremely serious. You can only be reformed by giving a full confession telling us how you conspired with the British imperialists in their scheme to undermine the People's Government. Are you going to confess?"

"I have never done anything against the Chinese people and government. The Shell office was here because the Chinese government wanted it to be here. The order to allow Shell to maintain its Shanghai office was issued by the State Council and signed by no less a person than Premier Zhou Enlai. Shell is full of goodwill for China and the Chinese people and always observed the laws and regulations scrupulously. It is not Shell's policy to meddle in politics . . ."

Even though I spoke in a loud and clear voice, no one in the room could hear a complete sentence, for everything I said was drowned by angry shouts and screams of "Confess! Confess!" and "We will not allow a class enemy to argue!" At the same time, the hysterical Red Guards and Revolutionaries crowded around me threateningly, shook their fists in my face, pulled at my clothes, and spat on my jacket while yelling, "Dirty spy," "Dirty running dog," "We will kill you," and so on. Several times I had to brace myself to stand firmly when they pushed me very hard.

Throughout the pandemonium, the men on the platform were smiling; the man in the tinted glasses seemed particularly pleased to see me suffer at the hands of the mob. What was I to do? It was useless to try to explain and worse than useless to try to resist. If I had made any move at all, the mob would have jumped me. I could only stand there looking straight ahead, with my eyes fixed on the distant wall, hoping their anger would soon spend itself.

Eventually the noise died down a little. The man said, "Our patience is exhausted. You are guilty. We could give you the death penalty. But we want to give you a chance to reform yourself. Are you going to confess?"

Everybody stared at me expectantly. I had stood there enduring their abuse for so long, I suppose I should have been filled with hatred for every one of them. Looking back, I remember distinctly that my predominant emotion was one of great sadness. At the same time, I longed to see my daughter. I was sad because I knew I could not reach out to these people around me to make them understand that I was innocent and that they were mistaken. The propaganda on class struggle that they had absorbed, not only since the beginning of the Cultural Revolution but also since 1949 when the Communist army took over Shanghai, had already built an impregnable wall between us. It was not something I could break down in a moment.

After staring at me for a few seconds and finding me silent, the man beckoned to a young man at the back of the mob. The crowd parted to let him through. He carried in his hand a pair of shiny metal handcuffs, which he lifted to make sure I saw them. When the young man came to where I stood, the man in charge of the meeting asked again, "Are you going to confess?"

I answered in a calm voice, "I've never done anything against the People's Government. I have no connection with any foreign government."

"Come along!" the young man with the handcuffs said.

I followed him out of the building into the street. The others came behind us. The cool night air was refreshing, and I felt my head clearing magically.

Parked in front of the entrance of the school was a black jeep, a vehicle of the Shanghai police department. It was a familiar sight to the people of Shanghai. During the height of every political movement, they saw it dashing through the streets with siren screaming, taking victims to prison. I stood beside the jeep with the Red Guards, the Revolutionaries, the ex-staff of Shell, and a number of pedestrians who stopped to watch.

"Are you going to confess?" the man in the tinted glasses asked again.

I was silently reciting to myself the Twenty-third Psalm, "The Lord is my shepherd; I shall not want . . ."

"Have you gone dumb?"

"Have you lost your voice?"

"Speak!"

"Confess!" They were shouting.

The man with the tinted spectacles and the man from the

police department were looking at me thoughtfully. They mistook my silence as a sign of weakening. I knew I had to show courage. In fact, I felt much better for having recited the words of the psalm. I had not been so free of fear the whole evening as I was in that moment standing beside the black jeep, a symbol of repression.

I lifted my head and said in a loud and firm voice, "I'm not guilty! I have nothing to confess."

This time there was no more shouting. The Red Guards and the Revolutionaries, as well as the onlookers, were perhaps awed by the solemnity of the occasion. After I had spoken, at a signal from the man in the tinted glasses, the young man from the police pulled my arms behind my back and put the handcuffs on my wrists. There was a deep sigh from an elderly man.

Suddenly, a girl pushed her way to the front and called in an agitated voice, "Confess! Confess quickly! They are going to take you to prison!" Her clear young voice was like a bell above the hum of the noisy street. It was the girl with the short hair and pale face who had sat by my desk guarding my jewelry when the Red Guards were in my house. Her impulsive effort to save me from going to prison was immediately checked by a woman who pulled her back and took her into the school building.

The driver of the jeep started the engine.

"Get in!" The young man gave me a push.

It was good to sit down. I looked out at the faces of the men and women watching this dramatic scene and saw relief in the eyes of the former staff of Shell. Perhaps they thought that with me out of the way they would be freed from pressure. Others of the crowd looked excited. To them, it was like watching the end of a thrilling drama, only better for their having taken part in it.

The young man from the police department got in with the driver, and the man with the tinted glasses sat down beside me. The jeep drove off into the dark streets.

II

THE
DETENTION
HOUSE

5

Solitary Confinement

THE STREETS OF SHANGHAI, normally deserted at nine o'clock in the evening, were a sea of humanity. Under the clear autumn sky in the cool breeze of September, people were out in thousands to watch the intensified activities of the Red Guards. On temporary platforms erected everywhere, the young Revolutionaries were calling upon the people in shrill and fiery rhetoric to join in the Revolution, and conducting small-scale struggle meetings against men and women they seized at random on the street and accused of failing to carry Mao's Little Red Book of quotations or simply wearing the sort of clothes the Red Guards disapproved of. Outside private houses and apartment buildings, smoke rose over the garden walls, permeating the air as the Red Guards continued to burn books indiscriminately.

Fully loaded trucks containing household goods confiscated from capitalist families were parked along the sidewalks ready to be driven away. With crowds jamming the streets and moving in all directions, buses and bicycles could only crawl along. The normal life of the city was making way for the Cultural Revolution, which was rapidly spreading in scope and increasing in intensity.

Loudspeakers at street corners were broadcasting such newly written revolutionary songs as "Marxism is one sentence: revolution is justified," "To sail the ocean we depend on the Helmsman; to carry out a revolution we depend on the Thought of Mao Zedong," and "The Thought of Mao Zedong glitters with golden light." If one heard only the marching rhythm of the music but not the militant words of the songs, if one saw only the milling crowd but not the victims and the Red Guards, one might easily think the scene was some kind of fair held on an autumn night to provide the people with entertainment, rather than a political campaign full of sinister undertones designed to stir up mutual mistrust and class hatred among the populace.

Both my body and my mind were paralyzed with fatigue from continued stress and strain, not only from the last few hours of the struggle meeting but also from the events of the preceding two and a half months. I had no idea where I was being taken, and I did not speculate. But I was indignant and angry about the way I was being treated, because I had never done anything against the People's Government. The accusation that I had committed crimes against my own country was so ludicrous that I thought it was just an excuse for punishing me because I had dared to live well. Clearly I was a victim of class struggle. As my friend Winnie had said, since Shell had closed its Shanghai office, the Maoists among the Party officials in Shanghai believed they should bring me down to the level of the masses.

Whenever the police vehicle in which I was being transported was forced to halt momentarily, a curious crowd pressed forward to peer at the "class enemy" inside; some applauded the victory of the proletariat in exposing yet another enemy, while others simply gazed at me with curiosity. A few looked worried and anxious, suddenly turning away from the ominous sight of another human being's ill fortune.

In Mao Zedong's China, going to prison did not mean the same thing as it did in the democracies. A man was always presumed guilty until he could prove himself innocent. The accused were judged not by their own deeds but by the acreage of land once possessed by their ancestors. A cloud of suspicion always hung over the heads of those with the wrong class origins. Furthermore, Mao had once declared that 3 to 5 percent of the population were enemies of socialism. To prove him correct, during the periodically launched political movements, 3 to 5 percent of the members of every organization, whether it was a government department, a factory, a school, or a university, must be found guilty of political crimes or heresy against socialism or Mao Zedong Thought. Among those found guilty, a number would be sent either to labor camps or to prison. Under such circumstances, the imprisonment of completely innocent persons was a frequent occurrence. Going to prison no longer carried with it the stigma of moral degeneration or law infringement. In fact, the people were often skeptical about government claims of anybody's guilt, and those unhappy with their lot in Communist China looked on political prisoners with a great deal of sympathy.

From the moment I became involved in the Cultural Revolution in early July and decided not to make a false confession, I had not ruled out the possibility of going to prison. I knew that many people, including seasoned Party members, made ritual confessions of guilt under pressure, hoping to avoid confrontation with the Party or to lessen their immediate suffering by submission. Many others became mentally confused under pressure and made false confessions because they had lost control. When a political campaign ended, some of them were rehabilitated. Many were not. In the Reform through Labor camps that dotted the landscape of China's remote and inhospitable provinces, such as Gansu and Qinghai, many innocent men and women were serving harsh sentences simply because they had made false confessions of guilt. It seemed to me that making a false confession when I was innocent was a foolish thing to do. The more logical and intelligent course was to face persecution no matter what I might have to endure.

As I examined my own position, I realized that the preliminary period of my persecution was drawing to a close. Whatever lay ahead, I would have to redouble my efforts to frustrate my persecutors' attempt to incriminate me. As long as they did not kill me, I would not give up. So, while I sat in the jeep, my mood was not one of fear and defeat but one of resolution.

When the jeep reached the business section of the city, the crowds became so dense that the car made very slow progress and was forced to stop every few blocks. The man in the tinted glasses told the driver to switch on the siren. It was an eerie wail with a pulsating rhythm changing from high to low and back again, rising above the sound of the revolutionary songs and drowning all other noise as well. Everybody turned to watch as the crowd parted to make way for the jeep. The driver sped up, and we proceeded through the streets with no further hindrance. Soon the jeep stopped outside a double black iron gate guarded by two armed sentries with fixed bayonets that glistened under the street lamps. On one side of the gate was a white wooden board with large black characters: No. 1 Detention House.

The gate swung open and the jeep drove in. It was completely dark inside, but in the beams of the jeep's headlights, I saw willow trees on both sides of the drive, which curved to the right. On one side was a basketball court; on the other side were a number of man-sized dummies lying near some poles. They looked like human bodies left carelessly about. It was not until several months later, when I was being taken to a prison hospital, that I had an opportunity to see the dummies in daylight and discovered that they were for target practice by the soldiers guarding the prison compound.

I knew that the No. 1 Detention House was the foremost detention house in Shanghai for political prisoners; from time to time it had housed Catholic bishops, senior Kuomintang officials, prominent industrialists, and well-known writers and artists. The irony of the situation was that it was not a new prison built by the Communist regime but an old establishment used by the former Kuomintang government before 1949 to house Communist Party members and their sympathizers.

A detention house for political prisoners was an important aspect of any authoritarian regime. Up to now, I had studied Communism in China from the comfort of my home, as an observer. Now I was presented with the opportunity to study it from an entirely different angle, at close range. In a perverse way, the prospect excited me and made me forget momentarily the dangerous situation in which I found myself.

The jeep followed the drive and went through another iron gate, passing the guard barracks and stopping in front of the main building in the courtyard. The two men jumped out and disappeared inside. A female guard in a khaki cap with its red national emblem at center front led me into a bare room where another uniformed woman was waiting. She closed the door, unlocked the handcuffs on my wrists, and said, "Undress!"

I took my clothes off and laid them on the table, the only piece of furniture in the room. The two women searched every article of my clothing extremely thoroughly. In my trouser pocket they found the envelope containing the 400 yuan I had intended to give to my gardener.

"Why have you brought so much money?" asked one of the guards.

"It's for my gardener. I was waiting for him to come to my house to get it. But he didn't come. Perhaps someone could give it to him for me," I said.

She handed me back my clothes except for the brassiere, an article of clothing the Maoists considered a sign of decadent Western influence. When I was dressed, the female guard led me into another room across a dimly lit narrow passage.

A man with the appearance and complexion of a peasant from North China was seated there behind a counter, under an electric light bulb dangling from the ceiling. The female guard indicated a chair facing the counter but a few feet away from it and told me to sit down. She placed the envelope with the money on the counter and said something to the man. He lifted his head to look at me. Then, in a surprisingly mild voice, he asked me for my name, age, and address, all of which he entered into a book, writing slowly and laboriously as if not completely at home with a pen and having difficulty remembering the strokes of each character. That he was doubtless barely literate did not surprise me, as I knew the Communist Party assigned men jobs for their political reliability rather than for their level of education.

When the man had finally finished writing, he said, "While you are here, you will be known by a number. You'll no longer use your name, not even to the guards. Do you understand?"

I nodded.

We were interrupted by a young man carrying a camera with a flash. He walked into the room and said to me, "Stand up!" Then he took several photographs of me from different angles and swaggered out of the room. I sat down again, wishing they would hurry up with the proceedings, for I was dead-tired.

The man behind the counter resumed in a slow and bored

manner, "Eighteen-oh-six is your number. You will be known henceforth as eighteen-oh-six. Try to remember it."

I nodded again.

The female guard pointed to a sheet of paper pasted on the wall and said, "Read it aloud!"

It was a copy of the prison regulations. The first rule was that all prisoners must study the books of Mao Zedong daily to seek reform of their thinking. The second rule was that they must confess their crimes without reservation and denounce others involved in the same crimes. The third rule was that they must report to the guards any infringement of prison rules by inmates in the same cell. The rest of the rules dealt with meals, laundry, and other matters of daily life in the detention house.

When I had finished reading, the female guard said, "Try to remember the rules and abide by them."

The man told me to dip my right thumb in a shallow inkpot filled with sticky red paste and make a print in the registration book. After I had done so, I asked the man for a piece of paper to wipe my thumb.

"Hurry up!" The female guard was getting impatient and shouted from the door. But the man was good-natured. He pulled open a drawer and took out a wrinkled piece of paper, which he handed to me. I hastily wiped my thumb and followed the woman out of the room and the building.

My admission into the No. 1 Detention House had been done in a leisurely manner; the attitude of the man and of the female guards was one of casual indifference. To them my arrival was merely routine. For me, crossing the prison threshold was the beginning of a new phase of my life that, through my struggle for survival and for justice, was to make me a spiritually stronger and politically more mature person. The long hours I spent alone reexamining my own life and what had gone on in China since 1949 when the Communist Party took power also enabled me to form a better understanding of myself and the political system under which I was living. Though on the night of September 27, 1966, when I was taken to the detention house I could not look into the future, I was not afraid. I believed in a just and merciful God, and I thought he would lead me out of the abyss.

It was pitch-dark outside, and the ground was unevenly paved.

As I followed the female guard, I breathed deeply the sweet night air. We walked around the main building, passed through a peeling and faded red gate with a feeble light, and entered a smaller courtyard where I saw a two-story structure. This was where the women prisoners were housed.

From a room near the entrance, another female guard emerged yawning. I was handed over to her in silence.

"Come along," she said sleepily, leading me through a passage lined with bolted, heavily padlocked doors. My first sight of the prison corridor was something I have never been able to forget. In subsequent years, in my dreams and nightmares, I saw again and again, in the dim light, the long line of doors with sinister-looking bolts and padlocks outside, and felt again and again the helplessness and frustration of being locked inside.

When we reached the end of the corridor, the guard unlocked a door on the left to reveal an empty cell.

"Get in," she said. "Have you any belongings?"

I shook my head.

"We'll notify your family in the morning and get them to send you your belongings. Now go to sleep!"

I asked her whether I could go to the toilet. She pointed to a cement fixture in the left-hand corner of the room and said, "I'll lend you some toilet paper."

She pushed the bolt in place with a loud clang and locked the door. I heard her moving away down the corridor.

I looked around the room, and my heart sank. Cobwebs dangled from the ceiling; the once whitewashed walls were yellow with age and streaked with dust. The single naked bulb was coated with grime and extremely dim. Patches of the cement floor were black with dampness. A strong musty smell pervaded the air. I hastened to open the only small window, with its rust-pitted iron bars. To reach it, I had to stand on tiptoe. When I succeeded in pulling the knob and the window swung open, flakes of peeling paint as well as a shower of dust fell to the floor. The only furniture in the room was three narrow beds of rough wooden planks, one against the wall, the other two stacked one on top of the other. Never in my life had I been in or even imagined a place so primitive and filthy.

The guard came back with several sheets of toilet paper of the roughest kind, which she handed to me through a small square window in the door of the cell, saying, "There you are! When you get your supply, you must return to the government the same number of sheets. Now go to sleep. Lie with your head towards the door. That's the regulation."

I could not bring myself to touch the dust-covered bed. But I needed to lie down, as my legs were badly swollen. I pulled the bed away from the dirty wall and wiped it with the toilet paper. But the dirt was so deeply ingrained that I could only remove the loose dust. Then I lay down anyhow and closed my eyes. The naked bulb hanging from the center of the ceiling was directly above my head. Though dim, it irritated me. I looked around the cell but could not see a light switch anywhere.

"Please, excuse me!" I called, knocking on the door with my hand.

"Quiet! Quiet!" The guard hurried over and slid open the shutter on the small window.

"I can't find the light switch," I told her.

"We don't switch off the light at night here. In future, when you want to speak to the guards, just say, 'Report.' Don't knock on the door. Don't say anything else."

"Could you lend me a broom to sweep the room? It's so dirty."

"What nonsense! It's past two o'clock. You just go to sleep!" She closed the shutter but remained outside and watched me through the peephole to make sure I obeyed her orders.

I lay down on the bed again and turned to face the dusty wall to avoid the light. I closed my eyes to shut out the sight of the wall, but I had to inhale the unpleasant smell of dampness and dust that surrounded me. In the distance, I heard faintly the crescendo of noise from the crowds on the streets. While it no longer menaced me, I worried about my daughter. I hoped my removal to the detention house would free her from any further pressure to denounce me. If that were indeed the case and she could be treated as just a member of the masses, I would be prepared to put up with anything.

Suddenly a horde of hungry mosquitoes descended on me. I sat up and tried to ward them off with my arms, but they were so stubborn and persistent that I was badly bitten. The itchy welts greatly added to my discomfort and annoyance.

Just before daybreak, the electric light in the cell was switched off. In the darkness, the dirt and ugliness of the room disappeared. I could imagine myself elsewhere. It was a moment of privacy and relief; I felt as if a tight band around me had been loosened. But not for long. Soon the narrow strip of sky turned gray and then white. Daylight slowly poured into the cell, bringing its ugly features into focus again. However, during all the years I spent in that prison cell, the short time of darkness after the light was switched off and before daybreak was always a moment when I recovered the dignity of my being and felt a sense of renewal, simply because I had a precious moment of freedom when I was not under the watchful eyes of the guards.

Footsteps in the passage approached. "Get up! Get up!" It was the voice of the same guard calling at the door of each cell. I could hear the muted sound of people stirring all over the building, and whispering voices and movements in the cell above mine.

The shutter of the small window on the door was pushed open. A young woman called, "Water," and pushed the spout of a watering can through the opening.

When I told her I had no utensil for the water, she withdrew the can but pressed her pale young face against the opening to look at me. When our eyes met, she smiled. A few days later, I caught a glimpse of a square piece of white cloth pinned on her jacket front stating that she was a prisoner serving a sentence of Labor Reform. After that, whenever there was an opportunity, we would smile at each other to acknowledge the painful fate we shared as prisoners of the state. This silent contact and the flicker of a smile I observed on her pale face came to mean a great deal to me in the years I spent in the detention house. When she disappeared, perhaps having completed her sentence, I experienced a deep sense of loss and felt despondent for days.

The shutter opened again. An oblong aluminum container appeared. A woman's voice said impatiently, "Come over, come over!"

When I took the container from her, she said, "In future, stand here at mealtimes and wait." She also handed me a pair of bamboo chopsticks that were wet and worn thin with prolonged usage.

The battered container was three-quarters full of lukewarm watery rice porridge with a few strips of pickled vegetables floating on top. I wiped the edge of the container with a piece of toilet paper and took a tentative sip. The rice tasted smoky for some reason, and the saltiness of the pickled vegetables made it bitter. The food was worse than I could possibly have imagined, but I made a determined effort to drink half of it. When the woman opened the small window again, I handed her back the container and the chopsticks.

In a little while, another female guard came. She said, "Why didn't you eat your rice?"

"I did eat some of it. May I see a responsible person?" I asked her. Chinese Communist officials did not like to be called "officials" unless they were addressed by their exact titles, such as "Minister Wang" or "Director Chang." Generally speaking, the officials were known as *ganbu*, which the standard Chinese-English dictionary translates as "cadres." Minor officials were usually referred to as "responsible persons," which could mean cadres or just clerks.

"What's the hurry? You have only just arrived. When the interrogator is ready, he will call you. What you should do now is to consider the crime you have committed. When he calls you, you must show true repentance by making a full confession in order to obtain lenient treatment. If you denounce others, you'll gain a point of merit for yourself."

"I've never committed a crime," I declared emphatically.

"Ah, a lot of you say this when you first come here. That's a foolish attitude to assume. Just think, there are ten million people in this city. Why should you have been brought here rather than someone else? You have certainly committed a crime."

It seemed pointless to argue with her. But her words convinced me that I was going to be there for some time. The dirt in the cell was intolerable. I simply had to deal with it if I was to live in that cell for another night. Besides, I had always found physical work soothing for frayed nerves. Since I was deeply unhappy to find myself in prison and terribly worried about my daughter, I asked her whether I could borrow a broom to sweep the floor.

"You are allowed to borrow a broom on Sundays only. But since you have just come, I'll lend you one today."

A few moments later she came back with an old, worn broom, which she squeezed through the small window to me. I pulled the bed around the cell and stood on it to reach the cobwebs. When I brushed the walls, the cell was enveloped in a cloud of dust.

The shutter opened again. A sheet of paper was pushed through to me. Looking out, I saw a male guard standing there.

"The money you brought here last night has been banked for you. This is your receipt. You are allowed to use the money to buy daily necessities such as toilet paper, soap, and towels," he said.

"That's just what I need. Could I buy some now?" I asked him.

"You may buy what you need," the man said.

"Please get me a washbasin, two enameled mugs for eating and drinking, some sewing thread, needles, soap, towels, a toothbrush and toothpaste, and some toilet paper. Am I allowed to buy some cold cream?"

"No, only necessities."

Soon he returned with a washbasin decorated with two large roses, six towels with colorful stripes, a stack of toilet paper, six cakes of the cheapest kind of laundry soap, two enameled mugs with lids, a toothbrush, a tube of toothpaste, and two spools of coarse cotton thread. He told me that prisoners were not allowed to have needles in the cell but they could borrow them from the guards on Sundays.

The guard had to open the cell door to hand me the washbasin. While it was still open, another male guard brought me the clothes and bedding left me by the Red Guards, as well as *The Collected Works of Mao Zedong* and the Little Red Book of Mao's quotations. After I had signed the receipt for these things, the two guards locked the door and departed.

I looked through everything very carefully, hoping to find a hidden note from my daughter. There was nothing. I sat on the edge of the bed, weary with disappointment and sadness. I longed for a moment with my daughter and prayed for her safety. After some time, I felt more peaceful. I decided to tackle the dirty room. What I needed was some water.

"Report!" I went to the door and called.

It was another female guard who pushed open the shutter and said sternly, "You don't have to shout! Now what do you want?"

I knew from her tone of voice that she would probably refuse whatever I might request. To forestall such a possibility, I quickly recited a quotation of Mao that said, "To be hygienic is glorious; to be unhygienic is a shame." Then I asked, "May I have some water to clean the cell?"

She walked away without saying a word. I waited and waited. Eventually the Labor Reform girl came and gave me enough water to fill the new washbasin as well as the one brought from my home with my things. First I washed the bed thoroughly; then I climbed onto my rolled-up bedding to wipe the dust-smeared windowpanes so that more light could come into the room. After I had washed the cement toilet built into the corner of the cell, I still had enough cold water left to bathe myself and rinse out my dirty blouse. When hot water for drinking was issued, I sat on the clean bed and drank it with enjoyment. Plain boiled water had never tasted so good.

The midday meal was dry rice and some boiled green cabbage. With a portion of the rice I made a paste that I used to glue sheets of toilet paper onto the dirty wall along the bed so that I and my bedclothes would not touch it while I was sleeping. After that I felt much better. When the guard came to tell me to walk about in the cell for exercise, I said, "May I return the broom, please?"

She opened the small window to accept the broom and saw the toilet paper I had pasted onto the wall.

"It's against regulations to make changes in the cell," she said. I remained silent, wondering how best to deal with the situation if she should order me to remove the paper. But she only picked up the broom and closed the shutter. A moment later, I heard her upstairs calling from cell to cell, "Exercise! Exercise!"

I could hear footsteps of many people walking around and around in the room above mine. When the guard called for everybody to sit down at the end of the exercise period, I heard many prisoners flopping down onto the floor. Evidently in the multiple cell upstairs there were no beds; the inmates were sleeping and sitting on the bare floor. The wall between the next-door cell and mine was too thick for me to hear any sound, but I could hear quite clearly every word spoken aloud in the cell above. The sound of the women prisoners moving overhead and the murmuring of their voices when the guard was not near somewhat mitigated my acute feeling of loneliness and isolation.

The contrast of color and shape and the blending of different sounds that please the senses in normal life were completely absent in prison. Everywhere I looked I saw ugly shapes and a uniform shade of depressing, dirty gray. There was nothing other than the guards' cold and indifferent voice of authority to break the ominous silence. Sitting in the cell, I found my gaze straying often to the window. I would stare at the narrow strip of sky through the iron bars for hours at a time. It was not only that light and fresh air came in through the window to sustain my life; the window was also the only channel through which I maintained a tenuous link with the world outside. Often, while my body sat in the cell, my spirit would escape through the window to freedom. One of my most vivid memories of prison life is watching the shifting shadow of the window bars on the cement floor. With its slow movement across the cell, I watched the passage of time while I waited and waited day after day and year after year, sometimes for the next meal, sometimes for the next interrogation, but above all for some political development that would curb the power of the Maoist Revolutionaries.

Daylight faded, and the electric light was switched on. I ate another portion of rice and green cabbage. The guard on night duty was another woman. She handed me the newspaper. Putting her face to the small opening on the door, she shouted, "What have you done to the cell?"

"I cleaned it according to Chairman Mao's teaching on hygiene," I answered.

"If you heed the teaching of our Great Leader Chairman Mao, why are you locked in a prison cell?" she yelled. "Did the Chairman tell you to commit a crime?"

"I've never committed a crime. There has been a mistake. It can be cleared up by investigation and examination of the facts," I said.

"You have a glib tongue, that I can see. You're trying to bring your capitalist way of life into this place, aren't you? I advise you to think less of your own personal comfort and more of your criminal deeds. Give the matter serious consideration. When you are called, be sure to give a full confession so that you can earn lenient treatment." She closed the small window so that I could not answer back.

I was getting very tired of this talk of confession and how it could earn lenient treatment for the prisoner. Perhaps it was true, I thought, that a really guilty person could earn a lighter sentence by confessing voluntarily. But I was not guilty. It was infuriating to be told so often that I had committed a crime when I had not.

I picked up the newspaper and stood directly under the feeble light to read it. Like other newspapers in China, the *Shanghai Liberation Daily* was published, financed, and completely controlled by the People's Government. The journalists were officials appointed by the Party's propaganda department; their job was to select and often distort news, especially foreign news, for propaganda purposes and to write articles praising government policies. The newspaper is used everywhere in China, including in the prisons, for the education of the people.

The Chinese people had long ago learned that the only way to read the newspaper was to read between the lines and pay attention to the omissions as well as to the printed items. In fact, the real source of news for the Chinese people was not the newspaper at all, but political gossip passed from one person to another in low whispers, often in the language of symbols and signs, with no names mentioned. This was called "footpath news," meaning that it did not come openly by the main road, that is, official channels. In the past, before the Communist Party took control of the country, its underground organizations had used "footpath news" effectively to undermine the Chinese people's confidence in the Kuomintang government. Now they themselves were plagued by it. When the people mistrusted the official newspapers and could not obtain news freely, they were naturally more than eager to listen to and believe in whatever they could pick up in the way of political gossip.

In the detention house, the *Shanghai Liberation Daily* was my sole source of information about what went on outside the prison walls. I read it very carefully, sometimes going over the same news item or article twice, in order to follow the course of the Cultural Revolution and evaluate the political development that was taking place. From the way items of news were presented, the subjects of special articles, the tone of the editorials, and the quotation of Mao Zedong selected for use on a certain day, I could often discern what the Maoists hoped to accomplish or what had not gone according to plan. However, my full understanding of the details of the struggle for power within the Communist Party came only after my release. I succeeded then in gathering together a collection of uncensored Red Guard publications and had the opportunity to question young people who had taken part in the revolutionary activities.

When Sunday came around, I asked the guard for the loan of a needle. I joined two of the newly purchased towels to make a seat for the cement toilet, sewed together layers of toilet paper to make a cover for one of the washbasins I used for storing water, and cut up a handkerchief to make an eyeshade to cover my eyes at night. When I asked to use scissors, the guard stood at the small window to watch me, taking them back as soon as I had finished cutting. Doing something practical to improve my daily life made me feel better. I found sewing, in particular, a soothing occupation.

Several days passed. I made a request every day to see the interrogator, without result. One sunny morning, the prisoners were told to get ready for outdoor exercise. The guard went to each cell calling, *"Fangfeng!"* ("Out to get air!")

Eager for sunshine and fresh air, I jumped up, laid down the book of Mao's I had been reading, and rushed to stand by the door. But I had to wait for quite some time before being let out. The No. 1 Detention House had an elaborate system to prevent inmates of different cells from meeting one another. I had to wait until the prisoner in the cell next to mine turned the corner and was out of sight before being allowed to leave my cell. Guards were posted along the route to watch the prisoners and to lead them to the exercise yards.

The exercise yard I was locked into was spacious but in a state of dismal neglect. Broken plaster on the walls exposed the bricks underneath. The ground was covered with dirt and loose gravel. I saw something green in one corner and discovered a cluster of resilient weeds struggling to keep alive. Pleased to see something growing in this inhospitable place, I went over to examine it closely and saw tiny pink flowers at the tip of each stem. Every flower had five perfectly formed petals that were no bigger than a seed. In the midst of dirt and gravel, the plant stood proudly in the sunshine giving a sign of life in this dead place. Gazing at the tiny flowers, which seemed incredibly beautiful to me, I felt an uplifting of my spirit.

"Walk about! Walk about with your head bowed! You are not allowed to stop walking!" a guard shouted at me from the raised platform on the walls of the exercise yard. There were two pavilions on the platform, one open and one enclosed with glass windows. As the weather was fine, the guards were watching the prisoners from the open pavilion.

I started to walk around in the exercise yard; gradually the heaviness on my chest loosened, and I breathed more easily. The autumn air was cool and dry; the sun was warm on my face. Time passed slowly in prison, with each day endlessly long. But not so during outdoor exercise periods. Even in the depths of winter when my clothes could not keep my starved body warm and I shivered incessantly in the bitter north wind, the outdoor exercise period passed altogether too quickly for me.

The male guard who led me back to my cell could not find the right key for the door. While he was trying one key after another, I took the opportunity to make another request to see the interrogator.

"I've been here such a long time already. May I see the interrogator?" I asked him.

"A long time already?" He straightened up and turned to face me. "You talk nonsense. I know you've been here less than a month. A month is not a long time. There are people who have been here for years, and their cases are not yet resolved. Why are you so impatient? You are always asking to see the interrogator. What are you going to say to him when you do see him? Are you ready to make a full confession?"

"I'll ask the interrogator to investigate my case and clarify the misunderstanding."

"What misunderstanding?" He appeared genuinely puzzled.

"The misunderstanding that brought me here," I said.

"You are here because you committed a crime against the People's Government. There is no misunderstanding. You mustn't talk in riddles."

"I've never committed a crime in my whole life," I said firmly.

"If you have not committed a crime, why are you locked up in prison? Your being here proves you have committed a crime."

His logic appalled me. It was based on the assumption that the Party and the government could not be mistaken. I could not argue with him without appearing to offend the Party and the

People's Government, so I merely said, "Honestly, I have never committed a crime. There has been a mistake."

"Perhaps there was something you did that you don't remember. Prisoners often need help and guidance from the interrogator to confess."

"I don't think I could forget if I had committed a crime," I told him. I recalled hearing of cases where the interrogator fed the prisoner with things to say while confessing. All of it was written down and held against the prisoner eventually.

"Perhaps you did not realize you were committing a crime at the time. You are probably still quite muddled," the guard said. He seemed quite sincere.

Could it be possible that what I considered innocent behavior had really been interpreted by others as criminal deeds against the state? Although I had followed political and economic developments in China carefully and tried to acquire an intelligent understanding of events, I had never studied the Communist government's penal code. I decided to make good this omission without further delay. So I said to the guard, "In that case, I'll study the lawbooks to see if I have indeed committed a crime inadvertently. Will you please lend me your lawbooks?"

"What lawbooks? You talk just like the capitalist intellectuals who are being denounced in this Cultural Revolution. You think in terms of lawbooks, rules, and regulations. We are the proletariat, we do not have anything like that." He seemed highly indignant, as if my assumption that they had lawbooks were an insult.

"If you do not have lawbooks, what do you go by? How do you decide whether a man has committed a crime or not?"

"We go by the teachings of our Great Leader Chairman Mao. His words are our criteria. If he says a certain type of person is guilty and you belong to that type, then you are guilty. It's much simpler than depending on a lawbook," he said. To him, it was perfectly good and logical to have the fate of men decided arbitrarily by the words of Mao Zedong, which varied depending on his priorities during a particular period and were often so vague that local officials could interpret them to suit themselves. The absolute infallibility of Mao's words was a part of his personality cult. But I wondered how the guard would have felt if not I but he had been the victim.

After he had locked me into the cell again, I made no further request to see an interrogator. Instead I settled down to study assiduously and seriously *The Collected Works of Mao Zedong*. I wanted to know how his words could be used against me, and I wanted to see if I could not use his words to refute my accusers. I thought I should learn to speak Mao's language and be fluent in using his quotations when the time came for me to face the interrogator.

Many weeks passed. One day merged into another. Prolonged isolation heightened my feeling of depression. I longed for some news of my daughter. I missed her terribly and worried about her constantly. Often I would be so choked with emotion that breathing became difficult. At other times, a heavy lump would settle on my stomach, so that I had difficulty swallowing food.

Outside the prison walls, the Cultural Revolution seemed to be increasing in intensity. The loudspeaker of the nearby high school was blaring all day long. Instead of revolutionary songs, angry denunciations of local officials and prominent scholars were pouring out. I strained my ears to listen to them, trying to catch a word here and a phrase there when the wind was in the right direction. Within the gloomy cell, I studied Mao's books many hours a day, reading until my eyesight became blurred.

One day, in the early afternoon, when my eyes were too tired to distinguish the printed words, I lifted them from the book to gaze at the window. A small spider crawled into view, climbing up one of the rust-eroded bars. The little creature was no bigger than a good-sized pea; I would not have seen it if the wooden frame nailed to the wall outside to cover the lower half of the window hadn't been painted black. I watched it crawl slowly but steadily to the top of the iron bar, quite a long walk for such a tiny thing, I thought. When it reached the top, suddenly it swung out and descended on a thin silken thread spun from one end of its body. With a leap and swing, it secured the end of the thread to another bar. The spider then crawled back along the silken thread to where it had started and swung out in another direction on a similar thread. I watched the tiny creature at work with increasing fascination. It seemed to know exactly what to do and where to take the next thread. There was no hesitation, no mistake, and no haste. It knew its job and was carrying it out with confidence. When the frame was made, the spider proceeded to weave a web that was intricately beautiful and absolutely perfect, with all the strands of thread evenly spaced. When the web was completed, the spider went to its center and settled there.

I had just watched an architectural feat by an extremely skilled artist, and my mind was full of questions. Who had taught the spider how to make a web? Could it really have acquired the skill through evolution, or did God create the spider and endow it with the ability to make a web so that it could catch food and perpetuate its species? How big was the brain of such a tiny creature? Did it act simply by instinct, or had it somehow learned to store the knowledge of web making? Perhaps one day I would ask an entomologist. For the moment, I knew I had just witnessed something that was extraordinarily beautiful and uplifting. Whether God had made the spider or not, I thanked Him for what I had just seen. A miracle of life had been shown me. It helped me to see that God was in control. Mao Zedong and his Revolutionaries seemed much less menacing. I felt a renewal of hope and confidence.

My cell faced southwest. For a brief moment, the rays of the setting sun turned the newly made web into a glittering disc of rainbow colors, before it shifted further west and sank below the horizon. I did not dare to go up to the window in case I should frighten the spider away. I remained where I was, watching it. Soon I discovered it was not merely sitting there waiting for its prey but was forever vigilant. Whenever a corner of the web was ruffled or torn by the breeze, the spider was there in an instant to repair the damage. And as days passed, the spider renewed the web from time to time; sometimes a part of it was remade, sometimes the whole web was remade.

I became very attached to the little creature after watching its activities and gaining an understanding of its habits. First thing in the morning, throughout the day, and last thing at night, I would look at it and feel reassured when I saw that it was still there. The tiny spider became my companion. My spirits lightened. The depressing feeling of complete isolation was broken by having another living thing near me, even though it was so tiny and incapable of response.

Soon it was November. The wind shifted to the northwest.

With each rainy day the temperature fell further. I watched the spider anxiously, not wishing to close the window and shut it out. It went on repairing the wind-torn web and patiently making new ones. However, one morning when I woke up, I found the spider gone. Its derelict web was in shreds. I felt sad but hopefully kept the window open in case it should come back. Then I chanced to look up and saw my small friend sitting in the center of a newly made web in a corner of the ceiling. I quickly closed the window and felt happy to know that my friend had not deserted me.

Towards the end of November one morning, I woke up with a streaming cold and a severe headache. Blowing my nose and feeling miserable, I sat on the edge of the bed wondering whether I should ask for some medicine. When the watery rice was given to me, I made myself drink it up, hoping the warm liquid might give me some relief, but I could not eat the dry rice and boiled cabbage at noon. I returned it to the woman from the kitchen untouched. Throughout the afternoon, the guard on duty came frequently to watch me through the peephole. She made no attempt to speak to me until evening, when she suddenly pushed open the small window and said, "You have been crying!"

"Oh, no," I said, "I have a cold."

"You are crying. You are crying because you are not used to the living conditions here. You find everything quite intolerable, don't you? We have been watching you trying to improve things. Also you are crying because you miss your daughter. You are wondering what's happening to her," the guard said.

"No, really, I just have a cold. May I have an aspirin?"

"Aspirin isn't going to help you. What's bothering you is in your mind. Think over your own position. Assume the correct attitude. Be repentant," she said.

I sat in the cell for the rest of the evening with my face averted from the door and tried not to blow my nose or wipe my eyes. When rice was given to me in the evening, I ate some and tipped the rest into the toilet, pouring water in to wash it away. Nevertheless, so firmly did the guards believe I was crying because I could not endure the hardship of prison life that they seized on what they thought was a psychologically weak moment and called me for interrogation the next day.

6

Interrogation

T HE MORNING DAWNED BRIGHT and sunny. When I opened the window, frosty fresh air flowed into the cell. Winter was not far off, I thought. The guard was going from cell to cell calling the inmates to take their sheets off their beds for laundering, a routine that took place once a month on a sunny day. Extra cold water was issued to the cells. The inmates soaked their sheets in it, rubbed soap on the wet sheets, and then pushed them out of the small windows of the cells, to be collected by the Labor Reform girls, who finished washing them in the laundry room.

While I was rubbing soap on my wet sheet, a male guard unlocked the cell door, threw it open wide, and yelled, "Come out!"

"I'm doing my laundry," I said.

"Don't argue. When I say come out, just come out."

The female guard on duty also came to the door. She said, "You can do your laundry later. Now you must go for interrogation."

Interrogation! At last it seemed I was to come face to face with my antagonist. I hurriedly wiped my hands on a dry towel.

"Hurry up! Bring your book of Chairman Mao's quotations," the male guard said impatiently.

I followed him out of the cell through the courtyard of the

women's prison into an area at the back of the prison compound. He led me into a building past a large white wooden board on which was written in black characters, "Lenient treatment to those who confess frankly. Severe punishment to those who remain stubborn. Reward to those who render meritorious service."

My heart palpitated with excitement; my footsteps were eager with expectancy. The long-awaited opportunity to answer questions and to have my case examined dispassionately was here at last. I believed a government interrogator couldn't possibly behave like a hysterical Red Guard or a Revolutionary. He must be a trained man with a sense of responsibility, able to distinguish a guilty person from an innocent one.

Several guards were lolling on wooden chairs in a small room beside the entrance to the building. I was handed over to one of them who led me through a long corridor with many interrogation rooms ranged on either side. Most of the doors were closed. But I heard the muffled sound of voices and an occasional shout from some of them. The guard stopped in front of one of the rooms, threw open the door, and shouted, "Go in!"

The room was narrow and long and rather dark, with only a small window, like the one in my cell, high on the back wall. Two men, dressed in the baggy and faded blue cotton Maoist uniform worn by nearly all men in China except senior officials, were seated behind a wooden counter under the window. About two yards away, facing the window, was a heavy wooden chair for the prisoner. The room was very dark, but the little light that came through the window was focused on the spot where the prisoner sat. I noticed that the walls were dusty, the cement floor was black with damp, and the wooden counter and chair had been rubbed into a neutral color of gray.

After I entered the room, one of the men said, "Read the teaching of our Great Leader Chairman Mao from your book of quotations." The quotation he selected was the same one used by the Red Guards when they came to loot my home.

" 'When the enemies with guns are annihilated, the enemies without guns still remain. We must not belittle these enemies.' " I read the quotation in a firm voice, conscious of the fact that the two men were watching me closely. I tried not to show any sign of nervousness lest it be interpreted as a sign of guilt.

"Sit down," the man said, pointing to the prisoner's chair.

As I turned to sit down, I saw a small window rather like the one in the door of my cell, only perhaps a little larger, in the wall behind the prisoner's chair. I concluded that the interrogations carried out in the room were monitored by someone in the corridor.

I sat down on the heavy wooden chair and looked at the two men behind the counter. They had the pale faces of men who worked indoors with little chance for exercise. Unlike the man who registered my arrival, these two men, despite their rather shabby appearance, exuded an air of authority and self-confidence common to men of official position. They were quite relaxed, almost casual; of course, interviewing a prisoner was just routine work to them. I assumed the one who spoke to me was the interrogator and the one with sheets of paper in front of him was the secretary.

After I was seated, the interrogator looked past my shoulder at the small window behind me and gave a barely perceptible nod. It seemed my initial perception was correct; a man was indeed outside listening in on my interrogation. Disappointment overwhelmed me for a moment. It seemed the interrogator was just an intermediary and I was not going to see my real antagonist after all. How I wished I could deal face to face with the man who had treated me so unjustly and have his features carved on my memory, never to be forgotten!

In a low voice that was almost bored, the interrogator asked me my name and other personal particulars. Then he looked up, raised his voice, and asked firmly, "Do you know what this place is?"

"I suppose it's some sort of prison or concentration camp, since everybody is locked up."

"You are quite right. This is the Number One Detention House, a prison for political prisoners. This is the place where counterrevolutionaries who have committed crimes against the People's Government are locked up and investigated."

"In that case, I should not have been brought here," I declared firmly.

He was not perturbed by my remark but went on calmly, "You are locked up here precisely because you have committed a crime against the People's Government."

"There must have been some mistake," I said.

"The People's Government does not make mistakes."

"You are not an irresponsible Red Guard. You are a government representative. You can't make wild accusations like that."

"It's not a wild accusation."

"You will have to provide some evidence to prove what you are saying." I was deeply disappointed that the long-awaited interrogation was turning out to be just like the sessions I had had with the Revolutionaries before my imprisonment.

"Of course we have the evidence," the interrogator bluffed shamelessly.

"Produce it, then," I said sarcastically, calling his bluff. "Why waste time having an interrogation? Why not just produce the evidence and punish the culprit?"

"You must not underrate the masses. The Red Guards and the Revolutionaries can obtain all the evidence we need. Nothing can be hidden. Those who have made mistakes or committed crimes are making confessions and providing denunciations of others. They want to earn lenient treatment by confessing and to receive rewards by incriminating others."

"I don't believe you could possibly have any evidence against me, not because I fail to understand the nature of the Proletarian Cultural Revolution or because I underestimate the power of the masses. It's because I don't think you, or anybody else for that matter, could have something that simply doesn't exist. I have never committed any crime; how could there be any evidence to show that I have done so?" Because he had lied about having evidence, I had gained a moral advantage over him. It reinforced my self-confidence.

"It would be an easy matter to produce the evidence and punish you. But that is not the policy of our Great Leader. The purpose of this interrogation is to help you change your way of thinking and to give you an opportunity to earn lenient treatment by confessing frankly so that you can make a clean break with your criminal past and become a new person."

"I'm not a magician. I don't know how to confess to something that did not happen."

"Perhaps you are not ready yet. We are patient. We can wait." He fixed his gaze upon me and spoke slowly so that his implied threat of long imprisonment would sink in.

"A million years would make no difference. If something didn't happen, it just didn't happen. You can't change facts, no matter how long you wait." I also spoke slowly and firmly to make him see that he had failed to frighten me.

"Time can change a person's attitude. A woman like you would not last five years in this place. Your health will break down. Eventually you will be begging for a chance to confess. If you don't you will surely die."

"I would rather die than tell a lie."

"Not at all. To want to live is the basic instinct of all living things, humans included."

"I will obey our Great Leader Chairman Mao's teaching. He said, 'Firstly, do not fear hardship, and secondly, do not fear death.' "

"That quotation was not for the likes of you. That was for the Liberation Army soldiers," he said indignantly.

"Marshal Lin Biao said, 'The teachings of our Great Leader have universal significance and are applicable in all circumstances.' " A subtle change had taken place in my mood since the interrogator had given me the moral advantage by lying. I was beginning to enjoy this interrogation now. It was a lot better than being left in a dark, damp cell with no one to talk to.

There was a moment of silence. The interrogator again looked past my shoulder. Then he said, "You are audacious. But you can't talk your way out of your difficulties. The only way out for you is to assume a correct attitude of sincerity. It's my duty to help you come to a full understanding of the policy of the government and realize that you have no alternative to showing sincerity of repentance by giving a full confession. Do not belittle the Dictatorship of the Proletariat! This interrogation room is the equivalent of the People's Court. You must take everything said here extremely seriously."

"Am I not to expect justice from the People's Government?"

"Justice! What is justice? It's a mere word. It's an abstract word with no universal meaning. To different classes of people, justice means different things. The capitalist class considers it perfectly just to exploit the workers, while the workers consider it decidedly unjust to be so exploited. In any case, who are you to demand justice? When you sat in your well-heated house and there were other people shivering in the snow, did you think of justice?"

"You are confusing social justice with legal justice. I can tell you that it was precisely because my late husband and I hoped that the People's Government would improve conditions in China so that there would never be anybody suffering cold and hunger that we remained here in 1949 rather than follow the Kuomintang to Taiwan," I told him.

"In any case, we are not concerned with the abstract concept of justice. The army, the police, and the court are instruments of repression used by one class against another. They have nothing to do with justice. The cell you now occupy was used to lock up members of the Communist Party during the days of the reactionary Kuomintang government. Now the Dictatorship of the Proletariat uses the same instruments of repression against its own enemies. The capitalist countries use such attractive words as 'justice' and 'liberty' to fool the common people and to prevent their revolutionary awakening. To assume a proper attitude you must get all that rubbish out of your head. Otherwise you will get nowhere."

What he said was not new to me or to anybody who had lived in China and followed events since 1949. It was the accepted Marxist theory of class struggle. "The army, the police, and the court are instruments of repression used by one class against another" was said by Mao Zedong in his essay "On the Dictatorship of the People's Democracy." In the fifties Mao Zedong and his propaganda machinery used "the Dictatorship of the People's Democracy" to describe the Communist regime in China. The facts of history have demonstrated, however, that the Communist regime in China was a dictatorship by Mao Zedong until his death in 1976. Mao's essay "On the Dictatorship of the People's Democracy" was published on July 1, 1949, to celebrate the anniversary of the founding of the Chinese Communist Party in 1921. That essay actually heralded and justified a series of political campaigns and large-scale arrests of men and women suspected of being hostile to the new Communist regime.

I saw that the interrogation was getting nowhere. As long as the interrogator did not ask concrete questions, nothing could be clarified. There was no point in my engaging in theoretical arguments over Marxism. One either believed in it or one did not. There was no middle way. My own outlook and my values had been formed long ago. I did not believe in dividing people into rigid classes, and I did not believe in class struggle as a means to promote progress. I believed that to rebuild after so many years of war, China needed a peaceful environment and the unity of all sections of society, not perpetual revolution. I could not change these beliefs. Unfortunately the interrogator would not see that, at least not at the moment. At the moment, he hoped to confuse me, to overcome my resistance with a combination of threats and arguments. The session was going to be protracted and tedious. My head was throbbing from my cold. I decided to let him talk on and hear him out.

After a moment's silence, the interrogator went on. "The first requisite to confession is an admission of guilt. You must admit your guilt not only to the People's Government but also to yourself. The admission of guilt is like the opening of the flood-gates. When you admit sincerely that you are indeed guilty, that you were opposed to the People's Government even though you pretended not to be, your confession will flow out easily."

He stopped for a moment and looked at me searchingly to see my reaction. He had said "opposed to the People's Government." Of course I had been opposed to some measures of the People's Government, such as large-scale arrests of innocent people, declaring a man an enemy just because of his class origin, etc. But I never talked about any of these things to anybody. And certainly I never tried to do anything about them. I only hoped that when the regime achieved maturity and experience, it would mellow. The interrogator was trying to instill in me a feeling of guilt because he knew very well that every citizen in every country opposes some measures of his or her government at one time or another. He hoped to manipulate me psychologically. But I saw through him at once, so I just sat there without any expression on my face. In my mind I thought of all the aspects of the People's Government's work that I fully supported, such as the improvement in public hygiene and the resettlement of the homeless. On the whole, I thought of myself as a supporter of the People's Government. This assessment of my own positive attitude towards the Communist regime bolstered my courage to resist the interrogator's attempt to promote a sense of guilt in my mind. It proved invaluable in all the years I spent in prison.

The interrogator continued. "The thing for you to do is to look over your own life and examine your family background.

Find your correct place in the political and economic structure of our socialist state. Where do you stand? With the working people and the Revolutionaries or with the class enemies? You do not need me to tell you that you came from a feudal family that owned an enormous amount of rich agricultural land. For generations, your family exploited the peasants and lived off the riches they created. Your grandfather, your father, and your husband were all senior officials of reactionary regimes that cooperated with foreign imperialism, exploited the people, and opposed the Communist Party. You yourself decided to work for a multinational foreign firm though you were offered the opportunity to become a teacher at an educational institution of the people. It's seventeen years since the Communist army liberated Shanghai. Scores of Chinese with backgrounds like yours have changed their mode of life and fallen in line with us. What did you do? You just went on as if nothing had happened. You carried on arrogantly in your old lifestyle, wore the same bourgeois clothes, and even dared to speak English in public and maintain friendly contact with a large number of foreigners here and abroad.

"Did you think your attitude of intransigence could pass unnoticed? The proletariat has been watching you for years. Our Great Leader said recently, 'The eyes of the masses are clear and bright as snow.' Do you still think you can hide anything from us?

"You are an intelligent woman. Do you honestly think we would let you out of here without succeeding in completely transforming your way of thinking?

"You have been here nearly two months already. I must admit you surprised us with your adaptability. Nevertheless, no matter how nonchalant you appear, you must find the living conditions in the prison cell extremely trying. Winter will soon be upon us. I do not believe you have ever passed a single winter in an unheated room in your whole life. That cell is going to be very cold. Then there is the coarse food you often find difficult to swallow. We have observed that. And what about your daughter? Do you not miss her? Do you not often wonder what is happening to her?"

He paused again. But when I continued to maintain silence, he went on. "First of all, we want you to write your autobiography. Nearly everyone in the country has done it, but we could find nothing like that in your file. Write everything down clearly. Do not try to whitewash yourself. Do not try to hide anything. We will check what you write with the material we already have about you. If you omit anything, we will think you are not sincere. Write in chronological order, starting with your family. We will make an assessment of your political standpoint and your sincerity from what you write."

The man taking notes got up and handed me a roll of paper. After I had accepted it, the interrogator said, "If this paper is not enough, the guard on duty will give you more. She will also give you pen and ink. You are not allowed to make a draft. You are not allowed to throw away the paper on which you make a mistake. Hand it in with the rest when you finish."

He looked at me with great seriousness and said, "Think over carefully everything I have said today. When you have finished your autobiography, give it to the guard on duty. We will call you again."

The door of the interrogation room opened, and a guard appeared. I followed him through the long corridor back to my cell. I had no way of knowing how long I had been gone, but it seemed ages. I was hungry, tired, and very disappointed.

My wet sheet was spread on the stacked beds, which I used as a table. I picked up the cake of soap to rub on it. When I had finished, I called to the guard on duty, "Report!"

She came to the small window and handed me a pen and a bottle of ink.

"May I have my sheet washed now?"

"Laundry time is over. You can keep it for the next time."

"But it's wet, and I have soaped it. It's not hygienic to keep a wet sheet for a whole month," I said.

She did not wait for me to finish speaking but banged the small window shut and walked away.

During the afternoon, however, she came repeatedly to the peephole to look into the cell. After several trips, she opened the small window and asked me, "Why are you not writing?"

"How can I write? I'm worried about the wet sheet. It will smell. I haven't another sheet to use."

Perhaps to ensure my getting on with writing my autobiography as the interrogator wanted, she relented and got the Labor

Reform girl to take the sheet. It was returned to me the next day, clean and dry.

The guard continued to come regularly to the peephole to look into the cell. To give the appearance of writing, I laid one of Mao's books on my lap, placed a sheet of paper on it, and put the ink bottle beside me. After that, the guard left me alone.

Before writing anything, I had to ascertain what the interrogator hoped to achieve by ordering me to write my autobiography. His excuse that all other Chinese had done it was not a valid one. Although I had never been asked to write an autobiography, I believe the police in my district had a detailed record of my life already, as they had for everybody else who lived there. Obviously the interrogator hoped that the autobiography would provide some material they could twist and use against me.

A point that puzzled me was that I was not the only Chinese woman in Shanghai who had carried on with a comfortable lifestyle, worn traditional Chinese dress instead of the Mao suit, and kept foreign friends. But I had been singled out for imprisonment. No doubt the others had suffered at the hands of the Red Guards and probably had their homes looted. Maybe they had been beaten up. But I did not think they could all have been arrested. There was in fact much in the situation that was still a mystery to me. It would be foolish to plunge in and write frankly about myself and my life, revealing my innermost thoughts and standpoint. Besides, I had known cases of men being asked to write autobiographies over and over again. When discrepancies were found, the men were enmeshed in deep suspicion. Obviously the only thing I could do was to write a simple record of my life giving the bare facts in chronological order. If I was asked to write my autobiography again, I would have no difficulty in producing an identical version.

In the evening there was a sudden drop in temperature. By nightfall a strong wind was blowing. The window of the cell was so badly fitted that it rattled. Cold air came through the gaps in sharp gusts. I folded sheets of toilet paper into strips and pushed them into the gaps to stop the wind. By then the web of my small spider friend was already torn. Instead of making a new web promptly as it always had done in the past, the spider descended from the corner of the ceiling on a long silken thread. When it reached the floor, it crawled across the room very slowly and with difficulty. I crouched down to watch it closely, wondering what it was going to do. My small friend seemed rather weak. It stumbled and stopped every few steps. Could a spider get sick, or was it merely cold? Watching anxiously, I saw it go from corner to corner, probably looking for a sheltered place away from the wind. Finally it disappeared into the corner where the cement toilet was joined to the wall. There, in the crevice, it made a tiny web, not as well done or beautiful as the ones before, but the layered threads were thicker, forming something rather like a cocoon. I thought my small friend was well protected. When I had to use the toilet, I carefully sat well to one side so that I did not disturb it.

Next morning, I wrote my autobiography rather quickly on a few sheets of paper and finished it in the afternoon. Then I went to the window and called, "Report!"

The same guard who had been on duty the day before came to the window. I handed her what I had written, together with the remaining blank sheets of paper.

"You have finished writing already?" she asked doubtfully, eyes fixed on the five sheets of paper covered with my handwriting.

"Yes, I have finished," I answered.

"It seems so short. Have you put everything down?"

"Yes."

"Why is it so short?"

"Oh, is it too short? In any case, I did put everything in."

She said nothing more and walked away. I half expected some sort of immediate reaction. When nothing happened, I became rather lighthearted. For the whole evening I watched the small spider, for it had abandoned its newly made home and was again crawling with difficulty across the room, stumbling and stopping frequently. Finally it headed straight in my direction. When it came close to my feet, I wondered if it intended to climb up my leg for warmth. But it continued past my feet and disappeared under the bed. I waited for it to come out again, but hours passed and nothing happened. Perhaps the most sheltered place in the cell was under the bed and my little friend had decided to remain there for the winter.

Next morning, when the guard called me to get up, I looked carefully on the floor to make sure the small spider was not there before putting my feet on the ground. In fact, while I ate my watery breakfast my eyes strayed continuously to the area of the cement floor next to the bed, where I hoped to see the spider emerging with renewed vigor. But again nothing happened. Looking up at the ceiling, I found the torn web gone. No trace was left of the life of the small spider at all; I might have imagined the whole thing. Yet while it was there, it had worked and lived with such serious effort, making and remaking its web. The small spider had obeyed its natural instinct for survival. I should do the same. As long as I was in the No. 1 Detention House, I would fight on resolutely and seriously to the best of my ability.

My thoughts were interrupted by the sound of the cell door being unlocked. A male guard shouted, "Come out!"

I picked up Mao's book of quotations and followed him, bracing myself for a stormy session with the interrogator, who I guessed would probably share the woman guard's view and consider my autobiography not up to expectations.

I was led to the door of another interrogation room, identical with the previous one. The same two men were seated just as before, except that their uniforms bulged with sweaters that were peeping out over their collars and cuffs. The room was icy and damp. Outside, the strong northwest wind from Siberia lashed the city relentlessly, rattling the window and whistling through the gaps. The interrogator looked at me with knitted brows. When he told me to read the quotation by Mao, he spoke sharply and stared at me sternly to register displeasure. I knew he was deliberately putting on an act to impress and frighten me.

I ignored the attitude of the interrogator, which I thought rather childish and amusing, but read the quotation in a clear and firm voice just as I had the day before. " 'The imperialists and their running dog, the reactionary clique, will not readily accept their defeat in China. They will continue to conspire and use every available means to oppose the Chinese people. For instance, they will send agents into China to make trouble. This is a certainty. They will not forget this kind of work,' " I read from the Little Red Book of Mao's quotations.

He did not tell me to sit down but asked, "Do you understand the meaning of this quotation?"

"It seems quite clear to me."

"Explain what you understand it to mean."

"This is a quotation familiar to all Chinese people, taken from a speech made by Chairman Mao at the preparatory meeting of the New Political Consultative Conference held on June 15, 1949, in Beijing. He warned the Chinese people to be vigilant because he believed the imperialists and the Kuomintang would not accept their failure in China but would send agents into the country to make trouble."

"Quite right! Events of the past seventeen years have proven that the warning of our Great Leader was both timely and correct." He stared at me for a moment and asked, "What do you think?"

Obviously I could not very well say Mao was paranoid and oversuspicious. At the same time, I could not agree with what he said without implying some knowledge of such activities by the regime's enemies. So I answered diplomatically, "Oh, I believe every word of our Great Leader Chairman Mao, whatever it is. He's always correct, isn't he?"

The interrogator glared at me. After a moment he said, "Sit down!"

I heard the wooden cover of the small window behind me being opened. The interrogator looked at me to observe if I had noticed the slight noise. I simply looked straight ahead at the window behind him as if lost in thought. I did not want him to think I was watchful and alert to every sound. From the behavior of the interrogator, I realized that they did not want me to know that someone in the corridor was listening to my interrogation.

The autobiography I had written was in front of him. The interrogator picked it up and said, "Do you call this a serious effort at self-examination?"

Since there was nothing I could say, I remained silent.

"You gave a statistical record of your life like someone writing down an account of daily expenditures. Do you call this writing your autobiography?" He waved the few sheets of paper in the air in my direction.

"Is it no good? I'm afraid I have never written an autobiography before," I said innocently.

"You have never written an autobiography, but you have read many of them. On your bookshelves there were autobiographies by both Chinese and foreign writers," the interrogator said.

"Yes. It's true I have read many autobiographies of important people. All of them have achieved a great deal in one sphere or another. I have done nothing worth speaking of. Except for the last nine years since my husband died, I was just a housewife."

"A housewife, were you?" the interrogator asked sarcastically. He snorted and went on. "Did you spend your time sewing, knitting, or cooking? No, you studied Marxism, read every sort of magazine and newspaper, copied down speeches by our Party and government leaders, and kept a file of resolutions passed at Party Central Committee meetings. When the Red Guards went to your house to take revolutionary action against you, they found your bookshelves full of political books and your desk drawers full of notes in your handwriting. You had a powerful shortwave radio in your bedroom. Your servants said you were in there regularly to listen to foreign broadcasts. What housewife did all that? A housewife's concern is for her family and her home. Your concern was for politics. You were never a simple housewife by any stretch of the imagination."

"I'm not ashamed that my interests went beyond the house and my family. I thought the People's Government and the Communist Party encouraged women to study Marxism and to take an interest in political affairs. I merely did what I thought was the right thing to do, since women in China were liberated by the Communist Party," I told him.

"We encourage women to study Marxism under our guidance and direction. If you were so keen to study Marxism to raise your political consciousness, why did you not join an indoctrination class? We were told you never took part in any of the activities organized by the Residents' Committee in your district for the indoctrination of women living there. If you were interested in politics because you wished to be a good citizen, why did you turn up two hours late to cast your vote in an election for the Shanghai People's Congress? Was that the behavior of a woman conscious of her own liberation? Don't smear gold paint on your face to make yourself look like a harmless Buddha. Why not admit that your interest in politics had an ulterior purpose?"

"I did not take part in the indoctrination classes organized by the Residents' Committee simply because I could study better by myself. Besides, they took place in the afternoons. It was not possible for me to join them after I started working for Shell. As for being late to cast my vote, I admit I simply forgot to go until someone called to remind me. I did not think my vote was important. I didn't know that all Shell staff members had to vote together, so that by being late I was holding everybody up. In any case, there was only one candidate appointed by the Party. He would have been elected whether I voted or not," I explained.

"You dare despise the election process of the People's Government! You did not think it was important! What was important to you was to do the dirty work of the imperialists!" the interrogator said heatedly.

"That's a wild accusation, and an irresponsible one too," I said, shaking my head at his outburst.

He picked up the five sheets of paper again.

"I told you to write an autobiography. You produced this. Why? Because you have something to hide!"

"Please tell me what you have in mind. I didn't intend to hide anything. If there's something about my life you want to know, whatever it is, I'll be only too glad to tell you about it."

"That's good. This is the first time since the interrogation began that you have shown sincerity. I hope you now realize the hopelessness of your situation and will make a full confession."

"You are again talking in riddles. I said I would be glad to tell you everything about my life because I believe facts are more eloquent than arguments. I believe when you are in full possession of all the facts you will know that I am innocent. I have never done anything to harm the People's Government and the Communist Party."

"I want a full and frank answer to all my questions. If you want to earn lenient treatment, don't try to hide anything," he warned.

"I promise you I have nothing to hide. I understand fully the power of the People's Government and the ability of the interrogator to get at the truth. In fact, I count on you to clear me of the unwarranted accusation flung at me and to restore my reputation," I told him.

"I accept your declaration of sincerity. You may now go back to your cell. This afternoon you can tell me about your dealings with the British agents Scott and Austin, the truth about the company you worked for, and the person responsible for intro-

ducing the White Russian double agent to your general manager."

I could hardly believe my ears. I started to speak, but the
interrogator silenced me with a gesture and stood up.

"Don't say anything now. We will give you ample opportunity
to confess this afternoon."

A guard was already standing at the open doorway waiting to
take me back to the cell.

I was so stunned by what the interrogator had said that I did
not remember how I got back to the women's prison.

Instead of sitting in her small room at the entrance, the female
guard on duty was standing in the cold wind waiting for me to
return. She had her hands in her pockets, and her shoulders
were hunched as she shuffled her feet impatiently. From the
moment I came in sight, all the way to the door of the cell, she
was constantly throwing glances at me as if watching every expression on my face. After locking me in, she remained at the
peephole to observe me. From her behavior, I understood that
she had been instructed to observe my reaction to what the
interrogator had said. That was why he had terminated the
interview and sent me back to the cell. Although I was greatly
shocked to hear the interrogator call two of my British friends
"British agents" and refer to the White Russian secretary to the
general manager of the Shell office in Shanghai as a "double
agent," I knew that it was vital that I behave normally. Any sign
of agitation on my part would certainly be interpreted as a sign
of guilt.

I poured some water into the washbasin and refreshed myself
by washing my face and hands. Then I picked up a volume of
Mao's works and sat down near the window, bending my head
over it and turning its pages from time to time to give the
impression of reading with absorption. After standing at the
peephole for quite a long time, the guard went away. But a
minute later another guard took her place. When it was time for
the midday meal, I ate the rice and cabbage rather quickly because I was hungry. After the woman from the kitchen collected
the container, I heard her say to the guard, "All eaten up." After
the prisoners had walked about in the cells for the usual ten
minutes' exercise, the guard went from cell to cell to tell everybody to sit down. She came to me last and took up her position

at the peephole at once. Although she moved very quietly, I had been in the detention house long enough to identify every kind of noise and could easily sense her presence. But I pretended I did not know she was there. I lay against my rolled-up bedding, closed my eyes, and feigned sleep. Sleeping in daytime was strictly against regulations and usually incurred the wrath of the guards. I had often heard them scolding prisoners for the offense. So anxious was she that I should not know I was being watched that she did not shout for me to get up.

After an hour or so, I was called again to the interrogation room. I had to read the same quotation I had read in the morning.

"Let's start with MI5 agent Scott. How did you meet him? Did you know him before he came to China? What information did you give him?" asked the interrogator.

"Before I give you an account of how I met Scott, I think I should point out to you that I knew him only as a British diplomatic officer."

"You may point out anything you like. Whether we believe it or not is another matter. Proceed with your account."

"I first met Scott in September 1961 at someone's dinner party. I no longer remember who the host and hostess were," I said.

"Your host was the Indian consul general. We have the guest list. But that's not important. Did you know Scott before you met him at the Indian consul general's dinner party?"

"No."

"You went to Hong Kong shortly afterwards. And while you were in Hong Kong you were in contact with another MI5 agent who was a British air force officer during the Second World War. He was well known in Hong Kong as a British spy though he assumed the cover of a businessman. Did Scott send you to that man to receive instructions?"

"I met many people socially in Hong Kong. I was not aware any one of them was an agent. My trip was arranged before I met Scott. I went to Hong Kong every two years. As you know, everyone needs a travel permit from the police to go to Hong Kong. I made my application to my police station long before I met Scott," I said.

"You want me to believe your meeting with Scott was accidental, but the facts tell a different story. Scott came to Shanghai just before you went to Hong Kong. He returned to Beijing as soon as you left. But he came back again before you returned and stayed several months. When the ship you traveled on was delayed on the river by a typhoon, he came on board to see you several times. That is not the usual behavior of two people who have just met at a dinner party. Moreover, when he was in Shanghai you went out together a great deal. He always drove the car himself when he went out with you, but he used the chauffeur when he went out with others.

"The gossip of the foreigners in Shanghai was that you were having a decadent love affair, but none of the people assigned to watch you reported anything to indicate that this was the case. We believe your relationship with Scott was a political one. You deliberately created the impression of a liaison to mislead those around you.

"The British are racially arrogant. And the discipline of his organization would not have allowed its agent to form a sentimental attachment to a native woman of the country in which he was operating. In fact, we know that while he was in Shanghai he was having an illicit relationship with the wife of a British bank manager.

"Now that you see how much we know about this odious business, do you still hope to avoid telling the truth? Confess what Scott asked you to do and what you actually did for him!" The interrogator concluded his accusation and sat there glaring at me.

"You are making a perfectly ordinary situation sound suspicious," I said. "I did see Scott rather frequently, mainly because he led an active social life and entertained a great deal. Often he showed British films after dinner. That's always an attraction because we did not have the opportunity to see films like that. I remember on several occasions he invited officials from the Foreign Affairs Bureau to those film shows. It's customary to return hospitality. I had a collection of porcelain. I would have a dinner party and invite several friends including Scott to see my newly acquired pieces. And he taped quite a number of my records. The Red Guards must have told you that I had a large collection of records. I think he did drive himself more than other Europeans in Shanghai, probably because he speaks Chinese and so was not afraid. As for the fact that he arrived in Shanghai just before I left for Hong Kong and came back again just before I returned, that was pure coincidence. When the typhoon delayed my ship, he came on board not to see me but to see the captain. There was another passenger from Shanghai. I think he was a Danish businessman. They drank and talked together. I did not join them. When foreign vessels are on the river, many soldiers and customs officials remain on board. Why don't you ascertain from them whether he came on board to see the captain or me?" I said.

"Your relationship with Scott was more than a casual acquaintance," the interrogator said.

"Whatever it was, your interpretation of the situation is far-fetched and incorrect."

The interrogator glared at me and said, "My advice to you is not to try to get out of your difficulties by claiming you did have a love affair with Scott. A Chinese woman degrading her country by having a love affair with a barbarian from the West deserves incarceration in a Reform through Labor camp."

Chinese throughout the ages have suffered from racial arrogance. Those who never went out of the country and had no close contact with other nationalities often thought of people in other lands as alien, therefore uncivilized creatures with strange habits and called them "foreigners" or even "foreign devils." The self-imposed isolation during Mao Zedong's reign and Party propaganda on the evils of capitalism greatly reinforced the Chinese people's unfortunate state of self-delusion. When Deng Xiaoping threw China's door open to the rest of the world and a flood of well-meaning and obviously affluent "foreigners" came to China with money to invest and ideas to share, the Chinese people suffered such a traumatic awakening that they sank into shame and self-reproach, only to emerge with an eagerness to jettison everything Chinese in order to become thoroughly "civilized."

There was nothing I could say to the interrogator really, though I realized by his stance that sending me to a labor camp was not satisfactory unless I could be sent as a "spy." This was interesting, and I asked myself why. Normally when the Party picked a victim to be punished, the Party didn't much care what excuse it used for imposing sentence. Indeed, sometimes the excuses were extremely vague or nonexistent. To punish was the aim. In my case, to judge from the attitude of the interrogator, it seemed that I had to be punished as a "spy," not for some other reason. Why? I was not to know until much, much later.

"I see you are not attempting to tell more lies. Now confess what Scott said to you when you were together," the interrogator said.

"You cannot expect me to remember conversations that took place several years ago. There was nothing of any significance. We talked about books, music, Chinese porcelain, places we both knew, our families, and so on."

"Your conversation never touched politics at all?"

"Well, we probably exchanged views on current affairs sometimes, mostly international affairs. Scott was a diplomat. He would not have wanted to comment on anything that was going on in China to a Chinese."

To all the Europeans I had met, whether diplomats or businessmen, China under Mao Zedong was a fascinating subject mainly because the closed-door policy of the Communist Party shrouded the country in mystery. There were also some who came to China because they were interested in Chinese culture. When they had an opportunity to meet a Chinese with whom they could talk, naturally they asked questions. But these questions had nothing to do with political secrets. As a Chinese I believed that helping people from other lands understand China, her history, her cultural heritage, and her aspirations was not a bad thing. But the Communist Party officials of the radical faction did not see things in this light. They assumed that any Chinese not parroting the official propaganda line was hostile to the regime and everybody coming to China was trying to find fault with the Communist system. So they were always suspicious of the Chinese who worked in foreign firms and had contacts with the Europeans.

Before the Cultural Revolution, my feeling of safety had rested on the fact that I knew no Chinese of any significance in the official world and was not in a position to learn of anything that could possibly be considered a state secret. And I took great care never to ask questions on sensitive subjects when I saw my Chinese friends and relatives, especially when they happened to be Party members. In the end this policy paid off, because during the Cultural Revolution, when my friends and relatives were cross-examined, they could honestly say that I never showed any interest in state secrets.

"Scott was an intelligence officer. It was his duty to find out things. What did he ask you to do? Did he not ask you to get information for him?" persisted the interrogator.

"Never! How could I get information for him? I worked for Shell, a foreign firm. I knew nothing more than the foreigners knew."

"It's not possible for an intelligence officer to refrain from trying to gather information useful to his government."

"Are you sure he was in fact an intelligence officer?" I asked the interrogator.

"Do not doubt our information."

"Then why did you not arrest him or declare him persona non grata and expel him from China?"

"It was much better that he did not know we knew. We put him under close surveillance, and we knew everything he did. The British were working not only for their own country but also for the United States, since the Americans could not come here openly. The United States cooperates closely with the Kuomintang, so the British were helping the Kuomintang also."

Raising his voice and abandoning his matter-of-fact manner, he went on. "In 1962, when Scott came to Shanghai for the second time, the Kuomintang were preparing for an attack against us. Scott chose to establish contact with you because you were connected with the Kuomintang."

"Nonsense! I was never connected with the Kuomintang."

"Your husband was a senior official of the Kuomintang government. But that's not the whole story. Your class origin dictated that your sympathy would be with the Kuomintang. The teaching of our Great Leader on class struggle is like a telescope as well as a microscope. Armed with Mao Zedong Thought, we see through the superficial phenomena and get to the heart of the matter."

I knew that the official propaganda line of Beijing in 1962 was that the Kuomintang was about to launch an attack against the mainland. But none of the newspapers and magazines I got from abroad ever hinted at any sign of military preparation in Taiwan. Besides, I was sure that Taiwan would not undertake an attack against the mainland without the consent of the United States and that in 1962 the United States was unlikely to allow such a venture. In Shanghai, however, I heard frequently of movements of Chinese troops to, and the withdrawal of families of military personnel from, Fujian province facing Taiwan. Many people believed that Mao planned military action against Taiwan, not the reverse. The gossip in Shanghai was that only the economic collapse caused by the failure of Mao's Great Leap Forward, along with dissension in the Party leadership, compelled him to shelve his plan.

As I tried to recall whether anybody in the foreign community, including Scott, had asked me about Taiwan during that time, I became thoughtful. The interrogator, observing me closely but misunderstanding the reason for my thoughtfulness, seized the moment to say, "Whether you confess or not, we have a complete record of what you said to Scott."

"In that case, you would know for a certainty that we never talked politics," I told him.

"You are obviously not ready to confess right away. You need time to think and to recollect. That's perfectly all right with us. We'll give you plenty of time to prepare for a full and frank confession. After today, you should know it's useless for you to try to evade. Now we will talk about that female agent Austin. Give an account of your dealings with her."

"As you know, Mrs. Austin was the wife of a businessman. My contact with her was purely social. We played bridge together and dined with each other."

"You brought her into contact with an ex-Kuomintang army officer!"

"What! Who was that?" I was genuinely shocked, and I showed my surprise. The interrogator, watching me, relaxed visibly.

"The Chinese doctor of traditional medicine you took to her apartment was a ranking officer of the Kuomintang army before he practiced medicine."

"I knew nothing of his background. I knew only that he was a very good doctor of Chinese traditional medicine. Mrs. Austin confided to me that she was unhappy because she could not have children. She had been to European doctors who could not find anything organically wrong. I was sorry for her, so I asked the doctor if Chinese medicine could do something for her. Since

he said that he could not be certain without seeing her, I introduced them to each other. You could easily get confirmation of
what happened from the doctor himself."

"He committed suicide soon after the Red Guards started
their revolutionary action against him."

Had the Red Guards tortured him because he had had contact
with a British agent? God, why did I introduce him to her? How
stupid I had been not to realize fully the complexity of life under
Mao! Since good intentions and sympathy for others often led
people into trouble, the Chinese people had invented a new
proverb that said, "The more you do, the more trouble you
have; the less you do, the less trouble you have. If you do
nothing whatever, you will become a model citizen." Why did
I not heed the experience of others? I felt greatly saddened by
the death of this poor man.

"Besides taking the doctor to see her, you also traveled to
Beijing with her. What did you do there and whom did you see?"

"The tomb of Ming emperor Wanli had been newly opened
in Beijing in 1959. In 1960 we went to see it. Traveling with
foreigners, I could stay in a good hotel, but as a Chinese citizen,
I would only be allowed to stay in a third-rate guesthouse. So
I went with Mrs. Austin and another British woman friend. For
them it was convenient to take me because I knew Beijing well,
having lived there in my childhood, and I spoke the language."

"Did you introduce her to anybody in Beijing?"

"No, I don't know many people in Beijing myself."

"What about your brother? He visited you at the hotel, we
know."

"On the day my brother came, the two British ladies went to
the Jade Temple without me. My brother did not want to meet
them."

There was a slight noise behind me. The interrogator looked
past my shoulder and then at his watch. After a few whispered
words with the man taking notes, he stood up and said, "You
may go back to your cell. When I call you again we will talk about
the dirty work you did for the company that employed you and
the reason your office engaged as secretary the White Russian
woman who was also a Soviet agent. I don't think you will find
it easy to deny your involvement with the affairs of the firm that
employed you."

After a momentary pause, he went on. "Think carefully about

your relationship with Scott. Remember, we already know he used you to gather information, and we have a good idea what you told him."

"I couldn't have told anybody more than I knew myself. Since I knew nothing, how could I have been of use to him?"

"Well, we think he came to Shanghai to see you, both before you went to Hong Kong and after you came back. He wouldn't have done that if it hadn't been worth his while."

A guard opened the door of the interrogation room. The interrogator told me to go. I realized that he was not interested in prolonging the session after the man listening at the small window had departed.

Back in the cell, I was continuously watched by the guards. My mind was troubled, as I felt responsible for the death of that poor doctor. And I wished I had never met Scott or Austin. Were they really British agents? Even if they were, it still did not explain why I was in prison now. Both the foreign residents in Shanghai and the senior Chinese working in foreign firms were under constant observation by their servants at home and by other Chinese staff members at work. In public places, there were always policemen and uniformed sentries, as well as plainclothes operatives working for the police and zealous activists eager to report any unusual behavior. Personal privacy did not exist in Shanghai as it does in other cities of the world. If the People's Government had been suspicious of my relationship with Scott and Austin, the Shanghai police should have acted years ago. Indeed there was much in the situation I did not as yet understand. It seemed quite likely that the interrogator would go through the whole list of my foreign friends and declare them all secret agents. Scott and Austin were merely the first two being named to frighten me. I realized that I was being drawn into a quagmire. I would have to watch my step to avoid sinking into its depths.

Ever since I had been brought to the No. 1 Detention House, I had been wondering why I was arrested. This was the question that puzzled me most. Who was behind my arrest? Did they really suspect me of having done something criminal, or did they merely hope that I would be frightened into providing them with a false confession they could use against me? Winnie seemed to think that because Shell had closed its Shanghai office, it was my turn to be punished. Was she correct?

As I sat in the cell thinking of my encounter with the interrogator, I couldn't help recalling all the cases of innocent men and women sentenced to terms of imprisonment and hard labor that I had heard of. My spirit of bravado deserted me, and I became really frightened, not because I was burdened with a sense of guilt but because I feared that the task of defending myself might be beyond my ability.

In the evening, I composed myself for that quiet moment of daily prayer, but the stern voice of the interrogator intruded. I felt lost and unhappy, almost as if God had turned away from me as well.

That night, I had a nightmare, the first of many during my imprisonment. I dreamt I was standing on the narrow ledge of a sheer rocky cliff by the sea. The roaring waves of the incoming tide were rising higher and higher to engulf me. It was pitch-dark, I was utterly alone, and I was petrified.

Instinctively, I pulled my quilt over my face to stifle a cry of terror. I opened my eyes to find the electric light glaring down at me. My eyeshade had slipped to the floor. Remembering the guard standing forever outside the door with her eyes glued to the peephole, ready to interpret any sign of restlessness as a sign of guilt, I froze in fear and apprehension. But the sound of a heavy bolt being driven in place somewhere upstairs told me that she was temporarily elsewhere, putting a newly arrived prisoner into a cell.

7

The January Revolution
and Military Control

I WAITED FOR THE INTERROGATOR to call me again. However, several days passed and nothing happened. I felt tension in the atmosphere; the guards looked harassed as they dashed up and down the corridor. Something was happening in the world outside, I felt sure. Often I would stand by the door hoping to hear what the guards were talking about in their little room at the other end of the corridor, but all I could discern was an unusually excited, high-pitched intonation in their voices. Sometimes they seemed to be arguing about something, other times they lowered their voices to an almost inaudible whisper. Even though the prison was deadly silent, I could not make out what they were talking about. My inability to find out what was actually going on frightened me.

Early in December, not long after my first interrogation, the guards stopped giving me the newspaper. Since the newspaper was considered important material for the prisoners' indoctrination and the guards always told us to read it carefully, this was very strange. After waiting for a few days, I asked for it. At first the guard ignored my request. When I asked again, the guard simply said impatiently, "Don't you know there's a revolution going on?"

By the middle of December, winter came in earnest. A pene-trating north wind swept the city with icy blasts, lowering the temperature daily until it was hovering around freezing. The window and door of my cell rattled with each strong gust. The folded strips of toilet paper I had pushed into the gaps to stop the wind were often blown onto the floor. I had already put on both my sweaters and a padded jacket, but still my teeth chat-tered as spasms of shivering shook my body. In the icy room, my breath made white, cloudy puffs, and I had to stamp my feet and rub my hands to bring blood to my toes and fingers.

One cold day the guards yelled for the prisoners to get ready for outdoor exercise. I thought they must hate to have to leave their stove on a day like this. In spite of the wind, it was in fact a little warmer outside than in the damp cell. Besides, walking improved my circulation. But the strong wind whirled the dust and gravel into the air so that I could hardly keep my eyes open.

Suddenly I saw all the guards rush out of the closed pavilion on the raised platform from which they had been watching us, dash down the steps, and disappear from view. At the same time, the noise from the street grew louder and louder, as if a mob of several thousand were storming the detention house. In the sentry box overlooking the exercise yards, a soldier holding a rifle stiffly by his side was craning his neck in the direction of the prison entrance, but he did not abandon his post. A woman prisoner in a neighboring exercise yard said in an excited whis-per loud enough for all the prisoners to hear, "It's probably the Red Guards trying to get in to rescue their comrades imprisoned by the municipal government!"

Immediately, the voice of a young girl shouted from one of the exercise yards, "Let me out! Let me out! I'm a Red Guard! Long live our Great Leader Chairman Mao!" Her urgent entreaty for freedom was accompanied by the sound of her fist knocking on the heavy door of the exercise yard.

The commotion at the entrance of the detention house went on until we heard gunshots, probably fired by the soldiers on guard duty. The sound of the mob receded. After a while the guards came back to let the prisoners out of the exercise yards. Obviously the attempt by the Red Guards to break into the detention house had given our guards quite a jolt. When the guard unlocked my exercise yard, he seemed rather subdued, did not shout, "Come out!" as usual, but waited by the door for me to walk out.

In the following days, I observed a marked change in the behavior of the guards. They neglected their duties and were often absent from their posts. Frequently there was no sight or sound of any of them for hours at a time. Fortunately the woman from the kitchen continued to bring the prisoners their food and hot drinking water, and the girl doing Labor Reform gave out cold water for washing as usual. When the guards did come on duty, they gathered in the little room, holding excited discussions. From the occasional word I overheard, I concluded that they were being drawn into the Proletarian Cultural Revolution and were forming their own revolutionary organizations so that they too could join the ever swelling ranks of the Revolutionaries. For the prisoners, the relaxed interest of the guards was like the lifting of an enormously heavy weight. Sometimes I heard the whispering voices of the inmates rise to the normal tone of conversation, and occasionally I even heard giggles.

When the newspaper stopped coming on December 2, I started to make light scratches on the wall to mark the passing days. By the time I had made twenty-three strokes, I knew it was Christmas Eve. Though the usual bedtime hour had passed, the guards were not yet on duty to tell the prisoners to go to sleep. While I was waiting in the bitter cold, suddenly, from somewhere upstairs, I heard a young soprano voice singing, at first tentatively and then boldly, the Chinese version of "Silent Night." The prison walls resounded with her song as her clear and melodious voice floated in and out of the dark corridors. I was enraptured and deeply moved as I listened to her. I knew from the way she rendered the song that she was a professional singer who had incurred the displeasure of the Maoists. No concert I had attended at Christmas in any year meant more to me than that moment when I sat in my icy cell listening to "Silent Night" sung by another prisoner whom I could not see. As soon as she was confident that the guards were not there to stop her, the girl sang beautifully without any trace of nervousness. The prison became very quiet. All the inmates listened to her with bated breath.

Just as the last note of her voice trailed into space, the guards' footsteps echoed on the cement floor. They rushed from cell to cell asking, "Who was that? Who was singing? Who was breaking the rules?" None of the prisoners replied.

A few days after the New Year, the loudspeaker in the corridor was switched on, and all the prisoners were told to sit still to listen to an important announcement.

A man's voice read a proclamation by the Shanghai Workers Revolutionary Headquarters. It stated that the Red Guards and the Revolutionaries in the city, acting with the approval of the Cultural Revolution Directorate in Beijing, had seized power in Shanghai on January 4 and had overthrown the "reactionary" Party Secretariat and municipal government, which for a long time had "opposed the correct policy of our Great Leader Chairman Mao and pursued a revisionist line in order to revive capitalism in China."

It was subsequently revealed in newspaper articles that the "hero" of this coup was a former security chief of a textile factory, Wang Hongwen, who had succeeded in affiliating all mass revolutionary organizations that had sprung up all over the city into one organization called the Shanghai Workers Revolutionary Headquarters, with himself as its head. He was backed by Zhang Chunqiao, longtime associate of Mao's wife Jiang Qing and representative of the Beijing Cultural Revolution Directorate in Shanghai. Eventually, Jiang Qing, Zhang Chunqiao, Wang Hongwen, and the well-known left-wing writer Yao Wenyuan were to form a tightly knit political faction, the notorious "Gang of Four."

It seemed that while anyone who was not a class enemy could join a revolutionary organization and become a Revolutionary, the leadership of such organizations was now firmly in the hands of approved Maoist activists.

The man also read a document from the State Council giving approval to the rebels' action but urging the workers not to neglect production. This statement by the State Council, the office of the prime minister, gave the unprecedented revolutionary action by the Maoist radicals a semblance of legality. That Prime Minister Zhou Enlai should have given the rebels his support and approval shocked me. I simply could not believe he truly agreed with their action. However, I thought his call for the workers not to neglect production was at least a note of sanity in the atmosphere of madness. It wasn't until after my release from prison that I learned of the tremendous pressure put on Zhou Enlai by the radicals, who persistently tried to dislodge him from his position as prime minister. It was only by skillful and subtle handling of the situation and by always identifying himself with Mao's designs that Zhou Enlai managed to survive the Cultural Revolution and give protection to a few of the old guard in the Party.

A few days after the announcement of the coup, the guards handed me a copy of the *Shanghai Liberation Daily*, which reappeared under new revolutionary publishers. Under banner headlines printed in red ink, it reported that on December 2 the Red Guard and the Revolutionaries had seized the newspaper after a prolonged struggle, as a preliminary to the overthrow of the municipal government.

Reading the news items and reports carefully, I learned that final victory for the Revolutionaries was made possible only when two senior officials of the Shanghai municipal government were persuaded to switch allegiance. At a public rally to indict the former chief secretary of the Party and the mayor of the city, the two turncoats, anxious for their own acceptance by the Maoists, had demonstrated their firm stand on Mao's side by slapping the faces of their former colleagues, to the loud and prolonged cheers of assembled Red Guards and Revolutionaries. (These two officials, Ma Tianshui and Xu Jingxian, were to rule Shanghai on behalf of the Gang of Four until Mao's death and the Gang's arrest. In 1982, both were sentenced to long terms of imprisonment for crimes, including murder, committed at the order of the Gang of Four. Subsequently Ma Tianshui went mad.)

The overthrow of the Shanghai municipal government by the radicals shattered any hope I had of a quick solution to my own predicament. I realized that my case would have to wait for the reorganization of all the departments of the new Shanghai government, including the Public Security Bureau, which held jurisdiction over the No. 1 Detention House. This process would take time, especially if there was overt and covert resistance to the new officeholders. I also thought the viability of the new Shanghai government and its smooth functioning depended on how quickly the rest of the country could be taken over by the Revolutionaries. From the numerous articles denouncing officials in other cities of China, I could see that elsewhere the Revolutionaries and the Red Guards were meeting stronger resistance than they had encountered in Shanghai.

In the spring of 1967, the *Liberation Daily* published Mao Zedong's call for the army to support the leftists. It included a quotation of Mao stating that the People's Liberation Army was not only a military organization but a political one as well. From the statement, it seemed obvious to me that the Red Guards and the Revolutionaries had been unable to take over many local governments in other parts of China by their efforts alone. However, intervention by the military did not immediately produce the desired result. In many instances, the military was quite unable to distinguish between the Red Guard and Revolutionary organizations led by Maoist activists and those organized by Party officials whom Mao wished to topple, since both sides claimed to be dedicated to Mao's policy. Furthermore, many military commanders were concurrently local administrators, as in Tibet and Xinjiang. They simply declared themselves the true leftists and turned their troops on the Red Guards and the Revolutionaries. In the bitter struggle that ensued there was much bloodshed. In many regions, fearful of committing a political error, the military turned a blind eye when different factions of self-styled leftists raided their arsenals. However, when the dust settled, it appeared that in most parts of the country the aid given by the military substantially helped one or another group of rebels to seize power.

The prominent part played by the military in assisting the Red Guards and the Revolutionaries to seize power raised the prestige of the army and its commander in chief, Defense Minister Lin Biao. Numerous photographs of him walking with or standing beside Mao appeared in the press, a sure sign of enhanced status. He was referred to as "the close comrade-in-arms of our Great Leader Chairman Mao," a phrase elevating him to second place in the Party hierarchy, after Mao and before Premier Zhou Enlai, who was now caught by the photographer's camera walking behind Lin Biao in third place. Lin Biao lost no time in purging the army command of his possible opponents and replacing them with his cronies. The newspaper reported the successful exposure of an anti-Mao group of officers in the former army high command. A list of new names appeared for the posts of chief staff officer of the army, navy, air force, and logistics. Lin Biao was heartily congratulated by the rebel-controlled press for the change.

In Shanghai, the Red Guards and the Revolutionaries began taking over subsidiary organizations one by one. Daily the newspaper revealed not only that they had to contend with stiff resistance and sabotage by those they wanted to overthrow, but also that they themselves broke into conflicting factions struggling for the spoils of office. Actual fighting took place in every district of the city. Control of organizations changed hands frequently. The city was in a constant state of upheaval. The noise of yelling mobs reached my cell from the streets. In the exercise yards, I could hear the broadcast speeches of denunciation clearly. The sound of mob fury conjured up terrible scenes of death and destruction, and I greatly feared for the safety of my daughter.

Instead of trying to control the violence and bloodshed, the rebel leaders seemed to be encouraging it. One day I read a newspaper article entitled, "It's an honor to have our hands stained with the enemy's blood." Another day there appeared a statement attributed to Lin Biao: "There are casualties in all revolutions, so let us not exaggerate the seriousness of this situation. Many people have committed suicide or been killed. But these deaths are fewer than those incurred during the war of resistance against Japan or the Civil War, or even during natural disasters. Thus, our gains are greater than our losses." These callous words made me sick with apprehension for the safety of my daughter. I could no longer eat or sleep normally.

One evening, after I had again refused the rice, a guard came to the small window and pushed it open.

"What's the matter with you? Are you sick?" she asked.

"I'm worried about my daughter. Could she be brought here to stay in this cell with me?"

"Of course not! She hasn't committed any crime. Why should she be locked up in prison?" the guard replied.

"I haven't committed any crime either, but I'm locked up in prison just the same," I told her.

"I have no time to argue with you about that. Whether you have committed any crime or not, I don't know. In fact, I don't know anymore what's a crime and what's not a crime. But since you are here already, you must just wait. Someone will deal with you one day. You're not so badly off. You get eight hours' sleep every night and have rice to eat. We have to attend meetings after work and don't get eight hours' sleep." She banged the window shut and walked away.

The behavior of the guard astonished me. This was the first time a guard had revealed herself to me as a normal human being. She certainly sounded discouraged and grumpy. I concluded that the struggle within the Party leadership was having a demoralizing effect. To work in such sensitive jobs, the prison guards must have been firm believers in the Party and its leadership. It must be disheartening, if not downright shattering, for them to learn that according to Mao Zedong so many of their superior officers were no more devoted to the ideals of Communism than the man in the street and some of them were in fact working to revive capitalism in China. They lost interest in their work. The prison gradually degenerated into a disorderly place, with prisoners shouting, crying, fighting with each other, and banging the floor when the guards were not in evidence. One night I was awakened by low hysterical laughter coming from another solitary cell in the dark recess of the long corridor. The guard on duty, if there was one, made no effort to stop the prisoner.

I began to observe the guards more closely and to see them as individuals. I noticed that many looked unhappy and subdued. A few younger ones appeared wearing the red armband of the Revolutionaries, and these swaggered in and out insolently, full of self-importance. They assumed an air of authority, not only shouting orders to the prisoners but also speaking in a commanding voice to the other guards.

During 1967, while anarchy ruled the city of Shanghai, control gradually disintegrated in the No. 1 Detention House. By autumn the guards, split into rival factions, were fighting among themselves. When the prisoners were allowed outdoor exercise, I saw their civil war slogans scribbled on the walls and the paved walks of the courtyard. From my cell, I would often hear the familiar voices of the guards at the women's prison shouting with other voices in argument, and once or twice even the sound of scuffling. The points of contention seemed to be what constituted Mao Zedong's policy and who among the officials were "capitalist-roaders" to be overthrown.

Often guard duty was taken over by prison administrators and interrogators, who, because they were considered "intellectuals," were excluded from revolutionary organizations. During the Cultural Revolution, all intellectuals, whether Party members or not, were denounced as "the stinking ninth category." The eight other categories of enemies were landlords, rich peasants, counterrevolutionaries, bad elements, rightists, traitors, foreign agents, and "capitalist-roaders." The ninth category, the intellectuals, included not only people with degrees working as professors or research fellows but also schoolteachers, technicians, and white-collar office workers. The word "stink" used as a Chinese slang word also meant "unjustified pride." Because intellectuals were often thought to be arrogant and proud of their superior knowledge or training, and because they enjoyed positions of honor in traditional Chinese society, the Revolutionaries called them the "stinking" ninth category to show their contempt for both the intellectuals and the Chinese tradition.

At the beginning of my second winter at the detention house, I again developed a bad cold, which refused to clear up in spite of aspirin tablets the young prison doctor gave me. When my cold turned to bronchitis, my body shook with spasms of coughing, particularly severe during the night when the cell became extremely cold. One night, lying under my quilt almost fully dressed, with two sweaters and a pair of knitted long johns to keep warm, I could not control persistent fits of coughing. It was after midnight. The prison had long ago settled down to complete silence. No matter how I lay on that hard bed in the cold room, I coughed and sneezed continually. To ease the irritation in my throat, I drank some of the water left in my mug. The cold liquid actually made me worse. I covered my head to muffle the sound of coughing and hoped the warmth of the quilt would give me some relief.

I heard the small window being opened. The sound was different from the usual loud bang made by the guards. I then heard a man's voice saying quietly, "Come over here!"

I got out of bed, pulled on my slacks, and threw my padded jacket over my shoulders, wondering what the man wanted of me in the depth of night. When I walked to the small window and looked out, I was astonished to see my former interrogator standing there, holding a thermos flask in his hand.

"Have you a mug? Bring it over," he said.

I took the mug to the window, and he poured some hot water into it.

I had been waiting for over a year for him to continue the interrogation. This seemed a good opportunity to ask him, so between fits of coughing I said, "When are you going to clarify my case?"

After a moment's hesitation he said, "When the Revolutionaries are ready, they will call you. More important issues are at stake right now. You must be patient. Now drink the hot water. That should ease your cough. Tomorrow, report to the doctor. He'll give you some medicine."

He seemed to be saying that he was no longer dealing with my case. I wondered if he still thought I was guilty or indeed if he had ever really thought I was guilty. Suddenly I thought, How perfectly ghastly to have to work as an interrogator in such circumstances, when you knew a person was innocent and yet it was your job to find the person guilty. I drank the hot water quickly but was seized with another fit of coughing and vomited.

"Never mind, never mind! I'll give you some more hot water." The interrogator opened the small window again. He was joined by another man with dark-rimmed glasses whom he addressed as Director Liang.

"May I borrow a mop to clean the floor?" I asked between coughs.

"You can clean it tomorrow. Is it dirty? Is there anything else besides water?" Director Liang asked.

I looked down at the floor. Indeed there was only water, which was already being absorbed by the cement. Certainly Director Liang was in an excellent position to know how empty the stomach of a prisoner was. After all, he had been the director of the No. 1 Detention House before the Red Guards and the Revolutionaries reduced him to guard duty.

They both remained there until I drank more water. Then they closed the small window and went away.

I got back into bed and reflected that the Cultural Revolution was certainly producing some strange phenomena. For the director and interrogator of the detention house to give a prisoner hot drinking water from their own thermos must be one of them. Such humane behavior had to be in direct contravention of their belief that the No. 1 Detention House was "an instrument of repression used by one class against another," as I had been told by the interrogator. Perhaps as the Red Guards and the Revolutionaries expanded the scope of their revolutionary action, they were alienating potential supporters and pushing Party intellectuals into the enemy camp.

Next morning the doctor gave me some sulfadiazine tablets. But I continued to waken during the night with coughing when the cell became unbearably cold. It was in the small hours of one morning that I overheard a whispered conversation outside my door. A former female interrogator was on guard duty. She had given me my medicine for the night and told me to go to sleep. Now I heard her talking to the woman locked in the cell opposite mine. Though their voices were very low, the prison was very silent, and I got the gist of their conversation. I was shocked to discover that the woman in the cell was an official of the Public Security Bureau and a former schoolfriend of the interrogator when they were both at the College for Public Security Officers. They were talking about the violent struggle at the office of the Shanghai Public Security Bureau after Mao's wife Jiang Qing called upon the Red Guards and the Revolutionaries to "smash the security, prosecution, and law enforcement agencies." They were saying that this person jumped out of a window, that person was beaten to death, someone else was taken to the hospital . . . It was obvious that the Public Security Bureau was in disarray and unable to function at all.

After listening to their conversation, I decided that the Cultural Revolution was going to be a long-drawn-out affair, with the Party officials Mao wanted to remove fighting for survival with cunning and desperation. For the time being, the radicals seemed to be winning because they enjoyed the support of Mao and the army. But unless the ousted officials were all to be killed, which was an impossibility, they would be bound to wait for a chance to stage a comeback. In the meantime, they would probably do everything within their power to sabotage every move made by the radicals. I thought the situation was extremely complicated and would surely remain unsettled for a very long time to come.

A few nights later, just before the prisoners' bedtime, the guard on duty came to the cells again to tell the prisoners to sit quietly and listen to a broadcast. Through the loudspeaker, a man's voice announced that the No. 1 Detention House had been placed under military control.

"All of you prisoners listen attentively! The revolutionary situation is excellent! The true supporters of our Great Leader Chairman Mao and the followers of his close comrade-in-arms Vice-Supreme Commander Lin have overcome all obstacles and have already overthrown the reactionary municipal government of this city! We are now in the process of taking over the whole country and will continue to exterminate all our enemies. The sludge and filth left by the old society have been thrown onto the rubbish heap of history. Our achievement is great, great, great! Our losses are small, small, and small! Some people say we have created chaos. Chaos is an expression of class struggle. Our Great Leader Chairman Mao has said, 'A revolution is not a dinner party, or writing an essay, or painting a picture, or doing embroidery; it cannot be so refined, so leisurely and gentle, so temperate, kind, courteous, restrained, and magnanimous. A revolution is an insurrection, an act of violence by which one class overthrows another.' There is nothing wrong in sowing chaos to confuse the enemy. Some people say we have killed too many. Nonsense! We have killed fewer people than during the war against the Japanese imperialists and the war of liberation. In fact, we have not killed enough. There are still enemies lurking in dark corners. We'll get them. Don't underestimate our determination or belittle our ability to exterminate our enemies. We are Revolutionaries! We are not afraid of chaos and killing. They are the natural outcome of a revolution. They inspire our own side and send terror into the hearts of the enemy. We won't fear even the collapse of heaven. The teachings of our Great Leader Chairman Mao will prop it up again.

"Our dear comrade Jiang Qing told us, 'Smash to pieces the security and law enforcement agencies.' We have done it! The Shanghai Public Security Bureau and all its subsidiary organizations are now under our control. This detention house was run by the revisionists and capitalist-roaders of the Security Bureau. It's absurd the prisoners here should have such good treatment. You eat rice three times a day. You live better than the poor peasants. That proves the revisionists at the Security Bureau love the counterrevolutionaries better than the peasants. This is because they themselves are also counterrevolutionaries. From now on your ration will be cut to conserve grain. You do not labor. Two meals a day is ample. And you will eat sweet potatoes and other grains rather than rice. You won't die. But if you do, it is no loss to the Revolution. We have plenty of people in China. We will not miss a few counterrevolutionaries!

"A lot of you have been here a long time already. But some of you have not confessed. You hope to slip through the net. This is sheer wishful thinking. The iron fist of the Dictatorship of the Proletariat will crush you without mercy if you don't confess. Let that be a warning to you all!

"The policy of our Great Leader Chairman Mao is 'Lenient treatment for those who confess, severe punishment for those who remain stubborn, and reward for those who render meritorious service by denouncing others.' Tonight we will deal with some of the outstanding cases here to give expression to our Great Leader Chairman Mao's policy."

After a moment's silence, he called out one name after another of prisoners sentenced to death because they had not confessed to their crimes. He gave such particulars as their age, address, occupation, and "reactionary" family background and described the "crimes" the prisoners had committed, all of which came under the category of "revenge against the proletarian class." Those so-called crimes were in fact no more than statements of opposition to the Cultural Revolution or disparaging remarks against Jiang Qing, Lin Biao, or Mao Ze-dong himself. Then the man shouted at the top of his voice, "Take him out! Immediate execution!"

His voice was an inhuman roar, charged with cruelty. In spite of my rigid control, I shivered involuntarily.

The list of names of people to be executed went on and on. It was followed by a list of those sentenced to life imprisonment or to terms of twenty-five or more years in jail, all examples of "severe punishment" dealt out to prisoners who had not confessed fully or whose confessions were not considered adequate or sincere. Finally he read out a list of people given "lenient treatment" because they not only confessed but also rendered meritorious service by incriminating others. A woman was ordered to be released immediately because she had provided information leading to the arrest of several other people who had plotted to escape to Hong Kong. Others received short sentences of three to five years.

After the loudspeaker was switched off, the threat in that man's voice reverberated in my ears. Never in my life had I heard anything so shocking. The thought that this person was now in charge of the No. 1 Detention House and of my own fate frightened me. The night, already icy, seemed to get even colder. Spasms of shivering ran through my body while I waited for the guard to tell me to go to bed. The other prisoners, I thought, were probably frozen with fear too, as there was not the slightest sound of movement anywhere.

The door at the other end of the corridor banged, and I heard the sound of leather boots echoing down the passage. The small windows of the cells along the corridor were being opened and shut. There were shouts of "What about you? Have you confessed? Did you confess everything?" The heavy footsteps drew nearer and nearer. I braced myself for an unpleasant encounter. The footsteps stopped outside my cell. The shutter of the small window was pushed open. I heard the sound of rustling paper and the voice of a male guard saying, "It's this one."

"Come over!" The guard sounded even more severe than usual, perhaps to impress the Military Control officer.

Through the opening, I could see only a pair of black leather boots and the lower part of the uniformed body of an air force officer, not his face or head. But I pictured him in my mind's eye as having what we Chinese call a villain's face with "horizontal flesh." We believe a man's face reflects the life he has led, so a wicked man would end up having an unpleasant face with "horizontal flesh." Somehow, thinking of him in these terms encouraged me. I felt that whatever he was going to say, I could cope with it.

"Why haven't you confessed?" It was the voice of the man who had made the broadcast.

"I haven't committed any crime. How can I confess?" I replied.

"Nonsense! You are a spy of the imperialists. Do you want to be shot?"

"I expect the new authority of this detention house to release me after examining the facts and finding me innocent."

"You are dreaming! Do you think we are fools? You'll never

be released if you do not confess! Didn't you hear the other cases of those who did not confess? They are dead," he shouted vehemently, "dead! Do you hear?" Then he said something to the guard, who took out his bunch of keys and unlocked the door.

"Come out!" the guard shouted.

I stepped out of the cell, uncertain what the man in the air force uniform was going to do to me. He was already halfway down the corridor heading for the entrance. I followed the guard after him, but before we had taken more than a couple of steps, there was a heavy thud and commotion overhead. Several voices called, "Report! Report!" Others were yelling, "Come quickly! She is bleeding!"

Low hysterical laughter came from another direction, rising to a shrill cry. With the corridor shrouded in shadows under the dim light, the scene took on a sinister aspect. The guard stopped abruptly, pushed me back into the cell, snapped the lock, and hastened upstairs.

I heard footsteps of several guards running to the cell above mine. "Take her out!" the voice of the air force officer shouted overhead. "How dare you threaten the Dictatorship of the Proletariat with suicide! Did you think you could get out of confessing by bashing your head on the toilet? Your act proved you are guilty. You will be punished without mercy."

There was a girl's voice sobbing and mumbling, and the sound of people moving about. Then silence.

After some time, a female guard came to order everybody to bed. When she came to me, she said, "Why are you standing here?"

"I'm waiting to be called for questioning," I said.

"No more questioning. Go to bed!"

It seemed that I had been forgotten in the commotion overhead. I wondered what unpleasant fate would have awaited me if the girl upstairs had not chosen just that moment to bash her head on the cement toilet. While the method she used could not have resulted in her total escape from persecution, it demonstrated how desperate her mood was after listening to the broadcast. In fact, attempts at suicide were seldom successful at the No. 1 Detention House. The only person I heard of who actually did succeed was a young and talented surgeon, Dr. Song, the son of a vice-mayor of Shanghai. I was told that he painstakingly sharpened the handle of his toothbrush by grinding it on the cement floor and then used it to pierce his artery. It was revealed after Mao's death that the Revolutionaries had put the young doctor in the detention house and tortured him to make him denounce his father.

Next day, the prisoners were not given any food until mid-morning. It was dry rice with boiled cabbage. In the afternoon, a portion of boiled sweet potatoes was pushed through the small window. On subsequent days, this alternated with strips of moldy dried sweet potato boiled in water. Since I found this impossible to eat or digest, on those days I had to be content with only the midmorning meal. After some time, hunger became a permanent state, no longer a sensation but an ever present hollowness. The flesh on my body slowly melted away, my eyesight deteriorated, and simple activities such as washing clothes exhausted my strength.

Some of the guards disappeared. New guards came to work wearing the red armband of the Revolutionaries. Early in the morning, at midday, and at night, I would hear them shouting to each other, "Long live our Great Leader Chairman Mao," and chanting his quotations. The newspaper reported a new ritual observed by all Chinese people: "Ask for instructions in the morning, check your action with Chairman Mao's teachings at noon, and report everything at night." Apparently everyone went through this formality in front of an official portrait of Mao. To ask for instructions was to read passages from the Little Red Book, to check was to read again from the same book, and to report was also to read from the same book. In short, three times a day, every day, every Chinese, except babies, had to read from Mao's book of quotations. The newspaper published articles discussing whether one should do it when one was alone at home on Sundays. The conclusion was that one should not neglect going through the ritual even when one was lying in bed sick. Fortunately for us, this absurd practice was the privilege only of the approved "masses" and was not allowed for class enemies locked in prison!

Military Control had restored discipline. There was no more fighting or arguing among the guards. And they came on duty promptly. But it also created a frigid atmosphere. The guards no longer chatted with one another as they had done before. If one guard was alone with the prisoners, he or she seemed more relaxed. But whenever two were on duty together, they seemed to be on guard, almost as if each one feared that the other would report his or her behavior to the Military Control Commission.

There were new schedules for the prisoners besides the changed mealtimes. Every morning, the entire prison listened to news bulletins, first from the Central Broadcasting Service in Beijing and immediately afterwards from the Shanghai Broadcasting Station. Frequently, the prisoners were lectured through the loudspeakers. At such times, lists of those getting "lenient treatment" and "severe punishment" were read out to encourage the rest of us to confess. Whenever the loudspeaker was switched on, the guards walked from cell to cell to make sure the prisoners were listening.

One of the loudspeakers was just outside my door. The din was deafening. With the guard watching, I could not put my hands to my ears to shut out the noise. When Sunday came around, I asked for scissors, cut up a tiny piece of cloth, rolled the broken fibers into two small balls, and used them as earplugs when there was a broadcast. While they did not stop the noise altogether, it was sufficiently muted to be bearable.

From time to time, I was called to the interrogation rooms for special indoctrination and questioning by militant guards who seemed to enjoy the confidence of Military Control. Only selected prisoners received this treatment, I noticed. Whether we were the most hated class enemies or the most intransigent, I had no way of knowing. The guards used these occasions to abuse me verbally, calling me a "dirty exploiter of peasants" or a "running dog of foreign imperialists." They attacked me for my family background, for my job with Shell, and for my "resistance to reeducation" in not confessing to my "crime" readily. They would bombard me with questions but did not wait for me to give any answers. They would tell me I would be shot soon or that I would be kept at the detention house for the rest of my life.

I soon discovered that there was no need for me to do anything except listen, as the guards never stopped speaking once I entered the room. After several similar sessions, it dawned on me that their performances were solely for the purpose of establishing themselves as bona fide Revolutionaries. I was placed there merely as a necessary stage prop for their act. I concluded that even the militant guards who appeared so confident felt insecure in the atmosphere of suspicion created by the Cultural Revolution, when long-trusted Party leaders were suddenly condemned as "hidden enemies of Communism" who had "raised the red flag to oppose the red flag."

One day, the prisoners were allowed outdoor exercise. When I stepped out of the door of the women's prison, I saw ex-director Liang and several other men digging up the flower beds. This sight did not surprise me, for the day before I had read in the newspaper that Mao had said flowers and decorative plants were a softening influence that undermined the revolutionary spirit of the masses. The same report also said that in Mao's own garden in the former imperial palace, Zhongnanhai, only apple trees and sunflowers were grown since they had practical economic value. During this period of the Cultural Revolution, Mao's personality cult was such that every word of his, no matter how insignificant, was applied and implemented with alacrity. Conversely, nothing could be done if Mao had not pointed the way.

In the distance, I saw other men and women sweeping the drive and carrying buckets of water towards the kitchen. From their appearance and the rather clumsy way they were working, I knew they were the Party intellectuals of the detention house, like ex-director Liang, being reformed by physical labor. Mao had said that the more knowledge a man had, the more reactionary he would become, unless he purged himself through arduous physical labor.

Years later, I heard that during the Cultural Revolution millions of men and women had been ordered to give up their jobs in the cities and settle in rural areas to receive reeducation through physical labor. Those intellectuals allowed to remain in the cities were assigned the work of common laborers in their organizations. It was the practice of that time to have medical doctors emptying bedpans in the hospitals, professors cleaning toilets in the universities, and artists and musicians building walls and repairing roads. While they were doing all these things, they had to attend struggle meetings and political indoctrination classes at which they had to abuse themselves by "confessing" to their "crimes." Indeed Mao's abuse of intellectuals reached an unprecedented level of cruelty during the Cultural Revolution. It very nearly destroyed China's tradition of respect for scholarship. During that time, anywhere in China, a man found reading a book other than Mao's four slim volumes ran the risk of being labeled an opponent of Mao.

When I reached the exercise yard, the guard told me to weed the ground with my bare hands. Since it was winter, only a small patch was growing at the foot of the wall facing the sun. But the ground was frozen hard. It was slow work to get the weeds out without tools. When the guard returned, he kicked the small pile of dead weeds at my feet and yelled, "Is this all you have done? You didn't dig out the roots."

"I have nothing to dig the roots with."

"You have hands. You could get the roots out with your fingers. You are just lazy!" He kicked the pile of weeds again, sending them flying in all directions.

When I stood up, dark shadows blinded my eyes and I felt dizzy. However, I managed to stagger after him back to the cell.

Two soldiers were in the corridor. The door of my cell was open. I saw a militant female guard going through my things. My sheets, quilt, and blanket were already on the dusty floor. She was tossing other things out of my canvas bag. When she saw me, she grabbed the front of my padded jacket and pulled me roughly into the cell.

"Unbutton your jacket!" she yelled. When I unbuttoned it, she pulled it off my back and threw it on the floor. Holding my shoulders, she pushed me to a corner of the cell and turned me to face the wall. I stood there shivering and coughing.

"Take off your trousers!" she yelled when she had finished examining my jacket.

"Please let me put on my jacket before I take off my warm trousers. I already have a bad cold."

"You are still soft and pampered. Prison life hasn't done you any good, has it? You haven't changed one little bit. I don't think you will die of cold if you take off both your jacket and your trousers. Take them off!"

I sneezed and coughed while she looked over my trousers. Then she threw them on the floor too and frisked me. She tore the toilet paper off the wall by my bed and deliberately walked over my bedclothes. Pushing my eyeshade along the floor with her foot, she kicked it out of the cell and locked the door. I heard her unlocking the door of the cell next to mine and shouting to the inmate, "Come over!"

I picked up my padded jacket and trousers and put them on. Then I had to sit down on the bed to calm myself and wait for my heartbeat to slow down before collecting my things from the floor and cleaning them as best I could. Next day, when rice was given to me, I used some to make a paste to replace the toilet paper on the wall—quite a sacrifice now that every grain of rice was precious to me for survival. To make another eyeshade, I had to wait until Sunday to borrow the needle.

Searching prisoners' cells became an established practice. It was done at irregular intervals by the militant female guard or others like her. I replaced the toilet paper on the wall many times and made many eyeshades; many a time I counted the grains of rice individually so that I used just enough to paste the paper but not a grain more than was necessary.

After coughing all night and being unable to sleep because of a terrible headache, I could barely get out of bed the next day. I went to the window and called, "Report!"

It was a mild guard who opened the small window.

"I think I'm sick. May I see the doctor?" I requested.

She brought a thermometer and put it into my mouth. After a few minutes, she took it out, looked at it, and said to me, "You have a fever. It's quite high." She gave me two aspirin tablets and told me to drink plenty of water. I waited for the doctor, but he did not come. Just before the guard went off duty, I asked for the doctor again.

After a moment's hesitation, she said, "The doctor has gone to the countryside to receive reeducation through physical labor. I don't know when he will be allowed to come back. Maybe someone will come to take his place. Report again tomorrow. If you feel unwell, you may go to bed now." She gave me two more aspirin tablets.

It was good to be allowed to lie down, but I had a splitting headache. When my body shook with spasms of cold shivers, I knew my temperature was going up.

I heard the night duty guard arrive and the two guards exchange shouts of "Long live our Great Leader Chairman Mao."

Then the night duty guard walked along the corridor towards my cell, inspecting the prisoners in cells along the way. She walked briskly and stopped briefly at each peephole.

"What? Lying in bed already? You know how to be comfortable, don't you? Get up! It's not bedtime yet," she shouted when she reached my cell. From her voice, I knew she was the same guard who had searched my cell the previous afternoon.

"I'm ill. The guard who just left told me to go to bed." Unless I was dragged out of bed, I intended to stay there. She didn't bother to come in. In a moment, I heard her upstairs scolding another prisoner.

Next day, a young man came in response to my request for medical attention. After I told him I had a fever and had been coughing for nearly two months, he declared, "You probably have hepatitis. There is a lot of it going around in this detention house. I'll examine a specimen of your blood."

I was astonished. Any ignoramus with no special medical knowledge would know I had bronchitis, possibly verging on pneumonia, not hepatitis, an inflammation of the liver with symptoms entirely different from mine. What sort of "doctor" was this young man? I bent down to look at him through the opening of the small window. I saw a country lad no more than twenty years of age in a soldier's uniform. I realized he was not a trained doctor at all but had been given the job because Mao Zedong had said, "We must learn swimming from swimming," when referring to appointing unskilled workers who were politically reliable to do technical jobs. The young man was simply carrying out Mao's order to "learn to be a doctor by being one."

There were many reports in the newspaper of cases where untrained hospital coolies were said to have performed operations successfully after mastering Mao's quotations. During an operation, Revolutionaries anxious to prove the magic of Mao's words remained in the operating room reciting quotations from the Little Red Book while the untrained "doctor" struggled with the patient. However, when Mao himself or one of the other radical leaders needed medical attention from experts other than their own personal doctors, those experts, trained in Western universities before the Communist Party took over China, were bundled into special planes and flown to Beijing, often

hastily removed from the countryside where they had been exiled to perform hard labor.

The young "doctor" took me to the room reserved for the
guards. In the warm room, where a stove was burning, my head
cleared and I stopped shivering. After he had unwrapped his
instruments and taken out the syringe, he told me to take off my
jacket and roll up my sleeve. When he plunged the needle into
my arm, he could not locate my vein. After several attempts, a
bruise appeared under my skin and my arm became very painful.
He was visibly agitated. Beads of sweat appeared on his forehead, and his hand trembled.

I felt sorry for this poor creature who had been given a job
beyond his ability. I knew that if I did not calm him, he might
easily inflict worse damage on my arm.

"I have very small veins. All doctors have trouble taking blood
from me," I said, trying to give him confidence and steady his
hand.

He looked at me with what might be called a grateful glance
and tried again while I held my breath. Finally he managed to
locate the vein and fill the syringe.

Several days passed; my fever got so high that I no longer felt
the cold in the cell. The guard told me to stay in bed. Twice a
day, the Labor Reform girl was allowed to come in, under the
watchful eyes of the guard standing at the open doorway, to
bring me liquid rice and hot drinking water. I slept most of the
time, in a state of semiconsciousness, with fantastic dreams of
myself floating in and out of the cell through the iron-barred
window as if I were an ethereal spirit.

One morning, the young man came back and said, "You don't
have hepatitis. It's probably TB. A lot of prisoners have TB. Get
dressed. You may go to the hospital to have a fluoroscope."

Though I was sure I did not have TB, I welcomed the idea of
going to a hospital.

In the afternoon, a female guard unlocked the cell door and
took me out. My legs felt wobbly, and I was weak, but she did
not shout or urge me to walk faster. At the entrance of the
detention house, a male guard was waiting with a pair of handcuffs. The female guard shook her head and whispered, "Too
ill." I did not know whether the female guard meant I was too
ill to escape en route, so that the handcuffs were unnecessary,

or I was so ill that they had to show me consideration. In any case, the male guard put the handcuffs away.

A black jeep was waiting just inside the second gate. The female guard and I got into it.

How changed the drive of the detention house appeared from that night over sixteen months ago when I had been brought there! The place was now ablaze with color and activities. Red boards mounted on sticks, bearing Mao's quotations dealing with the suppression of class enemies, were placed alongside the willow trees that lined the drive. The quotations were written in large characters with yellow paint. The boards were arranged to face the front entrance, probably to create an impact of fear on the prisoners being driven into the detention house. On a large banner of red cloth suspended over the soldiers' barracks were three slogans written in white paint: "Down with the U.S. Imperialists," "Down with the Soviet Revisionists," and "We must liberate Taiwan." Dummies dressed in Western men's suits with the names of the president of the United States, the general secretary of the Soviet Communist Party, and the leader of the Kuomintang in Taiwan pinned on the front of the jackets were tied to wooden poles. Soldiers were practicing bayonet charges on them. As one uniformed figure after another rushed forward to sink his bayonet into the dummies, all soldiers present yelled, "Kill!"

Under an overcast sky, the streets of Shanghai were almost deserted. On the long drive across the city from the detention house to the prison hospital at Tilanqiao, I saw only a few people bundled up in their padded winter jackets struggling against the sharp north wind. I felt very ill, but it was so long since I had seen the streets of the city that I made a special effort to observe the changes caused by the Cultural Revolution. Somehow, I had hoped that what I saw would give a hint of my daughter's life under the new circumstances.

There was evidence of destruction everywhere: scorched buildings with blackened windows, uprooted trees and shrubs, and abandoned vehicles. Debris whirled in the wind. Gray, bent figures were digging hopefully through heaped rubbish. Traffic lights were not operating. Slogans and quotations covered the walls of every building we passed. They were even plastered on the sides of buses and trucks. Some were chalked on the sidewalks. Instead of policemen, armed soldiers patrolled the streets. We passed several truckloads of helmeted Revolutionaries armed with iron rods and shouting slogans, probably on their way to carry out revolutionary actions against some rival factions. Large portraits of Mao on wooden boards several feet high stood at main street corners. Painted to make the old man look extremely youthful, healthy, and fat (a sign of well-being in China), these pictures provided a mocking contrast to the thin, pale-faced pedestrians walking listlessly below them.

Tilanqiao was a district of Shanghai in which the city's main prison was located. In time, the name was used to denote the prison itself. The prison complex was enormous, covering many acres of land. Prisoners who had already passed through the various detention houses of the city and had been sentenced were sent there. There were political prisoners as well as common criminals considered unsuitable for labor camps, either because they were too ill or too old for heavy physical work or because their special skills could be better utilized in the numerous workshops run by the prison. No one knew for certain how many prisoners were in this large compound, but it was widely believed that over twenty thousand men and women labored in the various workshops, producing goods that ranged from primitive computers to buttons, some for the export market.

The prison hospital was situated inside the Tilanqiao prison compound. I noticed that security was more strict here than at the No. 1 Detention House. The jeep passed through two checkpoints where its papers were carefully scrutinized before it was allowed to drive through a heavy iron gate guarded by more soldiers. The guards who looked into the jeep had revolvers at their belts.

The prison compound looked extremely bleak, with not a single tree or plant in the entire place. It included many workshops with the sound of motors moving at high speed, a row of houses for interrogation and administration, all marked with written notices, and a lot of brightly colored slogans denouncing class enemies and urging hard work in production as a means of reform. In the distance, enclosed by a tall, steep fence, stood six huge buildings with windows covered by black wooden boards, just like mine, so I surmised that those buildings were the living quarters of the prisoners.

The guard led me into the hospital building. The walls inside were covered with slogans, quotations, and large posters of Mao. Whoever had done the decoration had done a thorough job; even the glass windowpanes were painted with Mao's face. Some had a red heart pierced with an arrow underneath his face, others had the Chinese character for loyalty—*zhong*—written beside them.

The waiting room of the prison hospital could only be described as a scene of hell, though no one was being devoured by wild beasts, burning in a roaring fire, or drowning in a boiling sea. This was a hell of poverty and silent suffering, full of emaciated human beings draped in tattered clothes, with pain and agony clearly written on their wasted faces, waiting patiently for the end. Whether ravaged by illness or hunger or both, they appeared to be past the stage where the skill of a medical doctor could make them whole again. I had heard of the high mortality rate at Tilanqiao. Now I was having a glimpse of the cases that would shortly contribute to the next statistic.

Besides the hunched figures on the benches, there were others wrapped in patched quilts lying on dirty canvas stretchers on the cement floor. On one of these stretchers, right in front of where I was told to sit, was an old man with a bald head. Except for spasms of quick and jerky breathing through his half-open mouth, he seemed already dead, with sunken closed eyes and transparent skin tautly stretched over his waxen face.

With all the windows closed, the air in the room, smelling of a mixture of disinfectant and human decay, was foul and stifling. I closed my eyes to shut out the depressing sight and tried to hold my breath while I waited for my turn to see the doctor.

"Eighteen-oh-six!" A nurse in a gown that had been white but had been worn and washed into a neutral, dingy gray called at the door of the waiting room.

I followed her into the clinic, where the female guard who had brought me was talking to a middle-aged woman doctor. In the middle of the large room there was a stove with a kettle boiling on it. Around the stove were small tables behind which sat doctors in the process of examining patients. There was no concession to customary Chinese decorum. Men and women undressed in full view of others in the room, and the questions and answers exchanged by the doctors and patients could be heard by everyone. At the time, I thought this crude practice was due to the fact that prisoners were not generally looked upon as human beings. But after my release, I was to discover that all hospitals in Shanghai had degenerated to a similar low standard during the Cultural Revolution.

While I was busily thinking how best to respond if the doctor should ask me to undress, she handed me a thermometer. I put it in my mouth. Fortunately that was all she wanted me to do. When she looked at the thermometer, she said to the female guard, "She had better stay here for a few days. Her temperature is very high. The ward is on the fifth floor. I don't think she should walk up. She had better be carried on a stretcher."

"Please let me try to walk," I pleaded with her. The very thought of lying on one of those dirty stretchers was unbearable.

The doctor had a deeply lined face with graying hair at her temples. Her soft eyes were kind and full of understanding. Perhaps she realized my reluctance to come into contact with a dirty stretcher, for she said to the guard, "You may use the staff elevator. It's quicker than waiting for a stretcher. She is really very ill, probably with pneumonia."

The female guard went with me to the ward on the fifth floor. After cautioning me not to discuss my case with anybody, she told me that my washbasin and face towel would be brought over from the detention house when the guards came again with other sick prisoners. Then she handed me over to a young woman with a Labor Reform badge pinned on the front of her jacket. A soldier on duty stood a few feet away watching us.

The ward was a small room with five beds in it. The two near the door were occupied. I was given the innermost one against the wall, separated from the other two women by two empty beds. The Labor Reform girl told me to undress and lie down.

How good it was to rest my feverish, aching body on a real bed again! The unbleached calico sheets were rough but quite clean. Though the room was icy cold, the quilt was thick. I took off my jacket and trousers and lay down in my sweaters and long knitted pants. The girl brought another quilt and laid it across the bed. I soon fell asleep.

For the next few days, I drifted in and out of consciousness, sometimes faintly aware of my surroundings but mostly in a dream world of my own. When my mind came into focus again,

I found my arm bound to the side of the bed. A needle in my vein was attached to a long rubber tube that led to a bottle hanging upside down on a tall stand. I was being fed intravenously by the liquid dripping through the rubber tube into my arm. The Labor Reform girl was pushing a thermometer into my mouth to take my temperature. When she saw that I was fully awake, she untied my arm, removed the needle, and took everything away. Though I seemed to have regained full consciousness, I felt languid and drowsy.

After a while, she brought me a bowl of steaming liquid. "Drink it!" she said.

Although my arm was stiff, I held the bowl quite steadily. Lifting my head from the pillow, I drank the liquid. It tasted rather strange. Then I realized that it was soybean milk with quite a lot of sugar. Since I had not had sugar for a long time, I did not immediately recognize its sweet taste.

I seemed much better. The dizziness had gone, and my head was clear. I put my hand on my forehead. It felt cool and moist with perspiration. The young woman came back with a small syringe filled with a milky liquid. She told me to turn on my side. I braced myself, remembering the experience with the young medical soldier. But I felt no pain, for she gave the injection swiftly and expertly. She worked like a professional nurse, she held the syringe like a professional nurse, and she walked in the pert way that only a professional nurse, confident of her skill, walks. I was sure that in real life she had been a professional nurse. I wondered with a deep feeling of sadness what had brought her to do Labor Reform in the ward of a prison hospital.

For the evening meal, she gave me a bowl of soft cooked rice and a plate of vegetables with a whole yellow fish on top cooked in oil and soy sauce with scallion and garlic. The fish was only a tiny one, no longer than six inches, but it tasted more delicious than anything I remembered. I ate it all up. My toilet things were on a chair beside my bed. On the floor were a bedpan and a chamber pot. I managed to get out of bed and give myself a badly needed wash.

After the young woman had taken away the empty dishes, a soldier locked the heavy steel door of the ward and retired to his room some distance away. One of the women occupying one of the other beds came over to chat with me.

"You were unconscious for six days. They thought you were going to die. Do you feel better now?" She was as thin as a reed, with hollow cheeks, colorless dry skin, but burning bright eyes. Her padded jacket was patched and patched again. She looked over sixty, but her voice was that of a young woman of thirty. She spoke in low whispers, constantly glancing at the door.

I nodded and smiled at her, glad to have her company but still too weak to enjoy talking. She sat down on the edge of my bed.

"Have you just been transferred to Tilanqiao? When did you receive your sentence?" she asked me.

Remembering the warning of the female guard not to discuss my case with anyone, I said nothing but merely smiled again.

"Don't be afraid. I won't report you. Here we prisoners have to protect each other, you know," she told me. After a moment's pause, she asked, "Have you got TB? This is a TB ward. That's why we get better food. But I go back to the cell tomorrow because I no longer cough blood. When my condition deteriorates and I cough blood again, they will let me come back here to have a rest and receive streptomycin injections. They don't bother to cure us, but they don't let us die either," she sighed.

"I'm sorry you have TB." I felt a surge of sympathy for her.

"Nearly everybody gets it sooner or later at this place. It's inevitable really. We catch it from one another. Twenty people in one cell, sleeping within inches of one another—how can we avoid it? And there is the poor diet and hard work."

"Do you work? What do you do?" I asked out of curiosity.

"Sewing. Ten hours and more a day, six days a week, I sew buttons and make buttonholes on cardigans. They are for export, so the work must be good. It earns me a few yuan a month for soap and toilet paper. My husband cannot afford to send me any money. We have three children." Talking about herself depressed her. She bowed her head, almost in tears. But she continued to sit by my side. I thought she wanted someone to talk to. As for me, after being in solitary confinement for so long, I found her presence by my side strangely comforting.

"I was an accountant in a factory where my husband is a technician. It was a good job, but I carelessly threw it away," she said.

"Did you do something wrong with the money in your charge?" I asked her.

"No, nothing like that. I criticized our Party secretary. Someone reported me during the Elimination of Counterrevolutionaries Campaign in 1955. I was denounced, but I fought back. Instead of apologizing to the Party secretary, I said more. I was so inexperienced! The Party secretary got angry and included me in the list of counterrevolutionaries he was drawing up for our factory. I was arrested and sentenced to twelve years."

"Could you not appeal to a higher court? To criticize your Party secretary is not so serious a mistake. Twelve years is a long sentence."

"What's the use? A higher court would only refer the case to my Party secretary again. The Security Bureau always cooperates with Party secretaries. You know the Chinese saying, 'An official is always on the side of another official.' "

"Well, you have been here a long time already. The worst is behind you. You will soon be reunited with your family." I tried to comfort her.

"It won't be long now. I hope when I see them again my children will still recognize me and my husband hasn't got involved with another woman."

"Don't they come to see you on visiting days?" I knew that once a prisoner was sentenced and sent to Tilanqiao, he or she was allowed a monthly visit by a family member. In fact, prisoners left for a long time in various detention houses often made false confessions to get sentenced so that they could see their families.

"No, I asked them to sever their relationship with me as soon as I was sentenced. That was the only way to make sure my husband retained his job and to protect the children. You know how badly the families of counterrevolutionaries are treated. My husband and I were very much in love. Ours wasn't an arranged marriage. When I told him to divorce me and never come to see me again, he cried bitterly and told me that he would pretend to divorce me but in fact wait for me."

I felt terribly sad for her, but I could find nothing to say that might lighten her burden. She was again lost in thought. After some time, she changed the subject.

"You are lucky to have that nice doctor. She is highly qualified, a graduate of a world-famous medical college in the United States, I heard. She's very kind and considerate of others. When

I first came here, she was still a prisoner like us. After her release, she came back to work here. I heard she volunteered to come. It's very hard to go back to the outside world after being here. People outside don't want to associate with ex-prisoners. Your superior doesn't dare to assign you to a decent job, and there is no hope of promotion. You are a marked person, always singled out for insults and criticism. Once a counterrevolutionary, always a counterrevolutionary. You suffer for it in prison, and you suffer for it afterwards. Your family suffers for it too. I have seen others in our factory treated like that. Now I'm one of them. Sometimes I dread going out of here back into the world again."

I was shocked to the core to hear that the woman doctor had been a prisoner at Tilanqiao. It never occurred to me that behind her kind face there was a sad story, but then, she did have a very special expression in her eyes, not just kindness and understanding. It was almost as if she had some special knowledge of life that made her extremely wise and tolerant.

"She came back to China in response to the People's Government's call for patriotic Chinese from the United States to serve the people. I understand she had a good job there. But she gave it up and returned. Even when I first met her, she was always speaking frankly, like a foreigner. Of course, she got into trouble."

In the early 1950s, the People's Government mounted a quiet propaganda campaign through their agents and sympathizers among overseas Chinese to persuade Chinese intellectuals living in the United States to return to China and "help with national reconstruction." The real purpose of the campaign was to attract physicists who could help China to build the atomic bomb, but it was conducted in general terms to avoid attracting attention. Strong appeals were made to the patriotic feelings of all Chinese intellectuals living abroad everywhere, but especially in the United States. Quite a number in different professions responded. They abandoned good jobs and comfortable living standards to answer the call of the motherland and returned to China, only to find that they were not really wanted. The Communist Party officials' deep suspicion of anyone with what they called "foreign connections" and their prejudice against all intellectuals added to the difficulties of the returnees. Since the strained relationship between Washington and Beijing made it impossible for them to return to the United States, they had to put up with the conditions in China as best they could. A few lucky ones made their way to Hong Kong. But the majority remained inside China and accepted whatever jobs the Party was willing to give them. Many suffered persecution during one political campaign after another, especially the Anti-Rightist Campaign of 1957. Those who survived to 1966 were virtually all caught up in the net of the Proletarian Cultural Revolution. Only the physicists working on China's nuclear arms program were protected by Prime Minister Zhou Enlai. It was a sad story of callous disregard for human rights and another instance of the readiness of the Chinese Communist Party to sacrifice individuals for political purposes.

We sat in silence in the hospital ward, each with her own thoughts. The patient in the other bed began to groan and cough. At the sound of a door opening in the distance, the prisoner sitting on my bed became nervous. She said good night to me and slipped into her own bed.

I lay there wide awake. My thoughts were with my daughter. Where was she at that moment? Was she well and managing to cope with the complicated situation of the Cultural Revolution? I prayed to God to guide and protect her.

Next morning, I got out of bed just to put my feet on the floor. I was still very weak, and my heart palpitated wildly when I moved about. Afterwards, I took a few steps each day until I could walk around the ward easily. With nutritious food and medication, I gradually became stronger.

There were now only two of us in the room. The other woman was very ill and never left her bed. Once I walked to her side, but she did not open her eyes and seemed unaware of my presence. Beside her pillow was a container half full of sputum and blood. Her face was like old parchment, and she lay there without moving, except when she coughed. At mealtimes, the Labor Reform girl fed her with a spoon.

I never asked the Labor Reform girl any questions, and she did not venture to speak. But we smiled at each other to convey our friendly feelings. Although she brought nutritious food to me, I noticed that she herself had only the usual rice with cabbage or boiled sweet potatoes. She was poorly dressed and seemed always cold, with her lips blue and her shoulders hunched. I tried to give her one of the sweaters I was wearing. I took it off when she wasn't in the room, and when she came in, I offered it to her without speaking because of the soldier outside. However, she was too frightened to accept. She looked nervously at the prostrate form of the woman at the other end of the room and pushed the sweater back to me.

A year later, when I was ill and back in the hospital again, she was no longer there. I liked to think she was now working on the ward of an ordinary hospital in Shanghai, walking pertly, syringe in hand, ministering to the sick.

After another week, when my temperature was normal, the doctor told me I could return to the No. 1 Detention House. She spoke softly, and her eyes were full of kindness, as if she saw something good and lovable in me that I was not aware of myself. There was something saintly about this woman, I thought. I did not believe she came back to work at the prison hospital because she could not cope with the outside world after imprisonment. I believed she came back because she knew the prisoners needed her. She had found a mission to which she could devote her life even though her position was not honorable or rewarding in the eyes of the world. She seemed to possess great spiritual strength. She had obviously become a finer person because of her suffering.

A few days later, when a guard brought more prisoners to the hospital, he took me back to the No. 1 Detention House.

8

Party Factions

THE BOUT OF PNEUMONIA I suffered in the winter of 1967 marked the beginning of rapid physical deterioration. The prolonged lack of nutritious food, sunshine, and fresh air made full recovery impossible and caused the body's aging process to speed up. It also reduced my mental powers to such an extent that I often found it difficult to concentrate on one subject for long. To think logically and analytically required a great deal of conscious effort. I was beginning to understand why abject poverty produces a vacant stare and lethargic movements. In fact, I knew I was experiencing all the symptoms of mental and physical exhaustion that could lead to a breakdown. The prospect of losing my ability to think clearly frightened me more than the fact that my hair was falling out by the handful, my gums bled, and I had lost a great deal of weight. The psychological effect of total isolation was also taking its toll. Often my mood was one of despair. Sometimes I had difficulty swallowing the meager food I was given, even though I was desperately hungry.

Outside the prison walls, the general situation remained confused. In spite of military control, violence and factional wars among the Red Guards and the Revolutionaries continued well into 1968. It seemed that after unleashing the Red Guards and the Revolutionaries to serve his political purposes, Mao Zedong was no longer able to control them. The detention house could not resume normal working order as long as the political situation remained unsettled. No one was in a position to deal seriously with my case, and I was left in the cell waiting. The fear that I might die before my case could be clarified became a real one.

One day after the Labor Reform girl had given me cold water, I could hardly carry the filled basin from the small window to its usual spot only a couple of feet away. My hands shook, and my heart palpitated wildly. My legs were so wobbly that I had to place the basin on the floor and sit down.

While I sat on the bed panting to catch my breath, I thought that if I was going to survive the Cultural Revolution, I must discipline myself with physical and mental exercise. Inspired by my own resolution, I stood up rather abruptly. Dark shadows almost blinded me, and I had to sit down again. But from that day onward, I devised a series of exercises that moved every part of my body from my head to my toes and did them twice a day. At first, the exercise exhausted me, and I had to interrupt it with frequent periods of rest. Also I had to avoid the prying eyes of the guards, as exercise other than the few minutes of walking in the cell after meals was forbidden. Nevertheless, I managed to exercise each day and after a few months recovered my physical strength somewhat, as well as my feeling of well-being.

For mental exercise, I first tried to memorize some of Mao's essays, which I thought would enable me to understand his mentality better and to use his quotations more fluently when I had to face an interrogator again. I liked best of all his essay on guerrilla warfare, in which he advocated seizing the initiative whenever and wherever possible so that a small band of poorly equipped guerrillas could cause havoc and defeat a well-equipped army. Although Mao was a hateful dictator who had killed millions of Chinese people and imprisoned more with his political campaigns, and although he had several times brought the nation's economy to the brink of ruin with his disastrous economic policy, I had to concede that he was a brilliant strategist of guerrilla warfare. His essays on Marxist principles were often half-baked, but his essay on guerrilla warfare was, I thought, a masterpiece of clear thinking based on the experience of the Communist army. But in the last analysis, to study Mao's books for many hours a day was in itself a depressing occupation for me, his victim, because it constantly reminded me of his evil power prevailing over my own fate and of my own impotence to overcome it.

I turned instead to the Tang dynasty poetry I had learned as a schoolgirl. It really amazed me that I was able to dig out from the deep recesses of my brain verses that had lain dormant for decades. Trying to remember poems I thought I had forgotten was a joyful occupation. Whenever I managed to piece together a whole poem, I felt a sense of happy accomplishment. The immortal words of the great Tang poets not only helped to improve my memory but also transported me from the grim reality of the prison cell to a world of beauty and freedom.

My persistent efforts to maintain sanity had a measure of success. But there were still moments when I was so burdened with hunger and misery that I was tempted to let go my tenuous grip on the lifeline of survival. At those times, I had to depend on conflict with the guards to stimulate my fighting spirit.

"Report!" I would walk to the door of the cell and call out with all my strength.

"What do you want?" Shuffling footsteps approached my cell as the guard spoke lazily. "How many times do I have to tell you not to shout?"

"How long do I have to wait for the government to investigate my case? It's illegal to lock up an innocent person in prison. It's against Chairman Mao's teachings." In fact no mention was ever made in his four volumes of such practice, but I was pretty sure that the semiliterate guard had not read Mao's books thoroughly.

"Hush! Don't shout! The government will deal with your case in due course. You are not the only one."

"But I have been here such a long time already. I want to see the interrogator!" I would raise my voice deliberately.

"Lower your voice! You mustn't shout! The interrogator is busy." I knew very well that there was no interrogator working at that time. She knew I knew it, but we kept up the pretense.

The prison was exceptionally silent. Our voices carried to the four corners of the building. I knew the other prisoners were listening, as they had nothing else to do. I also knew that they

probably enjoyed my defiance, just as I felt encouraged whenever I heard another prisoner brave enough to answer the
guards back. The knowledge that the other prisoners were listening to my exchange with the guard forged a link between
them and me. I no longer felt alone. Heartened by what I was
sure was their silent approval, I acted with renewed effort,
though I was already fatigued by my own shouting.

"I'm innocent. I've never committed any crime. I've never
done anything to oppose the People's Government. You have
no right to lock up a law-abiding citizen! I demand rehabilitation
and an apology!" I yelled at the top of my voice.

"Have you gone mad? Keep quiet!" The guard was now
shouting in anger.

"I'm not mad. The person who ordered my imprisonment was
mad."

"Do you want to be punished for creating a disturbance?"

I heard urgent footsteps. Another guard had come to join her.
The second guard said, "You are committing a crime at this
moment by creating a disturbance."

"Our Great Leader Chairman Mao taught us, 'Lay out the
facts; speak with reason.' I'm merely following his instructions.
I'm innocent. I have not committed a crime. I should say so,"
I argued in a loud voice.

"Come out!"

The guard would unlock the door of the cell and lead me into
a room in a remote corner of the prison compound where we
could continue to shout at each other without being heard by the
other prisoners. I would give in and stop talking when I became
utterly exhausted. Sometimes my endurance outlasted the
guards' patience. When that happened, they resorted to physical
violence to silence me, either hitting my body or kicking my legs.
They called me a "hysterical old woman" and often deplored my
"mad fits," but they never knew my real purpose in provoking
them. During my six and a half years of solitary confinement, I
deliberately caused scenes such as this many times. Whenever
deep depression overwhelmed me to the extent that I could no
longer sleep or swallow food, I would intentionally seek an
encounter with the guards.

Though my arms became bruised and my legs bear to this day
scars inflicted by their heavy leather boots, I always enjoyed a

period of good humor and calm spirits after fighting with the guards. Then tension would gradually build up in me again. I believed that what I needed was human contact; even encounters with the guards were better than complete isolation. Besides, fighting was a positive action, much more encouraging to the human spirit than merely enduring hardship with patience, known as a virtue of the Chinese race. Many of my friends and acquaintances survived their ordeal during the Cultural Revolution by that virtue. But for me, only the positive stimulant of fighting buoyed up my spirits.

On August 6, a particularly stifling summer's day, the newspaper came very late. I overheard the male guard who brought copies of the newspaper to the women's prison saying to the female guard on duty, "Very important news!" I wondered what it was. But I had to wait until nearly bedtime for the newspaper to reach my cell.

On the front page in large characters, with banner headlines printed in red, was a news item. The day before, Mao Zedong had sent a basket of mangoes to the workers and peasants engaged in indoctrinating the students at the famous Qinghua University in Beijing. The mangoes had originally been a gift to Mao from Pakistan's foreign minister when he came for an official visit. The newspaper reported the jubilation and excitement of the workers when Mao's gift was brought to them. According to the report, the workers and peasants cheered with joy and wept with gratitude. Chanting Mao's quotations, they pledged their loyalty to the Leader.

Although I did not know that Mao had disowned the Red Guards a few days before, when he had called together their leaders in Beijing and criticized their violence, I recognized immediately that his well-publicized action had important political significance. Undoubtedly the workers and peasants had been sent to Qinghua, one of China's leading universities, where the Red Guard had been especially militant and unruly, to restrain the young revolutionaries. To make a present to the workers and peasants there was a clear and eloquent warning to the Qinghua Red Guards not to resist the disciplinary actions of those sent to tame them.

For the next few days, the newspaper reported the organization of "Mao Zedong Thought Propaganda Teams" all over the country. Photographs of these men marching into universities and schools appeared daily. Although named "Workers' and Peasants' Propaganda Teams for Mao Zedong Thought," the teams included no peasants and few workers. They were composed mainly of military men in civilian clothes and Party officials considered loyal by the Maoist leaders, such as Mao's wife Jiang Qing and Defense Minister Lin Biao.

Although Communist totalitarianism in China was in essence military dictatorship, from the inception of its power in 1949 the Chinese Communist Party was always careful to keep the gun in the background and to create an impression of civilian rule by persuasion. Political indoctrination was the preferred method used to bend the will of the populace. Only in extreme cases of mass armed uprising in remote areas inhabited by minority races had troops been called out. To use the Workers' and Peasants' Propaganda Teams to overcome the resistance of the Red Guards and restore order by nonmilitary means rather than the speedier method of sending in contingents of soldiers illustrated once more how anxious Mao was to preserve this carefully cultivated image of a benign government.

While the Red Guards were being dealt with, the Maoist leadership in Beijing continued its efforts to organize provincial and municipal Revolutionary Committees (a new name for the provincial and municipal governments) and new Party Secretariats. The newspaper frequently published lead articles expressing the hope that this process would be speeded up so that conditions would be felicitous for the convening of the Ninth Party Congress. I concluded that the Maoists who had seized power were anxious to give themselves official status by being elected to the Party Central Committee and the Politburo, and to have the old officials they had ousted from office expelled from the Party so as to remove any possible future threat to their own power.

Time dragged on, and it was again autumn. With each rainy day, the temperature dropped a few degrees. I thought that by adhering to a regimen of mental and physical exercise I had stalled the rapid deterioration of my health. So it was quite a shock when something new and alarming happened. I had been losing an unusually large amount of blood at each menstrual period. When I began hemorrhaging every ten days or so, for several days at a time, I became very frightened. Yet remembering my experience with the untrained orderly, I did not dare to ask for medical attention. Depression once again overtook me; I often had nightmares from which I would waken sweating and panting for breath.

One night in October, while I was still struggling with my own physical problems, the guard went again from cell to cell to order the prisoners to sit quietly and listen to a broadcast. A man's voice came through the loudspeaker to make the startling announcement that at a Central Committee meeting presided over by Mao, a resolution was passed to expel Liu Shaoqi, the chairman of the Chinese People's Republic, from the Chinese Communist Party and to strip him of all his official positions.

Liu Shaoqi, a longtime Communist Party leader, was second only to Mao Zedong in the Party hierarchy. When Mao was leading the armed struggle from the Chinese soviet in Jinggang-shan in the early thirties, Liu was directing the Communist underground in Kuomintang-held areas. After 1949, when Mao occupied the twin positions of chairman of the Central Committee of the Communist Party and chairman of the Chinese People's Republic, Liu Shaoqi was the general secretary of the Communist Party. The two men worked in close collaboration, and there was no sign that Liu was trying to usurp Mao's power. Indeed, the term "Mao Zedong Thought" was coined by Liu Shaoqi in his report as Party secretary at the Seventh Party Congress in 1945. However, in 1960, after Mao's Great Leap Forward Campaign pushed China's fragile economy to the brink of ruin, Mao Zedong relinquished the position of chairman of the People's Republic in favor of Liu Shaoqi. The rumor that reached the Chinese people was that there had been fierce debates within the Party leadership and Mao had been obliged to make a humiliating gesture of self-criticism in front of a meeting of seven thousand leading Party officials.

Liu Shaoqi immediately adopted a series of policy reversals to save the rapidly deteriorating economic situation. When his economic policy succeeded where Mao's had failed and Liu Shaoqi became increasingly popular with Party members and the Chinese people, eclipsing Mao Zedong in influence and importance, Mao became alarmed. He carefully plotted to destroy the man who threatened his position, for he feared losing not only everything he had believed in and worked for but also his place in history.

While the Great Proletarian Cultural Revolution was different things to different people, this gigantic struggle lasting ten full years was essentially a contest between two conflicting Party policies personified by Mao Zedong and Liu Shaoqi. The irony is that although Mao Zedong had Liu Shaoqi persecuted to death and seemed to have won during the Cultural Revolution, after his own death, Deng Xiaoping led China along the route of economic liberalization pioneered by Liu Shaoqi twenty years earlier, and went much further than anybody in China or the rest of the world could possibly have imagined during the days of the Cultural Revolution.

In the resolution passed by the Central Committee, Liu was declared "a traitor, a hidden agent, and a scab." However, no evidence was offered to substantiate the accusation, and, as was customary in Communist China, the victim was not allowed to defend himself. Furthermore, Liu's expulsion by the Central Committee rather than the Party Congress was not strictly legal. But at the zenith of his power, Mao could afford to ignore this fine point.

After the announcement of the Central Committee resolution against Liu Shaoqi, the nation's propaganda machinery was mobilized to denounce him. Day after day, the newspaper was filled with articles listing Liu Shaoqi's "crimes," the foremost of which always seemed to be that he "opposed the policies of the Great Leader." The newspaper also described mass meetings held all over the country for the people to voice their "strong and unanimous support" for the resolution and their deep hatred of Liu. I concluded that the primary objective of the radical-controlled press was to frighten those who might sympathize with Liu Shaoqi and to silence them. Therefore, while the newspaper gave the impression that the whole nation hated Liu Shaoqi, I knew it was not true, because long ago I had learned how to read the Communist press, like so many of my compatriots. Having lived in China since the Communist Party assumed power, I knew that probably most non–Party members were indifferent because they had no special feelings for either Mao Zedong or Liu Shaoqi, while Party members, except for a small group of Maoists, were doubtless embarrassed by this development because it exposed the ugly nature of Party politics.

When the cold wind again swept down from the north and frosty nights left the iron bars on the window glistening with moisture in the mornings, a "Workers' and Peasants' Propaganda Team for Mao Zedong Thought" came to the No. 1 Detention House to assist the Military Control Commission in conducting the Cultural Revolution. There was no formal announcement of their arrival on the loudspeaker, as there had been when the detention house was placed under military control. However, when the prisoners were given outdoor exercise, I saw strips of colored paper with slogans of welcome pasted on the walls of the prison compound. "The working class must exercise leadership in everything"—a Marxist slogan used by every organization to herald the arrival of a Workers' and Peasants' Propaganda Team—was in prominent display.

A few weeks later, interrogations began again. With hope and expectation I heard the familiar clanging of heavy bolts as prisoners were taken back and forth from their cells. I asked the guard's permission to write a letter to the Workers' and Peasants' Propaganda Team for Mao Zedong Thought, half expecting her to refuse. But to my surprise she handed me a sheet of paper, a pen, and a bottle of ink. I wrote a polite letter requesting investigation of my case, using quotations from Mao's Little Red Book, now the usual practice to demonstrate a writer's correct political standpoint. Every article in the newspaper was sprinkled with them. After I had handed the letter to the guard, I waited for the resumption of my long-interrupted interrogation.

One day, I had another hemorrhage that stained my underclothes. I was washing them when a female guard came to the peephole.

She opened the small window and said to me, "What's happened to you? How did your trousers get stained with blood?"

"It's just my period."

"There's such a lot of blood. Is this normal?" She unlocked the door and came into the cell. The toilet was full of bloody toilet paper I was going to wash down with the water I was using to wash my underclothes.

"Why did you not report your condition?" She stood there

staring at me for a while before leaving the cell and locking the door behind her.

Later, she brought the young doctor, who seemed to have got his job back again.

After asking me my age, the doctor said, "You are probably having your menopause. But you might also have a growth. You should be examined by a gynecologist, but there isn't one at the prison hospital. I'll give you some injections to stop the bleeding."

The injections he gave me were effective. But I was left with the nagging fear that I might have a growth and that the growth might be malignant. More than ever, I was anxious to leave the No. 1 Detention House.

It was a bitterly cold January day in 1969, over two years after my last interrogation at the end of 1966, when things finally started moving for me again.

I was seated on the bed in my usual posture with a volume of Mao's works on my lap when the door of the cell was unlocked and two Labor Reform girls came in. Behind them, the militant female guard who had searched my cell positioned herself in the open doorway, with her hands on her wide hips, watching. Another guard was hovering behind her in the shadows. The Labor Reform girls removed my things from the top of the two stacked beds I was using as a table and placed them on the floor. Then they carried the top bed to the window.

"Pick up your things! Do you think your old servants will come here to pick them up for you?" the militant female guard shouted sarcastically.

While I was putting my things back on the remaining bed, the Labor Reform girls brought in a bedroll and a washbasin. A female prisoner in her early thirties followed them into the cell. She walked in slowly with her head bowed in the manner required of all prisoners, carrying in her hands a few articles of clothing.

The Labor Reform girls withdrew from the cell, and the guard locked the door.

After living in isolation for so long, I was as thirsty for human contact and companionship as a man lost in the desert is thirsty for water. My first reaction to the arrival of another prisoner in my cell was a lightening of spirit and a readiness to show her welcome. But my awareness of the Maoists' fondness for devious practices warned me not to accept the situation at its face value. I returned to my seat and again bent my head over my book while I tried to assess this rather unexpected development. Since military control had been imposed and the Cultural Revolution had entered a new phase, the work of the detention house seemed to have slackened. There was no large influx of new prisoners. In fact, I detected a thinning down of the prison population when I noticed fewer footsteps in the cell overhead during exercise periods. The arrival of another prisoner in my cell did not appear to be due to overcrowding. I waited for events to enlighten me.

The new arrival was arranging her things on the bed, but from time to time she stole glances in my direction, as if hoping to catch my eye.

"How long have you been here already? Is it very bad? Do they beat people?" Finally she came over to sit beside me while she whispered.

I was surprised at the implication of her remarks. She did not look like a newly arrested person fresh from freedom and a full rice bowl. Her face had that unhealthy pallor tinged with gray peculiar to prisoners who have been locked up for quite some time. Her hair was thin, brownish, and dry as straw from lack of protein in her diet, and her clothing hung on her starved body in the same way as mine did. She looked at me with lackluster eyes that were desperate and frightened.

"We mustn't talk. It's not allowed," I told her. I shot a glance at the peephole and caught sight of a black eye before it hastily disappeared from view. It was strange that the guard did not open the small window to scold her when she moved over to sit beside me on my bed, I thought.

When we were given our evening meal, she ate her portion of sweet potatoes very quickly. Seeing that I took only a few pieces to put into my mug to eat, she grabbed the container and tipped the rest into her own. While she was eating, she muttered, "We mustn't waste food."

While I did not object to her having what was left of my portion of sweet potatoes, the episode proved to me beyond doubt that she had been lying when she implied by her initial question that she had just been arrested. She was much too hungry.

If I had been familiar with prison practice, I would have suspected her role immediately. But it was years later that I learned it was a rule of the Security Bureau never to put two prisoners in one cell. The minimum number for multiple cells was three because the prison authorities believed that it was more difficult for three prisoners to conspire together than for two.

I sat on my bed waiting to see what she was going to do next. But apart from using my soap and toilet paper, she made no further attempt to speak to me.

Next morning, after the news broadcasts, she again came to sit next to me.

"I just hate this terrible Cultural Revolution, don't you? My home was looted by the detestable Red Guard. Was your home looted too?"

I had heard frequently from the loudspeaker that people were sentenced to long terms of imprisonment just for criticizing the Cultural Revolution and the actions of the Red Guards. I knew such criticism was regarded as an extremely serious offense. It was extraordinary for her to express her feelings so freely, unless, of course, she had been told to do so by the guards as a means of prompting me to agree with her. So I just answered, "You shouldn't complain. Why don't you read Chairman Mao's books rather than just sitting here chatting? If the guard sees us talking to each other, we will be punished."

I looked around the cell and discovered that though she had her own clothes and bedding, she did not have a set of Mao's books. Since the beginning of the Cultural Revolution, Mao's books had become an essential part of every Chinese, as important as his shirt or trousers and just as necessary, because having or not having Mao's books was taken as a test of political reliability. Besides, I remembered that one of the prison rules I had been told to read aloud when I arrived at the detention house stipulated that every prisoner must study Mao's books. How could she have been brought to prison without them? The only explanation seemed to be that she had been removed from another cell rather hastily into mine. There hadn't been time to gather up all her things. That was probably why she had been obliged to use my soap and toilet paper the night before.

"Where are your books by Chairman Mao? Did they not make you bring them with you when you were brought to the detention house? How could they have overlooked that?" I exclaimed.

me:

Her face went red. I offered to lend her mine, but she pushed them away.

"I don't want to read his books. I hate him. He destroyed my home. I think the Kuomintang was a great deal better than the Communist Party, don't you?"

Instinctively my eyes went to the peephole. No one was watching us. It was such a serious offense to praise the Kuomintang that I was more than ever convinced that she had been given a mandate to do so by the militant guard, probably a Maoist activist anxious to incriminate me. I said, "You mustn't talk wildly. I may report you, you know."

But she ignored my caution and continued to try to make me talk. "Were you not living in Shanghai before 1949? Wasn't the Kuomintang much better?" she persisted.

"I really have no idea what life was like before 1949. I was abroad," I said.

"How lucky for you to have lived abroad! I hate living in China under the Communist Party! We have no freedom at all. Don't you hate the Communist Party?" She tried again.

"I'm a Christian. A Christian is supposed only to love and never to hate anybody. We even forgive those who have wronged us," I told her.

I could see she was skeptical that I could forgive those who had wronged me, because she smiled in a rather supercilious manner. Then, perhaps to gain my confidence, she suddenly declared, "I'm also a Christian!"

"That's good! Let's say the Lord's Prayer together. 'Our Father who art in heaven . . .'" She did not join in but looked completely lost.

"You shouldn't pretend to be a Christian when you are not," I said. "But never mind, I'll teach you the Lord's Prayer."

She shook her head, missing the opportunity to report me for spreading religious propaganda. I realized she did not have the intelligence to know that the Maoists who sent her would have been just as pleased to catch me teaching her the Lord's Prayer as to catch me saying derogatory things about the Communist Party. While the Communist Party claimed to allow the Chinese people religious freedom, to spread religious propaganda, that is, to talk about religion or to teach religious rites, was strictly forbidden even before the Cultural Revolution. Since the begin-

ning of the Cultural Revolution, the penalty for religious ob-
servance in any form was very severe. Almost the first act of the
Red Guards was the destruction of all temples and churches and
the punishment of nuns and monks.

In the afternoon, the same tough female guard unlocked the
door and called my cellmate's number. "Come out for interrogation!" she yelled.

I waited rather anxiously to see what would happen when they
found that she had failed to incriminate me. After a couple of
hours, she came back, wiping her eyes as if she had been crying.
The sight of a tearful person always upset me; I was sorry she
had to suffer because I had refused to fall into their trap. But I
refrained from trying to comfort her, for I did not want to give
her the opportunity of tricking me into saying something inadvertent. I expected her to try again. But I was surprised to find
that she showed no more interest in talking to me.

For the whole of the next day, she did not try to engage me
in conversation but looked out of the window as if lost in
thought. However, a couple of times when she thought I was
absorbed in reading, I caught her looking in my direction.

In the afternoon, she was called for interrogation again, and
again she came back wiping her eyes. This went on for three
successive days. On the fourth day, she did not come back.
When the woman from the kitchen came to give us our evening
meal, she gave me only one container of sweet potatoes. When
I asked her for another for my roommate, the woman merely
shook her head. However, I kept some of my sweet potatoes for
her in my mug.

The loudspeaker was switched on. One guard followed by
another came to my small window to make sure I was seated and
ready to listen to the broadcast. An announcement was made of
the sentences passed that afternoon on a number of prisoners.
One death sentence was declared "carried out immediately."
The number of the prisoner was the same as that of the girl who
had shared my cell. The announcer said that she had been a spy
for the imperialists and the Kuomintang, "hidden in our midst"
for many years but uncovered by the Red Guards and the Revolutionaries during the Cultural Revolution. She had been given
the opportunity to confess and to earn lenient treatment, but
she did not confess because she had hoped "to slip through."

Now she had been punished by "the iron fist of the Dictatorship of the Proletariat," which had "crushed her to powder."

My first reaction was one of shock; the announcement of any death sentence was rather terrifying. I raised my head and caught sight of an eye glued to the peephole observing me. Like lightning, the realization struck me that she was neither a spy for anybody nor had she ever been accused of being one. If I should show fear or nervousness at the announcement, the Maoists would interpret it as a sign of guilt. I stared straight at the door as if I were listening carefully to the broadcast while leaning against my bedroll in a relaxed posture.

When the loudspeaker was switched off, the guard opened the small window and called me over.

"Did you hear the announcement of the death sentence?" she asked.

"Yes."

"What do you think of the case of your former cellmate?"

"Since she was a spy for the imperialists and the Kuomintang, she deserved to die," I said casually.

"You should consider her fate in relation to your own position," the guard pointed out.

"I don't see the connection. She was a real spy. I'm not. I expect the People's Government to clarify my case and give me full rehabilitation in due course," I answered.

"You are not being realistic."

"I don't agree. What could be more realistic than to trust the People's Government?"

She closed the small window but remained at the peephole to watch me. I picked up one of Mao's books and sat down at my usual place on the bed, calmly reading.

Just before bedtime, the militant female guard opened the door of the cell. The Labor Reform girls came in and removed my former cellmate's things. They stacked the beds up again and left. This indicated that the girl was indeed alive. It was a bitterly cold night. The girl needed her quilt if she was not to freeze. They had to come to get it for her.

Since the guards had trusted her enough to let her undertake the task of trying to incriminate me, she must have been a prisoner they felt they could control and manipulate at will. She was probably promised some favor if she was successful in getting me to say something wrong. When she failed, they changed their tactics and pretended to sentence her to death in order to frighten me.

After the Labor Reform girls had left the cell, the militant female guard came in.

"Stand up!" she shouted threateningly, standing only a foot or so away from me.

When I stood up, she slapped my cheek with the back of her hand. The sting brought tears to my eyes, but I blinked them back. I just stood there looking straight ahead as if nothing had happened and she weren't there. This seemed to infuriate her further. She slapped me again and kicked my leg with her heavy boot.

"Remain standing! You are being punished. You are smart, aren't you? The imperialists trained you well, didn't they? Well, you won't get away with it. The proletariat is going to destroy you. Remain standing!"

She banged the heavy door shut, locked it, and stumped down the corridor to the exit of the women's prison.

After the night guard came, she made her routine check of each cell. When she came to me, she asked, "Why are you standing here?"

"I'm being punished by the other guard."

"Which guard? The one on day duty?"

"No, another one."

"You are imagining things. Go to bed!"

She did not seem to be in the picture at all. Perhaps the scheme to trap me was the work of only a few Maoists in the detention house. "I'll never know the truth," I said to myself. But I was glad I did not have to stand there all night.

One of the kicks had landed on my ankle, which was unprotected by my padded trousers. The bruise was throbbing, and the skin was broken. The woolen socks I was wearing were not very clean; my only other pair hadn't dried in the damp cell. I was afraid the bruise might get infected. "What to do?" I asked myself while my eyes searched the bare cell and my meager belongings. When I saw the tube of toothpaste, I decided it might contain some ingredients that were antiseptic. So I smeared a thin layer of toothpaste over the wound and laid on it a piece of cloth torn from an old shirt. Then I tied my ankle up with the only handkerchief I had left.

My ankle was so painful that I had a restless night, waking

frequently from fragments of dreams in which I was either crippled and unable to move or was being kicked again and again by the same female guard.

The misery of hunger and cold, the interminable days of waiting, the persistent yearning for freedom, the nagging worry for my daughter, and this latest abuse by the female guard produced the cumulative effect of making me very angry. When I got out of bed next morning, I was no longer depressed; I felt as if something inside me were about to explode. I told myself that in my present circumstances such civilized virtues as tolerance, forgiveness, and even a sense of humor were luxuries I could ill afford. The Maoists were deadly serious in their design to destroy me. I must be equally serious in my efforts to frustrate them.

Although I was tired because of lack of sleep, I was wide awake. My ankle was swollen and painful, but I paced the cell restlessly in urgent strides, impatient to seek an encounter with the Maoists. The more I thought of what Mao Zedong was doing to me, my friends, and a multitude of unknown fellow sufferers, the angrier I got. I swore I would hit back at the Maoists somehow.

Suddenly the cell door opened. It was almost as if God had speedily granted me my wish for an encounter with the Maoists. "Come out for interrogation!" a male guard shouted.

I picked up Mao's Little Red Book of quotations with alacrity and followed him down the corridor, limping hurriedly to keep up with him.

The loudspeaker was broadcasting a lead article from the *People's Daily* explaining Mao's latest directive: "Dig deep tunnels, store grain everywhere, and never seek hegemony." The announcer's reverent tone of voice followed me from loudspeaker to loudspeaker as I followed the guard through the prison compound. While I listened to the words of homage to Mao, I remembered Mao's awesome power, like a blanket over China threatening to smother whomsoever he chose. I reminded myself to be careful not to say anything that could be interpreted as opposition to Mao, the Communist Party, or the People's Government. If I did, I would become a "counterrevolutionary" and the Maoists would have won a victory over me. My tactics must be to insist that the officials in charge of my case were mistaken in their understanding of Mao's policy though the policy itself was correct. If necessary, I would lie and declare that I supported Mao, even revered him, as so many other Chinese were doing daily in order to survive. To fight was not enough; I must fight well and intelligently, I warned myself.

A heavy quilted curtain of blue cotton covered the entrance to the interrogation building. The guards were no longer lolling on chairs in the small room at the entrance. They stood to attention, while armed soldiers patrolled the corridor. Several blue-uniformed men went in and out of the interrogation rooms, which had their doors open. It seemed the day's work had just begun and I was among the first to be called. Remembering what had happened the night before, I knew I was going to have an unpleasant encounter. The Maoists had hoped to trick me into saying something wrong and to frighten me. They had failed. While I cautioned myself to be alert and to be brave, I was eager to hear what they had to say. Whatever it was, they would reveal themselves to me. The more they revealed themselves to me, the more chance I would have of finding out what they really wanted of me and why. There was still much in the situation that was puzzling to me.

The guard opened the door of one of the rooms and shouted, "Go in!"

The walls of the interrogation room had been whitewashed; it was a bit brighter and much cleaner. On either side of the window were two long banners made of red cloth. Written on them in white paint were two slogans: "Long Live the Dictatorship of the Proletariat" and "Long Live Our Great Leader Chairman Mao." A large reproduction of the official portrait of Mao was on the wall.

Five men, one of them in army uniform, were seated facing the door. I tried to assess their background and status. Since the abolition of military insignia by Defense Minister Lin Biao in 1963, all military personnel wore similar baggy, loose-fitting uniforms in a revival of the old guerrilla tradition. It was difficult to identify the rank of the round-faced young man sitting astride a chair in the gloomy interrogation room, but I saw his uniform had four pockets. This indicated that he was an officer, as soldiers were allowed only two pockets on their jackets. The other four wore the usual faded blue Mao suits. One was much older than the others. His face was deeply lined, and the hands resting on top of the table were the calloused hands of an industrial worker. I assumed that the young man in uniform represented the Military Control Commission, the older worker and perhaps one or two of the others represented the Workers' and Peasants' Propaganda Team for Mao Zedong Thought, and one might be the representative of the Revolutionaries who had taken over the Public Security Bureau of Shanghai.

As I looked at the five men in the room, I knew that they were all beneficiaries of the Communist Revolution of 1949. Their attitude towards Mao Zedong and the Communist Party could not be expected to be the same as mine. I knew also that the old worker probably had only bad memories of the days before the Communist Party came to power, and the others were hardly old enough to have any clear memories at all. Therefore, I could expect them to see me, the widow of an official of the former regime and the daughter of an affluent family, as an enemy. Furthermore, because China had closed her doors since 1949 and isolated herself from the Western world, I knew that whatever these men knew of the West was simply the repeated criticism of capitalism and imperialism fed them through official propaganda, including virulent attacks against the Western nations in general and the United States in particular during the Korean War and the recent fighting in Vietnam. My heart sank at the formidable task of having to break down this iron wall of prejudice and ignorance. If I wanted to walk out of the No. 1 Detention House free and cleared of the accusation against me, I had to try.

After entering the room, I stood beside the prisoner's chair, holding the Little Red Book in my hand, waiting for them to tell me which quotation to read. The interrogator indicated Mao's portrait on the wall with a wave of his arm. "Bow to our Great Leader Chairman Mao and apologize to him for your crime!" he said.

Apologize to Mao for my crime? I decided to use this opportunity to show resistance and disrupt their procedure. "I have not committed any crime. I can't apologize for something I haven't done," I replied, remaining upright.

"What! You have the audacity to refuse to bow to our Great Leader! How dare you! Everybody in China bows to the portrait of our Great Leader morning and night. You dare to refuse?" the interrogator shouted sternly, half rising from his chair. The others glared at me with astonishment and disapproval. For the first time that morning I felt really good.

"You misunderstood me. I merely said that I haven't committed any crime. I can't apologize for something I haven't done. I did not say I would not bow to Chairman Mao's portrait. I can bow to his portrait to show my respect for him, of course." I spoke in a calm voice as I became more relaxed.

"Do it, then! What are you waiting for?" the interrogator shouted and sat down again.

I bowed to the portrait. My resistance was not in vain; at subsequent sessions no one mentioned apologizing for my crime anymore. Whenever I entered the interrogation room, the interrogator merely waved his arm in the direction of the portrait without speaking.

The quotation the interrogator chose was the same one I had read before. It was a much-used favorite of the Cultural Revolution. " 'When the enemies with guns are annihilated, the enemies without guns still remain. We must not belittle these enemies,' " I read. Then he asked me to read one about the army. It said, "Without the People's Army, the people would have nothing." The frequent use of this quotation at this period of the Cultural Revolution reflected the ascendancy of the military and of Defense Minister Lin Biao in the power structure of the Party.

I sat down in the prisoner's chair. In front of me, a few feet away, was the outside panel of the counter behind which the interrogator sat. It was now painted white. Freshly written on it in large characters was "Lenient treatment for those who confess; severe punishment for those who remain stubborn." On either side of the official portrait on the wall were other messages urging the prisoners to confess.

I heard the small window behind me slide open softly and saw the interrogator look over my shoulder and give a barely perceptible nod before speaking.

"You wrote a letter requesting an interview with the Workers' Propaganda Team. Are you now ready to give a full confession?"

"I requested the Workers' Propaganda Team to investigate

my case and clear me of the false accusation against me. I understand that the Workers' Propaganda Teams represent Chairman Mao. I expect you to implement the correct policy of Chairman Mao of distinguishing the innocent from the guilty. I have been held here for over two years already. Isn't that long enough for an innocent person to be incarcerated in a detention house?"

"You have been here more than two years already, but your attitude has not improved. You are still hoping to slip away. Don't you realize that a great victory has been won by the Proletarian Revolutionaries? The situation is now very different from the time of your last interrogation. Did you not hear the announcement of the resolution passed by the Central Committee against Liu Shaoqi? Even he could not slip through the net of the Proletarian Revolutionaries. What hope have you of escaping?"

"I have nothing to hide. All I request is that you get at the facts," I said.

"We'll get at the facts about you just as we did about Liu Shaoqi. He was the agent of the imperialists abroad, the Kuomintang in Taiwan, and the capitalist class in China. He was the number one capitalist-roader and the backstage boss of all of you. Now you should understand fully that the whole intrigue to destroy socialism in China is exposed and defeated."

"Who wanted to destroy socialism in China? I don't know what you are talking about," I told him.

"All of you who belong to the capitalist class are actual or potential agents of the imperialists and the Kuomintang. Liu Shaoqi and his clique were hidden agents who infiltrated the leadership of the Communist Party," the interrogator said.

His argument was so absurd and the accusation against Liu Shaoqi was so ridiculous that I felt disgusted. Mao Zedong and the other radical leaders insulted the intelligence of the Chinese people when they expected them to believe the Central Committee resolution against Liu Shaoqi. Furthermore, I looked upon these men seated in front of me with contempt because they were obviously cowardly enough to want to be a part of Mao's despicable scheme against Liu Shaoqi. My one wish at that moment was to irritate them. Pretending to be stupid, I said, "I always had the greatest respect for Chairman Liu Shaoqi. I'm not at all sure he is really guilty of the charge against him. Perhaps there was some mistake. It's well known that he fought against the imperialists, the Kuomintang, and the capitalist class and risked his life doing so."

I was pleased to see that my seemingly innocent remarks had the effect of a bombshell. All of them stood up and shouted at me, "How dare you defend a traitor to the Communist Party! How dare you oppose the Central Committee resolution! How dare you oppose our Great Leader Chairman Mao!"

They were behaving as required by their position as representatives of the Revolutionaries, but strangely, only one of the younger workers and the military officer appeared really angry. The other three were staring at me with curiosity and amusement, definitely not anger or disapproval. I thought they looked quite pleased to hear me defend Liu Shaoqi and surprised that someone who was supposed to be opposed to the Communist Party could feel so strongly about their deposed leader.

Intrigued by the discovery that among the seemingly ardent supporters of the radicals there were some who harbored sympathy for Liu Shaoqi, I decided to prolong this dialogue a bit further. "I do not oppose the Central Committee resolution, and I do not oppose Chairman Mao. Who would dare to do that? I merely suggested that the evidence against Chairman Liu Shaoqi might not be completely reliable," I said.

"Shut up! You are not allowed to refer to a traitor as 'chairman,'" the young worker shouted vehemently. The interrogator was gazing at the paper in front of him, and so was the man taking notes. The old worker seemed to be enjoying the situation. The ghost of a smile hovered at the corners of his mouth.

"You are not allowed to refer to somebody denounced by the Central Committee as 'chairman,'" said the interrogator.

"I did it from habit," I said. "For sixteen years, in the newspapers, in daily broadcasts, and in books published by the government printing press, Chairman Liu . . ." I paused when I caught sight of the interrogator glaring and saw the young worker stand up.

"Liu Shaoqi," I continued, "was always presented to the Chinese people as a revolutionary hero who had made a tremendous contribution to many aspects of the work of the Communist Party, including the development of the Party apparatus and the education of its members. I have found in Chairman Mao's books several complimentary references to Liu Shaoqi. It's so difficult to turn around now and think of him as totally bad. Perhaps he has just made a mistake. If that is the case, I hope Chairman Mao will forgive him. After all, they were close comrades for many years."

"You are dreaming! Chairman Mao will never forgive him!" the young worker said.

"Well, the outside world must be laughing at us now. How could such an important man who was chairman of the Chinese People's Republic suddenly be discovered to have been a traitor all these decades? It's incredible that he could have fooled all the other leaders, including the Great and Wise Leader Chairman Mao himself. It just doesn't make sense. Doesn't this make Chairman Mao lose face too?" I asked them.

"We don't care what the imperialists and capitalists in other countries say. They don't have anything good to say about us anyhow. What happens in China is none of their business," the young worker replied heatedly. "To defend Liu Shaoqi is a criminal offense. He's a counterrevolutionary and so are you!"

"I'm not a counterrevolutionary, that I know. I'm a supporter of the People's Government and the Communist Party. I have the greatest respect for our Great Leader Chairman Mao. I challenge you to produce concrete facts to prove that I have ever done anything or said anything against the People's Government or the Communist Party," I said calmly but firmly.

"You think you can slip away through bluffing. That's the game you are playing. Who do you think you are to challenge the People's Government? Even if you have never committed any crime, you are still just a dirty exploiter who has lived all her life on the blood and sweat of the laboring class. In any case, we have irrefutable evidence that you are a spy for the imperialists," the interrogator declared, and he banged the table.

I got so angry and disgusted with them that I marched up and banged the table right in front of him. All of them stood up, surprised by my action.

The soldier pulled his revolver from its holster. Pointing the gun at me, he shouted, "What do you think you are doing?"

I stood in the middle of the room and faced him squarely. I said, "You may shoot me if you can prove me guilty with concrete evidence." There was stunned silence in the room as we confronted each other.

"Quiet! Quiet! You are a hysterical woman given to mad fits, I have heard already. Try to control yourself. Go back to your chair. If you dare to get out of that chair again, I'll have you chained to it." The interrogator raised his arm to order me back to the prisoner's chair. The soldier pushed his gun into its holster while he continued to glare at me.

During the commotion, the only one who remained calm was the old worker. He looked at me with an expression akin to sympathy. Perhaps he was beginning to realize that I could really be innocent.

I returned to the prisoner's chair and sat down. The interrogator assumed an air of gravity and gave me a few words of education.

"To defend someone denounced in a resolution of the Central Committee of the Communist Party is a very serious offense. On that account alone I could sentence you to several years of imprisonment. But in consideration of the extenuating circumstance of your having had no opportunity to follow developments of the Cultural Revolution, so that your understanding has not caught up with events, we will overlook your mistake this time.

"The Revolutionaries under the leadership of our Great Helmsman Chairman Mao are determined to expose all hidden enemies of socialism in our midst, no matter how senior their rank or how cleverly they are disguised. You should have no doubt on this point. You must cast away your illusions and realize you cannot escape," the interrogator said.

"I understand the situation perfectly. And I think it quite right to punish the real enemy. But you should not mistake for enemies innocent people who have not opposed the People's Government. I request you to make a thorough investigation of my case. If you should find real evidence that I have lied and I have indeed committed crimes against the People's Government or the Communist Party, you can give me the death penalty. But if you find that I am indeed innocent, the People's Government must apologize to me and you must have the apology published in the newspaper for everyone to see," I said with sincerity.

"You want an apology?" the young worker sneered. "Who do

you think you are? You have an inflated idea of your own importance."

"All men are equal in the eyes of the law. Although I am not an official, I'm a citizen of this country."

"You have just repeated a statement of the revisionists. No wonder you defended Liu Shaoqi. He was truly your backstage boss. Men are not equal. Men are divided into conflicting classes. The victorious class imposes its will on the vanquished class. As long as there are classes, there cannot be true equality," the interrogator said.

"Do you mean to say that you will ignore the law and punish an innocent person simply because that person is a member of the bourgeois class?"

"Why not? If it's necessary to punish somebody, we will certainly do so. The bourgeois class is our enemy. We hope to reeducate most of its members and make them labor for their food. Those who resist and oppose us will certainly be eliminated. In any case, the victorious proletarian class makes the law to suit its purpose and to serve its interest."

"Well, that seems to simplify matters greatly. Since you have already classified me as a member of the bourgeois class and I'm too old and weak to labor for my food, why not just shoot me and be done with it? Why waste time having an interrogation?"

"We want you to confess because others are involved. You yourself are of no importance. We couldn't care less whether you are dead or alive," the interrogator said with an air of indifference.

He said others were involved. Whom did he mean? I became more than ever puzzled at the situation in which I found myself.

"Who is involved? Do you mean the ex–staff members of the Shanghai office of Shell?"

"No, of course not! They are completely unimportant, like you. We are interested in those who made it possible for you and others like you to undermine the security of China on behalf of the imperialists."

"Who do you mean? Do you mean Liu Shaoqi? I assure you I have never met him."

"Liu Shaoqi was one of them. But he doesn't matter anymore. There are others who are still raising the red flag to oppose the red flag. They are yet to be exposed. It's their policy which made it possible for you to carry on your dirty work against China on behalf of the imperialists."

How incredible! It seemed that their persecution of me and the denunciation of Shell was not simply due to their antiforeign attitude or their adherence to the principles of class struggle. The problem was much more complicated than I had thought. Their targets, I saw, were the Party officials whose policy permitted foreign companies to operate in China. If they could make me and others like me confess to being foreign spies, they could claim that allowing foreign firms to operate in China was providing a safe haven for the intelligence activities of foreign agents. Whether I liked it or not, I was a pawn in the struggle between the two irreconcilable policies of the Communist Party. When I argued and fought back, I was defending some officials in the Communist Party whom I did not know and who did not know me. This bizarre situation was too ridiculous! It was like a surrealist painting, understandable only to the initiated.

The voice of the interrogator cut short my speculations. "Now, cast your mind back to 1949, just before the People's Liberation Army took over Shanghai. Under what circumstances did the Kuomintang order your husband to remain in Shanghai? Did they order him to work his way into the People's Government and undermine it from within?"

"My husband stayed in Shanghai because he hoped the People's Government would rescue China from economic chaos and political confusion after so many years of war and build a strong and prosperous country for all the Chinese people. Both my husband and I were idealistic and ignorant. We knew nothing of class struggle. Essays written by Chairman Mao were being circulated in Shanghai by the Communist Party underground. Our friends who were professors at various universities gave them to us to read. None of these essays mentioned class struggle. Chairman Mao talked about the formation of a united front and cooperation with all patriotic Chinese," I pointed out.

"That was the correct policy at that time. It was meant to win the support of the bourgeois class and to undermine the Kuomintang. After the Kuomintang was successfully overthrown, naturally that policy was no longer needed. In every circumstance, we unite the lesser enemies to fight the major enemy. When the major enemy is overcome, one of the lesser enemies will become the new major enemy. So the struggle goes on. That's dialectical materialism."

There was nothing for me to say. The interrogator had put the philosophy of Mao's regime in a nutshell. It was entirely my own fault that I had not understood it before. After a moment, the interrogator asked, "Did your husband discuss his plan to remain in China with anyone? Perhaps he discussed it with some of his foreign friends?"

"No, it was entirely his own idea. Early in 1949, my daughter and I were in Hong Kong. My husband asked us to come back to Shanghai. After my return, he told me that he had decided to remain in China. It seemed he was influenced by his old university friends in the Democratic League. As you know, the Democratic League supported and cooperated closely with the Communist Party and helped to foster friendly feelings for the Party among intellectuals and Kuomintang officials with a liberal outlook. I knew quite a number of intellectuals who decided to remain in China at that time because of the efforts of the leading members of the Democratic League."

"The Democratic League was an instrument of the American imperialists. Its leaders wanted to establish parliamentary democracy in China and share political power with the Communist Party. They were absurd dreamers with absurd ideas. Without an army, what can politicians achieve? In 1957, during the Anti-Rightist Campaign, most of the league's leaders were exposed as rightists. They deserved it."

"They did render service to the Communist Party in 1949," I reminded the interrogator. The fate of the leaders of the Democratic League was a chilling example of Mao's habit of using people and then ruthlessly discarding them when they were no longer needed.

"Circumstances changed . . ." The interrogator started to explain dialectical materialism again.

"I understand. It's another case of the application of the theory of dialectical materialism to real life," I said hastily to save myself from another lecture.

"It's our conclusion that your husband remained in Shanghai under orders from the Kuomintang and the imperialists in order to infiltrate the Ministry of Foreign Affairs of the People's Government."

"Zhang Hanfu, who later became vice-minister of Foreign Affairs in Beijing, was the man who took over my husband's office in Shanghai when the Liberation Army came into the city. When he was about to go to Beijing to take up his new appointment as vice-minister, he asked my husband to join the People's Government and go with him to work at the Ministry of Foreign Affairs. My husband refused Zhang Hanfu's invitation. If my husband had wanted to infiltrate the Ministry of Foreign Affairs, why did he refuse to go to Beijing in 1950?"

While I was answering him, I was thinking of the few former Kuomintang diplomats who did go to Beijing to join the Communist Ministry of Foreign Affairs. A former ambassador to Burma was imprisoned as a counterrevolutionary. All the others suffered persecution during one political campaign or another. I used to feel deeply thankful that my late husband had refused Zhang Hanfu's invitation.

"Zhang Hanfu is a member of the dirty Liu Shaoqi clique. When he was arrested by the Kuomintang before Liberation, he betrayed Communist Party secrets. He is now under arrest." I was shocked by this revelation because I knew Zhang Hanfu was a follower of Prime Minister Zhou Enlai.

"The fact remains that he was vice-minister of Foreign Affairs when he invited my late husband to go to Beijing to work at the Ministry of Foreign Affairs of the People's Government. My husband refused. You can check the record. If my husband had wanted to infiltrate the Ministry of Foreign Affairs, would he have refused to join it?"

The point I made was such simple logic that even the interrogator was momentarily at a loss for words. I took the opportunity to settle the issue once and for all.

"In fact, by remaining in Shanghai and not following the Kuomintang to Taiwan, my late husband demonstrated his goodwill towards the Communist Party. He was an official of the Kuomintang government. Yet he disobeyed their orders. It's the Kuomintang in Taiwan who should loot our home and put us in prison. They are powerless to do so. You have done it for them. Now who is acting for the Kuomintang?"

Being accused of acting for the Kuomintang was an intolerable insult to the Revolutionaries. I could see the face of the interrogator turning pale, and the veins on his temple stood out as he tried to control his temper. The soldier stood up and made a gesture of pulling out his revolver again.

"Shut up!" he shouted.

But the old worker said in a conciliatory voice, "It's all right for you to state your point of view. Our Great Leader said, 'Lay out the facts and speak with reason.' We permit you to defend yourself. But you mustn't malign the Revolutionaries and accuse them of acting for the Kuomintang."

The interrogator looked at his watch and whispered something to the others. Then he said to me, "You may go back to your cell now. We'll resume in the afternoon."

I had been called for interrogation before the first of the two daily mealtimes for the prisoners. Now I was hungry and exhausted. When I stood up, the room whirled and everything went black in front of my eyes. I had to steady myself by holding on to the arm of the prisoner's chair. My legs were so wobbly that I did not think I could walk away steadily. But I did not want the men to misinterpret my unsteadiness as a sign of nervousness, so I pointed at my swollen ankle and said, "I want to lodge a protest against a guard who came into my cell and kicked me last night."

"Nonsense!" the interrogator said. "The guards are not allowed to kick or beat prisoners."

"This one certainly did." I hobbled out of the room behind a male guard.

I was famished and feared that I had missed the only meal of rice of the day. The evening meal of potatoes always caused me indigestion. But while she led me towards my cell, the female guard on duty at the women's prison told me that my portion of rice was being kept warm for me. "If you want, I can give you some hot water to drink," she said.

Even though she was one of the nicer guards whom I always thought of as the "mild" ones, such humane consideration was unheard of. I found the container of rice and cabbage wrapped in a towel and a blanket. It was not yet completely cold. The guard came to the small window with her thermos of hot water and poured a generous amount into my mug. I sat down on the edge of the bed to eat my rice while trying to sort out the impressions of the morning.

The interrogator was definitely the best educated and most

intelligent of those five men. Judging by his air of self-confidence, I thought he must be a seasoned Party official. Whether he was a true Maoist or not I couldn't tell. But he was certainly acceptable to the Maoists, because he had been given the job as interrogator. The old worker was not a true Maoist. I thought he had probably been chosen because he was an old industrial worker of many years' standing, the sort of man put on the Workers' Propaganda Teams for cosmetic purposes. The young man who took notes appeared indifferent. He merely participated as a secretary; that was probably his job. I detected no real annoyance in his voice or in his expression when I spoke up for Liu Shaoqi. The young worker and the military man were the true Maoists. They looked and behaved like Mao Zedong–era young people from poor family backgrounds who had received so much political indoctrination that they had completely lost the ability to think for themselves.

The behavior of the guard on duty at the women's prison was the most strange. What had I done that morning to earn her goodwill? That was the question I puzzled over as I chewed the tough cabbage leaves. The only thing I had done that could be considered unusual was speaking my few words in defense of poor Liu Shaoqi. Did she reward me because I had said what she thought but could not say because of her position as a prison guard?

Personal relations had always been important to the Chinese, in a tradition that dated back thousands of years. The Communists were no exception. When a Communist leader fell from grace, all those who had ever worked with him were disgraced, no matter how remote the connection. Since the entire Public Security Bureau had been denounced by the Maoists, there must exist in the No. 1 Detention House a number of men and women whose fate was linked to that of Liu Shaoqi and who would be sympathetic to him. If my defending Liu Shaoqi would earn me better treatment and more humane consideration, it was worth doing. To improve my chance of physical survival must be my primary concern. However, this was a situation I had not anticipated when I impulsively defended Liu Shaoqi because my sense of justice was outraged.

When I was called to the interrogation room again in the afternoon, the interrogator waved his arm towards Mao's portrait. I bowed. Then he selected the following quotation for me to read: "All reactionaries are paper tigers. Superficially the reactionary clique looks strong, but in actuality the reactionary clique does not have great strength."

After I had finished, the interrogator said, "You may go on with your account. Describe the circumstances under which your husband joined the British spy organization."

"My husband never joined any spy organization. Shell is an international oil company of good repute," I said.

"Its Shanghai office was a spy organization."

"It was not."

The interrogator took a stack of papers from under the counter and started to read in silence while the two workers watched me closely. Every now and then, when the interrogator turned a page, he would look at me and shake his head disapprovingly as if he had found something about me that shocked him. I knew he was acting, and the paper he was pretending to read might be about astrology for all I knew, so I assumed a blank expression and quietly waited for the interrogator to speak again.

After a while he laid the papers down and said, "The other members of your staff are more enlightened than you are. They know where their interests lie. They have already confessed everything." He pointed to the papers and continued, "These are some of their confessions. The ones written by the various heads of departments, including your ex-chief accountant, give very interesting details of the spy activities of your office."

"All right, then. Since you have got what you wanted, why bother to press me to make a false confession?" I said.

"Each of you must speak for himself."

"If you want me to speak, I can tell only the truth. Shell is a trading firm. It has nothing to do with politics. Shell was in China because Shell wanted to develop trade with China. In any case, it was here in Shanghai because the People's Government allowed it to be here. Both my late husband and myself were given the impression by the officials we dealt with that the People's Government encouraged Shell to maintain an office in Shanghai."

"Exactly. The capitalist-roaders in the Communist Party tried to shield a foreign spy organization. It's obvious," the interrogator said.

"I advise you to be careful about what you are saying. It was the State Council that gave permission for Shell to remain in China."

What I did not mention was that the order permitting Shell to retain its head office in Shanghai had been signed by Prime Minister Zhou Enlai. The interrogator must have been aware of this. I couldn't help wondering whether Prime Minister Zhou was one of the leaders the Maoists hoped to topple next. But they would never dare to come out with an accusation openly as long as Zhou remained the prime minister.

"Shell is a multinational corporation. As such, according to Marxism, it is the worst form of capitalist enterprise. It exploits the working class of many countries. Politically such companies are invariably the most anti-Communist and reactionary. It should never have been allowed to remain in China after Liberation," the interrogator said.

"I don't agree with you. I think it was an extremely clever and subtle move to allow a British oil company to remain in China when the United States was imposing an oil embargo against China. It created dissension in the enemy camp. What could be more clever than that? I understand from reading Chairman Mao's books that he advocates creating dissension and friction among the enemies as an effective tactic of class struggle," I said.

The young worker joined in. "Our Great Leader Chairman Mao taught us to be self-reliant. We do not need foreign companies."

"Our Great Leader Chairman Mao said, 'We do not refuse foreign aid, but we rely chiefly on our own strength.' He did not rule out accepting aid from friendly sources."

"You cannot classify trading with a company like Shell as aid from a friendly source," the interrogator said.

"For years Shell did not trade with Taiwan or maintain an office there. What could be more friendly to the People's Government than that?"

"You certainly have a glib tongue. First you defended Liu Shaoqi. Now you defend a reactionary multinational organization. Even if you have never committed any other crime, what you have said in this interrogation room today is enough for us to pass sentence on you," said the interrogator.

"Everything I have said is the truth. Everything you have said is just wild accusation based on imagination. Yet you are supposed to be an enlightened Revolutionary representing the People's Government and the Communist Party, and I'm merely a backward old woman."

Angered by my remark, the interrogator banged the table again. "You are forgetting yourself! This is the interrogation room of the Dictatorship of the Proletariat!"

"Stand up! Stand up! Remain standing! You must be punished for showing contempt for the Dictatorship of the Proletariat," the young worker joined in excitedly.

I stood up.

"Give an account of the circumstances in which your husband joined the British spy organization," the interrogator said.

"If you put it like that, I simply cannot answer you."

"You are very careful, aren't you? The imperialists trained you well, didn't they? You do not concede a single point," said the interrogator.

The old worker said, "Answer the question the interrogator asked you. We'll leave the matter of 'spy organization' aside for the time being."

"Exactly! Conclusion should come after investigation. That's what Chairman Mao taught us also. He said, 'Without investigation, you have no right to speak,' " I told them.

The interrogator banged the table again and shouted, "Did we ask you to lecture us? You are impertinent. You seem to forget that you are a prisoner and we are the representatives of the People's Government."

"I expect the representatives of the People's Government to be reasonable, to abide by the law, and to get at the truth of my case," I said.

"That's exactly what we are trying to do. But you refuse to confess."

"It would be irresponsible of me to make a false confession. I do not believe a false confession serves the interest of the government or anybody else. It would only create confusion. I have never done anything against the law. To help you ascertain the true facts, I will be glad to answer any question you may wish to ask me. I'll speak the truth. If I lie and try to cover up, you may punish me severely. In fact, I'll gladly sign a statement to that effect, if you will give me a sheet of paper."

After checking with the interrogator, the secretary held out a sheet of paper to me. I walked up to the counter and wrote down the following: "I am a patriotic Chinese and a law-abiding citizen. I've never done anything against the People's Government. If the investigators of the People's Government should ever find anybody in the whole of China from whom I have tried to obtain information of a confidential nature, I'm prepared to accept the death penalty. At the end of the investigation of my case, when I am found to be completely innocent, the People's Government must give me full rehabilitation, including an apology to be published in the newspaper."

I signed my name and wrote down the date before handing the paper over to the interrogator. He read it and passed it on to the others. The old worker took out his reading glasses, carefully wiped the lenses, and put them on. He read my pledge while nodding with approval. Pointing to the chair for the prisoner, the old worker said to me, "Sit down, sit down!"

Both the soldier and the young worker refused to read my pledge. The young worker said with a sneer, "You are just bluffing like a poker player!"

The interrogator handed my pledge to the secretary, who stored it in a folder.

"In what circumstances did your husband become the general manager of the Shanghai office of Shell?" the interrogator asked.

"To invite a national of the country in which it operated to be general manager was a policy adopted by Shell after the Second World War," I told them.

"Was it not because they believed that being a Chinese national, your husband would be able to obtain information more easily than a British manager?"

"The only advantage my husband had over a British manager was that he did not need an interpreter when he talked with a representative of the Import and Export Corporation of the People's Government."

"Your husband made trips to Hong Kong several times, and both of you went to England and Europe in 1956," the interrogator said. "We are especially interested in your trip to Europe because we know you received instructions from the headquarters of the British intelligence organization."

"You are getting things mixed up. We went to London to visit the head office of Shell. Then we traveled to The Hague for the same purpose, because half of Shell's head office was there. My husband held discussions with the directors about trade prospects in China. The Import and Export Corporation as well as the Chemicals Corporation in Beijing were anxious for him to make the trip. They wanted to purchase many things from Shell. Trade prospects looked promising, and British experts were invited to come to China to help Chinese organizations with research. But soon after we came back the Anti-Rightist Movement was launched. This was followed by the Great Leap Forward Campaign. Everything had to stop. The Beijing officials who were so enthusiastic could no longer make decisions. Shell experts already on their way to China had to turn back. Nothing further could be done."

"How did you obtain your passports? Who gave you permission to go to Europe? Private people are usually not allowed to make trips abroad," the interrogator said.

"My husband applied for our passports at the Foreign Affairs Bureau in Shanghai. We were given permission to go, I suppose, because the government considered his trip useful to China's interest."

I remembered accompanying my husband to Beijing when he was invited by the Import and Export Corporation to discuss the supply of insecticides and chemical fertilizers to China by Shell. Mao Zedong wanted a dramatic increase in China's grain output to prove the superiority of the agricultural cooperatives formed in 1955 as his first step towards the collectivization of agriculture. The day before we were due to return to Shanghai, my husband went to the Import and Export Corporation for a last interview. The man there, with whom he had had pleasant business discussions for a week, informed my husband that our passports were approved and waiting for us at the Foreign Affairs Bureau in Shanghai. Then he added in a confidential manner, "The prime minister personally gave approval to issue you passports." Normally Party officials did not give more than the bare minimum of information when dealing with an outsider like my husband. We thought the official mentioned Prime Minister Zhou's personal approval of our trip to encourage my husband to obtain from Shell in London all the things the corporation wanted.

The interrogator had alleged that our trip to London was "to visit the headquarters of the British intelligence organization to receive instructions." If that had really been the case and I was made to confess to it, the prime minister's approval to issue us passports would have been tantamount to facilitating spy activities, to put it mildly. Was it possible that the Maoists were hoping to cast doubt on Prime Minister Zhou Enlai? The whole thing seemed farfetched and absurd. But the allegations against Liu Shaoqi were equally farfetched and absurd. When the interrogator said that he wanted me to confess because others were involved and that there were officials who were still "raising the red flag to oppose the red flag," could he possibly mean to include Prime Minister Zhou Enlai? I could only speculate. I would probably never know, I said to myself. But I did not think it out of character for either Lin Biao or Mao's wife Jiang Qing to wish Zhou Enlai out of the way. Every Chinese knew that Jiang Qing hated Zhou Enlai. Lin Biao probably considered the prime minister an obstacle to his ambition.

The voice of the interrogator brought me back to the interrogation room again. He was saying, "Your trip was not useful to China's interest."

"The officials my husband saw in Beijing gave him to understand that he would be rendering service to China if he could obtain what China needed from Shell. They also said that trading with foreign countries was beneficial to China," I told him.

"That was the policy of the capitalist-roaders in the Party, and against the teachings of our Great Leader Chairman Mao," the interrogator said.

"You can't expect us outsiders to have known that. To my husband and myself, the People's Government was the government, and the officials representing the government were the people we had to listen to and believe in," I said.

"Give a truthful account of your activities in England and other European countries you visited, and confess what information you divulged."

"My husband visited the offices of Shell in London and in The Hague. He met several directors and others concerned with the Far Eastern area. He also visited factories and installations. We saw some old friends."

"Did you see any British government officials?"

"Yes, some of our friends were diplomats we used to know."

"Did they not ask you about conditions in China?"

"Conditions in China in 1956 and 1957, before the Anti-Rightist Campaign, were very good. We were very happy to tell them about it. For the first time, after many years of war, inflation was brought under control. The first five-year plan was successfully accomplished. People were contented. There was peace. They all knew it."

"There must have been something you told them that they did not know already. You must confess everything," said the interrogator.

"What could we have told them? If you bother to look into our friends and contacts in China, you will find we did not know anybody who could possibly tell us anything of any importance. Since we obviously could not get into a government office to steal documents, everything we knew must have come from our friends. If we did not know anyone who knew anything important, we couldn't tell our British friends anything important, could we?"

"It's not up to you to judge what is important and what's not important. It's up to us to judge. I want you to write a detailed account of your trip to Europe in 1956-57. Give a list of all the people you saw, and put down everything you said to them. We will see if you told them anything that was important."

"It's an impossible task that would serve no purpose. How can I remember every sentence we ever spoke ten years ago? Besides, I was not with my husband when he went to the office or to oil installations and factories. How am I to tell you what he said? And how are you to check what I have written? You can't carry your inquiry to England. What you should do is examine our Chinese contacts to see if we had any possible source of secret information inside China. I can assure you we did not know anybody who could possibly tell us anything that could be interpreted as 'intelligence.'"

"Are you conducting this investigation or am I?" the interrogator asked with irritation.

I knew, of course, that the interrogator hoped to trip me up. A seemingly innocent account could be made to look suspicious if a word was taken out here and a sentence taken out there. And when one is writing about mundane affairs, one is not on guard. So I merely said, "Of course you are the interrogator, and, as you told me yourself, you are the representative of the People's Government. I'll do whatever you say. But it seems a waste of time."

"We do not mind wasting time if we can expose agents of the imperialists. It's our belief that all foreign firms operating in China have double status. They trade to make money because money is God to the capitalists. But they also gather information for their governments.

"The capitalist countries will never give up trying to subvert China because China is a socialist country. We are now powerful. They cannot hope to destroy us by military means. So they pin their hope on internal dissension. All of you trained in their universities or working in their offices are their potential allies. Britain was the first imperialist power to invade China. She still occupies Hong Kong. While she recognizes the People's Government, she votes with the United States at the United Nations to prevent our taking China's seat in that world organization. While the United States is openly supporting the Kuomintang, the British are playing a two-faced game that is more dangerous because people can be fooled by it.

"You exaggerate," I told him.

"You had better not try to defend the British imperialists. That will put you in a worse position than you are in now," said the interrogator.

It was obviously futile to engage him in a debate on international relations. I kept quiet and waited to hear what else he had to say.

"Before you write your confession, you should correct your thinking about Liu Shaoqi. You should realize that the capitalist-roaders are finished. Those who are already exposed will never be able to stage a comeback, and we are going to get at those who are yet to be exposed. Victory belongs to the policy of our Great Leader. So your only way out is to confess everything and come over to the side of the Proletarian Revolutionaries. It would be a big mistake for you to think China might go back to pre–Cultural Revolution days and those of you with foreign connections would again be protected by the capitalist-roaders," the interrogator said.

I was quite pleased with the day's interrogation because I had been given the opportunity to speak and I thought I had clarified several points. Now I decided to use the opening he had given me to defend Liu Shaoqi further. I needed to see whether I was right in thinking that mixed with the Maoists in the detention house there were also a number of Liuists.

Resuming my air of innocent stupidity, I said, "Honestly, I still don't understand what Chairman Liu Shaoqi did wrong and why Chairman Mao wants to punish him. In his books, Chairman Mao praised Chairman Liu in several places. I counted them when I was studying Chairman Mao's books. I do hope Chairman Mao will forgive Chairman Liu Shaoqi. Don't you think that would be best for China and for the Communist Party? Besides, wasn't it Chairman Liu who first used the term 'Mao Zedong Thought' and urged the Party members to study Chairman Mao's books? Surely that showed he did respect Chairman Mao."

"You are not allowed to refer to a traitor as 'chairman'! You are not allowed to defend Liu Shaoqi!" they shouted.

When they had quieted down, I said, "Of course I do not dare to defend Liu Shaoqi if he is really guilty. But I do wonder if the material on which the Central Committee based its judgment was really reliable. You know how people can easily be frightened into making false confessions. I suppose it happens all the time."

I couldn't resist making this dig at them. It was small revenge for the things they were doing to me. Actually what I had said probably touched a sensitive spot. From the traces of fear I saw on each of their faces and from the way they quickly tried to shut me up, I was sure they knew, or at least suspected, that the so-called evidence against Liu Shaoqi was indeed manufactured by the Maoists.

(After Mao's death in September 1976 and the subsequent arrest of his widow Jiang Qing, the people of China were told officially in a Central Committee document just how a special committee set up by Jiang Qing and Defense Minister Lin Biao manufactured the evidence against Liu Shaoqi. The document said that Maoist activists selected by Jiang Qing and Lin Biao rounded up Liu's associates and tortured them to make them provide the necessary false evidence. To prove that they had carried out their assignment faithfully, the activists taped the tortured cries of their victims and played them for Jiang Qing and Lin Biao.)

"Shut up! Shut up! You are a madwoman!" the interrogator shouted, seemingly terrified by my candid remark. He quickly added, "Liu Shaoqi was guilty and you are too!"

"I'm not guilty, that I know for sure. As for Chairman Liu Shaoqi, I have a feeling he is innocent too," I said.

"Shut up! Shut up! Close your lips. You are not allowed to speak again," ordered the interrogator.

I heard a loud noise behind me. This time no attempt was made to soften the sound from the small window behind the prisoner's chair. It seemed that the man listening outside was tired of the game. He shut the small window with a loud bang to show his displeasure. The interrogator hurriedly got up and went out of the room.

When he came back, he did not resume his seat but handed me a roll of writing paper.

"Go back to your cell and write about your trip to England and other European countries. Put down the names of all the people you saw and everything you said to them. Give a full confession."

A guard was already standing in the open doorway. I followed him out.

Hot drinking water had been issued during my absence. It had been kept warm for me, like the rice earlier in the day. Such kindness and consideration were extraordinary. Was I correct in thinking their kindness to me was due to my defense of Liu Shaoqi? Or did the Maoists think I could be moved by gestures of kindness into doing their bidding? Such thoughts were in my mind as I sat on the edge of the bed drinking the hot water. Hot water may mean very little under normal circumstances, but in that prison cell, in the middle of winter, it tasted very good indeed.

Suddenly the small window in the door of the cell was pushed open. The voice of the young doctor said, "Come over!"

"What's the matter with your ankle?" he asked.

What a surprise! I had never heard of the doctor coming to a prisoner without his visit being requested. Often I would hear a prisoner's voice, anxious and urgent, as she repeatedly made a request to see the doctor.

The guard was standing outside. After I had explained that I had a bruise on my ankle that seemed to be inflamed, she opened the door of the cell. The doctor stepped in. He examined my ankle and pressed the swollen flesh.

"No bone is broken. It's just superficial inflammation. I'll give you some bandages and ointment."

Later, the guard on duty handed me a tube of Aureomycin and a roll of bandages. Before I could recover from my surprise at this change in my treatment, I was handed a container of rice and cabbage instead of the usual sweet potatoes for the evening meal. When I returned the container and chopsticks to the woman from the kitchen, she murmured, "Doctor's orders for you to have rice."

Thinking over the day's events and going through the interrogation carefully several times in my mind, I felt quite pleased. The new interrogator was a Party official but not a professional interrogator like the first man. I thought he was not too unreasonable, under the circumstances. At least he listened to what I had to say, and everything was recorded. Even though I knew that the Maoists would do everything within their power to make me confess to something I hadn't done, I was now hopeful that at least those who were not diehard Maoists would in time realize I was innocent. When I prepared for bed, I was in a calmer mood than I had been for a long time. However, the exertion and excitement of a full day's interrogation and debate were too much for my weakened body. That night, I had the worst hemorrhage ever. In a short while, all the toilet paper and towels in the cell were used up; there was blood everywhere, even on the cement floor. I was alarmed and called the guard, who quickly summoned the doctor. He gave me an injection and told me to lie perfectly still on a plastic sheet. At daybreak, I was taken to the prison hospital in an ambulance.

9

Persecution Continued

THE ANTIQUATED AMBULANCE SPED through the streets of Shanghai, accompanied by the loud and continuous clang from the bell hanging on its side. I lay on a stretcher on the floor of the vehicle, with a female guard perched on the folding seat. The interior of the ambulance was by no means clean. I kept my eyes closed, partly to avoid looking at the guard, who hovered over me in the confined space, and partly to be alone with my thoughts.

I was deeply disappointed that I had had another hemorrhage just as the long-awaited interrogation seemed to have begun in earnest. I wondered whether I had a malignant growth. I thought of death. It did not seem frightening. After all, my death was the natural and unavoidable result of my having lived. In any case, being a Chinese, I believed that my own death would be only an interval in the continuity of life, for I would go on living in my child and her children, generation after generation, a flowing stream without end. But thinking of my daughter always caused my heart to contract with pain and worry. How was she living? What sort of future would she have after the Cultural Revolution?

The ambulance jerked to a sudden stop. I heard a loudspeaker in the distance broadcasting Mao's directive, "Dig deep tunnels, store grain everywhere, and never seek hegemony." When the stretcher was lifted out of the ambulance, I caught sight of a group of young male prisoners with shaven heads being led by a guard in front of the hospital. They all carried spades, shovels, and large baskets; their Little Red Books of Mao's quotations were slung over their shoulders on a string. They seemed to be on their way to "dig deep tunnels" somewhere behind the prison hospital; Mao's directives always had to be obeyed immediately. But they looked so emaciated that I did not know how they could perform heavy physical labor. Their pathetic appearance, dejected air, and bowed heads reminded me forcefully that I was just like them, a nonperson without any rights, quite unable to control my own fate. I turned my head to avoid looking at the sad spectacle of human ruin, and for the first time I was glad that being in a cell by myself without a mirror, I could continue to entertain an illusion of self-esteem.

I was put in a ward with surgical cases. In the small room, beds were placed next to each other with only a few inches of space between. My bed was by the door, through which a cold draft blew in a vain effort to dispel the odor of blood, urine, disinfectant, and unwashed humanity. On the other side of my bed was a woman groaning and muttering in a state of semiconsciousness, obviously just returned from the operating room. I wondered why I was put there among the surgical cases and whether it meant that the doctors at the prison hospital intended to operate. This prospect was extremely alarming, because in a rigidly stratified Communist society prisoners of the state certainly would get the worst medical care.

However, for several days, I was only given injections. The hemorrhage was brought under control, and I felt stronger because of bed rest and better food. One evening a small banana that had gone soft and brown appeared with my supper. I was surprised by my own positive reaction to that sad-looking banana and the pleasure I got from eating it.

A few days after my hemorrhage stopped, the same woman doctor I had seen when I had pneumonia in the winter of 1967 came to see me in the ward. She took me to a small office and told me that she had been trying to arrange for me to be examined by a gynecologist in a city hospital. But at that time the hospitals in Shanghai, controlled by the Red Guards and the Revolutionaries, were refusing to give medical treatment to "class enemies."

"What do you think I am suffering from?" I asked her.

"It may be a growth, or it may be nothing more than the menopause."

"Could it be a malignant growth?"

"It's hard to say without a biopsy."

"I'm not afraid to die," I said. "But I mustn't die before my case is cleared up. I can't let a cloud of suspicion remain with my daughter for the rest of her life. It would ruin her happiness. Besides, I long to see her again. I've missed her so very much." My voice quivered, and I couldn't go on.

She laid a hand on my arm in a gesture of sympathy. "In my report to the Number One Detention House, I will stress the need for you to have better nourishment."

"Please, Doctor, tell me what I can do myself to prolong my own life," I asked her.

"Eat everything that's given to you. Even the most unpalatable food has some nourishment. Try to be optimistic."

Bitterness had so eaten my heart that I had lost the ability to cry. But the doctor had tears in her eyes when she murmured, "May God bless you!"

A week later, I was brought back to the No. 1 Detention House. I was then given rice twice a day, and a small piece of pork or fish appeared with the rice and cabbage for the mid-morning meal. Often the pork was mostly fat. Sometimes the skin was not altogether free of half-plucked hairs. And the fish was never really fresh. But remembering what the doctor said, I ate everything.

The young doctor at the detention house gave me written permission to purchase vitamin pills with the money I had deposited when I arrived. A male guard came with my banking record and bought me cod-liver oil capsules and vitamin B complex tablets. Vitamin C, so vital for my bleeding gums, was unobtainable in Shanghai.

The reaction of the guards to my improved treatment was by no means the same. The militant Maoists could not conceal their displeasure at the decision of the prison authorities to give me extra food and vitamins. They were always shouting at me or manhandling me whenever there was an opportunity. When I left the cell for exercise or interrogation, they would give me a hard shove that sent me stumbling, pinch my arms, or kick my legs. If I asked them for permission to replenish my supply of vitamin pills, they would refuse and shout, "Do you eat vitamin pills like rice?" or "Do you think this place is a health sanatorium?"

The mild guards obeyed the doctor's orders without question. They bought me vitamin pills whenever I could show them that I had no more. But they bought one or two bottles at a time. The few guards I thought of as Liuists, however, would buy several bottles at a time when they were on duty. Once or twice, they even brought me bags of glucose powder as well as vitamin pills and pushed the lot quickly through the small window into my cell before another guard could see it.

The day after I returned from the prison hospital, the guard on duty handed me a pen and a bottle of ink. She said, "Get on with writing your confession! The interrogator is waiting for it."

I picked up the roll of paper the interrogator had given me and saw that instead of the blank sheets I received in the winter of 1966 when I was told to write my autobiography, page 1 had a special quotation of Mao. It was enclosed in a red-lined square under the heading "Supreme Directive," and it said, "They are allowed only to be docile and obedient; they are not allowed to speak or act out of turn." At the bottom of the sheet, where the prisoner usually signed his name, was written, "Signature of Criminal."

My immediate reaction was anger at the insulting word "criminal" and determination not to sign my name after it. However, after several minutes of consideration, I devised a scheme to exploit the situation and fight back at the Maoists.

Under the printed quotation of Mao, I drew another square, over which I also wrote "Supreme Directive." Within the square, I wrote another of Mao's quotations. It did not appear in the Little Red Book, but I remembered it from his essay "On the Internal Contradiction of the People." The quotation said, "Where there is counterrevolution, we shall certainly suppress it; when we make a mistake, we shall certainly correct it."

Then I wrote an account of the trip my late husband and I had made to Europe in 1956, with a list of the countries we visited, the activities I could recall, and the names of the people we saw. On the subject of conversations we had, I included general topics of no political significance. When I had nearly finished writing, I suddenly remembered two important events that had taken place in the world during the time we were in England: the Hungarian uprising and the Suez War of 1956. I couldn't very well comment on the first, but I could with impunity include the second as a topic of conversation with friends, as it did not concern China or Communism. At the bottom of the page, following the printed words "Signature of Criminal," I added, "who did not commit any crime," and signed my name.

I handed the papers to the guard on duty. That very afternoon, I was called for interrogation.

The same men except for the soldier were in the room. A dark scowl was on each face, a reaction I had anticipated when I decided to contest their assumption that I was a criminal when I was not. I did not wait for a signal from the interrogator but bowed to Mao's portrait immediately. The quotation the interrogator chose for me to read was "Against the running dogs of the imperialists and those who represent the interests of the landlords and the Kuomintang reactionary clique, we must exercise the power of dictatorship to suppress them. They are allowed only to be docile and obedient. They are not allowed to speak or act out of turn."

In front of the interrogator were the pages I had written. After I had sat down, he banged the table while glaring at me. Then he banged the table again and shouted, "What have you done here?" He pointed at the papers. "Do you think we are playing a game with you?"

I remained silent.

"Your attitude is not serious," the old worker said.

"If you do not change your attitude, you will never get out of this place," said the young worker.

Before I could say anything, the interrogator threw my account on the floor, scattering the pages, and stood up. He said, "Go back to your cell and write it again!"

A guard appeared at the doorway and shouted, "Come out!"

I followed him back to the cell. The roll of paper I was given was the same as before. It had the same first sheet with the printed quotation enclosed in a red square at the top and "Signature of Criminal" at the bottom. Since I had embarked on this course of action, I decided I had to carry the fight to the finish. I did not hesitate but wrote the same quotation and again added the words "who did not commit any crime" before my signature. The account I wrote could not be exactly the same as the first one, but I have an excellent memory, and it was more or less the same. The next day, I handed the paper to the guard. Again I was called almost immediately. Again the interrogator threw my account on the floor, scattering all the pages, and told me to write another.

This was repeated once more. Then the interrogator said to me, "Are you mad? Perhaps we should send you to the mental hospital and have you locked up with the crazy people."

"I'm not mad. If you are not satisfied with what I have written, you can point out my mistakes. I would be glad to correct them."

"Why did you add a quotation under the printed one? Why did you write a qualifying phrase before your signature?" the interrogator demanded.

"I was only trying to make my account reflect the true facts more accurately," I said. "I wanted to remind you that our Great Leader Chairman Mao said that we should correct our mistakes. I hope you will carry out Chairman Mao's directive and correct your mistake in my case. As for the added phrase before my signature, it's appropriate. I did not commit any crime. If you must call me a criminal, then I am the criminal who did not commit any crime."

"Instead of confessing your crime, you spend your time arguing," answered the interrogator, no longer shouting.

"I've never committed any crime. If you insist I have, you will have to prove it."

"We'll certainly prove it. But we want to give you a chance to confess so that you can earn lenient treatment."

"Have I not told you over and over again I've never committed any crime? Have I not signed a pledge that you can shoot me if you can prove I've committed a crime?"

"You are bluffing! Don't you worry. We'll shoot you when the time comes," the young worker said heatedly.

"Go back to your cell and write the account again," said the interrogator.

The secretary handed me another roll of paper, and I followed the guard back to my cell.

When I looked at the paper, I found that this time the first page with the printed quotation and the "Signature of Criminal" at the bottom was not included. All the sheets were blank. Again I wrote down my account. Two days later I gave it to the guard on duty.

To people who have not dealt with such men as the Maoists, my persistent effort to fight back against my persecutors may seem futile and pointless. But the Maoists were essentially bullies. If I had allowed them to insult me at will, they would have been encouraged to go further. My life at the detention house would have become even more intolerable than it was already. Besides, every word I uttered in that interrogation room was recorded. Being an eternal optimist, I hoped that one day a just man would be appointed to investigate my case and that what I had said would help him to arrive at the right conclusion.

Several days passed. Daily I waited for the interrogator to call me and go on with his questioning. But I was never called. Finally, one morning, a militant male guard and the militant female guard who had kicked me came to the door of my cell. "Come out!" they threw open the door and shouted.

When I bent to pick up the Little Red Book of Mao's quotations, the female guard stepped into the cell and pushed me roughly. This was so unexpected that I nearly fell down.

"You won't need this where you are going!" She snatched the book out of my hand and tossed it onto the bed. Then she twisted my arms behind my back. The male guard came in and clamped a pair of handcuffs on my wrists. The female guard again gave me a shove. I stumbled. When I regained my balance, she gave me another push.

"Hurry! Hurry!" she shouted.

I followed the guards out of the women's prison and through the main courtyard to the front entrance. The interrogator, the young worker, and another man were waiting at the second iron gate. Parked in the drive was a white sedan with the engine running.

"Get in! Sit in the middle," the interrogator said.

I climbed into the back of the car and sat in the middle of the seat. With my hands pinned at my back, I had to sit upright. My first impression was surprise at how soft the seat of the car was. It was a long time since I had sat on a soft seat with springs.

The interrogator and the young worker sat on either side of

me. The other man sat with the driver. The car moved slowly along the drive and, gathering speed, drove out of the prison gate.

Where were they taking me? Were they going to carry out their threat and have me confined to a mental hospital? I did not think they were taking me for execution, because surely such extreme measures were carried out on the prison premises under cover of darkness. Besides, once they had killed me, they would have no hope of extracting a confession from me. To keep me alive but make my life difficult was their probable aim. I thought a mental hospital was the more likely destination. It would be difficult to continue my fight from a mental hospital. The shrieks and cries of the mentally ill would be depressing. However, I soon discovered that the car was not going towards the road that led out of town to the mental hospital.

Through the fluttering silk curtains that covered the windows of all official cars, I could see that we were passing through Shanghai's downtown business section and were speeding towards the western suburbs. There were few pedestrians and little traffic. The familiar streets evoked a flood of memories. We crossed an intersection only a block from my house. And there was the No. 1 Medical College. It seemed a lifetime ago that I had met Winnie coming out of its gates in the evening twilight when I first got involved with the Cultural Revolution in the summer of 1966. I wondered how she was faring and whether she had had to go to one of those Cadre Schools I had read about in the newspaper.

The car slowed down and entered the drive of the technical school where I had attended the first struggle meeting against our former chief accountant, Tao, and from where I was taken to the No. 1 Detention House on the night of September 27, 1966. It was now already early March 1969, and the unwarranted accusation that I had betrayed my country still hung over my head.

Several men were standing in the pale spring sunshine. One of them opened the door of the car and led me into a small room. Another man behind me was pushing my head down, so that all I could see were the legs of the man walking in front of me. I heard the turning of the lock on the door as soon as I entered. I was left there alone.

There was only one solitary wooden bench in the dusty place. Paper pasted on the window prevented me from looking out. The walls were covered with Big Character Posters from ceiling to floor. There were more piled up in one corner of the room. The ones on the walls did not look freshly written. Some were torn; all were stuck on the walls in a haphazard manner, overlapping one another. When the door was opened to admit me, a gust of air blew several onto the floor.

I sat on the bench and let my eyes wander over the posters. Gradually I realized that they had been hastily pasted on the walls entirely for my benefit. They were old Big Character Posters used during the past two and a half years. Now they were on display again to undermine my fighting spirit. The signatures on them were those of Shell's ex–staff members. Some were written by one man, while others were signed by several names. The messages on them denounced Shell, my late husband, and myself. The "crimes" listed were numerous. Some were distortions of facts or misinterpretations of events. Others were pure imagination. Names of our friends and the three British managers who succeeded my husband were all listed as "foreign intelligence officers" with whom I was supposed to have worked in close cooperation. The names of Scott and Austin appeared on several posters. The White Russian woman employed as secretary at our office was denounced as a double agent for Britain and the Soviet Union.

I closed my eyes to shut out the obnoxious lies. After waiting for a long time, I thought I should try to find out what was going on outside. I listened. When I heard footsteps, I knocked on the door.

"What do you want?" the voice of a man asked.

"May I go to the bathroom?"

The door was unlocked by a woman, who led me to a courtyard at the back. We passed through an area used as a dormitory, with rows of bunk beds jammed into the rooms. Later I learned that the ex-staff of Shell had been confined there since 1966, undergoing endless indoctrination and writing confessions while doing physical labor. Now there was no one about. In the distance I could hear the voice of a man addressing a meeting. I thought that whoever lived in the dormitory must be at the meeting.

When I came out of the bathroom, I was not taken back to the small room with posters, but to the hall where the struggle meetings against Shell's former chief accountant and myself had been held in 1966. Again a man came behind me and placed his hand on my head to bend it low. Two women held my arms, straining them forward to hurry me on, so that the handcuffs cut into my wrists painfully. They were behaving in an exaggeratedly militant manner, as women trying to appear revolutionary often did in China.

I was taken to the front of the room and half thrown, half dropped onto the floor as if I were a sack. The man kept his hand on my head so that I could not look around. When I sat down on the floor, he sat down right behind me, with his hand firmly exerting pressure.

Just before I sat down, out of the corner of my eye, I saw that the room was filled with people sitting on the floor. This arrangement implied insult, as according to Chinese tradition only slaves, condemned criminals, or enemies captured in wars sat on the floor. The people in the room were shouting slogans long familiar to my ears. For a full minute, it seemed, they shouted demands for my downfall and destruction. I heard footsteps coming to the front of the room. When the noise of slogan shouting died down, a young man's voice addressed the meeting.

"Here she is!" he shouted in a loud scream. I imagined him pointing a finger at my bowed head. "We have brought her here so that she will be exposed for what she is. We'll let her see that we know all her secrets. All of you were involved in the scheme of the imperialists to destroy socialism in China too. To a certain extent, you are also guilty, because you also worked for the firm that exploited the Chinese people from the beginning of this century. It was also a spy organization that gathered information to be used for the imperialists. The more senior you were, the more guilty you are. The more management valued your work, the more guilty you are. We, the Revolutionaries, are very fair-minded. If you are thirty percent guilty, we do not punish you for fifty percent. But of course we have our own standard of evaluation. It's the standard set up in accordance with our Great Leader Chairman Mao's teaching.

"During the past two and a half years we have given all of you an intensive course of reeducation combined with physical labor. Many of you have made good progress in improving your socialist awareness. You shed your inhibitions and came forth with your exposure of the enemy. That's to be commended. Others of you are still hesitant. You are like a tube of toothpaste. When we squeeze, something comes out. When we squeeze hard, more comes out. When we do not squeeze, nothing comes. Well, if you continue to maintain a negative attitude, naturally we'll squeeze very hard until you are dry.

"Very soon we are going to let some of you return home. This is good news for you. But remember, only those we consider ready will be allowed to go. The others will have to continue with reeducation. When or whether you will be allowed to go home and how long you must continue with reeducation and physical labor depends entirely on yourselves."

The speaker was just a voice to me. But it was the voice of an uneducated young man, perhaps a worker who had become a Revolutionary of some standing because of his close adherence to the Maoist doctrine. These Revolutionaries were the most ardent supporters of the Cultural Revolution because it gave them undreamt-of opportunity for personal advancement. They looked upon Maoist leaders like Jiang Qing as redeemers who had elevated them from the mundane existence to which their mediocre intellect and lack of ability had condemned them.

From what the speaker had said, I knew that the people sitting on the floor in the room were mostly ex–staff members of my former office. Now he called on them to "expose" and "condemn" me as a means to redeem themselves. They readily complied. But I knew it was all arranged beforehand and that the speakers had been selected and told what to say. And the drafts of their statements had been approved by the Revolutionaries. Even before the Cultural Revolution no one in China could make a public statement without first having it approved by his or her Party secretary. During the Hundred Flowers Bloom and Hundred Thoughts Contend Campaign of 1956, and later during the period of the Democracy Wall of 1978–79, the Party ordered the people to speak and write Big Character Posters. In both instances, because the Party did not or could not censor each and every statement and poster and the people exceeded what the Party wanted them to say, the situation quickly got out of hand and the Party had to clamp down again.

The men I used to see daily and worked with for over eight

years stood up one after another to repeat what was written on the posters I had seen in the small room. Their hesitant and frightened voices were telling lies so outrageous, using words so alien to them, that I knew they were suffering shame and anguish. My own emotion was one of deep sorrow that the high-handed Maoist Revolutionaries had degraded all of us to such an extent. But I listened carefully, trying to fathom the intention of the Maoists from the words they had put into these men's mouths.

The floor was hard, and my neck was aching from having my head pushed down by the heavy hand of the man behind me. I shifted my position and drew up one leg. Then I rested my head on my knee. In this posture, I could see a corner of the blue jacket of the man seated on my left and nothing more. Since I made no attempt to look up but appeared content to bend my head down, the man behind me gradually relaxed his grip.

The statements made by Shell's ex-staff became more fantastic by the hour. What they were saying was absurd and unbelievable to anybody who had some knowledge of the world outside China. The sum total of the accusations was an amateurish attempt at a spy drama without a convincing central theme, beginning, or end.

I heard the voice of the young man calling on our former chief accountant, Tao.

The corner of the blue jacket disappeared from view as the man next to me stood up. I wondered why the Maoists had placed Tao next to me on the floor.

Tao was saying in a faltering voice, "As everybody knows, I was arrested at the beginning of the Cultural Revolution and taken to the Number Two Detention House. While I was there, the interrogator and the guards most kindly gave me reeducation to help me raise my socialist awareness. Gradually I realized the seriousness of my crime against socialism and the Party. A desire to earn lenient treatment was born in my heart. At that juncture, the kind and understanding Revolutionaries brought me back here and allowed my family to visit me . . ." He was evidently overcome with emotion and unable to go on.

"My eldest son is a Party member, and so is my daughter-in-law. My son received his higher education entirely due to the opportunity given him by the Party and the People's Government. My whole family is eternally grateful to our Great Leader Chairman Mao. I cannot describe the remorse I experienced when I saw my wife, my son, my daughter-in-law, and my baby grandson . . ."

He drew a long breath, broke down, and sobbed.

There was dead silence in the room. The pale spring sun cast a shifting shadow of the window on the floor in front of me. I had been watching it move across the floor. Now I wondered how much longer the meeting was going to last. I was getting tired and hungry. But I warned myself not to relax vigilance. Somehow I did not think Tao was called upon merely to set an example for me to follow. After all, I did not have a child specially educated by the Party.

When Tao resumed, he seemed to be making an effort to speak, like a man utterly exhausted. His voice was unsteady as he declared, "My wife, my son, and my daughter-in-law talked to me. The Revolutionaries talked to me. The cadres representing the Party and our Great Leader Chairman Mao talked to me. They showed that I must obey the teachings of Chairman Mao. There is no other way for me to turn. I can't let them down. I'm going to confess and make a clean break with the past. I want to go home and be with my family. To confess fully is the only way." He again paused for a moment, almost as if he were reluctant to go on. Then he plunged in and said in a loud and firm voice, "I was a spy for the British imperialists. I joined the British spy organization through the introduction of this woman's husband, the late general manager Cheng. After he died, this woman became my boss. At the beginning of the Cultural Revolution, she warned me not to confess and promised me a large sum of money if I would hold out."

A denial or an argument with Tao would serve no useful purpose. But I must put a stop to this farce. I jerked my head up and laughed uproariously.

My reaction was not what anyone had expected. There was a moment of stunned silence. Then several men rushed to my side. The man behind me pushed my head down again. Another man shouted, "What are you laughing at?" Someone else said, "How dare you laugh!"

The sound of people moving about came from the back of the room. There was even a noise that was like suppressed giggles.

The tense atmosphere of a moment ago had collapsed like a burst balloon.

The voice of the young man in charge of the meeting was shouting at me amidst the noise, "Why did you laugh? Answer me!"

"If you put on a comic play, you must expect the audience to laugh. It's the natural response," I answered. With my head pressed down, I had to talk to the floor. But I raised my voice and spoke clearly so that every person in the room could hear me. I wanted to show our ex-staff that there was no need to be frightened of the Maoists.

"Take her out! Take her out!" the young man yelled. Then he led the others in the room to shout slogans against me.

I was forcibly dragged out of the room, pulled through the courtyard like a sack, and pushed into the waiting car. A woman Revolutionary kept her hand over my mouth to prevent me from speaking, while the man did not relax his pressure on my head. I was pinned on the back seat of the car in an awkward position, with the woman perching on the edge of the seat and the man squatting in the narrow space between the front and back seats. But I was lighthearted. I thoroughly enjoyed breaking up their carefully planned meeting. I wondered what would have happened if I had sat there quietly. I did not rule out the possibility that Tao had been instructed to talk to me and incriminate me in some way to validate his lies. There must have been a reason, I thought, for the Maoists to have placed me next to him.

It was my bad luck to find the militant female guard on duty when I returned to the cell. Needless to say, she had not kept rice for me. She did not take the handcuffs off my wrists. As soon as she unlocked the door, she gave me a hard shove that sent me lurching into the room, where I collapsed on the bed. Almost immediately, running footsteps could be heard in the corridor. The same male guard who had escorted me from the car came back to call me for interrogation.

The guard was in a great hurry; it was difficult to keep up with him. When I reached the interrogation room, I was out of breath and my heart was beating wildly.

There were no fewer than eight men in the small room, four seated on chairs placed along the wall opposite Mao's portrait, the others crowded around the interrogator.

The interrogator waved his arm towards the portrait. I bowed and nearly lost my balance. The floor heaved, and I closed my eyes.

"Remain standing!" someone said, but his voice seemed to come from very far away.

"Explain yourself! Why did you laugh?" another voice said in the distance.

I tried to say something, but no word came. I must have fainted from hunger. When I opened my eyes, I found myself sitting on the floor supported by a female guard. My arms were freed from the handcuffs. The sleeve of my left arm was pulled up. The young doctor was standing over me, unscrewing the needle from a large syringe. He nodded to the interrogator and left the room. The female guard pulled me up and pushed me into the prisoner's chair. She also left the room.

My heart was still palpitating, and my lips were parched. But I felt better.

"Now answer my question. Did you not see for yourself that the others are more enlightened than you are? They are coming over to the side of the Proletarian Revolutionaries. They have confessed everything. What are you going to do? Are you going to do the same and admit your guilt?" the interrogator asked.

I was feeling stronger by the minute. What did the doctor give me? Was it just an intravenous injection of glucose, or was there something else in the syringe? Perhaps there was a stimulant. I was now wide awake, ready to fight.

Before I could answer the interrogator's question, someone interrupted. 'What were you laughing at? Why did you laugh? It's no laughing matter. To be accused of being a spy for the imperialists is a very serious matter." It was the voice of the young man who had led the meeting at the technical school. I looked at him with curiosity.

To my surprise, he did not look like the young industrial worker I had assumed him to be from his voice and vocabulary. He wore a jacket like that of an army officer, but without the red patches on the collar that denoted a member of the Liberation Army. His trousers were dark gray, made of good-quality worsted that would cost at least 30 yuan a yard, twenty days' pay for an industrial worker. His hair was plastered down with grease, and his black leather shoes were carefully polished. On the wrist of his left hand a gold watch peeped from under the cuff of his shirt sleeve. He was a young man of about twenty-five with an air of self-importance. I was puzzled who he was and how he dared to appear so well dressed during the Cultural Revolution; the clothes he was wearing were denounced as the habitual attire of the capitalist class. Was he not afraid to be mistaken for a class enemy?

Years later, I was to learn that his appearance was typical of the sons of senior army commanders. The khaki jacket was a hint that the wearer was connected with the armed forces and therefore above the law. The status of their fathers gave these young men the privilege of looking different from the other Revolutionaries they attempted to lead. Direct access to the seat of power through their family connections set them apart. In time they became the Mafia of Communist China as they plundered wealth, raped women, and organized black market and gambling activities.

Those whose fathers were very senior in the military hierarchy became China's biggest "back-door men" and "fixers." They could arrange anything, from housing and jobs to import and export trade, because they could get things done through their own network of cronies without going through the established bureaucracy. Even merchants from Hong Kong anxious to get a good contract in China had to bribe these swaggering young men, often by giving them "jobs" enabling them to travel to and from the British colony and smuggle gold, silver, and antiques out of China, and TV sets, recorders, and watches into the country.

"Answer! Answer!" the well-dressed young man shouted. I looked at him, and then I looked at the interrogator. But the latter was staring at the paper in front of him, seemingly annoyed that the young man had taken over the job of questioning me.

"I laughed because it was funny," I told him.

"What was funny?"

"The whole thing you arranged was funny."

"Explain yourself."

"Well, don't you see? Tao was lying, and lying very badly. But you believed him, and you were going to let him go home to his family. Isn't that funny?"

"Tao wasn't lying."

"Wasn't he? Then you mean he was a real spy? In that case, you were going to let a real spy go home instead of punishing him with the death penalty or a stiff sentence? That's even funnier."

"Never mind what's going to happen to Tao. What about yourself? Don't you want to go home?"

"Of course I want to go home. I want full rehabilitation. I want an apology from the People's Government to be published in the *Liberation Daily* in Shanghai and in the *People's Daily* in Beijing. But I won't lie. I'll achieve all that by adhering only to the truth," I said.

I was looking at this well-dressed but rather stupid young man intently, wondering how he could have failed to realize that I laughed merely to break up his carefully arranged meeting. Suddenly he stood up and shouted in an excited voice, "Bow your head! Bow your head! I won't let a class enemy stare at me with eyes like a pair of searchlights!"

The man seated next to him, obviously a lackey, quickly stood up, walked over to me, and stretched out his hand to push my head down.

"It's my habit to look at the person I speak to. If I made you nervous, I apologize. Would you like me to sit with my back to you?" I turned my body to face Mao's portrait on the wall, as the prisoner's chair was nailed to the ground and could not be moved. From the corner of my eye I caught a glimpse of the interrogator. He was biting his lip to stifle a smile.

"Now answer my question. Were you or were you not a spy for the British? Are you or are you not going to confess?" asked the young man.

"I'm not a spy for anybody. I have nothing to confess," I said firmly to the wall from which Mao's portrait looked down on me. As I gazed at Mao's face wearing what was intended as a benign expression but was in fact a smirk of self-satisfaction, I wondered how one single person could have caused the extent of misery that was prevailing in China. There must be something lacking in our own character, I thought, that had made it possible for his evil genius to dominate.

"You are a spy!" the young man shouted angrily.

"I'm not." I shook my head.

"We have evidence you are."

"Produce it, then." I turned to face him once more.

"Didn't you hear your ex–staff members this morning?"

"That was no evidence. Just empty words of accusation made under duress."

"Don't you worry. We'll show you concrete evidence. One, two, three, four . . . a very long list of things you said and did. But by then it will be too late for you to win lenient treatment."

"A real spy shouldn't be given lenient treatment. A real spy should be shot, whether he confesses or not," I declared.

The interrogator stood up and took over. "Go back to your cell now and think over everything you heard at the meeting this morning. They were not all lies. Some are serious matters. The situation you are in is no laughing matter." He got up and walked out of the room. A guard came to lead me back to the cell.

As I approached the women's prison, I saw the woman from the kitchen in her white apron pushing the huge cart with layers and layers of containers of sweet potatoes for the prisoners. She was being helped by two Labor Reform Girls. Apparently another inmate was also being given rice; the two containers of rice and cabbage stood out amid the golden brown color of the potatoes. As soon as I was back in my cell, my portion of rice was pushed through the small window.

My gums were now bleeding almost continuously. I had to rinse my mouth before taking food, or the food tasted of blood. Chewing had become more and more difficult. The cabbage was usually very tough. It took me a very long time to finish a meal. Because I had to return the chopsticks with the container before I could finish eating, I had been allowed to purchase a plastic spoon from the prison shop. Now I sat on the edge of the bed, scooped the rice and cabbage into one of the mugs, washed the aluminum container and chopsticks to give back to the woman from the kitchen, and started to eat my only meal of the day with the plastic spoon. While I ate, I reviewed what had happened during the day.

In spite of being knocked about and handcuffed, I thought that on the whole the day had not been wasted. I had learned what had happened to the former members of the company's staff and could see my own predicament in better perspective.

I regretted that so many of them had succumbed to pressure, which must have been great, but I worried about others whose names I did not see on the Big Character Posters and who were not among the speakers denouncing me. I wondered whether they were still in this world.

As for our chief accountant, Tao, I considered his behavior dastardly. But I had to forgive him, I believed. The sound of his sobbing was still in my ears. It was the cry of a tortured soul who had reached the end of his tether.

The weather was decidedly warmer, and I had stopped shivering several days earlier. I wondered whether I should wash the warm woolen sweater I was wearing and put it away. I felt I must take great care of all my winter clothing, as goods like that were not available in the prison shop. God knew how long I would have to remain in the detention house. The struggle between the Maoists and myself was in fact a war of endurance. I simply must not die.

Soon after I had got into bed, the guard on duty came to the small window. She pushed open the shutter gently and said in a whisper, "Would you like to take a hot shower?"

What an unexpected and welcome offer! Prisoners were allowed one hot shower a month. In the winter months, when it was too cold to wash in the cell with cold water, I counted the days from one hot shower to the next. That afternoon, when I came back from interrogation, I had noticed that the female guards were going to the shower room one after another. This continued throughout the whole evening. Now, it seemed, they had all finished, so the guard was offering me the chance to use up the hot water that was left in the pipes.

I jumped out of bed, grabbed my soapbox and towels, and followed her to the shower room. While I stood under the spray of warm water, washing my hair and my body, I marveled at the changed attitude of some of the guards since the day I had been bold enough to defend their former leader, Liu Shaoqi. When I emerged from the shower room, I slipped into the cell quietly. Soon afterwards, the guard came and snapped the lock.

It rained the next day, not the chilly drops of winter that crystallized into ice on the ground, nor the angry torrent of summer thunderstorms. It was the gentle drizzle that softly soaked the earth to awaken the trees and flowers, warning them

of the approach of spring. I had always loved that wet smell of
the earth after a day of spring rain. It seemed so full of hope and
the promise of beautiful scented flowers and green shady leaves.
The departure of winter, the relatively better food and vitamin
pills, and the relaxed attitude of some of the guards combined
to make me feel less on edge. I found myself more optimistic
about my chances of surviving the ordeal and less worried about
the future.

My feeling of euphoria continued the next day. When I was
called again for interrogation, I walked with almost sprightly
steps. This time only the well-dressed young man and the young
worker were seated behind the counter.

After I had entered the room and the guard had closed the
door, the young man raised his arm in the direction of Mao's
portrait. I bowed. He told me to read the following quotation:
"A revolution is not a dinner party, or writing an essay, or
painting pictures, or doing embroidery; it cannot be so refined,
so leisurely, and so gentle, so temperate, kind, courteous, restrained, and magnanimous. A revolution is an act of violence
with which one class overthrows another."

"Do you love England better than you love China?" he asked.

"I'm a Chinese citizen. Of course I love China better," I
answered.

"If we leave out the matter of citizenship, would you still love
China more?"

"Chinese blood flows in my veins. Of course I love China
more. I have always been a patriotic Chinese."

"Were you in the United States in 1940?"

"Yes, I was there for a few months."

"Did you make speeches when you were there?"

"Yes, I made some speeches about the Japanese invasion of
China."

"We have information that you also made speeches in praise
of the British war effort. You spoke on a radio program in New
York. You were heard by some of your former Yanjing University friends who have now confessed and provided us with this
information. Probably you also spoke at other places. In any
case, when you returned to Chongqing, you made a propaganda broadcast from the Kuomintang radio station. You said
the British imperialists were heroic people with great courage

who would never give up until they won the final victory. Did
the British government ask you to make propaganda for them?
Were you already recruited by the British in 1940? Answer
me!"

"I went to New York from England on a British passenger
steamer. A number of the passengers were interviewed on a
radio program. The interviewer asked me questions about Britain. Naturally I answered truthfully," I said.

"You made propaganda for Britain."

"During the war, Britain and China were on the same side."

"Not in 1940. The British were helping the Japanese then.
What you did proves beyond doubt that you were a British spy
as long ago as 1940."

"Nonsense. I was just a Chinese visitor in Britain who was
moved by the courage and resolution of the British people in the
face of overwhelming odds when Britain stood alone to resist
Hitler's plan to conquer all of Europe."

"Listen to you! You are at this moment echoing the propaganda line of the British imperialists. We think you love Britain
better than China."

"You can think whatever you want to, but you will have to
prove your accusation against me."

"We will prove it. We will prove that your claim of patriotism
is false. It's for the purpose of covering up your evil deeds."

He took a small brown folder from under the counter and
held it up to look at. All I could see was the back of the folder;
I wondered what it was that he was looking at with so much
assumed concentration. Suddenly he turned the folder around.
I saw that it enclosed a black-and-white photograph of myself
dancing with a Swiss friend in the early fifties, when the French
Club was still in existence in Shanghai. An unemployed photographer snapped pictures of the guests of the club and offered
them copies for a yuan each. To help this man, we all bought
the pictures. When the Red Guards came to my house, the
photographs were in the storeroom. They must have taken them
all. My Swiss friend was an excellent dancer who knew many
fancy steps. In the picture, he was teaching me something new
and we were both laughing.

"Do you call that patriotic?" the young man said severely, as
if I had been caught doing something terrible.

"What has dancing got to do with patriotism?" I was genu-inely puzzled.

"You were dancing with a foreigner. And you looked quite happy dancing with a foreigner. That's decidedly unpatriotic."

"Is dancing with a foreigner unpatriotic?" I was rather taken aback by his line of attack. But I recovered in a moment and saw how I could turn the argument in my own favor. I went on, "I didn't know dancing with a foreigner was not patriotic. But I must accept your superior judgment, as you are an enlightened Marxist and a Revolutionary. However, if I was not patriotic, at least I was useful. That's to my credit, don't you think?"

"What do you mean, you were useful?"

"Well, as you have just said, dancing with a foreigner was not patriotic. By dancing with my Swiss friend, I was making him unpatriotic, because to him surely I was the foreigner. If by the simple act of dancing I can make others unpatriotic, isn't that being useful? Think of the possibilities from that point on. You can simply send me to dance with all China's enemies all over the world and let me make them unpatriotic. Then, without firing a single shot, all of them are done for. How could anybody be more useful than that?" I was so overcome with mirth that I had some difficulty speaking the last few words clearly.

But the young man was not amused. His face flushed in anger. Pointing to the door of the interrogation room, he shouted, "Get out! Get out! I'll have you shot!"

He looked so threatening as he advanced towards me that I fled the room in haste. But in the corridor there was no guard to lead me back to my cell. I waited, trying to stifle my giggles. I did not think it seemly or prudent to break out in laughter in that grim place. They might really think I was mad and consider themselves justified in sending me to the mental hospital.

However, it did not pay to laugh at the expense of someone in authority. This was made amply clear to me the very next day.

I was called to the interrogation room just before the prison-ers' midmorning meal. After the preliminaries, the same young man handed me the fourth volume of *The Collected Works of Mao Zedong,* opened to a page reprinting a letter broadcast from the headquarters of the Communist army to a group of Kuomintang generals. The letter was drafted by Mao Zedong in December 1948, when Kuomintang troops were encircled by the Communist army on the north bank of the Yangzi River near Nanjing, the Kuomintang capital. It pointed out the hopelessness of the Kuomintang position and urged the generals to surrender.

"Remain standing and read the letter aloud," the young man ordered.

I read the text aloud. When I had finished and was about to hand him back the book, he said, "Read it again! Let the words sink into your stupid mind."

I read it again. When I had finished it for the second time, he said, "Did the words sink in? Do you understand the hopelessness of your position? You are surrounded just like those Kuomintang generals. No help is coming! The only way out is to surrender."

I said nothing. He glared at me for a moment and then yelled, "Read it again!"

When I had finished reading, we stared at each other. Then he shouted impatiently, "Read it again! Let the words sink into your granite head!"

There I stood in the interrogation room for hours that day, reading the letter over and over again until I was dizzy, my voice hoarse and my legs badly swollen. By late afternoon, I was so weary that my voice was barely audible and I read the words haltingly. Since by this time I knew the text by heart, I no longer had to look at the book but spoke the words slowly with my eyes closed. Gradually my arm holding the book dropped to my side. Whenever I stopped or hesitated, the young man yelled, "Are you going to surrender?" He would wait for me to answer. When I did not answer, he would yell, "Read it again!"

At first the young worker stared at me while I read. Now I saw that he had lost interest. With his head on his folded arms, he seemed to be dozing. The two of them took turns to go out to eat. I had to go without food. Hungry and exhausted, I was in a daze. My mouth was so dry that my voice became a low murmur. Still, each time I finished reciting the text, the young man yelled, "Repeat!"

I was allowed to go back to my cell only when it was getting dark. Though I couldn't be sure how long I had stood in the interrogation room reading that letter drafted by Mao, it must have been more than seven hours. No food was kept for me. Throughout the whole day I had only water to drink in the morning before I went to the interrogation room and in the evening after I came back to the cell. To give myself some nourishment, I swallowed a handful of cod-liver oil capsules and B complex tablets.

This routine went on for three days, except that on the second and third day I was allowed to return to the cell in time for the afternoon meal. The guard on duty at the women's prison cooperated with the young man. She prolonged the evening exercise period, during which she took up position outside my cell and saw to it that I walked around and around for an hour. After I went to bed, the night duty guard came repeatedly to my cell to open and shut the small window with a loud bang or kick the door with her heavy boot to disturb my sleep. In spite of being awakened by her several times during the night, on the whole I slept soundly.

At the end of the third day, I was again on the verge of collapse. I thought this might be apparent to the two young men. At the end of the afternoon, they both asked me, "Are you going to surrender?"

I tried to speak. But I was very weak, and my throat was so dry that only a hoarse whisper came.

"Speak clearly! Are you going to surrender?" the well-dressed young man asked.

I made a great effort. With all my strength I managed to say, "Not guilty!"

"You will surely be shot!"

He left the room in a fit of temper and banged the door. I sat down in the prisoner's chair to rest and to wait for the guard.

The young worker stared at me with a puzzled frown on his brow. After a while, he said, "What can you be thinking about? What is it you pin your hope on?"

I said nothing. A guard came to lead me out of the room.

Days passed. But I was not called again. Many times a day I thought of the exchanges I had had with all the interrogators, including the well-dressed young man. Over and over again I went through the questions they had asked me and the answers I had given. Could I have done better? Could I have done otherwise? I came to the conclusion that although they sometimes appeared to be trying to find out the actual facts of what had happened, all the interrogations were in fact simply part of the attempt to find me guilty. The questions were asked to elicit answers in which they could find something to use against me. At the same time, they used the sessions of interrogation to show their power over me so that I would eventually be frightened into submission. Interrogations were not going to help resolve my case. They were used solely to add to my hardship. In fact, there was no point in my hoping for more interrogations.

With the coming of warmer weather my general health seemed to have improved somewhat. One piece at a time, I washed my winter sweaters and socks and laid them out to dry. I cleaned the collar and cuffs of my padded jacket and put it away. Be prepared for a long stay in the detention house, I told myself. As long as I could keep alive, I still had hope. The philosopher Laozi once said that when events developed to the extreme, the trend would be reversed. I must wait. I did my daily exercise and spent many hours reciting poetry to myself. Often I would sit there with Mao's book on my lap as if I were absorbed in reading his essays, but actually my mind was filled with the stanzas of Li Bo or Du Fu.

On April 1, 1969, two and a half years after my arrest, the long-awaited Ninth Party Congress opened in Beijing. The newspaper reported that Lin Biao delivered the important political report, praising the Cultural Revolution and promising unrelenting efforts at class struggle. Among the fifteen hundred delegates were a large number of his supporters from the army, navy, and air force. In the new Party constitution, Lin Biao was officially named Mao's successor. Both Lin Biao and Jiang Qing succeeded in placing their associates in the new Central Committee of 279 members. Many old, well-known Party officials were dropped. Some few, like Prime Minister Zhou Enlai and Foreign Minister Chen Yi, maintained their positions. But as a group the influence of the old guard was greatly diminished. In the final photograph published in the newspaper, Mao stood in the middle. On his left were all the Maoist leaders, such as Lin Biao and Jiang Qing. On his right were the few members of the old guard headed by Prime Minister Zhou Enlai.

While the Ninth Party Congress was in session, the newspaper reported daily displays of enthusiasm and support by the populace. In the detention house, prisoners were obliged to listen from morning till night to broadcasts of speeches and news bulletins, including long lists of names of delegates. Familiar names disappeared. New names appeared, reflecting the power realignment that was going on in the Party leadership. On the day Lin Biao gave his political report, all prisoners were roused from sleep and told to get dressed and listen to a tape of it.

One day, just as I had settled down to eat my rice in the morning, the cell door was unlocked. A male guard yelled, "Come out!"

I ignored him while I quickly swallowed mouthful after mouthful of rice without chewing.

"Come out!" he yelled again. But he did not come into the cell.

My chopsticks were flying as I swept the rice into my mouth. I was determined to face whatever was in store for me with some food in my stomach. I suspected they always timed the interrogations to make me miss my meals.

"Come out!" he yelled for the third time and came into the cell. Calmly he took the mug of food from my hand and placed it on the table. "You can eat it when you come back," he said.

Quickly I dipped the other mug into the washbasin full of cold water and drank several mouthfuls to wash down the hard rice lingering in my esophagus.

"Hurry up! You are so slow," he said.

"Please go outside. I have to use the toilet."

He had to leave the cell. The female guard on duty came in to watch me. I washed my hands and wiped my mouth. As I was picking up the Little Red Book of Mao's quotations, the mild female guard shook her head and murmured, "No need to take it." I put the book back on the bed and followed her out of the cell.

The militant female guard ran into the corridor and shouted breathlessly, "What are you doing? Why are you so slow?"

I followed her out of the women's prison to the courtyard. Another male guard was waiting with a pair of handcuffs. The female guard twisted my arms back and put the handcuffs on my wrists. Then she gave a hard shove that sent me staggering. As soon as I recovered my balance and started to walk normally, she gave me another hard shove. Thus, by fits and starts, I reached the front entrance of the detention house. The same white sedan was parked there with the driver in his seat. He had his hand on the horn, emitting intermittent bursts of sound until he saw me coming. The well-dressed young man was pacing to and fro, and the old worker was standing nearby.

When they saw me, they both walked over. I knew from the expression on the young man's face that what was going to happen to me this day was a punishment for my intransigence. He said through clenched teeth, "You are going to a meeting to celebrate the successful conclusion of the Ninth Party Congress and the election of the new Central Committee. Be sure to behave yourself. Abandon your arrogant manner! Otherwise the Revolutionaries will tear you apart." He relaxed somewhat, almost as if the prospect of my being torn apart by the Revolutionaries was pleasing to him.

"Here in the Number One Detention House, we have rules and regulations about the treatment of prisoners. We have been extremely tolerant and restrained towards you. Outside this gate, the situation is different. The revolutionary masses can do whatever they want. You had better be careful. Don't speak out of turn. In fact, you had better be docile and obedient, otherwise they will kill you. Many people have been killed already in that way," the old worker said.

Were they really concerned about the preservation of my life? I thought not. They were simply anxious to avoid the criticism that they had failed to tame the prisoner under their control. Possibly senior officials were to be present at this meeting, on whom they would want to make a good impression.

"Do you understand the situation?" the young man asked me.

"I will not answer back if I am not provoked," I told him.

"Perhaps we should really teach you a lesson before we go," he said, curling his fingers into a fist and waving it in front of my eyes.

"You should know by now I am not to be silenced by physical violence. The more you provoke me, the more I'll answer back."

"All right, then. We shall let the masses teach you a lesson. You better look out. They will kill you if you answer back."

"Do you mean to say I must remain silent even if someone asks me a question?" I wanted to get the situation clear.

"Yes, just bow your head and admit your crime."

"I would rather die than admit something that is not true."

"Keep silent, then. Whatever they say to you, just keep quiet," said the old worker, who seemed decidedly the better person of the two.

"All right. I'll keep silent, no matter what they say. But that doesn't mean I admit I'm guilty."

"It's not for the masses to decide whether you are guilty or not," the old worker assured me.

The young man told me to get into the car. I sat down on the back seat with the old worker and another man. The young man sat beside the driver. As the car emerged from the drive onto the streets, another sedan with all the others who had taken part in my last few interrogations followed.

April was a beautiful month in Shanghai. The polluted air of this industrial city was freshened by the young leaves of plane trees lining the streets. There was a sense of renewal after the rigors of winter. The windows of the car were open; the brown silk curtains fluttered in the breeze, so that I could see something of the streets. We were heading north right across town. At intersections we were frequently held up by parades organized to celebrate the conclusion of the Ninth Party Congress. The red banners, the slogans on colored paper, the drums and gongs, and the portraits of Mao were the same as had been used in other parades at the beginning of the Cultural Revolution. But I noticed that the people taking part now looked very different from the excited crowds of three years ago. Instead of the animation I remembered, people looked bored. Their steps were slow and dragging; their voices shouting slogans were weak and flat. Some did not join in at all. They seemed to be suffering from revolutionary fatigue after nearly three years of unremitting enthusiasm for class struggle. Or, perhaps more likely, they were simply disillusioned by the developments of the Cultural Revolution. Many of them probably had children who had been Red Guards, to whom they now had to send food and clothing since nearly all former Red Guards had been dispersed to the rural areas. Others might have found the confusion and shortages created by the Cultural Revolution a heavy burden added to their already straitened living conditions.

Normally streets in Shanghai were filled with loitering people. But on this spring day, apart from the paraders, there were few idle onlookers. I was puzzled, because I had not fully realized to what extent the violence by the Red Guards and the Revolutionaries had driven the people off the streets. Stray bullets had claimed many victims during the factional civil wars, and the Red Guards and Revolutionaries had beaten people up at random just to keep themselves in a state of readiness for further action.

When the car reached the area of the universities and the military airport on the outskirts of the city, an air force parade came towards us. At the end of the line was a contingent of strikingly beautiful, slender young girls in uniform. They looked more like glamorous females in a film version of the air force than the real thing. Later, after my release, when the Lin Biao affair had officially been made the subject of public criticism, I learned something about these young women. The Chinese people were told that when Lin Biao made his son, Lin Liguo, second in command of the Chinese air force at the age of twenty-five, fresh out of some military college reserved for sons of senior officers, followers of Lin Biao sent Lin Liguo beautiful girls from all over China to form his "three thousand beauties in the inner palace," in imitation of the selection of concubines for the emperor's heir in the old days. The girls were offered jobs in the air force as an enticement. Because membership in the armed forces was a guarantee of higher prestige and better treatment, with special consideration for their families, the girls enrolled eagerly without realizing that they were chosen for Lin Liguo's pleasure. Then they were brought to Shanghai, where Lin Liguo had an elaborate secret establishment. The girls were sorted out under the pretext of physical examination. Those who did not catch Lin Liguo's fancy were assigned jobs in the air force. These were the girls I saw taking part in the parade.

The car turned into the gates of a large compound of red-brick buildings. There was no signboard to indicate the nature of the place, and no sentry to guard the entrance, only a solitary man to admit the cars and close the gate after us. He followed the cars inside. The atmosphere was rather mysterious, and I decided to observe everything closely. It almost seemed as if they did not want me to know where I was being taken.

After passing between trim lawns and budding willow trees, the car stopped in front of one of the buildings. Two husky-looking women in blue Mao uniforms with the red armband of the Revolutionaries were waiting. One of them opened the door of the car. The old worker jumped out. I was preparing to alight when the second woman stretched out her hand and pulled me out roughly. The two women put their hands under my arms and hoisted me up to take me into the building, almost as if they thought I might try to run away. We entered a small room, and they pushed me into a corner.

"Face the wall! Don't move!" one of the women yelled.

I heard the women sit down heavily. No one uttered a word. After what seemed a long time, I heard the door being opened; a man's voice mentioned food. After whispered consultation, one of the women left the room. When she came back, the other one went out. All the time I stood with my face to the wall.

More waiting in complete silence. I shifted my weight from one leg to the other for the hundredth time. Suddenly the door opened again. A man's voice said with an air of awe and mystery, like a servant in the home of a Chinese high official speaking of his important master, *"Lai-la!"* This meant someone had arrived. From the messenger's tone of voice, it was someone important.

The two women shot out of their chairs like lightning, grabbed my arms again, and half carried, half dragged me out of the building. We passed beside a deserted basketball court along a tree-lined path and entered another building. My feet hardly touched the ground; my armpits were bruised by the women's iron fingers.

My curiosity increased by the minute. What could this place be? The layout was like that of a university compound. But the clean buildings and trim lawns seemed to indicate this was no ordinary institution of higher education. The men who came with me were walking a few steps ahead of me. They had an air of restraint and caution. I decided, in spite of the absence of armed sentries at the gate, that the place was either the site of a government department of some importance or a military installation. Chinese people usually tread gingerly in the vicinity of power and firearms.

We entered a meeting hall where about a hundred people were assembled, sitting in two sections facing each other. In the space between, against the wall, was a raised platform. A number of people in civilian clothes were seated there in a semicircle behind a table. The men from No. 1 Detention House joined them. On the walls were the usual Cultural Revolution slogans written in white paint on red cloth. They proclaimed the victory of the Maoists and the utter destruction of the "capitalist-road-ers" in the Party. The "historical" meeting of the Ninth Party Congress was declared a great success for the promotion of Marxist-Leninist–Mao Zedong Thought. I noticed that the por-trait of Lin Biao, the official successor to Mao, appeared beside the official portrait of Mao.

Everything in the room was neat and clean, indicating that the building belonged to an organization with a generous budget and a high degree of discipline. That could only mean the mili-tary. I looked at the audience. The people seemed to me rather better dressed than the usual crowd on the streets. There were many jackets and trousers made of wool or Dacron, not the sea of faded blue cotton at an ordinary Shanghai meeting.

The women deposited me in front of a microphone opposite the platform. One of them pushed my head down so that I was forced to look at the floor. Within my view were some tangled wires leading from the microphone. One of the wires must lead to an electric outlet, I thought. Where did the others lead? Was it possible that men in another room were listening in on the struggle meeting? Who could they be? Why should they behave in such a mysterious manner? Perhaps they did not want me to see them? Apart from my local policeman and the young woman in charge of the section dealing with foreign firms at the Shang-hai Industry and Commerce Department, I knew few govern-ment officials by sight. At diplomatic receptions of the few West-ern missions in Shanghai to which I had been invited, I had seen one of the vice-mayors and some officials of the Foreign Affairs Department. Surely they must have become victims of the Cul-tural Revolution when the Shanghai municipal government was overthrown. The only possible explanation was that Lin Biao's men had taken over my investigation. The men listening to the struggle meeting were men in uniform. What they did not want me to see was not their faces but their military apparel.

The audience was shouting slogans and waving Little Red Books in the air. After the "Long live our Great Leader Chair-man Mao" came "Good health to our Vice-Supreme Comman-der Lin, always good health!" This seemed to me not only a reflection of the elevated position of Lin Biao after the Ninth Party Congress but also testimony to the fact that those who had organized this meeting were his intimates, anxious to promote Lin Biao's personality cult.

Two legs came into my limited field of vision. A man's voice spoke in front of me. He introduced me to the audience by giving an account of my family background and personal life. I had noticed already that each time my life story was recounted by the Revolutionaries I became richer and my way of life became more decadent and luxurious. Now the farce reached fantastic proportions. Since I had promised not to answer back but to remain mute, I was much more relaxed and detached than at the previous struggle meeting in 1966. However, the audience jumped up from their seats when the speaker told them I was a spy for the imperialists. They expressed their anger and indignation by crowding around me to shout abuse.

To be so maligned was intolerable. Instinctively I raised my head to respond. The women suddenly jerked up my handcuffs. Such sharp pain tore at my shoulder joints that I had to bend forward with my head well down to ease the agony. They kept me in this position during the rest of the man's denunciation of me. Only when the people were again shouting slogans did they allow my arms to drop back. I was to learn later that I had been subjected to the so-called jet position invented by the Revolutionaries to torment their more recalcitrant victims and to force them to bow their heads in servile submission.

Another man took over. He spoke about what he called my "disobedience" to the command of the Revolutionaries, who represented the Communist Party, to confess. I realized for the first time that my failure to provide a confession of guilt was interpreted as an act of defiance against the Party. The audience was now even more angry. Perhaps disobeying the Party was a more serious offense than being a spy? I did not have time to decide on an answer before I was pushed and fell to the floor. However, the female giants by my side pulled me up with their strong arms, and I was restored to my previous position behind the microphone.

A third man spoke. He denounced my defense of Liu Shaoqi. After the Central Committee resolution against him and the amount of propaganda that "proved beyond doubt" that Liu was everything the resolution named him to be, the subject of Liu Shaoqi became one that demanded a strong display of anger from anyone who did not want to get into political trouble. When one tries to show emotion one does not genuinely feel, one tends to exaggerate. This audience was no exception. The women were always prompt and ready to pull me up again. Once or twice they even raised an arm to ward off a blow aimed at me.

The people in the audience soon worked themselves into a state of hysteria. Their shouts drowned out the voice of the speaker. Someone pushed me hard from behind. I stumbled and knocked over the microphone. One of the women tried to pick it up, tripped over the wires, and fell, dragging me with her. Because my arms were pinned behind me by the handcuffs, I fell in an awkward position. My face was pressed on the floor; many others fell on top of us in the confusion. Everybody seemed to be yelling. There was pandemonium. Several minutes passed. Finally I was pulled up again.

Utterly exhausted, I longed for the meeting to end. But the speeches continued. It seemed everyone sitting around the table on the platform wanted to make a contribution. They had ceased to denounce me; instead they were competing with each other to sing the praises of Lin Biao in the most extravagant flattery the rich Chinese language could provide. Their efforts to register their devotion to Lin Biao could be explained, I thought, only by the probable presence of Lin Biao's loyal lieutenants listening in an adjacent room.

Suddenly the door behind me opened. A man's voice shouted, "*Zuo-la!*" This meant that somebody had departed. The two simple words produced an electric effect. The speaker stopped in mid-sentence. Since the important person or persons listening in another room had gone, there was no more need to go on with the performance. Some of the audience were already on their feet, while others were collecting their bags and jackets. Hastily the speaker led them to shout slogans. He was largely ignored. Only a few responded while walking out of the room. It seemed the people were no longer angry with me; though they did not smile, the glances directed at me were indifferent. I was just one of the many victims at whose struggle meetings they had been present. They had done what was required of them. Now it was over. Once when a man brushed against me, someone behind him even stretched out a hand to steady me.

The room cleared in a moment. I could hear members of the

departing audience chatting as they left the building. "Getting rather chilly, isn't it?" "Where are you going for supper?" "Not raining, is it?" etc., etc. They sounded no different from an audience departing after a show in a cinema or theater.

The tense atmosphere dissipated like the escaping air from a burst balloon. The two women led me to the waiting car. This time they allowed me to walk by myself. For them also the show was over.

The "celebration" of the Ninth Party Congress went on for several weeks. Every few days I was taken to a different struggle meeting, sometimes less well organized than the first one. When the audience was very violent, I suffered much. Afterwards, I would be called for an interview in the interrogation room and asked whether I was ready to confess. I would either say, "I have nothing to confess" or "I'm not guilty," or simply remain silent. Then I would be taken to yet another struggle meeting. This exposure to one struggle meeting after another, called "rotating struggle," was a mind-numbing experience. Day after day, my ears were filled with the sound of angry, accusing voices, my eyes were blurred by images of hostile faces, and my body ached from rough handling and physical abuse. I no longer felt like a human being, just an inanimate object. Sometimes my spirit seemed to leave my body to look on the scene with detachment. Though I stopped thinking or observing what went on and withdrew into myself after a time, I was never really confused or frightened.

My personal experience of "rotating struggle," painful though it was at the time, was a comparatively mild one. After Mao Zedong's death in 1976, people became vocal about their experiences in the Cultural Revolution. I met one wizened old man who talked about his experience with a great sense of humor. He told me that he had been struggled against "more than a hundred times," frequently with a heavy iron chain around his neck, used to punish victims who refused to bow their heads voluntarily. Only when he told me some of his friends and colleagues had died during the struggle meetings did he display emotion. I asked him about the "jet position," which inflicted so much pain on the victims. He lightly brushed it aside, saying that it was used on everyone.

10

My Brother's Confession

WHEN THE SERIES OF ROTATING struggle meetings was over, summer was upon us. Before the humid heat of July started in earnest, Shanghai had a month of rain that the weathermen called the *huangmei,* named after the yellow plum that ripened in June. Dampness filled the cell and blackened the cement floor. After a particularly heavy downpour, water overflowed from the drain to seep through the base of the walls, forming murky puddles in the corners of the room. The pervading odor of mustiness and decay made each breath an unpleasant experience. Green mold formed on my stored winter jacket, padded trousers, and even the shoes I left overnight on the damp floor.

While I always welcomed the warmer weather with eagerness because I no longer had to shiver in the cold and huddle into all my clothes, I was dismayed to find the dampness causing me pain in the joints, which became red and swollen. When cool winds accompanied rainfall, my joints became so stiff that I had difficulty getting out of bed in the morning. At the same time, the inflammation of my gums became much worse. They bled all the time, not just when I brushed my teeth. I had to rub the gums, press out the blood with a finger, and rinse my mouth before eating any food. Even then, the contact of salty food with the inflamed gums sent shivers of pain through my body. I had to wash the vegetables with cold water in an effort to get rid of the salt. When the pain of my gums became too severe, the young doctor gave me sulfa drugs to reduce inflammation. But he told me that there was no dental department at the prison hospital.

My already difficult existence became a constant struggle to keep one step ahead of my body's steady deterioration. Life had never been so demanding or so meaningless. However, despite the physical pain and discomfort, I was in a calmer mood than I had been for some time. This was because I was going through a series of interrogations that again led me to hope for the eventual clarification of my case. Every few days I was called to the interrogation room, where the interrogator of the Workers' Propaganda Team questioned me about my relatives and friends, one by one. Between interrogations, I was asked to write lengthy accounts about each one of them and to describe all our contacts. I knew that what I wrote would be checked against the accounts of my friends and relatives about me, our contacts, what they had said to me, what I had said to them, etc. The interrogator and his fellow workers would compare what we had written to find discrepancies that might be used to cast doubt on my honesty. Therefore it was important to write accurately, giving all facts but not elaborating on them, in case I contradicted what others had said. Sometimes the interrogation sessions were stormy, with the interrogator voicing threats and dissatisfaction with what I had written or said. At other times, I would be urged to provide incriminating evidence against this one or that one of my relatives and friends. Then I knew the person in question was in serious trouble.

On the whole, to answer questions about my relatives and friends and to write about them gave me the opportunity to speak on their behalf. From what I knew of the nature of their occupations and their past lives, I could generally guess the sort of problems confronting them during the Cultural Revolution. I searched my memory for what they had done and said that might help to improve their standing in the eyes of the Revolutionaries. And I put what I had to say in language familiar and acceptable to the Maoists.

One of the outstanding characteristics of educated Chinese of my generation was our keen sense of patriotism, born of our knowledge and experience of the outside world and our concern for China's comparative backwardness. We were acutely conscious of the fact that China's recent history was the record of a great civilization that had been in steady decline for a century. In fact, it was the naive belief that the Communist Revolution might provide China with the impetus for progress that led so many of us to remain in, or go back to, China around 1949. So in my accounts I could truthfully speak of my friends' and relatives' deep love for China and their service to the country. But all of it fell on deaf ears. Determined to find fault, the Revolutionaries refused to see virtue. Furthermore, the Maoists confused the concepts of nation, which means "people having common descent," and state, which means "an organized political community under one government." If a man had made an important scientific or artistic contribution to China's cultural life before the Communist Party came to power, he was supposed to have served not China but the Kuomintang regime. Therefore, he was guilty of helping to sustain the rule of the enemy. This point of view was so narrow-minded and absurd that I engaged in frequent arguments with the interrogator about it. However, I soon discovered that I was dealing not with the prejudice of the few Maoists in charge of my case but with the accepted view of the Communist Party.

The interrogation sessions started in the rainy season. Often I arrived in the interrogation room with a wet face, wet, matted hair, and soaked socks and shoes. I had no raincoat, but fortunately it was still cool enough for me to wear several layers of clothing so that I was not drenched through. The interrogations went on into the hot summer months, when dampness and rain gave way to oppressive heat and mosquitoes. Sometimes other men, obviously from organizations dealing with the persons I had been asked to provide material on, joined my interrogator to question me. Then I would know that my friends or relatives were also undergoing investigation, just as I was. I would worry about them and watch closely the language and attitude of the strangers. If they looked fairly mild and seemed reasonable, I would be relieved; if they looked particularly stupid and menacing, I would be apprehensive.

In the autumn, I had a grueling time when a member of the

Military Control Commission of the People's Art Theater came to question me about their director, Huang Zuolin. Huang and his wife, Danni, a beautiful and talented actress, were old friends of my husband's and mine from our student days in London. When the Communist army took over Shanghai, Huang was already a well-known and successful film director. It was believed that the couple had been invited to remain in China by the Communist Party underground in Shanghai. Both of them were accepted by the new regime at once; when the People's Art Theater was formed, Huang was named its director and became a Party member. Their careers flourished; together they put on the Shanghai stage many first-rate plays, including translations of Shakespeare's comedies and other works by contemporary European and American writers that satirized the capitalist system. It was largely through the efforts of these two that the Chinese audience was made aware of the fact that playwrights of other lands were allowed to present their own societies in a critical light. Huang was considered a first-rate director by the public and the Party leaders in charge of cultural affairs. It was also obvious that he was different from those who followed closely the Maoist line of "art serving politics" and "art for the glorification of the workers, the peasants, and the soldiers."

Before this particular interrogation, I had already read numerous articles in the newspaper criticizing Huang's film *Fighting for Shanghai,* made in the early fifties to eulogize the Communist takeover of the city. The film was a very successful propaganda effort carried out with skill; at the time it came out, it was hailed as a great achievement. Now the newspaper devoted several days and many columns to criticizing the film, alleging that Huang had made the Kuomintang defenders of the city "heroic," thereby slighting the Communist soldiers. The critics also claimed that when he depicted the destruction of the city and the sufferings of the people, he exposed himself as a man opposed to armed struggle in general and the War of Liberation by the Communist Party in particular. It was clear from the avalanche of criticism directed against him in the press that he had been singled out as a victim.

Why had a man like Huang Zuolin, who had served the Communist regime effectively and well, become the target of severe attack? Like many others, he was a victim of the internal power struggle within the Communist Party leadership. The men who gave him his positions and Party membership were old enemies of Jiang Qing in the thirties in Shanghai. At that time, she was a minor film actress struggling for recognition, while they were the leaders of the Left-Wing Cultural Movement, which was the rallying point of China's left-wing writers and artists and a part of the Chinese Communist Party underground directed by Liu Shaoqi. Apparently these left-wing intellectuals largely ignored her, thinking of her as a woman of easy virtue and little talent. Jiang Qing had nursed her resentment throughout the years. When she gained power over the Cultural Department of the Party during the Cultural Revolution, she had all these men arrested and denounced as members of the Liu Shaoqi faction. Since patronage was a part of Chinese political life, the downfall of any official always brought about the downfall of his subordinates.

"Do you know Huang Zuolin, the comprador?" the Military Control representative from the People's Art Theater, seated beside my interrogator, asked me as soon as I sat down in the prisoner's chair after reading one of Mao's quotations.

I gathered from his question that since they had failed to find anything wrong in Huang's personal behavior, they were digging into his background.

A comprador was a man who acted as liaison between foreign firms and Chinese officials. The system had been invented by the Qing dynasty at the end of the last century in order to control foreign traders. With the advent of modern business methods, the system died out gradually in the thirties. But big firms like Shell did not fire their compradors. They simply stopped appointing new ones after the old ones died. The Chinese Communist regime regarded former compradors as the most reactionary members of the bourgeois class. After the Communist army took over Shanghai, those classified as members of the "comprador-bourgeois class" all suffered imprisonment or heavy fines. Huang's father had been Shell's comprador in Tianjin; he died during the Sino-Japanese war.

"I know Huang Zuolin, the well-known director of films and plays," I answered.

"He was also a comprador of Shell!" said the uniformed man from the People's Art Theater. "We know all about you. You are a diehard reactionary and a spy of the imperialists. We are not surprised you try to evade my questions.

"Huang Zuolin is in serious trouble. He is a class enemy who wormed his way into the Party. If you try to shield him, the consequences will be extremely serious. Your own position will become much worse. If you are clearheaded and cooperative, it will count in your favor as a contribution to the Cultural Revolution," my interrogator said.

"I'll speak the truth," I said.

"If you speak the truth, you will say he was a comprador of Shell," the military man said.

"It was his father who was a comprador of Shell. Huang Zuolin has an unfortunate family origin," I said.

"He took over the job when his father died," the man insisted.

"The position of comprador was abolished long ago. When his father died, it had ceased to exist," I told him.

"Then what is this?" The man threw a document on the table. The interrogator handed it to me. It was the deed for a piece of land in Tianjin bearing Huang Zuolin's seal as the owner. I saw the serial number on it and recognized it as a document taken from a Shell office file.

"That's an old document," I said.

"Old or new, it shows that Huang Zuolin was a Shell comprador, a fact he hid from the Party."

"I can tell you the whole story, if you will listen," I said.

"Go ahead," said my interrogator.

"I don't know the date, but long before the war the Kuomintang government proclaimed a new regulation forbidding foreign ownership of land in China. All the foreign firms owning land transferred their deeds to their compradors' names. Shell did the same. When Huang's father passed away, Huang inherited the family's property holdings. This took place during the war; Tianjin was under Japanese occupation, and Huang Zuolin was not there. Shell was not there either. It had ceased operation after Pearl Harbor. I suppose whoever was Huang Zuolin's agent just put his seal on the deeds of all his father's properties, including this piece of land belonging to Shell. That doesn't mean Huang Zuolin was ever employed by Shell as its comprador."

"He was paid by Shell for his services," said the military man from the People's Art Theater.

"I know nothing about that," I answered.

"Your husband actually made the payment as Shell's general manager."

"He did not mention the matter to me." I decided it was best to deny knowledge of the transaction so that they would think I could not help them to incriminate Huang and would leave me alone. Actually my husband did tell me that Shell wanted to give Huang a sum of money to show the company's appreciation of what his father had done for Shell, even though the land was confiscated by the Communist government during the Land Reform Movement of 1950. Such a generous gesture did not fit the image of foreign exploitation projected by Communist Party propaganda.

"You are lying. Your servants said you and your husband talked about everything together."

"He did not mention this matter to me. Perhaps he did not consider it important," I said. "Certainly we did not discuss everything that took place in his office."

"We don't believe you."

"That's as you please. I know nothing about any payment. But that doesn't mean you can't find out. You can look at our office files, or you can ask our accounts department."

"We have already done that. Do you think we would overlook anything like that? I have all the proof that he was paid by your husband."

"In that case, the fact that I do not know anything makes no difference."

"We want you to admit that Huang Zuolin was a comprador of Shell. He was paid for his services. You are the most senior of Shell's Chinese staff. You can confirm what we know already. Huang Zuolin belongs to the comprador-bourgeois class. The comprador-bourgeois class is the most reactionary of all. He will be expelled from the Party. You and your husband were friends of his. You know him well. You could provide valuable information against him," the military man said.

To be expelled from the Communist Party was the worst possible fate for a Party member. He could not again become one of the masses. His position in society would be little better than that of a counterrevolutionary; he would be discriminated against at all times. And his family, including his children and their children, would have to suffer with him. For me, it was tragic and unjust that such a future awaited Huang Zuolin, who had devoted his life and talents to the Communist cause. The whole situation made me angry. I said firmly, "As far as I know, Huang Zuolin was a loyal member of the Communist Party. He was never a comprador. When his father died, Shell no longer had any comprador in Tianjin."

"You are uncooperative," said my interrogator. "Don't you want to earn a merit point for yourself?"

"I have to adhere to the truth," I said.

They became angry. The representative of the Military Control Commission of the People's Art Theater went red in the face and stared at me with disappointment and disgust. My interrogator said, "We want you to write an account of Huang Zuolin, the comprador. Put down everything you know about him. If you try to cover up for him, the consequences will be extremely serious for you. If you provide information that is useful, you will make a contribution to the Cultural Revolution. And you'll get a merit point. Try to remember everything he said to you and your husband, and put down what you know of his life and his views. He's a class enemy. You should expose him and denounce him. This is your opportunity to declare your standpoint. If you expose him effectively, we will think you have made an improvement in your own reform."

"If you want to earn a merit point for yourself, denounce Huang Zuolin," added the military man from the People's Art Theater.

What they said was an insult to my integrity. But it was the standard pronouncement made to encourage lying to suit the political campaign of the moment. How many people succumbed to such pressure I did not know. In the present instance, it only strengthened my resolve to speak the truth.

When I had written down everything I knew and remembered of Huang Zuolin's life and views, including his firm belief that the Chinese Communist Party represented progress and enlightenment for China, they threw the account back to me and threatened me with severe punishment because I had failed to state that Huang was a Shell comprador in Tianjin. I was threatened and warned in stormy sessions, and had to write the account over and over again. But I stuck to my story and refused to accede to their demands. After a few weeks the matter was dropped, and the man from the People's Art Theater disappeared just as suddenly as he had appeared.

Later, after my release from the detention house, I learned that the Revolutionaries never succeeded in classifying Huang Zuolin as a member of the comprador-bourgeois class and expelling him from the Party. Huang was merely denounced as a member of the Liu Shaoqi camp. He and his wife spent the years of Cultural Revolution being struggled against at numerous meetings and working at various tasks of heavy physical labor, including carrying loads of earth and bricks at a building site in severe winter weather and scorching summer heat. Huang's health was damaged, and his beautiful wife became an old woman.

After Mao's death and the arrest of the Gang of Four in 1976, the political situation changed in China. Both Huang Zuolin and his wife were rehabilitated.

One of the most ugly aspects of life in Communist China during the Mao Zedong era was the Party's demand that people inform on each other routinely and denounce each other during political campaigns. This practice had a profoundly destructive effect on human relationships. Husbands and wives became guarded with each other, and parents were alienated from their children. The practice inhibited all forms of human contact, so that people no longer wanted to have friends. It also encouraged secretiveness and hypocrisy. To protect himself, a man had to keep his thoughts to himself. When he was compelled to speak, often lying was the only way to protect himself and his family.

While I was being pressured and urged to provide incriminating material against others, those others were at the same time being pressured and urged to provide incriminating material against me. I could usually guess what my relatives and friends had said or written about me from the questions the interrogator asked. It was not difficult to discern whether a certain person was still cool-headed and holding his own or had become panicky and confused. Towards the end of 1969, I went through a rather difficult time because of a "confession" made by my brother in Beijing. It illustrated once again how a perfectly intelligent and well-educated person could break down under pressure so that he no longer knew the demarcation line between fact and fiction.

Amid fanfare and celebration, Mao had made another new pronouncement. It appeared in red print in the newspaper and was elaborated in a lead article by the joint editors of the *People's Daily* and the *Red Flag* magazine, both Party organs, and the editors of the *Liberation Army Daily*. Mao had declared, "The Proletarian Cultural Revolution is a great political revolution of the proletarian class against the capitalist class. It is the continuation of the class struggle by the proletarian class against the capitalist class. It is also the continuation of the class struggle by the Communist Party against the Kuomintang."

After the publication of this piece of wisdom, a campaign was initiated to "root out the dregs of the Kuomintang." Daily, the newspaper reported the exposure of undercover Kuomintang agents, hidden Kuomintang military personnel, and sympathizers of the Kuomintang regime in Taiwan. So many enemies were unearthed in such a short time that it seemed that China was suddenly full of men and women secretly longing for the Kuomintang. The years of Communist propaganda against the former government seemed a wasted effort. A tense atmosphere of extreme nervousness had been deliberately created. It provided the excuse for another round of witch-hunts and legitimized the escalation of class struggle to create fear in the general public. The only way for a man to prove his innocence was to display exaggerated support for Mao and the Party, to shout slogans louder, to work harder in a spirit of self-sacrifice for no material reward, and to be extra cruel to the class enemies. The newspaper urged members of the proletariat to be vigilant and to watch for unusual activities and strange behavior among their neighbors and fellow workers. They were also to increase surveillance of class enemies not incarcerated in prisons.

The next call for interrogation came as no surprise to me. My persecutor could not afford to leave me out of another round of class struggle if he wished to appear to be following Mao's directives closely. After all, I was the widow of a Kuomintang government official.

The interrogator told me to read the latest directive of Mao as soon as I entered the interrogation room and had bowed to his portrait. When I had finished reading it, he told me to read it again. Then the interrogator said, "We are to expose the dregs of the Kuomintang. You are one of them."

Two other men were in the room. Suddenly the younger of them shouted, "Confess!"

"To what?" I asked.

"Don't pretend to be calm and innocent. Confess your relationship with the Kuomintang!"

"I have no relationship with the Kuomintang."

"You are a loyal supporter of the Kuomintang."

"I doubt very much the Kuomintang would agree with you," I said. While I was speaking I observed the two men. From their clothes and their short hairstyle, I thought they were from North China. All Chinese are supposed to speak Mandarin, the national spoken language based on the Beijing dialect. However, natives of Beijing like the young man who had just spoken often retained certain recognizable intonations of their original dialect. I wondered why two men from Beijing were taking part in my interrogation. In the earlier stage of this series of interrogations, when I was going through the members of my family, I had already written about my brother and sister-in-law in Beijing, and provided the interrogator with an account of our contacts throughout the years.

"You are a loyal supporter of the Kuomintang. It's useless to deny it."

"Please prove your accusations," I said.

"Of course we have proof, otherwise we wouldn't have come such a long way to question you," said the older of the two men, who seemed to be senior in position. He looked and spoke like an industrial worker with little education, a true member of the proletariat. The younger man looked like a student.

"Have you ever had your photograph taken in front of a Kuomintang flag?" asked my interrogator.

"Maybe I have. I can't remember for sure," I answered. I thought he was asking me about the days during the Second World War, long before the Communist Party came to power in China, when my late husband was a diplomat at the Chinese embassy in Canberra, Australia.

"How could you not remember! You can't get out of your difficulty by simply claiming loss of memory," said the young man from Beijing.

"It was so long ago," I said. "If there was a photograph, the Red Guards who came to my house should have it. They took all my photographs."

"You must have destroyed the photograph. It's not there," the older man said.

"Why should I destroy a photograph like that? Everybody knows my late husband was a diplomatic officer of the Kuomintang government when we lived in Australia."

"What are you talking about? Who is asking you about those days?" the interrogator said with impatience.

"Aren't you asking me about the time when we lived in Australia?"

"Nonsense. We are asking you about the present time, after Liberation. Have you had a photograph taken in front of a Kuomintang flag since Liberation? Answer truthfully. Confess everything!" the young man from Beijing leaned forward and said to me.

I was astonished that they thought it possible for anyone in China to have had a photograph taken in front of a Kuomintang flag since the Communist Party came to power. I asked, "How could there be any Kuomintang flag in China after Liberation? Where is it?"

"Never mind about the flag. Just confess why you did it. Was it to show your loyalty to the Kuomintang?" the interrogator asked.

"I never had a photograph taken in front of a Kuomintang flag after Liberation," I stated categorically, deciding to end this absurd conversation once and for all.

"Now, don't be so sure. You will regret it. You'll miss the opportunity to earn lenient treatment," the older man from Beijing said.

"You had better assume a serious attitude. Someone else has already confessed, so we know what we are talking about. We are determined to expose all Kuomintang supporters. There is no escape for you," said the younger man from Beijing.

"I don't know what you are talking about. I'm not a supporter of the Kuomintang. If I were, wouldn't I be in Taiwan now?" I asked them.

My interrogator whispered something to the two men and then said to me, "You had better return to your cell now and think about the whole matter. You have been here long enough to know the policy of the People's Government. You should know it's quite useless to deny something that can be proved."

I was taken back to my cell, where I continued to puzzle over this extraordinary affair. The men seemed so serious. They must have something on which to base their accusation. Was it someone's malicious plot to incriminate me? I had already been accused of being a spy for the imperialists. Why this sudden diversion?

Three days later, I was called again. I was again pressed to confess; I gave the same answers as I had the first time. Then I was sent back to the cell and told to think it all over again. For three weeks, I went back and forth to the interrogation room every two or three days. The atmosphere became very tense in the interrogation room, but I was quite unable to guess what they had in mind.

During this time, to add pressure, the guards refused to give me the sulfa drug so necessary for keeping the inflammation of my gums in check. The condition rapidly deteriorated. Not only the gums but the lining of my mouth were so inflamed that I could no longer eat the food given to me. I requested liquid rice so that without chewing I could still get some nourishment into my body to keep alive. My gums were now so painful that I was completely preoccupied with them. When I was in the interrogation room, I had difficulty concentrating on the proceedings. I could understand how some prisoners gave in under such conditions simply because physical suffering had weakened their willpower. I warned myself to keep a clear head in spite of the pain.

My request for liquid rice gave the Maoists the opportunity to reduce my ration. What was handed to me at mealtimes was no more than a half-container of gray-colored water with a few grains of rice floating on top. After a few days of this diet, I fainted. It was a mild guard who called the doctor. He gave me an intravenous injection of glucose and sent me with the guard to the prison hospital. I did not know what the guard said to the doctor privately, but the doctor gave her a written order. When I was brought back to the detention house, the regular dosage of sulfa drug was resumed and I was given a thick rice porridge with a piece of steamed bread at mealtimes.

When I was again called to the interrogation room, the interrogator told me to read Mao's latest directive three times. After I finished and sat down, he asked me, "Do you fully understand what our Great Leader Chairman Mao has said?"

"I think I do," I answered.

"Explain."

"I think Chairman Mao wants everybody to know that the Great Proletarian Cultural Revolution is a political revolution, not simply a revolution limited to the field of culture."

"That's correct. What about the two continuations?"

"The Cultural Revolution is the continuation of the class struggle the proletarian class has been carrying on against the capitalist class. It's not a new struggle but the continuation of the same struggle that has been going on," I explained.

"What about the part concerning the Kuomintang?"

"The Cultural Revolution is also the continuation of the class struggle carried on by the Communist Party against the Kuomintang, which has been going on since 1927."

"Yes, since you understand that, you should realize the seriousness of the situation. The Kuomintang is our enemy. After its defeat by our army, it took refuge on the island of Taiwan, protected by the United States. Until we have liberated Taiwan and brought the island under the banner of our Great Leader Chairman Mao, the struggle against the Kuomintang will continue. The Kuomintang must be destroyed to complete our Revolution. Our Great Leader is determined to liberate Taiwan, and our Vice-Supreme Commander Lin is confident we will succeed. But the capitalist-roaders led by Liu Shaoqi opposed them. They said the Taiwan problem was for the next generation. That's a defeatist attitude. Our Great Leader believes the Taiwan issue is for our generation. It must be resolved now while the seasoned military leaders such as our Vice-Supreme Commander Lin, who have had the experience of defeating the Kuomintang before, can still lead our army to victory. The class struggle against the capitalist-roaders of the Liu Shaoqi clique is linked to the class struggle against the Kuomintang. Now that we have thoroughly defeated the Liu Shaoqi faction and power is once again concentrated in the hands of our Great Leader, we will deal with the issue of the Kuomintang. That's why we must expose all Kuomintang sympathizers in our midst to prevent the formation of a fifth column for the enemy. The dregs of the Kuomintang must be isolated and watched closely so that they will not be able to do harm," said the interrogator.

"Your husband was a senior Kuomintang official," added the older man from Beijing.

"Not senior, only middle-ranking. But in any case, he elected to remain here when the Kuomintang went to Taiwan," I pointed out.

"Yes, yes, many Kuomintang officials did that. Some of them were deliberately planted here by the Kuomintang to do mischief. Each one of them will be closely examined."

"When my late husband became Shell's general manager in Shanghai, his appointment had to be approved by the Shanghai municipal government. Surely the Party had already examined his case thoroughly at that time," I told them.

"That's not enough. The man who gave approval might have been a capitalist-roader. We, the Revolutionaries, must examine everybody on behalf of the Party now," said the interrogator.

"As early as the days of the Chinese soviet, before the Long March, our Great Leader had already formulated a whole set of effective methods to deal with class enemies before our army started an offensive against the Kuomintang forces. At that time we put the important class enemies in prison, as we have done now during the Cultural Revolution. The others were given to the revolutionary masses to watch. We have also done that during the Cultural Revolution." The young man from Beijing was obviously a student anxious to display his knowledge of Mao Zedong's books. He was referring to Mao's account of the preparations made by the Chinese Communist Party before military engagements against the Kuomintang's encirclement campaigns, described in a 1936 essay entitled, "The Strategy of China's Revolutionary War."

"You should understand your own position in the struggle between the Communist Party and the Kuomintang. You are on the side of the Kuomintang by virtue of your family background and your husband's association with them," the older man from Beijing said.

"I'm afraid you are quite wrong. I'm not involved in the struggle between the Kuomintang and the Communist Party at all. I regret that the Communist Party and the Kuomintang had to fight each other, killing innocent Chinese people and destroying our national wealth in the process. As a Chinese I hope for peace and unity of the two political parties to work for the common good of the country," I declared.

"We will achieve unity after we have crushed the Kuomintang," said the student.

"If you are not a sympathizer of the Kuomintang, if, as you say, you are not involved in the struggle between the Kuomintang and the Communist Party, why did you have your photograph taken in front of a Kuomintang flag?" asked the interrogator.

"I have no idea what you are talking about. I've tried very hard to guess, but I simply can't. Why don't you tell me what it's all about? There must be some misunderstanding," I said with sincerity.

"Think back to 1962. What happened in 1962?" asked the interrogator.

"I don't know what happened in 1962, except that was the year I lost my mother."

"That's right!" declared both men from Beijing. "You had better confess and tell the whole story."

"Do you mean you want to hear about my mother's death?" I asked them incredulously.

"Yes, tell the whole story. Confess everything," said the interrogator.

I was puzzled. I had no idea what they were driving at. But since they wanted to know, I told them about my mother's death.

"I was called to Nanjing by my mother's neighbor, who telephoned me. When I got there, I found my mother unconscious after suffering a heatstroke. It was July, and the temperature was persistently about ninety-five degrees. We called an ambulance and rushed her to the hospital. At first she got better. But she developed pneumonia and died of heart failure."

"Did your brothers come to Nanjing too?"

"Yes, they came with their wives."

"What did you do after your mother died?"

"Being the eldest, I arranged her funeral."

"You indulged in superstition. That's another proof you're a real reactionary," said the younger man.

"Superstition" is the word habitually used by Communist officials when they refer to any kind of religious practice.

"My mother was a devout Buddhist, so I arranged for her to have a Buddhist funeral," I said.

"You must have done something illegal. The Buddhist temples were all closed after the Great Leap Forward Campaign, and the monks dispersed. Yet you managed to get several monks for your mother's funeral," said the interrogator.

"I got the monks with the help of the man in charge of the Buddhist Research Institute in Nanjing."

"They are only allowed to perform religious services for foreign visitors from Southeast Asia, not for Chinese."

"The man I saw decided to help me because I begged him," I said. How well I remembered my prolonged negotiation with the man at the Buddhist Research Institute in Nanjing! I obtained the services of the monks by making a large donation, which I was not sure was allowed officially. Finally he agreed to provide me with six monks to recite the sutras at my mother's funeral.

"You are guilty of reviving superstition at your mother's funeral. Your brothers and sisters-in-law are guilty too because they did not stop you. You also put the names of your sisters in the United States on your mother's tombstone. You failed to draw a line between yourself and the traitors who chose to live abroad. All of these things prove beyond doubt you are a reactionary," the young man said.

"My sisters in the United States are also my mother's daughters. It's a Chinese custom to put all the children's names on the tombstone."

"We'll talk about all that later on. Now tell me, what did you do after your mother's funeral? After you left the cemetery, where did you go?" my interrogator asked. All three of them now seemed to become excited. The two men from Beijing were staring at me intently.

"We returned to her house to sort out her things."

"Before you returned to her house, where did you go?"

"Nowhere. We returned to her house directly."

"Did you not go to the Sun Yatsen Memorial after your mother's burial?" asked the older man from Beijing.

"No, we were all so sad and exhausted."

"Confess!" The young man suddenly banged the table.

"What do you want me to confess? The funeral of my mother has no political significance."

"The funeral of your mother has no political significance, but your going to the Sun Yatsen Memorial with your brothers to have your photograph taken in front of a Kuomintang flag had a great deal of political significance. You wanted to pledge your loyalty to the Kuomintang. At that time, in 1962, the Kuomintang was planning to attack the mainland," said the young man.

The allegation was so absurd that I wanted to laugh. But I knew the situation was in fact very serious. To talk to these ignorant men was a strenuous effort, and I had so little strength because of my poor health and inadequate diet. Throughout each interrogation, I was suffering severe pain in my mouth. Already I was so exhausted that I felt faint. But I had to go on talking to try to clear myself, even though I had no idea how they had formed their absurd suspicion of me in the first place.

"Please be reasonable. First of all, are you sure there was a Kuomintang flag at the Sun Yatsen Memorial? If there was no flag there after the Kuomintang left Nanjing, you will know we couldn't possibly have had a photograph taken in front of one. Secondly, even assuming there was a flag and assuming you are correct in your allegation that I wanted to impress the Kuomintang in case they came back to the mainland, would the Kuomintang accept my declaration of loyalty simply because I could show them such a photograph? The Kuomintang officials are not fools. Wouldn't they become extremely suspicious of my motives, since they knew very well my late husband and I had elected to remain here in 1949 and did not follow them to Taiwan?"

"They would believe you. You are already an agent for the Kuomintang," the young man declared.

"If indeed I were already an agent of the Kuomintang, I would have no need to prove my loyalty to them. You contradict yourself in your allegation."

Both the men from Beijing shouted, "You must confess that you did in fact have a photograph taken with your brothers in front of a Kuomintang flag at the Sun Yatsen Memorial in Nanjing."

"Please ask my brothers and sisters-in-law. They'll tell you it did not happen. We never went to the Sun Yatsen Memorial in Nanjing at all."

"We did ask your brother at the Foreign Trade Institute in Beijing. At first he also tried to deny everything. But when the Revolutionaries made him see the right path to take, he confessed everything. He said it was your idea to go to the Sun Yatsen Memorial. He also said it was your camera that was used to take the photograph. You had the film developed in Shanghai and sent him a copy of it. Do you still dare to deny it?" the young man shouted.

My heart sank. It was pure fabrication, of course. What had the Maoists done to my poor brother to make him lie like that? I could imagine the agony he must have gone through before he succumbed to their pressure.

To meet this extremely serious situation, I enlisted the help of Mao's Little Red Book. Raising it in my hand, I said, "Our Great Leader Chairman Mao taught us, 'Rice must be eaten one mouthful at a time; a journey must be undertaken a step at a time.' I beg you to obey his teaching in this case. Please go to the Sun Yatsen Memorial in Nanjing and see for yourselves. The Sun Yatsen Memorial is managed by a government department in Nanjing and visited by foreigners. There simply couldn't have been a Kuomintang flag there so many years after the Kuomintang left Nanjing. Please go there and see for yourselves. If you should find a Kuomintang flag, then come back and punish me. I can't run away."

The two men from Beijing simply stared at me while the interrogator stood up and said, "You may now go back to your cell and think the matter over."

Perhaps, I thought, he at last understood the logic of what I had said and decided that the only way to resolve the problem was for the two men to go to Nanjing to see for themselves. I hoped they would do just that. When they found no Kuomintang flag at the Sun Yatsen Memorial, they would return to Beijing to report. Perhaps that was what actually happened, for many weeks passed and I was not called again.

During the Cultural Revolution, the Revolutionaries traveled all over China at public expense to "investigate the crimes of the class enemies" under their charge. They used the opportunity for sightseeing and visiting friends and relatives. Some of them prolonged their trips or took roundabout routes to include famous scenic spots on their itinerary. Since Shanghai was a favorite city for shopping for all Chinese, the Revolutionaries always wanted to come to or pass through it. When the two men from Beijing came to Shanghai, they actually passed through Nanjing. I thought they had deliberately avoided stopping there to check the matter of the flag at the Sun Yatsen Memorial because they were afraid they might have to turn back if they found there was no Kuomintang flag. Each session of my interrogation took only a couple of hours at the most. They had the rest of the day free. Since their travel expenses and hotel accommodations were paid for by the Revolutionary Committee at their place of work, they enjoyed a free holiday for over a month. In fact, the opportunity to travel was one of the perks given to the more aggressive Revolutionaries to encourage their loyalty to the Maoist leaders.

Alone in my cell, I could not help thinking over and over again about this strange episode. At first I was indignant that my own brother should have behaved so badly under pressure. But when I thought of his life since the early fifties, the difficulties he had had to endure for so many years, and the degree of persecution a man like him must have been subjected to during the Cultural Revolution, my sense of outrage evaporated. A deep feeling of sadness and compassion for this unfortunate man took its place in my heart. I could only assume that some Revolutionaries, overzealous to unearth as many sympathizers of the Kuomintang as possible, had invented the story and planted it in my brother's mind for him to confess. But before they succeeded in doing that, they must have really damaged his reasoning powers. Normally my brother was neither stupid nor disloyal.

My brother had worked as an economics expert in the Ministry of Foreign Trade in the early fifties, one of a group of outstanding young economists the Communist Party invited back from British and American universities where they were doing research. His job was to analyze and write reports on world economic conditions. He was given senior rank and good treatment. However, it soon became apparent that although his work was appreciated by other experts working in a technical capacity in the Foreign Trade Ministry and its agencies abroad, he failed to satisfy the requirements of the Party, which through the Party secretary of his unit controlled his life. The reports he wrote did not bear out the Party propaganda line that predicted impending doom for the capitalist world. Those were unhappy years for my brother. In trying to find a compromise between the facts as he knew them and the lies he was required to tell to justify the Party line, he became a very silent man, speaking very little and smiling very seldom. It seemed that no matter how hard he tried to please, unless he fell in with the Party line completely, the Party secretary was always exasperated with him. Once the man declared bluntly, "I simply can't afford to allow optimistic reports on the economy of any capitalist country to be sent out from this office. You are subverting the Party if you go on writing like this."

When the Anti-Rightist Campaign started in 1957, the Party secretary saw it as an opportunity to get rid of my recalcitrant brother. Much was made of the fact that he had done graduate work in England and for a brief period of time had worked as personal assistant to a senior Kuomintang minister. He was subjected to many grueling hours of struggle meetings, isolated in his office for several months, not allowed to go home, and questioned continuously by a throng of Party activists, day and night, without sleep, in what was known as the tactic of "exhaustive bombardment." The Party activists did not succeed in making him a "Rightist," mainly because they could find no evidence that he had criticized the Party, but the ordeal left him a broken man with an ulcer. The last trace of a smile left his face, his hair turned gray, and he acquired a faraway look in his eyes. He was then only thirty-seven.

Realizing that he was unwanted at his office, my brother asked to be transferred to another job. Angered at his failure to brand my brother a Rightist, the Party secretary of his unit declared that my brother was too proud and needed a period of time with the peasants to improve his socialist understanding. He was sent to a village outside Beijing to raise chickens. Living conditions were primitive; he was allowed to go home only once a month. But he enjoyed being away at last from the Party bureaucrats. He took the job of raising chickens seriously and soon established a reputation for having chickens that were fatter and produced more eggs than anyone else's. Whenever he returned to the village after visiting his family in the city, he would bring back an armful of books and cases of equipment for various experiments to improve his work. The peasants flocked to his dwelling, anxious to get his advice and to talk over their problems with him. This situation offended the Party boss of the village. He urged the Ministry of Foreign Trade to send my brother elsewhere.

At the time the Maoists were retreating after the failure of the Great Leap Forward Campaign and the ensuing acute economic crisis. Generally at times of real difficulty like this, the Party made some concessions to the intellectuals. The ministry took the unprecedented step of asking my brother what he wanted to do. My brother requested a job as an English teacher and was assigned to the English Language Department of the Foreign Trade Institute as a professor. He gave his new field of work the same serious attention he gave everything else he had undertaken. At the time of the Cultural Revolution he had already become a recognized authority on English language teaching and was conducting training classes for young teachers. He had also published books and articles on the subject.

Later, after my release from prison, I tried to get in touch with my brother. He refused to correspond with me, saying that my former contacts with the Western world made me a "dangerous person." It was not until the winter of 1976, after Mao died and the Gang of Four had been arrested, that my brother invited me to visit him in Beijing. I found him completely shattered by the cruel treatment he had received as a professor during the Cultural Revolution. He and his wife also spent several years doing physical labor in a Cadre School where living conditions were extremely hard. I did not have the heart to ask him what made him say that we had been to the Sun Yatsen Memorial to have our photograph taken in front of a Kuomintang flag. I did not want him to think I blamed him for succumbing to pressure. He had suffered too much for too long.

After being closed for several years, the Foreign Trade Institute was reopening. He was busily engaged with other professors in putting the English Language Department together again. He seemed content to be doing something worthwhile after so long. His small apartment was always full of people coming to talk to him. I did not want to remind him of the Cultural Revolution. However, just before my departure, he suddenly mentioned the subject himself.

He said, "You did send the photograph to me in 1962, didn't you?"

"I sent you a photograph of Mother that I had enlarged at Wan Xiang, the photographic studio in Shanghai," I told him. "That was the only photograph I sent you in 1962."

"Was it simply a photograph of Mother? I remembered receiving a photograph from you. The Revolutionaries insisted it was a photograph we had taken at the Sun Yatsen Memorial in front of a Kuomintang flag. They seemed very sure and were able to tell me exactly what we did. I couldn't remember a thing. But as they repeated it over and over again, I got a picture in my mind. Finally, it seemed to me that what they described did happen."

"No," I said angrily, "it did not happen. We never went to the Sun Yatsen Memorial at all. The Revolutionaries were liars. They wanted to incriminate us. They wanted to prove we were loyal to the Kuomintang so that they could punish us."

He laid a hand on my arm and said calmly, with resignation, "Don't get excited and angry. It's useless to get angry with them. They have the last word always. If they say something happened, it happened. It's useless to resist. I've learned this from my personal experience. I'm sure you learned all that too during your imprisonment."

"Not at all. I haven't learned a thing. What's more, I do not intend to learn."

"You will learn to accept. We all have to. I have seen it happen to so many. And it happened to me. It will happen to you too."

"I won't let it happen to me."

"I'm sorry to hear you say that. Deeply sorry. You'll get hurt, badly hurt, I'm afraid."

My sister-in-law came into the room then to tell me that my taxi to the airport was waiting. When I said goodbye to my brother, I was trembling. I did not know whether it was because I was angry at the terrible system under which we had to live or because I was sad that we could not do anything more effective than blindly resist to maintain our dignity. From inside the taxi, I turned to wave to my brother; he had already gone in. I somehow thought he was disappointed in me. I had not behaved like wise Chinese who "bend with the wind to survive the hurricane."

I went out to Arizona to see my brother again in March 1984, when he came to the Thunderbird Campus of the American Graduate School of International Management as an exchange professor from the Institute of Foreign Trade in Beijing. I found that he was now an old man suffering from emphysema, looking a good ten years older than his age. But the twinkle of humor returned to his eyes when he told me that at last he had been reinstated as a professor of economics and had come to the

United States to lecture on China's new economic policy. When I asked him what would happen when the Party's policy swung left again, as it had done from left to right and right to left like a pendulum for over thirty years, he took a deep breath and sighed. After a while, he said, "I'm a very sick man. Each cycle of change takes a number of years to complete. Let's hope that when the time comes for another change, I won't be around to see it."

11

A Kind of Torture

AFTER THE EPISODE INVOLVING my brother, the interrogator continued with his inquiry about all my relatives and friends. This series of interrogations lasted nearly seven months, until the end of 1969. Then I was no longer called to the interrogation room. I waited and waited. A month passed, and then another. When there was still no sign of the interrogation being resumed, I spoke to the guard and requested to see the interrogator.

"What do you want to say to the interrogator?"

"I want to ask him when he is going to clarify my case."

"He can't clarify your case for you. He just asks the questions and assembles the material. The government will make the decision about your case."

"When is the government going to do that? I've been here such a long time already. I'm not well, I need medical attention," I said.

"You are all right. We give you medicine and special food."

"I'm not all right. My condition gets worse every day. I have had several more hemorrhages recently, and my gums are very painful. The sulfa drug I am obliged to take is bad for my kidney. I have only one kidney, you know. When I had my operation, the doctor warned me not to take too much sulfa."

The guard did not speak for a moment. Then she said, "The difficulty about your case is really your own doing. You have to stay here because you won't confess."

"I haven't done anything wrong. What am I supposed to confess? The interrogator has examined my whole life and my contacts with all my relatives and friends. By now the government should know all about me. How can anyone still think I am guilty of anything?" Frustration and disappointment made me raise my voice. But the guard merely closed the window and walked away.

During the past few months and the many sessions of interrogation, I had formed a distinct impression that when my life and activities had been examined, I would be released. Now I could not understand what was holding things up. The guard had said that it was up to the government to make the decision. This made sense to me because it was the usual working method of the Communist Party. What I did not know was on which level of authority my case was to be decided, and why it was taking so long. If my hopes had not been raised, perhaps my disappointment would not have been so great. As it was, I was plunged into renewed despair.

The misery of my life in the winter of 1969–70 was beyond imagination. Looking back on those months of heavy snowstorms, intense cold, and constant physical pain, I marvel that I could have lived through it all.

One day when I asked the guard to buy soap, I was given something that did not lather. The guard told me that soap was rationed and each person was allowed only one cake per month. When I requested permission to buy a little more because I had to wash my underclothes more frequently, the guard became annoyed and shouted, "When are you going to get rid of your capitalistic way of wanting more than other people? You are lucky to be allowed one cake per month. In many places the people are only allowed one cake per family."

The toilet paper made of processed rice straw was replaced by something even coarser, made with old newspaper, string, and old cloth; bits of these were clearly visible on the rough gray sheets, stiff as a board. This substitute for toilet paper was rationed also. The cod-liver oil and vitamin pills I was allowed to purchase were often not available. A small lump of fat rather than meat often appeared with my rice. The severe shortages seemed to affect the guards as well. Several of them lost a good deal of weight, and even the militant guards who used to stride in and out energetically now looked rather subdued and peaked. It was all too apparent that the country was going through another period of economic crisis that invariably followed each political upheaval.

The newspaper printed reports of peasants "voluntarily" reducing their already meager rations and rural Party secretaries offering to increase the quota of grain the communes sent to government purchasing agencies. This was a repetition of the hunger and shortages of the early sixties, immediately after the failure of the Great Leap Forward Campaign. In such times of hardship, there were daily stories in the newspaper about heroes who increased production output and decreased their consumption of food and other commodities. However, half a sheet of the *Shanghai Liberation Daily* was still given over to criticism of the "capitalist-roaders," who were also called "revisionists." The subject of contention now was Mao Zedong's military theory of the People's War versus the capitalistic concept of the importance of military skill and modern weapons. Two ousted and disgraced military leaders, former defense minister Peng Dehuai and former chief of staff Luo Ruiqing, were the main culprits. Daily newspaper articles read to us over the broadcasting system accused these two of believing that advanced weapons rather than men armed with Mao Zedong Thought were the most important factor in deciding the outcome of war. Since both men had been removed from office several years earlier and handed over to the Red Guards and the Revolutionaries for persecution, the continued campaign of criticism could only mean that their viewpoint was shared by others in the Party and military leadership.

Prolonged hardship and privation were eroding my mental powers in a frightening way. The stalling of my investigation produced in me a deep feeling of despondency. Not being able to keep clean because of insufficient soap and toilet paper was demoralizing. Even the evidence in the newspaper of differences of opinion, or perhaps fierce debate, in the Party and military leadership failed to rouse me from lethargy. Every day I sat on the wooden bed, leaning against my rolled-up bedding, too tired and too ill to move.

In early spring, I again became ill with pneumonia and was

taken to the prison hospital. There I made a slow recovery. When I returned to the No. 1 Detention House, just before May First, the weather had become warmer. Even though conditions continued to be extremely hard, the milder weather made life easier to endure. I felt I had somehow survived another crisis and been mysteriously brought back to life from the brink of death. When I was allowed outdoor exercise on a warm and sunny day and saw the young leaves unfolding on the plane tree over the wall, I thanked God for the miracle of life and the timely renewal of my own.

Since the conclusion of the Ninth Party Congress and the formation of Party Secretariats in each province and municipality, the Party's tight control of every aspect of life had been reestablished. It became much harder than before to find out what was going on outside the prison walls through reading the newspaper. In the turbulent years of the height of the Cultural Revolution, vehement denunciations of the "capitalist-roaders" often revealed internal struggles in the Party leadership. In explaining Mao's "correct" policy, the revolutionary writers, often non–Party men, would sometimes inadvertently state facts kept from the Chinese people. Now articles like that had disappeared altogether from the *Shanghai Liberation Daily*. Denunciations continued to appear, but I could tell that they were now written by professional Party propagandists. They were using the same stale language and timeworn quotations that were the stock-in-trade of Party men anxious to say the right thing but even more anxious not to say it in any way that might bring criticism on themselves.

I had my first inkling of another round of power struggles at the top when I saw in the newspaper a list of members of the standing committee of the Politburo. Missing was the name of Chen Boda, one of the radical leaders who had charted the course of the Cultural Revolution from its very beginning. Soon articles of criticism, without mentioning his name, were denouncing a "fake Marxist" who had declared himself a "humble commoner." The sudden omission of a prominent man's name without explanation almost always meant he was in disgrace. The criticism of a "fake Marxist" seemed to me to point to someone renowned as a theorist of Marxism. Chen Boda was just such a man.

I was greatly puzzled by this unexpected development because Chen Boda was known to the Chinese people as a faithful follower of Mao and his longtime confidential secretary. In fact, it was often whispered in China that many essays purportedly written by Mao Zedong were actually from the pen of Chen Boda. Though he did not seek the limelight like other radical leaders such as Jiang Qing or Lin Biao, the Chinese people knew him to have been one of the small elite group of Marxist theorists Mao relied upon.

After my release from the No. 1 Detention House a good deal later, I questioned several friends and acquaintances about the downfall of Chen Boda. It seemed that at the second plenary session of the Ninth Central Committee held at Lushan at the end of August 1970, the new Constitution of the Chinese People's Republic was discussed. An important issue was whether to abolish the post of chairman of the Chinese People's Republic, left vacant by the downfall of Liu Shaoqi. Chen Boda proposed that the post be maintained and nominated Lin Biao as the new chairman. Already alarmed by the rapid expansion of Lin Biao's power since the Ninth Party Congress only a year and four months earlier, Mao was not keen to give Lin Biao added power and position. He declared that he favored the abolition of the post of chairman of the People's Republic and suggested giving the ceremonial function of the head of state to the chairman of the Standing Committee of the People's Congress. In a heated debate, Mao denounced Chen Boda's proposal as a counterrevolutionary move designed to reestablish pre–Cultural Revolution conditions.

Another subject under discussion at the Central Committee meeting was China's relations with the United States after President Nixon expressed, through third-country intermediaries, the desire for a rapprochement with Beijing. Premier Zhou Enlai had convinced Mao that if the United States could be induced to recognize the Chinese People's Republic rather than the Kuomintang government in Taiwan, Communist China would receive recognition from most other countries in the United Nations. This would not only enable Communist China to take China's seat at the United Nations, but it would make the eventual liberation of Taiwan much easier and less costly. Both Lin Biao and Chen Boda expressed opposition to any move for a rapprochement with the United States. They argued that as the leader of the capitalist world, the United States was inherently socialist China's main enemy.

But all my informants agreed that the downfall of Chen Boda was really Mao's warning to Lin Biao. It was not lost on the military man, who correctly concluded that the days of his own usefulness to Mao were numbered. This eventually led to Lin Biao's unsuccessful attempt to wrest power from Mao. In any case, later developments proved that the second plenary session of the Ninth Central Committee was an important one. It ended the brief Lin Biao era and marked a drastic deterioration in Lin Biao's power position relative to that of Prime Minister Zhou Enlai.

In 1970, when I was still in my cell in the detention house, I recognized the downfall of Chen Boda as something important, and I watched for events that might throw some light on the situation. In the autumn of that year, the newspaper published a photograph of the American writer Edgar Snow standing beside Mao on the balcony above the Gate of Heavenly Peace, Tiananmen, on China's National Day. Though Mao had often stood there with other prominent visitors to China, this was the first time an American had been given such an honor. Snow was an old friend of the Communist Party and Mao Zedong. His book *Red Star over China*, published in the thirties, did much to legitimize the Chinese Communist Party in the eyes of the world. Since I had learned that everything Mao did or said had meaning, often a subtle one, I pondered the significance of his having an American with him on the balcony of the Gate of Heavenly Peace on China's National Day while he reviewed tens of thousands of enthusiastic men and women carrying his portraits, shouting his slogans, and chanting his quotations.

Soon after National Day, the newspaper reported that Beijing had reached an agreement with Canada to establish full diplomatic relations based on the following five principles: mutual respect for territorial integrity and sovereignty, nonaggression, noninterference in each other's internal affairs, equality and mutual benefit, and peaceful coexistence. Canada undertook to sever diplomatic relations with the Kuomintang government on Taiwan and to recognize Beijing as the sole legitimate government of China.

I thought Mao was using the case of Canada to say something to the United States. I believed his message was that he was ready to be friends if the United States would agree to abandon Taiwan. The establishment of diplomatic relations with Canada was the opportunity for him to declare his conditions for a similar arrangement with the United States. I became quietly excited and hopeful. That Communist China might move closer to the West seemed too good to be true.

The northwest wind started to blow again, but this time it did not dampen my spirits. For the first time since the Cultural Revolution began, something seemed to be happening in the right direction. When a gust of wind blew a withered leaf of the plane tree into my cell, I picked up the bright yellow leaf and looked at it for a long time, thinking it was a symbol of hope and a good omen.

A calmer mood took the place of anxiety while I waited in my cell for further developments. I thought I had reached the bottom line of suffering and things would get better when they started to move again. I was wrong.

One afternoon in January 1971, I was summoned to the interrogation room. The call was so unexpected that my heart was pounding with excitement as I followed the guard through the courtyard; I hardly noticed that a blizzard was beginning. At the door of the interrogation room, the guard suddenly gave me a hard shove, so that I staggered into the room rather unceremoniously. I found five guards in the room. As soon as I entered, they crowded around me, shouting abuse at me.

"You are the running dog of the imperialists," said one. "You are a dirty exploiter of workers and peasants," shouted another. "You are a counterrevolutionary," yelled a third.

Their voices mingled, and their faces became masks of hatred as they joined in the litany of abuse with which I had become so familiar during the Cultural Revolution. While they were shouting, they pushed me to show their impatience. I was passed around from one guard to another like a ball in a game. Trying to maintain my balance, I became dizzy and breathless. Before I could gather my wits together, a young male guard suddenly grabbed the lapels of my padded jacket and pulled me towards him. His face was only inches from mine, and I could see his eyes glistening with sadistic pleasure. Then he bit his lower lip to show his determination and gave me a hard push. I staggered backwards and hit the wall. But before I collapsed onto the floor like a sack, he grabbed my lapels again and pulled me forward, and again he bounced me against the wall. He did this several times with lightning speed, in a very expert manner. All the time, the other guards continued to shout at me. I became completely disoriented. My ears were ringing, my head was splitting, and my body was trembling. Suddenly my stomach heaved, and I vomited. Water from my mouth got on the guard's hands and cuffs. He became furious. Pushing me into the prisoner's chair, the guard swore under his breath.

My heart pounded as if it were going to jump out of my throat. My breath came in gasps. I collapsed into the chair and, trying to recover my equilibrium, closed my eyes. Suddenly a stinging blow landed on my cheek. The voice of a female guard shouted, "Are you going to confess?"

Another sharp blow landed on my other cheek as several voices joined in to shout, "Are you going to confess?"

I remained in the chair with my eyes closed and ignored them. That was my only way to defend myself.

Someone grabbed my hair from behind and jerked my head up. I was forced to look up and found all five of them staring at me expectantly. It seemed that they really thought I would change my mind simply because they had beaten me up. But then, people who resort to brutality must believe in the power of brutality. It seemed to me that these guards at the detention house were rather stupid not to know me better after watching me day and night for so many years. I knew, however, that they were merely carrying out someone else's orders.

One of the female guards was the militant young woman who had made trouble for me on many previous occasions. Now she said, "Are you going to confess, or do you want more punishment?"

When she saw that I remained silent, she gave my cheek another smart slap, took my arms, and draped them around the back of the chair on which I was seated. The young male guard who had pushed me against the wall grabbed my wrists and clamped a pair of handcuffs on them.

"These handcuffs are to punish you for your intransigence. You will wear them until you are ready to confess. Only then will we take them off. If you confess now, we will take them off now. If you confess tomorrow, we will take them off tomorrow. If you do not confess for a year, you will have to wear them for a year. If you never confess, you will have to wear them to your grave," said the militant female guard.

"Think about it! Think about the situation you are in!" a male guard shouted.

"If you decide to confess now, we will take off the handcuffs right away and you can return to your cell," another female guard said.

"What about it? Are you ready to confess? Just say yes, and we will take the handcuffs off," another male guard said.

"Speak! Speak!" several of them shouted.

I looked at them all and said in a feeble voice, "I've done nothing wrong. I have nothing to confess."

"Louder! Louder! Speak louder!" they yelled.

Though I spoke in a low voice, each one of them inside the room had heard what I said. Someone must be listening outside in the corridor. They wanted this person to hear my answer. From where I sat I could not see whether the small window behind the prisoner's chair was open. But I did notice the guards glancing in that direction when they were pushing me around.

I pulled myself together with an effort and stated in a clear and loud voice, "I'm innocent. You have made a mistake. I have nothing to confess."

I heard the small window behind the prisoner's chair close with a loud bang. My tormentors waited a little while before opening the door to usher me out, perhaps to make sure the person outside had time to get out of sight. When I stood up, the militant female guard came behind me and put her hands around the handcuffs to tighten them a few notches so that they fitted snugly around my wrists.

The blizzard was now in full force. Whirling snowflakes were falling from the darkened sky, and the strong wind nearly knocked me over when I stepped out of the interrogation building. The guard said, "Follow me!"

He did not return me to the women's prison but led me in another direction into a small building in a corner of the prison compound. When he opened the door and flipped the switch to put on the dim light, I saw that the place was in an even worse state of neglect than the rest of the prison compound. A thick layer of dust covered the floor and the walls. When we moved down the corridor, cobwebs floated down from the ceiling. The guard unlocked a small door and said, "Get in!"

The room was very dark. I waited for him to switch on the light, but he just closed the door after me. Standing outside, he asked, "Are you going to confess?" When I did not reply, he snapped the lock and went away.

I stood just inside the door in total darkness, trying to make out where I was. An unpleasant odor of staleness and decay assailed my nostrils. Gradually I realized that the tiny room in which I was locked had no windows. However, the door fitted badly; a thin thread of light seeped through the gap. When my eyes became accustomed to the darkness, I saw vaguely that there was a wooden board on the dusty floor and a cement toilet in the corner. Actually I was standing in the only space left, for the room was no more than about five feet square. Something soft dropped on my forehead. I was so startled that I experienced a moment of panic. With my hands tied at my back, I could do nothing to brush it away. I shook my head hard, and it slid down my face to my jacket. Perhaps not many insects could live in this dark room, I thought. It must have been a cobweb from the ceiling.

My heart was still beating very fast. In spite of the unpleasant smell in the room, I breathed in and out deeply and slowly to try to calm down and slow my heartbeat. When I felt better I sat down on the wooden board and tried to look around in the dark. I was relieved not to see anything that suggested blood, excrement, or vomited food left by previous prisoners. I was so tired that I put my head on my drawn-up knees and closed my eyes to rest. The only compensation for being locked in a cement box, I thought, was that without the window to admit the cold air and wind, the place was decidedly warmer than my cell.

The handcuffs felt different from the others I had worn before. I examined them with my fingers. Indeed, they were different, much heavier and thicker, with a square edge, not rounded like the others. My hands felt hot, and my fingers were stiff. I tried to exercise my hands by moving them as much as the handcuffs allowed.

"Are you going to confess?"

The sudden sound of a voice startled me. Had the guard been outside all the while, or had he just come into the building? How was it that I had not heard him?

There was really no point in exhausting what little strength I had, so I did not answer him but remained where I was with my head resting on my knees. I tried to take my mind off the present by recalling beautiful scenes and pleasant experiences of the past. But it was very difficult. The ugly reality was all too real and overpowering.

Other guards came at intervals to ask me the same question. I listened for their footsteps. Some came quite stealthily, others did not bother to soften their tread. When they opened the door of the building to come inside, I could hear the howling wind and the sound of the guards stamping their feet to get rid of the snow. I supposed they were told to come and see if I had succumbed to their new form of pressure. Some of them lingered for a moment after asking their question; others did not wait for my answer but left almost immediately.

Apart from the guards, there was no sound whatsoever. I must have been the sole occupant of that building on that day. If there were other prisoners, surely I would have heard a sigh or a moan long ago.

I did not know how long I sat there. In a dark room, in complete isolation, time assumed a different meaning or had no meaning at all. I only knew that my legs felt stiff and my head ached. But I refrained from moving as long as the guards continued to come. When a guard switched off the light in the corridor on his departure, I thought they might have decided to retire for the night. But I still waited for a while before standing up. It was not possible to walk because there was simply no space and I was afraid to bump into the dirty wall in the dark. So I shuffled my feet to try to restore circulation to my legs. My arms ached from being held at my back in the same position for so long, and my hands felt very hot. I tried to get some relief by moving my shoulders up and down.

After standing for a while, I sat down again. With my head on my knees, I rested. Perhaps I had snatches of real sleep, or perhaps I just dozed while murmuring prayers. Then I would stand up again to repeat my newly devised exercise. I felt very weak. My natural inclination was to move as little as possible, but

I compelled myself to do the simple exercise, for I knew that was the best way to keep going. In the past I had not suffered from claustrophobia, but there were moments during the night when I felt myself getting tense. My breathing became difficult, and I had the sensation that the walls were falling on me. To prevent myself from getting into a panic, I would stand up quickly and move my body as much as possible in that confined space. And I would breathe very slowly and deeply until I felt calm again.

The best way for me to snap out of fear was always to take the initiative in doing something positive. Even the simple act of moving my body around made me feel better immediately. If I had just sat there feeling dejected and let my imagination run wild, I could easily have become terribly confused and unable to cope with the guards. Of course I was hungry and my throat was parched. But when I thought of the cement toilet coated with dust and grime, I was reconciled to not having any food or water that might force me to use it.

The night dragged on very slowly. More and more I felt that I was buried in a cement box deep underground. My hands became very hot and uncomfortable. When I found it difficult to curl my fingers into a fist, I knew they were swollen. My hands became my sole preoccupation. I feared that the brutal and ignorant guards, intent on getting what they wanted from me, might inadvertently cripple me. I knew that when a Communist Party official tried to achieve an objective during a political campaign, he went to excess to carry out his orders and ignored all possible complications. Trained to obey promptly by such slogans as "Wherever Chairman Mao points, there I will run," and fearful of the consequences of appearing hesitant or reluctant, he exaggerated everything he had to do. If the victim suffered more than was intended or was left a cripple, that was just too bad. I had seen this happen again and again. Hands are so important. If my hands were crippled, how would I be able to carry on with my daily life when the Cultural Revolution was over?

I pressed my fingers in turn. At least they were not numb. But I could tell they were badly swollen. I wondered how long I would remain manacled like this and how long I could live without food or water. Vaguely I remembered reading in an article that a human being could live for seven days without sustenance. In my present weakened state, perhaps five days, I thought. In any case, hardly twenty-four hours had passed. At that moment I did not need to think of the threat to my life, only the threat to my hands. What could I do to lessen possible damage to them? It seemed to me the swelling was caused by the tight handcuffs fitted firmly around my wrists, preventing proper circulation. When the militant female guard put her hands around the cuffs to tighten them, she knew exactly what she was doing. If she had not tightened them but had left them as they were, perhaps the state of my hands would not have been so bad now. The guard who first put the handcuffs on had not tightened them, so they had probably not been instructed to do so. In that case, a mild guard might be persuaded to loosen them a little. I decided to show my hands to the guard who came in the morning and request that the handcuffs be loosened.

When finally I heard the sound of a guard coming through the outside door and saw the thin line of light appear again around the cell door, I stood up.

"Are you going to confess? Have you thought over the matter?" It was the voice of a male guard.

"I would like to speak to you for a moment," I said.

"Good! So, you have decided to confess at last."

"No, no, it's not about confession. It's about my hands."

"What about your hands?"

"They are badly swollen. The handcuffs are very tight. Could you loosen them a bit?" I asked.

"You are feeling uncomfortable now, are you? That's good! Why don't you confess? If you confess, the handcuffs will be taken off."

"Can't you loosen them a bit now?"

"Why don't you just confess like the other prisoners? You have brought this on yourself. It's not the fault of the handcuffs."

"Please look at my hands. They are badly swollen."

"I can't do anything about that. If you decide to confess, I will unlock this door and take you out. That's all I can do," the guard said.

"Could you not report to your superior that my hands are very badly swollen?"

"No. If you decide to confess, I will take you out."

It seemed useless to go on. I sat down on the wooden board again.

"Are you going to confess?" he asked me once again. I did not answer. He remained there for a moment longer before going away.

The fact that my hands were badly swollen was no surprise to the guard. Of course he knew the effect of the handcuffs. I could not have been the first person they had done this to. He was probably telling his superior at that moment that I was getting worried and agitated about my hands. From that his superior would think I was nearer to doing what he wanted. They would never loosen the handcuffs to prolong what they regarded as the period of waiting for me to confess. I decided it was useless to ask the guards to loosen the handcuffs. I must just trust God to preserve my hands.

"Come here!" the voice of a female guard said.

I stood up. I was already right by the door. She had turned up rather quickly, I thought.

"I've come to give you some advice," she said in a normal voice, as if she were talking to another guard, not in the harsh tone the guards habitually used to address the prisoners. "You are not a stupid woman. Why don't you do the intelligent thing and confess? Why punish yourself by being stubborn?"

I didn't say anything.

"You are worried about your hands. That's quite right. Hands are very important to everybody, but especially to an intellectual who must write. You should try to protect your hands and not let them be hurt. You can do that easily by just agreeing to confess."

I still did not say anything.

"You know, when they said they would never take the handcuffs off until you agreed to confess, they really meant it. They will do it too. The Dictatorship of the Proletariat is not something to be trifled with, you know."

I continued to remain silent.

She waited for quite a long time. Then she said, "Well, you think carefully about what I have just said. It's good advice I have given you. I'm sorry for you. Think about what I said."

When I heard her footsteps going away from the door, I sat down again.

I was angry with myself for being so stupid. How could I have thought for one moment that they would loosen the handcuffs? Now that I had shown them my weakness, they would be glad and think I might indeed succumb to their pressure out of concern for my hands. I said to myself, "I'll forget about my hands. If I have to be crippled, then I'll accept being crippled. In this world there are many worthy people with crippled hands or no hands at all." I remembered that when my late husband and I were in Holland in 1957, we had bought a painting by a veteran of the Second World War who had lost both his hands. He used his toes to hold the paintbrush, I was told. I used to treasure this painting as a symbol of human courage and resourcefulness. It was slashed by the Red Guards when they looted my home. But the thought of this artist whom I had never met inspired me with courage and helped me to become reconciled to the possibility of losing the use of my hands after this ordeal.

The female guard was followed by others. All of them lectured me on the advantage of obeying the Dictatorship of the Proletariat and confessing. Now that they knew I was suffering discomfort and worrying about my hands, they did not dash away but lingered hopefully outside the door waiting for my answer. After being so long without food and water and not having had much sleep at all, I felt very weak and faint. My intestines were grinding in protest, and I had spasms of pain in the abdomen. But I just continued sitting on the board with my head on my knees waiting for the guards to go away.

The day seemed interminable. Patiently I waited for their next move. At last the door was unlocked. A female voice called, "Come out!"

The icy-cold fresh air in the courtyard miraculously cleared my head, and I felt a surge of life to support my wobbly legs. The guard led me back to the same interrogation room in which they had beaten me up the day before.

The militant female guard and the young male guard who had put the handcuffs on me sat in the place of the interrogator behind the counter. After I had entered the room and bowed to the portrait of Mao, the female guard told me to recite a quotation from memory.

" 'First, do not fear hardship. Second, do not fear death,' " I said. It was the first quotation of Mao that came into my head and, under the circumstances, certainly appropriate.

"That quotation is not for the likes of you! Chairman Mao said that to the revolutionary soldiers," the female guard said indignantly.

But they let it pass. They did not ask me to recite another quotation, although I had one about overcoming ten thousand difficulties to strive for final victory ready to recite if they gave me the opportunity to do so.

"What are you thinking about now?" asked the male guard.

"Nothing very much," I answered.

"Don't pretend to be nonchalant. You are worried about your hands. You would like the handcuffs to be loosened," he said.

I did not say anything.

"What you should think about is why you have to wear them in the first place. It is entirely your own fault. Do we put handcuffs on all the prisoners kept here? Of course not. If you find the handcuffs uncomfortable, you should think why you have to wear them. They can be taken off if you decide to confess. It's up to you entirely," he said.

"Are you going to confess?" asked the female guard.

When she saw that I said nothing, she got angry and shouted, "You deserve all you are getting. You are tired of living, I am sure. I have never seen a prisoner as stubborn and stupid as you!"

"Have you lost all reason? Have you lost the wish to protect yourself? You are being extremely stupid. You are like an egg hitting a rock. You will get smashed," declared the male guard.

A year or two ago, I would have shouted back at them and taken pleasure from it. Now I was too ill and too tired. I no longer cared.

They looked at each other, and they looked past my shoulder at the small window behind the prisoner's chair. Then they stood up.

"Take her out! Take her out! Let her go to see God with her granite head!" the male guard shouted.

It might seem surprising that a guard in a Communist prison should have spoken of God, but what he said was in fact a quotation from Mao Zedong. Referring to political indoctrination and hard labor as a means to change the thinking of intellectuals allegedly opposed to the Communist Party, Mao had declared that the Party's purpose was reform of the enemy rather than annihilation. Then he added, "If some still want to go to see God with their granite heads, it will make no difference." Since the publication of his remark, "to go to see God with his granite head" was generally used to denote a man refusing to change his mind or accept the point of view of the Party.

A guard flung the door open. Although I felt dizzy, I made an effort to walk steadily and followed him out of the room. The icy air outside was like a knife cutting through my clothes. I shivered violently. The guard led me back to the women's prison and my cell. When I passed the small room used by the female guards, I saw from their clock that I had been locked in the cement box in the other building for almost twenty-four hours.

The guard unlocked the door of my cell and said to me, "Now you will continue your punishment in here."

When I was called to the interrogation room the day before, drinking water had just been issued to the prisoners. The water was still in the green enameled mug on the edge of the table where I had hastily placed it. Now I bent over the mug, removed the lid by gripping the knob on top of it with my teeth, and placed it on the table. Then I caught the edge of the mug with my teeth, gradually lowered my body to a squatting position, and tipped the water into my mouth. By this method, I succeeded in drinking quite a bit of water. After that, I moved over to the cement toilet, stood with my back to it, lowered my body, and removed the lid with my imprisoned hands. I strained my hands to unzip my slacks. I was able to sit on the seat I had made with two towels joined together and to relieve myself. But to strain my hands to one side to unfasten the zipper made the handcuffs cut severely into my flesh. It was very painful.

I sat down on the edge of the bed. The cell was very cold and seemed to get progressively colder. But the familiar cell was not as dirty and stuffy as the cement box where I had spent the previous twenty-four hours. When the second meal of the day was delivered to the prisoners, the woman from the kitchen pushed the aluminum container through the small window in the usual manner. Even though I was famished, I had to refuse it, for I simply did not know how I could eat with my hands tightly tied behind my back.

No one came to ask me if I was going to confess. But I knew I was under observation, for I could hear the guards come to the peephole to look into the cell. At bedtime, the guard called at each cell for prisoners to go to bed. She came to my cell as if nothing unusual had happened and said, "Go to sleep!"

With my back to the wooden bed, I unrolled my quilt and blanket and spread them over it. It was slow work and strenuous for one who had not eaten any food for so long. But I managed it. Then I lay down on the bed. First, I lay on one side with my body weight pressing down on one shoulder and arm. It was extremely uncomfortable; my arm ached. Then I tried to lie on my stomach with my face turned to one side. I found this position impossible on the hard wooden bed because my body weight was on my breasts. After lying like this for a little while I had to give up. In any case, I could not cover myself with the blanket. While I was performing these acrobatics with my hands in handcuffs behind my back, I never stopped shivering. The room was bitterly cold. Finally I decided lying down to sleep was out of the question. I should try to get some sleep sitting up. I sat across the bed with my legs up and my back leaning on the toilet-paper-covered wall. Then I closed my eyes, hoping to doze off.

It was such a cold night that there was ice on the window-panes, and the snow piled against the window did not melt. Inside the cell, the feeble light shone through a haze of cold air. Every breath I took was a puff of white vapor. My body shook with spasms of shivering. My legs and feet were frozen numb. I simply had to get up from time to time and walk around the cell to restore circulation to my limbs. The weight of the hand-cuffs dragged my hands down, and I tried to hold the cuffs up with my fingers while walking slowly in the cell. They seemed to get tighter and tighter, and my hands seemed to be on fire. I tired so easily that after walking around for only a little while I had to sit down again. Then I got so cold that I had to walk some more. Perhaps I managed a little sleep from time to time when I sat against the wall with my feet up, but the long night was a night of misery and suffering.

However, it came to an end, as everything in life must do, no matter how wonderful or unpleasant. I saw the light of dawn creeping into the room and heard the guard calling outside each cell, "Get up! Get up!"

Soon afterwards the Labor Reform girl pushed the spout of the watering can through the small window to offer me cold water for washing. When she did not see my washbasin, she peered into the cell and looked at me inquiringly. I turned my body a little so that she could see my handcuffs. Quickly she closed the small window and went away.

Under the circumstances, being unwashed was the least of my worries. I could receive water in the empty mug with my back to the window and drink by gradually squatting with the mug in my teeth, but my empty stomach protested with spasms of gripping pain that refused to be assuaged by water. My hands were so hot that I was in a constant state of restless agitation.

On the third day, the pain in my abdomen miraculously stopped. But I felt very weak. My eyes could no longer focus, and the usual sound of prison activities seemed to grow fainter and fainter.

That night, I again sat on the bed, leaning against the wall with my hands crossed to hold the handcuffs with my fingers in an effort to reduce their weight. Though I shivered with cold, I no longer had the strength to get up and walk around the room.

After the prisoners had settled down to sleep, the small window was pushed open gently. I did not hear any sound until a voice that was almost a whisper said through the opening, "Come over!"

I wondered whether it was just another guard urging me to confess. But she had spoken softly, almost stealthily, as if she did not want others in the building to hear her.

With an effort I moved to the small window and saw the face of one of the older guards there. She was bending down to watch my faltering steps through the opening.

From the beginning of my imprisonment I had found this guard the most humane. At first she attracted my attention because she walked in that peculiar way of women whose feet had been crippled with foot-binding, an old custom that lingered into the 1930s in some remote rural areas of China. When the feet of these women were unbound, they were already permanently damaged. This guard was not a native of Shanghai, because she spoke with the accent of North China peasants. I thought she must be one of those country women who had been liberated by the Communist troops as they swept down the plains of North China and had joined their ranks and become a Party member. I observed that she carried out her duty in a matter-of-fact manner and did not seem to enjoy shouting at the prisoners as the other guards did. When the weather got cold, if she was on night duty, I often heard her offering to lend bedding from the prison stock to prisoners who did not have sufficient covering. The last time I fainted because of lack of food, it was this guard who took me to the hospital and got the doctor to sign a paper ordering more rice to be given to me. Since it was the Maoists who had reduced my ration to pressure me on that occasion, I thought she couldn't be one of them.

"Why aren't you eating your meals?" she asked me.

I thought, "What a silly question! Doesn't she know I have got the handcuffs on?"

"They will not remove the handcuffs simply because you won't eat, you know. And if you should starve to death, you will be declared a counterrevolutionary. That's the customary procedure for prisoners who die before their cases are clarified," she added.

"I don't know how to eat without using my hands," I said.

"It's not impossible. Think hard. There is a way. You have a spoon."

She sounded sympathetic and concerned. I decided to ask her to loosen the handcuffs a little, as my tightly imprisoned hands were tormenting me. I was in a constant state of tension because of them. They occupied my mind to the exclusion of all else.

"My hands are swollen and very hot. My whole body feels tormented because of them. Could you please loosen the handcuffs a little bit?" I asked her.

"I haven't got the key to unlock the handcuffs. It is being kept by someone higher up. Just try to eat something tomorrow. You will feel better when you have some food inside you," she said.

A gust of cold wind from the other end of the corridor indicated that the door of the building was being opened and another guard had just entered. She slid the shutter quietly into place and went away.

I returned to the bed and sat there thinking. The guard was right. I should try to eat. To die was nothing to be frightened of. What really frightened me was the possibility that my mind might get so confused that I might sign something without realizing its significance. But how could I handle the food without my hands? The guard said there was a way and told me to think hard. She also mentioned that I had a spoon. My eyes strayed towards the table. First I saw the plastic spoon, and then I saw my clean towels neatly folded in a pile. A plan formulated in my mind, and I decided to try it when food was offered to me again.

The guard had said that the key to unlock the handcuffs was not kept by the guards but by "someone higher up." There was no hope the handcuffs could be loosened. I must think of some way to reduce the heavy weight of the handcuffs, which were not only dragging my hands down but also pulling my shoulders out of their sockets. With difficulty and very slowly, with my back to the bed, I managed to roll up the quilt. Then I pushed the rolled quilt to the wall. When I sat down against the wall, I placed my hands on the soft quilt. The weight was lifted, and I felt a surge of relief.

To have made plans and thought of some way to overcome difficulty gave me a new lease on life. Although I continued to be cold, hungry, and miserable, the long night seemed to pass more quickly.

At daybreak, when the guard called the prisoners to get up, I stood up to stretch my legs. I tried to hold the handcuffs with my fingers and, to my horror, felt something sticky and wet. Turning to the quilt on which I had rested my hands throughout the night, I saw stains of blood mixed with pus. It seemed the handcuffs had already broken my skin and were cutting into my flesh. I shuddered with a real fear of losing the use of my hands, for I realized I was powerless to prevent disaster.

When the woman from the kitchen offered me the aluminum container of rice through the small window, I went to accept it. I turned my back to the opening, and she placed the container in my hands. I took it to the table. With my back to it, I picked up a clean face towel from the pile and spread it on the table. Then I picked up the plastic spoon and tried to loosen the rice with it. Shanghai rice was glutinous. When it was cooked in the container, it stuck to it. I had to dig hard with the plastic spoon to push the rice and cabbage onto the face towel on the table. With each movement of my hands, the handcuffs dug deeper into my flesh. My whole body was racked with pain, and tears came into my eyes. I had to rest and take a deep breath. Nevertheless, I persisted in my effort to get the rice out of the container. When I succeeded in getting quite a bit out, I turned around, bent over the towel, and ate the rice like an animal.

I repeated this several times. When the woman came to collect the container, she did not immediately open the small window to demand it back but stood outside watching me struggling to get the rice out. Because of the pain and my fear of infection, I stopped after each scoop to take a deep breath. I was very slow. Still the woman said nothing, though normally she was always in a great hurry. As I blinked back tears of pain, I wondered if eating was really worth the effort. But I continued to try, simply because I had decided to stay alive. When I could not carry on any longer and had got nearly half of the rice onto the towel, I carried the container behind me and pushed it through to her with my wounded hands.

In the afternoon, when rice was given to me again, I found that the woman from the kitchen had already loosened it for me. I had only to tip the container and most of the rice fell out onto the towel and bare table.

My being able to consume food seemed to have infuriated the Maoists, for the guards came to the small window again to threaten me. They never mentioned the word "handcuffs," probably because they did not want the other prisoners within hearing to know what they were doing to me. But they continued to urge me to confess. Although the rice I managed to eat each day did in fact make me feel stronger, I was having difficulty walking. For some reason I could not explain, the handcuffs were affecting my feet. Like my hands, they felt hot and painful. My shoes became so tight and unbearable that I had to kick them off. Fortunately they were soft cloth shoes, so that I was able to press down the backs and wear them as slippers. Now I just staggered about, for my feet could not bear even the reduced weight of my emaciated body. The stains of blood and pus on the quilt became larger and more numerous as the handcuffs cut through more skin on my wrists and bit more deeply into the wounds. Either the weather suddenly got a lot warmer, or I was feverish; I no longer felt the cold but shivered from pain whenever I had to move my hands or stagger across the room.

One day when I was at the small window getting drinking water, my imprisoned hands holding the mug trembled so much that half of the water spilled down the back of my padded jacket and slacks.

"Your hands are very bad. The higher-ups don't know it. Why don't you wail? As long as you don't cry out, they will not know how bad your hands are," the woman from the kitchen whispered through the opening before hastily closing the shutter.

Though the Chinese people were normally restrained about showing emotion, they did wail to show deep grief at funerals or as a protest against injustice that involved death. The sight of someone wailing had always embarrassed me. It was like seeing someone strip himself naked. From childhood I had been disciplined never to show emotion. The memory of trying for many years to fight back tears lingered; gradually I came to regard crying as a sign of weakness. Should I wail now just to call attention to the fact that my hands were being crippled? I decided against it. For one thing, I did not think I knew how to emit that prolonged, inarticulate cry that was so primitive and animallike. For another, I did not want to do anything that might be interpreted as asking for mercy. "The man higher up" had ordered the handcuffs put on my wrists so that I would be tormented by them. He believed my suffering would eventually lead me to give a false confession to save myself. The best way to counterattack was certainly not to show that I could no longer endure suffering. So I ignored the kind advice of the woman from the kitchen.

Several more days passed. The handcuffs were now beginning to affect my mind, probably through their effect on my nervous system. I got muddled periodically and forgot where I was. I no longer remembered how many days ago I was first manacled. Life was just an unending road of acute pain and suffering on which I must trudge along as best I could.

During moments of lucidity, I tried to discipline my mind by doing simple arithmetic. I would repeat to myself, "Two and two makes four, four and four equals eight, eight and eight equals sixteen, sixteen and sixteen equals thirty-two . . ." But after only a little while my ability to concentrate would evaporate, and I would get confused again. The guards still came to the locked door. But what they said was just a jumble of words that made no sense to me.

After several more days, I became so weak that I no longer had the strength to stagger to the small window for rice or water. I tried to refuse when they were offered to me, but whether words came out of my mouth or not I did not know. Perhaps the woman from the kitchen was urging me to take the rice or the drinking water; I did not hear her voice, only sensed that she stood there waiting for something. Most of the time I was so far away that I did not know what was happening around me. After drifting in and out of consciousness like that for some time, I passed out altogether.

When I opened my eyes again, I found myself lying on the dusty floor.

"Get up! Get up!" a man's voice was shouting very near me. "You are feigning death! You won't be allowed to get away with it."

My arms were still bent to my back, but they were no longer held together by the handcuffs.

"Get up! Get up!" a female voice joined in.

I pulled myself together and looked up to find the militant female guard and the young man who had put the handcuffs on me standing over me. The cell door was wide open. Dangling in the hands of the female guard was the pair of heavy brass handcuffs they had removed from my wrists. The handcuffs were covered with congealed blood and pus. Probably the guard considered them repulsive, as she was holding them gingerly by the chain with just two fingers.

"Don't think we are finished with you! There are other ways to bring you to your senses. Those who dare to oppose the Dictatorship of the Proletariat will not be allowed to get away with it," said the man.

The female guard gave my prostrate form a hard kick as they left the cell and locked the door behind them.

I remained on the floor, too exhausted to move. Although the handcuffs were gone, my whole body was aching and hot. Slowly I brought my left arm forward and looked at my hand. Quickly I closed my eyes again. My hand was too horrible to contemplate. After a moment, I sat up and looked at both hands. They were swollen to enormous size. The swelling extended to my elbows. Around my wrists where the handcuffs had cut into my flesh, blood and pus continued to ooze out of the wounds. My nails were purple in color and felt as if they were going to fall off. I touched the back of each hand, only to find the skin and flesh numb. I tried to curl up my fingers but could not because they were the size of carrots. I prayed to God to help me recover the use of my hands.

After a while, I tried to get up. But I had to stifle a cry of pain, for my feet could not support my body. As I was very near the bed, I managed to haul myself up to it. The woolen socks were stuck to my feet with dried pus. When I succeeded in peeling the socks off with my numb and swollen fingers, I saw that my feet were also swollen to enormous size. Under each toe was a large blister. I could not take the socks completely off because some of the blisters had broken and the pus had dried, gluing the socks to my feet. What was making it impossible for me to walk was the fact that some of the blisters had not broken. Obviously I needed a sterile sharp instrument such as a needle to break the blisters and let the fluid out. Also, to prevent infection, I needed bandages and some antiseptic medicine for the wounds on my wrists. I stood up. I almost sat down again immediately because the burning pain in my feet was unbearable. However, I resisted the impulse to sit down and, shuddering, remained standing. I thought that since I had to move about in the cell, the sooner I practiced walking on my swollen feet, the better. I moved one foot forward a couple of inches, shifted my weight onto that foot, and moved the other foot a couple of inches. Eventually I arrived at the door. Leaning against it for support, I called the guard on duty.

"Report!" My voice sounded feeble. But almost immediately the shutter on the small window slid open. The guard had been right outside the door, watching me through the peephole all the time without my knowledge.

"What do you want?"

"May I see the doctor, please."

"What for?"

"My wrists and feet are wounded. I need some medicine and bandages," I explained.

"The doctor does not give treatment when the prisoner has been punished," declared the guard.

"In that case, perhaps you could just give me some disinfectant ointment or Mercurochrome for the wounds?" I knew the guards kept a supply of these in their little room.

"No, not allowed."

"The wounds may become infected."

"That's your business."

"May I just have a roll of bandages to tie the wounds up?" I lifted my swollen hands to the window to show her the wounds on my wrists, but she turned her head the other way and refused to look at them.

"May I have some bandages?" I asked her again.

"No."

I got angry. "So, you do not practice revolutionary humanitarianism in accordance with Chairman Mao's teaching," I said.

"Revolutionary humanitarianism is not for you," she said.

"No, it's not for me because I'm not a real enemy of the Communist Party. And I haven't done anything against the People's Government. Revolutionary humanitarianism was applied to the Japanese invaders. The Communist Party gave the wounded Japanese prisoners of war medicine and bandages, according to Chairman Mao's books," I said sarcastically.

"Look at you! As argumentative and unrepentant as you were before. You learned nothing from the handcuffs. Perhaps you did not have them on long enough. If you argue any more, I am going to put them on you again." With that threat she retreated to the guards' room and remained there. I knew she had no authority to put the handcuffs back on my wrists again. It was just bluff. She knew I knew it too.

It seemed there was no alternative to relying on myself to deal with the wounds on my wrists and feet. With the help of God, I thought, I would find some way to prevent infection. Very slowly I shuffled to the table and drank up the water in the mug. I heard the woman from the kitchen entering the building with her heavy trolley, on which were two huge buckets of boiled hot drinking water for the prisoners. I waited for her at the small window. When she came to me, she gave me a generous portion, filling the large mug almost three-quarters full. I poured this water into the washbasin and with a clean towel carefully washed the wounds on my wrists and wiped away the dried blood and pus. Then I washed my feet in the same bloodstained water. The feel of hot water on my skin was good. I longed to drink some, but I thought it more important to clean the wounds.

While I sat on the bed drying my feet, I wondered what I could tear up and use as bandages. After so many years, my meager stock of clothing had become even more depleted because I often had to tear up a worn garment to patch those that were just beginning to develop holes. As I was searching my mind for an idea, I saw the pillowcase hanging on the clothesline. I had washed it the morning I was called to the interrogation room. It looked dry. It was the only pillowcase I had left, but I thought I could dispense with it; I could put the pillow under the sheet at night. I raised my arm to take it off the clothesline. To my dismay, I found I could not reach the pillowcase because my arm refused to be raised higher than the level of my shoulders. I supposed that after such long restraint the tendons were paralyzed. I resolved to restore the function of my arms by exercise. But that would take some time. For the moment, at any rate, I would have to leave the wounds on my wrists uncovered.

The Labor Reform girl came with cold water. She poured the water slowly into the washbasin as I held it up to the small window. As soon as she saw my hands shaking because they could no longer bear the weight, she stopped. The washbasin was barely half full. I poured some of the water into one of the mugs for drinking. With the rest, I washed my face. Then I tried to comb my hair. Since my right arm holding the comb could not reach the top of my head, I used my left hand to hold up the elbow of my right arm. With my head bent forward, turning first this way and then that way, I managed to smooth out my hair. I wanted very much to give myself a sponge bath and change my underclothes. But I was afraid I would catch cold in the icy room. In any case, I was already exhausted, and there was no more clean water.

The woman from the kitchen was again at the small window. She handed me the afternoon meal through the opening. The aluminum container was filled to the brim with rice and boiled cabbage. When I pushed the food into my mug, I discovered two hard-boiled eggs buried at the bottom of the container.

To forestall, I am sure, any possibility of my thanking her for the eggs, the woman did not open the window to collect the container as was her habit but shouted through the door as if she were angry, "You are always so slow! Hand the container over to the guard on night duty when you have finished! I can't stand here all night waiting for you!"

I sat down on the edge of the bed to eat. With each mouthful I swallowed, I felt a little strength flowing back to me. When I had finished, I washed the mug and stood up to exercise my arms. I was most anxious that I should be able to reach the pillowcase on the line as soon as possible so that I could make bandages to cover up the wounds on my wrists. I swung my arms up and down many times, each time raising them a little higher in the air to stretch the tendons. My feet were very painful, but I remained standing until I was exhausted. After a short rest, I resumed the exercise.

The guard on night duty came to the small window, handed me the day's newspaper, and took away the aluminum container. I looked at the date on the newspaper and discovered that only eleven days had elapsed since I had been called to the interrogation room and manacled. It seemed much longer. The guard came to tell the prisoners to go to bed.

This was the first time in eleven days that I had the chance of a full night's sleep. But it took me a long time to drop off. Somehow, the tight handcuffs had affected my nervous system. My whole body was aching and hot. No matter on which side I lay, it was painful and uncomfortable. The weight of the blanket and quilt seemed unbearable. Since I did not feel the cold, being feverish, I pulled the blanket off. I tried to arrange my feet and arms in such a way that the blood and pus would not stain the quilt. I soon found this impossible.

To put those special handcuffs tightly on the wrists of a prisoner was a form of torture widely used in Maoist China's prison system. Sometimes additional chains were put around the prisoner's ankles. At other times, a prisoner might be manacled and then have his handcuffs tied to a bar on the window so that he could not move away from the window to eat, drink, or go to the toilet. The purpose was to degrade a man in order to destroy his morale. Before my own imprisonment, victims and their families had simply not told me about such practices. But after my imprisonment, I became a member of that special group, so they did not hesitate to tell me of their experiences. However, since the People's Government claimed to have abolished all forms of torture, the officials simply called such methods "punishment" or "persuasion."

It took me many months of intense effort to be able to raise my arms above my head; it was a full year before I could stretch them straight above me. The minor wounds left no scar after healing, but the deeper wounds where the metal of the handcuffs cut through my flesh almost to the bone left ugly scars that remain with me to this day: a legacy of Mao Zedong and his Revolutionaries. The swelling of my hands and fingers subsided eventually, but the backs of both my hands had no sensation for more than two years. The nerves were so damaged that when I experimentally pricked the back of my hand with a needle to draw blood, I felt nothing whatever. Even now, after more than thirteen years, my hands ache on cold, wet days. In winter, even in a warm room, I have to wear gloves in bed. If I use my hands a little too much in cleaning, typing, or carrying heavy parcels, sometimes I find my right hand suddenly going limp and useless, unable to grip anything. My right hand sustained a greater degree of damage than my left hand, mainly because the zipper on my slacks was on the left side. Since I strained to the left of my body to unzip my slacks whenever I had to use the toilet, the handcuffs cut deeper into the flesh of my right wrist. The irony of the situation was that normally women's slacks in the clothes stores in China had the zipper on the right side. Since my slacks had been specially tailored, I had the zipper on the left, because I had worn it that way long before the Communist regime came into being. I suppose the interrogator would have said that this was another instance of my stubborn reluctance to change my old way of life.

Some of my friends exclaimed, "Why did you bother to zip up your slacks at all when you had your handcuffs on!" I suppose I could have left my slacks unzipped, but I would have felt terribly demoralized. That wouldn't have been good for my fighting spirit. Looking back on those years, I believe the main reason I was able to survive my ordeal was that the Maoist Revolutionaries failed to break my fighting spirit.

On the whole my feet fared better. Though they remained swollen and painful for many weeks after the handcuffs were taken off, there was no permanent damage. When Sunday came around again, I was able to borrow a needle to open the blisters and let the fluid out. After that, I was able to hobble along slowly without excruciating pain until the blisters gradually healed.

The morning after I was freed from the handcuffs, the guard called the prisoners for outdoor exercise. I went to the door to wait for her so that I could ask to be excused.

"May I be excused today? My feet are swollen. I can't get them into my shoes," I said when she opened the shutter.

She looked at my feet through the opening and saw that I was wearing cloth shoes with the backs pressed down.

"You can go out just as you are," she answered.

"I'm afraid it will be difficult for me to walk the distance to the exercise yard. My feet are very painful. May I be excused this time?" I requested again.

"No, you will have to go. Today, everybody must go."

She unlocked the door and stood there watching me. Each step I took was sheer agony. My body trembled, and I was very slow.

"Please, may I stay in today?" I asked again after going a yard or so.

"No, you have to go today," she said.

What did she mean? Why must I go today? What was so special about today? I was thinking while making slow progress. She was patiently following me out of the building of the women's prison. Since my cell was at the end of the corridor, I was always the last prisoner from downstairs to go out.

Suddenly, the militant female guard ran into the courtyard. "Why are you so slow? Walk faster! We can't wait for you all day!" she shouted.

I continued to shuffle along, trying very hard to bear the pain and walk faster. She gave me a hard push impatiently. I collapsed onto the path. The other guard pulled me up.

"You are acting! Hurry up! Hurry up! Can't you walk faster? Walk faster!" she yelled and then dashed off in the direction of the exercise yards.

"I can't walk any faster. To fall down only delays me," I said to the other guard.

"Never mind. Do the best you can." She seemed much more reasonable.

Finally I reached the exercise yard. Instead of being locked into my usual place with the plane tree over the wall, I was put into an exercise yard directly below the pavilion on the raised platform from which the guards watched the prisoners walking about below. The pavilion seemed to be closed. All the guards were standing in the wind on the platform. As soon as the door of the exercise yard was locked, I leaned against it for support and to take the weight off my feet, which were burning with pain. I thought I would remain there until the exercise period was over.

"Start walking!" shouted the voice of the militant female guard on the platform above me.

I had reached the end of my tether, so I ignored her and remained beneath the platform, leaning against the heavy iron door.

"What are you doing there? Start walking!" she called again.

"I can't walk. My feet are excruciatingly painful. Can't you see my arms and hands? My feet are just the same. They are badly swollen and wounded. Blood and pus are coming out of the wounds." I was so angry that I shouted back at her. I fully expected her to come down and hit me, as prisoners were not allowed to talk about what happened to them in the hearing of other prisoners. My voice was loud enough for everyone in the area of the exercise yards to hear clearly. But she did not rush down from the platform to punish me. It almost seemed that what I had just said was exactly what she wanted to hear, for she moderated her tone of voice when she said, "Just stand in the middle of the exercise yard."

I hobbled to the middle of the yard and stood facing her.

"Turn around! Face the other way!"

Why did she want me to face the other way? It seemed she wanted me to be seen but not to see what went on on the platform where she stood. It suddenly dawned on me that some-one, probably the so-called higher-up, was on the platform. But I saw only the guards who were familiar to me. The man could be inside the pavilion. It had glass windows. If he was inside, he could see my wounded arms and hands easily. I supposed he had come in person to verify the damage done me by the handcuffs. What I had said to the militant female guard was tantamount to a description of my condition. That, I decided, was why the militant female guard was pleased to hear it. She probably hoped to impress the "higher-up" with the good job she had done in inflicting damage on my wrists and feet. But why did the "higher-up" not stand with the guards on the platform? Why did he have to hide in the enclosed pavilion? I turned my body slightly so that I could see the entrance to the pavilion from the corner of my eye. After a little while, three men in khaki military topcoats came out of the pavilion and disappeared down the steps followed by the female guard. Although I had been outside hardly more than ten minutes, I was now told to go back to my cell. On my way back no one urged me to walk faster.

The same guard who had accompanied me out walked back with me. When she opened the door of the cell, I showed her the wounds on my wrists. They were once more covered with blood and pus.

"Please look at these wounds. I need to bandage them up to prevent infection. Could you please help me to take down that pillowcase on the clothesline so that I can tear it up to make bandages?" I asked her.

Without a word she stepped into the cell, pulled the pillowcase down, and handed it to me.

The pillowcase was not new in 1966 when I first came to the detention house. Now it was paper-thin and fragile. I had no difficulty tearing it into strips. It made two sets of bandages.

The prison was very quiet. I did not hear the guards calling the prisoners upstairs to go for outdoor exercise after I came in. It seemed they had stopped the outdoor exercise—something that had never happened before. I thought probably the whole so-called outdoor exercise in which I had participated was arranged solely for the three military men to see the state I was in. It had not been a routine outdoor exercise at all.

When drinking water was given to me again, I washed the wounds and bandaged them up. Very quickly the blood and pus seeped through the cloth. It was out of the question to change the bandages immediately. In the cold and damp cell, a wet bandage would take a long time to dry. I simply had to find a way to dry the bandages more quickly. Perhaps, I thought, I could dry the bandages by wrapping them around my mug whenever boiling water was given to me. That would enable me to change the bandages at least twice a day. And if I washed the bandages just before going to sleep and left them to dry after rolling them in a towel to take out the excess moisture, they would probably be dry by morning. In this manner, I might manage to change the bandages three times during each twenty-four hours.

When hot drinking water was next given to me, I wound a strip of wet bandage firmly on the outside of the mug. It pleased me to see steam coming from the damp cloth, which quickly turned lighter in color as it dried.

For the next few months I devoted my whole attention to caring for the wounds and gave the newspaper only a cursory glance. But I had the impression that there were fewer articles of denunciation of a military nature and many articles demanding that Communist China take her rightful place at the United Nations. It also seemed that Lin Biao's name was mentioned less frequently, while Premier Zhou Enlai seemed to have become more prominent than he had been for years.

Because of my poor physical condition, the wounds were slow to heal. It was many weeks before even the most superficial wounds formed scabs. At the same time, my old trouble of inflamed gums and hemorrhages persisted. It amused me to see the young doctor giving me treatment for these while stringently ignoring the wounds on my wrists.

To add insult to injury, several of the guards came to examine my wounds when they were on duty at the women's prison. Though most of them made no comment, a few militant Maoist guards told me I deserved the punishment.

I did not expect to be called for interrogation, as everything about my simple life seemed to have been scoured with a fine-tooth comb. I thought probably the Maoists would come up with some other way to torment me. But I did not try to anticipate what it might be.

12

Release

Wᴴɪʟᴇ ɪ ᴀᴛᴛᴇɴᴅᴇᴅ ᴛᴏ my numerous physical problems and waited for the next move by the Maoists in 1971, spring and summer came and went. The golden autumn days were upon us. The most important event of the year, the National Day of the People's Republic of China, was celebrated in the autumn on October First. It was a national holiday. The celebration of the National Day had been observed by the People's Government ever since its inception. Everyone received extra food rations, was given the opportunity to enjoy free shows in public parks, and was allowed to purchase scarce consumer goods in the state-owned shops.

The major event, organized by the authorities, was a parade held in each city. Colorful floats displayed diagrams, figures, and pictures of economic and cultural achievements of the previous year. Tens of thousands of workers, peasants, students, and even housewives marched in procession to pledge their loyal support for the People's Government by shouting slogans specially composed by the Communist Party Propaganda Department for the occasion. The parades were carefully planned and reviewed by prominent Party and municipal officials in each locality.

In Beijing the parade was held at Tiananmen Square in front of the old Forbidden City and reviewed by Mao Zedong and other Politburo members and leading government officials from the balcony above the Tiananmen. Special stands on either side of the balcony were filled with foreign dignitaries and diplomats. At night there was an elaborate fireworks display.

The spectacle of hundreds of colorful floats with impressive displays and tens of thousands of men and women marching past the review stand waving red flags, shouting slogans, and holding aloft reproductions of Mao's official portrait was an affirmation of Mao's power and triumph. It must have been an intoxicating moment for the old man to see the adoring faces turn to gaze at him as the marchers passed and to hear their thundering voices wishing him a long life of ten thousand years (in the same words historically used for Chinese emperors). The smiling photograph of Mao splashed on the front pages of China's newspapers all over the country on October 2 attested to his genuine happiness on this important occasion.

Everybody in China knew that for Mao Zedong, the peasant from Shaoshan, the National Day of the People's Republic of China was a great day of personal satisfaction. Therefore it was most astonishing to find that on October First, 1971, there were no celebrations at all. When the morning broadcast did not mention anything, I was surprised. In the afternoon, I waited eagerly for the newspaper. When it came, I saw only Mao's official portrait on its front page. The date, October First, and "Nation Day" were printed in red, but there was no mention of any activities by leading officials or any special events. While I was still puzzling over this extraordinary omission, a guard suddenly pushed open the shutter on the small window.

"Hand over your book of quotations!" she demanded.

It seemed such a strange order that for a moment I thought I had inadvertently done something to damage the book and she was going to use it as an excuse to punish me. Hastily I picked up the book and, with a brief glance to make sure it looked all right, handed it to her. After she had closed the shutter, I heard her going upstairs to demand the book from other cells. Then I knew that she had been instructed to collect the book of quotations from all prisoners.

She did not give the book back to me until she called me to

go to bed. I examined it to try to find out why she had demanded it in the first place and was greatly astonished to discover that she had torn out the preface. This book of Mao's quotations was first compiled and published by the People's Liberation Army for its semiliterate soldiers to use in studying Mao Zedong Thought, on the orders of Lin Biao after he became defense minister.

The preface had been written by Lin Biao himself. In it he praised Mao as "the greatest living Marxist of our time, who developed the doctrine of Marxist-Leninism and successfully applied it to the specific conditions of China." He exhorted the Liberation Army soldiers to study the quotations of Mao contained in the book and apply them to their daily tasks so that they could "blend Mao Zedong Thought into their bloodstream" and become soldiers who "study Chairman Mao's books, obey Chairman Mao's orders, and become Chairman Mao's good fighters."

There was nothing in the wording of the preface that could be considered objectionable by Mao. In fact it was such blatant flattery that many people found it embarrassing to have to memorize and recite it, a practice made obligatory during the Cultural Revolution. I felt the only possible explanation for the removal of the preface was that its author was in disgrace, as it was the practice of the Communist Party to obliterate from all its records the name and writings of a disgraced official as if he had never existed. Obviously the guard was under orders to collect the books from the prisoners and to deal with them. My realization that Lin Biao might be in disgrace was so stupendous that I stood there with the Little Red Book in my hand, lost in thought.

"Why are you not in bed?" the voice of the guard said outside the door.

Not wishing to give her the impression that I was interested in what had happened, I quickly arranged my bedding and lay down. But I did not get much sleep that night.

A few days after the guard had torn the preface out of my copy of the book of quotations, the newspaper came out with denunciations of someone "sleeping by our bedside." No name was mentioned. To a Westerner, "sleeping by our bedside" would mean a spouse. To the Chinese, the expression meant someone very close. The same expression had been used for Liu Shaoqi when he was denounced. It implied that Mao did not know that very near him was an enemy who wished him ill. Other articles talked about the duplicity of a man Mao had trusted, who had voiced support for Mao while plotting Mao's death. There were also frequent mentions of Party history and military engagements during the War of Resistance against Japan and the War of Liberation against the Kuomintang. The Chinese people, including myself, were familiar with Lin Biao's personal history because it had been so frequently glorified when he was being built up as a suitable successor to Mao Zedong, just before the Ninth Party Congress. I now had no doubt that he had been ousted, though at the time I didn't know any details of the struggle between him and Mao Zedong. Watching events closely and reading every word in the newspaper with meticulous attention, I noticed with relief that the name of Lin Biao's man in charge of Military Control of the Public Security Bureau in Shanghai had disappeared. Since the No. 1 Detention House was a part of the network of prisons under the jurisdiction of the Shanghai Public Security Bureau, this man was also the highest officer of the detention house. If my assumption was correct that the motivating force behind my own persecution was the military representative of Lin Biao in Shanghai, then I had good reason to hope that the downfall of Lin Biao would benefit me. On the other hand, I warned myself to continue watching developments. I thought it was premature to rejoice, for I had no idea whether the power vacuum created by Lin Biao's downfall would be filled by the radicals headed by Jiang Qing or by the old guard headed by Zhou Enlai.

One night late in October, the guards once again called the prisoners to sit quietly to listen to a special broadcast. The loudspeaker was switched on, and a man's voice lectured the prisoners on "the excellent situation created by the Great Proletarian Cultural Revolution." The central theme of his speech was the announcement that President Nixon was to visit China in February of the following year. He told us that the Proletarian Cultural Revolution had so raised China's importance in the world that the United States of America, which had hitherto adopted a policy of hostility towards the People's Republic, was now on the point of realizing the futility of that policy.

"What is the significance of the forthcoming visit of Nixon, the head of the strongest capitalist country in the world? Would he have decided to come if China were weak and impotent? Of course not! Nixon has decided to come to China to pay his respects to our Great Leader because he has to face the fact that China, under the wise leadership of our Great Leader Chairman Mao, after being purified and strengthened by the Great Proletarian Cultural Revolution, is invincible. Don't forget that the United States is the most reactionary capitalist country in the world and our foremost enemy. The forthcoming visit of the president of the United States is a great victory for the Chinese proletarian class. It's a reflection of the great achievement made by the Cultural Revolution. It bears out the fact that the decadent capitalist system is on the decline while our own socialist system is increasing in vigor and influence in the world.

"At first, when he offered to come, many of our comrades thought we shouldn't welcome a man who represents imperialism against Vietnam, exploitation of the workers in the United States, and long-standing hostility against the People's Republic of China. But our Great Leader is magnanimous. He said, 'Let him come. Let's receive him with courtesy and hear what he has to say. If he admits past mistakes and sincerely wants to change, we'll welcome it. We are Marxists. We give a man a chance if he is honestly repentant.' Our Great Leader is so wise! He is right! We'll receive Nixon. And for the next few months we will educate all our comrades about the new situation and help them to see that by accepting Nixon's visit, we are not surrendering our principles but accepting the surrender of the wrong policy of the United States government. Nixon's visit is a great victory for us!

"In this connection, I want to give a word of warning to many of the prisoners confined in the Number One Detention House. Many of you are here precisely because you worshiped the capitalist world of the imperialists and belittled socialist China. You placed your hope in the capitalist world and believed that one day capitalism would again prevail in China. Let the forthcoming visit of the American president be a lesson to you all. Think carefully. If the reactionary Kuomintang had not been thrown out of China, if the United States troops had not been defeated by the Chinese People's Volunteer Army in Korea, if the United States army were not bogged down in Vietnam, and if we had not become stronger as a result of the Great Proletarian Cultural Revolution, would Nixon have wanted to travel across the world to Beijing to pay homage to our Great Leader?"

The speech was long-drawn-out, gloating repeatedly over the proposed visit by the president of the United States. I have given the gist of it. After my release from the detention house, I learned that the same interpretation was given to the visit when it was announced to the general public. Discussions were held in every factory, commune, and Residents' Committee meeting to "prepare" the people for the forthcoming visit and to use the occasion to create the impression that Mao Zedong was now the most important leader in the world.

I was elated by the new turn in China's relations with the United States and believed that it could have a decisive effect on the power balance in the leadership of the Communist Party. At least, I thought, Zhou Enlai's position would be strengthened for a considerable time to come. Perhaps the moderate forces in the Party leadership would gain the upper hand. If so, the end of my own ordeal might be approaching. However, I knew from experience that everything in China developed slowly. The effect of a major switch of policy in Beijing often took months, if not years, to be felt at the base level where I was. I also knew that the radical faction headed by Jiang Qing had a strong hold on Shanghai and that her longtime associate Zhang Chunqiao was the chief party secretary here.

After living for so many years without real hope, I became quietly excited by the new development. For weeks I watched the newspaper and waited. The guards appeared preoccupied, as they had been in the days after the Revolutionaries and the Red Guards took over the Shanghai municipal government in January 1967. I thought they were probably undergoing intensified political indoctrination about the downfall of Lin Biao.

Winter was again approaching. The holes at the elbows of my sweaters and at the knees of my knitted longjohns were beyond repair. The filling of my padded jacket and quilt had fallen to the bottom, leaving patches that were no more than two layers of cloth. The only shirt I had left was so patched that it was no longer possible to tell which piece of cloth was the original shirt. Obviously, if I was to survive another winter at the detention house, I desperately needed some additional clothing. Though my past requests for clothing had always fallen on deaf ears, I decided to try once more and see whether the changed circumstances might not bring forth a different response.

"Report!" I called at the door.

"What do you want?" A guard's lethargic footsteps stopped outside my cell, and the shutter was pushed open.

I held my sweater out to show her the holes and said, "The weather is getting cold. My clothes and quilt are so worn that they are no longer warm. Please look at this. It's full of holes. I also need a padded jacket and another shirt. Please look at my clothes. You will see I do need warm clothes for the winter."

"How long have you been here already? How many years altogether?"

"This will be the sixth winter I am here. I came in September 1966. The clothes and bedding given me by the Red Guards were not new then. After so many years without the padding being renewed, they are no longer warm," I said.

Now that I could see a glimmer of light at the end of the dark tunnel in which I had been confined for so long, I was determined to survive to the day when that glimmer might guide me out into daylight. Probably my voice showed my anxiety. This seemed to annoy her. She closed the shutter and walked away.

Undaunted by her cold indifference, I repeated my request for warm clothing and bedding to each guard who came on duty for several successive days. Finally one of them said impatiently, "All right! All right! You need warm clothing. We know about it already. Your request is being considered."

A week passed, and then another. The weather got colder and colder. I decided to try once more.

"Report!" I called.

"What do you want?" a guard asked through the closed door.

"May I see the interrogator?"

"What for?"

"I want to make a request for warm clothes."

"Haven't you got warm clothes already?" The guard opened the shutter, and I saw through the opening that it was the older woman who had urged me to eat when I was manacled. I had not seen her since that night.

"My winter clothes are worn out. Please come into the cell and look at them. I'm so afraid I might get ill again this winter if I do not get some warm clothes," I said.

She unlocked the cell door, came in, and examined my clothes and the quilt. Then she said, "I'll report to the authorities. Would you like to borrow some prison clothes for now?"

The thought of wearing prison clothes filled me with horror, not only because I thought they might have bugs, but also because it seemed the final surrender of my dignity and independence.

"No, thank you. I do not want to borrow prison clothes. I want to get permission to buy new winter clothes with my own money that is now in the hands of the government."

She appeared to be thinking over the problem, so I added, "My money was taken by the Red Guards when they looted my home. One of their teachers told me the government would keep the money for me if it had not come from exploitation. I have no shares in any factories or land in the countryside. When I explained this to the teacher, he told me that the money would not be confiscated."

"I'll report to the authorities," she promised.

A few days later, I was called to the interrogation room. The older guard was nowhere to be seen. In the place of the interrogator sat the militant female guard who had always taken a lead in persecuting me. She was flanked by two other female guards, including one I considered mild. The sight of the militant female guard was both a surprise and a disappointment for me. Had the new situation in Beijing brought no change at all in the No. 1 Detention House? With this woman in charge, what hope had I that my request would fall on sympathetic ears?

After I had bowed to Mao's portrait and read a passage from the mutilated book of quotations, I sat down on the prisoner's chair and waited for her to ridicule my request. I was unprepared for her normal, almost kind tone of voice when she said, "What is this request of yours about winter clothes? Haven't you got winter clothes already?"

"They are worn out," I said. To prove my point, I pulled off my blue cotton jacket to reveal the padded jacket underneath, with its holes and tufts of cotton escaping through them. I raised my arms to show her the frayed cuffs.

"All right! All right! Put on your jacket," she said.

"The government is holding my assets. I want to ask permission to use some of my own money to buy some much-needed clothes," I said, laying emphasis on the words "my own money."

"Which government department is holding your money?" she asked. "Have you a receipt?"

"The Red Guards took the money when they looted my house. They didn't give me a receipt."

"You mustn't use the word 'loot' when you refer to the revolutionary action taken by the Red Guards. They were acting on our Great Leader's instruction to rid socialist China of the Four Olds and to deal with the exploiting class," she said.

"I'm not a member of the exploiting class. According to Marxism, only those who live on the interest from their stocks and shares in factories or on rent collected from the peasants are 'members of the exploiting class.' My money was mostly my salary, which I earned legally, and my family inheritance, which was guaranteed by the Constitution," I said heatedly. If I had spoken like this a year ago, she would have exploded. Now she just ignored me.

"Did the teachers of the Red Guards who came to your house to take revolutionary action against you tell you which government department would be holding your money?"

"No, they merely said the money would be held pending a decision by Chairman Mao."

"Exactly. All personal assets taken by the Red Guards are frozen and cannot be touched before the Chairman makes a decision," she said.

"I also have a foreign exchange account with the Bank of China," I said.

"Foreign exchange accounts are frozen too."

"All right, then. Let me borrow an English typewriter. I will write a letter to my bank in Hong Kong and get them to send me some money."

"That won't be allowed. You are not allowed to communicate with anybody outside China," she said. "How do we know what you might write?"

"Before posting the letter, you will naturally read what I have written."

"You might send a coded message out of the country. That wouldn't do at all. What we'll do is to report your request to the senior authorities and see to it that you get some warm clothes when it gets really cold. Now you must go back to your cell and study our Great Leader Chairman Mao's books really diligently."

I was dismissed and led back to the cell. Throughout the interview, the militant female guard had spoken in a normal voice, almost sympathetically. The change was startling. I supposed she was a typical example of those Party members who "follow the Party line closely." The Chinese people called them "chameleons," as they changed attitude and behavior according to circumstances just as rapidly as the chameleon changes color. Such Party members were the survivors and achievers. They never questioned the policy of the Party but followed it promptly and carried it out. They were mindless robots, unburdened by the capacity for independent thinking or a human conscience. They made the best cadres for any Party secretary in any organization, as they were always willing and ready to serve him without question as long as he represented the power of the Party and could give them promotions. But should he fall into disgrace, they were always the first to denounce him. They were the new type of successful people produced by the Communist Revolution in China. Because they seemed to maintain their positions through every twist and turn of the Party's policy, they became the example for the young generation of Chinese to emulate. The result was a fundamental change in the basic values of Chinese society.

A week later, a large bundle was deposited on the floor of my cell by a male guard. After I had signed the receipt, he locked the door and departed. I took the bundle to my bed and untied it. To my great astonishment, I found in the bundle the padded jacket, the fleece-lined winter coat, the two sweaters, and the pair of woolen underpants the Red Guards had allowed my daughter to keep for her own use after they looted our home in 1966. Also included was the winter quilt for her bed. Wrapped among the clothes were several towels and a mug she used for tea. One of the towels was a rose-colored Cannon face towel I had brought back from Hong Kong, which she was using when I was taken to the No. 1 Detention House. It looked exactly the same as it had in 1966. I examined the padded jacket of navy blue woolen material lined with maroon silk. It was new in 1966, and it looked new now. I picked up the white porcelain mug with trembling hands and found it was stained faintly brown inside. It had not been washed, and the tea had dried.

My heart thumped faster and faster as I examined each article and realized its appearance was an ominous message of disaster.

Hateful though the idea was, I could not help thinking that something terrible had happened to my daughter not long after I was arrested. She had probably died. That was why the clothes had hardly been worn and the face towel remained unused and new-looking. Perhaps her death had happened rather suddenly and unexpectedly, so that she did not have time to wash the mug she had used for tea. My legs were shaking so violently that I had to sit down quickly.

The No. 1 Detention House allowed families of inmates to send them articles of clothing and daily necessities such as soap and towels on the fifth day of each month. It was always the loneliest day of my imprisonment as I listened to the guards carrying parcels to other prisoners but never to me. At first I wondered why my daughter never sent me anything. Later I believed that because she was a member of the Communist Youth League, she had been compelled to renounce me. While I missed not having this tenuous link to my child through monthly parcels, I was glad she was spared the unpleasant task of coming to the prison gate and lining up for hours to hand over a parcel. Now, deep in my heart, I knew the reason I had never received any parcels was that she had died.

"Report!" I rushed to the door, hoping to find out the truth from the guard.

"What do you want?" The guard opened the shutter and looked at me through the opening.

"These things you have just given to me—they are my daughter's clothes and quilt," I said.

"Yes," answered the guard.

"What's happened to my daughter?"

"Nothing has happened to her," she replied.

I bent down to look at her face through the small window. She appeared quite normal and calm.

"The clothes look as new as they did in 1966. Has she not used them during the past few years?"

"How do I know? She probably bought new clothes. She works, doesn't she? She has her own salary. She can buy new clothes, can't she?"

"Do you mean to tell me that you know for a fact my daughter is alive and well at this moment?" I hoped so much for reassurance.

"I haven't seen her, if that's what you mean."

"But you do know, don't you?"

"Why should she be otherwise?" The guard closed the shutter and walked away.

Was I being hysterical? Had prison life made me oversuspicious and sensitive? I examined everything again carefully. As I touched each item of her clothing, I became more and more convinced that she had indeed died. The message came to me clear and strong that she was no longer in this world. Yet I needed concrete proof because I was accustomed to dealing with facts and was suspicious of feelings I could not understand or explain. There was also a block in my mind that prevented me from accepting such a terrible possibility as her death, which would have rendered my years of struggling to keep alive meaningless. Death came to old people, not to someone as young and healthy as she was. I kept on trying to convince myself she was all right in spite of what I saw.

But I could not explain the unusual look of her things spread out in front of my eyes. They seemed to say time had suddenly stood still not long after my imprisonment. The navy blue jacket looked new. But when I examined the silk lining I saw that it had creases at the armpits and that there was a handkerchief in one of the pockets. It seemed to me she had worn that jacket, but certainly not for more than one winter at the most. My mind was racing with speculations as I tried to imagine what could possibly have happened. What the guard said seemed to indicate she was alive and well. Yet she did not specifically say so. An idea came into my head. I went to the window again.

"Report!" I called.

No one came. I called again and again. Still no one came. Yet I heard the guards talking in their room at the other end of the corridor. When the guard on night duty came to tell me to go to bed, I tried to talk to her. But she did not come near my cell, only called out from a distance her order to go to bed.

I was not able to sleep. I became more and more anxious. The first thing next morning, I called the guard again.

"Report!"

No answer. I decided to wait for the daytime guard to come on duty. When she came, I called again, "Report!"

She came quite promptly. "What do you want?"

"These things of my daughter's the guard brought me yesterday make me very uneasy. I can't understand why my daughter doesn't seem to have used them. The Red Guards left each of us only one padded jacket. Why hasn't she worn hers during the past few winters? To prove my daughter is alive and well, I request you to ask her to write me a few words in her own handwriting."

"Prisoners in a detention house are not allowed to communicate with their families," she said.

"Perhaps she could just write 'Long Live Chairman Mao' or one of Chairman Mao's quotations or even just her name," I pleaded.

"No, that's not allowed. I have told you already, prisoners in a detention house are not allowed to communicate with their families," she said firmly.

"But I have been here such a long time already," I said.

"That makes no difference."

I repeated my request to every guard who came on duty during the next few days. I was more and more convinced that my daughter was really dead, because they were either evasive or simply kept silent. One or two of them looked definitely embarrassed when they refused my request to see my daughter's handwriting. They did not look at me but averted their eyes or simply looked at the floor.

My mind was in turmoil and my heart in anguish. I longed to know the truth while I was afraid of it. One moment I was convinced that she had died. The next moment I believed I had become oversensitive and too pessimistic because of prolonged imprisonment.

After a few weeks of anxiety, with little food and hardly any sleep, I became sick once more, with a high fever and delirium. I was again taken to the prison hospital. My body was so resilient that in spite of the fact that I no longer had the will to live, I survived. I was brought back to the No. 1 Detention House just before Christmas.

Throughout the years of my imprisonment, I had turned to God often and felt His presence. In the drab surroundings of the gray cell, I had known magic moments of transcendence that I had not experienced in the ease and comfort of my normal life. My belief in the ultimate triumph of truth and goodness had been restored, and I had renewed courage to fight on. My faith had sustained me in these the darkest hours of my life and brought me safely through privation, sickness, and torture. At the same time, my suffering had strengthened my faith and made me realize that God was always there. It was up to me to come to Him.

Under the watchful eyes of the guards, I could not pray openly in the daytime. The only way I could be certain of being left alone with my prayers was to bend my head over a volume of Mao Zedong's books while I prayed to God from my tormented heart. As I spoke of my daughter, I relived the precious years from the time of her birth in Canberra, Australia, in 1942 until our forcible separation on the night of September 27, 1966, when I was taken to the struggle meeting and arrested. I felt again and again the joy she had given me at each stage of her growth and knew I was fortunate to have received from God this very special blessing of a daughter. Day after day I prayed. More and more I remembered the days of her living, and less and less I dwelled on the tragedy of her dying. Gradually peace came to me, and with it a measure of acceptance. But there was something more. While I could no longer cling tenaciously to the hope that I would see her alive and well on the day I walked out of the No. 1 Detention House, I knew there was much I still had to do both before and after my release. My battle was by no means over. It was up to me to find out what had happened to my daughter and, if I could, to right the wrong that had been done to her. My life would be bleak without Meiping. But I had to fight on.

In February 1972 President Nixon came to Beijing. The newspaper devoted whole pages to reports of the visit and published large photographs of his arrival, the banquet of welcome, and his visit to Mao Zedong at the latter's home. As I looked at the smiling face of Mao while he was shaking the hand of the American president, I thought the moment was indeed Mao Zedong's finest hour. In that moment his years of humiliation, of being denied recognition, were wiped away. And I was certain that he relished the meeting with the American president not only for its significance to himself and the Chinese Communist Party but also for what it meant to his lifelong foe, the Kuomintang in Taiwan.

In all the photographs and reports, Zhou Enlai figured prominently. The newspaper reported that Prime Minister Zhou Enlai accompanied President Nixon to Shanghai, whence the American president was to return to the United States. It said the departure of the president was slightly delayed, hinting that there was some last-minute difficulty about drafting the text of the final communiqué. However, eventually it was signed. The published version included an acknowledgment by the United States that Taiwan was an integral part of China. This commitment would render it impossible for the United States to recognize an independent Taiwan state, the event the Chinese Communist government feared most. Furthermore, in the communiqué the People's Government did not renounce the use of force for future reunification of the two Chinas. This was decidedly a victory for Communist China. It seemed Communist China had gained a great deal from the president's visit, while the price she paid was no more than a display of elaborate hospitality. The policy of rapprochement with the United States seemed more than justified. I felt that the personal position of Prime Minister Zhou Enlai had been greatly enhanced by his successful and skillful diplomacy.

Now there was a respite from class struggle; a more peaceful atmosphere prevailed. The tone of the newspaper was no longer belligerent. Even the guards seemed to behave more like normal human beings. In March I was called for interrogation. The interrogator I had when I first came to the detention house was back at his job. He started from the beginning, as if the intervening years had not existed, and asked me to write another autobiography. Then he questioned me about my family, my relatives, and my friends, as well as my personal life and activities, going once more through everything I had already covered with the interrogator from the Workers' Propaganda Team in 1969. When I became impatient and pointed out to him that I had already answered all these questions, he merely said, "You have to answer them again." I did not think he was trying to trap me into saying something different so that he could charge me with lying. It was more likely that the official interrogator of the No. 1 Detention House and the interrogator of the Workers' Propaganda Team served different masters.

This series of interrogations lasted several months. I did not remember how many times I was called to the interrogation room or how many quotations I read from Mao's book. There was no more shouting or argument. But I was sick and tired and found the sessions extremely tedious.

One day in the autumn of 1972, the interrogator produced a letter, obviously taken from our office file, and asked me whether I had written it. I saw it bore my name, so I said yes.

"This is proof of your illegal activity. But at the same time, it may only be a political mistake," he said.

I was astonished. "May I see the letter again?" I asked him.

He handed the letter to me. I saw that it had been written soon after my husband died in October 1957. I had gone to the Shell office to take charge because the Bank of China had refused to cash the company's checks unless someone was made responsible for the office and had his or her personal seal registered with the bank. I remembered the circumstances very well. That morning I had received a telephone call from the general manager of Shell's Hong Kong office. He told me that a general manager had been appointed to succeed my late husband but he could not get to Shanghai until March of the following year. He said, "London wants to know if it is all right with you." I told him it was all right and I would inform the Industry and Commerce Department of the Shanghai municipal government. Then he asked me to draw up a list of things the new general manager and his wife should bring with them. In particular they wanted to know whether they should bring a supply of wheat flour, as they knew the Chinese people ate rice.

Because our secretary at that time was a British woman, I thought she would know best what advice to give, so I asked her to draw up the list and write a covering letter, which I signed. In her zeal to help her compatriots, she gave rather a long list that included items from buttons to detergents. But from a political point of view, the letter seemed to me completely innocuous.

"I can't see anything political in this letter," I said.

"Nothing political? You divulged information about the grain supply situation in Shanghai," he said.

"Really? Let me see the letter again." By now I realized that he had been instructed to find some excuse for my imprisonment in order to avoid having to declare at the time of my release that I was innocent. I knew the Communist Party loathed admitting mistakes, since it had declared itself to be "the great, glorious, and correct Chinese Communist Party."

He handed me the letter again and said, "Read the passage about grain rations."

I read, " 'The Shanghai government allows everyone twenty catties of grain per month. One can buy either rice or flour. It is more than enough.' " I asked the interrogator, "What's wrong with that?"

"That's divulging information concerning the grain supply situation," he said.

"The grain ration is given to everyone, including all the Europeans living in Shanghai. It's not a secret. What's there to divulge when it is a fact known to everyone?"

"Your letter was sent abroad," he said.

"Do you mean to say the Europeans in Shanghai will not tell people abroad about it when they go back to their own countries? What about all the overseas Chinese who come back for short visits? Don't they know what grain rations their family members get? Do they conveniently forget it when they leave China?"

"That's their business. This letter is your business. Do you or do you not admit you wrote this letter?"

"The letter was not actually written by me. But I accept full responsibility for it, as I signed it and it was sent out of the office when I was the responsible person. The point with which I disagree is that stating the fact of a ration of twenty catties of rice or flour per person per month constitutes 'divulging information.' "

"It's illegal to divulge information about the grain supply. But we can consider it only a political mistake since you were ignorant of the regulations," he said.

"Nonsense! It's not a mistake, political or otherwise. Show me the regulations, if you have any." I was angry. But he just ignored me and adjourned the interrogation.

When winter came, the prisoners were again given three meals a day; I got fish or meat with my midday meal. But my health had deteriorated to such an extent that these measures made no difference. I had another bad hemorrhage. When the bleeding was brought under control, I was taken by the militant female guard, dressed in civilian clothes, to the Zhongshan Hospital of the No. 1 Medical College for an examination. An appointment was probably made beforehand, as we went straight to the gynecology department and were admitted into the doctor's office ahead of all the other waiting patients.

I was surprised to find the "doctor" a young woman in her early twenties, with an armband of the Revolutionaries. She was clumsy during the brief examination, and afterwards she told the guard I had cancer of the uterus. I did not believe her because I was sure she was not a qualified doctor. I thought she was one of those who had learned to be a doctor by being one, just like the young medical orderly I had encountered before. But apparently the guards and others at the detention house believed her. My treatment improved. Some of the guards looked at me with pity in their eyes. After my release, I learned that the officials in charge of my case looked for housing for me in earnest after my visit to the hospital. Eventually it was decided to allow me an apartment with two rooms and a bathroom because it was assumed that since I did not have any children to look after me I would need a live-in nurse towards the end of my life.

On March 27, 1973, after the midday meal, while I was walking about in the cell, a guard opened the small window and said, "Pack up all your things."

"All my things?" I asked her.

"Yes, all your things. Don't leave anything behind."

Soon afterwards the door opened and two Labor Reform girls came into the cell. They collected all my things and took them away. A guard in the corridor said, "Come out!"

I looked around the cell, my "home" for exactly six and a half years. Without my washbasin and towels, it already seemed different. I noticed the sheets of toilet paper I had pasted on the wall by the bed and wondered if I should tear them off so as not to leave any impression of myself behind. But I decided to leave them for the next unfortunate woman who was to occupy the cell. As I stood in the room looking at it for the last time, I felt again the cold metal of the handcuffs on my wrists and remembered the physical suffering and mental anguish I had endured while fighting with all the willpower and intellect God had given me for that rare and elusive thing in a Communist country called justice.

"Come along! What are you doing in there? Haven't you stayed there long enough?" the guard called.

I followed her to the front courtyard and into the room where I was registered when I arrived at the detention house in 1966. There was no one inside. I sat down on the chair.

The young doctor followed me into the room. He stood by the counter, half leaning on it in a casual manner, and said, "I want to tell you the medication I have been giving you so that you can tell your own doctor when you leave here." He named several medicines.

"Thank you very much," I said.

"Well, you are going to be released shortly. Are you glad?" the doctor asked me.

"It's high time, isn't it? Six and a half years is a long time to lock up an innocent person," I said.

He winced but went on as if he had not heard me. "I want to give you some advice before you leave. It's for your own good. During the time you have been here, you haven't exactly behaved in an exemplary manner. In fact, in all the years of the detention house, we have never had a prisoner like you, so truculent and argumentative. When you leave this place, you must try to control yourself. Be careful not to irritate the masses. Shanghai is no longer the same city it was before the Cultural Revolution. You must show some respect for the proletariat. Otherwise you will suffer. You are a sick woman. You don't want to be brought back here again, do you?"

I did not say anything. He stayed a few more minutes and then departed. Obviously he had been told to talk to me. But why, I could not tell. In fact, I wasn't listening to him very carefully. What occupied my mind was simply whether I would find my daughter alive after all.

My bundle of clothing was thoroughly searched by two male guards. When they had finished, I was escorted to one of the interrogation rooms. There was no more bowing to Mao's photograph or reading quotations. The interrogator merely pointed at the prisoner's chair. I sat down.

Another man I had never seen before sat beside him. This man said, "You are going out today. We feel the time has come for you to go out. I will read to you the conclusion arrived at by the People's Government on your case. However, after you have heard it, you are allowed to express an opinion, if you have any."

He took a couple of sheets of paper out of a folder. Then he said to me, "Stand up to listen to the conclusion."

I stood up.

He read out my name and other personal particulars such as age and place of birth. Then he went on, " 'The above-named person was brought to the Number One Detention House on September 27, 1966, for the following reasons. One, in October 1957, in a letter to England, she divulged the grain supply situation in Shanghai. Two, she defended the traitor Liu Shaoqi and opposed the Central Committee resolution passed on Liu Shaoqi. These are serious matters that deserved punishment. However, in view of the fact that she is politically backward and ignorant, we decided to give her a chance to realize her mistakes. After six and a half years of education in the Number One Detention House, we observed a certain degree of improvement in her way of thinking and an attitude of repentance. We have, therefore, decided to show her proletarian magnanimity by refraining from pressing charges against her and allowing her to leave the detention house as a free person.' " When he had finished reading, he lifted his head and looked at me.

I was livid. Anger and disgust choked me. While I despised their blatant hypocrisy and shamelessness, I knew deep in my heart that the real culprit was not this man but the evil system under which we all had to live. I would have to fight, whatever the price, I told myself. I stared back at him and sat down.

"Haven't you something to say? Aren't you grateful? Aren't you pleased that you can now leave as a free person?" the man said.

I tried my best to control the rage that made me tremble and said, "I can't accept your conclusion. I shall remain here in the Number One Detention House until a proper conclusion is reached about my case. A proper conclusion must include a declaration that I am innocent of any crime or political mistake, an apology for wrongful arrest, and full rehabilitation. Furthermore, the apology must be published in the newspapers in both Shanghai and Beijing, because I have friends and relatives in both cities. As for the conclusion you have just read, it's a sham and a fraud. I was brought to the Number One Detention House long before Liu Shaoqi was denounced. How could you have anticipated that I would speak on his behalf? As for divulging information about the grain supply situation, it's just your invention to save face. I never divulged anything, and you all know it."

They looked at each other. Then the interrogator said, "The Number One Detention House isn't an old people's home. You can't stay here all your life."

"It doesn't have to be all my life. I'll stay here until you give a proper conclusion to my case. If you are ready to give one tomorrow, I can leave tomorrow."

"We have already heard your opinion. As I have said, we allow you to express your opinion. It's noted down. We'll forward it to the senior authorities. You can leave now," the other man said.

"No. The moment I leave, you will forget the whole thing. The wrong conclusion will go into my personal dossier. I'll stay here," I said.

The interrogator stood up. He said, "I have never seen a prisoner refusing to leave the detention house before. You must be out of your mind. In any case, when the government wants you to go, you have to go. Your family has been waiting for you since early this morning. How much longer do you want to delay your departure?"

Did he mean my daughter was out there waiting? Oh, how I longed to see her! Suddenly two female guards came into the room. One on each side, they dragged me out to the second gate.

In the distance, standing beside a blue taxi, was the figure of a young woman. She was shorter than Meiping, and I realized with a sinking heart that she was my goddaughter Hean.

III

MY
STRUGGLE
FOR JUSTICE

13

Where Is Meiping?

I STOOD STILL AND my eyes searched the driveway. Apart from the armed sentry in the distance, there was only my goddaughter Hean coming towards me with her arms outstretched.

"Meiping is dead! That's why she isn't here to meet me. Meiping is dead! Meiping is dead . . ." My ears buzzed and my eyes misted, blurring the scene before me. Even though in the back of my mind I still hoped for some tangible explanation for my daughter's absence, my whole body was weakened by grief and I could not move my legs. Hean grasped my arm and guided me to the waiting cab.

"Where is Meiping?"

I feared the answer, but I had to ask.

Hean didn't reply but merely tightened her grip on my hand. I could not bring myself to say, "Is Meiping dead?" Putting it into words would make it real.

We sat in the car in silence as it drove through the familiar Shanghai streets. Release from the No. 1 Detention House was not bringing me a feeling of relief, only a new anxiety in the place of the old one.

The taxi stopped in front of a narrow black wooden gate set in a cement wall. Hean paid the driver and knocked on the gate.

A middle-aged woman dressed in a blue cotton tunic and loose-fitting trousers like a servant opened the gate and helped Hean with my things.

What must have been a small garden at one time was now covered with rubble. Except for a single elm tree struggling in the midst of broken tiles, bricks, and dirt, there were only clusters of weeds. The house before us looked shabby and neglected, the downstairs rooms unoccupied. A thick layer of dust lay on the terrace. The front door opened into a small hall, and we went up the stairs. The hall and staircase had been swept and washed with a wet mop, but the walls were gray. Hean preceded me into a large room at the top of the stairs. A bed with clean white sheets and a floral quilt, a chest of drawers, a small desk, a table, four chairs, and an easy chair were in the room. The furniture was the standard set, mass-produced and identical in design, usually rationed to newly married couples.

"These two rooms up here are allocated to you. The Security Bureau issued me a certificate to buy these few pieces of furniture for you." Hean hugged me and exclaimed, "Oh! It's good to have you back again!"

She put her face against mine and held me for a long moment. I realized that she found it difficult to talk about Meiping. I would have to give her time. The fact that she did not explain Meiping's absence proved beyond doubt that Meiping was dead. I felt an overwhelming depression and painful anxiety. But I would have to let her come to the subject in her own good time.

"They gave me five thousand yuan of your money. I did not dare to spend it all. I thought you would need some of it to live on. That's why the walls are dirty and the curtains are so skimpy," explained Hean. "Mother was coming with me to get you, but at the last moment, while we were waiting for the taxi, she was told to go to a meeting of her study group to listen to an official document about Lin Biao. You know about that, don't you?"

"I suppose he is in disgrace, since his name has disappeared from newspaper reports."

"He's dead! In a plane crash while escaping to the Soviet Union! Premier Zhou is now the man next to Chairman Mao. That's why things are getting better. That's why you are saved! Oh, I'm so happy to see you! If only . . ." She didn't finish her sentence, and what she was going to say turned into a sob. Tears streamed down her face, and she bowed her head.

I thought she was going to tell me about Meiping. But we were interrupted by the maid entering the room with two cups of hot tea.

Hean quickly pulled herself together and blinked back her tears, almost as if she were afraid of the maid.

"This is A-yi," Hean introduced her. "She is here to look after you. She will sleep in the other room."

"Thank you, A-yi," I said to the maid while accepting the teacup from her. She was a wiry little woman of about fifty with coarse skin and sinewy hands. As she handed me the teacup, her eyes were summing me up.

"Shall I boil hot water for a bath?" she asked me.

"No, thank you. Not just yet. I'll tell you when I'm ready for a bath."

When she had left the room and closed the door, I asked Hean, "Are servants still allowed?"

"Why not? There are so many unemployed people. If someone is ill or there are babies, nobody will say anything. In our case, it was the man from the Security Bureau who suggested that I find a maid for you. He said you were ill and would need an operation. He led me to think you were more ill than you are. Though I must say, you look terribly thin," said Hean, looking at my emaciated body with wrinkled brows.

"Don't worry, it's a matter of food. I'll be all right. How did you find A-yi?" I asked Hean, wondering if the Security Bureau had sent the maid.

"Mother found her through a friend. But"—Hean lowered her voice—"she isn't the same as Chen-ma. Be careful what you say to her."

I nodded.

"I think the government wants to be nice to you now that the situation in Beijing is different. You have been given these two rooms with your own bathroom. And yesterday when I was here hanging the curtains a man came from the tree-planting section of the Housing Bureau to tell me that he was sent to plant trees in the garden for you. He even asked me what kind of trees you liked."

Because I was given two rooms with a private bath and the

tree-planting section of the Housing Bureau offered to plant trees in the garden, Hean had come to the conclusion that the People's Government wanted to be "nice" to me. Since the government was the sole arbiter of their fate, the Chinese people were sensitive to every little sign from government agencies, interpreting them as indications of their position in the eyes of the authorities.

Hean seemed more relaxed and was smiling. So I decided to ask her about Meiping. "Are you now ready to tell me what has happened to Meiping?"

She looked at me searchingly, as if she weren't sure whether I could take what she was going to tell me. Then she seemed to decide to face the issue. "I wasn't in Shanghai at the time. As you know, I graduated from the Conservatory of Music in 1966 just when the Cultural Revolution started. When I came to Meiping's birthday party in August, I was waiting to be assigned work by the authorities. In December of that year, I was sent to Guiyang. Soon after I got there, I was told to go to an agricultural commune near Guiyang to be 'reeducated.' In the summer of 1967, Mother wrote me to say that Meiping had committed suicide."

So, Meiping was really dead, just as I had suspected when her clothes were sent to me in the No. 1 Detention House. Yet how desperately I had clung to the hope that I would somehow find her alive when I came out of prison. Now my last spark of hope was snuffed out. Now there was nothing left. It would have been less painful if I had died in prison and never known that Meiping was dead. My struggle to keep alive and to fight against adversity, so vitally important at the time, suddenly seemed meaningless. I felt that I had fallen into a void and become disoriented. Hean's arms were holding me up. Together we wept for Meiping.

What did they do to Meiping that she had to commit suicide? It was not the sort of thing a healthy young woman would even think of if she wasn't pushed to the point of no return.

"Her name was included in a list of suicides read at a meeting of the entire film studio, I was told. Yesterday, the Security Bureau man told me not to say anything to you. He said the representatives of the Revolutionary Committee of the film studio would come to notify you tomorrow," Hean told me.

"Did they announce why she committed suicide?"

"I have attended meetings when suicides were announced. Usually the announcement just said the persons concerned were 'unable to assume a correct attitude towards the Proletarian Cultural Revolution.' "

"That means nothing at all," I said.

"Exactly. I wonder whether we'll ever know the facts. I'm sure no one will dare talk about it," she added.

I would find out how she died, I told myself. It would take time, but I would not rest until I found out. However, I would have to be careful, because if the authorities found out my intentions they would want to stop me. Nobody must know what I intended to do, not even Hean.

"Are you now working in Shanghai?" I asked Hean.

"Oh, no! I was called back by the Shanghai Security Bureau. They sent a letter to my unit in Guiyang, which gave me a month's leave. That was nearly two weeks ago. At first the Security Bureau man wanted my mother to get things ready for you. But she had a heart attack a year ago and cannot stand in lines at the shops. So the Security Bureau decided to get me to do it. I'll have to go back to Guiyang soon. The children need me. I'm married and have a girl and a boy." Hean smiled happily and took a snapshot of the family from her bag.

"Congratulations!" I said.

The snapshot showed a pretty girl of five and a fine baby boy, with her husband and herself smiling towards the camera.

"His name is Li Tong. He was also sent to work in Guiyang after graduating from the Beijing College of Dramatic Art. The Cultural Department of the Guiyang municipal government was in disarray. The senior officials were all denounced as 'capitalist-roaders.' The Revolutionaries were fighting each other to gain control of the department. Nobody knew what to do with the graduates assigned to them, so they just sent us all to the same agricultural commune to receive 'reeducation' through physical labor. Li Tong and I became friends almost at once. Work in the commune outside Guiyang was very hard because the land is cut from the sides of huge mountains and terraced. We had to carry heavy loads of water and fertilizers up and down many hundreds of steps each day. The peasants were crude and unpleasant to us. They resented our being there to eat their meager ration of grain, but they didn't dare refuse to take us. So they were very unpleasant. No matter how hard I worked, they said I didn't do enough. I was so frightened of them. Sometimes I thought I would die from exhaustion and would never come home again. Li Tong used to help me and protect me from the peasants when they got nasty. He is a scriptwriter, so he knows a lot of old Chinese stories. He used to keep me going with his good humor and funny stories."

I looked at Li Tong in the photograph again and saw a skinny man, not at all strong or distinguished-looking, but he had a twinkle in his eyes and a sardonic smile. Standing beside him in the photograph, Hean, softly feminine with her round face and small stature, looked like a child.

"Are you quite happy with Li Tong?"

"Oh, yes! We are very happy together. He looks after me and the children. You know, he is secretly writing a play about the Cultural Revolution. It's called *Madness,* a satire."

"Goodness! What will happen if the manuscript falls into the hands of the Revolutionaries? I suppose you live in rooms assigned to you by the government." I was alarmed that he was taking such a risk.

"Li Tong said he had to write, otherwise his head would burst. Besides, the Revolutionaries in our organization are very friendly with him and are not likely to search our rooms. Li Tong is a sort of underground writer for the Revolutionaries, who have had very little education and have never read a single book on Marxism. They recite Chairman Mao's quotations, but they have not read his books. They ask Li Tong to write their speeches for them so that he can include quotations from books by Marx and Lenin as well as Chairman Mao. That makes the audience think the Revolutionaries are knowledgeable. Sometimes Li Tong even plans their strategies when they have a factional fight with other Revolutionaries," Hean told me.

"Why on earth would he want to do that?"

Hean laughed so hard that she could barely get the words out. "Li Tong says that since he cannot very well kill the Revolutionaries himself, the next best thing is to let the Revolutionaries kill each other in their factional wars."

I was speechless with consternation. Asking Hean about Li Tong's family background, I learned that his bitterness was the result of family suffering. His eldest brother, a middle-school teacher who believed in the Communist Party, was denounced as a Rightist in 1957. His sister-in-law committed suicide. His father died of a heart attack after the Red Guards accused him of having been a landlord, put him in a sack, and kicked him around.

"I gather you are no longer at the agricultural commune?"

"No, we were called back to Guiyang when Chairman Mao invited the American table-tennis team to visit Beijing. All of a sudden, the Revolutionaries were very nice to me because I was born in Australia. They thought Australia and the United States were one and the same place." Hean was laughing heartily. "Everyone must follow the correct line of Chairman Mao. The Revolutionaries watch Beijing closely. The visit of the American table-tennis team told them China wants to be nice to the United States, so they decided they must be nice to those born in the United States. Some people say that when the Politburo in Beijing takes a deep breath, the rest of the country feels a gust of wind."

"What work do you do now?"

"I play the piano as an accompanist for the Guiyang Song and Dance Ensemble."

Hean's mother arrived. My old friend had aged so much that I could hardly recognize her. An expression of defeat and resignation was written on her deeply lined face. She embraced me and exclaimed, "You look much better than I imagined. Oh, it's good to see you!"

My memory moved back in time and space to Sydney, Australia, over twenty-six years before. Then we were two happy young mothers walking side by side, following our two little girls in frilly sunsuits, who were running ahead of us with toy buckets and shovels to look for a spot on the wide expanse of golden beach to build a sand castle. We did not know that we were living in a sand castle ourselves and how near collapse it was. Hean's father was working in the Chinese consulate general in Sydney. All of us were about to return to China, and we were looking forward to it.

Obviously Hean's mother was also thinking of Meiping. She said, "You must be brave. What's happened has happened. We can't undo that. There's your own life to think about. You are not well. Too much grief is not good for you. You must try to be philosophical."

Then she told me of their experience during the Cultural Revolution. Their humiliation and persecution had not been very different from the suffering of millions of others who had worked for the previous government or lived abroad. She told me that she had been allowed to retire from her work as a schoolteacher but Hean's father was still working in the bank. Because they had never been classified as members of the capitalist class, they were still living in their own home. The Red Guards had merely burned their books and confiscated their "valuables."

I thanked her for her help in preparing living quarters for me. She said, "Things are getting better now with Premier Zhou in charge. Quite a lot of people are being released from detention."

"Were many people put into detention houses?" I asked her.

"Oh, yes. Almost all the senior members of foreign firms were locked up. We know the number one Chinese with the Hong Kong–Shanghai Bank, and our neighbor is a relative of the man with the Chartered Bank. Both these men were locked up at the Number One Detention House. One was released at the end of last year, and the other man is due to be released soon. One of them lost his wife when the Red Guards looted their home. The poor woman was so scared that she jumped out of the window of their sixth-floor apartment."

I was thinking of what she had just told me when she said, "The most important thing is to get medical treatment for you. Most of the doctors now working at the outpatient departments of hospitals aren't really trained doctors at all. You need someone with experience. The man from the Security Bureau told us you have cancer of the uterus."

"I don't think I have cancer," I said. "I've had a bleeding problem for a long time. It started several years ago. It hasn't worsened. If it was cancer, I should be feeling pain by now."

"That's good. I hope you don't have cancer. What you need is a good doctor to give you an examination."

"Is it possible to find such a doctor? I wonder what's happened to my old doctor, Guo Qing at the Second Medical College Hospital?"

"I'm afraid Dr. Guo is very ill. He suffered a lot during the Cultural Revolution. I'll see what I can do to find someone else. We'll probably have to do it through the 'back door.' "

"What's a back door?" I asked her.

"That's a new way to get things done. It means making arrangements to see a doctor or to buy something one needs urgently through friends or acquaintances rather than going through the regular channels," she explained. "Of course, back doors generally cost more because we have to give presents, not money, to those who make the arrangements. But in many instances, it's the only way to get things done nowadays."

"Isn't that illegal?" I asked her. I remembered how the Party used to frown on such practices and how fearful the people were of doing anything like that. Before the Cultural Revolution, except for the very privileged, nobody dared to make private arrangements for anything.

"All laws and regulations have been declared tools of the 'capitalist-roaders' against the people. No one knows what's legal and what's illegal anymore. I suppose when one gets caught, it's illegal. When one gets away with it, it's legal. People using the back door seem to get away with it, so everybody does it."

A-yi came in with food. I went into the bathroom to wash my hands. For the first time in six and a half years, I looked at myself in a mirror. I was shocked to see a colorless face with sunken cheeks, framed by dry strands of gray hair, and eyes that were overbright from the need to be constantly on the alert. It was a face very different from the one I once had. But after all, six and a half years was a long time. I would have aged in any case. I looked at myself again. I hoped that in time my cheeks would become rounded and my eyes would look at the world with calm appraisal rather than anxious apprehension.

Hean and her mother were already seated at the table. A-yi had prepared a good dinner of chicken soup, sliced pork, and tender green cabbage stir-fried in oil. The steaming rice was soft. I had not seen food like that for a long time, but I had no appetite, and the pain in my gums precluded chewing. I drank some soup and swallowed a few mouthfuls of rice.

"Perhaps I should see a dentist before I see a gynecologist," I said.

"I'll take you to my cousin. She is a dentist at the Number Six People's Hospital," Hean offered.

"You had better contact her first and make some arrangements," Hean's mother reminded her daughter.

"Yes, I'll go see her tomorrow morning. Then I'll come tell you what she says," Hean said to me.

When Hean and her mother left, I helped A-yi carry the dishes down the narrow back staircase to the kitchen. Then I went to look at the smaller bedroom where A-yi was to sleep. There was only a single bed with her things on it, no other furniture at all, and the windows were uncurtained. Obviously Hean didn't have either enough money or enough furniture to furnish both rooms. I took one of the chairs from my room and placed it next to A-yi's bed.

I called down to A-yi in the kitchen to heat some hot water for me to have a sponge bath. I had already noticed that the bathtub was ringed with yellow stains and there was nothing to clean it with. Besides, it was still quite chilly at night, and there was no way I could heat the bathroom.

To have even a sponge bath in Shanghai was quite an undertaking. To get enough hot water, A-yi had to boil the kettle many times and fill the thermos flasks first. Then she had to heat water in a large pot. While I waited for the water, I discovered some paper and envelopes Hean had placed in the desk drawer. I wrote a short note to Meiping's friend and old classmate Kong, an actor at the film studio. I thought he was the one most likely to throw some light on Meiping's death. I requested him to call on me as soon as possible.

I heard A-yi coming up the back staircase. She was staggering under the weight of a large pot of boiling water. I quickly picked up the enameled washbasin I had brought back from the detention house and told her to put the pot in the washbasin before she spilled hot water on her hands. Then we each took one side of the basin and carried the water into the bathroom.

With no guards to hurry me, I washed myself thoroughly, using up all the water in the large pot and the six thermos flasks bought by Hean. When I came out of the bathroom, I stood on the balcony and looked down on the street bathed in the feeble light of street lamps to get my bearings.

The house I was assigned to was one of many in a large

residential compound. It was actually at the end of a row of semidetached houses, all uniform in design and in need of a coat of paint. I could see a similar row of houses in front of me, separated from my garden fence by a cement road six feet wide. From one end of the balcony I could also look into the garden of my immediate neighbor and see laundry fluttering on bamboo poles. Once these houses were homes of Shanghai's middle class. But since 1949 the population of the city had more than doubled, and the government had built very few houses. It was Mao's policy to build up cities in the interior rather than the coastal regions. Now several families had to inhabit each of these houses, sharing kitchen and bathroom and using the same hallway. Never in my life had I lived in conditions like that. I wondered whether there was any way to get my own house back.

Even though there was not a soul on the street, I didn't think it was very late. However, I was physically and emotionally exhausted, so I closed the door and lay down on the neatly made bed. It had been a long day. But sleep eluded me. A heavy weight seemed to be pressing on my chest as I tried to suppress my emotion while Hean and her mother were here. Now, with no guard to watch me and A-yi already asleep, in the first really private moment for many years, I let my grief take possession and poured out my sorrow in tears.

Next morning, two men called on me. They told me they were members of the Revolutionary Committee of the Shanghai Film Studio, sent to inform me of the death of my daughter by suicide on June 16, 1967.

"We were told by the Security Bureau that you were to be released for health reasons. We understand that shortly you may have to enter a hospital. We decided to come right away to notify you officially of your daughter's death so that her case can be considered closed," said one of the men.

For the entire interview, he alone spoke. The other man just sat there.

It was a surprise to hear him say that I was released for health reasons. However, that was not a point I could pursue with them. So I merely said, "I would like to know the circumstances of my daughter's death."

"She jumped out of the ninth-floor window of the Shanghai

Athletics Association building on Nanjing Road in the early morning of June 16, 1967."

"Why was she in the Shanghai Athletics Association building?"

"She was taken there for questioning by the Revolutionaries."

"Why was she questioned?" I asked him.

"That's not important," he said, brushing aside my question.

"Of course it's important. It has a bearing on her death," I said firmly.

"No, it has no bearing on her death. She committed suicide. Her death was her own responsibility," the man said in a stony voice. "In any case, we were sent to work at the Shanghai Film Studio with the Workers' Propaganda Team in 1968, long after your daughter died."

"Did the film studio make an investigation of her death either before or after you went there to work?" I asked. Though I was indignant at the man's bureaucratic attitude, I remained calm and polite.

"How could we do that?" he answered impatiently. "There have been so many suicides. We have so many problems that are urgent and pressing right now. In any case, according to our Great Leader Chairman Mao, committing suicide is an attempt to resist reeducation and reform. It's a crime against socialism. Those who commit suicide are really counterrevolutionaries, though we do not call them that posthumously."

"Are you quite sure my daughter did commit suicide?" I asked.

"Her name was on the suicide list when we took over at the film studio. Your daughter's ashes are stored at the crematorium. When you are ready to take possession of them, you must come to the film studio to get a letter of authorization."

"Is it not the law that before the body can be cremated the coroner's doctor must examine it?" Speaking of my daughter like this made me ill, but I had to maintain my composure and pursue the subject. "I would like to see a copy of the coroner's report."

"Don't you realize that your daughter committed suicide at a time when there were widespread disturbances and law and order had broken down completely?" The man was exasperated with me. "There were many other cases of suicide, perhaps hundreds in one day at that time."

"Do you mean to say there was no examination before she was cremated?"

"We don't know whether there was or not. In fact, we know very little of the circumstances of her death except that she committed suicide."

"I would like to make a formal request to the Revolutionary Committee of the Shanghai Film Studio that the death of my daughter be investigated," I said to both of them.

They glared at me in silence. Then they got up to leave. The other man took from his bag an envelope and several hardcover notebooks that I recognized as Meiping's and laid them on the table.

The spokesman said, "In the envelope you will find a sum of money the film studio normally pays to the family of a deceased worker. And these books are a part of your daughter's diaries. We were told by the Revolutionary Committee to return them to you."

I stood there watching them go to the door of the room. He turned back to look at me and said, "From what we heard at the film studio, your daughter was well thought of by her colleagues and fellow workers. We regret that because of her unfortunate family background she could not assume a correct attitude towards the Great Proletarian Cultural Revolution."

The two men walked downstairs followed by A-yi, who locked the front gate after them.

I stood there staring at the books of Meiping's diary but could not bear to touch them. In time, I would derive real comfort from their pages. But just then, the wound was too raw and my sense of loss was too overwhelming for me to read them. I was thinking of what the man from the film studio had told me. He had not said very much, but I had learned something of Meiping's death. I was more than ever determined to pursue my inquiry discreetly, and I believed that eventually I would get at the truth of the matter. I picked up the letter I had written to Kong and asked A-yi to take it to the post office.

Following A-yi downstairs to bolt the front gate, I thought I should buy a spring lock for the gate and another one for the door leading into the house. There seemed so many things to be done. The walls needed to be whitewashed, the rubble in the garden should be carried away, and additional furniture should be bought. I wondered again if I could get my own house back. The government would probably say it was too large for one person. If I had to live in this place for any length of time, I thought, I would have to move the second-floor bathroom downstairs and install a kitchen for my own use in the space. That would prevent whoever eventually came to live downstairs from coming up to use the bathroom. The change would also save A-yi from having to carry food and water up and down the back staircase. To ensure my privacy and to avoid contact with people downstairs, I should also put a door on the back stairs and build a wall to divide the front hall into two portions. To do all that I would need material and labor. And I would need a large sum of money. How was I to manage it?

When I reached the landing upstairs and turned the corner to go into my room, I saw, through the uncurtained windows of the corridor, several of my neighbors in the row of houses behind mine leaning on their windowsills watching me. At night, when the lights were switched on, I would be like a goldfish in a bowl whenever I stepped out of my room. In fact, one of the windows faced the door of my room. If the door was open, the people leaning out of their windows could look right into my room. I decided to make some curtains for those windows immediately. That was one sum of money I had to spend.

I heard someone knocking on the front gate. It was too soon for A-yi to be back. I ran to the balcony and looked down. A man dressed like a worker said in a loud voice from below, "I'm from the tree-planting section of the Housing Bureau. I'm to tell you about planting trees in the garden."

I went down and opened the gate for him.

"Are you the new tenant?" he asked me.

"Yes."

He walked around the garden and kicked at the rubble. "You will have to clear away all this rubbish before I can plant trees. They won't grow with all that around."

"That's a job for the Housing Bureau. I can't be held responsible for the rubble. It was all here already when I arrived," I told him. "Besides, I haven't got the strength to cart all that out."

"What about the young woman I saw the other day? Isn't she your daughter?"

"No, she doesn't live here. My daughter has died."

There! I had said it. "My daughter has died." It was an acknowledgment I would have to make often as long as I lived. Each time I said it, my heart would contract with pain, and I would see my beautiful girl lying in a pool of blood on Nanjing Road.

In spite of my effort to maintain a calm expression, tears ran down my cheeks. I took out my handkerchief and averted my face to wipe my eyes, feeling very ashamed that I had broken down in front of a total stranger.

The man avoided looking at me, however. With his head bowed, he said in a quiet voice, "I'll report to my unit and see whether we can't find some young men to carry the rubble away," and left.

In the afternoon, Hean came to tell me that she had arranged for her dentist cousin to give me an examination at the No. 6 People's Hospital the next morning.

"It's the back door, so we won't have to go there at dawn to line up for a number. I've already given her your name and other particulars. She'll fill in the card for you and pay the twenty-cent registration fee. When she gets to her clinic, she will put your card on top of the others as if you were the first one registered at the outpatient window. Then when we get there you will be seen right away," Hean told me.

"Is that really legal? I would hate to get your cousin into trouble," I said, rather worried.

"No, she won't get into trouble. It's done all the time by everybody. Every doctor has a number of back-door patients. Party members and officials all bring their relatives and friends through the back door too."

It seemed China had changed during the years I was in the detention house, and the change was not in the direction the Cultural Revolution was supposed to lead the nation. When I went with Hean the following morning to see her dentist cousin, everything was just as she had said. Although the waiting room was packed and a number of patients had no seat, we were taken straight into her cousin's clinic. Other back-door patients were also called in by other dentists. The most astonishing thing was that no one protested. The others just sat there watching us, seemingly content to let us go in ahead of them although they had already waited for a long time and we had only just arrived.

When I asked Hean why they accepted the unequal treatment with equanimity, she said, "They have other back doors even though they don't have one at the dental department of the hospital. Under other circumstances, somewhere else, they may enjoy priority treatment while we have to wait our turn."

"What about those who have no back door?"

"They'll just have to create some. As long as you have friends and relatives, you'll have back doors," she informed me.

That was my first encounter with the new back-door system. In time I also became quite an expert at using it, teaching English without charge in return for favors. The rapprochement between China and the United States and the importation of scientific and technical materials in the English language created a demand for English teachers. Ambitious young men and women who hoped to find jobs as interpreters with delegates going abroad for government agencies, as well as others who planned to emigrate, also wanted to learn. Requests for lessons flooded my mail.

When Beijing decided to release all frozen foreign-exchange accounts to encourage the resumption of remittances from overseas Chinese, I recovered quite a large sum of money I had brought into China to pay for scarce commodities obtainable only through the Overseas Chinese Shop, where purchases could be made only in foreign exchange. I used to buy coal for central heating and wood for house repairs. Since I was allowed to use less than 20 percent of the foreign exchange for such purposes, the money I did not use had accumulated over the years. With this large sum returned to me, I had no more financial worries and could reward those who opened the back door for me in a practical manner.

But all that was later. When Hean took me to the clinic of her dentist cousin, I felt acutely uneasy and rather less than honorable as I walked in ahead of all the others in the waiting room.

Hean's cousin examined my teeth and told me I had a very serious case of gum infection that had been neglected for so long that it was beyond ordinary treatment. She said, "Although your teeth are good, they will all have to come out."

She looked at my wasted body and added, "You are not strong enough for daily extraction. Come every other day. In the meantime, I'll give you a certificate to enable you to buy milk. Have several eggs each day too, if you can get them. When your general health improves, I can speed up the extractions."

After we came out of the hospital, Hean and I went to a shop where I could buy a much-needed clock. Outside the shop, there was an old man seated on a low stool with scales before him. For 3 cents, a passerby could step onto the battered scales and weigh himself. I weighed myself and found that with all my clothes on I weighed only 85 pounds, 30 pounds less than my normal weight. After that I weighed myself regularly on the old man's scales right up to the time I left China.

As my health improved, the dentist was able to extract one or two teeth every day. When it was all over, she told me that the gums had to be allowed to heal and harden before dentures could be fitted. I was very disappointed because I found it difficult to speak clearly or eat anything other than liquids without teeth. And every time I looked into a mirror, I got very depressed by my appearance. So I took to wearing a gauze mask over my mouth, even at home.

Hean told me that since I was now well enough to move about the city alone, she would return to Guiyang to rejoin her husband and children. I was grateful to her for what she had done for me and sorry to see her go.

Kong came to see me one Sunday morning. We sat on the balcony in the warm sun. He wasn't able to tell me much about what had actually happened to Meiping, but he was skeptical about the official version of suicide.

"I've known Meiping for a long time, ever since we were in our teens. She was not the type to commit suicide. Besides, what was she doing at the Athletics Association building, and who took her there? It wasn't the Revolutionaries from our film studio, that's for sure. They would have questioned her in the film studio."

"Do you think she was taken there because she was once a member of the Women's Rowing Team some years ago?" I asked him.

"No, not at all. The Shanghai Athletics Association was disbanded. The building was taken over by a subsidiary organization of the Shanghai militia. I heard a secret court had been set up in there. The place sounds sinister," Kong said.

He got up from his chair and went to the door leading to A-yi's room to make sure she was out of earshot.

When he returned to his seat, I asked him anxiously, "Do you mean there were torture chambers and things like that?"

He did not speak for quite some time. But after I asked him the same question again, he said, "Well, Meiping wasn't the only person taken there who died in mysterious circumstances."

I saw Meiping now in my mind not only lying in a pool of blood on Nanjing Road but also with her slim body mutilated from torture. The image was so painful that I shuddered.

"All her friends feel very bad about her death," Kong said. "One day we'll get to the bottom of it. For the moment, nothing can be done. The political situation is still so uncertain."

"Isn't Premier Zhou in charge of things now in Beijing?" I asked him.

"Since Lin Biao's death, Premier Zhou's position has become stronger. But Jiang Qing and her group are still there. They will not rest until they obtain supreme power. When the Lin Biao affair blew up, they had to lie low because of their close association with him during the early days of the Cultural Revolution. Besides, Premier Zhou is very ill. People from Beijing visiting the film studio say the premier is suffering from cancer."

"Oh, that's bad," I said.

"The former secretary-general of the Party, Deng Xiaoping, has been rehabilitated. The announcement will be made in a few days. He'll become Premier Zhou's assistant. Zhou probably wants him to take over as premier eventually. But Jiang Qing and her group are determined that one of them will succeed Premier Zhou."

"What about Chairman Mao? Won't he have to make the decision?"

"He will have to decide. But will he make the right choice? He's very ill, and Jiang Qing is trying to isolate him from direct contact with other leaders, I hear. This is a time of change and turbulence. I'm supposed to be an actor, but I spend all my time attending political indoctrination classes or working in an agricultural commune. I never have a chance to act. I feel my life is being wasted."

"There are still many aspects of the Cultural Revolution I don't understand. A few days ago, Hean gave me some Red

Guard publications to read. I find them very interesting. Have you any that you could also lend me?" I asked him.

"I have some at home that you may find interesting. Because they are not censored, they reveal a lot about the power struggle within the Party leadership. Of course the aim of the Red Guard publications was primarily to expose the 'capitalist-roaders,' but inadvertently they exposed the whole Party leadership. The stories that circulated by mouth were worse than those in the publications. You missed all that. However, the major portion of the content of those Red Guard publications is just revolutionary hyperbole. I'll sort them out and bring you the more interesting ones."

Kong took his leave. I walked with him to the stairs. A flake of plaster floated down from the ceiling. "Why didn't Hean get this place whitewashed?" he asked me.

"There wasn't enough money. They gave her only five thousand yuan of my money to do everything."

"You should write a petition to ask for more money. This is a good opportunity, now that things are more relaxed. In a few months the situation may become tense again."

"Won't the officials holding my money use the opportunity to humiliate me and give me a lecture?" I said. "I would rather borrow some money from my brothers than get in touch with the Revolutionaries who are holding my money."

"Well, next weekend I'll come with a couple of friends to give these walls a coat of whitewash," Kong offered.

"Oh, no! I can't let you do that."

"We are all Meiping's friends. It's our duty to help you."

"How am I to thank you, then? And the others. I don't even know them."

"Perhaps one day you'll be in a position to do something for them. As for me, I've enjoyed the hospitality of your house for so many years that it's only right I should now do something for you in return."

For the small sum of 15 yuan, which was the cost of the whitewash, Kong and two other young men from Meiping's film studio spent a whole day painting the two rooms, the balcony, and the corridor with tools and a ladder from the studio. They told me it was the standard practice for members of any organization to use the tools of that organization for private projects as long as they were put back afterwards. Kong also brought me a stack of old Red Guard publications.

Hean's mother found me a woman doctor, Dr. Wu, who agreed to give me an examination. She told me Dr. Wu was a graduate of the former Beijing Union Medical College, so she had had long and good training. She had succeeded my old doctor Guo Qing as the head of the gynecology department of the Second Medical College Hospital.

"Dr. Wu is a friend of the daughter of a friend of mine. Once a week, on Thursdays, she sees patients whose cases are too complicated for the young doctors at the outpatient department to deal with. She'll see you next Thursday. To avoid the young outpatient doctors, my friend's daughter will take a day off from her work to accompany you to the hospital and introduce you to Dr. Wu."

"I can't let your friend's daughter take a day off just to take me to see Dr. Wu. Can't I go by myself?"

"She wants to meet you. When I told her you had been to a university in England, she was most enthusiastic. She hopes you will give her English lessons when you are stronger."

I could see I was getting entangled in the back-door network step by step. But what else could I do? If I went through the normal procedure, not only would I have to line up outside the hospital at dawn, but also I would not be able to see a senior doctor like Dr. Wu.

On Thursday, when I went to see her, Dr. Wu told me that I did not have cancer at all but was suffering from "acute hormone disturbance," probably caused by prolonged stress and abnormal living conditions, her polite way of referring to my imprisonment. She suggested that I have a hysterectomy rather than prolonged treatment, which might be interrupted if the work of the hospital was disturbed again by political developments. I saw that, like Kong, she anticipated more political struggle and regarded the relatively calm atmosphere now prevailing only as a lull.

A week later I was successfully operated upon. I stayed three weeks in the hospital in a crowded ward with twenty-five other women, some suffering from cancer. Our beds were only a foot apart. The sight of their emaciated bodies and the sound of their groans were as depressing as anything I had seen or heard in the detention house. In fact, when I awoke from the effect of the anesthetic, for a moment I thought I was back in the prison hospital.

While I was in the hospital I received notification from the Bank of China that all foreign exchange accounts were unfrozen. Being financially solvent again gave me a wonderful feeling of independence. I sent Hean and her husband a belated wedding present and invited them to come to Shanghai with their children for the Chinese New Year.

When I returned home, I went to the dentist again and was fitted with dentures. As soon as I had them in my mouth, I felt sick. The discomfort was so unbearable that my impulse was to tear the dentures out. I felt as though I had two enormous plates jammed inside my mouth and that I was choking. The dentist told me to take them out at night to get some relief. But I decided to wear them twenty-four hours a day so that I could get used to them sooner and shorten the time of agony. At night, when I couldn't sleep because of the discomfort, I took sleeping pills.

Now that I had sufficient money, I proceeded to carry out the plan to make my portion of the house self-contained. A door was put at the foot of the back stairs, and the bathroom fixtures were transferred downstairs to make a bathroom in the pantry. In the space where the former bathroom had been, at the end of the corridor, I installed a sink and a gas cooker. The work was carried out by three workers from the local section of the Housing Bureau, which charged me a fee. With the help of Kong and his friends, I was able to get the sink, the wood for the door, and tiles to fill in the space left by the bath. All done through the back door.

The workers, regular employees of the Housing Bureau on a fixed monthly wage, earned nothing extra for the work they did for me. In such circumstances, their attitude was perfunctory. They would ignore the quality of the work and prolong the time they spent on the job. It was against the law for me to offer them money. I had to encourage them to work well and efficiently with what was called by the Chinese people "treatment." It included cartons of the best-quality cigarettes and elaborate meals with wine and beer. Kong, A-yi, and their friends helped me to obtain the provisions by lining up at various shops and opening back.

doors. When the job was finished, I gave the three young men each a present. I told them I wanted to build a wall to divide the hall space but was unable to obtain bricks. While none of them knew of a back door for bricks, they offered to build the wall for me in their spare time if and when I could get the bricks.

One afternoon, while I was sitting in my room sewing curtains for A-yi's room, three ladies called on me.

"We are from the Residents' Committee of this area. My name is Lu Ying. I'm in charge of your unit," one of the women introduced herself. Then she pointed to a stout woman and said, "This is our Party secretary."

The third woman said, "I'm her deputy."

I stood up to welcome them and invited them to be seated. A-yi brought each a cup of tea.

The Residents' Committee of each district was an extension of the police department, working under its supervision. Officers of the Residents' Committee dealt directly with the people and reported to the police. The organization was responsible for the weekly political indoctrination of the residents, running the day-care centers, distributing ration coupons, allocating birth quotas, and arbitrating disputes between neighbors. In some instances, officers of the Residents' Committee even helped the police solve crimes and capture criminals, as they had such an intimate knowledge of the life of the people in their charge.

Most of the officers of the Residents' Committees were retired workers on government pensions, receiving no pay for their present work. Only in special cases, when the retirement pension was low, were the officers given an additional allowance. These ladies (and a few men) enjoyed great power over the people. Their reports on each individual were treated as confidential and were written into the dossiers kept by the police. In fact, the Residents' Committee system enabled the police to remain in the background while maintaining close and constant surveillance of the entire population.

As we took our seats, the Party secretary gave a broad smile and said to me, "We have come to see you because we heard you have recently moved to our area. We also want to invite you to join our study group meetings on Tuesday and Friday afternoons."

"Thank you very much for taking the trouble to come. I

should have come to you to register my arrival. But I've been busy with medical treatment and getting my life in order," I said politely.

"What was the nature of your illness? Was it . . ." The Party secretary hesitated to finish her sentence.

"Nothing serious. The operation was successful," I said.

"Didn't you have cancer?" The deputy Party secretary was less tactful.

"Oh, no! Nothing serious like that," I said quickly, realizing they had been told by someone connected with the detention house, probably the police, that I had cancer.

They exchanged glances, seemingly surprised. But very quickly they regained their composure and looked impassive.

"Can you join our study group meetings two afternoons a week?" asked Lu Ying.

"I would like to. But could I have a couple of months' vacation so that I can recover further from my operation? The doctor was very firm that I should rest in the afternoons until I am fully recovered."

The Party secretary got up and walked to the balcony. She exclaimed, "What a wide balcony!" She looked into the bathroom and exclaimed, "A bathroom to yourself!" She even opened the door of the cupboard and peeped inside while she exclaimed, "What a spacious cupboard!" Then she sat down again and said to me, "Two large rooms for one person! You have been given very special consideration, you know," looking at me in earnest as if inviting me to agree with her.

"Normally a single person doesn't get so much living space," added her deputy.

She couldn't very well compel me to go to the indoctrination meetings of the study group, because they were supposed to be voluntary, and yet she was displeased that I asked for a few months' holiday. Making a person feel guilty of ingratitude when they want that person to comply with their wishes is a common practice of Party officials.

"I appreciate what the government has done. I hope you will convey my thanks to the appropriate authorities," I said.

The Party secretary and her deputy both nodded approvingly, pleased with my words.

"Of course, one day I hope to live in my own home. Do you

know what the government policy is concerning private houses?" I thought I might as well remind her that since the government was using my house, giving me a little more room than others was not much of a consideration.

The smile disappeared from her face. She said rather stiffly, "I'm afraid I'm not very clear on that point."

Lu Ying said, "You must get well quickly and join our study group activities to improve your socialist awareness. We all need to study Marxist-Leninism and Chairman Mao's teachings. Members of the capitalist class need it more than others. I live here in this compound, only three houses away from you. I'll come often to visit you and see how you are getting on."

"That would be very nice," I said politely.

"I have one room, which I share with my son and daughter. There are three other families in the same house." Lu Ying was telling me about her own living conditions to illustrate further how very special was the "consideration" shown me by the government. I also gathered from her tone of voice and facial expression that she did not quite approve of my being given so much living space. Since she was the head of my unit, I would have to deal with her on a regular basis. I hoped she wouldn't be difficult and create trouble for me.

Chinese society under the Communist Party was stratified according to the treatment given each person by the Party. Before the Cultural Revolution, I did not mix with the "masses." Lao-zhao represented our household in all our dealings with the Residents' Committee ladies. The United Front Organization of the Shanghai Party Secretariat took charge of people like me and treated us with courtesy. The special treatment we received helped the People's Government project an image of tolerance in the eyes of the outside world, for we all had visitors from abroad frequently. But the Cultural Revolution changed all that. I had now become a part of the masses. My life after my release from the No. 1 Detention House until my final departure from Shanghai provided me with a deeper understanding of the life and problems of the average Chinese.

My visitors stood up to leave, but the Party secretary had a few last words to say. "You must study Chairman Mao's books. They will help you to assume a correct attitude towards your recent experience."

I didn't say anything. What was there for me to say? Would she believe me if I said I had enjoyed being in the detention house? She seemed to be waiting for some answer. When I continued to be silent, the deputy Party secretary looked at Lu Ying. Lu Ying said, "Oh, yes, I have brought you your coupons for cotton cloth, knitting wool, sewing thread, and quilt fillings. I already gave your oil, meat, and tofu ration coupons to A-yi the other day."

I thanked them, and they moved towards the door. Etiquette required that I see them to the front gate. But they insisted that I remain in my room and called A-yi to go with them to lock the front gate. Realizing that they probably wanted a private word with A-yi, I didn't insist on going down.

I took the teacups to the kitchen and returned to my sewing. When A-yi came back, she asked me, "Have you taken away the teacups already?"

"Yes, but I'm afraid I didn't wash them. I really want to finish these curtains so that you can have them on your windows before nightfall," I said.

A-yi threw her arms in the air and exclaimed, "You are not a bit like what they told me!"

I didn't know who "they" might be, but I suspected it was either someone from the police or someone at the Residents' Committee. I thought it best to say nothing, but I smiled.

"You are really a nice person. You helped me carry hot water on the very day you came back from that awful place, when you were really very ill. You gave me one of your chairs to use when you saw I had no chair. You spent a lot of money moving the kitchen upstairs so that I wouldn't have to go up and down the back stairs. When you got your foreign exchange account back, you raised my wages, and now you are making curtains for me. You are very kindhearted."

"Thank you, A-yi. I'm afraid I haven't done anything extraordinary at all."

"Well, I won't let you down. You are a decent person. By the way, how do you feel about the Cultural Revolution?" she asked.

I realized that my answer to the last question was what the Residents' Committee ladies wanted her to find out. They, in turn, probably had been told by the police to report on my attitude.

"Well, from my personal point of view, the Cultural Revolution was a disaster. I was imprisoned and my daughter died. But from the point of view of the whole nation, which is of course more important, perhaps it is good and necessary," I said diplomatically, knowing exactly what the Residents' Committee ladies would like to hear.

She clapped her hands and exclaimed, "You are so right! You are so enlightened! Why didn't you tell the Party secretary all that? She would have thought well of you for assuming such an enlightened attitude."

"They didn't ask me what I thought of the Cultural Revolution," I said.

"The Party secretary did talk about your assuming a correct attitude. Remember? Never mind! I'll tell her what you said when I see her at the market tomorrow morning. She gets milk for her grandson every morning," A-yi told me. Then she went into the kitchen to get supper.

A-yi was a simple soul. She had unwittingly revealed where she was to report to the Party secretary about me. It seemed that although I had been released from detention, I was still under surveillance. Probably as long as I lived in Shanghai I could not relax vigilance.

That night as I sat in the quiet of my room alone, the idea that I should leave China for good came to my mind for the first time. To be freed from the atmosphere of political intrigue and the necessity of being constantly on the alert would be true liberation indeed. With my daughter dead, there was nothing to keep me in Shanghai. Although at the moment the idea of leaving China seemed outlandish and impossible, I knew I had to hold on to it and work towards its realization.

It almost seemed God had lifted my downcast eyes to enable me to see the distant green hills on the horizon.

14

The Search for the Truth

FREQUENT NIGHTMARES IN WHICH I saw my daughter bru-
tally beaten, tortured, and killed in a blood-spattered room left
me gasping for breath. My heart would palpitate wildly as I lay
in the dark conjuring up still more fearful scenes in my imagination. I decided I should make a trip to Nanjing Road to have a
close look at the Shanghai Athletics Association building. I believed I must take this painful step as soon as I was physically
fit so that I could have a clear picture of the place where Meiping
died and if possible make some inquiries. I could not tell A-yi
my intention because she would probably tell the Residents'
Committee ladies. What I could do was to set out at the usual
hour for my daily walk but take a bus to Nanjing Road instead.
So I prolonged the time of my walk gradually until I was often
away from the apartment for two hours.

"What long walks you are having these days! You must be
getting really strong. Your cheeks are quite flushed. Come and
sit down! I'll bring you a cup of tea," A-yi would exclaim upon
my return.

When my daily long walk had become an established routine
and A-yi made no more references to the length of absence, I
thought the time had come for me to carry out my plan.

Nanjing Road was the main thoroughfare of Shanghai, running across the city from the downtown section by the river to the western suburb. Before the Communist army took over the city in May 1949, the Shanghai Athletics Association building was the headquarters of the International YMCA. It stood in the middle section of Nanjing Road, facing the People's Park, formerly the racetrack. From where I lived it was half an hour's journey on the bus. As was always the case in Shanghai, the bus was packed. Not being able to squeeze myself further inside, I stood by the door with my body flattened by the crowd. At times, the woman next to me was pressing so hard on my chest that I thought she must feel my thumping heart. I was intensely nervous, fearful of what I might discover. While my mind told me I must go, my emotions wanted me to turn back. When finally the bus reached my stop, I hesitated. But so many people were getting off that I was carried out by the pushing passengers and found myself standing on the sidewalk.

I walked along, mingling with the crowd and forcing my eyes to look at the buildings on the other side of the crowded street. Next to the Athletics Association building were the Park Hotel and the Grand Cinema, both built in the thirties but still landmarks of Shanghai. The buildings were decorated with Cultural Revolution slogans on red banners. "Politics is in command," "Do not forget class struggle," etc., fluttered in the autumn wind. On the roof, neon lights spelled out another message urging the people to "carry the Revolution to the end." To the people around me, my upturned face indicated that I was a visitor from another part of China admiring the urban wonders of Shanghai. No one paid me any special attention. When my footsteps faltered as my eyes counted the floors and searched for the windows of the Athletics Association building, I was rudely pushed by the thick crowd of pedestrians.

At the gate of the People's Park, men and women with children were lining up to buy entrance tickets; others were waiting for their friends and families. I stopped among them and looked up at the building across the street again, for I had counted up to eight floors and then saw no ninth floor but only the slanting roof. To avoid attracting attention, I paced up and down as if I too were waiting rather impatiently for someone. Then I looked up again. I simply could not see the ninth-floor window from which I had been told Meiping had jumped. While I was absorbing the significance of my discovery, I strolled past the People's Park. It was only when I turned around to go back that I saw the ninth floor and the windows on the side of the Athletics Association building. They did not face Nanjing Road at all but were above an alley with low two-story dwellings. The windows were very narrow, with vertical iron bars. Whether there was enough space between the bars for a person to squeeze through was something I could not tell from street level.

What I had discovered was very different from what I had been told. I wanted time to think it all over, so I bought a ticket for the park and walked in. From a bench in a quiet corner I could see the top floors of the buildings across the street. I stared at those narrow windows with iron bars and wondered what was the truth about my daughter's death. I felt sure there was something more to it than what I had been told. The sun felt warm, and a slight breeze was rustling the autumn leaves overhead. I could hear the hum of traffic and the sound of human voices. But in my grief I was utterly alone, as alone as a man isolated on a desert island.

Should I cross the street, knock on the door of the Athletics Association building, and attempt to make inquiries? I asked myself repeatedly, unable to decide. A little girl on a tricycle pedaled into view around the corner of the footpath. Her mother was walking behind her. As she gathered speed, the mother called, "Go slowly! Be careful!" But the child pedaled faster. Her black eyes were mischievous as she looked back at her mother. They passed in front of me and disappeared behind a cluster of shrubs.

As I left the park and walked towards the bus stop, I saw Meiping everywhere; every young woman and every little girl on the street looked like my daughter. My heart was bursting with pain, and I felt more desolate and helpless than I had felt at any time in prison. At the bus stop, a crowd was gathered. A bus passed without stopping. I pulled myself together and boldly turned to the intersection to cross the street. At the entrance of the narrow alley beside the Athletics Association building, I saw a young woman sitting on a low stool knitting.

"Do you live here?" I asked her.

She nodded and went on with her knitting. A few people went by on the sidewalk, but no one was looking in my direction. I saw that the houses were lean-tos built against the wall of the Athletics Association building, taking up half the space of the alley.

"Are you looking for someone?" the girl looked up from her knitting and asked.

"I'm from Beijing," I lied. "I heard a young actress of the Shanghai Film Studio committed suicide by jumping out of a window of this building in 1967. Do you know anything about it?" I pointed at the Athletics Association building behind her.

She looked up and shook her head. "Not in 1967. That was the year after the Cultural Revolution started, wasn't it? The building was being repaired then. There was scaffolding all around it. I remember it because we moved in here not long before the Cultural Revolution started. The workers made a mess of this alley, and then they left without finishing the work."

"I must have made a mistake," I said quickly and left. A vital piece of information had just been given to me. It seemed certain my daughter couldn't have committed suicide in the way described to me.

I must have walked in the wrong direction on Nanjing Road, for after a while I found myself further from home than I should have been. A bus came along, and I boarded it. After a rough ride, I was back on my street again. When I opened the front gate, I saw two bicycles parked in the garden. There were voices in the downstairs rooms.

A-yi met me in the corridor with the news that the downstairs portion of the house had been allocated to a family by the name of Zhu. She was telling me about the Zhu family, but I wasn't listening, for I was preoccupied with my discovery on Nanjing Road.

The death of my daughter continued to be a mystery, and I was no nearer to the facts than before. But that she was questioned by the Revolutionaries and died at their hands seemed certain. If she had been murdered and did not commit suicide, somehow I must find the murderer and see that he was punished. In China, the punishment for murder was the death penalty. I no longer saw Meiping in my mind lying on Nanjing Road in the pale light of dawn on a summer morning in June when the busy street was temporarily deserted. But in my dreams, and whenever I was alone, I saw her colorless face and lifeless form. And I heard her cries and groans. I swore to God that I would seek vengeance.

A few days later, the Zhus moved in. While I was wondering whether I should go down to greet them and say a few friendly words of welcome, Mrs. Zhu came up the stairs to see me. She was a woman of about my age, with dyed black hair carefully greased and held in place with a mock tortoiseshell comb. A cigarette was dangling from a corner of her mouth. I invited her to sit down. A-yi brought her a cup of tea and an extra saucer for an ashtray.

"My daughter Ye was in the same school as your daughter Meiping." She was effusively cordial. "They were good friends."

"Is your daughter living here with you in Shanghai?"

"Ye is my eldest daughter. She's in Beijing with the Liberation Army Song and Dance Ensemble. Because my husband was a capitalist, we were thrown out of our home and had to live in a garage when the Red Guards looted the house. Can you imagine seven of us all living in the space of a garage? We had to walk more than two hundred yards to get water and to go to the toilet. The Red Guards made me sweep the streets, and my husband was beaten up and struggled against I don't know how many times. We are only a small, insignificant capitalist family. We didn't have a lot of money. My husband had a small workshop making face cream at the time of Liberation. That was all." She became very tense as she spoke and took repeated sucks on her cigarette.

"Since your daughter was with the army, you should have been spared all that. Isn't your family considered an 'Honored Household'?" I asked her. The title of "Honored Household" was given to all families with sons or daughters in the armed forces. They were given special rations and privileges by the Party.

"The Red Guards ignored all that. But now it's recognized. Our status is restored, and we have been allocated these rooms here."

"I hope you will be happy living here," I said politely.

She patted my hand and said, "I mustn't talk about myself all the time. You had a worse time than we did. You had to go to the detention house, and your beautiful daughter is dead. As soon as I heard Meiping had committed suicide, I wrote to Ye in Beijing. We were all so sad!"

I did not want to talk to her about Meiping, and it would have been unwise to complain about what had happened to me, so I did not say anything.

She smiled, put out her cigarette on the saucer, and lit another. After drawing deeply on the cigarette and exhaling the smoke, she said, "I really have come up for a little discussion about the electricity bill. I always believe in getting everything clarified at the very beginning, don't you? Then there won't be any misunderstanding. My son-in-law is an electrician. He noticed that there is only one electricity meter for this house. Would you agree that we share the electricity bill fifty-fifty since you have half of the house and we have the other half?"

Before I could answer her, A-yi, who must have been listening in the corridor, came in and said, "Oh, no, Mrs. Zhu. We should pay the electricity bill according to the number of persons in each household. You have seven people, and we are just two. We'll divide the bill into nine portions. You pay seven portions, and we'll pay two portions."

"Oh, no, although we have seven persons, we don't have more space. The bill should be divided half and half." Mrs. Zhu was very annoyed with A-yi.

"Since you have more people, you are bound to have more lights. Half and half is not fair," argued A-yi.

I decided to mediate. "Why don't we find out how others divide the bills. I'll go to see Lu Ying. She is the leader of our unit. She lives in a house with other families. We'll ask her."

"That won't be satisfactory at all. Everybody except you has been allocated equal living space. You have been given more space than others. If each of these two rooms were allocated to one family, there would be six or seven of you living here," Mrs. Zhu said heatedly.

She crushed her cigarette in the saucer and stood up. "I'll ask my husband to talk to you." She left the room and went downstairs muttering to herself, without waiting for me to say whether I wanted to see her husband or not.

I couldn't understand why she was so worried about the electricity bill. In the few months I had lived there, the bill had never been more than a few yuan per month.

I heard footsteps on the stairs. A minute later, the door was pushed open. Mr. Zhu walked in. He was a florid man with a flabby face; he had probably once been quite fat. Almost immediately A-yi came back into the room and stood beside me protectively.

"What's this my wife tells me about your not wanting to shoulder your part of the electricity bill?" Mr. Zhu said boldly.

Since he had entered the room in a rude manner without knocking, I did not get up to greet him but remained seated by my desk.

"In future, if any of you wishes to see me, you must first knock on the door. You must not barge in without knocking. People with self-respect should behave in a civilized manner," I told him.

He went red in the face and looked ill at ease. "Do you want to discuss the arrangement for paying the electricity bill?" he asked.

I said firmly, "No, I'm tired of discussing the payment of electricity bills. I'll pay half of next month's bill. In the meantime, I'll install a meter so that there won't be any further argument. The sum involved is insignificant. I can't think why you want to make a fuss about it."

He sat himself down on the chair and blurted out, "You don't know what the fuss is about? The fuss is about money! The Red Guards have confiscated my bank account. I'm not working. We get only twelve yuan [about $6 at the exchange rate of that time] a month each for my wife and myself to live on. One of my sons is unemployed. The other one makes only forty yuan a month. We have to look after our grandson. His parents are in the northeast. There is very little food there. We also have to send them food parcels."

I stood up to indicate the interview was over and said, "I'm sorry about all that. In consideration of your difficulties, I'll pay half of the next electricity bill."

Mr. Zhu made a grimace and muttered, "I haven't come for charity," and left the room.

Watching the stooped figure of Mr. Zhu leave the room, I felt sorry for the Zhu family and thought how terribly demoralizing was poverty.

Next day, I applied to the Housing Bureau for a permit to buy a meter. But the bureaucrats there ignored my application. Each time I went there to inquire, I was told my application was under consideration.

One day, I met one of the workers who had moved the bathroom for me. He said, "You won't get a permit from them. Your best chance to get a meter is through the back door."

A few days later, as I was going out, I was accosted by Mrs. Zhu's son-in-law, the electrician. He seemed to have been waiting for me in the garden. He offered to get me a meter through the back door and quoted a price that was several times the official price. We bargained. Finally we agreed on a price double the official one.

"Is this meter you are offering me from the stock of your place of work?" I asked him point-blank because I felt sure he had stolen it from his organization. Pilfering was common in Communist China's state-owned enterprises, as the Party secretaries were slack in guarding properties that belonged to the government and the poorly paid workers felt it fair compensation for their low pay. The practice was so widespread that it was an open secret. The workers joked about it and called it "Communism," which in Chinese translation means "sharing property."

"Why should you care where the meter comes from? You want to buy a meter, don't you?" the young man said impertinently.

I hesitated, wondering if I should really buy a piece of stolen property.

"I'll install it for you," he said.

"How much are you going to charge me for the work?"

"I really should do it for free because you are so nice to us all. But I'm very badly paid by the government, and I need the extra money. Would six yuan be too much?" he asked me.

I looked at this rather unsavory individual standing in front of me. He seemed quite intelligent, though undernourished and ill clad. I realized that he was just a victim of the system like all of us. Under different circumstances, given the opportunity to earn a decent living, he could have been a young man with self-respect. He was looking at me imploringly. I said, "Six yuan is quite all right."

A-yi was furious with the Zhus about the whole affair, and she was angry with me for what she called my "weakness" in dealing with them. She predicted that the Zhus would take advantage of me henceforth, declaring, "You don't know people like them."

The grandson of Mrs. Zhu was a lively boy of six waiting to enter primary school. He was very spoiled and had no manners. Several times a day, he would run up the stairs and slip into my room, especially when I was not there. He would open my drawers and help himself to whatever he fancied. Sometimes when I came home from my walk, I would find him drawing pictures by my desk with my pen and paper. At other times, he would bring a ball with him and bounce it against my clean walls. Often he would just run in and out of the room yelling some unintelligible war cry to work off his excess energy. When A-yi was cooking, he would help himself to the food, and if she left small change on the table, it was sure to disappear when the boy had been in the room. I talked to Mrs. Zhu about him several times, and she would always say, "I'll tell him not to go up. But it's so difficult for me to watch him. I've got all this housework and cooking to do."

One morning, I opened my door and heard someone yawning at the foot of the stairs. Looking down, I saw the unemployed son of Mrs. Zhu getting out of bed. During the night, while I was asleep, the Zhus had taken over the hall and converted it into a bedroom. The bed was against the wall on their side, but on my side was a small table and a chair, leaving me a passage to the door that was no more than a foot in width. In fact, they had even claimed the last few steps of the staircase by putting several bags on them. I called A-yi to come and see what had happened. She wanted to go down at once to have a row with Mrs. Zhu. I had to restrain her.

After breakfast, I went to the office of the Housing Bureau.

"I'm a resident of Number One Taiyuan Road," I told the man sitting behind the desk.

"I know who you are, I recognize you," he said.

"I'm sorry to bother you with an inquiry. Could you tell me how much space the Housing Bureau has allocated to me?"

"You have the use of the upstairs rooms," he said.

"What about the entrance hall downstairs?"

"The hall downstairs and the garden are half and half. Your rent covers half of the garden and half of the hall space."

I thanked him for the information and returned home. Mrs.

Zhu was on the terrace hanging out her laundry. I said to her, "I notice your son is now sleeping in the hall."

"Yes, there is no room inside," she answered casually and went on hanging the clothes.

"I've just been to the Housing Bureau office to verify that half the space of the hall belongs to you. The other half belongs to me. Will you please tell your son to move his things to your side of the hall and not to block the staircase?"

"He did leave space for you to go in and out. You are only a slim person. How much space do you need to go in and out?" She was disgruntled.

"How much space I need is not the point. The point is how much space belongs to me. Please tell him to remove his things from my side of the hall," I said firmly and went inside.

"There are seven of us. My daughter is coming to pay us a visit. We don't have the space to put another bed inside," Mrs. Zhu said.

A-yi stood on the balcony to listen to our conversation. When I got to my room, she whispered to me, "We will just have to build a wall. There is no other way to prevent them from encroaching on your part of the house."

"But we can't find anywhere to buy bricks," I said.

"Would you give me a few days off so that I can go home to Suzhou to see if I can find someone with old bricks for sale?"

"Of course! You should go home for a visit in any case." I was pleased that A-yi suggested going home for a few days. Although she had a day off every week, she seldom went anywhere.

The morning after A-yi went home, I got up early to go to market with her shopping basket. Although it was only five o'clock and the sky was still dark, the street leading to the marketplace was already full of hurrying people buttoning their jackets as they headed towards the food stalls. It was a scene of milling crowds going in all directions. The sound of voices could be heard from a long way off.

Because A-yi and I had already consumed our small ration of pork and eggs, I hoped to get a chicken, which was not rationed, to make some soup. And I had to get vegetables and buy our monthly ration of tofu before the ration ticket expired. Also I had to get my bottle of milk. Since chicken was more scarce than vegetables, I went to the chicken stall first. There was already a long line. Apart from the people standing there, there was also a motley collection of objects such as broken boxes, old hats, stools, and tin cans arranged in a line with the shoppers. Whenever the line moved forward a few steps, the women near the odd objects would move them forward too, as if they were a part of the line. From the conversation of the women around me I realized that placing an object on line was as good as being there as long as a friend or acquaintance was ready to move it along for you. With this arrangement, one person could stand in two or three lines at the same time. In fact, it was a mutual assistance scheme like the back door; while I moved your object forward in one line, you could do the same for me in another line. When a certain object was nearly to the stall, the friend would shout to the person in the other line to come at once and make her purchase. The person would quickly put an object down to maintain her position in the second line, dash across to the first line, and make her purchase. Everybody was obliging because everybody needed to be helped by someone else. Under such conditions shopping became a highly organized operation that was extremely exhausting.

I must have waited for nearly an hour, when at last it was my turn. There were only five chickens left in the huge basket, as far as I could see.

"Where is your ration card?" the man asked me.

"Is chicken rationed?" I asked him in surprise.

"Hurry up! Hurry up! Others are waiting! Show him your ration card!" Voices of the women behind me were shouting impatiently, and I was being jostled forward.

I quickly took the ration card from my purse and held it out to the man.

"What? Only two persons in the household? You can buy only a chicken of two catties. All I have left are large ones. Come early tomorrow! The smaller ones go very fast." The man was already turning his attention to the woman behind me. "Show me your ration card!"

I decided to go to the vegetable stall. I wasn't too sorry not to be allowed a chicken, because I was already tired from standing in line and listening to the shrill voices of the women around me. If I had gotten a chicken I would have had to join another line to have it killed and cleaned up. Even the best chicken soup did not seem worth such a great deal of effort, I thought.

As I walked through the crowd towards the vegetable stall, I

heard a man's voice behind me calling, *"Taitai! Taitai,"* a form
of address used for a woman of the upper class by her servants.
I was indeed surprised to hear it after the propaganda of the
Cultural Revolution, and I wondered who the *taitai* might be.
The voice seemed to be following me. In a moment, my old
gardener was standing beside me. Tears filled his eyes, and his
voice broke as he said, "You are still alive! You are still alive!
You look quite well. But Meiping . . ."

People were looking at us with curiosity, and a few stopped
to listen. I quickly gave my gardener my address and told him
to come see me later in the morning.

I lost all interest in obtaining food. I had a loaf of bread and
a tin of jam as well as some pickles at home. I thought I could
survive on that for one day. So I got only my bottle of milk and
returned home to wait for my old gardener.

How glad I was to see the old man! I had looked for him ever
since my release! I owed him money. His gratuity had been in
my pocket when I was taken to the detention house.

He was equally glad to see me. He had put on a new suit and
was beaming when I ushered him into my room.

"I'm so glad to have run into you at the market. I want to pay
you the gratuity I have owed you all these years," I told him.

"Oh, that! Meiping gave me the money long ago. She came
to see me after you were taken to . . ." He couldn't quite bring
himself to mention the word "prison."

Meiping's salary was small, and I knew the Red Guards had
left no more than a few hundred yuan in her savings account.
She must have given the gardener all the money she had at the
time. I was proud of what she had done.

"Do you know anything about her death?" I asked the old
man.

"I heard she committed suicide. Except for the day she
brought me the money, I did not see her." The old man bowed
his head. "But Lao-zhao saw her. I met Lao-zhao on the street
once. He told me he was seeing Meiping regularly."

"Do you think you could find Lao-zhao and tell him to come
see me?"

"Certainly! I'll find the cook too. They will be so happy to
know you are still alive and well."

"Do you know if Lao-zhao and Cook are working?"

"Yes, they have both been given jobs. I think Cook is at a factory and Lao-zhao is working as gatekeeper at a school. You know, the Red Guards beat him up and broke his arm. It was badly set. He is crippled," my old gardener said.

I was shocked and saddened by the news of Lao-zhao. I asked whether the gardener was working.

"I was unemployed for many years. To plant flowers was supposed to be bad, if not counterrevolutionary. But now things seem to have changed a bit. I sometimes get odd jobs now. Even the local police station asked me to plant some flowers for them. It must be all right again, don't you think?" The old man was obviously puzzled by all these ups and downs in what was all right and what was not.

I was wondering if I could ask him to come and do something with the garden here. It certainly looked empty and deserted, even with the trees planted by the Housing Bureau's tree-planting section. He seemed to be thinking the same thing, for he said, "Would you like me to come every now and then to tidy up the garden down below? I notice the hedge needs clipping and you have nothing except trees."

"That would be wonderful! Can you get seedlings for some flowers? Is it possible to make a lawn?" I asked him eagerly.

"I'm afraid it's not possible to get grass anymore. I grow seedlings in boxes at home. My fingers itch if I don't plant something, you know. When the Red Guards were everywhere, I hid my seedling boxes under the beds," he chuckled.

When I accompanied him downstairs to show him the garden, Mrs. Zhu was there. I introduced the gardener and told her that he was going to plant some flowers.

"Only on your side. We don't want flowers on our side. Don't you know our Great Leader Chairman Mao is against flowers?"

Mrs. Zhu was obviously not informed about the changed situation regarding flowers. I did not bother to enlighten her since the situation might easily change again. I just asked her, "Would you want the hedge on your side of the garden clipped?"

"As long as I don't have to pay your gardener. We have no foreign exchange account and no foreign connections. We can't afford to pay for a gardener."

She was making an unkind dig at me when she mentioned "foreign connections." She was referring to my imprisonment.

Two days later, A-yi came back, carrying a basket in which were a large fish, a fat chicken, and some eggs that she had obtained in Suzhou through the back door. As was her habit, she entered the house by the back entrance. Mrs. Zhu was in the kitchen and saw A-yi with her basket.

"What have you bought on the black market in Suzhou?" Mrs. Zhu asked A-yi.

"Who said I bought anything on the black market? These are presents from my husband and son. In any case, it's none of your business." A-yi was very annoyed to be greeted with an accusation.

I heard her and came out of my room to meet her. A-yi went into our kitchen and said to me, "That old woman is a nuisance. How did you get on at the market? Were you able to get vegetables?" After putting her basket on the kitchen table, A-yi went into the bathroom. I took the eggs from the basket and wondered whether I should take a few down to Mrs. Zhu as a present. To buy things on the black market was illegal. But as long as the purchase was not reported, officials generally ignored it; they knew there was nothing they could do to stop the practice.

I heard footsteps on the stairs, and Lu Ying appeared on the landing. I walked over to welcome her.

"It's such a long time since I was here. You must be well enough to join our study group meetings now," she said as she took a seat in my room.

"Thank you very much for your concern. I'm getting stronger every day."

"Many people have remarked that you should come. They see you going out and walking fast. They know you are fit."

"Indeed, I am now quite fit."

"We are studying the crimes of Lin Biao. It's very important. It helps us to clarify our understanding of this criminal who tried to harm our Great Leader Chairman Mao. You had better join us next week." She spoke firmly in the voice of authority.

"All right. I'll gladly come next week." Since I could no longer hide behind the excuse of ill health, I might as well be pleasant about it.

When A-yi came out of the bathroom, Lu Ying said to her, "I hear you have been away."

"I went home to visit my old man for a couple of days," A-yi said.

"Did you buy anything on the black market?" Lu Ying asked.

"Of course not! We have a Residents' Committee in Suzhou too. The things I brought back are presents from my family. We have cousins in the country. They raise chickens and catch fish in the river. They gave these things to my husband."

"You know buying things on the black market is illegal. Everybody has a duty to report to us when they see such activities. Be sure you don't buy things on the black market." Lu Ying was quite rude to A-yi because she could not prove A-yi had really bought those things on the black market. She had lost face and was angry.

A-yi left the room. Turning to me, Lu Ying said, "Incidentally, I hear many people in this neighborhood comment on your clothes. They say you pay too much attention to your clothes. Your clothes are not only expensive but they are all new."

"Indeed, I dislike wearing new clothes. Nothing would please me more than to get my old clothes back again, but unfortunately I don't know how to find the Red Guards who took them when they looted my home. Perhaps you could help me get them back?" I said to Lu Ying.

She was visibly embarrassed that she had forgotten about the Red Guards taking all my clothes away. But she wasn't going to give up criticizing me. "Next time you buy clothes, buy something ready-made in navy blue drill such as we all wear. Then you'll look more like one of us and won't appear so different in your gray woolen suits."

When Lu Ying had gone, A-yi and I both realized Mrs. Zhu had reported A-yi to the Residents' Committee and perhaps was also the one who had gossiped about my clothes.

I asked A-yi what she had found out about the bricks.

"My old man will make discreet inquiries. When he locates them, he'll let us know."

The next Sunday, both Lao-zhao and Cook came to see me. After asking about their work and the members of their families, I questioned them anxiously about Meiping.

Lao-zhao said, "Soon after the Revolutionaries took you away, they gave her a room in a house that belonged to a Professor Chen of Tongji University. The professor was denounced by the Red Guards and made to move with his family to the attic. The rest of his house was allocated to other families. I used to go to see her every ten days or so. She seemed well but worried about you. After she died, I asked Mrs. Chen what had happened. Mrs. Chen told me Meiping was abducted from the house by a group of Revolutionaries in the middle of the night. Mrs. Chen did not think those men were from the film studio. She said when she heard Meiping's voice refusing to go with them, she came to the landing to listen. But in the end, the men made Meiping go."

"What about the other people who had rooms on the same floor as Meiping?"

"I made inquiries. No one would say anything. They seemed afraid."

I asked Lao-zhao for the address of this house. He wrote it down for me but warned, "You mustn't go there. You won't find out anything. I got the impression they had all been told not to talk about it."

"It's better not to make inquiries yourself. If the police hear of your making inquiries, it won't be good," the cook said.

"Did you say this professor is at Tongji University?" I asked Lao-zhao because I thought Winnie's husband Henry, also a professor at Tongji, might introduce me to the Chens.

"Yes, Mrs. Chen told me herself. She is a very nice lady. Meiping used to tell me she was good to her."

"Do you know what's happened to my friends Professor and Mrs. Huang?"

"They had a lot of trouble and were locked up by the Red Guards, but they are all right now, except that Mrs. Huang is very ill."

"Do they still live in the same apartment?"

"I think so."

Lao-zhao and Cook also told me dear Chen-ma was dead.

"You can't imagine what Shanghai was like in 1967 and 1968," said the cook. "The Red Guards and the Revolutionaries went mad. They ran wild in the city, looting and abducting people at will, torturing them in secret courts, and killing them in every cruel way imaginable. It wasn't safe for anyone to go out on the streets. They even used ambulances to abduct people when there weren't enough vehicles for their purposes. There were so many suicides! And many people went to the police stations begging to be taken to prison for protection."

"Not long before I saw her for the last time, Meiping told me she was going to marry Sun Kai, but they wanted to wait until you were released. She seemed confident that you would be released soon because she said she knew you had done nothing wrong. Do you want me to find Sun Kai?" Lao-zhao said.

"Do you know his address?" I asked him.

"He gave me his address in 1968 and told me to let him know if I had news of you."

Nineteen sixty-eight was five years ago. Would Sun Kai still be concerned for me? Since he was likely to know of Meiping's life during that crucial period just before she was abducted, I was naturally anxious to see him.

"Please try to find him. Just give him my address. If he is married now, don't mention Meiping in front of his wife," I told Lao-zhao.

Then I asked Lao-zhao to get a letter of authorization from the film studio and go to the crematorium to bring Meiping's ashes to me.

A few days later, Lu Ying came again to remind me of the Residents' Committee study group meeting on Tuesday afternoon and told me I must be there.

"Bring a stool with you. There are not enough benches at the meeting place," she added.

On Tuesday afternoon, I put on a navy blue cotton jacket with my gray flannel trousers. I hoped the jacket would make Lu Ying feel she had gained face because I had taken her advice. But my jacket was specially tailored by my old tailor, quite different from the badly cut ready-made ones worn by most other Chinese women. I wanted Lu Ying to see that I had taken her advice, but I didn't want to encourage her to give me advice too often. While I would not do anything to imply disrespect for her authority, I also had to make sure she did not think she could do whatever she liked with me. That was the best way to deal with people like Lu Ying.

The Residents' Committee premises were similar to the house I was living in. For the meeting, three downstairs rooms had been opened into one. It was already two-thirds full of blue-clad people with toddlers running underfoot, and others were coming into the room steadily to join the crowd. I was met with stares of undisguised curiosity, leading me to believe that my reputation as an ex-inmate of the No. 1 Detention House had preceded me.

Mrs. Zhu, with whom I walked to the meeting place, led me

across the crowded room to a group of women under the window. She gestured me to put my stool down and sit among them. Nobody greeted us. Everybody maintained an impassive face, as if afraid to be betrayed by a carelessly assumed expression. I was to learn some weeks later that the group of women I was sitting with were all members of the denounced capitalist class and intellectuals, the outcasts of the Cultural Revolution, considered undesirable and suspect by the proletariat. We sat with the others in the same room, yet we were apart from the others. Even when the room was packed, a few inches of space separated our group from the stools of the workers.

This segregation was not ordered by the Party or the police. It was the result of political propaganda on "classes" that had been fed to the people over the years. Once, several weeks later, I arrived when the speaker had already begun. I hastily placed my stool by the door and sat down among the proletariat. Almost as if an electric shock had hit them, the two workers closest to me immediately moved their stools away so that I sat there isolated in the crowded room. Though I was really more amused than embarrassed, I dashed across the room with my stool when the speaker paused to take a sip of water. Mrs. Zhu and the other ladies, with whom I felt by now an invisible bond, welcomed me with nods and approving glances while their facial expressions remained impassive.

The meeting room was decorated with familiar Cultural Revolution slogans and reminded me of my own struggle meetings. But it also had many large posters with messages of a more peaceful nature. These extolled the country's economic achievement since the Cultural Revolution, which was supposed to have liberated the forces of production and increased productivity. Of course, the Cultural Revolution had done just the opposite. Official lies like this, habitually indulged in and frequently displayed by the authorities, served no purpose except to create the impression that truth was unimportant. In fact, the posters were meant to show the Residents' Committee's support of the Cultural Revolution and Mao's policy. It was a display of the political *savoir-faire* of our Party secretary and her co-workers.

Right in front of us, occupying the most prominent position in the room, were the slogans denouncing Lin Biao, the target of our criticism. Large sheets of paper held cartoons and lists of Lin Biao's crimes against Mao and the Party.

The meeting started with all of us standing up to sing "The East Is Red," a song eulogizing Mao Zedong as the rising sun of the East. It had taken the place of the national anthem since the Cultural Revolution. When we sat down, a man whose name and official status were not revealed to us made a virulent attack on Lin Biao for his crimes. He started with the days of the Long March, went through Lin Biao's entire career as an army officer, and ended with Lin Biao's attempt to kill Mao. He reversed the propaganda we had been fed during the Cultural Revolution while Lin Biao's star was rising. Everything Lin Biao did that we had been told was good now turned out to be bad after all. All Lin Biao's virtues had been turned into vices. And the vices we weren't told about were now exposed. However, hardly anybody was listening. Many women had brought their knitting and mending, while the men were either smoking in a relaxed posture or dozing. The study group meeting was a mere formality. People came to it because they had been told to by officials they could not disobey. It was not a serious effort to indoctrinate the people, and the result was nil. Nobody became more pro-Communist or anti-Communist as a result of attending study group meetings.

After the man had finished talking, several members of the audience stood up to support the view expressed by the speaker, who on such occasions represented the Party, no matter how lowly his official rank or status. Everything had been prearranged. The residents who spoke read from bits of paper pulled out of their pockets. Their texts had already been approved by the Residents' Committee.

At the end of the meeting, everybody stood up to shout slogans expressing our collective disapproval of Lin Biao. Though to hear him condemned gave me some measure of satisfaction, I did not join in. In fact, very little noise came from our corner. Perhaps, like me, the others felt that since we were not considered a part of the people, we were merely spectators. When we trooped out into the fading light of the chilly November evening, we definitely walked a great deal faster towards our homes than we had when we came to the meeting.

In the feeble light of the street lamp outside my front gate, I saw a tall young man standing there. When I came nearer, I recognized him as Winnie's son. He had changed from a husky teenager into a thin and rather delicate-looking young man, but his features were recognizable. I led him into my room and asked him about his parents.

"We were very pleased to get your letter and to know you had survived the detention house. Mother is very anxious to see you. I'm afraid she is very ill. It's a strange disorder of the skin that is incurable. My father is also unwell. He has heart trouble and high blood pressure." The young man spoke quietly and looked sad and troubled.

"Tell me more about your mother's illness. Has she seen a skin specialist?" I asked him.

"It's called scleroderma. The skin becomes hardened and rigid. The internal organs are affected too so that they cannot absorb nutrition," he said. "She has been in and out of the hospital, but none of the doctors seems to be able to do anything more than give her intravenous feeding."

"I'll come to see her tomorrow," I told him.

"Be prepared to see a great change in my mother. She doesn't look the same as she used to."

"What about yourself and your two brothers? Are you all working now?" I asked him.

"I was in college when the Cultural Revolution broke out. I was sent to Sichuan. Because of the famine conditions prevailing there, I got TB and was allowed to come back. My two younger brothers were sent to the countryside to be peasants. But after the Lin Biao affair, they were allowed to come back. One is now a delivery man for a shop. But the youngest is unemployed."

I told him again I would visit his mother the next day.

It rained heavily during the night. The damp cold made my arthritis-ridden joints so painful and stiff that I had difficulty getting out of bed. After breakfast, I set out with a heavy heart to see my old friend Winnie.

Dressed in raincoat and galoshes, with a large umbrella in my hand, I splashed through the water and mud of the badly drained Shanghai streets to Winnie's apartment building. Preoccupied with thoughts of Winnie, I walked past my old home without seeing it. It was only when I had reached my destination and was folding my umbrella that I realized where I had been.

Even now, after more than ten years, the shock of seeing Winnie's rigid form and the once beautiful face so mercilessly wasted by this frightening and mysterious disease remains vivid in my memory. She was already dying when I saw her. She could no longer move her frail body without the aid of her son. I had to bend over her so that she could see me and I could hear her faltering words.

Her eyes told me that she was happy to see me. But they clouded over when she murmured, "Meiping is dead. My boys have no future. We could have gone away in 1949, couldn't we? We were fools to have stayed here." She closed her eyes, out of breath with the strain of speaking.

I took her hand in mine. It was just a skeleton hand, and icy-cold. "We couldn't have known! Don't think that way, dear friend!" I said to her, bending down to her ear.

She sighed. I put her hand down inside the quilt and stood there fighting back tears that I did not dare to shed for fear of making her sadder than she was already. As I looked down at her shrunken form under the quilt, her son gestured for me to leave. I bent down again and kissed her brow. She opened her eyes, and her lips moved. Slowly and hesitantly the words came. "Try to go abroad! You can still make it!" That was her last advice to me.

Outside her apartment, I could no longer control my tears. In the dark passage, I sobbed for Winnie, for her sons, for Meiping, for myself, and for all the thousands and thousands of innocent men and women who were mercilessly persecuted by the Maoists. "Oh, God! Why this waste of our lives?" I asked.

I wiped my eyes hastily when I heard the sound of someone walking with labored steps up the stairs. Puffing to catch his breath, an old man stood before me. It was Winnie's husband Henry. His hair was snow white, his face was deeply lined, and his expression was one of despair. I greeted him by name. For a moment he did not appear to recognize me. When he did, he didn't smile, only nodded and said, "It must have been terrible. But you survived it. Wonderful!" I asked him about Winnie's illness. He confirmed what their son had already told me. When I asked him about himself, he shook his head and sighed. Finally he told me that he was allowed to do translation work now because of his heart trouble. Before that he had done manual labor. I asked him whether he knew a Professor Chen of Tongji

University, in whose house Meiping had spent the last few months of her life.

"I know him well. But don't attempt to see him or his wife now," he urged. "Wait until the situation is better. Then they will be able to speak more freely."

"Is the situation going to get better?" I asked him.

"Oh, yes, it's already better. You must be very strong to have survived your ordeal. You can afford to wait."

Early in December, A-yi's husband came with the good news that he had located some bricks for me. Two peasant brothers agreed to bring the bricks to Shanghai on a wooden boat on the Suzhou River and land them at a jetty under a certain bridge where such wooden boats were allowed to anchor. The question was whether I could find a truck to take the bricks when the boat arrived. I sent A-yi to notify Kong, with whom I had already discussed the project. When he came that evening, he told me that he could introduce me to a young man at the power company who drove a truck to transport repairmen to repair street lamps.

I sent A-yi's husband back with an initial payment for the bricks and asked him to wait for a message from me before shipping them to Shanghai. He had measured the width and height of the hall and made calculations. He assured me that the number of bricks available was ample. But he told me I must locate an iron bar to be placed across the floor to support the weight of the wall and prevent the floor from sinking.

Although I was most anxious to have the wall built as soon as possible, I thought it important to ensure that the Zhus would not oppose my plan. And to give it a semblance of legality, I should obtain approval from the Housing Bureau office. The best plan was for me to write a petition to the Housing Bureau, signed by both Mrs. Zhu and myself.

A-yi and I joined in a conspiracy to prepare the Zhus. I changed the time of my daily walk from afternoon to early morning, and A-yi went to the market not through the back door but through the hall and the front door. We would carelessly leave the door slightly ajar when we passed the sleeping figure of Mrs. Zhu's son so that a jet of cold air hit the very spot where he was sleeping. Sometimes he would get out of bed to close the door, only to find it left open again half an hour later. Whenever he complained, we would apologize profusely. But we went on leaving the door slightly open morning after morning. Two weeks later, when I thought a sufficiently strong impression had been created, I invited Mrs. Zhu to come up for a cup of tea.

"What do you think of the idea of building a wall to divide the hall space so that your son would have a small bedroom? Then he would not be sleeping in a draft whenever A-yi and I go out in the morning," I said.

"That would be good, but it would be very costly," Mrs. Zhu said.

"I'll pay for the whole thing: the bricks, the cement, and the labor."

"Would you really? I feel uneasy about letting you do it. But you do have more money than we do."

"I would like to do it, if you agree."

"Of course, it's a good idea."

"I'll write a petition to the Housing Bureau," I told her. "We can both sign it, and I'll take it to them tomorrow morning."

She signed the petition I wrote. To prevent my request from falling into the bottomless pit of bureaucracy, I sought out the young workers who had moved the bathroom for me. They could smooth the way with the officials at the Housing Bureau, I thought. I asked them if they still wanted to build the wall for me after working hours, to earn extra money. When they showed enthusiasm, I told them I had located the bricks and had written a petition. I requested that they speak to the officials before I presented the petition at the office. I handed them a carton of the best brand of cigarettes and left it to them to decide whether to give it to the officials or keep it for their own use. They said, "No problem. We'll speak to the man who belonged to the same faction of the Housing Bureau Revolutionary organization as we did. He won't refuse us."

When they gave me the signal, I took the petition to the Housing Bureau office. The man there put the official seal on it without hesitation. With that I went to a special shop and obtained the cement and the iron bar, which Kong's friend Little Fang transported to my house in his power company truck.

He came after depositing his repairmen at their destination where the street lamps needed repairs. I was waiting for him outside the front gate and climbed in beside him at once. We were able to get the things back to my house before he was due to pick up his repairmen. I asked him whether the mileage and gas consumption of the truck were checked. He laughed and told me that all rules and regulations were abolished by the Cultural Revolution. Then he said, "Don't forget, in a socialist state everything belongs to the people. You and I are a part of the people." However, he accepted a carton of cigarettes from me so that he could distribute them to the repairmen. "I'm supposed to wait for them at the place of their work," he explained.

I sent A-yi home again to organize the delivery of the bricks. I asked her to send me a letter to tell me the date they could set off on the river. The journey would take two days. I would arrange with Little Fang to go with me in his truck to the designated bridge to wait for the boat.

On the day the boat was expected to arrive, Little Fang took me in his truck early in the morning to wait for it, since the exact time of its arrival could not be anticipated. I took some sandwiches for our lunch. While we were munching, I asked Little Fang about the repairmen. He told me that he had arranged with another truck driver to take care of them so that he could have the day off. Of course, I had to thank his colleague as well as his repairmen. Again, no money was given, only presents, so that it was not illegal. I did not think using a truck that belonged to the power company in the way I was doing was exactly legal, but I didn't ask Little Fang about it. I just assumed that the whole affair landed somewhere in the narrow but ever widening gap between what was legal and what was illegal. When I appeared concerned, Little Fang said, "Don't worry, 'politics must lead economics,' Chairman Mao has said. Economics is not important at all as long as we think the correct political thoughts."

"Should we shout 'Long live our Great Leader Chairman Mao' to show that we are thinking correct political thoughts?" I asked him jokingly.

Taking me seriously, Little Fang shook his head and said, "No need. My Party secretary is not within earshot." Then he looked at me and asked, "Were you really locked up in the Number One Detention House for over six years?"

"Yes, it's true."

"Do you know why you were locked up?"

"They accused me of being a spy for the imperialists."

"No, you were locked up because you don't understand China. I think you had better learn quickly. You have so many old-fashioned ideas about what's legal and what's illegal. And you worry unnecessarily."

"Well, to tell you the truth, I feel uneasy about using this truck for my private purposes. I don't really think it's right."

"We have public ownership in China. Right? What's public ownership? Everything belongs to the public. Right? Who is the public? We are. Right?" Little Fang said rather impatiently.

I couldn't tell whether he was serious or just joking.

In the afternoon, we sighted A-yi standing in the bows of a small wooden junk sculled by two peasants. It was slowly approaching the dilapidated jetty beside the bridge. I waved to A-yi. She waved back. Little Fang backed the truck to the landing. When the boat pulled alongside, I saw that the bricks piled on board looked very old. As far as my eyes could see, there was not a single one that wasn't broken. Many had already crumbled into dust during the journey. I wondered if they were any use at all, but as he jumped off the boat A-yi's husband whispered to me, "The good ones are hidden underneath to avoid attracting attention."

The two peasants, Little Fang, A-yi, her husband, and I worked frantically to load the bricks onto the truck. When it was done, I paid the two peasants, who immediately set off on their return journey.

The landing by the bridge was crowded with people getting on and off the few wooden junks using the jetty. Most of the people carried more baskets, bundles, and cases than they could easily manage. Many had shoulder poles with baskets at each end containing a variety of goods, most of which I was sure would end up on Shanghai's black market. They were so intent on their own neither legal nor illegal business that none of them paid more than casual attention to our activities. Nevertheless, I heaved a sigh of relief when we drove away from the place. Whether warranted or not, I had a guilty conscience and hoped I would never have to come to this jetty again.

When we got home, we unloaded the bricks and stacked them in a corner of the garden. The entire Zhu family came out to watch us, but not one of them offered to help. Though I was utterly exhausted, I felt I simply had to take Little Fang, A-yi, and her husband to a restaurant to give them a good dinner. Little Fang was in high spirits and toasted our success repeatedly with many bottles of Shanghai beer and warm Shaoxing wine. When I thanked him for his wonderful help, without which we couldn't have managed, he raised his glass to toast himself and said, "Long live the working class!" and quoted the Marxist slogan "The working class must exercise leadership in everything!" Then he laughed uproariously. Little Fang was obviously one of those cynical individuals who took nothing seriously.

I was so tired that I slept soundly. The next morning, when I went to the garden to look at the bricks, I discovered that quite a number were missing. The Zhus told me that they had heard noises at night and suggested that perhaps someone had climbed over the garden wall to steal the bricks. But A-yi told me the missing bricks were actually taken by the Zhus and hidden in their rooms. Soon after the wall was built, the Zhus made a flight of steps at the end of their terrace with them.

I went to the Housing Bureau to look for the young workers. They came in the evening after work to start building the wall. Working from five-thirty to eleven o'clock each night with only half an hour's break for dinner, they completed the job in three nights. A-yi had the foresight to bring sufficient provisions from Suzhou to enable her to provide them with good meals. I supplied them with coffee, cakes, and cigarettes after A-yi had gone to bed and sat on the staircase to chat with them and be hospitable. Though they were less articulate, essentially they shared Little Fang's philosophy and casual attitude towards work and government property. The implements they used all belonged to the Housing Bureau. When I offered to pay for them, they laughed at me and called me a "foreigner who did not understand China."

The building of the wall ensured my privacy and completed the process of my physical rehabilitation. I spent the morning of Christmas Day in prayers of thanksgiving and meditation. I could neither understand nor be reconciled with the death of my daughter. But each day I lived without her, I was a day nearer to acceptance.

Many people, mostly strangers, had come to my aid to help

me regain my good health and establish a home. Although I gave them presents and tried my best to return their kindness, I knew that what I was able to give was no match for what I had received. The demand on their time and service, especially in the case of the doctor and dentist, was great. They did not have to choose me as the beneficiary. Besides, when they opened the back door to help me, they exposed themselves to risks that could have led to serious consequences. Even though the authorities turned a blind eye to the practice for the present, back doors were illegal. Government policies often changed abruptly, and Party officials liked to settle old scores.

In the last analysis, they chose to help me because they had pity for a woman who had suffered injustice and the loss of an only child. My tragic misfortune had touched their hearts. For so many years, the official propaganda machinery had denounced humanitarianism as sentimental trash and advocated human relations based entirely on class allegiance. But my personal experience had shown me that most of the Chinese people remained kind, sensitive, and compassionate even though the cruel reality of the system under which they had to live compelled them to lie and pretend.

The Proletarian Cultural Revolution, ushered in with so much fanfare and promise for the Chinese masses, had not really changed their lives or given them new opportunities for development. The Chinese people continued to struggle against poverty, shortages, and lack of choice. The Cultural Revolution had merely created a new set of circumstances to which at least the young workers were adjusting with cynicism and audacity.

15

A Student Who Was Different

A FEW DAYS AFTER the New Year, I took a long bus ride to Fuzhou Road, where the major bookshops were located. I first visited the Foreign Language Bookshop hoping to find some English textbooks I could use for teaching my students who were to start their lessons after the New Year. Besides the single clerk and myself, the spacious shop was empty. On the bookshelves lining the walls were displayed only the English, German, French, and Russian translations of Mao Zedong's four volumes of collected essays and the complete works of Marx, Engels, Lenin, Stalin, Kim Il Sung of North Korea, and Enver Hoxha of Albania. There were no other books. Near the entrance, a collection of Communist Party newspapers from other parts of the world was gathering dust on a counter. I looked at a copy of the British *Daily Worker* and found it was nearly two months old.

I went up to the clerk and asked, "Is there any way I can get some English textbooks?"

She merely shook her head.

Then I went to the main Xinhua Bookshop, the government agency for selling all publications, to get a copy of *Three Hundred Tang Poems.* I wanted to check the poems I used to recite in prison to see if my memory of them was correct.

The Xinhua Bookshop was more lively. A small crowd stood in front of the counter of technical books, and the clerks were busy. Quite a number of customers were buying children's comics, which in China were illustrated propaganda stories about the lives of revolutionary heroes, the suppression of bad landlords, and the unmasking of Kuomintang counterrevolutionaries. The large middle section of the bookshop was for the display of Mao's books. His collected works, his book of quotations, and his slim volume of poetry in cloth or paperback filled the shelves. I remembered that when I was in the detention house, I had learned from a newspaper report that as many as one hundred and fifty million copies of his collected works and seven hundred million copies of his book of quotations had been printed to enable each Chinese family to possess one set of the collected works and each individual to have one copy of the quotations. Also, the shelves contained Chinese-language versions of the complete works of Marx, Engels, Lenin, Stalin, Kim Il Sung, and Enver Hoxha. Though this female clerk presided over the most fully stocked shelves, she had no customers.

In a corner of the shop, I saw under the label "Literature" a few books lying flat on the shelves. I could not see their titles. I went up to the clerk and asked her, "Have you a copy of *Three Hundred Tang Poems*?"

She shook her head and said, "No, of course not."

From her tone of voice I understood that *Three Hundred Tang Poems* had been banned by the radicals. She probably thought me very stupid even to ask for it.

Pointing to the books lying flat on the shelves behind her, I asked, "What are those books?"

Without speaking, she picked up a copy and turned it around to let me see the title. It was *The Song of Ou Yanghai*, the story of a soldier who was killed by a passing train when he tried to save his mule. His courage and spirit of self-sacrifice were attributed to the fact that he had studied Mao's books diligently and therefore was fearless. The story had been approved by the Maoist leaders, especially Jiang Qing. Tens of thousands of copies of the book were printed, and the author was made a Central Committee member at the Ninth Party Congress.

"I've already read that. Have you anything else? What about that?" I pointed to the lower shelf.

She patiently picked up the book and showed it to me. It was just another copy of the same book.

"Have you any other book?"

"There is *The Diary of Lei Feng,*" she said.

Lei Feng was another soldier who died and was declared a national hero and a model of self-sacrifice by the Maoists. He had been eulogized before the Cultural Revolution in a nation-wide campaign called "Learn from Lei Feng," when the indoctrination of all Chinese people with Mao's books was intensified. Passages from Lei Feng's diary, such as "Read Chairman Mao's books, obey Chairman Mao's orders, and be Chairman Mao's good warriors," were widely quoted by newspaper articles and Party leaders including Lin Biao. The case of Lei Feng was used by the Maoists in the army to illustrate their assertion that political indoctrination was more important than the modern weapons and combat skill advocated by military leaders subsequently purged during the Cultural Revolution.

"I've already read that. Have you any other books?" I asked.

She shook her head again.

I walked out of the Xinhua Bookshop and boarded a bus to go home. I thought that the Cultural Revolution could be more aptly named Cultural Annihilation.

Since I could not obtain English textbooks, I could not teach beginning students but had to accept only those who had studied English already and were equipped with books. I had six students and gave either a morning or an evening to each from Monday to Saturday. After the lesson, we would chat over a cup of tea. My students brought me news and gossip that was not printed in the newspaper. It was largely through my students that I was kept informed of the volatile political situation in China during that time.

My most interesting student, and the one who stayed with me for many years, was a young man who had been a leader of the Red Guards in the early years of the Cultural Revolution. Da De had rather an unfortunate personal background. His father deserted his mother when he was only a few months old and disappeared in Hong Kong, never to be heard of again. There was little money. His mother, his two sisters, and he lived in great poverty for many years before his mother obtained a job teaching English at the Shanghai Foreign Language Institute.

Her salary was small. Even though they no longer had to sell their belongings to buy food, they remained poor. His mother's youngest sister, however, married a general in the Communist army in the early fifties when, flushed with victory, many Communist Party leaders discarded their peasant wives and married attractive city girls.

His family connection with the elite of the army and his intense hatred of anybody who was rich catapulted him into leadership positions, first in the Red Guard organization of his own school and later in the Red Guard organization of the city. He took part in all the Red Guard activities: plundering the wealthy, torturing class enemies, fighting factional wars, and killing innocent people. When we practiced English conversation and I asked him to tell me stories in English, he would talk about his exploits during the Cultural Revolution in a matter-of-fact voice, as if he were talking about the weather. He was not proud, or ashamed, of what he did. I thought Da De was amoral. And I wondered why he wanted to learn English from me when his own mother was an English teacher. Once, I asked him point-blank. He merely shrugged his shoulders and said, "You mustn't ask anyone a direct question like that. In any case, you can't afford to believe the answer, whatever it is."

Da De told me that he had lost his leadership position in the Red Guard when his uncle by marriage, the general, was buried alive at the order of Lin Biao. This happened after the Ninth Party Congress when Lin Biao was made the official successor of Mao Zedong. His uncle, a longtime Party member and much-decorated war hero, had voiced doubts about Lin Biao's suitability because of Lin Biao's addiction to heroin.

"Can I afford to believe what you have just told me?" I asked him half jokingly.

"Yes, definitely. Because believing it will do you no harm. However, you may foolishly choose to trust me more because I'm no longer a leader of the Red Guards and my uncle has died. But I'm sure you know trusting anybody at all is ill-advised," he said, blithely dispensing wisdom as if he were an old sage.

The name Da De means "great virtue." I couldn't think of anyone I had ever known who was more indifferent either to virtue or to vice. Intelligent and self-taught, he was extremely egotistical. In fact, it was his overdeveloped ego that prompted him to tell me from time to time what he knew of the power struggle within the Party hierarchy. And he loved conflict of any kind. When he talked about the political intrigues of the Party leaders, he glowed with excitement. He seemed to relish other people's misfortune and despised victims simply because they had failed to win. To him, there was glamor in success no matter how it was achieved. It was difficult to know where his loyalty lay. Once I asked him, "Which side are you on?"

Pointing to his chest, he said, "Of course, here, on my own side."

One day he saw a copy of a Red Guard publication on my desk. "Why do you bother reading such childish rubbish?" he asked me disdainfully.

"I want to know what went on during the Cultural Revolution when I was locked up in the detention house."

'I can tell you everything, from beginning to end, and more," he boasted.

"Won't you get into trouble for doing that?"

"Why should I if you do not tell anybody? And if you do tell somebody, you'll get into trouble just as fast as I will."

"What if the authorities find out anyhow?" I asked him.

"How can anybody find out if neither of us talks about it? Your room isn't bugged."

"Are you sure?"

"Of course I'm sure. You are not important enough for mechanical devices that are in short supply, only for human effort," he said, laughing uproariously.

Da De became my student through what I later realized was an elaborate maneuver. When I first started to give lessons, one of Meiping's friends, a violinist with the disbanded Shanghai municipal orchestra, became one of my students. His mother was a fellow student when I was at Yanjing University. She asked me if I would take on her son because the young man hoped to emigrate to the United States, where his uncle was a tenured professor. Because I was under the impression that the young violinist was very anxious to learn English, I was extremely surprised to find he was not attentive during lessons and did no homework. In fact, he often did not come at all at the appointed hour.

One day I was waiting for him and feeling increasingly exasperated when Da De turned up. He introduced himself and said, "I've come to apologize for Zhang. He has just been called to the police station to get his passport and can't come today."

He sat down across the table from me, opened the book he was carrying, and said, "I'm sorry to bother you. I'm trying to study English by myself. Could you explain this passage for me?"

I looked at the book. It was *The Gathering Storm* by Sir Winston Churchill.

"Where did you get this book?" I asked him.

"I borrowed it," he said, laying emphasis on the word "borrow." "There was a whole set, but I was able to borrow only this one volume."

"Were you a Red Guard?"

"Oh, yes!" He smiled at me and said, "You are very quick-witted, just as I have heard. I have also heard that your spoken English is the best in Shanghai."

The book had actually been stolen by him when he went with the Red Guards to loot homes. The other volumes had probably been burned.

A few days later, the violinist came with Da De to bid me goodbye and asked me to accept Da De in his place.

A-yi was always excessively polite to Da De when she brought us tea, though her attitude towards my other students was one of indifference. A-yi's attitude and Da De's maneuver to become my student aroused my interest in this lanky young man. Also he seemed anxious for my company. In addition to the mornings designated for his lessons, he took to visiting me almost every day under one pretext or another. He told me that he had plenty of time since he was "waiting for employment"—an expression used by the People's Government for "unemployment," which was not supposed to exist in a socialist state. He also said that he wished to render service to me in order to repay me for the free lessons.

He often accompanied me on shopping trips. Then he would stand on line with me, push through the crowd when it was disorderly, and tell me what commodities were available on the counter, because he could see over the heads of the other shoppers. Sometimes he even stretched out his long arm to take something from the shop assistant before the other customers could get it. If we failed to find what I wanted after visiting several shops, he would offer to get it for me through the back door. On the bus, he would shield me from the jostling crowd and elbow people to make room for me to get on and off. When I thanked him after an exhausting day, he would say, "I enjoy shopping with you. You always buy the best of everything. That makes me feel good."

Very soon I discovered that he liked good food but could not afford to go to good restaurants. So when he accompanied me on shopping trips, I would treat him to a really good lunch in a restaurant of his choice. On the first occasion, he asked me, "Do you want to go to one of the best restaurants?"

"I'll take you to whichever restaurant you want," I told him.

"Never mind the cost?"

"Never mind the cost."

He ordered enough food for four people and finished everything. That was when I realized that he was thin because of undernourishment. I felt sorry for him even though I was aware of the likelihood that he was an informer planted by those who wished me ill.

I would be a hypocrite if I did not admit that I hoped to make use of Da De. If he had indeed been planted by someone who wanted me under constant observation so that he could make use of a careless word or an inadvertent action to incriminate me, Da De was likely to know the truth about my daughter's death. At an opportune moment, I meant to ask him. That moment had to be one when such divulgence would not be detrimental to his own self-interest. In the meantime, I thought I could use him to convey an image of myself I wished his peers to have.

Long before there was any possibility of my leaving China, I tried to create the impression that I could not live without servants. Once, in my hearing, Da De told Kong, "She hates housework of any kind and can't even boil rice!" I was sure he despised me as a parasite and probably told everybody so. In fact, the impression I deliberately created of wishing to live in China because I liked having servants probably contributed in the end to my being given a passport to visit my sisters in the United States. Those who decided to give me the passport probably thought I was sure to return after a few months because I could not manage without servants.

Early in 1974, having recovered from my operation and improved the apartment, I was in euphoric mood. Teaching prevented me from brooding over my daughter's death. I felt more peaceful and relaxed than I had been for a long time.

As the Chinese New Year approached, A-yi told me that special rations for the festival, first cut back and then abolished by the Revolutionaries, were being distributed again. Unrationed food items were also more plentiful in the shops. It seemed to me that the effort made by Deng Xiaoping and his lieutenants to restore China's economy had been fairly successful, in spite of resistance by the radicals. The political wind in China had certainly veered to the right since the Tenth Party Congress as more and more former senior Party officials, denounced as "capitalist-roaders," were reinstated.

My students brought me reports of drastic measures, including arrests, being taken against the more intransigent Revolutionaries. One of them told me that the newly rehabilitated minister of railways went to Xuzhou, a vital junction linking Guangzhou (Canton) and Shanghai to Beijing, to restore service. When the Revolutionaries, who had occupied the railway junction and paralyzed its work, refused to obey his order, the minister of railways, Wan Li, called a mass meeting. He condemned the leading Revolutionaries in front of their followers and had them taken out and shot. Such decisiveness by an old Party official was encouraging to the long-suffering people who cheered him and his action. Unfortunately it also hastened the next round of struggle as the radicals saw their hard-won position being eroded under their feet. However, the old Party officials were careful not to repudiate the Cultural Revolution openly. They found enough quotations from Mao's old writings to justify their efforts to restore order and to prevent any accusation that they were against Mao's policies.

The Chinese New Year celebrations were traditionally linked to ancestor worship. When I was a child they lasted a full month, with preparations beginning fifteen days before the New Year and lasting until the Lantern Festival on the fifteenth of the first lunar month. Even though life had become much simpler under socialism and family reunions had taken the place of ancestor worship, the Chinese people still prepared seriously for the Chinese New Year celebrations. On New Year's Day everything in the home had to be clean, so A-yi and I spent days cleaning the apartment, taking everything out of the cupboards, waxing the floor, polishing the furniture, and washing the windows. There had been a time when we wore a completely new set of clothes on New Year's Day. Not everybody could afford a new suit of clothes now, not because of the price but because there was rationing of clothes coupons. All I could manage was to get A-yi a padded jacket. But it was a more stylish one than she normally wore. We both stood in numerous lines to get the food we were going to serve to our visitors. I expected all my students to come to wish me a happy New Year, as it was the custom. For those who might bring children, I prepared good-luck money wrapped in red paper. As she watched me getting it ready, A-yi became nervous and asked whether the Residents' Committee ladies might accuse me of trying to revive an old custom. I told her I would give the money only to those who were not likely to report to anybody.

With my returned foreign exchange account I was obviously a great deal better off than most people, so I decided to be generous to everybody. I even bought a large cream cake and two catties of chocolates for the Zhus as a New Year's present. Deep in my heart, however, I was very sad, because while others were surrounded by their families, I was alone. Scenes of past New Years I had spent with my daughter and my husband were always in my mind. But I was determined not to let anyone know how I really felt. I wanted the Revolutionaries to think I had assumed a fatalistic attitude towards my daughter's death.

Two days before the Chinese New Year, Hean came home with her husband and children to spend the holiday with her family. I was very happy to meet her extremely intelligent husband and to hear his version of the power struggle going on in Beijing. Their two children were adorable. Being too young to feel the political cloud over all our heads, they were completely carefree and happy.

Hean was fortunate to have her husband and children with her. Many young people in China were sent away from their families to work in other parts of the country, thousands of miles away, and allowed short "marital leave" only once a year. Children grew up hardly knowing their fathers, while women faced the dual responsibility of bringing up the children single-handed and holding demanding jobs. The Party inflicted this mindless cruelty on China's young people in the name of "the needs of socialism" and "serving the people." The hypocrisy of the claim was exposed by the fact that Party officials and their children were seldom asked to make such sacrifices. Instead, they received "special consideration" and were given jobs in the same city as their spouses.

The news of my release had spread among Meiping's friends. During the holiday period, many of them came to visit me, including those home on marital leave. Much of their conversation was about job transfer. They were anxious to take advantage of the present rampant use of the back door to get themselves transferred to places near their loved ones. Those who had already started the process of negotiation were anxious to exchange information and experiences with one another when they met at my place. From their conversations, I learned of the widespread practice of bribery and corruption in all parts of China among the lower-ranking Party officials.

"How do you account for the collapse of idealism among Party officials when the purpose of the Cultural Revolution was to purify Chinese society and promote socialism?" I asked one of Meiping's friends who was on marital leave from Wuhan and was trying to get herself transferred to somewhere near Shanghai, where her husband was.

"The new Party officials promoted during the Cultural Revolution were never idealists in the first place," she said. "They saw the Cultural Revolution simply as an opportunity for personal advancement and joined the Revolutionaries to realize their ambition. The old Party officials who have been reinstated might have been idealists when they joined the Party a long time ago, but they are now thoroughly disillusioned by their humiliating experiences during the Cultural Revolution. They feel that they have been treated unfairly by the Party and that their sacrifice during the war years was for nothing. All they are concerned with now is their political survival in future power struggles and a comfortable life for themselves and their children."

"When you give the officials expensive presents or money in order to get permission for a job transfer, are you not afraid you might get into trouble?" I asked her.

"Of course, there's a risk. But I'm desperate. Anyway, I think such instances are too numerous to be investigated. One day the Party leadership may clamp down, but at the moment they are too busy fighting each other. We must seize the opportunity."

Our conversation was interrupted by the arrival of Da De, who had taken upon himself the task of supplying me with freshly baked pies and cakes from the bakery. I knew, of course, it was just an excuse for making sure that he could pay me a daily call to see who was visiting me. While he was putting the cakes away in the kitchen, I accompanied Meiping's friend downstairs, carrying her baby's paraphernalia while the baby slept quietly in her arms. When we were at the front gate and she saw that no one was around, she whispered to me, "Be careful of that student of yours. He seems to me like a plain-clothes policeman."

"He's just an unemployed youth," I told her.

"Don't believe it! Be careful what you say to him" were her parting words.

Sun Kai, the young man my daughter was going to marry, found out my address and came to see me on the last day of the Chinese New Year holiday. He told me that he was no longer working as a mathematics teacher, since the school had been closed. Instead he was in a research institute designing precision instruments.

"In 1966 when Meiping told me you had been arrested, both my parents and I thought Meiping and I ought to get married right away so that she could move into our place and not have to live alone. But she wouldn't agree. She insisted on waiting for your release and said that she couldn't get married without your being present. Of course, at the time we all thought the Cultural Revolution would be over in a year," Sun Kai said.

"Did you see her often before she died?" I asked him. I felt terribly sad to see this handsome young man who might have been my son-in-law if my daughter had not been killed so ruthlessly.

"I saw her two or three times a week. We tried to be together as much as we could manage. You know my father was denounced as a Rightist in 1957. I was labeled 'the family member of a class enemy,' and since I was a teacher, I also belonged to 'the stinking ninth category' of enemies. Meiping had to take part in the film studio Cultural Revolution activities. She didn't seem to have any trouble there. Then, out of the blue, some unknown people abducted her."

"Please tell me about it," I begged him.

"She was supposed to have dinner at our house on June sixteenth. When I went to pick her up in the afternoon, Mrs. Chen, the wife of the professor whose house Meiping was living in, told me Meiping had committed suicide that very morning. I went immediately to the film studio. No one seemed to know anything about it. Then I went to the crematorium. I was not allowed to see their records because I was not a family member. But when the attendant saw how distraught I was, he told me that the body of a young actress of the Shanghai Film Studio had been brought in for cremation that morning." Sun Kai broke down and wept.

"Do you believe she committed suicide?" I asked him.

"No, of course not! I went to see the place where she was supposed to have done it. It's not possible."

"Are you talking about the scaffolding?"

Sun Kai looked at me in alarm and said, "How did you know about that? Who told you? You mustn't let anybody know you know." Then he added, "If those people responsible for Meiping's death think you do not believe she committed suicide, they may do things to endanger your life. You must be extremely careful. They are completely ruthless and cruel."

"I understand. I won't talk about it," I assured him. But I asked, "Do you know who was responsible for her abduction?"

"I'm not sure. But I think it had something to do with the men conducting the investigation of your case. Whoever they were, they were acting on the orders of some leaders in Shanghai."

"How did you find that out?"

"As you know, the Athletics Association was closed by the Red Guards at the beginning of the Cultural Revolution, and the Revolutionaries took over the building. But the defunct Athletics Association retained one floor for storage of documents. It was from one of their men that I learned that the men who abducted Meiping were acting on orders from above."

"Do you think you could arrange for me to see this man from the Athletics Association?"

"That would be dangerous for you."

"I'm prepared to take any risk to find out the truth."

"So many years have passed, I don't even know whether he is still there. Why not wait until the political situation clarifies?" Sun Kai seemed reluctant to accede to my request.

Indeed, many years had passed since Meiping died. One could not grieve forever. Sun Kai did not visit me again. The following year, I heard that he had married the daughter of a senior Party official. The man agreed to his daughter's union with the son of a Rightist because he wanted to take a young wife himself after being widowed. He thought that an unmarried daughter of the same age as his new wife would be an embarrassment. I understood why Sun Kai wanted to marry a girl from an official family. After what had happened, it was natural that he should wish to make sure that the woman he married would never become a victim of political persecution. Besides, married to the daughter of a senior Party official, he would no longer have to suffer the stigma of being the son of a Rightist, a burden he had borne with courage since he was a boy.

Sun Kai's visit made me so sad that I told A-yi I would lie down in my room to rest. A-yi went to clean up the kitchen. Suddenly I heard the sound of knocking on the front gate. The entire Zhu family was out. I called A-yi, and she went out to the balcony to find out if the visitor had come to see them.

She came back from the balcony and said to me, "It's an elderly man. He asked me if you lived here. Shall I go down?"

"Please do," I told her, wondering who this visitor might be. I quickly straightened the cover on the bed and made the room tidy. Then I went to the landing to see who my visitor was.

"Mrs. Cheng! Don't you recognize me? How glad I am to see you!" said the man coming up the stairs.

I realized by his voice and the formal manner in which he addressed me that my visitor was Mr. Hu, my husband's old friend, whom I had not seen since he paid me an unexpected visit at the beginning of the Cultural Revolution in the summer of 1966.

The hand he stretched out to me was calloused, and his little finger was bandaged. Otherwise he seemed little changed. I greeted him warmly, remembering the kind advice he had given me in 1966.

After ushering him into my room, I invited him to be seated. "I'm really happy to see you again. And you look very well;

perhaps, if I may say so, much better than one has the right to expect, under the circumstances," Mr. Hu said.

"How are you and your family? Are you still living in the same house?" I asked him politely.

"Oh, no! I was thrown out of my home by the Red Guards just like all of us," Mr. Hu told me. "And I have had my share of misfortune. But we mustn't dwell on the past. We must look ahead and be thankful that we have survived. Many of our loved ones didn't. I know about Meiping, of course. I suffered the loss of my dear wife and my beloved mother. Both died of heart attacks during the most terrifying period of the Cultural Revolution. The hospital refused them treatment because they belonged to the family of a capitalist and I was under investigation." Mr. Hu sighed and seemed for a moment to be almost in tears. But he quickly regained control. Taking a handkerchief out of his pocket, he blew his nose.

"How did you find my address?" I asked him.

"It was sheer luck. I met your old servant Lao-zhao on the street this morning and was overjoyed to hear that you were free. I had visitors all afternoon, but as soon as the last one departed, I came on my bicycle."

"Are you still working?"

"Yes. I could retire, but there is no point in sitting at home. It's good to do heavy physical work. At night I am so tired that I sleep soundly. I'm now living in my mother-in-law's home. The Red Guards left her one room. We had it partitioned, and I moved in. She is well over eighty. I'm glad to be able to take care of her."

"What about your children?"

"With a capitalist as a father, they were all sent to work in other parts of the country. My eldest son is married and has a baby girl."

"When you visited me in the summer of 1966, you very kindly gave me some advice. I'm very grateful to you. When I was in the detention house, I often thought of what you said. What do you think of the political situation now?"

"It's infinitely better, of course, but one can't help wondering how long it's going to last."

"Do you think there will be more power struggles at the top?"

He looked at the half-open door and nodded. After a while,

he asked me, "Would you care to go with me to Nantao tomorrow? I hear the old flower shop is open again and they have narcissus bulbs."

"I can't go tomorrow. I have a student in the morning, and I must do some laundry in the afternoon. A-yi is going home for a short holiday. She has worked very hard the last few days."

"May I come help you with the laundry tomorrow afternoon? I have an extra day's holiday because I volunteered to work on New Year's Eve," Mr. Hu said. I didn't want him to help me with the laundry, but I also knew he wanted to talk. I decided that if I wanted to hear what he had to say, I must go out with him.

"Perhaps the laundry can wait. Let's go to the flower shop. It would be nice to have some narcissus bulbs," I said.

Mr. Hu beamed at me for accepting his invitation. I had forgotten how much Chinese men enjoyed having a woman do exactly what they wanted. It almost seemed that my innocent acceptance of his invitation to go to a flower shop had brought our relationship a step more intimate than it had been when he first crossed the threshold. Not only did he hold my hand a fraction of a moment longer than necessary when he took his leave, but he actually felt encouraged enough to offer me money.

Taking a package from his jacket pocket, he said, "I know how stringent the living allowance is for people like us. I'm getting a regular monthly remittance from my cousin in Japan. May I offer to share it with you?"

I was so taken aback that I was momentarily at a loss for words. He held out the package to me and added, "Please accept it. I would be so happy if you would accept."

"Thank you very much for your kindness. It's good of you to offer to help me. But I'm not living on an allowance from the government. My foreign exchange account has been unfrozen, and I have no financial difficulties at all," I said quickly.

He seemed crestfallen but recovered in a moment. He said, "I have always had the highest regard for you. You cannot imagine how happy I am to see you again. It's a miracle that you came through your ordeal so well. You are a woman of exceptional courage and fortitude."

I thanked him for his kind words and followed him down the stairs. As I stood in the garden watching Mr. Hu push his bicycle towards the front gate, I was conscious of Mrs. Zhu watching us through the window. It seemed they had returned from their outing while Mr. Hu was upstairs.

"I'll call for you at two-thirty tomorrow afternoon," Mr. Hu said.

"That will be fine," I said.

So curious was Mrs. Zhu about my visitor that she questioned A-yi closely when A-yi went through the back door to take out the garbage. I supposed Mrs. Zhu would report to the Residents' Committee ladies in the morning and it would become known that I had had a male visitor during the holidays. The ghost of feudalism lingered in China. Although men and women worked together, they did not become friends in private life. Mr. Hu's visit to me would become the subject of gossip, I was certain.

Nantao was the walled city of Shanghai. The walls had been torn down long ago, but the Nine-Twists Bridge over the pond and the pavilion made famous by the blue-and-white willow pattern of English dinner services remained. Nantao was now a marketplace with narrow, winding lanes and hundreds of small shops and stalls selling a great variety of commodities, from wigs to live frogs for medicinal purposes. It used to be said that one could get everything one wanted in Nantao except a coffin. There were also numerous restaurants offering special food unobtainable elsewhere. In the middle of the market-place, near the pond, was a Ming dynasty garden, Yu Yuan, with ornate artificial rockeries and many courtyards sur-rounded by pavilions and studios. The Red Guards did not destroy Yu Yuan because an antiimperialist revolutionary or-ganization of 1853, the Little Sword Society, had used the place as its secret headquarters.

The street near Nantao was closed to motor traffic because of the crowd visiting the marketplace during the holiday period. Mr. Hu and I got off the bus several blocks away and walked towards one of the entrances of the market. We were literally carried along by the crowd, there were so many people. When we got to the flower shop, there were no flowers left. But the shop was jammed with men, women, and children buying or just looking at the Yixing teapots and cups on the shelves. There were also attractive porcelain figures, animals, vases, and flower-pots at a reasonable price. All these products had only recently reappeared after being destroyed and banned by the Red Guards at the beginning of the Cultural Revolution. I bought a Yixing teapot in light brown earthenware decorated with the traditional motif of mountains and trees. I also bought a celadon flower vase that could be made into a table lamp.

When we got out of the shop, Mr. Hu said, "You must be tired. Maybe we could find somewhere to sit down in the Ming garden."

But when we approached the Ming garden, we found a long line of people waiting to purchase entrance tickets and another line waiting to enter the enclave with tickets in hand. An officious-looking man wearing a red armband was there to keep order. He allowed only as many people to enter the garden as came out.

"Why don't we take the bus and go to Zhongshan Park? We shall be able to sit down and have a quiet chat. There won't be many people at this time of year," Mr. Hu suggested.

Perhaps it was the effect of my solitary confinement for so many years that I felt nervous and exhausted whenever I was in a crowd for some time, even when the crowd was not hostile. So the deserted park with its wintry scene of bare tree branches and frozen pond was a welcome sight. Mr. Hu paid for our twenty-cent tickets, and we walked in.

Even though it was a windless day, the February air was icy and seemed colder now that we were not surrounded by people. Both Mr. Hu and I were bundled up in many layers of padded winter garments, like everybody else in Shanghai, but my face tingled in the cold as we walked along the path. A holly bush with a profusion of red berries caught my eye. When we approached it, we found a seat behind an artificial rock formation. It seemed a good spot for Mr. Hu to tell me what he wanted to say. But I couldn't help wondering how many people in the world would understand that we had to take such elaborate precautions just to have a perfectly innocent private conversation.

After silently observing me for some time, Mr. Hu said, "You have had a terrible time. I shouldn't remind you of your unpleasant days in the detention house, but I just wonder whether you found out why you became the target of persecution."

"I suppose it was because I worked for Shell. They said the

Shanghai office of Shell was a 'spy organization' and my late husband and I were British agents. In fact, they never accused me of anything concrete. They just pressured me to confess." Once again I remembered those days of shouted accusations by the interrogators and my efforts to cope with everything.

"From the questions they asked you, did you not discern anything concrete?"

"I thought what happened to all of us probably had something to do with the so-called struggle between the two lines within the Party," I told him.

"That's true. I think you will find what I'm going to tell you interesting," said Mr. Hu. "When the Red Guards and the Revolutionaries took over our factory after the January Revolution of 1967, the Revolutionaries demoted my Party secretary to the position of an ordinary worker and accused him of being a 'capitalist-roader.' He was assigned to my unit. As you know, we used to get along very well together before the Cultural Revolution when I was looking after the technical work of the factory and he was the Party secretary. Now we were both working as coolies. Often, during lunch breaks, when there was no one around, he would talk to me quite frankly. It was my former Party secretary who told me that your arrest was due to the so-called conspiracy of foreign companies and government departments."

"How did your Party secretary know about me?"

"Before you were taken in, the Red Guards came to our factory to question me about you. The Party secretary was in charge then. He was present at the interview. Being a film actress, Meiping was well known. When she died, the tragic news was the talk of the city. Your case was frequently mentioned in connection with her death," Mr. Hu said.

"What else did your Party secretary tell you?" I asked him.

"It seems one of the departments supposedly involved in the so-called conspiracy was the United Front Department, which was accused of shielding class enemies. Its director, a protégé of Premier Zhou, died in mysterious circumstances after a struggle meeting. It was alleged that he committed suicide by putting his face to the gas burner. But when his body was found, the windows were open and there was little gas in the room," Mr. Hu said.

"Perhaps his suicide was faked?" I was thinking of my daughter and wondering when I would find out the truth.

"That's what his family claims. In Beijing, Premier Zhou's adopted daughter, Sun Weishi, the director of the People's Art Theater, was put in prison and tortured to death simply because Jiang Qing regarded her as an enemy. Two well-known Beijing opera actors, Ma Lianliang and Cheng Yanqiu, were beaten to death because they refused to confess they were Kuomintang spies. I heard these two actors had been invited back from Hong Kong by Premier Zhou, who was also their sponsor when they joined the Party. There are many cases of scientists accused of being spies for the imperialists who were invited back to China by the premier too. Just think, if any one of these people had confessed to being a spy, the radicals could have then cast doubt on the premier, if not actually accused him of shielding spies," Mr. Hu said.

"Do you mean to say that your Party secretary was of the opinion that I and other senior Chinese employees of foreign firms in Shanghai were put in prison and pressed to confess just because someone, either Lin Biao or Jiang Qing, wanted to use our confessions, if we made them, to discredit Premier Zhou's policy of allowing foreign firms to operate in China?" I asked him.

"Yes, my Party secretary implied as much. Lin Biao and Jiang Qing both regarded Premier Zhou as the major obstacle to their ambition after Liu Shaoqi was overthrown. In their eyes Premier Zhou was difficult to deal with because unlike Liu Shaoqi, he had never opposed Chairman Mao. So they had to formulate an outlandish scheme. Premier Zhou was not a single person alone. Behind him stood a large group of Party leaders and the senior members of the bureaucracy. It's a formidable force in the power structure."

"Now that Lin Biao has died, Premier Zhou has become the most powerful man after Chairman Mao. Isn't his position secure?" I asked Mr. Hu.

"Strengthened, but not secure, because Jiang Qing and her associates are ambitious. Premier Zhou is ill. The question is who will succeed him."

"Isn't Deng Xiaoping going to succeed Premier Zhou?"

"That's by no means certain. Deng Xiaoping is not a subtle

person like Premier Zhou. He wants quick results. The radical leaders will feel threatened. That would hasten the next round of struggle," said Mr. Hu.

It was really getting very cold in the deserted park since the sun had gone down. In the distance, several desultory figures were walking towards the exit. I suggested that we leave too. Mr. Hu asked me if I would go with him to a restaurant for an early supper, but I was depressed and tired. We took a bus home.

Outside the front gate, Mr. Hu said goodbye and told me that he would like to visit me again when he had his day off. "It's ages since I have enjoyed an excursion as I did today. It's good to see you looking so well. You mustn't stay by yourself and brood. I'll come and try to cheer you up."

I opened the gate to find Mrs. Zhu standing in the cold on the terrace. I supposed she came out when she heard us.

Taking her cigarette out of her mouth, she said, "Did you have a nice outing?"

She probably hoped I would tell her where I had been so that she could report to the Residents' Committee. Resisting an impulse to be rude, I merely said, "Don't you find it cold standing there?" and went upstairs.

The next day, my old friend Hean's mother arrived while I was still with my student. By the time the lesson ended, she had prepared a simple lunch for both of us. While we were eating, she mentioned the Chinese New Year celebrations several times and kept on bringing the conversation around to the guests I had until I suddenly realized that she was hoping I would tell her about Mr. Hu. But how did she know Mr. Hu had been to see me? Shocked and disappointed, I came to the reluctant conclusion that she had been asked to visit me by those who were having me watched. I went cold all over. I decided to be candid with her so that no one would think I was trying to hide anything.

"Besides all the young people, an old friend also came to see me. Apparently Lao-zhao met him on the street and gave him my address. I went with him to Nantao yesterday and bought a Yixing teapot and a vase," I said.

"Is he married?"

"He is a widower."

"Have you known him long?"

"He was really my husband's friend."

"What does he do?"

"He used to have a paint factory."

"Is he interested in you personally?"

"What do you mean?" I asked her, feeling rather annoyed.

"If you'll forgive my saying so, Chinese gentlemen of our generation don't ask Chinese ladies to go out with them unless they are interested in them personally," my old friend said.

I said to her, "You mustn't jump to conclusions. I think it's possible he feels lonely and he enjoys my company." I was thinking perhaps it was just as well that Mr. Hu's visit to me was seen in this light rather than as something political. "I'm an old lady now. I consider him only an old friend who is trying to be kind," I told her.

"You are an attractive old lady. It's strange that in spite of your terrible experience, you still look years younger than your age. I have no doubt your gentleman friend will eventually ask you to marry him, if you give him the chance."

"I really don't know Mr. Hu very well. It's premature to think our relationship will develop into anything at all."

"Speaking as an old friend, I would like to see you married. It's not good to be alone in this society. You need someone to discuss things with and to look after you," she said with sincerity.

After she had left, I drew the curtains and lay down on my bed. It was depressing to know I was being watched so closely. And it saddened me to have Hean's mother join the ranks of informers. When would I be able to live a normal life again? I asked myself. As for Mr. Hu, I had no idea what his plans were beyond enjoying my company on his days off. In any case, I would not marry him or anybody else. It was still my intention to leave China for good when circumstances permitted.

Since President Nixon's visit, the Shanghai police had resumed issuing exit permits for private people to go abroad. Though the waiting period remained long and there were many rejections, since my release I had heard of several people actually being granted passports to leave the country. I continued to examine Mao's photograph closely whenever it appeared in the newspaper, just as I had in prison, and I wished for his death no less ardently than when I was in the detention house. I knew that unless there was a change in the political situation, I had no hope of being allowed to leave. To keep myself fit and well so that I could survive still seemed the sensible thing to do.

I heard heavy footsteps on the cement path that ran the length of the house, followed by knocking on my door at the foot of the stairs. Since I was in no mood to see anybody, I didn't get up to open the door. After a while, I heard Da De talking to Mrs. Zhu beneath my window.

"Isn't A-yi here?" Da De said.

"She has gone to visit her family," Mrs. Zhu's voice said.

They stood in the garden talking in low whispers for a little while. Then Da De knocked again. Again I didn't get up to open the door.

In the evening, Mrs. Zhu came up with a plateful of fish she had cooked, followed by her grandson.

"I know you don't like to cook, so I prepared something for your supper," she said. She didn't mention Da De's visit, so I didn't say anything either. I knew she was using the fish as an excuse to come up and find out if I was really sound asleep and hadn't heard Da De or if I didn't wish to see him.

I offered her grandson some sweets and invited them to be seated. He held an armband of the militia in his hand. Jokingly I said to him, "Have you joined the militia?"

He held the armband out and said, "This belongs to my uncle. He is training under Uncle Da De."

"Is Da De in the militia?" I asked him. Though I was surprised, I kept my voice as casual as I could.

In spite of Mrs. Zhu's effort to divert his attention to the sweets, he said, "Oh, yes! He's a captain."

"Isn't that wonderful!" I exclaimed. "I bet when you grow up you would like to be in the militia just like your uncle and Da De!"

The child had obviously said something I was not supposed to know, because Mrs. Zhu was not only embarrassed but frightened as well. She said to the boy, "You are talking nonsense. Uncle Da De isn't in the militia at all."

The child retorted, "He is! He is!"

Hastily Mrs. Zhu stood up and said good night to me. As she went down with her grandson, she was still muttering to him for talking out of turn.

Since the militia was a subsidiary of the army, it used to be under Lin Biao's men in Shanghai. After Lin Biao's death, the control of the militia fell into the hands of Jiang Qing's associates in the city. In 1974 and 1975, the radical leaders did a great deal to expand and strengthen the Shanghai militia, hoping to develop it into their own private army.

If Da De was a militia captain, he could not have been an "unemployed youth" as he claimed, because members of the militia were recruited among the activists in factories and government offices. I did not think Da De was a factory worker, because he was too interested in books and his hands were too clean. He must have been an activist in an office of the Shanghai government. In other words, his masters were Jiang Qing's associates in Shanghai. I was glad to know at last Da De's true status. Was he with the police or some other organization? It really made no difference to me or to the situation. I had long suspected that he was more than what he seemed.

Time went on and spring came to Shanghai again. I had been out of the No. 1 Detention House a whole year. But I could hardly say I was free. Certainly my material life had greatly improved. I seemed to have no health problems other than arthritis.

Early in the morning I would stand on the balcony and look down at the garden. The metasequoia trees planted by the Housing Bureau had grown very fast. Now tiny buds of delicate green dotted the branches. In the short period of a few days they would burst into clusters of young leaves. My old gardener had made two beds of roses and planted a border of mixed spring flowers. He had also put in rambler roses at the base of the pillar of my balcony and made a latticed frame for them to climb on. An increasing number of sparrows were making the garden their home, and in the early mornings I sometimes heard a cuckoo singing in the trees.

As the days got warmer, the balcony became my living room. I would sit there with my students for our English lessons. Often I would have my meals out there, sitting in the sun among pots of jasmine, lilies, ferns, and other plants I had collected or my students had given me. A beautiful dwarf tree in an ornamental flat vase with a rock arrangement and moss-covered earth was the pride of my possessions. I succeeded in borrowing a copy of

Three Hundred Tang Poems and spent many pleasant hours copying the poems into an exercise book and reciting them to improve my memory.

Mr. Hu came to visit me from time to time. I noticed that if we sat on the balcony, Mrs. Zhu would be right there below us on her terrace; if we stayed in the room, A-yi would be within earshot.

One day in August, when daylight lingered until evening and the temperature was hot, Mr. Hu called on me. He wanted me to go out with him to a restaurant. But since A-yi had already prepared dinner, I invited him to stay and share it with me. When dinner was ready, we ate on the balcony in fading daylight in the evening breeze. Mr. Hu was in a happy mood, chatting to me about his childhood years in Hangzhou. After A-yi had cleared the table, Da De turned up. He always had a good excuse for coming to see me. This time, it was to give me a bag full of luscious Wuxi peaches, which he said would have spoiled if he had waited until the following morning to bring them. I introduced him to Mr. Hu. It was getting dark. There was no light on the balcony, so A-yi took the table lamp from my desk and placed it on the windowsill. She also handed Da De a large plate. When Da De took the peaches out of the bag and laid them on the plate, I saw that each was without blemish and was ripened to exactly the right degree. They were better than any I had ever been able to buy from the shops even before the Cultural Revolution.

"Where did you get the peaches?" I asked him.

"I have many back doors. In fact, though I didn't go to college, I'm a Ph.D. of back doors," Da De joked. Then he went to the kitchen to wash the peaches.

Da De's sudden appearance seemed to have disconcerted Mr. Hu, who became silent. However, he allowed an interval of time to pass and complimented Da De on the excellent peaches before he politely took his leave. I walked downstairs with him and saw him to the front gate. The Zhus were nowhere to be seen, as was always the case whenever Da De was with me. They behaved as if they no longer had to pay attention to me when he was there.

"I'll come again tomorrow, if I may," said Mr. Hu as he shook hands with me.

When I returned to the balcony, Da De said to me, "He is a capitalist, isn't he?"

"How do you know?"

"I can tell by his bearing. Besides, he exudes the bad odor of money, like all capitalists," said Da De with vehemence.

"You are still very much the leader of the Red Guards, I see."

"No! When I was a leader of the Red Guards, I was just a hotheaded fanatic. Now I'm a Marxist."

"Are you a Party member?" I asked him.

"Not yet. I'll join the Party one day in the not too distant future."

"Since you hate the capitalists so much, why do you want to study English with me? Don't you find me as repugnant as the capitalists? Don't I exude the bad odor of money too?"

"You are different. Actually I don't think you would make a good capitalist, as you are rather careless with money. The trouble with you is you are naive enough to believe in kindness, charity, generosity, and all that rubbish preached by the ruling class of the capitalist nations to fool their people and undermine their revolutionary spirit," Da De said.

"What do you know about the capitalist nations anyway? You have never been to one."

"And, more's the pity, I have no hope of going."

"Do you want to go if you have the chance?" I asked him.

"Of course I would go! In the United States or in a European country I could work hard and create my own life. I would probably do quite well," he said wistfully.

"You puzzle me. A moment ago you wanted to join the Communist Party. Now you say you would like to go abroad if you have the opportunity. Are you perhaps thinking of starting a revolution in a capitalist country?" I asked him.

"Of course not. I want to join the Communist Party because I have to stay here. If I could go abroad to a capitalist country, I would try to become a capitalist," he said impatiently, almost as if he thought I was too stupid to see his perfect logic.

"What! I thought you hated the capitalists!"

"I hate them now. But if I were one of them, I wouldn't hate them, would I?"

"Won't you be uncomfortable if you become something you hate?"

"Why should I? Don't you understand dialectical material-ism?"

After Da De left, I sat there on the balcony for a long time thinking of this rather strange young man. Never in my life had I met anyone quite like him. Marxists believed a man's character was formed by environment. Was he the typical product of the Chinese Communist Revolution? In fact, I felt rather sorry for him. He was extremely intelligent and hardworking. If he had the chance to live and work in a free society, he would probably do well. I did not think he would have much of a future in China, even as a Party member. With his overdeveloped ego and self-confidence, Da De was essentially an individualist. The Communist Party was not very tolerant of individualists. And with his uncle dead, he had lost his entrée to the proletarian elite.

Mr. Hu came again after work the next day. This time I went with him to a noisy restaurant. After we were seated, Mr. Hu said, "That student of yours seems to have access to food reserved for senior government officials. I don't think anyone less than a deputy Party secretary of the Shanghai Revolutionary Committee could get hold of those peaches he brought you."

"You don't think he got them through the back door?"

"No, definitely not! Peaches like those are not for sale through front or back doors. They are reserved for senior officials, who do not have to pay for them."

"No wonder he couldn't tell me what I owed him."

"The question is why he was given those peaches to bring to you." Mr. Hu sounded worried.

"Perhaps it was just an excuse to come to see me right away. He had to bring something not easily obtainable and not easily kept fresh without refrigeration." Actually I thought he came because Mr. Hu was there, but I did not want to alarm Mr. Hu by telling him that.

"Do you think you are under observation?"

"Yes, I'm pretty sure that is the case."

"To have you under such close surveillance is anomalous. What did they say to you when you were released?" Mr. Hu asked me.

"Nothing very much. No mention that I was found to be innocent. They just said that I had been reeducated and had shown a certain degree of improvement in my thinking." I was remembering my last interview in the interrogation room of the detention house.

While Mr. Hu was thinking over what I had said, I remembered the man from the film studio.

"The man from the Shanghai Film Studio said that I was released for health reasons," I told him.

"Really? Did he say that? Do you think they would have kept you there longer if you had not been ill?" he asked me anxiously.

"They thought I had cancer."

"Perhaps your case is not closed and no decision has been made about the so-called conspiracy. That would explain why you are being watched so closely," Mr. Hu said.

"If they are looking for an excuse to take me back to the detention house again, they won't succeed," I said.

"Have you tried to get in touch with Shell in London or Hong Kong?"

"No. I don't think I should try to contact anyone abroad when the political situation here is so uncertain."

"What if they try to get in touch with you?"

"I have already thought of that. If I receive any letter from anybody abroad, I will take it to the police and ask them whether I should respond."

"That's wise. The political situation is not good. Jiang Qing is making a comeback. Have you noticed that there are many more reports about her activities in the newspaper lately? I also heard that Chairman Mao is relying on her more than ever," Mr. Hu told me.

"Why do we have to suffer so much just because there is a power struggle in the Party? We are not even Party members!" I exclaimed helplessly.

In spite of the heat, the restaurant was crowded. Mr. Hu and I were able to talk freely in the din of voices filling the large room.

The night was hot and oppressive. I suggested that we walk back instead of taking a bus full of passengers. The streets we passed were crowded with people sitting on stools fanning themselves or sleeping on cots. Their homes were so hot and overcrowded that they had to go to the streets for a breath of air. The population of Shanghai had increased from under four million to ten million since the Communist Party took over the city. Yet little additional housing had been provided by the government, and private individuals had not been allowed to build. The result was several families sharing a house, several generations sharing a room, and the rooms being partitioned again and again. In the feeble light of the low-voltage street lamps, the street scene of Shanghai was one of depressing poverty, rather like a refugee camp.

Mr. Hu was correct when he said that the political situation was deteriorating. In the latter half of 1974, the name of Jiang Qing appeared with increasing frequency in newspaper reports from Beijing, a sure sign of increasing power. She received foreign dignitaries on Mao's behalf or in her own capacity as a revolutionary leader and a Politburo member. She played hostess to visitors from abroad, inviting them to special performances of her model plays, and held conferences with them to discuss affairs of state. Almost every day there was either her picture or an account of her activities prominently displayed on the front page of the paper.

The "Criticize Lin Biao Campaign" became a campaign to criticize both Lin Biao and Confucius. Jiang Qing personally directed the campaign through her control of the press and all major publications. Maoist writers were organized by her associate Yao Wenyuan to supply the newspapers with a steady flow of articles, and the entire population was mobilized through their indoctrination study groups to take part in the campaign. Scant attention was paid to Confucius's philosophy. Article after article stressed the little-known fact that when Confucius was fifty years of age he was made an official in the Kingdom of Lu and for a short time undertook the duties of the prime minister. It was claimed by the Maoist writers that Confucius was a retrogressive upholder of conservatism and therefore a hindrance to progress.

The Chinese people were left in no doubt that Jiang Qing's campaign to criticize Confucius was in fact a campaign against Prime Minister Zhou Enlai. The name of the ancient sage was used as a code name for the ailing prime minister. The anti-Confucius articles further claimed that in Confucius's time there existed in China another school of thought that was progressive, the legalists. The struggle between these two schools of thought was compared to the struggle between the Revolutionaries and the "capitalist-roaders."

Weary of the power struggle among their leaders, the Chinese people, including the rank-and-file Party members, were on the side of their prime minister. Rumors about Jiang Qing abounded, many no doubt invented to discredit her. She was such an unpopular figure that outlandish tales of her private life of self-indulgence and sexual promiscuity became the whispered entertainment of the masses. The more serious-minded worried that Mao Zedong seemed to be siding with his wife and the other radical leaders. They thought that perhaps he was alarmed by the speed with which Zhou Enlai, through Deng Xiaoping, was reversing the trend of the Cultural Revolution and that he feared a total repudiation of himself and what he had advocated during the Cultural Revolution.

With the increased political tension caused by the campaign to criticize Confucius and a revival of the Cultural Revolution hyperbole, several of my students dropped out. They were afraid that learning English was going to be taboo again. The Residents' Committee also stepped up its activities. One hundred percent attendance rate at study group meetings was required. Knitting was no longer allowed. More and more people were organized to stand up and support the Criticize Confucius Campaign. The Lin Biao part was dropped. A-yi reminded me to wear only my cotton jacket when I went out so as not to attract attention. Our daily fare became leaner and leaner as she became more and more reluctant to patronize the peasants who snuck into the city with their eggs and chickens for sale.

At the beginning of winter, an extraordinary event warned me of the fact that I was again in danger of being incriminated.

Among Meiping's friends who came to visit me during the year was a young woman peasant by the name of Chen Lan. Before she started working at the Shanghai Film Studio, my daughter had to spend six months at the Malu People's Commune outside Shanghai to "experience the life of a peasant" in accordance with a decision of the State Council. She lived with Chen Lan's family, sharing their life and work. The two girls became good friends. According to Chen Lan, Meiping taught her to read and write, opened her eyes to the larger world outside her narrow existence, and introduced her to such girlish pleasures as cold cream and shampoo. Chen Lan told me that Meiping once saved her mother's life when the woman was suddenly taken ill. There was no one else at home. In a boat

borrowed from their production brigade, Meiping rowed her
mother through the creeks to the county hospital in time for an
emergency operation. After that Chen Lan's family treated
Meiping as a daughter, and the two girls became sworn sisters.

When she came to see me, Chen Lan brought me a large
photograph of Meiping taken with her and several other peasant
girls of the village. Through her tears, Chen Lan said, "This is
my most treasured possession. But since you lost all your photographs, I want you to have it."

I told her that I would get copies made and then return the
original to her. But for several months I could not find a photographer's shop willing to do this simple work. One day I was on
the point of going out to try the shops at the other end of the
city across the Suzhou creek when I heard knocking on the door
at the foot of the stairs. Presently A-yi went down. Then I heard
a man's voice saying, "I'm her daughter's friend."

A moment later, A-yi came into my room followed by a stocky
young man of medium height.

I put down the photograph I was looking at and stood up.

"My name is Liu Xing. I'm Meiping's friend," the young man
introduced himself. Then he held out a gift-wrapped box and
continued, "I heard that you were out of detention, so I have
come to see you to find out if there is anything I can do for you.
This is Changbaishan ginseng. It's unobtainable in Shanghai. I
was in the northeast on business, so I got a box for you."

A box of Changbaishan ginseng was a very expensive gift. It
would cost a worker a full month's wage. I wondered what he
hoped to get from me in exchange for such an expensive gift.
I said, "It's very kind of you to think of bringing me ginseng, but
I never use it. How did you get my address?"

"The Revolutionary Committee of the Shanghai Film Studio
gave it to me when I went there to inquire."

This was an obvious lie, because Chinese officials never
obliged private individuals like that. Somehow I did not believe
he was Meiping's friend. He did not look or speak like the type
of young man my daughter made friends with. Why had he
called on me? What did he want? I was curious and wanted to
find out. Deep in my heart, at the same time, I had the feeling
that he was probably sent by those who wished me ill.

"A-yi, will you please bring a cup of tea to our guest?" I went to the door and called to A-yi in the kitchen. My polite gesture was reassuring to my visitor, who smiled and relaxed. He sat down on the chair I indicated and placed the box on the table.

I sat down too and asked him, "Did you come to our home before the Cultural Revolution? How is it that I don't recall seeing you? And Meiping never mentioned your name to me. She used to tell me about all her friends."

"You were very close, mother and daughter, weren't you? You were devoted to each other, everybody knows that. That's why I have come to discuss a very important matter with you." He leaned forward and said in a confidential manner, "I know some people who could help you hit back at her murderers. These people do not want any money or reward. They feel sorry for you. They simply want to help you."

What an extraordinary offer, I thought. The correctness of everything that had taken place during the Cultural Revolution had been repeatedly reaffirmed by official propaganda during the campaign to criticize Confucius. For me to try to do anything at all about my daughter's death was certain to take me right back to the No. 1 Detention House. Quickly I said, "I'm not interested in hitting back at anybody. I'm very sad my daughter had to die as she did. It was entirely unjustifiable and unnecessary. But she has died. Nothing will bring her back."

"How can you be so magnanimous! It's your duty as her mother to avenge her death," he said.

"I believe her death will be avenged. I believe the government will carry out an investigation when the time comes. I have full confidence in the People's Government. You haven't told me where and when you knew Meiping."

"I met her when she was at the Malu People's Commune. She lived with a peasant family there. I used to visit her and have a chat."

"Were you at the Malu People's Commune?"

"Yes. I was doing some scientific work there. That's when I met her."

Was he really Meiping's friend, as he claimed? Did he really meet Meiping at the Malu People's Commune? I thought I could check his story. I said, "Since you were at the Malu People's Commune and met Meiping there, you must know Chen Lan, the girl Meiping was very friendly with."

"Oh, yes, indeed. I used to see them together," he said hastily.

I picked up the photograph of Meiping with the group of peasant girls and handed it to him. "Someone gave me this photograph. I have never met Chen Lan. Could you tell me which one of these girls is Chen Lan?"

He examined the photograph and pointed at the girl with her arm around my daughter's shoulder. It was a good guess, but the girl he pointed out was not Chen Lan. Chen Lan was standing at the end of the row, not near my daughter at all.

His mistake was proof that he had not known my daughter at the Malu People's Commune, if at all. Why had he come? Was it just to persuade me to attempt to avenge Meiping's death so that I could be induced to do something wrong? Or was there something else he hoped to achieve? Because I did not speak, he thought he had made the correct guess. Emboldened by his success, he said, "I'll come to see you often and let you get to know me really well. I'm interested in world affairs. I'm sure I can learn a lot from you. You can learn a lot from me too because I'm a scientist. If you do not want to meet those people I told you about face to face, I could be your emissary."

"Why should you want to do that? Isn't it dangerous to oppose those involved in my daughter's death? Are they not Revolutionaries backed by powerful people?" I asked him.

"I loved Meiping. Ever since I heard she died, I can't stop thinking of her. I hate her murderers no less intensely than you do. I would be glad to do anything to have her death avenged," he said with mock sincerity, pretending to be very sad.

"You loved Meiping? You must have known her quite well, then. It's strange that she never mentioned you to me."

He went red in the face. "I loved her from a distance. She did not know it. It was a case of 'one-sided longing.' "

"I can see you are a romantic. But I think we should wait for the government to avenge her death. No matter how angry we are, we have no legal right to act."

"The present government will never do anything! They are behind the murderers, can't you see? How can you expect them to do anything?" He raised his voice impatiently, perhaps feeling disappointed that I had not swallowed the bait.

"Please calm down. You mustn't malign the government. To say the government is behind the murderers is counterrevolu-

tionary. I cannot allow my guest to talk like that in my home,"
I warned him in a stern voice.

"You are a careful woman. It doesn't matter what we say in
private. After what happened to Meiping and to yourself, you
must hate the Communist Party and the People's Government,
even though you don't say so."

"You are quite wrong. I do not hate the Communist Party or
the People's Government. But I'll think over what you have said.
If I change my mind, I'll get in touch with you. Will you please
show me your work pass so that I can verify your identification
and copy down your address?" I asked him.

"There is no need for you to see my work pass. I'll write down
my address for you." He seemed flustered by my request.

"I must see your work pass if you expect me to trust you," I
insisted.

Reluctantly he took out his work pass and handed it to me. I
put on my reading glasses and examined it. The pass was issued
by a factory identified by a number only. Everyone in China
knew that such factories belonged to the army. And stamped
across the pass was the word "confidential." He seemed to be
a technician engaged in some sort of confidential work at a
weapons factory.

My strongest defense during my imprisonment was the fact
that I did not know anybody who knew government secrets. To
be in contact with someone doing confidential work in an army
factory would not only make it impossible for me to leave China
but would also open the way to all sorts of false accusations
against me.

I opened the door of my room and called A-yi. When she
came, I said, "I want you to be a witness to what I'm going to
say to our guest."

Turning to the man, I handed his work pass back to him and
said, "Liu Xing, I forbid you ever to come to see me again. I have
'foreign connections' and have been wrongfully accused of
being a spy of the imperialists. As a scientist at a factory doing
confidential work, you have committed a serious mistake by
coming to see me. When you go back to your factory, you must
report to your Party secretary at once and confess your mistake.
You must report to him exactly what you said to me and what
I said to you." He just stood there, looking embarrassed.

"A-yi! This is a serious matter. You must never open our door to admit this young man to our house."

Opening the door wide, I said again to Liu Xing, "I presume you are a Party member since your work is confidential. I'm astonished that you did not know better. I should really denounce you to the police. Now go! Don't ever come back."

He went without a word. But I discovered he had left the box of ginseng on the table. I sent A-yi to give it back to him, but he had already disappeared on his bicycle.

I was furious about the whole episode and abandoned my plan of going out. A-yi brought me a cup of tea and said, "Don't be angry. It's not worth it."

A little while later, Da De dashed up the stairs and said rather breathlessly, "Ah, you are home! That's good!"

"You know very well I'm home," I said to him.

"What's wrong? Are you angry about something?" He professed surprise.

"You know exactly what's wrong." I handed him the box of ginseng and said, "Take it back. And tell them to stop their stupid tricks."

"I'll take away anything you don't want. But I won't tell anybody to stop their stupid tricks. Why should I? Why not let people play their tricks? Why not have a good laugh? Why should you be afraid of tricks? Aren't you smart enough to see through any trick and make the people playing them uncomfortable?" Da De said in his cynical way.

"It's so dishonest!" I said.

"Why assume anybody should be honest? After what you have gone through, you should know that to be honest is suicidal. Dishonesty is the best policy nowadays!"

"Please go, Da De! I'm not in the mood to listen to your nonsense," I told him.

"I'm only trying to cheer you up. Well, I'll come when you feel better tomorrow." He went, taking the box of ginseng with him. I wasn't at all sure he would return it to wherever it came from. I had a sneaking suspicion that he took it home and gave it to his mother as a present. Da De was that sort of person.

16

The Death of Mao

Liu xing's visit was not an isolated incident. He was followed by a series of visitors all claiming to be my daughter's friends. A few I knew by name, but I had met none of them in our home before the Cultural Revolution. They did not come together but one at a time. And they sometimes came at night. After talking about Meiping's death for an hour, I was sure to have a sleepless night.

"A-yi, do you mind not opening our door to so many visitors who claim to be my daughter's friends? All they want to talk about is what she must have gone through at the hands of her murderers and how I must try to avenge her death. I'm tired of hearing the same thing day after day."

"I have to open the door as long as I'm here. I know you are being harassed by these visitors. After you have talked to them, you always look quite ill. But what can I do? Perhaps you had better discharge me. You can easily manage on your own," she said, looking distressed.

"Can you find another job?" I asked her.

"Frankly I like being here with you. I'm not likely to get another job with the same pay and working conditions," she said.

I did not want to discharge her. But she had obviously been told to admit visitors who called on me. As long as she was here, she could not refuse to open the door. I would have to think of some way out.

"If I paid the rent, could you find some other place to live?" I asked her. The housing shortage was an extremely serious problem in Shanghai.

"I have a recently widowed cousin. She might take me in and let me share the rent. Do you want me to sleep out?"

"Good! We'll arrange it this way. You go to live with your cousin and come in the mornings only. I'll pay you the same wage and the rent. How about that?"

"That's a good arrangement. You can have quiet afternoons and evenings. If you don't open the door, no one can blame me for it," she said happily.

That weekend A-yi made the arrangement with her cousin and moved out. I got a piece of cardboard, wrapped it in a sheet of red paper, and secured it with tape. Then I pasted a piece of white paper in the center, leaving a red border. On the white paper I wrote the following message: "Because of advanced age and indifferent health, I need rest. Visitors without previous appointments will not be admitted. Representatives of the government on official business are welcome anytime." I signed my name, hung the cardboard notice outside my front door at the foot of the stairs with a red ribbon, and locked the door.

Next morning when I opened the door to go into the garden, I saw that my carefully made cardboard notice had been torn up and was lying on the ground. Mrs. Zhu was on the terrace. I picked up the pieces and confronted her with them.

"Did somebody in your family tear up my notice?" I asked her.

"Oh, no! Of course not! We never go near that door. As you know, when I come up to see you, I always come up the back stairs."

Her unemployed son came out to lend his support to his mother and said, "Somebody must have climbed over the wall again last night. We lost two shirts that were hanging on the clothesline on the terrace."

"You know there have been several cases of theft in this neighborhood. Don't you remember the Party secretary warning us to be extra careful at our last study group meeting?" Mrs. Zhu joined in.

I did not believe a thief had climbed over the wall at all, so I asked them, "Have you reported your loss to the police?"

"No." Mrs. Zhu's son threw a glance at his mother and said quickly, "But we will certainly do so."

"I'll go to the police now and report it," I said, glancing at my watch to see that it was after eight o'clock.

"Please don't bother. I'll go later," Mrs. Zhu's son said.

"I'll go now," I said.

With the pieces of cardboard in my hand, I walked to the local station at the end of our street. I thought it would be interesting to find out if the police were behind my harassment. If so, my local policeman, Lao Li, should know about it. I might discern something by watching his reaction during the interview.

The police station of our district was formerly the private residence of a wealthy Shanghai merchant who had fled to Hong Kong just before the Communist takeover. It was one of the largest houses in the area, with an attractive garden. I walked up the steps and entered the house. The large living room had been partitioned. In the front section, a man and a woman in uniform sat behind a counter. There were a few tables and benches scattered about the room. An elderly man with his resident's book in hand was registering the arrival of his son on home leave from another province.

I stood by the counter and waited until the policewoman asked me, "What's your business?"

"I'm a resident of Number One Taiyuan Road. I've come to see Comrade Lao Li, who is in charge of our street," I answered.

"Did he tell you to come see him?"

"No. Something happened last night. I've come to report to him."

"Everybody is at a study group meeting this morning. Come another time," she said.

"I'll wait for him."

"They may be a long time. Sometimes the study group meetings last the whole morning."

Determined not to be put off, I said, "I don't mind waiting, if it's all right."

She didn't say anything, so I sat down on one of the benches.

Several people came to register births, deaths, arrivals, and departures. I watched the routine work of the police department and from time to time looked up at the clock on the wall. The hands seemed to move very slowly that morning, but I was determined to see Lao Li. Soon after eleven o'clock, the door leading to the inner section opened, and a man in uniform came out.

"Tell Lao Li there is someone from Taiyuan Road to see him," the policewoman said to the man.

He went inside. After a while Lao Li came out. He was a burly man with a relaxed manner. Unlike most other policemen, he did not wear a habitual scowl on his face, nor did he let me know by his attitude that he thought me an undesirable character. I rather liked Lao Li and respected him as someone down-to-earth and fair. Behind his mild appearance, he was shrewd and alert. On his few visits to my apartment, he was always polite. But I knew he took in the situation at once just by a casual glance at the room. Certainly he was very different from the young policeman who had spat on my carpet as he strode into my living room in the early days of the People's Republic.

When Lao Li entered the room, I stood up to show him respect. He told me to sit down and took a seat opposite me across the table.

"I'm from Number One Taiyuan Road," I introduced myself.

"I know who you are," Lao Li said impatiently with a glance at the clock. "What is it you want to see me about?"

"I've come to report that a thief climbed over the wall at our place last night."

"Is anything missing?"

"The Zhus downstairs said they lost two shirts. I only had this torn up." I placed the pieces of my cardboard notice on the table. Lao Li put them together and read it. The frown on his brows deepened.

"What's this all about? Why did you write this?" He looked genuinely puzzled, so I knew that he did not know anything about my stream of visitors. The police department as a department was not involved in harassing me, but I could not rule out the possibility that some individual officials, most likely Maoist Revolutionaries promoted to official positions during the Cultural Revolution, were behind it all. During the entire 1970s, Maoist Revolutionaries and the rehabilitated old officials coexisted side by side in every government department in China. In the atmosphere of hostility and noncooperation, very little got done. The already clumsy bureaucracy became truly unwieldy. If a project had been formulated by the Revolutionaries, the rehabilitated old officials would most likely not know anything about it. At the same time, the Revolutionaries would make sure the rehabilitated officials did not recover all the power they had lost when they lost their jobs during the Cultural Revolution. In most cases, the rehabilitated officials found that though they had been given their old titles back, they had become simply figureheads. The Revolutionaries just carried on as if they were not there.

"So many people who claim to be my daughter's friends call on me at all hours to talk about her death. I am tired of seeing them. I'm an old lady. I've had a serious operation. I need to rest," I told him. He nodded and looked thoughtful.

"Why should a thief want to tear that up?" Lao Li asked me, pointing to the pieces of cardboard on the table. "It doesn't look like something a thief would do."

"The Zhus told me the thief did it."

"All right. I'll go over there to have a word with the Zhus this afternoon."

I thanked him and went home.

It seemed Lao Li did not know anything about my string of visitors. While I was no wiser as to who was behind the scheme to harass me, I derived some encouragement from the fact that Lao Li did not tell me to stop putting up cardboard notices. I decided to make another one and hang it up again.

When I got back, A-yi was already there. I told her where I had been and showed her the pieces of my cardboard notice. She said, "It must have been torn up by the Zhus. No thief came over the wall at all. It's just a pack of lies."

"Why should the Zhus want to do that?"

"Someone must have told them to do it," she replied in a low whisper, as if frightened, although no one could possibly overhear us.

"Who could have told them to do it?" I asked her.

"Who knows?" she said. But I thought she did know.

I had a peaceful afternoon. The second cardboard notice I

made was not disturbed, and no one came to the locked door.

On the following day, after A-yi had left, my resolution was put to the test. Hean's mother came to the door. I thought she would go away when she had read my notice. But she did not go away. Instead, she called me and knocked on the door. It was difficult to ignore my old friend. But I had to. She called me again. Then she left.

The day after that, my niece came with her baby. She was the daughter of my sister who had died. When the Cultural Revolution started she was only a teenager. Because of her family background, she was treated very harshly. The result was that she became nervous and timid, fearful of offending the Revolutionaries. Because I had been in the detention house, she had been reluctant to visit me. I had to send A-yi to urge her to come at Chinese New Year time. Therefore I was very surprised to hear her calling me outside my door. However, I ignored her. After a while she also went away.

I suspected that Hean's mother and my niece were both sent to test my resolve. But I could not be sure. I decided to visit my old friend.

After I had explained to Hean's mother why I could not open the door to her, I asked her, "Did you read my notice?"

"Yes, I did. But . . ." She hesitated, looking at me intently, unable to put into words what she wanted to tell me.

She could not bring herself to say that she had been told to come. Perhaps she felt ashamed, or perhaps she was afraid I might blurt it out to somebody. She bowed her head and seemed deeply embarrassed.

After a while, she said, "Wouldn't it be better just to put up with the visitors? You can always take a sleeping pill. Why seek a confrontation? Are you not afraid of them?"

"No, strange to say, I'm not afraid. I have to fight back, otherwise I will die of anger and frustration." Even as I was speaking, I felt anger welling up in my chest. Because of my daughter's death, I hated the Maoists a million times more than I had when I was in the detention house. To fight back at them at least gave me some consolation.

Hean's mother said to me, "We are such old friends that you should know I'm very fond of you. I hope you understand if I have said or done things I would not normally say or do. Living in the present circumstances, we can't always be our true selves."

"Oh, yes, don't worry! I understand perfectly," I told her and took my leave.

She accompanied me to the street. "Would you approve if I told everybody that I'm too ill to visit you? I do have rather serious heart trouble, as you know."

"Certainly. I would miss seeing you, but it's for the best. I don't want you to be placed in an awkward situation."

"I'm glad you understand. Let's hope it won't be for long. Take care of yourself." She sounded relieved.

I continued to be firm and refused to open my door to people without appointments in the afternoons. Da De never talked to me about my cardboard notice, but he would carefully make appointments with me when he wanted to visit me in the afternoons. After a couple of weeks, the visitors ceased to come.

But the attempt to harass me did not stop. It only moved from my room to the street. One day when I came home from my walk, suddenly a small group of schoolchildren yelled at me, "Spy! Imperialist spy! Running dog of the imperialists!"

I walked on, ignoring them. But two bolder ones blocked my way and continued to yell at me. I could not push the children aside without creating a scene, so I stopped and said to them calmly, "Come with me. Let's have a little chat."

They fled. I went to the Residents' Committee to complain. They told me that unless I could tell them the names of the children, they could do nothing.

This happened day after day, almost as if the children were waiting there to perform their act of insulting me. I varied the time of my walk. It made no difference. They were always there. And in the distance, there was always a man with a bicycle. As soon as the children started yelling, he would mount his bicycle and disappear.

Although the children were a nuisance and I was stared at by the few people who passed on our street, I did not give up my daily walk. I would just ignore the children and walk on as if I did not see or hear them.

A couple of weeks later, A-yi discovered that someone had written on our front gate with a piece of chalk, "An arrogant imperialist spy lives here." She was furious and wanted to wipe it off with a wet cloth.

"Please just ignore it, A-yi," I said to her.

"But it's so insulting," she said. "What will the people passing our front gate think?"

"Let them think whatever they wish to think. In any case, they must be used to such messages by now. Weren't a lot of these messages written outside people's homes during the early years of the Cultural Revolution?"

I went out at my usual hour of the afternoon and saw the same man with his bicycle across the street. He was close enough for me to see that he was about thirty, with a mop of thick black hair. Also I noticed that his bicycle had a rather bright yellow saddle cover. As soon as he saw me coming out, he mounted his bicycle and rode away. I closed the front gate without looking at the message and went on my walk.

A few days later, a heavy downpour obliterated the chalk writing on my front gate. Not long afterwards, the children also tired of their game. The most interesting thing was that although Da De could not have missed seeing what was written on my front gate, he made no reference to it at all when he came for his lessons.

I enjoyed a few peaceful days. The date March 27, 1975, was the second anniversary of my release from the No. 1 Detention House. I spent a quiet day sitting on the balcony in the pale spring sun knitting and reading Tang poetry. In the afternoon, I thought of the years I had spent in my cell, remembering the individual guards and the interrogations, and felt once again the cold, the hunger, and the torture I had endured. I looked at my wrists and saw the scars that would remain with me until I died. It seemed that although I was no longer confined in a prison cell, my struggle against persecution was by no means over. My enemy hovered on the periphery of my existence, and I must continue to be vigilant.

I was too depressed to go out, so I missed my afternoon walk. The next two days we had a steady drizzle. When the sun came out again, I was anxious for exercise.

"Are you going for your walk today? The weather is so nice," A-yi said as she was leaving.

"Oh, yes, I certainly will go today," I told her.

"Perhaps you can take the handle of the old wet mop to the co-op and get a new mop made."

"Do I have to take the old handle?"

"Yes, they are short of handles. They won't make one for you unless you bring the old handle."

At the usual hour of three o'clock, I set out with the handle of our old mop to go to the little cooperative store where a few housewives in the neighborhood did odd jobs to make a few extra yuan. If I was being followed, I didn't notice it. When I stepped off the sidewalk to cross the busy street in front of me, something suddenly hit me hard from behind. I shot out and landed flat on my back right in the path of an oncoming bus. Brakes squealed, and a man pulled me to the side. The bus slowly rolled over the handle of my old mop, breaking it. The conductor looked out of the window and shouted at me, "Why didn't you look where you were going? Do you want to kill yourself?" Then the bus gathered speed and pulled away.

Everything had happened so quickly and so unexpectedly that I was dazed. My heart palpitated wildly, and my knees were wobbly.

"A bicycle hit you. The man didn't stop," my rescuer said.

"You saved my life. How am I to thank you?" My voice was shaky. It sounded to me like someone else speaking.

"No, no. The bus stopped in time. You had better go to a hospital to make sure no bones were broken," the kind man said.

"I think I'm all right, just a little shaken. Please come with me. I would like to thank you in a concrete way with a present. Maybe you could accompany me to the police station to report the incident," I said.

"You didn't catch the man on the bicycle. The police won't do a thing. Anyway, I have a meeting to attend."

"Did you see the man who hit me?"

"Not really. But I noticed his bicycle had something bright on the saddle."

"Was it a bright yellow saddle cover?"

"He was sitting on the saddle. But something bright caught my eye."

"Was he a man with a mop of thick black hair?"

"Yes, do you know him?" the man asked me. "Is he a personal enemy?"

"No, I don't know him. But I've seen him before."

"Well, I have to go to my meeting. You had better be careful. He hit you deliberately. The street was empty. He didn't have to hit you. And he rode away quickly."

I thanked the man again, and he disappeared in the crowd.

When I managed to get home, I took two aspirin tablets and went to bed. It was only a little after four o'clock. I slept for about an hour. When I woke up, I found my whole body stiff as a board and aching so excruciatingly that I could hardly move. With difficulty I rolled out of bed and went to the bathroom. I thought a bath with a lot of hot water might help, but I couldn't manage to get the water ready without A-yi.

The night was terribly long, and I was most uncomfortable. Finally A-yi came and served me breakfast in bed. She was very distressed to hear of my accident. Perhaps she guessed that I was hit deliberately and felt partly responsible, for she had reported where I was going. The whole morning, she was on the verge of tears.

While she prepared a hot bath for me, I read Tang dynasty poems in bed. Suddenly I remembered that Mr. Hu had said he was going to call on me that very afternoon. Although I would have preferred to remain in bed, I got up and tidied up my room. I had no way of telling Mr. Hu not to come. After the revolutionary action of the Red Guards, no one in China was allowed a private telephone. To make a call, one had to go to a public telephone. The attendant took down the number one wanted to call and listened in to every conversation. Often she was not there at all, and the phone was locked up.

When Mr. Hu came at four o'clock, I served him tea and biscuits that A-yi had ready in the kitchen. Then I told him I had been knocked down by a man on a bicycle and had nearly been run over by a bus. I expected him to sympathize with me, show alarm, or maybe just say he was sorry. But he stared at me with great seriousness and said, "Please let me take care of you! If you would allow me to look after you, I would be so happy." He seemed to be under emotional strain, as his voice was not altogether steady.

Was this meant to be a marriage proposal? I wasn't sure. And because I had been preoccupied with what had been happening around me, he caught me by surprise. He seemed embarrassed by my silence. Hastily he added, "Do you think marriage is for young people only? Perhaps I shocked you with my blunt proposal?"

"Oh, no, not at all. I think it perfectly all right for older people to marry. And I'm sure many women would be proud and happy to be your wife. As for myself, though I am grateful to you and flattered by your proposal, I am bound by a vow I made to my late husband that I would remain Mrs. Cheng to the end of my life."

His kind face softened into a wistful smile. He took my hand in his and said reluctantly, "I don't know about other women. I have waited . . . But never mind! I must respect your resolution to remain faithful to your husband. I have always had the greatest respect and affection for him. He was a very fine person." He let go of my hand after giving it a gentle squeeze.

The awkward moment passed. I had not caused Mr. Hu to lose face by a flat refusal. That was not the Chinese way.

After his proposal, Mr. Hu continued to visit me from time to time. He was always pleasant and attentive. But the interval between his visits lengthened until he resumed his old practice of calling on me on Chinese New Year's Day only. In 1978, he came specially to tell me that he had been rehabilitated and restored to his former position as assistant manager and chief engineer at his factory. He was busily coping with post–Cultural Revolution problems and trying to resume full production.

"I'm working sixteen hours a day. I wish I were younger and could do more. There is so much to do and so much to learn. I have become rusty," he said, looking so happy that he seemed suddenly to have shed ten years of his age.

In 1980, when I was given a passport to leave China, I wrote to him to say goodbye. He came to see me at once and told me he had thought all along that I wished to leave China. But I do not think Mr. Hu ever understood why I had chosen the uncertain prospect of starting a new life in my old age in some foreign land rather than settling down quietly with a ready-made family in my native country.

To have received a marriage proposal from a worthy man at the age of sixty was pleasant, if not exhilarating. I was in a good mood in spite of my aching limbs when Da De came for his lesson next morning.

I had unlocked the front door and was just finishing breakfast when I heard him bounding up the stairs. I looked at the clock. Da De was twenty minutes early.

"You are early today," I said to him when he appeared at my door.

"I have something exciting to tell you." He came into the room with a big smile. "I may be going to Beijing in the not too distant future."

"Indeed. Have you been offered a job?" I asked him.

"Not yet. But I may have a wonderful opportunity." He sat down across the table from me.

"Would you like a cup of tea and a piece of toast?" I asked, as I knew Da De was always hungry.

"Some toast would be nice." He went into the kitchen and came back with four whole slices of toast, which he ate in no time at all. I wondered whether he had eaten breakfast, but I did not ask.

Taking a book from his bag, Da De asked me, "Do you think we could study this today?"

The book was Emily Post's *Etiquette*. "Why do you want to study that? The contents of this book are of no use to a Chinese."

"Not unless the Chinese is to become a diplomat stationed abroad," he said.

"I see. Is that your exciting news? Is that why you are going to Beijing? Are you going to the Foreign Affairs Institute to train as a diplomat? If that's the case, congratulations!"

A-yi arrived and came to my room right away. "Are you better today?" she asked anxiously. "Are you still sore all over?"

"Thank you, A-yi! I'm a lot better."

She cleared the table and left the room. Da De asked me, "Have you been ill?"

"I was knocked down by a man on a bicycle and nearly run over by a bus. I thought you knew already," I said.

Da De went red in the face and said indignantly, "How could I know? Do you think I'm behind every unpleasant thing that happens to you?"

"No, I don't think you are behind them. That would be giving you too much credit," I told him. Da De winced and looked ashamed for the first time since I had known him. "But I do think you are in the know; you are usually told. I think that whoever is behind all the unpleasant things happening to me trusts you."

"You don't understand. You think people are free agents. They are not. And the world isn't divided into good men and bad men. In any case, good people are often compelled to do bad things, and bad people can also do good things. You will never know the things I have done for you. It doesn't matter. I'll only say that I'm not a piece of stone. You have been decent to me. Often I think you are kinder to me than anybody I have known except my own mother. Do you think I would allow someone to knock you down with a bicycle and have you run over by a bus?" Da De said this in a wounded tone of voice.

"My goodness! You have gone soft! If you weren't told, that's bad. It wouldn't do, would it, if you were no longer trusted," I said sarcastically.

Da De asked, "Are you sure it wasn't just an accident?"

"The street was empty. He didn't have to hit me. However, the bus passing at that precise moment might have been coincidental."

"The whole thing could have been an accident," Da De argued.

"No, I have seen the same man before. The man who helped me up told me the man had a mop of black hair and a bright-colored bicycle saddle."

From Da De's expression, I thought he knew who the man was. After a moment's hesitation, he said, "Would you be angry if I give you a little advice?"

"Fire away!" I said, leaning back in my chair ready to listen to him.

"Do you realize there are people in positions of power who hate your guts? You make them think you despise them. They want to be looked up to, feared, and respected. But they think you laugh at them. Why don't you hide your contempt for them and just take it easy sometimes?"

"How do I 'take it easy'?" I asked Da De.

"Don't react when something happens. Don't get angry. Look at that notice you put down there outside your door. Nobody in China does a thing like that. A man's home may be his castle in England, but it isn't the case in China. When you don't allow people to come see you freely and you send A-yi away in the afternoons, naturally people wonder what you are up to. Do you realize the Housing Bureau could have put another family in your other room when A-yi moved out?"

"There is no bathroom. Another family cannot come through my bedroom to go to the bathroom, can they?" I asked Da De.

"You simply have no idea how people live in Shanghai," Da De said. "There are many families in this city living in rooms without bathrooms. The Housing Bureau didn't send another family here. It's a special consideration. You should realize it."

"You puzzle me. Why should I be harassed and persecuted on the one hand and be given consideration on the other?"

"I can't tell you more than to advise you not to look upon the situation in a simplistic way. In every government department, there are many people with power to do things. They don't always agree, especially nowadays. The situation is extremely complicated. Just remember, there are people who feel sorry for you. They know you have been victimized. They very much regret the death of your daughter. Please try to be meek and resigned. The political struggle has reached a crucial stage. Why suffer more than you have to?"

"All right! Wise Da De! I'll try to be meek and resigned, as you say. But life will be very dull, won't it?"

"No, life won't be dull. Many things are going to happen," Da De said.

"Such as Da De going to the Foreign Affairs Institute to train as a diplomat," I said, changing the subject.

"I'm not going to the Foreign Affairs Institute for training. Comrade Jiang Qing has said that the Ministry of Foreign Affairs must be reorganized. Young men and women faithful to our beloved Chairman Mao's teaching are going to be sent there. She said, 'Mix some sand in the sticky clay to loosen it up.' The Ministry of Foreign Affairs has been under Chen Yi and Premier Zhou for so long that it has become an independent kingdom full of capitalist ideas. The proletariat must now march in."

"Will you be going abroad right after getting to Beijing?" I asked him. From Da De's remark, I thought Jiang Qing wanted to take over the Ministry of Foreign Affairs.

"That I don't know. Comrade Jiang Qing wants some Revolutionaries in every embassy abroad. There will be resistance. It'll be a struggle. But backed by Chairman Mao, she will get her way. My name has been included in the list from Shanghai. I hope I'll be chosen. My English is a lot better than that of others on the list."

"I hope you will be chosen, Da De. It will be a break for you. Better than to stick around with the Revolutionaries you are mixed up with now. They seem to me to be a bunch of rascals."

Da De went red in the face again. But he did not argue with me and defend his comrades.

We spent the morning studying the elementary principles of etiquette. When Da De left, he was happy in anticipation of a brighter future. Having served the radicals for so many years, he believed he would be rewarded.

During 1975, the campaigns of denunciation in the press were like the tidal waves of the sea. When one subject was exhausted, another subject was introduced with a deafening roar. When the people's indignation against the ancient sage Confucius was deemed to have waned, other topics of denunciation were presented to stimulate their interest. In this way, the Maoists built up what they called "revolutionary momentum" and kept the pot boiling.

One day, the *Shanghai Liberation Daily* came out with a long article that occupied a full page of the newspaper, which had only four pages, denouncing a film about life in China made by a famous Italian filmmaker, Antonioni. At our study group meeting, the article was read to us, and Antonioni was condemned in no uncertain terms. None of us had ever heard of Antonioni, and we did not know that he had come to China and made a film. Furthermore, the film was never shown in any Chinese cinema, so that no Chinese had actually seen it. I carefully studied the long article, reprinted from the *People's Daily*, the official Party organ, as well as other articles published subsequently to echo its views. Gradually I realized that the denunciation of Antonioni was aimed at whoever had given him permission to come to China to make the film. The article alleged that every shot taken by Antonioni to show poverty, backwardness, and ugliness in China was a reflection of the reactionary thoughts of those who had made it possible for him to do so. What's more, it seemed the film had been used by several Chinese embassies abroad to entertain guests. Chinese politics operated by gossip and whispering campaigns. It was not long before I learned that the real targets of this attack on Antonioni were Prime Minister Zhou Enlai and First Vice-Premier Deng Xiaoping. It seemed they had given Antonioni permission to make the film, and they were of course responsible for the embassies abroad.

There were many other instances like the campaign against

Antónioni, too numerous to record here. All of the denunciations were in fact veiled attacks directed against either the prime minister or the vice-premier, who was working hard to restore production both in the factories and in the rural communes.

One day, I was told by my one remaining student besides Da De that Zhang Chunqiao, the Party boss of Shanghai, a Politburo member and a longtime associate of Jiang Qing, had said, "We would rather have socialism's lower production figures than capitalism's higher production figures." The radicals in the rural areas took up his statement and proclaimed, "We would rather have socialism's poor harvest than capitalism's abundance." Not to be left behind, other radicals declared, "We would rather have socialism's trains that are behind schedule than capitalism's trains that are on time." In such an atmosphere, the workers became fearful of doing too much, the peasants became reluctant to go into the field, and drivers of trains, buses, and even mules deliberately slowed down so that they could arrive behind schedule. The already strained economy took another tumble. With their controlled propaganda machinery and widespread network of radical organizations, which had been developed during the Cultural Revolution, the Maoist leaders succeeded in sabotaging Deng Xiaoping's effort to put China's economy back on its feet.

The newspaper headlines and the voices from loudspeakers screamed daily, "Hit back at the rightist wind of reversing the verdict of the Cultural Revolution!" What did the radicals mean by "the verdict of the Cultural Revolution"? They meant that Deng Xiaoping had been denounced as a "capitalist-roader" during the Cultural Revolution. This "verdict of the Cultural Revolution" should not have been reversed by Deng's rehabilitation in 1973. The atmosphere became increasingly tense. Anything that incurred the displeasure of the radicals was interpreted as "attempting to reverse the verdict of the Cultural Revolution." And they used this slogan to block any further attempt to rehabilitate old officials. Once again, the Chinese bowed their heads and walked on tiptoe, fearful of treading on dangerous ground or appearing less than totally submissive.

The program to modernize industry, agriculture, science and technology, and the armed forces, popularly known as the Four Modernizations Program, first proposed by Prime Minister

Zhou Enlai, had been adopted by the People's Congress. Oblivious of the radicals' propaganda war, Deng Xiaoping went on with his efforts to normalize life in China and implement the Four Modernizations Program. Entrance examinations for universities and colleges were reinstituted. But as a concession to Mao's ideology, the candidates for the examinations first had to complete a period of manual labor in a factory or rural commune. The radicals' answer to Deng's decision to restore entrance examinations was to announce the discovery of a young hero by the name of Zhang Tiesheng in Liaoning province. Zhang Tiesheng, according to press reports, did not answer any of the questions on the examination paper but wrote an essay on the back denouncing the effort by the "former capitalist-roaders" to take China backwards to pre–Cultural Revolution conditions. He declared in conclusion, "We must hit back at the rightist wind of reversing the verdict of the Cultural Revolution!"

Zhang Tiesheng became a hero the radical leaders urged the Chinese young people to emulate. He was sent on tours of the country to "warn" the people of the importance of "hitting back at the rightist wind." Since the Party secretary of Liaoning province, Mao Yuanxin, was Mao's nephew and a close associate of Jiang Qing, the Chinese people realized at once that the whole business of Zhang Tiesheng was manufactured by the radical leaders and that the young man simply acted according to their instructions.

Once again, to read a book or to study any subject at all became taboo, just as in the early days of the Cultural Revolution. My only other student besides Da De, a disabled girl, became very frightened. I told her to study at home but to come to visit me as a guest from time to time so that I could correct her essays. I also told Da De to stop coming regularly for his lessons.

One evening, I was in the garden cutting the last of the roses before the frost. I saw Mrs. Zhu's working son seeing a man off at the front gate. When he came back he asked me whether he could speak to me. I invited him upstairs.

"Did you notice the man I was seeing off? He is a great friend of Vice-Chairman Wang Hongwen. When Wang Hongwen organized the Shanghai Workers Revolutionary Headquarters to overthrow the municipal government and the Party Secretariat in January 1967, he was Wang's trusted lieutenant. They have remained close friends ever since. Whenever Wang Hongwen comes to Shanghai, he is always invited to wine and dine with him." He carefully watched my reaction as he told me this.

Obviously he was leading up to something, so I listened but made no comment.

"Well, he is going to Beijing in a few days' time at the invitation of Vice-Chairman Wang. He is in a position to help you. A word in the ear of the vice-chairman and all your troubles are over," he said.

"What trouble do you think I'm in?" I asked him.

"For one thing, you haven't been properly rehabilitated. And your daughter died in mysterious circumstances. I suppose you would like to see her death avenged. All of that can be done by a word from Vice-Chairman Wang."

"Do you mean to say that your friend can enlist the help of Vice-Chairman Wang Hongwen to 'reverse the verdict of the Cultural Revolution' for me?"

"To reverse the verdict of the Cultural Revolution is not allowed. It needn't be called that if Vice-Chairman Wang takes a personal interest in the matter. It would be called 'clarifying the case' or something like that. Of course, you'll have to pay for it, but not more than you can afford. Your money is in the People's Bank; they will know how much to charge you. And you can even get an exit visa to go to Hong Kong for as little as ten thousand yuan," the young man said.

While I was astonished to learn that the famous hero of the January Revolution that toppled the Shanghai municipal government and Party Secretariat, Vice-Chairman of the Chinese Communist Party Wang Hongwen, was indulging in large-scale corruption, I also realized the danger I was in if I should fall into this trap. So I smiled at him and said in as friendly a voice as I could muster, "You are really very kind to offer to help me through your friend. I'm most grateful. But at the moment I have no plans to go to Hong Kong. As for my rehabilitation and the death of my daughter, I expect the People's Government will do whatever needs to be done when the time comes. It would be presumptuous of me to trouble such an important person as Vice-Chairman Wang Hongwen with such a trivial matter."

"Don't you realize conditions in China have changed?" He was getting impatient and excited. He raised his voice to a high pitch when he said, "The government won't do a thing if you don't make arrangements privately with an official."

I looked at the open door and gestured to him to lower his voice. Then I said, "I have confidence in the People's Government. That can't be wrong, can it?"

"If you are sincere, you are a fool!"

He stormed out of my room, walking quickly down the stairs and banging my front door as he went out. He was plainly disappointed and annoyed that my refusal prevented him from getting his cut of the deal. I thought his offer was a straightforward case of corruption, but I could not rule out entirely that it was a trap to get me to take part in "attempting to reverse the verdict of the Cultural Revolution" so I could be found guilty of counterrevolution.

When Da De came a few days later, I said to him, "It's ages since I took you to a restaurant."

"We mustn't go to a restaurant now. In any case, all the good dishes have been taken off the menu. They are to be served only to visitors from abroad," he told me.

"It's too bad we only have cabbage and noodles today. Otherwise I would ask you to stay for lunch." I knew Da De's aversion to cabbage and noodles, which he had daily when he lived in poverty as a child.

"Would you like me to cook you a dinner?" he asked.

"There is hardly anything at the market," I said.

"I'll get the food through my friends. What would you like to eat?"

"Just get what you like," I told him and handed him three 10-yuan notes, more than two weeks' wages for a worker.

At five o'clock the following evening, Da De came with fish, shrimp, and a chicken, as well as a bottle of Shaoxing wine and two bottles of beer. I had asked A-yi to stay and help him. Between them they produced a really good dinner of several delicious dishes. Da De drank the Shaoxing wine with his meal and started on the beer while relaxing in my only easy chair.

Lazily he said, "Don't you think I'm a pretty good cook?"

"You are an excellent cook. I congratulate you! Now that you have been fed, may I ask you a few questions?" I said.

"Ah, I must pay for my dinner! Glad to tell you anything, as you know," Da De drawled.

"I need to be educated about the present situation. You needn't tell me anything you shouldn't. But I'd like to hear your analysis of the situation."

"I've told you already the struggle has reached a crucial stage. It concerns the future course of the Communist Party and the government. Are we going to preserve the fruit of the Cultural Revolution and proceed from there, or are we to go back to Liu Shaoqi's policies without Liu Shaoqi?"

"What are Liu Shaoqi's policies without Liu Shaoqi?"

"What Deng Xiaoping is doing."

"I thought the propaganda attack was aimed at Premier Zhou."

"Deng Xiaoping is acting on behalf of Premier Zhou, who is ill, as you know. The point of contention is who is to succeed Premier Zhou. Is it going to be Deng Xiaoping, or is it going to be Zhang Chunqiao? The premier himself and the old leaders like Chen Yun and Ye Jianying want Deng Xiaoping to succeed Premier Zhou. The present campaign is to impress upon the nation that if Deng Xiaoping becomes premier, he will reverse the verdict of the Cultural Revolution," Da De told me.

"What about Vice-Chairman Wang Hongwen? Is he going to succeed Chairman Mao?"

"Oh, no! He is just keeping the seat warm for Comrade Jiang Qing. She can't very well be appointed vice-chairman while Chairman Mao is still living. But she will become his successor when he dies. What Comrade Jiang Qing wants is to be the chairman of the Central Committee of the Communist Party and Zhang Chunqiao to be the prime minister."

I thought, Good God, don't let that happen! But to Da De I could not express such an opinion. Instead I told him about the offer made to me by Mrs. Zhu's son.

"Have you agreed to it?" Da De asked me, sitting up.

"No. It's illegal to bribe officials," I told him.

"If you have agreed to it, you won't see your money again and you won't get an exit visa for Hong Kong either. A lot of people have fallen into their trap already," Da De said and took another sip of his beer.

"What about the victims? Don't they complain?"

"It's a case of 'a mute swallowing bitter herbs.' He can't speak out. They are already guilty of bribery." Da De laughed heartily and drained his glass. He took the second bottle and opened it.

"It's a shame such things are going on," I said.

"Don't be a puritan! As long as money can buy the things people need, they will always want to get money. Of course, leaders in high positions are exempt from punishment. *Xin bu shang da fu*—punishment does not reach senior officials. That's China's tradition. You know that!"

"Shouldn't a socialist government have changed that?"

"Who would do the changing? The senior officials themselves? What a hope!"

Silently Da De drank the second bottle of beer. When he had finished it, he stood up to bid me good night and lumbered to the door.

However, he stopped suddenly and said casually, "I suppose you know Premier Zhou is dying of cancer in the Beijing Hospital?"

"Is it really true?"

"Yes, it's true. Since he will be removed from the struggle by dying, a lot of cases . . . such as the one about a conspiracy of foreign firms and government departments in Shanghai, you know what I mean? Somebody mentioned it to you, perhaps? And others, of course, there are others . . . In any case"—he waved his arm in the air—"all will be shelved!"

"Why only shelved and not clarified?" I asked him anxiously.

Da De seemed to sober up and pull himself together when he said, quite clearly, "Once an accusation is made by a senior source, it can never be clarified, only shelved. You don't expect the senior source to admit he made a false accusation or a mistake, do you?" He did not wait for my answer but sauntered out the door and down the stairs.

I stood there staring at his retreating figure, momentarily stunned by his message. Perhaps I should have felt relief that the so-called conspiracy of foreign firms and government departments in Shanghai in which I had become so unjustly involved was to be shelved. It could mean the end of my harassment and the beginning of normal existence. But all I was conscious of was a feeling of emptiness. I thought of the wasted years of my life and the senseless murder of my daughter. At the same time, my determination to leave China for good one day was strengthened by what Da De had said. I knew that when a case was "shelved" and not clarified, it could always be revived again when the political climate demanded it. Just because a senior Maoist Party official had made a false accusation and refused to admit he was mistaken, an innocent person like myself would have to live the rest of her life under a shadow.

The year 1975 drew to a close amidst rumors impossible to verify. I heard from one person that Mao Zedong had visited Zhou Enlai in the hospital. My informant said that when Zhou suggested that Deng Xiaoping be appointed prime minister to succeed him, Mao pretended not to hear Zhou's weakened voice. Another person told me that both Mao and Zhou were dying. Jiang Qing and her associates hoped Zhou would die first, so they withheld medical treatment to hasten his death. Yet another person said that Jiang Qing and Mao's nephew Mao Yuanxin had completely isolated the dying Mao Zedong from all Politburo members wishing to see him. All messages were transmitted through them, the story went, including directives to the Politburo that might or might not have originated from Mao.

In January 1976, Zhou Enlai died after serving as prime minister of the People's Republic of China since its inception in 1949. An enigmatic man, Zhou was a Communist leader with a difference. To the Chinese people, he resembled those few traditional prime ministers immortalized in history and legend because of their high moral caliber. Even Zhou's consistent efforts to mitigate the ill effects of, rather than to oppose openly, Mao's disastrous political campaigns, such as the Great Leap Forward and the Cultural Revolution, were considered "wise" by the long-suffering Chinese people. They were only too glad that Zhou Enlai was there to pick up the pieces afterwards. Because Zhou appeared reasonable rather than intransigent, subtle rather than bombastic, many people who had met him thought him less than a firm believer in Marxism. In actual fact, a close examination of his life and views, as reflected in the decisions he made and in his published speeches and writings, reveals that Zhou Enlai never wavered from the commitment he made to realize Communism in China when he joined the Party as a young man. He differed from the radicals only in his belief that foreign capital and intellectuals trained abroad could be utilized to achieve his ultimate aim.

In China, news traveled faster by word of mouth than through the newspapers, where the simplest fact could not be published without the approval of several bureaucrats. It was the sudden return of a heart specialist urgently called to the bedside of the prime minister, the gathering of local officials at an unusual hour, the cancellation of a major event, and a telephone conversation overheard by a subordinate that told the Chinese people that Zhou Enlai had died. When the *Shanghai Liberation Daily* finally came out with the news, in the afternoon, the people read it to learn not what had happened but how the newspaper presented the news, which they knew reflected Beijing's attitude toward the event.

A-yi came breathlessly up the stairs and into my room with a basket of vegetables still in her hand. "Prime Minister Zhou has died!" she exclaimed.

She handed me a piece of black cotton cloth and continued, "I got this for our armbands of mourning. It's already nearly sold out at the cloth shop at the marketplace. There is a rumor that the Shanghai Revolutionary Committee will not supply extra black cloth for armbands because they do not want the people to wear mourning for Premier Zhou. As soon as the people heard this, they abandoned shopping and mobbed the cloth shops."

At the demand of Party members living in our district, our Residents' Committee organized a memorial meeting for Prime Minister Zhou. The room was decorated with wreaths made by the residents. The flowers on the wreaths were made of colored handkerchiefs because crepe paper had been sold out in the shops and the Shanghai Revolutionary Committee refused to sanction additional supplies. Lu Ying's son made a frame of dried rice straw for the wreath presented by our small unit, and Mrs. Zhu and I provided the green leaves from the evergreen ilex hedge in our garden.

The memorial meeting was well attended. A bedridden woman was carried in on a chair, and several old men were assisted by their grandchildren. The people came spontaneously, and I thought their emotion was genuine. Many were weeping openly, and the words of tribute spoken with trembling voices were sincere. It was a simple but moving ceremony. For the first time, I had attended a meeting where everybody was himself and not acting the part that was expected of him.

Meiping's friend Kong called on me in the evening to tell me how the news of Premier Zhou's death had been received at the film studio. He said that someone close to the radicals had just returned from Beijing in the morning. This man said that upon being informed of Zhou Enlai's death, Jiang Qing had exclaimed, "Hitherto I was locked in a cage. Now I can come out to speak!"

"I thought she had been speaking all the time ever since the beginning of the Cultural Revolution. What do you make of such a remark by Jiang Qing?" I asked him.

"God knows what more she wants to say, unless it's to declare her ambition to become the chairman of the Central Committee of the Communist Party," Kong said. "The country is seething with rumors already, ranging from a plot to assassinate Deng Xiaoping to civil war."

"I suppose a successor to Prime Minister Zhou will be announced soon?" I asked him.

"The delay in making an announcement can only mean the struggle is still going on. There is a move in Shanghai to send a delegation to the Politburo to demand the appointment of Zhang Chunqiao. I heard that those close to Zhang Chunqiao are already preparing slogans and banners to be brought out the moment his appointment is announced. They seem to expect to win."

"What about Deng Xiaoping? At the moment he is the first vice-premier," I said.

"The old leaders are all for him, of course," Kong said.

"Isn't the army an important factor in the struggle?"

"Yes. Ye Jianying is the head of the Military Commission. But I hear a few of the area commanders are leaning towards Jiang Qing and her group."

On subsequent days, apart from reporting the Central Committee's memorial meeting for Zhou Enlai, the *Shanghai Liberation Daily,* controlled by the radicals, cut to the minimum the space devoted to his death. It wasn't until a documentary film of his funeral reached the city's cinemas that the Shanghai people saw the long lines in the capital waiting to pay their last respects outside the Beijing hospital where Zhou's body lay in state. And one million people braved the bitter January wind of North China to stand for hours along the route on which his body was taken to be cremated. Close-up shots showed men and women of all ages, some with toddlers in arms, weeping, watching intently, and murmuring words the camera did not record.

The people of Beijing defied more than the weather when they stood in the cold waiting for Zhou Enlai's cortege to pass; they were sending a message of defiance to the radicals, who, they thought, had treated Zhou shabbily. The film ended with a shot of a plane flying over the country. From that the people of Shanghai learned that Zhou Enlai had willed that his ashes be scattered over China's rivers and mountains. Zhou's wish not to be buried in an elaborate tomb at the Eight Precious Hill Cemetery reserved for top Party leaders gave rise to a host of rumors about a radical plot to desecrate his grave, Zhou's aversion to sharing the same ground with Kang Sheng and Xie Fuzhi, both collaborators of Jiang Qing, etc.

After Zhou Enlai's death, Jiang Qing became even more active and was constantly in the public eye. While denunciations of the attempt by the "capitalist-roaders" to "reverse the verdict of the Cultural Revolution" continued, more and more articles appeared in the radical-controlled press praising China's few female rulers in history. Attention was concentrated on Empress Lu (241–180 B.C.) of the Han dynasty and Empress Wu (A.D. 624–705) of the Tang dynasty, both of whom succeeded their husbands upon the men's death. The reigns of these women were described as prosperous and propitious to prove the virtue of female rulers. The Chinese people watched with dismay Jiang Qing's maneuvers to prepare public opinion for her acceptance as Mao's successor. They showed their contempt by circulating stories about her promiscuity and self-indulgence that defied the most fertile imagination. Once at our Residents' Committee meeting, a police official addressed us and told us that we must not pass on rumors about our leaders and must report to the police if we heard any. Although the man did not mention any leader's name, everybody knew that some of the rumors had gotten back to Jiang Qing and that she was trying to stop their circulation.

The festival of Qing Ming ("Bright and Clear") in March of

the lunar calendar generally took place in early April. The Chinese people traditionally visited the graves of their ancestors to pay their respects. After the Communist Party took over the country in 1949, Qing Ming was designated as Martyrs' Day, when schoolchildren were organized to present wreaths at the tombs of the revolutionary martyrs. A couple of days before Qing Ming in 1976, people came to the Monument of Revolutionary Heroes in the center of Tiananmen Square in Beijing to place wreaths and floral tributes to Zhou Enlai. Children tied single white paper flowers on the branches of the evergreen hedge around the monument, with endearing messages addressed to "Grandpa Zhou."

Zhou Enlai was childless, in China considered the greatest misfortune. It was said and generally believed by the Chinese people that when advised to take a younger wife so that he could have an heir, Zhou had refused and said, "All Chinese children are my children." For this the Chinese people admired him as a man of impeccable moral principle, the more outstanding because many other Communist Party leaders were discarding their older wives in favor of young women in the cities they had conquered.

The wreaths accumulated. They came by the thousands from factories and people's communes in and around Beijing, carried by workers and peasants in mourning in a solemn procession and laid down in a ceremony, with the men and women taking an oath of loyalty to the deceased premier. Soon the steps and the area surrounding the monument were covered. Those who brought the wreaths lingered, and others made special trips to watch the scene. The men and women read, sometimes with homemade loudspeakers, the poems and pledges they had written for Zhou Enlai while others listened and copied down the poems and messages attached to the wreaths and flowers. So many children had tied single white flowers on the hedge that it was entirely covered. It was estimated that by the day of Qing Ming several hundred thousand people had visited the monument and taken part in one form of ceremony or another, swearing allegiance to Zhou Enlai and what he stood for. The young people pledged emotionally to accomplish Zhou Enlai's unfinished task of rebuilding China through his Four Modernizations Program. By now, the wreaths had overflowed to cover the stands around the square. Increasingly, the poems for Zhou went beyond simple epitaphs of praise. Many of them compared the radical leaders unfavorably with the deceased prime minister and expressed concern about China's destiny falling into their hands.

As news of this astonishing activity spread to other cities, trains departing for the capital carried contributions of wreaths and poetry to Beijing. The more militant opponents of the radicals chalked slogans and put up posters against them outside the carriages. The train attendants did not wipe off the slogans but kept them fresh, so that each train that arrived at the Beijing railway station was a living protest against the radical leaders.

This mass display of sentiment for Zhou Enlai very quickly developed into a mass demonstration of resentment against the radicals, including Mao Zedong himself. No names were mentioned. But veiled comparisons were made to the first Qin emperor (259–210 B.C.), generally regarded by Chinese historians as a cruel ruler who persecuted scholars and destroyed books, setting back China's cultural development. The wording of the poems became less ambiguous, and the sarcasm against Jiang Qing and her associates became bolder. To go to Tiananmen Square became a must for the young people of Beijing. They not only copied poems down and listened to the writers' recitations but laughed heartily at the radicals and made speeches against them.

Such behavior was unheard of in Communist China, where every demonstration was organized by the government to express support for government policies. On the few occasions when Chinese people supposedly demonstrated outside foreign embassies, activists had always been there among them to direct everything. During the Cultural Revolution, except for the short time when things got out of hand, the Red Guards were controlled by Maoist Party activists. The radical leaders watched the scene at Tiananmen Square with increasing alarm and decided to take action. On the fatal night of April 5, the mayor of Beijing, a Jiang Qing collaborator, ordered the militia to surround the area. The police and the militia, both controlled by Jiang Qing and her associates, went in with clubs and pistols to drive the people away from the monument. As the people dispersed, the militia opened fire. Thousands of unarmed demonstrators were killed or wounded. Those found with poems were taken to the Security Bureau, condemned as counterrevolutionaries, and shot without trial. Tiananmen Square was cordoned off. It took the cleaners of Beijing two days to hose away the blood and remove everything including the corpses.

I was told long afterwards that Mao Zedong, terminally ill at home, heard only the version of the Tiananmen affair given him by Jiang Qing and Mao Yuanxin, who acted as his liaison with the Politburo. They alleged that Deng Xiaoping was behind the Tiananmen affair, designed to discredit Mao and to repudiate the Cultural Revolution. It was the "capitalist-roaders," they claimed, hitting back at the Proletarian Revolutionaries. In a fit of temper, Mao dictated a directive to a hastily called Politburo meeting, asking its members to pass a resolution to remove Deng Xiaoping from the position of vice-premier and to appoint Hua Guofeng, a relatively junior member of the Politburo, as acting prime minister and first vice-chairman of the Central Committee of the Communist Party. In effect, Mao Zedong had designated Hua Guofeng as his successor. Though an aged and dying man, Mao was astute enough to know that if he had appointed Zhang Chunqiao as premier, there would have been civil war in the country and the Communist Party would have been irrevocably split.

Hua Guofeng had joined the Communist Party as a guerrilla fighter during the Sino-Japanese War in his native province, Shanxi. He was relatively unknown to the Chinese people, and his career was undistinguished. Just before the Cultural Revolution, he was appointed Party secretary of Mao's native province, Hunan. At the beginning of the Cultural Revolution, he was denounced as a "capitalist-roader" but was soon rehabilitated when it was found that he had perpetuated Mao's personality cult and was in the process of building an irrigation system for the county where Mao's relatives lived. Hua was not a controversial personality and seemed to be acceptable both to the radical leaders and to the old guard. He was a compromise choice. Evidently Mao believed that with Hua in charge, his own position in Chinese history would be secure.

The Politburo resolution was quickly broadcast by the Shanghai Broadcasting Station and appeared in the newspaper the next day. The people were also notified through their Residents'

Committee study group meetings. The Tiananmen affair was officially declared a counterrevolutionary attempt to create disturbance. After that no further mention of it was made in the official press. But horrifying details of the massacre spread fast by word of mouth all over the country. Those who had escaped from Tiananmen Square on the day of the massacre secretly wrote down the poems from memory. Soon handwritten copies were circulating surreptitiously among the people.

The appointment of Hua Guofeng to the supreme position of leadership both in the government and in the Party created a temporary lull in the published rhetoric, but the struggle for power and position went on nonetheless. Public interest in Deng Xiaoping was kept alive by rumors of plots to assassinate him. Though his whereabouts were unknown, several people told me that he had been seen in Guangzhou living under the protection of the army.

"It seems so strange that interest in the fate of Deng Xiaoping has not flagged since his removal from office," I said to Da De one day when he was chatting to me about Hua Guofeng.

"People expect him to bounce back again, just as he did before," my student told me.

"Is it likely?" I asked him.

"Who knows?" Da De said.

My student seemed much more subdued since the Tiananmen affair. Though usually forthcoming with comments and information, he never talked to me about what had happened on April 5 at Tiananmen. Also, the appointment of Hua Guofeng seemed to have disconcerted him. While he gave me the facts of Hua Guofeng's personal background, he refused to be drawn into a discussion of the appointment itself. His half-smile and air of nonchalance disappeared. In its place was often a thoughtful, if not worried, expression.

We had long ago exhausted the book on etiquette and had gone back to a volume of short stories. As I opened the book, Da De suddenly brightened up and said to me, "Would you like to meet my girlfriend?"

"Have you got a girlfriend? Why haven't you told me before?" I exclaimed in surprise.

"I thought I should wait until we were engaged."

"Are you engaged now?"

"More or less. Her father still opposes our marriage. I suppose he thinks I'm too poor," Da De said, looking dejected.

"Is he someone important? Is he a senior official?"

"No, he is an ex-capitalist," Da De said, looking me straight in the eye as if he dared me to say something unpleasant. In fact, I was so surprised that I was quite speechless.

"Well, as you know, I didn't go to Beijing after all. They selected two people from Shanghai; both had connections with someone senior in Beijing. These two don't even know any foreign languages. I think the best course for me is to become an English teacher in a middle school, get married, and settle down in Shanghai. My mother thinks it's best too." Being bypassed seemed to have given him a jolt. I thought he was beginning to wonder whether he really had a future with the radicals.

"It would be nice to have you remain in Shanghai. You must love the girl very much to accept the handicap of being united with a capitalist family in marriage," I said.

"It isn't such a handicap. The Politburo has already passed a resolution to return with interest all private bank accounts frozen by the Red Guards ten years ago. Her father will recover quite a large sum of money. He has told the children that he will distribute his fortune to them as soon as he gets it back, and not wait until he dies. Of course, I'm not marrying her for her money, though her father seems to think so."

A few days later Da De brought his girlfriend to visit me. She was twenty-eight, two years older than Da De, not very bright or very beautiful, but quiet and self-assured, obviously in love with Da De, whose sharp intellect and vibrant personality must have seemed exciting to her. I congratulated her and asked when she was going to invite me to her wedding feast. She blushed and said, "That's rather uncertain. At the moment, my father refuses to give permission for me to marry Da De. It's not because he doesn't have money. It's because he is a Revolutionary."

Da De said quickly, "I'm going to become a teacher. The Foreign Language Institute is conducting a test to recruit English teachers for the middle schools. My mother has already put my name down for it."

In July, an earthquake registering 8 on the Richter scale hit Tangshan, an industrial and mining city in North China. There was no warning because the State Bureau of Seismology was embroiled in a new round of power struggles and its work was completely paralyzed. The city was 80 percent destroyed, and over a million inhabitants died or were severely wounded. The quake area included both Beijing and Tianjin, where, though casualties were not heavy, houses collapsed and thousands were rendered homeless. As the news of the earthquake spread all over the country, rumors of government ineptitude spread with it. At the same time, based upon intensive observation of animal and insect behavior, new and worse earthquakes in many parts of China were predicted. Frantically, the people in cities built temporary shelters, covering every inch of available space with makeshift huts of every shade and description. Everybody lived in a state of hysteria while waiting helplessly for disaster. In Shanghai, the Residents' Committee organized earthquake drills, and everybody was told to sleep with their doors open. There were false alarms when I stood with the Zhus in the garden in my pajamas waiting for earthquakes that never came. It was while the nation was thus preoccupied that Mao Zedong died in September.

Da De had, in the meantime, passed the test for middle school English teachers and had been assigned to teach twelve-year-olds in a school not far from where I lived. After the excitement of being a Red Guard and a Revolutionary, Da De found his new life tedious and dull. Although our regular lessons had ceased, he continued to drop in for a chat. He found in me a willing listener, and he knew that since I knew no one of political consequence, his words would not get back to Party men who mattered to him politically. Soon after Mao died he came to see me.

That afternoon, a memorial meeting for Mao was held at Tiananmen Square, attended by half a million representatives of workers, peasants, and soldiers. From the platform Hua Guofeng, in his capacity as the first vice-chairman of the Central Committee of the Chinese Communist Party, read the memorial speech. Beside him were Vice-Chairman Wang Hongwen in military uniform and Jiang Qing in dramatic black mourning clothes that covered her from head to toe. Our Residents' Committee organized people to view the proceedings at the homes of those with television sets. I was told to join the Zhus downstairs.

After the TV program from Beijing, we watched the Shanghai memorial meeting for Mao conducted by Ma Tianshui, who was a deputy of Zhang Chunqiao, the official head of the Shanghai Revolutionary Committee. Before the Cultural Revolution, Ma was a junior vice-mayor of Shanghai. He joined the radicals after the so-called January Revolution when the Red Guards and the Revolutionaries toppled the old Shanghai municipal government and Party Secretariat. Over the years, Ma Tianshui became a trusted servant of the radical leaders, taking over the day-to-day administration of Shanghai while Zhang Chunqiao remained in Beijing. The Shanghai memorial meeting was held at the People's Square and timed to follow the Beijing meeting.

Mrs. Zhu's television set was tiny, but she turned up the sound so that everybody in the room could at least hear the speeches. Normally, according to Communist Party tradition, Ma Tianshui's speech should have been similar to the speech given by Hua Guofeng, if not a complete repetition word by word. Therefore, I was surprised to notice that Ma Tianshui's speech differed from the one made by Hua Guofeng in two important aspects. First, Ma said, "We must carry on with Chairman Mao's already decided policy," while Hua Guofeng made no mention of any "already decided policy." Second, Hua Guofeng quoted a well-known statement Mao had made during the Cultural Revolution: "We want Marxism, not revisionism. We want unity, not dissension. We want to be open and aboveboard, not scheming and intriguing." Ma Tianshui had not mentioned it.

When the program was over, I thanked Mrs. Zhu and went upstairs. Soon afterwards, Da De came. He had watched the TV program at his school.

"Why didn't Ma Tianshui make a speech exactly the same as Chairman Hua's?" I asked him. "What did Ma Tianshui mean by 'already decided policy'?"

"The 'already decided policy' is for Comrade Jiang Qing to become Chairman Mao's successor, of course," Da De said.

"Do you mean to say that Chairman Mao decided that before he died?"

He shrugged his shoulders.

"If Chairman Mao wanted his wife to succeed him, why did he give Hua Guofeng the note that said, 'With you in charge, my mind is at ease'?" I asked him.

"Did any of us actually see the note?"

"It was reproduced in the newspaper," I reminded him.

"Can you say for sure it was written by Chairman Mao? Can you say for sure there are no other notes?" Da De asked me.

"It can't be a forgery, surely," I said, remembering the hard-to-decipher script, obviously written by a shaky hand.

"Towards the end of his life Chairman Mao lost the power of speech. He scribbled many notes, you know," Da De said.

"Goodness! So nothing is really settled," I exclaimed.

"Thanks to my future father-in-law's insistence that I cease to be a Revolutionary, I am out of all of it," Da De said.

"I have been told you are a captain in the militia. Are you still with that organization?" I asked him.

Da De was surprised by my question. For a moment I thought he was going to deny it. But he quickly recovered and said with an embarrassed smirk, "I suppose the Zhus told you. As a teacher, I'm now an intellectual. I don't qualify for the militia anymore."

"How did you qualify when you were an unemployed youth?"

"Well, I wasn't exactly an unemployed youth."

"You told me you were."

"It was a lie. I was told to lie to you."

"Did you have a job with a government organization?"

"Sort of. I was only a messenger. Temporary messenger, you might call it. Didn't you once tell me that unimportant people in unimportant jobs are often called small potatoes? Well, I was just a very small potato."

"Were you a small potato with the group dealing with the case of the so-called conspiracy of foreign firms and government departments?"

He nodded.

"Did you really believe there was a conspiracy?"

"At first." Da De looked at me beseechingly and said, "Don't you understand? I was told so by people I trusted. They claimed they had evidence against you and the foreign companies. But as time went on and I got to know you, I realized the whole thing was really a plot. You became a victim of the power struggle within the Communist Party, like so many other people, including me. I missed going to college and wasted all these years of my life. I became a sort of tool of those who had power over me."

"Now you are out of it all. The case is shelved and you have become a teacher."

"Correct."

"Did they let you go with good grace? Were they not annoyed that you wanted to marry a girl from a capitalist family?"

Da De laughed and said, "You haven't a clue what those people are like. They are only too glad that they don't have to find a job for me. My usefulness is over. They were pleased to get rid of me. And some of them actually envy me because I am marrying a girl with the prospect of getting a large sum of money. Why do you think people want to get involved in political struggles? To get better jobs, of course. And better jobs mean better living conditions and more pay. There is no way one can get ahead in China except through taking part in political struggles."

"Please tell me how my daughter died and who killed her. Did they do it for money?" I tried to keep bitterness out of my voice.

He hesitated for a moment and then said, "Haven't you been told that she committed suicide?"

"I don't believe it. Do you think I should believe it?"

"Her death was not intended. They overdid it, I was told. It was really an accident," Da De said. After a few minutes, he added, "I'm sorry. Please believe me, I'm terribly sorry it happened."

"Do you mean to say the men who abducted her weren't ordered to kill her but they did? Isn't that what you are saying?"

Da De nodded.

"Why was she abducted?"

Da De was reluctant to tell me at first. But after a long hesitation, he said, "It's the usual formula. Someone thought she should be made to denounce you since you were so stubborn at the detention house and refused to confess."

"What has happened to her murderers?"

"They are around."

"Are they in senior government positions?"

"I can't tell you any more. I have already said too much."

"I'm going to write a petition to the People's Court to request an investigation of my daughter's death. I want those men brought to justice."

"It's no use. They will be protected. You'll be ignored. It's really worse than useless. If you should write a petition now, they would know you do not believe the official version of suicide," he told me.

"Would they suspect you of having told me things you shouldn't?"

"They might."

"I think you should stop coming to see me."

"Yes, you are right. Perhaps I should not come anymore now that . . ." Da De did not finish his sentence, but I knew what he was thinking about. Hitherto he had come to see me as a part of his job. Once the case was shelved, he really should have stopped coming.

"I have several eggs. Will you stay for supper? I could make some scrambled eggs."

"I would like to stay, thank you very much," Da De said.

We had supper together. After helping me with the washing up, Da De said goodbye. I took 400 yuan from the drawer and said, "Da De, it has been a pleasure knowing you. You are a very intelligent young man. I hope you will have a happy life. This is my wedding present for you. Perhaps you can buy something useful with it." I handed him the money.

He didn't say a word, obviously overcome with emotion. After standing there for a moment, he accepted the money from me and left.

17

Rehabilitation

For so many years I had waited for Mao to die. When I was in prison, I was desperate enough to pray for it to happen. Now that he had really died, I did not know how to proceed. The prospect of having the men responsible for my daughter's death brought to justice was just as remote as ever.

While I watched the political scene closely, I resumed regular English lessons for my disabled girl student, who came every other day in the mornings. Crippled from childhood by poliomyelitis, she had been barred from regular schools but had learned to read and write from her mother, who was a nurse in a large hospital. After our lessons, she would thank me politely, pick up her crutches, and slowly make her way down the stairs and out into the street to return home on foot.

As I watched her struggling with her disability, I could not help thinking of the irony of life in China. The misfortune of her illness had insulated her from the mainstream of Chinese life and protected her from the political experiments of Mao Zedong. But healthy and normal young people, including my daughter, were led by the Great Helmsman on a twisted road of frustration and anguish as they struggled to become a part of Mao's socialist new society. Scores of them like my daughter had died, while others, including ex–Red Guards like Da De, had been victimized. Being disabled, my student did not go to school and was bypassed in the agonizing search for China's destiny. Consequently she was mercifully spared.

My student hoped to become an English teacher at a secondary school, as Da De had done, to earn a living for herself.

"I can't depend on my mother all my life. She'll retire soon. My teacher's salary would be a great help to supplement her pension," she said to me when she asked me to help her prepare for the teacher's examination.

Teaching her became my main occupation. But I was watching and waiting for an opportunity to petition the People's Government to investigate the death of my daughter. I had long ago made a draft of the petition I wanted to send and had written it in the language of socialist China. Since then I had looked at it many times, changing a word here and adding a sentence there. The question was when and to which organization I should submit the petition.

On the morning of October 8, I awoke at my usual hour of six o'clock. I opened the door to the balcony and saw that it was a fine, crisp autumn morning with a few tufts of white cloud floating in the blue sky. Looking down, I saw my disabled student standing outside the front gate. When she saw me, she gestured for me to come down.

Quietly I went down the stairs, walked to the front gate, and opened it. My student's visit to me at this early hour was most unusual. I thought it best not to disturb the Zhus. When I stepped outside, she came close to me and whispered, "I've been waiting for you. I don't want the Zhus to know I'm here, so I didn't knock on the door. My brother in the militia was called suddenly for emergency muster last night. There is going to be a war. I thought I should warn you to stay at home."

I looked up and down the street and saw that it was deserted. I asked her, "War? War with whom?"

"I don't know. Last night several men came and told my brother to go with them immediately. They told my mother that the militia had been put on alert. We are not supposed to tell this to anyone. But my mother and I thought I ought to come and warn you, as you are alone."

I thanked her and watched her hobble away before returning to my apartment.

The news brought by my student was really extraordinary, I thought. I could not imagine any country attacking China or China initiating an armed conflict against any country at this time. Yet she had told me that the militia had been put on alert.

I had a Shanghai-made transistor radio. Sometimes at night when the weather was good, I could get international news bulletins from either the BBC or the Voice of America if I pressed my ear right against the set and listened carefully. I took the radio to the bathroom, closed the window and door, flushed the toilet to cover the initial noise of the shortwave, and switched on the set. Apart from static, I could not get anything at all. When A-yi came, I questioned her about conditions at the market. She made her usual complaint about shortages. I tuned the radio to the local station, hoping that if there was an announcement I would not miss it. Then I took out my notebook and spent the morning copying down and reciting Tang dynasty poems, a wonderful occupation, I had found, to take myself away from my immediate surroundings.

The day passed uneventfully. After supper, I heard Mrs. Zhu calling me in the garden. When I went to the balcony, she told me that the Residents' Committee had called a meeting; we were to go over immediately. I hastily picked up my stool and joined her to walk across the street.

The room was packed, and the atmosphere was rather tense. It was so unusual for the Residents' Committee to call a meeting at night that people sensed something extraordinary had happened. Everyone waited expectantly for enlightenment. There was none of the usual whispering and yawning; even the smokers were refraining from lighting their cigarettes.

After everybody had arrived, a middle-aged official of the District Party Committee got up and read a resolution passed by the Politburo. The gist of it was that "revolutionary action" had been taken on October 6 by the 8341 Regiment stationed at Zhongnanhai (the Central South Sea, former winter palace of the Manchu emperors, at present homes and offices of the Party Politburo members) to arrest Jiang Qing and her three close associates, known collectively as "the Gang of Four." The document said the decision to take action had been made by the acting chairman of the Central Committee, Hua Guofeng, with the agreement of the defense minister and senior statesman of the Communist Party, Ye Jianying. The arrest followed a Politburo meeting at which the decision had been approved unanimously, in order to preserve Party unity and prevent the disruption of the work of building socialism. The statement claimed that when Mao was alive he had already perceived the problem presented by the Gang of Four and had declared that it must be resolved. This part of the resolution seemed to me solely for the purpose of forestalling criticism that punitive action was taken against Mao's widow only twenty-six days after his death by men who had cooperated with her while Mao was alive. The wording of the document stopped just short of claiming that Hua Guofeng was carrying out Mao's orders when he arrested Mao's widow.

The resolution was not long. As soon as it was read, we were told that since it was late, discussions would take place next time. We could go home. There were no cheers, no boos. Nobody said a word. We trooped out of the room just as we had come in—with passive faces, heads slightly bowed to avoid unwittingly speaking with our eyes, moving slowly so as not to show excitement. We behaved as if we had no feelings one way or another because we were afraid. The news we had just heard was too startling, almost unbelievable. We were accustomed to sudden reverses of policy by the Party, but nothing like this had ever happened before. To play safe, it was best not to appear to react. Besides, Shanghai was in the hands of the radicals, as we all knew. Most of the local officials were their followers. Perhaps even the man who read the document to us was a Jiang Qing appointee. Shanghai people were wily; they did not wish to risk trouble by untimely laughter or cheers.

Mrs. Zhu and I walked home together in silence, each with her own thoughts. When we opened the front gate, we saw her militia son standing on the terrace.

"You are home already?" asked the mother.

"Yes, it's all over," answered the son.

I entered my part of the house and locked the door. As I walked up the stairs, I started to smile. By the time I entered my room, I was thanking God fervently. But I cautioned myself not to be overoptimistic. Obviously the arrest of the Gang of Four was the result of a power struggle within the Party leadership. It did not necessarily mean that Hua Guofeng was going to repudiate the policy of Mao. I very seriously doubted he knew any other way to govern China. Nevertheless I spent a restless night speculating on the future and composing petitions seeking my own rehabilitation and the investigation of my daughter's death.

Next morning, Mrs. Zhu told me that Lu Ying had called. "There is going to be a citywide parade in support of the Politburo resolution to arrest the Gang of Four. We are to assemble this afternoon at two o'clock at the Residents' Committee office to pick up flags and slogans," Mrs. Zhu informed me.

I had never taken part in a parade before. The very idea of marching in formation carrying little flags and shouting slogans was abhorrent to me. I resented being herded and used in such a manner; I considered it an infringement on my privacy, if not an attempt to compromise my personal dignity. Of course, I had been able to maintain such a lofty stance all these years simply because no one had asked me to take part in a parade. Now that I was told to join one, I suddenly found it difficult to put my objections into language others could understand. While I hesitated, wondering how best to refuse, Mrs. Zhu added rather impatiently, "You will come, of course. Everybody is joining in. No one wants to be taken for a supporter of the Gang of Four, you know."

"I don't think I can walk nonstop for several hours," I said rather lamely.

"We old ladies are required only to parade in our own district. It won't be for more than an hour, Lu Ying told me."

Wouldn't it be a great joke if the radicals in Shanghai who, Da De told me, "hated my guts" were to turn against the Gang of Four and denounce me because I refused to join a parade to demonstrate the Shanghai people's support for their arrest? The nimble-footed Party activists were very good at assuming new stances when the Party suddenly reversed its course. Many of them were known to hop right on the new bandwagon and become the guiding light for new directions, though of course there were some inevitable casualties. I realized I had no alternative. I had to take part in this parade, my very first and, I hoped, my last.

The Residents' Committee ladies must have worked very hard overnight to get the flags and slogans prepared. When I got to the committee premises at two o'clock, they were piled high on the table, ready for paraders to pick up. Lu Ying told me to line up with the ladies who generally sat in our corner. It was the shortest line and the quietest. Nearly all of us and our families had been victims of the Cultural Revolution. Perhaps we had more reason to rejoice than the retired workers, the members of their families, and the young people waiting for employment. But none of us was even smiling. We had been knocked about, kicked around, and told so often that we did not belong but were merely tolerated in the shining new society of socialism that we no longer felt a part of what went on around us. We knew that in the eyes of good Communists we were an ill omen and harbingers of dangerous ideas, so that we had to be consigned to permanent isolation. Even in a parade, we had to be organized in a formation of our own. However, under our seemingly wooden exterior of unconcern, there was in fact a heightened sense of alertness born of the instinct for self-preservation.

The parade started. Our contingent brought up the rear. As we passed through the door to go into the street, each of us accepted a paper slogan attached to a bamboo stick. Mine was a simple message saying, "Down with Jiang Qing." In the street, we halted for a moment to be addressed by a young activist. He told us that he would walk beside our group; whenever he shouted slogans from his sheet of paper, we were to repeat them after him. Then several young people with red banners, flags, drums, and gongs took up position at the head of the column. At a signal from the young activist, we started marching four abreast, shouting slogans after him. The contingent of workers and youths soon left us to join other paraders in the center of the city; we remained circling the area in which I lived.

We met a group similar to ours from a neighboring Residents' Committee. Otherwise we just walked through the quiet, shabby streets without attracting attention or creating a stir. Perhaps we did not have revolutionary charisma; our demonstration was definitely not a success. The young activist gave up on us after a little over an hour, and we were allowed to return to the empty Residents' Committee office. There we hastily laid down our slogans and fled home, not waiting for further orders.

"Did you know we were nearly in a civil war?" Mrs. Zhu asked me after we gained the seclusion of our garden and closed the front gate.

"Really? When?" I asked her.

"The militia was mobilized and issued weapons. They were to march to Beijing to rescue Jiang Qing. But news of a possible uprising leaked out. The regular army surrounded the city. They had to give up. My son told me it was touch and go."

"It's lucky he didn't have to fight," I said.

"Indeed. Wouldn't it have been tragic if our son had died for Jiang Qing after what we went through during the Cultural Revolution?" she said.

Soon afterwards I heard that the radical leaders in the city had been removed from office. Some people said they were taken into custody pending investigation; others said they were merely confined in a special place to write confessions that would be used against the Gang of Four at a public trial. Not long after these rumors, new leaders were appointed to head the Shanghai Revolutionary Committee and Party Secretariat. These men's fate during the Cultural Revolution had been very similar to that of Hua Guofeng. They had suffered denunciation by the Red Guards in the initial sweep but were soon reinstated and "came to the side of Chairman Mao's correct policy line." This phrase meant that they had confessed and denounced Liu Shaoqi and Deng Xiaoping. After that, they were given positions as senior officials and collaborated with the radical faction headed by Jiang Qing. Their appointment was symbolic of Hua Guofeng's brief four years in power, during which no real change of policy took place and radicals occupying official positions at the base level were not removed.

The Eleventh Party Congress was held in August 1977, while the entire country was engrossed in a campaign of denunciation against the Gang of Four. At this Party Congress, Hua Guofeng reached the zenith of his power. Not only was he elected chairman of the Party's Central Committee but he also became the chairman of the Party's Military Commission, the official commander in chief of China's armed forces. His portrait now hung side by side with that of Mao Zedong in public places. In the newspaper reports, he was referred to as "Wise Leader Chairman Hua" to differentiate him from the late "Great Leader." Clearly a new personality cult was in the making, carefully promoted by the remaining radicals in the Party and government, who saw in Hua Guofeng a possible protective shield for their survival.

The Party Congress reaffirmed that it would "hold high the

great red flag of Mao Zedong Thought," and Hua Guofeng pledged that he would carry out "all Chairman Mao's policies" and obey "all Chairman Mao's directives."

At the same time, the Party Congress named the commander of the 8341 Regiment responsible for the arrest of the Gang of Four, Wang Dongxing, a vice-chairman of the Central Committee. It was a reward for his contribution to Jiang Qing's downfall. It was said that the three men of the Gang were told to attend an urgent Politburo meeting and were arrested upon their arrival at the meeting hall. But Jiang Qing had refused to attend. Wang Dongxing had to go to her home and personally put the handcuffs on her.

Wang Dongxing was a longtime bodyguard of Mao. He was given command of the ten-thousand-man 8341 Regiment guarding Mao and other Politburo members living at Zhongnanhai because of his loyalty and devotion to Mao. It was said that his most outstanding service to Mao was bringing to his master's attention an exceptionally beautiful woman, Zhang Yufeng (Jade Phoenix), whom he placed on Mao's special train. She became Mao's concubine and was given the official title "secretary in charge of daily life."

Zhang Yufeng was the last of a succession of young females who had shared Mao's bed. The Chinese people knew but never dared to talk about the fact that their "Great Leader" was a womanizer. In his dotage, the self-styled successor of Marx and Lenin, and the symbol of progress and enlightenment, believed, as some Chinese emperors had believed, that sexual liaisons with young virgins enhanced longevity in an old man.

Hua Guofeng was not a strong ruler. Relatively junior in the echelons of power, and until recently almost unknown to the public and the Party rank and file, he had neither grass-roots support nor a group of trusted administrative assistants to place in key positions. Without such a power base he could not rule effectively.

During 1977, China was in effect split into pockets of power controlled by local military commanders and Revolutionaries who interpreted Mao Zedong Thought in their own way and ignored directives from Beijing. At the same time the country was paralyzed by economic stagnation. The people had lost confidence in the Party as they watched ten years of infighting and listened to the official denunciations of one leader after another.

The arrest of the Gang of Four was like the lifting of the tight lid of a boiling cauldron. Very quickly it overflowed. People with grievances came out to demand redress. There were demonstrations and protests by both individuals and groups. Crowds gathered outside government offices, sometimes all night long, waiting to be received by reluctant officials. Buildings were besieged. Angry young people exiled to the rural areas demanded the right to return to the cities. The walls of public buildings were covered with Big Character Posters relating personal tragedies and demanding justice. These were eagerly read by the people, who added large posters with stories of their own grievances.

At the second plenum of the Central Committee, Hua Guofeng made two concessions. He agreed to the demand made by Ye Jianying and other members of the old guard to rehabilitate Deng Xiaoping and appoint him a vice-premier. And he promised that the Party and government would review all cases of victims of the Cultural Revolution.

I made many trips and wrote many petitions to the People's Court, the Public Prosecutor's Office, and the Public Security Bureau. This activity lasted the whole of 1977. Though the junior officials appointed to receive the public and hear their petitions at the Prosecutor's Office listened with patience to my story, all they said to me each time was that I must write everything down and send in my report. There was no response from either the People's Court or the Public Security Bureau. In short, I was getting nowhere at all. The crowds I had met waiting outside those places fared no better than I did.

In March 1978, a man from the Public Security Bureau came to see me, accompanied by Lao Li from my local police station.

After they were seated, the middle-aged man in a faded blue Mao suit leaned forward, looked at me earnestly, and, with a frown on his brow, said, "I'm from the Public Security Bureau. You have sent many letters and petitions to both the Public Security Bureau and the Prosecutor's Office, haven't you?"

"Yes, I've sent a few petitions," I said.

"Not a few"—he shook his head—"a great many!" The frown on his brow deepened as he added, "Why did you have to write so often? Don't you trust the People's Government? Have you no patience at all?"

The man spoke to me irritably. Lao Li fixed his gaze on the floor. Neither of them touched the tea A-yi had brought them.

"It's over eleven years since I was wrongfully arrested, and it is over ten years since my daughter was murdered. I think I have been very patient. I don't mind telling you that while I trust the Communist Party and the People's Government, my confidence in some individual officials who claim to represent the government has been severely shaken by my experience during the Cultural Revolution," I said to him firmly.

"I have come here today to tell you to stop writing petitions. In due course your case will be reviewed, since it is the policy of the Party and government to review all cases of the Cultural Revolution."

"How much longer will I have to wait?" I asked him.

"Do you know how many cases we have to deal with in Shanghai? Ten thousand people died unnaturally in this city. Their deaths were all related directly or indirectly to the Gang of Four and their followers. Many times that number were imprisoned. Many are still detained. Our first priority must be to examine these cases immediately and to release the innocent people. Then we will examine the cases of those who are out of prison and are still living, like yourself. After that we will come to the cases of those who are dead, like your daughter. There are many people working very hard to clarify all the cases. You must wait patiently. We'll get to you and your daughter eventually."

What he said seemed reasonable. I had not realized the magnitude of the problem facing the officials charged with reviewing the cases.

"It's good of you to take time off to visit me today. I want to thank you and the government you represent. I must say your visit has somewhat restored my confidence. You are very different from the officials I have had to deal with during the past ten years."

"Of course I'm different. I've only recently been rehabilitated myself," the man said with a twist of his mouth that might have been a bitter smile.

"If you have experienced persecution yourself, you understand how I feel."

"Of course I understand. But when you think of your own losses and suffering, try to think of the losses and suffering of others too. Think of the Party leaders who fought and sacrificed for the Revolution all their lives, such as Liu Shaoqi, Peng Dehuai, He Long, . . . and many others who died in tragic circumstances. And think of cadres like myself who joined the Party during the War of Resistance against Japan and worked hard for the Party without any consideration of personal gain. Because I did not fall in with the wishes of the Gang of Four, I was accused of having an anti-Party attitude and put in jail. Do you know that Mrs. Liu Shaoqi has only recently been released from prison? You must try to see the whole situation and put your own problems in perspective," he told me.

I looked at this man seated in front of me and wondered what his true feeling for the Party was now. The cuffs of his faded blue cotton jacket were frayed, and his black cloth shoes were worn. His face was pale and thin. He had had a hard life; his appearance showed it. Dedicated lower-middle-ranking officials like this man were the foundation of the power of the Communist Party. When their faith in the Party was shaken, the Party could not govern effectively. No matter how correct or timely the policy decided upon by the Politburo in Beijing, its success or failure depended on officials like this man who implemented the policy.

"I'm grateful to you for coming. I shall not write any more petitions but will wait patiently for you to get in touch with me again," I told him.

The man seemed pleased that he had accomplished his mission. When the two took their leave, I followed them to the front gate and saw the man from the Public Security Bureau get on his old rusty bicycle and ride away.

I was reassured by the official's visit. It seemed my petitions had reached their destination and in due course I would be rehabilitated. At the same time, I also realized that I would be granted rehabilitation simply because the policy of the Party had changed. It had nothing to do with redressing injustice. In fact, in newspaper reports and in the documents concerning the review of cases, the word "justice" was never mentioned. When the Gang of Four was accused of committing crimes against the Party, the government, and the people, "crimes" referred not to their breaking the law but to their perverting the Party's policy to further their own ambition. In Communist China, there was no law independent of Party policy.

A few months later, in the summer of 1978, eleven years after my daughter had been killed by the Revolutionaries, three members of the Shanghai Film Studio called on me.

"We have come on behalf of the newly reestablished Party Secretariat of the film studio to offer you our condolences for the death of your daughter and our fellow worker Cheng Meiping," said the middle-aged man who introduced himself as the head of the personnel department.

The retired actress who had been Meiping's teacher at the film school took my hands in hers and with tears in her eyes said, "All of us were terribly sad. We want you to know that we feel deeply for you." The once famous actress, a graduate of Yanan's Lu Xun Art Institute, looked at me as if a camera were on hand to record the scene. Although I had not met her until that moment, I knew that she was the wife of the assistant director of the Shanghai Film Studio.

The third person, a young man, introduced himself and said, "I was Meiping's classmate at the film school. I have come on behalf of her former schoolfriends at the studio to express our sympathy."

I invited them to be seated, and A-yi brought them tea. The director of personnel said to me, "Wang Kun here is on the committee to review all the cases of the film studio. We have had twenty-nine cases of death. Many others, including some of our foremost artists, were denounced as counterrevolutionaries and imprisoned. There is a lot of work to be done to review all these cases."

"How did my daughter die? Who was responsible for her death? Do you know?" I asked all of them.

The young man named Wang Kun said, "We hope to get the cooperation of the Public Security Bureau to work on her case, because it involved people outside the film studio."

"How long do you think the investigation will take?" I asked him.

"We are working very hard. Government policy is very clear. We must clarify every case, and where a mistake was made we must correct it," Wang Kun said.

"Today we have come to convey to you the condolences of the

film studio and to tell you that we are concerned for you," the wife of the assistant director said to me. "If you have financial difficulty, you are entitled to assistance by the film studio."

I thought her offer of assistance so many years after my release from prison rather hypocritical, but I realized she had been instructed by the Party secretary to make it. I said politely, "Thank you very much. I have no difficulties at all." Then I addressed all three of them. "I hope it will not be too long before you will be able to bring the killer of my daughter to justice."

"The real culprit is the Gang of Four. We must direct our anger against them," said the personnel director in the tone of voice all Chinese bureaucrats used when they were embarrassed.

"That's true, of course. But the man who actually committed the murder must be brought to justice," I said.

"According to our records, your daughter committed suicide. Until we find evidence to the contrary, we must not assume her death was due to any other cause." The personnel director obviously did not want to hear me say my daughter was "murdered."

Perhaps Wang Kun saw that I was getting angry, for he said quickly, "I would like to come and talk to you again very soon. When would it be convenient?"

"Any afternoon would be all right," I told him.

They got up to leave. The wife of the assistant director again expressed her sadness at my daughter's death. Either her emotion was genuine, or she was an extremely good actress; she made me cry with her.

Wang Kun came to see me several times. Gradually I came to realize he was trying to prepare me to accept the rehabilitation document the film studio had already drafted. From my point of view, this document was not satisfactory because it failed to state clearly how my daughter had died. While it no longer insisted on the verdict of suicide, it merely said that she "died as a result of persecution." I was sure someone somewhere was trying to protect my daughter's murderer. I fought for the clarification of this point with the film studio to no avail. Wang Kun merely told me that politics was a complicated matter and the time was not yet ripe to get to the bottom of many things.

While I was still arguing with the Shanghai Film Studio, representatives of the Public Security Bureau called on me again in October 1978. There were three of them, including the man who had come with Lao Li to tell me to stop writing petitions.

Pointing to his associates. a short man of about fifty and a young woman, he said to me, "This is Director Han, and this is Xiao Li."

"We have come on behalf of the People's Government to apologize to you for the wrongful arrest and imprisonment you suffered during the Cultural Revolution. We also wish to extend you our condolences for the death of your daughter as a result of persecution," said Director Han in an official manner.

I invited them to be seated. Xiao Li took out her notebook to transcribe our conversation, as all official visits had to be put on record.

"I appreciate your coming today. There is no need to apologize. I feel no resentment against the People's Government. It was obvious to me that followers of the Gang of Four usurped the power of the government and put many innocent people, including myself, in prison. What I'm really concerned with is the fact that those responsible for my daughter's death have not been brought to justice," I said.

"You must trust the People's Government and the Security Bureau," the first man said.

"We have come today mainly to discuss your own rehabilitation," Director Han said. "We have read the record of your interrogations at the Number One Detention House. You were very brave when you defended the late chairman of the People's Republic, Liu Shaoqi. You spoke up for him when even veteran Party officials were too timid and afraid to speak up. You will be pleased to know that very soon Chairman Liu Shaoqi's name will be completely cleared by a Politburo resolution."

"I'm very glad the power to control the affairs of our country has once again returned to leaders who will pursue the correct line of Mao Zedong Thought," I said diplomatically.

The first man took a sheet of paper from his bag and laid it on the table. "This is the draft of your rehabilitation document. We would like to hear your opinion and suggestions before making it official."

The document gave my name, age, and other particulars before stating that my arrest on September 27, 1966, and subsequent detention was a mistake. Investigation by the committee charged with reviewing all cases of the Cultural Revolution had found me not guilty of any crime. Therefore, I must be rehabilitated according to the policy of the People's Government. I told them that I found the wording satisfactory.

"This document will be made official and given to the Residents' Committee. It will be read at one of their general meetings," Director Han said.

"Soon you will hear from the committee in charge of frozen bank accounts. Your deposits will be returned to you with interest," said the first man.

"I'll just accept the original sum. Since the country is having economic difficulties, I would rather not accept the additional interest," I told them.

"You will have to accept. It's government policy," Director Han said. Then he smiled and changed the subject. "Do you know I was rehabilitated and reinstated to my old job only a few months ago? I was imprisoned for three years. I didn't get the special food you were given in the Number One Detention House, you know."

"As I told you before, I feel no resentment about what happened to me. During the six and a half years I was at the Number One Detention House I had much time to study and to think. I have learned a great deal. But I do feel deeply disappointed that greater efforts have not been made by the Public Security Bureau to resolve the crime committed against my daughter and to bring the murderer to justice."

I addressed the above remarks directly to Director Han. But he refused to be drawn into a discussion of my daughter's case. He went on, "You were given very special consideration at the detention house, you know. The special food, the medical treatment, etc. If you had remained outside, perhaps you wouldn't have survived the Cultural Revolution."

It was really incredible, I thought, that this man could be trying to make me say I was grateful to the Party and the People's Government for putting me in prison. All the bureaucrats of the Party seemed to have an insatiable appetite for hearing words of gratitude from the people, even when they knew those words could not have been sincere. It was as if they needed reassurance that even when things went very wrong there was something good about the system after all. Perhaps it would have been diplomatic if I had spoken as he hoped and agreed with him. But I had been too wounded by my suffering and by the death of my daughter to go that far. I remained silent.

For an awkward moment, he waited for me to speak. Finally they took their leave.

I accompanied them to the front gate. As I opened it, I said to them all, "I would like to thank you again for coming today. I will wait for you to notify me when my rehabilitation document is finalized. And I would like to repeat my request that those responsible for my daughter's death be brought to justice."

In November 1978, twelve years and two months after my arrest, I was officially rehabilitated and declared a victim of wrongful arrest and persecution. The rehabilitation document was read at a meeting of the Residents' Committee. Then I was given back my bank deposits. Soon after that, the Shanghai Film Studio held a series of memorial meetings for the twenty-nine members of their staff who had died from persecution. Except for my daughter, the others were nearly all old artists who had known Jiang Qing during the thirties when she was a struggling actress in Shanghai. Among them were film directors who had refused to cast Jiang Qing in parts she coveted, actresses more talented and successful than she, and men with whom she had had love affairs.

The memorial meeting for Meiping, held at Longhua Crematorium, was attended by over two hundred of her friends and fellow artists, as well as representatives from the Shanghai Cultural Affairs Department and the Bureau of Motion Pictures. These two organizations and the film studio also sent wreaths in the name of the directors and the organizations. Kong and other schoolfriends of Meiping's decorated the hall. Although the growing of fresh flowers had only recently been revived in the rural areas around Shanghai, they managed to get enough to fill the front part of the hall, where an enlarged photograph of Meiping in a heavy black frame was placed. The rest of the hall was filled with evergreens and wreaths made of paper flowers.

The ceremony was simple and dignified. Meiping's teacher, the wife of the assistant director of the film studio, made the memorial speech, in which she recounted the story of Meiping's short life of twenty-four years, emphasizing the fact that Mei-ping had received many citations for outstanding achievement and service to other people. The veteran actress delivered the speech with feeling and sincerity, and she moved the audience to tears. The sound of sobbing could be heard throughout the proceedings, and at times it drowned the mourning music played on a tape in the background. At the end of her speech, led by the officials, everybody came up to bow to Meiping's photograph and to shake hands with me to express personal regret at Meiping's death.

Soon it was all over. Kong accompanied me home in the same car the film studio had sent to pick me up. Even as we were leaving, the organization that was to use the hall after us was already there unloading wreaths from a truck. Kong told me that all the auditoriums at the crematorium had been booked well into 1980. To accommodate as many memorial meetings as possible in the course of one day, two hours were allowed for each organization using the hall. In the following year, with more and more cases being clarified and more and more de-ceased being rehabilitated, it became necessary to combine me-morial meetings for several members of the same organization.

Kong carried Meiping's photograph upstairs into my room and took his leave. A-yi brought me a cup of tea. I told her to go home, as I wanted to be alone.

That night, I could not sleep. Lying in the darkened room, I remembered the years that had gone by, and I saw my daughter in various stages of her growth from a chubby-cheeked baby in Canberra, Australia, to a beautiful young woman in Shanghai. I felt defeated because I could do nothing to overcome the obstacles that prevented the complete clarification of her case. I blamed myself for her death because I had brought her back to Shanghai from Hong Kong in 1949. How could I have failed to see the true nature of the Communist regime when I had read so many books on the Soviet Union under Stalin? I asked myself.

Next morning, the newspaper printed a report of the memo-rial meetings of the film studio. Meiping was listed among the dead artists. The news of my own rehabilitation also spread as a result. During the following month of December and over the New Year holiday period, I had many visitors. Relatives who had kept their distance and avoided my daughter and me when our lives were under a cloud now claimed me as their dearest and nearest. They told me that they had worried about me and cried for Meiping. Some of them offered to live with me and take care of me, while others nominated their children for me to adopt so that I would not be childless. None of them attempted to explain why they had not shown us sympathy or given us help when we needed it. They felt no remorse for neglecting us, partly because some of them had had difficulties of their own and partly because they had behaved in exactly the same manner as millions of other Chinese living under the shadow of Mao Zedong. They thought I would understand.

Even minus a large sum that had somehow got lost after the Red Guards took my money away, the money returned to me from bank deposits was more than I could possibly use. Through the Party secretary of the Residents' Committee I learned that the Federation of Women had started a program to rebuild nursery schools and day-care centers that had been destroyed by the Red Guards. To help young working couples with small children seemed a worthy cause. I gave the Party secretary a donation of 60,000 yuan (about $40,000 at the exchange rate of 1978). And I distributed cash gifts to my husband's and my own relatives, the young people who had helped me after my release from prison, my old servants, and widows of former Shell staff members who had died since the Cultural Revolution. To absorb the large amount of cash that had been returned to the people, the government released on the market such household appliances as refrigerators and television sets imported from Japan, and organized a travel agency to offer sightseeing trips to scenic spots. The prices charged were very high. For instance, a twenty-inch Hitachi television set was priced at over 2,000 yuan. But the Shanghai people, starved for consumer goods, eagerly bought them. As for those who had large sums returned, they went on a spending spree.

On New Year's Day, 1979, China and the United States established diplomatic relations. This development triggered a terrific vogue for studying English. When I went to the public park to join a class for *taijiquan* exercise in the mornings, I saw young people on the benches, on the lawn, and in the pavilions reading English textbooks or spelling English words aloud. The daily English lessons broadcast by the Voice of America became very popular. The young people boldly purchased powerful radio sets and tuned in. The fact that they also listened to the *News Bulletin in Special English* following the lessons was incidental. As the government took no action to stop this trend, even people not learning English began to listen openly to the Voice of America broadcasts. To listen to foreign broadcasts had always been taboo in Communist China. Those of us who listened surreptitiously never dared to talk about what we heard, even before the Cultural Revolution. Now people not only listened to the Voice of America but discussed what they heard openly. In the schools, English became the first foreign language taught to the students. Even eight-year-olds were given English lessons. Now when I met the schoolchildren who used to yell, "Spy, imperialist spy!" at me, I was greeted with "good morning" or "good afternoon."

Early in the New Year, the Party secretary of the English Department of the Foreign Language Institute called on me to offer me a job as a teacher of English.

"I've come to invite you to join our department. There is now a great need to teach our young people foreign languages, especially English. We are expanding the department and hiring new teachers," he declared with a big smile, happy in the knowledge that he and his department had suddenly acquired prominence.

I had already heard that the former Shell doctor had been invited to teach English at the Foreign Language Institute. But I had no intention of getting myself involved and prejudicing my plan of eventual departure from Shanghai. Unemployed, I had a much better chance of getting a passport, for no one would be able to say I was needed for some kind of work and use it as an excuse to deny my application to go abroad. Since I was going to refuse his offer, I thought I should be extra polite to put him in a good mood. "I'm honored by your visit," I said. "You are the Party secretary of the department, with a lot of responsibility, yet you have taken the time to come to see me yourself rather than sending a deputy. I'm indeed most honored. But I'm afraid I am not well enough to take on a full-time job. I have had rather an unusual experience and a serious operation."

"I know all about that," he said. "I have already checked with the Public Security Bureau."

"Since you have been in touch with the Public Security Bureau, you know I have only recently been rehabilitated. I need time to get my personal affairs in order," I told him.

"Don't you want to serve the people?" he asked.

"To serve the people" was perhaps the most publicized slogan of the Chinese Communist Party. It was a phrase taken from an essay Mao Zedong wrote in 1944 to commemorate the death of a Party member, Zhang Side. Whenever the Party wanted a man to do something he did not want to do, the official would ask, "Don't you want to serve the people?"

It was impossible for me to say that I didn't want to serve the people. I thought a compromise was in order. "Would you agree to my teaching a few students here at my home?"

"You mean teaching them individually?"

"Yes."

"I'm afraid we've never had that kind of arrangement before. How are we to calculate your pay if you do not come to teach at the institute?"

"I would be quite happy to do it without pay. To serve the people, as you have said."

After thinking over my proposal for a few moments, he said, "I'll have to discuss your suggestion with my colleagues. I will let you know what we have decided."

He took his leave.

I never heard from him again. By offering an alternative he could not accept, I put the ball in his court and saved his face. Instead of my refusing him, he was refusing me. This was the only way to deal with people who hated to be refused.

The newly opened United States consulate general was located on Huaihai Road, a few blocks from the small park where I did my daily *taijiquan* exercise. On my way to and from the park in the early hours of the morning, I would see people in long lines outside the gate waiting patiently to apply for visas. And my students would bring me news of relatives and friends being given passports to leave the country. The major subject of discussion among young people was no longer how many lovers Jiang Qing had or how many innocent people had been killed during the Cultural Revolution but which Politburo or Central Committee member was sending his sons and daughters to America on the student exchange program. Now that China was welcoming visitors from abroad, overseas Chinese flocked into China to visit their relatives. They brought consumer goods with them as presents and offered to help with the education of family members who had missed going to college because of the Cultural Revolution. To go abroad, especially to go to the United States, became the most prestigious thing to do for young and old alike.

The political situation in China in 1979 was also good. Although Hua Guofeng continued to be the head of both the Party and the government, Deng Xiaoping was expanding his power and more collaborators of the Gang of Four were being ousted from Party leadership. There was an atmosphere of relaxation and hope in the country, reminiscent of the middle fifties, before Mao Zedong clamped down on the intellectuals with the Anti-Rightist Campaign.

I thought I must somehow get a passport before the Party tightened up again. The question was what reason I should give the authorities for my proposed journey abroad. It had to be good enough to ensure approval, because a refusal recorded in my dossier would prejudice future applications.

One night when I tuned in to the Voice of America's program of international news, I learned that China was applying to the United States for most-favored-nation status. Tucked away somewhere in a corner of my mind was a news item I once saw to the effect that the United States Congress would deny most-favored-nation status to countries that hindered family reunion. This was aimed at the Soviet Union, where a large number of Russian Jews were waiting to go to Israel. But I knew the Chinese Communist Party would take note of this condition. After I had switched off the radio, I thanked God that on this night the voice of the announcer had come through the atmosphere strong and clear so that I did not miss hearing the news. It was something unlikely to be reported in the Chinese press.

I had two sisters in the United States of America. When the Communist army took over China, they were students in American universities. Subsequently they married and settled in the United States. The younger of the two sisters was only a small child when I left home in 1935 to go to England. We had not seen each other for over forty years. My other sister, Helen, had accompanied her husband to Shanghai for a short visit a couple of years ago. Since then, I had maintained a sporadic correspondence with her. Now I sat down immediately and wrote her a letter requesting her to send me an invitation to visit both my sisters in California for "family reunion." Helen seemed to understand the situation perfectly. She quickly sent me a suitably worded letter signed by both sisters.

Early in March, when the warm current from the South Pacific began to reach Shanghai and the moisture in the wind reawakened the frozen sycamore trees lining the streets, I walked hopefully to the Xujiahui District Public Security Bureau, where the special office for passport and travel applications was situated. When I reached my destination, I realized that I should have come an hour earlier.

Though it was only a quarter to seven and the office did not open until eight o'clock, there was already a large crowd waiting. By the time the iron gate was opened at half past seven, I found myself in the first third of a long line that wound its way around the block. Slowly the line moved forward as the people were let into the waiting room. I was squeezed behind a young woman just inside the door. The rest of the line waited outside in the courtyard. The large waiting room was packed with people sitting tightly against each other on the narrow benches and standing next to each other in the aisles. Everybody was good-natured. When the door to the office opened at eight, there was no jostling for position. People went in one by one. Some came out with a smile and a blank form in hand. Others came out empty-handed and did not look so happy. After some time, the young woman ahead of me got a seat. As she moved on, I sat down beside her.

"Are you hoping to go abroad?" she whispered to me.

I nodded.

"Which country?" she asked.

"The United States," I said under my breath.

Her face lit up with a grin. "That's where I'm going too. To join my father, whom I have never seen. He left in 1949, a month before I was born."

"Has he sent for you?"

"Yes, he has a restaurant, and he said that he wanted to help me if I was willing to work for him."

"Have you a job in Shanghai?" I asked her.

"No, I'm waiting for employment. During the Cultural Revolution we had a hard time because my mother had not divorced my father. The Red Guards said my mother was an American spy. She died at the Cadre School. But recently she was rehabilitated," she said with tears in her eyes.

"I hope you'll be happy in the United States," I said.

"I'm rather scared because I'm not sure my stepmother will like me. Do you think the government will let me go?" she asked anxiously.

"Oh, yes. I think you'll have no difficulty."

"Have you been to the United States?"

"Yes, a long time ago."

"What do you think I should do to prepare myself for living there?"

"Study English, if you can find a teacher."

She nodded and said, "I'm working hard at it now."

As we chatted, we were moving towards the benches nearer to the door of the inner room. After more waiting, the young woman ahead of me went in. She wasn't there very long. When she came out, she was smiling. Bending down, she whispered, "I got it," and showed me the application form in her hand.

"Next!" a voice called from the room. I went in.

A rather stout middle-aged woman was seated behind a desk. There was a chair facing her, and a blank pad and a pencil on the desk. Otherwise the room was bare. She looked to be in an ill temper. It must have been a tedious way to spend a fine morning, interviewing masses of people eager to leave the country under one pretext or another.

"What is it?" she barked at me.

I sat down on the chair facing her and said, "I would like to make an application for a trip to the United States of America to visit my sisters, one of whom I have not seen for forty-four years."

"Why do you want to visit them?" she said.

"Family reunion. We are getting on in years. We would like to have a family reunion."

"Can't they come to Shanghai to see you? Many visitors are coming from the United States," she said.

"One of my sisters did come with her husband. But the younger sister I haven't seen for forty-four years is too busy. She can't spare the time to come."

"Which is your unit?" she asked.

"I have no unit," I said. "I'm not working."

"Which was your unit when you were working?"

"I used to work for a foreign firm before the Cultural Revolution."

"What's your name? What's the name of the foreign firm?"

I told her, and she wrote them down on the pad.

"During the Cultural Revolution I suffered wrongful arrest, but I am now rehabilitated," I told her.

She wrinkled her brow and stared at me, thinking. I knew she was in a quandary as to how best to deal with me; naturally she did not want to make a mistake. To prevent her from refusing, which would have been final and irrevocable, I said quickly, "I'm known to the senior authority at the Public Security Bureau. Director Han and other officials of the bureau have been to my home. Why don't you just let me make the application and leave it to them to approve or reject according to the policy of the government?"

After a moment's consideration, she said, "All right, I'll give you the application form. When you hand it in, you must present the required documents."

"I have a letter of invitation from my sisters," I told her.

"Bring your rehabilitation paper too and your resident's book," she said, continuing to stare at me. Her tone of voice had softened considerably since I mentioned Director Han. She must have been wondering how I knew her superior and whether she had not treated me too harshly. With her eyes fixed on my face, she pulled open one of the drawers, took out a form, and handed it to me.

I thanked her and left the room. In the waiting room, everybody watched me eagerly to find out whether I had been given a form. Their concern was later explained to me by one of my students who had been through the same experience. It seemed only a limited number of forms were given out each day. The more people coming out of the interview with forms, the fewer forms left for those waiting.

When I got home, to my surprise, I found the woman had given me an application for a travel document to Hong Kong by mistake. I had to go back to change it for a passport application. I quickly walked back. The waiting crowd kindly allowed me to go to the head of the line after I explained my problem.

The woman was rather disconcerted when I told her that she had given me the wrong form. But she changed it for me without saying anything.

Next morning I carefully filled out the application and handed it in with the required documents. I did not expect to hear from the Public Security Bureau for at least a year, the usual length of time for processing a passport application during 1979. But I also knew cases of people who had to wait several years just for permission to go to Hong Kong, before the Cultural Revolution. In any case, I was fortunate; the woman official did not refuse to give me the application form. If she had refused, there was absolutely nothing I could have done except to give up the whole idea of applying. Although her position in the bureaucratic structure could not have been very senior, the power she was allowed to exercise seemed frighteningly enormous.

Farewell to Shanghai

A FEW DAYS AFTER I had handed in my passport application, A-yi brought me an official-looking letter. It was from the "Bureau for Sorting Looted Goods," which I thought was a unique title for a government department. The letter invited me to go for an interview. Mrs. Zhu and her husband had received a similar call. She was given back a few pieces of costume jewelry, and her husband was told to go to a warehouse and search through the dusty volumes stored there to see if he could find some of his books. After being in the airless warehouse for over ten years, the books were rotting with mildew. When he picked up a volume, it fell apart in his hand and exuded a strong, unhealthy odor. He returned to the Bureau for Sorting Looted Goods empty-handed and agreed to sign a pledge relinquishing all claims to his looted property. Mrs. Zhu likewise had to sign a receipt for the costume jewelry. It listed "three rings, one brooch, etc." without identifying them as costume jewelry. When she asked the man for her rings of real diamonds and jade, he asked her to produce evidence to prove she actually had them when the Red Guards looted her home.

It seemed the things taken from the looted homes had not

been securely stored away. In the course of the ten years of the Cultural Revolution, many people must have had access to them. Now that the government had decreed that looted goods should be returned to their owners, the local officials had to make a show of doing so. Thus they organized this bureau to put on an act and invited us to take part. When a sufficient number of receipts for worthless objects had been collected and enough pledges made to relinquish claims, the work of returning looted goods to their rightful owners could be considered accomplished successfully.

While I was not hopeful that I would recover anything of value, I could not very well ignore a letter from a government department. Therefore I went at the time and on the day specified. I was received by a woman official who asked me right away if I would be interested in going to a warehouse to look for books and records.

"I'm pretty certain all my books were burned. As for records, it's possible a few were saved, but I'm not interested in getting them back. I'll sign a paper to that effect," I told her.

"I have some really good news for you," she said, laying emphasis on "good news" and "you."

After rummaging through the files on her desk, she took out a sheet of paper and said to me, "Some of your porcelain pieces have been located because they were in boxes bearing your name. These pieces are at a warehouse. However, the Shanghai Museum is interested in purchasing fifteen pieces from you. These fifteen pieces are at the museum. You can go to the warehouse and show the man in charge this letter of authorization."

She handed me a document identifying me as the owner of the pieces of porcelain contained in boxes bearing my name.

"What about the pieces displayed in my house and not put away in boxes when the Red Guards came on August 30, 1966?" I asked her.

"If there was no identification, it would be very difficult to find them."

"What about my white jade collection?"

"Items made of precious stones or semiprecious stones were put away with the jewelry. We are still trying to locate them," she said rather impatiently. I thought she was displeased that I had mentioned them. She was probably thinking that I should be satisfied that my porcelain pieces had been found.

"I ask only because there were some in boxes with my name on them," I explained.

"You may find a few pieces with your porcelain," she said.

"Thank you very much for locating my porcelain pieces. It must have been hard work."

"The Shanghai Museum helped us. They want to get in touch with you about those fifteen pieces."

I was overjoyed that some of my porcelain pieces had been saved, and when I got home I got in touch with Little Fang, asking him to help me get them back. It would seem my fight to save them in 1966 when the Red Guards were looting my home had not been in vain.

A few days later, Little Fang drove me in his power company truck to the underground warehouse at the other end of the city. After I had presented the letter to the security guard, we were allowed to enter the dark, cavernous interior. The man in charge told us to wait by a long, dusty table under a feeble light. Others were already gathered there. We waited with anticipation, moving restlessly in the airless room.

When the items were brought out and laid on the table, we were told to identify our things. There were scrolls, fans, boxes of various sizes, and containers tied together with string. Everything was covered with a thick layer of sooty dust peculiar to coal-burning, industrial Shanghai. A man sighed deeply and uttered a stifled exclamation that sounded rather like a sob when he picked up his antique fan to find that the paper, on which had been a valuable painting by a famous Ming dynasty painter, had rotted away with mildew. A woman standing beside him, perhaps his wife, murmured to him to throw away the now worthless fan. But he carefully took out his handkerchief and folded it lovingly around the fan to take it home.

Back home Little Fang helped me to carry my boxes upstairs to my room and took his leave. The odor from them was overpowering. I opened each box and took the porcelain pieces out. Then I took all the dirty and broken boxes out to the fresh air of the balcony. I saw that some of the vases, bowls, and plates were chipped or cracked; a few had been broken and then glued together again. All had identification numbers and other indecipherable writing on the delicate glaze. On a large plate of Ming celadon, some Revolutionary had expressed his hatred for the rich by declaring in writing that collectors were bloodsuckers. I was heartbroken to see the beautiful pieces so carelessly defaced. But I knew that they might easily have been smashed if someone somewhere hadn't succeeded in talking the Red Guards into taking them to the underground warehouse.

I filled the bathtub with lukewarm water, sprinkled a little soap powder in it, laid towels at the bottom of the tub, and placed the pieces there to soak. In the water the patched pieces disintegrated. I bent over the tub and washed each piece with a soft cloth to remove the markings. After rinsing, I placed them on a sheet spread on the floor of my room. It was already nightfall when I had finished. I realized that less than half of my original collection was left intact, including my Dehua Guanyin, covered with black ink stains but not broken. After washing, it was as gleaming and beautiful as ever. I placed it on my desk and sat down to enjoy looking at it. It was like being reunited with an old friend after a long separation.

I checked the list of the fifteen pieces the museum wished to buy and saw that it included what was left of my Xuande blue-and-white as well as an apple green (*fenqing*) Yongzheng vase I particularly liked. It had a raised pattern of a lizard with such a fluid line that it looked as if it were ready to slither off the vase. The Shanghai Museum also wanted my Zhengde chicken-fat-yellow plate and my best piece of Song dynasty Ding ware with an incised pattern of waterlilies.

Should I accede to the museum's request for the fifteen pieces, or should I refuse? Before the Cultural Revolution, when I was writing my last will, I had discussed the matter of my collection with my daughter. It was at her suggestion that I had willed my collection to the Shanghai Museum as a gift. Her death and the careless disregard for cultural relics demonstrated during the Cultural Revolution had cooled my enthusiasm for leaving my collection to the museum, a bureaucratic organization of the government, subject to political pressure. On the other hand, I had already decided to leave China. None of my collection was exportable. Would it not come to the same thing whether I left it to the museum or not? Therefore I decided I would give the museum the fifteen pieces they wanted rather than accept a token purchase price arbitrarily arrived at by some official who had no knowledge of the true worth of the pieces in question. However, I should get something out of the deal, I thought. All the blackwood stands that went with the pieces had disappeared. If I wished to enjoy looking at my collection until I left Shanghai, I must have stands to display it. I decided to ask the museum to make a few stands for me in exchange for my fifteen pieces. It was not an equal exchange by any means, but I did need the stands, and there was no other way to get them.

The Shanghai Museum sent me an invitation for an interview, and I went there to see them. The men received me with excessive politeness. They brought out my fifteen pieces, all beautifully clean and gleaming against the white satin lining of the new boxes in which they lay, and allowed me to examine each piece. Then we talked about them as if we were disinterested connoisseurs, pointing out a particular color or design and turning them over to examine the markings. When they deemed that sufficient courtesy had been shown me to establish themselves as civilized individuals and to put me in a receptive mood, they turned to the business at hand. The man who seemed to enjoy deference from the others said to me, "The museum has to work within the limits of a budget. We have to be very selective when we make purchases. You have many beautiful pieces in your collection, but we have decided, for the time being, to request you to sell us only these fifteen pieces."

"Of course. You can have the fifteen pieces you have selected. It's better to have visitors to the museum enjoying them than to leave them in my cupboard," I said.

They all beamed, and the man who had spoken nodded with approval.

"I'll make you a gift of all fifteen pieces if you meet my conditions," I added.

"What do you want us to do?" the man asked me.

"Nothing very difficult for the museum," I told him. "I would like the museum carpenter to make me some stands so that I can display the pieces that have been returned to me in my room and enjoy looking at them. I'll of course pay for the wood and the labor of your carpenter."

They looked at each other, surprised at the nature of my condition. Then they all laughed heartily.

"That's easy. I'll send our carpenter to your house to measure the pieces. How many do you want made? Do you want a stand for each piece?" the man asked me.

"No, of course I can't ask you to make so many stands. I think maybe ten or twelve will be all I want," I said.

"That will be perfectly all right," he promised readily.

"About your idea of making these fifteen pieces a gift to the museum, will you furnish us with a formal letter to that effect?" another man said.

"Certainly. I'll give it to the carpenter when he comes. Could he come tomorrow?"

"I'll get the carpenter now, and you can discuss the matter with him yourself," the man said and left the room.

When he came back with the carpenter in tow, the old man seemed unhappy to have this extra job thrust upon him.

"I have got a lot of work on hand just now," he muttered.

"It doesn't seem right to ask this old comrade to do this extra job for me during working hours. It might delay whatever he is doing for the museum. What about asking him to do my work in his spare time, and I will settle with him about payment?" I suggested.

"You can't do that," the museum official said firmly. Obviously he couldn't condone such a practice. But he had decided to let me have my stands, so he told the old carpenter to put aside whatever he was doing for the museum for the time being. We arranged that the carpenter would come to my apartment the next day to measure the pieces.

"We are holding an exhibition next week of our recently acquired items. All friends of the museum who have pieces displayed in the exhibition are invited to a special preview and a banquet afterwards. We hope you will come," the man said, handing me a gold-embossed invitation card. My name was already written on it. Evidently they had been quite certain I was going to let them have my fifteen pieces. Of course, since the Shanghai Museum was a government organization, their request to purchase was as good as a polite order to sell. Nevertheless, one doctor had refused to sell his collection of Tang porcelain pillows, as I was told by one of the Shanghai Museum officials with a great deal of regret and indignation.

The special exhibition was held in the hall on the ground floor of the Shanghai Museum. Strolling among the well-lit cases were the private collectors who had contributed the exhibits, their wives, and a large number of government officials, escorted by museum personnel. With each exhibit was a card giving a description of the piece and the name of the donor. Of my fifteen pieces, four were on display, including a large Xuande blue-and-white plate sixteen inches in diameter, with a pattern of grapes, and the Yongzheng vase with the raised pattern of a lizard. The museum official showing me around explained to me that due to the limited space, only token pieces from each collector were shown.

The most senior official present was a vice-mayor of the city, Zhang Chengzhong, who was concurrently the director of the Commission for the Administration and Control of Cultural Relics. He was surrounded by a large entourage and many museum officials ready to answer his questions. After everybody had looked at the exhibits, we were invited to sit down on chairs already placed in the center of the spacious hall. Vice-Mayor Zhang made a speech praising the patriotic spirit of the private collectors who had added to the collection of the Shanghai Museum. In particular he welcomed a young couple who had traveled to Shanghai from the United States to attend the ceremony as representatives of their grandfather, who had died during the Cultural Revolution and could not personally witness his own collection being included in this exhibition. After his speech, a representative of the museum invited the private collectors to come forward. As each man came to where Zhang Chengzhong was seated, the vice-mayor stood up to present him with a certificate of merit in a gold frame and a red envelope containing the purchase price. While this was going on, an official of the museum slipped into the seat next to mine and told me in low whispers that a separate ceremony would be held for me because I had donated my pieces. After everybody had been called, we were taken by special buses to the newly opened tourist hotel on Huashan Road and given an elaborate banquet in the large dining room.

The young couple from the United States and the collectors who had links with businessmen in Hong Kong were given the seats of honor at Vice-Mayor Zhang's table. Since the declaration of the new policy of attracting foreign investment, these individuals' personal importance in the eyes of the People's Government had increased a thousandfold. Until the government succeeded in establishing firm business ties with foreign countries, these men were useful for their ties with overseas Chinese in Hong Kong and elsewhere. The rest of us sat wherever we happened to find ourselves. At each table, an official of the Shanghai Museum acted as host. I knew no one at my table. We did not introduce ourselves or make conversation. And no one ate very much of the delicious food put in front of us. We were stiff and formal, patiently waiting for the banquet to end. The museum people were, however, in high spirits. They went around from table to table, wineglasses in hand, to toast each other.

Collectors do not like to part with their collections because they form a sort of sentimental tie with each item. Throughout the meal, I was thinking of the pieces I had surrendered to the museum. Though I did not regret having given them away, I felt rather sad. I thought the others were probably in the same frame of mind. It was true they had all been paid a purchase price, but they were not really in need of the money, and it was a certainty that the price represented only a fraction of the market value of the items.

When we saw Zhang Chengzhong preparing to leave, we quietly laid down our chopsticks too. The moment Zhang Chengzhong disappeared out the door with his entourage, we stood up to shake hands with the host at our table. Then we filed out to the elevators. Those at other tables behaved in exactly the same manner. It was only when we were on the street and about to mingle with the crowd, far from the aureole of officialdom, that we smiled at one another and said goodbye to those within earshot.

A week later, two museum officials took me in an official car to the Shanghai Mansions, an apartment hotel for foreign visitors. The ceremony of presenting me with the certificate of merit was to be held in the penthouse apartment reserved for official use. In the spacious lobby, an attendant led me to a table on which were an ink slab and several writing brushes. As I signed my name in the brocade-covered guest book, a cameraman took several photographs of me. The officials signed their names after mine. The attendant then threw open the double door leading to the reception room. Other officials of the museum, including the director, were introduced to me. I saw that my neighbors, Dr. and Mrs. Gu Kaishi, had been invited to make up the party. Dr. Gu was an eminent surgeon, and his wife a gynecologist at the No. 6 People's Hospital. He had given his family bronze collection to the Shanghai Museum.

After a little while, Vice-Mayor Zhang Chengzhong arrived. He sat down in the middle of the long sofa that had been left vacant for him. The attendant served us green tea while we chatted about the weather and politely inquired after each other's health. When the preliminary exchanges were over, one of the junior officials of the museum brought a framed certificate of merit and placed it on the coffee table in front of the vice-mayor. Zhang made a short speech praising my patriotic act of presenting the museum with pieces from my collection. Then he stood up, took the certificate of merit, and held it out to me with both hands. I stood to accept it and bowed to him. He also presented me with a scroll and said it was a gift from the Shanghai Museum to show their appreciation of my donation. I accepted and bowed again.

The scroll was taken out of its brocade cover and unrolled. It was a beautiful reproduction of the famous painting *A Lady with Peony*, by the great Ming dynasty painter Tang Yin. The original was one of the Shanghai Museum's proudest possessions. The scroll was about two yards long and twenty-eight inches wide, so perfectly reproduced that it was the exact replica of the original. It now adorns the wall of my Washington, D.C., condominium and is enjoyed by my friends.

When the presentation was over, Zhang Chengzhong sat down. I made a short speech expressing my pleasure at being able to add to the museum's collection. During the proceedings, the man with the camera took several pictures. These and the book containing the signatures of the guests were later given to me as souvenirs of the occasion.

The attendant announced that lunch was served. Led by the vice-mayor, we went into the adjacent dining room and were seated around the table. A sumptuous meal, the most elaborate I had ever had in socialist China, was served to us, with three kinds of wine, fruit, and dessert. The vice-mayor and everybody else were extremely polite and pleasant. During the meal, the vice-mayor told me that he himself had been incarcerated. When I expressed surprise and indignation, he said, "You are surprised that an old revolutionary like myself could be locked up by people who claim to be revolutionaries? Politics is a very complicated thing, you know."

Encouraged by the example of the vice-mayor, others also told me about their imprisonment. It soon emerged that among the ten people seated around the table, only three had escaped imprisonment.

"However, we are all rehabilitated now," one of the officials declared.

Led by the vice-mayor, we all raised our glasses and toasted the Chinese Communist Party, which had made our rehabilitation possible.

It seemed the People's Government in Shanghai wanted to put me in the right frame of mind. They could so easily have given me my certificate of merit when the others received theirs. They did not have to organize a separate ceremony and an elaborate party. I thought they were giving me the treatment usually reserved for foreign government visitors of senior rank mainly because I had applied to go abroad. They wanted me to leave Shanghai with a good impression of the post-Mao government. Even the vice-mayor's seemingly casual remark that he himself had suffered imprisonment was intended to make me look upon my own unfortunate experience in its proper perspective. He had tried to make me feel that I had somehow joined the distinguished company of veteran revolutionaries and senior officials of the government.

Next morning, in a corner of one of the *Shanghai Liberation Daily*'s four pages, a news item appeared stating that I had made a donation of porcelain to the Shanghai Museum. The report called it a patriotic act and added that I had not accepted monetary compensation. Since the *Shanghai Liberation Daily*, like all the other newspapers, was controlled by the government, which decided what was to appear in its pages, I felt that the Shanghai officials were continuing their efforts to put me in a good mood.

With the publication of this item of news, I became an instant celebrity. My friends and neighbors, including the Party secretary of my Residents' Committee, called to offer their congratulations and to examine the certificate of merit, which they told me should be hung up on the wall. People who had avoided me now crossed the street to greet me. Lu Ying, who had criticized my clothes only a few years ago, now complimented me on my neat appearance and asked me where I had bought them. It seemed I had come a long way from the days when I was a nonperson suffering insults and persecution. Yet I had not changed one iota. It was the Party's policy that had changed.

When the furor of congratulations had died down, Comrade He, a representative of the Shanghai Federation of Women, came to invite me to join their study group for women intellectuals. I readily accepted her invitation because it meant I would no longer have to attend the rather dull study group meetings of the Residents' Committee. I hoped the women at the federation would be more interesting and congenial.

According to China's Constitution, women and men enjoyed equal rights, but in practice there was a great deal of discrimination. Although in the cities there was no difference in pay or benefits for women doing the same work as men, the great majority of women remained in specialized occupations that traditionally employed women; they were textile workers, shop assistants, hospital nurses, and schoolteachers. The Chinese traditional attitude of a woman's position being determined by the position of her husband was still upheld. The widow of Marshal Zhu De was the president of the National Federation of Women. Among its local presidents and vice-presidents were wives and widows of other senior veteran Party officials. However, the women who did the actual work of the federation, such as Comrade He, were Party bureaucrats. Like other organizations in China, the Federation of Women was a government organization that orchestrated its members' activities.

"We are organizing two study groups," Comrade He said. "One group consists of pre-Liberation female factory owners and wives of prominent capitalists who used to have jobs in their husbands' factories. The other group consists of female intellectuals. In this group we also include wives of well-known scientists who have made a special contribution to socialism. After careful consideration, we have decided to put you in the latter group. We think you will find this group congenial."

"I hope you will convey to the senior authorities of the federation my appreciation of your invitation. I consider it an honor, and I look forward to coming to the study group meetings," I told her politely.

"We are having a joint session of the two groups at an inaugural meeting next Wednesday at two in the afternoon. It's going to be at the premises of the Shanghai Political Consultative Conference on Beijing Road West. We will be using their premises for our weekly meetings too, and they will invite all of us to their special events. There is also an 'internal' shop and restaurant for the convenience of our members," she added.

"I'll be there at two on Wednesday," I promised.

She took her leave. As I closed the front gate after Comrade He, I saw Mrs. Zhu coming out of her room to the garden.

"Was that Comrade He of the Federation of Women?" she asked me.

"Yes," I said.

"Has she come to invite you to join their study group activities?"

"Yes. But how did you know?"

"I've also been invited. But I'm going only to the one on the district level. You are going to the one on the municipal level, I suppose?"

"I've no idea which one I'm going to."

"If you are meeting at the Shanghai Political Consultative Conference premises on Beijing Road West, then you are going to the one on the municipal level," she said.

"Well, it's just another study group. It makes no difference what level it's on," I told her.

"Oh, it makes a lot of difference. On the municipal level you will be invited to many events that are not open to those on the district level. What's more, you can use the 'internal' shop and restaurant. You'll be able to get things not available to the general public, such as good cigarettes."

I was about to enter my part of the house when she added, "The reason you are invited to the municipal level is that your donation to the nursery school program is the second-largest in the city."

"You seem extremely well informed," I said dryly.

"You are the subject of gossip in many circles. People are saying you make fine gestures in order to buy a passport to leave the country," she said, watching my reaction.

"Do you mean to suggest that the People's Government is an agency for selling passports?" I asked, trying to appear incredulous. Actually I was rather amused by what she was telling me. The Chinese people are extremely sharp and cynical. They believe fine gestures and noble behavior are always motivated by selfish designs.

Rather alarmed, Mrs. Zhu said hastily, "Nobody is saying the People's Government would sell passports."

"Good! In that case, there is no point in trying to buy one, is there?" I did not wait for her reply but went inside.

I thought Mrs. Zhu was jealous because in her view I had somehow got ahead of her.

The Political Consultative Conference was a United Front Organization, a part of the campaign for national unity. The appointed delegates had no real voice in affairs of state. In theory they were there to be "consulted"; in practice they were there merely to add an affirmative voice to decisions already taken by the Party. The organization in Shanghai was housed in a large mansion that was once a part of the famous Zhang family garden. Other palatial mansions in Shanghai were often relics of the days of foreign domination. This particular house, however, enjoyed a certain revolutionary mystique, as it used to be the clandestine meeting place for prominent supporters of Sun Yatsen before the revolution of 1911, which established the Chinese Republic. The large garden with its lake and many pavilions had long disappeared. Other buildings had been added, and the mansion itself had been turned into an assembly hall on the ground floor and conference rooms upstairs. At the entrance to the lobby was the "internal" shop, and in a corner of the garden was the restaurant. Both establishments were non-profit organizations run by the state for the convenience of the delegates.

After I left Shanghai, I met many Europeans and Americans who thought Communist China was an egalitarian society. This simply is not true. The fact is that the Communist government controls goods, services, and opportunities and dispenses them to the people in unequal proportions. The term "internal" was used for goods and services available to officials of a certain rank and a few outsiders on whom for one reason or another the government wished to bestow favor. I have heard the term "internal internal" used to describe goods and services reserved for the very senior officials, especially in the military, who seemed to get the first choice and the lion's share of everything. Though the salary of a member of the Politburo was no more than eight or ten times that of an industrial worker, the perks available to him without charge were comparable to those enjoyed by kings and presidents of other lands. And the privileges were extended to his family, including his grandchildren, even after his death.

The members of the Federation of Women study group were not really important in the eyes of the government. We were courted by the Shanghai government to accommodate the new political trends: national unity embracing the capitalist class and the "open door" policy of the Four Modernizations. Nearly all of us had some ties with Chinese living abroad. The government was being kind to us in order to win the support of our relatives and to create an image of tolerance for the Western democracies. As far as those "perks" were concerned, they were minimal; even so, I became the envy of my friends and relatives. And they did not hesitate to ask me to buy things for them at the shop or to bring special food home from the restaurant. Soon I discovered that every member of our study group had the same problem. It was an embarrassment I was glad to leave behind when I finally departed from Shanghai.

A-yi was very proud that I had been invited to join the study group of the Federation of Women. She thought I had at last achieved the ultimate in respectability: not only received back into the ranks of the people but also raised by the government to a select group. On the day of the inaugural meeting, she served lunch early and hovered around me to make sure I wore clothes she approved of.

"I think the pale gray. You look so nice in that," she suggested.

"Not the navy blue?" I took the navy blue trouser suit out of the closet.

"No, pale gray is better. Much younger-looking. I wish you would dye your hair. You would look so much younger if you had black hair."

I put the navy blue suit back in the closet and took out the pale gray. She smiled with satisfaction and went into the kitchen. "Tell me all about it tomorrow," she said.

About seventy women, all middle-aged or older, were present at the inaugural meeting of the study groups. We sat in a large, clean conference room with high windows that admitted ample daylight and sunshine. We were served hot green tea in covered glasses. One of the vice-presidents of the federation welcomed us and spoke to us about the Four Modernizations Program, which, she said, had been first proposed by the late Prime Minister Zhou Enlai at the Tenth Party Congress and approved by the late Chairman Mao Zedong. Then she praised our Wise Leader Chairman Hua for smashing the Gang of Four and paving the way for the realization of the Four Modernizations Program. Like all official speakers, she repeated the same ideas, almost in the same language, contained in Party resolutions and speeches by leaders in Beijing.

After we had duly applauded the vice-president, a woman in her early fifties, smartly dressed in a black trouser suit, was introduced to tell us about her recent trip to the United States with her husband, a former capitalist. She apologized for being hoarse and said that she had lost her voice from making many speeches since her return from abroad. Her popularity as a speaker was explained by the content of her speech. She not only described life in the United States as rather less than desirable due to muggings, drugs, drunkenness, and costly medical service, but she also told the audience that in spite of being offered a lucrative job in America, her husband had decided to come back to China to continue his work as chief engineer of the factory he had handed over to the state. Her husband's greatest ambition was to serve the Four Modernizations Program and to do his part in the effort to make China strong, she said. When she had finished, we applauded heartily.

Obviously her speech was a political message the government wanted the people to hear, but I did not think its purpose was to malign the United States. The government was probably embarrassed by the crowds outside the American consulate general waiting to apply for visas. Her speech was useful to discourage would-be emigrants. In fact, the newspaper had already published several stories of young people who had gone to the United States as immigrants only to find that they could not get jobs or be assimilated into American society. Disappointed, they returned to Shanghai. To their surprise and joy, they found their old jobs waiting for them, and their Party secretaries gave them a hero's welcome. The stories invariably ended with the young people pledging to work hard for the Four Modernizations Program.

For over a year I was a member of the study group organized by the Federation of Women. We studied the same documents and speeches the Party gave out to study groups all over the country. We joined the delegates of the Political Consultative Conference to hear speeches by prominent officials on subjects ranging from cultural affairs to international relations. And we made use of the shop and restaurant with self-imposed restraint so that we did not appear too eager to take advantage of or abuse the privileges accorded to us.

There were thirty-two women in my study group; the average age was just below sixty. The leader was the seventy-year-old wife of a vice-mayor. Comrade He was one of two Party officials designated to oversee our meetings, take notes of the proceedings, and guide the discussion should it stray from its appointed course. But the vice-mayor's wife was an experienced chairman, and the rest of us were intelligent enough to know what was expected of us. Our study group activities went along smoothly, never causing Comrade He and the other young officials from the federation a single moment of embarrassment or anxiety.

Though I never once spoke at the study group meetings of the Residents' Committee, I had to say something every week at the federation meetings. The youngest member of our group, a writer of fifty, was called upon to read the government document we were to discuss. Then it was up to us, seated around a large conference table, to respond. To be overeager to speak was considered just as uncouth as a refusal to talk. If one spoke first, one might say the wrong thing; if one spoke last, one might find that all the right remarks had been made already.

The reading of the document was generally followed by a few minutes of silence while we gazed at our note pads as if seriously considering what we had just heard. Then our chairman, the vice-mayor's wife, would offer a few hints to guide our discussion. After another moment of silence, one of the bolder ladies would take a sip of tea and raise her head to speak. Others followed. Gradually everybody added something. I generally tried to make my banal remarks in the middle of the discussion, but sometimes I did not succeed. Then I would hope to be overlooked and get away with just listening. However, either

Comrade He or the other federation official would always ask me, "What do you think?" and I would have to make a contribution. To speak at the study group was an art. Obviously one could not afford to be original, and there were only a limited number of ways of saying the same thing over and over again. We generally chose to be boring rather than different.

As I got to know Comrade He better and found her free of the class prejudice that inhibited relationships between Party officials and people like myself, I tried to enlist her help to get Meiping's murderer brought to justice. She was extremely sympathetic and introduced me to a female official from the newly reestablished United Front Organization of the Shanghai Party Secretariat. Comrade He brought the official, Comrade Ma, to my apartment to see me one evening.

After I had told the whole story, Comrade Ma promised to discuss the matter with her superiors. A few days later, she came again with Comrade He.

"I've been instructed to inform you that your daughter's case will be dealt with in due course. There are many cases of mysterious death in Shanghai, and many families are appealing to the government for clarification. For instance, the former director of our department was supposed to have committed suicide. Now his family has raised doubts and provided evidence to show he was probably murdered. Cases like that, which happened so many years ago, are very difficult to clarify. Even when you can prove death was not caused by suicide, you still have to locate the person or persons responsible. Who is going to point an accusing finger at another man who might be working in the same organization? And even when someone is ready to step forth and denounce someone else, can we really believe him?"

"It does seem difficult," I conceded. "But I believe it isn't impossible to find the culprit if the government is determined to do so."

"You must trust the Party and the government. In the not too distant future, there will be an official verdict on the Cultural Revolution. After that, our work to clarify all residual problems will become easier," Comrade Ma told me. From what she said I understood that since the Cultural Revolution had not yet been officially repudiated, the Revolutionaries who had committed the crimes could not be denounced, because they committed the crimes in the name of the Cultural Revolution. What Comrade Ma did not say but everybody in Shanghai knew was that many Revolutionaries had joined the Party in the meantime and become officials. It is much harder to confront a Party official than an ordinary person.

The two ladies took their leave, and I accompanied them to the front gate. I thanked Comrade Ma for coming and promised her that I would wait patiently.

I did not see Mrs. Zhu standing in the dark on her terrace. After I had closed the front gate, she stepped off the terrace and came towards me. "Were you talking about your daughter?" she asked.

"Yes, as a matter of fact, we were talking about her," I said.

Since I had been bringing Mrs. Zhu special cigarettes from the "internal" shop at the Political Consultative Conference, our relationship had become more cordial.

"Well, my son told me that the man responsible for her death has been taken into custody. It seems he was involved in several other deaths too."

"How did your son know about it?"

"It seems his friends in the militia told him."

I was surprised by this information and wanted to verify its authenticity, so I asked that she send her son up to see me.

He came up later in the evening, but he refused to talk to me about Meiping's murderer and flatly denied having told his mother anything about the case. "My mother made a mistake. She got things mixed up," he said.

I did not give much credence to what Mrs. Zhu had told me, brushing it aside as mere gossip, for I thought if the man was in custody the Security Bureau would have informed me and Comrade Ma would have known. In fact, Mrs. Zhu's son had been correctly informed. A week after I left Shanghai, the man was publicly tried in the Cultural Square, with members of the families of his other five victims in attendance. *Da Gong Bao,* the left-wing newspaper in Hong Kong, reported the trial and stated that the man was sentenced to death but the sentence was suspended for two years.

One morning in Hong Kong I opened the newspaper, and there was this news item glaring at me, with my daughter listed as one of the victims. When the initial shock subsided, I realized that the Security Bureau had deliberately waited for me to get out of the country before holding the trial. The Cultural Square had seating for over a thousand people, and representatives from every walk of life were normally invited to attend such trials. Members of the families of the victims would occupy the front-row seats and would be invited to express agreement with the verdict and the sentence. China had not abolished the death penalty. According to Chinese law, a convicted murderer should suffer immediate execution after sentencing. The officials at the Security Bureau knew very well a suspended death sentence would not be acceptable to me. In every petition I had sent to the bureau I had stated as much. They had waited until I was out of the way to hold the trial so that I could not be there to protest the verdict. Meiping's murderer lives in China today, for a suspended death sentence meant that he could go free after two years.

The year 1979 was an important one for Deng Xiaoping and for Communist China. The adoption by the plenary session of the Central Committee in December 1978 of Deng's favorite Marxist adage that "practice is the only criterion for determining truth" opened the way for his plan to reform and restructure China's economy. His visit to the United States and the warm reception he received there established him as a leader of world stature. And the war "to punish Vietnam" for her border incursions rallied everyone around the Party in a surge of patriotism. It also helped to convince most of the military leaders, hitherto steeped in Mao Zedong's concept of People's War, of the need to modernize China's armed forces. Deng's position was further strengthened when four of Hua Guofeng's supporters were ousted from the Party leadership. Although for the moment Hua Guofeng remained chairman of the Central Committee and prime minister, he had become an isolated figurehead with power slipping out of his grip.

One of the measures of economic reform undertaken by Deng Xiaoping was to open China's doors to foreign firms. British Petroleum was the first oil company to open an office in Shanghai. Then I read in the *Shanghai Liberation Daily* that other oil companies, including Shell International Petroleum, had been invited to take part in offshore exploration. I became more hopeful that I would be given my passport in the not too distant future. In fact, I was so confident that I stopped giving English lessons. But it was another nine months before I could leave Shanghai.

When it was Chinese New Year again, in February 1980, I decided to have a big celebration for what might be my last Chinese New Year in Shanghai. I invited my students, the young people who had helped me, and their children to eat "foreign food" and watch fireworks with me. A-yi and I made pork hamburgers and cream of tomato soup for over thirty people. For dessert I ordered three enormous cakes topped with fresh cream from a former White Russian bakery, now state-owned but still producing the same cakes and pastry. My guests were jammed into my apartment. My bed had to be dismantled to make room, and we all sat on the floor to eat our supper. Then we took the large collection of fireworks I had bought into the garden, where for two hours my guests, especially the children, had a wonderful time letting off noisy firecrackers and illuminating the night sky with brilliant bursts of colorful stars and sprays. My neighbors opened their windows and leaned on their balconies to share the fun. The entire Zhu family also came out to watch. But I thought there must have been complaints too, for when I met Lao Li on the street a couple of days later, my policeman asked me, "What was this great noise you were making the other night?"

"Only fireworks to celebrate the Chinese New Year," I told him.

"Was it necessary to have so much of it?"

"Oh, it was a double celebration, in fact. We were also celebrating our victory in Vietnam."

I was with one of my young friends when I met Lao Li. After we had left the policeman, she said to me, "Have you heard what people are saying about the war in Vietnam?"

"No, what are they saying?"

"They are saying that Deng Xiaoping ordered the attack on Vietnam to avenge the defeat of the Americans. It was all arranged quietly between him and the American president, Carter, when he was in the United States," she told me in low whispers.

"That sounds like something put out by the remnants of the Gang of Four. Don't believe it and don't talk about it," I said.

Actually, from that time on until the present day, Deng Xiaoping has been plagued by such rumors circulated by opponents of his policy in the Party.

My young friend said, "Yes, you are right. Shanghai is still full of followers of the Gang of Four. But the people are with Deng Xiaoping. Have you seen the historical film *Jia Wu Naval Battle*?"

"No, what about it?"

"Well, when a naval commander by the name of Deng appears on the screen, the audience cheers and claps. That's the people's subtle way of saying they like what Deng Xiaoping is doing."

Greatly intrigued by what my young friend had told me, I went to the local cinema to see the film for myself a few days later. It was indeed just as she had said. The audience broke out in loud cheers when the naval commander appeared on the screen and was addressed by his subordinate officer as "Your Excellency Deng."

Before the Chinese New Year, I had received a large gold-embossed card from the Shanghai Revolutionary Committee, the Maoist successor to the municipal government, inviting me to a Chinese New Year celebration at the Shanghai Exhibition Hall, the Sino-Soviet Friendship Building back in the heyday of China's cooperation with her northern neighbor. The card admitted two persons, so I asked my young friend to accompany me. Since it was a fine day and buses were usually overcrowded during the Chinese New Year holiday period, we walked there in spite of the subfreezing temperature.

As we approached the exhibition hall, cars sped past us, enveloping us in clouds of dust, and we saw that the parking area outside the hall was full of chauffeur-driven cars. However, masses of other guests were on foot like us. It seemed everybody in Shanghai who was considered anybody at the time was invited. I presumed I was on the list submitted by the Federation of Women, since in the crowd I saw several other members of my study group.

We showed our invitation card at the door and were allowed to go in. The place was terribly hot, with central heating at full blast, the more unbearable because we had no heating at home and were not used to it. The hot air hit us like a tidal wave, and perspiration broke out on my forehead. We quickly shed our padded jackets and sweaters as well as our topcoats and added them to the mountain of similar garments discarded by others before us. My young friend was impatient to get to the "internal" shop at the exhibition hall, which was well known to the Shanghai public but inaccessible. She told me that she had boasted to her friends and neighbors that she was coming with me to the party; consequently they had all asked her to utilize the opportunity to buy them commodities they had long coveted but had been unable to obtain in the ordinary shops.

I told her that since we had come for the celebration, we should at least make a show of taking part in some of the planned activities before going to the shop. Meekly but impatiently, she followed me through the halls where games were being played, the theater where artists were performing, and the cafeteria where refreshments were being served. Then, because of the crowds everywhere, we were able to make our way in haste to the shop without attracting too much attention.

Much to my young friend's disappointment, when we got there we found that a large crowd had preceded us and that the staff was regulating admission into the shop. We had to join the line and wait. When we finally got in, half of the things she wanted were sold out. However, we still managed to spend several thousand yuan on items ranging from cashmere coat material to steel saucepans. We each had four shopping bags weighed down with her purchases, so that we barely managed to stagger to the front entrance to claim our coats and jackets. We tried to get a taxi without success, and there were no pedicabs. Then my young friend telephoned home to enlist the help of her two younger brothers, who were asked to come on their bicycles. As we stood in the icy air outside the exhibition hall waiting for her brothers, others similarly laden joined us. Those driving away in chauffeured cars could afford to depart in a dignified manner, without the encumbrance of parcels, because they had their own "internal" source of supply.

Soon after the holiday, almost overnight, temporary housing sprang up on both sides of our street. The structures were no more than makeshift shacks of old timber, bamboo poles, and broken pieces of brick, built against the walls of the existing houses and gardens. The trees on the sidewalk were enclosed in the structures or used as poles. Soon the leaves dropped and the trees died. Each shack was allocated to one family of several people. There were no washing facilities and no toilets. The Residents' Committee at first told us to keep our front gate open so that our garden taps would be accessible to the people outside. But after several households reported loss of personal property, taps were installed at each end of the street. A young woman sanitation worker came each morning to collect the night soil from buckets in each shack. The odor this operation created was overpowering.

Mrs. Zhu told me that the decision to house the people on our particular street was made by a female official promoted to the district government during the Cultural Revolution. The official said that she had selected our street to house the displaced people because it was too full of former class enemies and capitalists, too clean, and too quiet. To put a large number of proletarians in our midst would be "good" for us. I was astonished to hear this and asked Mrs. Zhu why the other officials did not oppose her. Mrs. Zhu said, "Nobody wants to offend former Revolutionaries promoted to official positions. They are afraid things will change back again."

We had a shack on each side of our front gate. At first, there was enough space left for us to go in and out. But as time went on, much of the space was taken up by the people in the shacks for storage of their odds and ends. These were covered with old plastic sheets and smelly straw mats to protect them from the weather. Our passage was reduced to a very narrow lane of no more than two feet in width. Boys urinated against our gate, and laundry dripped from a line across our entrance. From morning till night, incessant human voices mixed with the noise of several radio sets tuned to different stations. Our "too quiet and too clean" street was certainly no longer quiet, and far from clean. It was impossible to use the garden or sit on the balcony. But by tacit understanding the Zhus and I put up with the inconveniences without complaint. We were very conscious that the spirit of "class struggle" still lurked and that Party officials, steeped in Mao's philosophy, could not change easily. Their old working habits had already become second nature to many of them. They simply did not know any other way to discharge their responsibilities. Besides, because the Party leadership had not taken the bold step of totally repudiating Mao's philosophy, the diehard believers in Maoism could not be removed from office and new blood brought in. These disgruntled Party officials would inevitably make use of every available opportunity to assert their Maoist point of view and to sabotage Deng Xiaoping's new policy, which they regarded as a betrayal of socialism and Mao Zedong Thought. To this day, even though Deng Xiaoping's power has increased significantly as compared to 1980, the problem of recalcitrant Party officials remains the most thorny he has to face. And as long as this problem is not resolved, the situation in China will remain subject to sudden change when Deng Xiaoping departs from the scene.

The Zhus and I knew that although we were rehabilitated, our position in Chinese society was by no means secure. Therefore, we put up with our new neighbors and even extended all possible help to make their lives more tolerable. We allowed them to store food in our refrigerators and loaned them our mops and brooms. We were only too thankful that the female Revolutionary Party official had not ordered the shacks to be erected right inside the garden. If she had, there was simply nothing we could have done about it.

Perhaps other residents of our street who were not former class enemies or capitalists were not so restrained. Lu Ying called on Mrs. Zhu and me to have a chat, and the Residents' Committee officially informed everybody that a new apartment building was being built for the displaced persons. When it was completed, the people would be moved and our street would be restored to its old shape and condition again.

Since 1978 I had seen several visitors from abroad, including my sister Helen and her husband. As the news that I had survived the Cultural Revolution spread among my friends in Europe and North America, I began to receive letters from them. In July 1980, I got a letter from an old friend, Sir John Addis, telling me that he was coming to China and would be in Shanghai in August. He asked if I could see him. Sir John Addis was a Sinologist with a deep understanding and appreciation of Chinese culture. My husband and I had known him since the forties. When he was serving at the British chargé d'affaires office in Beijing in the fifties, he was a frequent guest in our house. During the years he served as British ambassador to Laos and the Philippines, we had kept in touch, and in 1965, when he came to China on vacation, he visited me in Shanghai. He was a knowledgeable collector of Chinese porcelain. His collection had been given to the British Museum. I was always interested in hearing his opinion of the pieces I had acquired.

In 1972, while I was in prison, I read about his appointment as the first British ambassador to Beijing. When I was released in 1973, the political situation was such that I could not get in touch with him. Then, in 1974, again from the newspaper, I learned he had left Beijing to retire. I certainly would like to see him again; on the other hand, I did not want to do anything that might be misunderstood by the government and so prejudice my chance of getting my passport. I decided to seek the advice of my policeman, Lao Li, before replying to John's letter.

I went to the police station and asked to see Lao Li. When he came out of the inner room and sat down across the table from me, I said, "I've received a letter from a former British ambassador to Beijing. He's an old friend. He's coming to Shanghai. In the letter he asks if he may come to see me." I took the letter out and translated it verbatim into Chinese for Lao Li.

Lao Li listened to my translation but said nothing. I asked, "Do you think I ought to see him?"

"That's entirely up to you. It's your private business," said Lao Li.

"Perhaps I should not see him?" I asked again.

"Wouldn't he think it rather strange if you refuse to see him?" Lao Li said.

"Do you mean to say you think I ought to see him?" I said, trying, of course, to find out what he really meant.

"I didn't say anything like that. It's entirely your own private business whether you see him or not," he said rather impatiently.

"I need advice from the government. Sir John Addis was an ambassador, not a schoolteacher or someone like that. He's a political person," I told Lao Li.

"I can't give you advice on your private life," Lao Li said.

"All right, in that case, I'll write and tell him I can't see him," I said.

"Did I tell you not to see him?"

"Perhaps I should see him?"

"It's entirely your own private business," Lao Li said again.

It suddenly dawned on me that I was putting Lao Li in a very awkward position by requesting his advice. I sensed that he was in favor of my seeing Sir John but did not want to be held responsible for saying so outright. I said, "All right, I'll write and tell him I'll see him."

Lao Li smiled and said, "It's entirely your own decision."

"Do you think I should invite him to dinner?" I asked.

"Can your A-yi cook a dinner suitable for an ambassador? Besides, what about those shacks outside your door? He has been to your home before the Cultural Revolution. What would he think of your living conditions now?" Lao Li became quite animated as he dispensed advice freely.

"All right, I'll take him to a restaurant. Thanks for the advice." I got up from the bench to leave.

Lao Li stood up also. "I didn't give you any advice," he said. "It's entirely your private business."

"Anyway, thanks for listening to me. I'll let you know when Sir John comes in August," I said and went home to answer John's letter.

On a hot summer's day in late July, I received a form letter from the Public Security Bureau calling me for an interview at the office where I had applied for my passport. When I got there, I found only one other person in the waiting room, a young man. He was obviously agitated, pacing among the benches, brushing past one and knocking against another. When he saw me, he said, "Have you come for an interview about your passport application?"

I nodded and sat down on a bench. He stood towering over me and said nervously, "Do you think you will get it, or do you think you will be rejected?"

"I'll soon know, I suppose," I said.

"Can one apply again if one gets rejected?" he asked.

"Please sit down and wait quietly. I don't know whether one can apply again or not. You can ask when it's your turn to go in," I told him.

He sat down but fixed his eyes on the door to the inner room. When it opened, he jumped up. But I was called. Obviously he had come much ahead of his appointed time.

After I had closed the door and sat down, I laid the printed form I had received on the desk. The official said to me, "You have applied for a passport to go to the United States?"

"Yes."

"What is the purpose of your trip?"

"To visit my sisters for a family reunion."

"Do you intend to visit other countries?"

"Yes, on my way there, I'll visit friends in Canada and Europe."

"Do you know many people abroad?"

"A few friends here and there."

He pulled open a drawer and took out the passport I had been waiting for. "Your application has been approved. Here is your passport. The People's Government wishes to facilitate family reunion. You may go to see your sisters in the United States, and you may visit your friends elsewhere. When you see them, encourage them to come to China. Tell them about the new conditions here and how we are building socialism. Tell them in Taiwan to come back and visit. They will be allowed to come and go freely."

"I don't know anyone in Taiwan," I said.

"Then tell your friends in Hong Kong to come and invest in joint ventures here. Encourage everybody to come and visit."

I nodded and picked up the passport, glancing at the photograph to make sure the man had not made a mistake.

"When you arrive in the United States, report to our embassy and register," he said.

"My sisters live in California. The embassy is not there," I told him.

"Is there no Chinese office where you are going?" He seemed not to believe me.

"No, my sisters live in the country," I said and left the room.

In his eagerness to come into the inner office, the young man collided with me in the doorway and nearly knocked me over.

My next job was to get a visa from the United States consulate general. To avoid having to line up outside the gate at an early hour of the morning, I paid a call on the local Chartered Bank manager, a Britisher interested in birdwatching. Taking the initiative to see a foreign resident was a bold move not lightly entertained by a Chinese not working for a foreign firm. It was after many days of consideration that I ventured to the bank's office on Yuanmingyuan Road. My late husband and I had banked with the Chartered Bank since the early forties, but we had dealt with its branches in Hong Kong and London.

Nevertheless, we were not unknown to the succession of managers who had come to Shanghai. Before the Cultural Revolution, they had been guests at our home. The young British manager received me with surprise and welcome, saying that the bank's officials in Hong Kong and London had been informed I had died during the Cultural Revolution. He also told me that my death had been recorded by the American correspondent Stanley Karnow in his book *Mao and China,* and by my former Yanjing schoolmate Han Suyin in one of her autobiographies.

I asked him to notify the bank in Hong Kong immediately that I was alive and well and to make an appointment for me with someone at the American consulate. He told me that several American officers of the consulate lived in his apartment building, set aside for foreign residents by the Chinese government, and that he would be glad to speak to them about my case.

Two days later I called at the American consulate general and was given a visa.

When Sir John Addis arrived in Shanghai early in August, I was able to tell him that I would definitely leave China in the autumn. We sat in easy chairs in the middle of the large, empty hotel lobby, in full view of the hotel clerk at the end of the room. Although he was really too far away to listen in to our conversation, I did not dwell on my imprisonment and my daughter's death; rather I talked mainly about my rehabilitation and the memorial meeting for Meiping. When I told Sir John that my collection of porcelain had been returned and I had donated fifteen pieces to the Shanghai Museum, he asked if he might come to my apartment to see the pieces I had left. Because the official banquet for him was to take place next day at noon, I invited him to dinner at the East Wind Restaurant, formerly the Shanghai Club, a famous British institution with the "longest bar in the Orient." I said, "I will see whether I can arrange for you to come to my apartment after dinner."

"I would like to see how you have been living during the last few years," John said.

When I told Lao Li that Sir John had arrived and that I had seen him, Lao Li asked, "Did you tell him everything that happened to you and your daughter?"

"He knows all about the Cultural Revolution already. He was

stationed in Beijing himself, so I wouldn't think it was a surprise to him to learn what happened to us," I told him.

"Still, it's somebody he knows personally," Lao Li said.

"He has many Chinese friends, including Party officials, I believe. I think he knows China very well indeed."

"Is he friendly to China?"

"Oh, yes, he is most friendly to China. Would he be invited back now if he weren't?"

Lao Li visibly relaxed. To him, the Chinese government's acceptance of Sir John as a friend made a great deal of difference.

"I've invited him to a dinner party at the East Wind Restaurant this evening. I've also invited the Chartered Bank manager and two Chinese friends to make up a party. Is that all right?" I asked him.

"Certainly, certainly, there must be a few other guests to show him due respect. He was an ambassador," said Lao Li.

"I'm afraid he wants to come and see my porcelain after dinner. What shall I say to him?"

Poor Lao Li was taken aback. "Oh . . ." He wrinkled his brow, stroked his chin, and looked thoughtful. I knew he was thinking about those shacks.

"You know, Sir John was stationed in Nanjing and Beijing for many years. He must have seen worse sights than the shacks outside my door," I reminded him.

"Yes, yes, you are right. In any case, you can't very well refuse to let a friend come to your home. Bring him after dinner. What time would you be coming?" Lao Li asked.

"Maybe nine o'clock or a little later," I told him.

When I brought John and the Chartered Bank manager to my apartment by taxi that night, I found the entire street cleared of people. No laundry was hanging outside the shacks, and no radios blared. The things that blocked our entrance had all been removed, and the sidewalk had been swept clean. When John stood on my balcony to look down at my garden, he commented on how peaceful and quiet the place was and said, "Your living conditions are much better than I had imagined." I didn't tell him that Lao Li had probably ordered the shack people to remain indoors and keep quiet for his benefit.

I have recorded John's visit here mainly because I think Lao

Li's behavior rather interesting. While he controlled my life, he did not want to appear to do so. It was up to me to anticipate his wishes and act accordingly. All Chinese Party officials behave in exactly the same manner towards the people. But of course not all of them are so touchingly human as my policeman, who was basically a very kind individual.

After obtaining visas from the embassies of the countries I wanted to visit during my trip, I rented a house for two weeks on Moganshan, near Hangzhou, and went up the mountain for a retreat. In spite of all that had happened, I was sad to leave China, never to return. All Chinese have this feeling of attachment to our native country. No matter how far we travel or how long we are absent, eventually we want to return to die in China. "The fallen leaves return to the root," we call it. But I had decided already that I would never come back. I would die elsewhere, in some country that would accept me. Now that my departure was imminent, I felt terribly sad. I wanted to sort out the conflicting emotions in my mind through prayer and self-examination before embarking on a new chapter of my life.

When I returned to Shanghai, a farewell tea party was arranged for me by my Federation of Women study group. After our leader announced that I was about to go abroad to visit my sisters, I made a short speech, thanking the Federation of Women for giving me the opportunity of joining such a distinguished group of ladies for my political studies. I praised their intelligence, their patriotism, and their high degree of socialist consciousness and told them that I had greatly benefited from their example. Several other ladies spoke politely too, urging me to tell my relatives and friends abroad about the new situation in China and to encourage them to visit. Comrade He informed everybody that I had booked a passage on a steamer of the newly opened shipping line linking Shanghai and Hong Kong, and she invited a few ladies from our group to join her to see me off.

On September 20, 1980, I left Shanghai. Because private individuals without official passes were barred from the waterfront, only Comrade He and the five ladies from the study group came to see me off in their capacity as representatives of the Federation of Women. They picked me up in a small bus recently imported from Japan. There were very strict rules governing the amount of luggage and money a traveler could take out of the country; I had only one suitcase and one grip. In my handbag was twenty U.S. dollars' worth of Hong Kong dollars, obtained through the Foreign Exchange Department of the Bank of China. My Chinese bank account and everything else, I had to leave behind.

A light rain was falling by the time we reached the wharf. In spite of Comrade He's official pass, the ladies were not allowed to go into the passenger waiting room. I said goodbye to them in the rain, and they returned to the bus. They wished me a pleasant trip and a happy reunion with my sisters, but none of them mentioned anything about my coming back. I think they knew that I was unlikely to return to the city that held for me such tragic memories.

After a long wait, the customs office opened and the passengers filed in. My suitcase and grip were thoroughly searched by two customs officials. They also looked in my handbag and counted the Hong Kong bank notes. When they were done, I followed the others into a bus that took us to the ship, anchored some distance downstream.

When the bus stopped alongside the ship, the light rain had become a heavy downpour, accompanied by thunder and lightning. I had neither a raincoat nor an umbrella. Hastily I staggered up the slippery gangway, my luggage dripping with rainwater. The ship was an old steamer of British origin bought by the Chinese government and refitted for the Hong Kong–Shanghai run. My first-class single cabin had a small shower. I warmed myself with a shower and put on dry clothes. Then I went on deck to have a last look at Shanghai.

The ship had lifted anchor and was sailing upstream in order to turn around. Through the misty curtain of rain, I caught a glimpse of the Shell building and the window of my old office. Already the past was assuming an unreal, dreamlike quality. The ship was gathering speed, sailing down the remaining stretch of the Huangpu River. When we reached the Yangzi estuary, the storm was over and rays of sunshine were filtering through the thinning clouds.

Many times in my life I had sailed from Shanghai to go abroad, standing just as I did now on the deck of a ship, with the wind whipping my hair while I watched the coastline of China receding. Never had I felt so sad as I did at that moment. It was I who had brought Meiping back from Hong Kong in April 1949, in response to my husband's request. The shocking tragedy of her death, I believed, was a direct consequence of our fatal decision to stay in our own country at that crucial moment of history. Therefore I felt guilty for being the one who was alive. I wished it were Meiping standing on the deck of this ship, going away to make a new life for herself. After all, it was the law of nature that the old should die first and the young should live on, not the other way around. Also I felt sad because I was leaving forever the country of my birth. It was a break so final that it was shattering. God knows how hard I tried to remain true to my country. But I failed utterly through no fault of my own.

Epilogue

M<small>Y REINTRODUCTION TO THE</small> Western way of life took place on a jumbo jet when I traveled across the Pacific on a first-class ticket: a gift from Shell, my former employer.

It was early afternoon in Hong Kong when I boarded the plane. After we took off, an attractive air hostess with shining blond hair bent over me and asked, "Will you have a bloody Mary or a screwdriver?"

I must have looked puzzled, for the young man standing behind her said, "Perhaps you would rather have champagne?"

It was then I realized that a bloody Mary was merely a drink and a screwdriver in this case was not for putting in or loosening screws.

As I stammered a polite refusal, the smiling air hostess handed me a glass of plain orange juice.

I spent nearly a year visiting friends and relatives and trying to find somewhere to live. Canada was the first country to offer me a home. For two years, I lived in Ottawa, its beautiful capital. But the northern climate of long winters and strong winds proved too severe for my arthritic limbs. In 1983, I moved south to Washington, D.C., as a legal immigrant sponsored by my sister Helen, who is a U.S. citizen. I bought a condominium and settled down. While I adjusted to my new life of freeway driving, supermarket shopping, and automated banking, I worked on my manuscript.

In Washington, I am free to do whatever I like with each day. I can travel anywhere without having to ask anyone for permission. Goods and services in abundance are available to me. Back doors in America lead only into people's kitchens. When I am with others, I can speak candidly on any subject without having to consider whether my remarks are ideologically correct or to worry that someone might misinterpret what I have said. I have not found the equivalent of either Lu Ying of my Residents' Committee in Shanghai or Lao Li, the policeman, in my new existence. In this atmosphere of freedom and relaxation, I feel a lightening of spirit, especially since I completed writing this book. What I enjoy more than anything else is the wealth of information available in the form of books, magazine articles, and newspaper reports on matters of interest to me, and the activities which bring me into the company of others of similar inclinations. I live a full and busy life. Only sometimes I feel a haunting sadness. At dusk, when the day is fading away and the level of my physical energy is at a low ebb, I may find myself depressed and nostalgic. But the next morning I invariably wake up with renewed optimism to welcome the day as another opportunity given me by God for enlightenment and experience.

The death of my daughter and my own painful experience during the Cultural Revolution can never be forgotten; even writing about it was traumatic. Often I had to put the manuscript away to regain my peace of mind. But I persisted in my effort. I felt a compulsion to speak out and let those who have the good fortune to live in freedom know what my life was like during those dark days in Maoist China. My many friends in England, Switzerland, France, Australia, Canada, and here in the United States encouraged me. I owe a special debt of gratitude to Peggy Durdin, a retired journalist and a dear friend of forty-five years. It was Peggy who first suggested that I put my experience down on paper, when I visited her and her husband Tillman in their beautiful home full of oriental treasures in La Jolla, California, in the winter of 1980. And throughout the time I worked on my manuscript, she gave me useful advice and urged me on.

The expiration date on my Chinese passport has passed. I did not have my passport renewed. The United States Immigration and Naturalization Service has issued me a document to enable me to travel abroad. I hope in due course to become a citizen of this great nation of open spaces and warm-hearted people where I have found a new life. The United States of America is the right place for me. Here are Jewish survivors of the Holocaust, dissidents of repressive regimes who had been imprisoned, boat people from Vietnam, and political refugees from tyranny. Among people like these, I do not feel alone. Since I settled in Washington, D.C., I have been accepted by the American people with unreserved friendliness. I have found old friends and made new ones. My only regret is that my daughter, Meiping, is not here with me.

While I have decided to become a citizen of the United States, I continue to be concerned with the situation in China. I am heartened by the news that unprecedented economic progress has been made since the implementation of Deng Xiaoping's new economic policy. Often I look back on the wasted years of the Mao Zedong era and the madness of the Cultural Revolution. I feel deeply saddened that so many innocent lives were needlessly sacrificed. I was glad when the Cultural Revolution was officially declared a national catastrophe, but I regret the Communist Party leadership's inability or unwillingness to repudiate Mao's policy in explicit terms.

From the point of view of the Chinese Communist Party, the greatest damage incurred by the Proletarian Cultural Revolution was the loss of the Party's prestige and its ability to govern. When Mao Zedong used the masses (the Red Guards and the Revolutionaries) to destroy his opponents in the Party leadership, he forced the Chinese people to witness and to take part in the ugly drama of a power struggle between himself and the so-called capitalist-roaders. The prolonged struggle and the denunciations of one leader after another enabled the Chinese people to stumble upon the truth that the emperor had no clothes. When Mao Zedong died in 1976, the country was in a state of political disintegration. Obviously if the Party was to continue to govern, it had to change course.

To the impoverished and disillusioned Chinese people, the promise of a Communist paradise in some distant future has become meaningless, and the time-worn revolutionary slogans seem vapid rather than inspiring. To rally the people and re-awaken their enthusiasm, the Party now appeals to their patri-otism. They are told to work for the modernization of China so that the country can regain her historical greatness and take her rightful place in the world. As reward, the Party promises the people an improved standard of living and no more politi-cal upheavals.

More than eight years have passed since Deng Xiaoping gathered the supreme power to rule China into his own hands and became the custodian of the fate of a quarter of the earth's population. His new economic policy of "opening the door to the outside world and invigorating the economy internally" has been generally successful. Businessmen, technical experts, teachers, and tourists from abroad pour into China in a steady stream. Foreign investment in joint ventures has reached sev-eral billion U.S. dollars. According to the 1986 World Bank report on world development, "China shifted from a major importer of food grains in the 1970s to being a surplus pro-ducer in the 1980s." There was a corresponding increase in cash crops, so that in most parts of rural China, where over 70 percent of the people live, the standard of living has dramati-cally improved. A number of hardworking and resourceful peasants have become "rich" by Chinese standards. Their two-story brick houses are replacing the traditional mud huts and changing the rural landscape of China.

Since 1984, reform measures are also being implemented in the cities. Party officials claim that eventually a new economic structure will emerge in China. It will include joint ventures with foreign capital and technology and Chinese labor, state-owned industries relying more on market forces than on rigid planning from Beijing, and small-scale private enterprises.

The implementation of Deng Xiaoping's reforms has not been without opposition. The old guard who have spent a lifetime in the Party viewed Deng's policy as a betrayal of Marxist principles and a threat to their position and privi-leges. The lower-ranking Party officials come largely from the peasantry, due to Mao's distrust of city-bred intellectuals. Their covert resistance to reform measures and hostility to-wards those better educated than themselves often render it impossible to make effective changes in work methods and personnel.

Since the Central Committee meeting in September 1986, there has been relentless debate and struggle for supremacy between the reformist leaders and the dogmatic Marxist old guard, with Deng Xiaoping assuming the role of arbitrator. Though activities and debates in the upper echelon of the Party are always shrouded in secrecy, deliberate leaks and casual gossip have provided the Chinese people with some information about what is going on. Powerless to intervene and denied any channel to freely express their concern, they watch with silent anxiety as their fate is being decided by men whose main concern is to retain personal power.

Only the youthful and impatient university students took to the streets in a brief demonstration to voice their demand for democracy in December 1986. This threat of rebellion provided the old guard with the opportunity to attack the reformists and gain a temporary advantage. The general secretary of the Communist Party, Hu Yaobang, was forced to resign. A number of well-known intellectuals supported by Hu were expelled from the Party or removed from office. The "antibourgeois liberalization" campaign was launched. Only firm and decisive action on the part of Deng Xiaoping and Zhao Ziyang averted a large scale witch-hunt reminiscent of the political movements of Mao Zedong's time.

The power struggle intensified in 1987 and lasted until the eve of the opening of the Thirteenth Party Congress on October 25, 1987. On that occasion, Deng Xiaoping voluntarily retired from the Central Committee and carried with him into retirement nearly all the old guard in the Party leadership. A younger new Central Committee of 175 members emerged and it in turn produced a Politburo of eighteen members. The five most senior members of the Politburo formed the new Standing Committee of the Politburo, which is the highest organ of decision-making. The appointment of Zhao Ziyang as general secretary was confirmed and he was also appointed senior vice-chairman of the Military Commission, with Deng Xiaoping retaining the post of chairman. This was an important step in establishing Zhao as the eventual successor to Deng, who is eighty-three. Because of Deng Xiaoping's skillful maneuver and the old guard's inability to produce a blueprint for the future that would take the place of reform, a page of Chinese history has been successfully turned without bloodshed or mass disturbances. But the composition of the new leadership represents a compromise rather than an outright victory for the reformists. The old guard had resisted retirement until men of whom they approved were installed in their vacated places.

In a lengthy report to the 2,000 delegates representing the 46 million Party members, Zhao Ziyang declared that China was in the "primary stage of socialism," thus legitimizing the adoption of capitalistic measures to revitalize the economy. The report thus contradicts Mao's assertion that in 1956, when the Party took over private enterprise, China had entered into the "advanced stage of socialism." Zhao also criticized the "leftist" thinking that has dominated China's economic and political life since the late 1950s, and blamed overconcentration of power for China's lack of economic progress. He said that the State should "regulate the market and the market should guide the state-owned enterprises." While he did not advocate the abolition of state ownership, he proposed the adoption of a scheme that would allow private individuals to sign contracts with the State to run state-owned shops or factories for profit.

Referring to the political reform demanded by China's intellectuals, Zhao expressly stated that "we shall never introduce a Western model of separation of the three powers—legislative, executive, and judiciary—nor would we accept a system of different political parties ruling China in turn." He reiterated the Party leadership's role in policy-making. But he proposed the separation of the functions of the Party and the government by making administrative officials and managers, rather than Party secretaries, responsible for day to day management and decision-making. In other words, if Zhao Ziyang's plan for political reform is carried out all over China, the Party secretaries will lose a great deal of their power. Without the old guard in Beijing to back them, the Party secretaries' position is definitely weakened. Nevertheless, China is a big country where the means of communication is poor. The power of the Party secretaries is deeply entrenched. To implement this policy will take time.

At its present stage, the emphasis of reform is still on changing China's economic system to free it from the rigidity of Maoist socialism. For the foreseeable future, China will remain a nation ruled by the will of a single leader rather than by institutions rooted in law. If the people want to have democracy, they will have to fight for it with a stronger voice and concerted action. They cannot expect the Communist Party to voluntarily abdicate. Perhaps one day, when the people's basic material needs are satisfied, they will join the intellectuals to fight for a more democratic form of government.

Constant change is an integral part of the Communist philosophy. For the entire thirty-eight years of Communist rule in China, the Party's policy has swung like a pendulum from left to right and back again without stop. Unless and until a political system rooted in law, rather than personal power, is firmly established in China, the road to the future will always be full of twists and turns. The wanton use of personal power such as Mao wielded during the Cultural Revolution may yet turn back the clock. Factional struggle for power among the new leaders is almost a certainty, though there will be an interval of superficial unity while each man consolidates his position. The Chinese people will continue to stand on the sidelines, allowed to speak only with an affirmative voice.

However, Communist China today is different from the past in one important aspect. She is no longer isolated and ostracized from civilized international society. World opinion and the China policy of the major powers can and do influence events in China. Anxious to project a good image, the better educated and more worldly new leaders will be sensitive to signals from abroad, especially from those countries which are the source of investment and trade.

Washington, D.C.
November 1987

Index

Addis, Sir John, 527–29, 531–32
American Graduate School of
  International Management, 299
Anti-Rightist Campaign (1957), 16, 20,
  25, 27, 29, 89, 200, 228, 236, 238,
  297, 499
Antonioni, Michelangelo, 458–59
Australia, 32, 35, 363

"Back-door" system, 365, 371–72, 376,
  390, 396
Bank of China, 377, 534
Beijing, 167, 206, 335, 467–72, 474
Buddhist Research Institute, 293

Canada, 306–7
Chen Boda, 304–5
Chen Yi, 5, 267, 457
Cheng Meiping, 3, 4, 29–36, 44, 51, 56,
  59, 60, 61, 68, 82, 87, 93–95, 98–99,
  101, 109, 112, 113, 115–16, 243,
  343–46, 357, 358, 360–61, 363,
  367–69, 383–87, 394, 397–99, 403–4,
  420–22, 423, 427, 438–41, 442, 444,
  448, 477–78, 487–88, 490–96, 520–22,
  535, 539
Cheng Yanqiu, 428

Chinese Communist Party, 23–24, 25,
  90, 198, 199–200, 279, 283–84,
  296–98; Congresses: Seventh, 208;
  Eighth, 50; Ninth, 207, 267–68, 269,
  273, 276, 304, 337; Tenth, 417, 518;
  Eleventh, 485–86;
  Thirteenth, 541
Communist Youth League, 105, 116
Confucius, 81, 437–38, 458
Constitutional Reform Movement, 88

Democracy Wall (1978–79), 253
Democratic League, 228
Deng Xiaoping, 38, 54, 374, 417,
  428–29, 438, 458, 459–60, 463, 465,
  467, 471, 472, 485, 487, 499, 522,
  523–24, 527, 539, 540–41
Du Fu, 267

Elimination of Counterrevolutionaries
  Campaign (1955), 16, 198

Fabian Socialists, 105
Federation of Women, 496, 514–15,
  517–20, 533
Fighting for Shanghai (film), 280
Formation of Rural Cooperatives
  Movement (1955), 16
Four Modernizations Program, 459–60,
  469, 517, 518, 519

Gang of Four, 173, 174, 285, 298, 481–92 passim, 523–24
Great Britain, 117, 160–62, 165–68, 235–38, 349–50
Great Leap Forward Campaign (1958–60), 38, 50, 54, 55, 166, 236, 292, 297, 465

Han (director of Shanghai Public Security Bureau), 492–94, 502
Han Suyin, 531
He Long, 489
Hong Kong, 6, 48–49, 101, 102, 105, 239, 461, 503, 510–11
Hong Kong–Shanghai Banking Corporation, 5, 364
Hua Guofeng, 471, 472, 474–75, 481–82, 485, 486–87, 499, 518, 522
Huang, Henry, 23–25, 28
Huang, Winnie, 22–29
Huang Zuolin, 280–85

Imperial Chemical Industries, 5

Jardines, 5
Jia Wu Naval Battle (film), 524
Jiang Qing, 34–35, 38–39, 54, 58, 98–99, 173, 181, 182, 207, 237, 240, 267, 281, 337, 339, 374, 428, 437–38, 457, 459, 463, 465, 467, 468, 470–71, 474, 475, 481–82, 484–86

Karnow, Stanley, 531
Kuomintang, 5, 16, 23–24, 42, 44, 49, 119, 128, 150, 165–66, 227–30, 264–65, 280, 286–88, 290–99 passim

Land Reform Movement (1950–52), 16, 88, 283
Lao Li, 446–48, 487–88, 523, 528–29, 531–33, 538
Laozi, 267
Let a Hundred Flowers Bloom Campaign (1956), 25, 253
Li Bo, 267
Li Zhen, 48–60 passim
Liberation Army Daily, 286
Lin Biao, 38, 39, 86, 149, 175–76, 181, 182, 207, 219, 221, 237, 240, 267–68, 271, 273–74, 290, 305–6, 333, 336–37, 358, 396, 400–401, 413, 428, 432
Lin Fengmian, 26, 72
Lin Liguo, 271
Little Sword Society, 425
Liu Shaoqi, 38, 53, 54, 208–9, 222–27, 231, 233, 239–41, 261, 274, 281, 290, 305, 336–37, 463, 489, 492

London School of Economics, 104
Lu, Empress, 468
Luo Ruiqing, 303

Ma Lianliang, 428
Ma Tianshui, 174, 475
Mao Yuanxin, 460, 465, 470
Mao Zedong, 9, 11, 12, 14, 16, 17, 21, 23–25, 35, 37–39, 45, 46, 49, 50, 53, 58–59, 62, 63, 86, 89, 110, 126–27, 174–75, 181, 182, 187, 203–4, 206–9, 218, 220, 222–24, 233, 234, 236, 240, 255, 259, 267, 276, 285, 286, 298, 303, 305–7, 315, 316, 335, 347, 374, 401, 413, 428, 437–38, 457, 463, 465, 470–71, 474–76, 479, 485–86, 499, 518, 522, 539–42
  Works: Collected Works, 96, 135, 142, 213, 264, 410, 411; "Fire Cannonballs at the Headquarters," 38; Little Red Book, 17, 96, 125, 135, 145, 146, 156, 185, 210, 218, 220, 244, 246, 249, 268, 295, 335–36; "On the Dictatorship of the People's Democracy," 150; "On the Internal Contradiction of the People," 246; "The Strategy of China's Revolutionary War," 291
Marx, Karl, 84, 104
Meiping. See Cheng Meiping
Military Control Commission, 181–93 passim, 220, 280, 284

Nixon, Richard M., 305, 337–38, 347–48, 430

Opium War, 14, 117

Peng Dehuai, 303, 489
People's Art Theater, 280, 284, 428
People's Bank, 65–66, 461
People's Daily, 97, 218, 259, 286
Political Consultative Conference, 50, 51, 55, 157, 515–16

Qi Baishi, 72
Qing Dynasty, 90, 281
Qing Ming festival, 468–69
Qinghua University, 206

Red Flag (magazine), 286
Red Guard News, 112
Red Guards, 58–122 passim, 171, 173–76, 206, 270–71, 364, 374–75, 394–95, 397–98, 426, 412–14, 415, 470, 475
Reform through Labor Camps, 127, 133
Residents' Committees, 378–82, 397,

399–401, 468, 471–72, 474, 481–82, 483–84, 496
Revolutionaries, 104–22 passim, 173–76, 269, 270–71, 397–98, 417, 475

Shanghai, 3–4, 23–24, 50, 62–63, 86, 94, 99–100, 125–26, 192–93, 195, 270–71, 277, 281, 349–50, 359–60, 366–67, 370, 387–94, 398, 425–26, 430, 456–57, 483, 488, 516, 523–26, 533–34
Shanghai Aluminum Company, 67
Shanghai Athletics Association, 367–68, 373, 383–86, 421
Shanghai Conservatory of Music, 48, 49, 53–60 passim, 360
Shanghai Film Studio, 6, 32–34, 112, 115–16, 360, 367–69, 386, 398, 421, 467, 490–91, 494–95
Shanghai Foreign Language Institute, 89, 412, 473, 497–98
Shanghai Liberation Daily, 96, 138, 174, 175, 259, 303, 304, 458, 466, 467, 513, 522
Shanghai municipal government, 4, 52, 85–86, 94, 98, 100, 113, 114–15, 171, 173–74, 273, 349, 461, 475, 524
Shanghai Museum, 76, 505–13 passim
Shanghai Public Security Bureau, 174, 180, 231, 337, 358, 359, 360, 361, 364, 487–89, 492–94, 497, 500–503, 521–22, 529–30
Shanghai Workers Revolutionary Headquarters, 173, 460
Shell International Petroleum Company, 5–6, 7, 9–10, 12, 19, 21–22, 27, 29, 42–43, 55, 69, 89, 117, 118–20, 126, 158–59, 232–33, 235–37, 281–84, 291, 349, 426–27, 436, 522, 537
Snow, Edgar, 306
Socialization of Capitalist Enterprises Campaign (1956), 39
Soviet Union, 47, 54, 495, 524
Sun Weishi, 428
Sun Yatsen, 516
Sun Yatsen Memorial, 293–95, 298–99
Suppression of Counterrevolutionaries Campaign (1950), 16

Taiwan, 117, 165–66, 290, 305, 347, 348
Tang Yin, 512
Tangshan earthquake, 473–74
Tao Yuanming, 72
Thought Reform Movement (1951), 24, 49
Three and Five Antis Movement (1953), 49
Tilanqiao prison, 193–201, 243–45, 303–4
Tongji University, 23, 397, 398, 404

United Nations, 117, 305, 333
United States, 49, 117, 165–66, 199–200, 305–7, 337–38, 348, 363, 496–97, 500–501, 538–39

Vietnam, 338, 522–23
Voice of America, 496–97, 499

Wan Li, 417
Wang Dongxing, 486
Wang Hongweng, 173, 460–61, 463
Wanli, Emperor, 167
Workers' and Peasants' Propaganda Teams, 206–7, 210, 220, 221–22, 231, 348, 368
Wu, Empress, 468

Xu Jingxian, 174

Yanjing University, 104, 262, 414, 531
Yao Wenyuan, 173, 437
Ye Jianying, 463, 467, 481, 487

Zhang Chengzhong, 510–13
Zhang Chunqiao, 98–99, 100, 173, 339, 459, 463, 467, 471, 475
Zhang Hanfu, 229
Zhang Tieshen, 460
Zhang Yufeng, 486
Zhou Enlai, 25, 95, 120, 173–74, 175, 200, 229, 233, 236–37, 267, 305–6, 333, 337, 339, 358, 364, 374, 427–29, 457, 458, 460, 464, 465–70, 518